THE ROUTLEDGE COMPANION TO SOCIAL MEDIA AND POLITICS

Social media are now widely used for political protests, campaigns, and communication in developed and developing nations, but available research has not yet paid sufficient attention to experiences beyond the U.S. and UK. This collection tackles this imbalance head-on, compiling cutting-edge research across six continents to provide a comprehensive, global, up-to-date review of recent political uses of social media.

Drawing together empirical analyses of the use of social media by political movements and in national and regional elections and referenda, *The Routledge Companion to Social Media and Politics* presents studies ranging from Anonymous and the Arab Spring to the Greek Aganaktismenoi, and from South Korean presidential elections to the Scottish independence referendum. The book is framed by a selection of keystone theoretical contributions, evaluating and updating existing frameworks for the social media age.

Axel Bruns is an Australian Research Council Future Fellow and Professor in the Digital Media Research Centre at Queensland University of Technology in Brisbane, Australia.

Gunn Enli is Professor of Media Studies and Head of the Research Project "Social Media and Election Campaigns" (SAC) at the Department of Media and Communication, University of Oslo.

Eli Skogerbø is Professor in Media Studies and Co-Head of the Political Communication Research Group at the Department of Media and Communication, University of Oslo.

Anders Olof Larsson is Postdoctoral Fellow at the Department of Media and Communication at the University of Oslo.

Christian Christensen is Professor of Journalism at Stockholm University.

THE ROUTLEDGE COMPANION TO SOCIAL MEDIA AND POLITICS

Edited by Axel Bruns, Gunn Enli,
Eli Skogerbø, Anders Olof Larsson,
and Christian Christensen

Routledge
Taylor & Francis Group

NEW YORK AND LONDON

First published 2016
by Routledge
711 Third Avenue, New York, NY 10017

and by Routledge
2 Park Square, Milton Park, Abingdon, Oxon OX14 4RN

Routledge is an imprint of the Taylor & Francis Group, an informa business

Library of Congress Cataloging-in-Publication Data
Names: Bruns, Axel, 1970– editor.
Title: The Routledge companion to social media and politics / edited by Axel Bruns,
    Gunn Enli, Eli Skogerbø, Anders Olof Larsson, and Christian Christensen.
Description: New York, NY : Routledge, 2016. | Includes bibliographical
    references and index.
Identifiers: LCCN 2015026472 | ISBN 9781138860766 (hardback) |
    ISBN 9781315716299 (ebook)
Subjects: LCSH: Communication in politics—Technological innovations. |
    Political participation—Technological innovations. | Social media—Political
    aspects. | Mass media—Political aspects. | World politics.
Classification: LCC JA85 .R68 2016 | DDC 320.01/4—dc23
    LC record available at http://lccn.loc.gov/2015026472

ISBN: 978-1-138-86076-6 (hbk)
ISBN: 978-1-315-71629-9 (ebk)

Typeset in Goudy
by Apex CoVantage, LLC

CONTENTS

CONTENTS

CONTENTS

FIGURES

FIGURES

TABLES

ACKNOWLEDGEMENTS

We offer our heartfelt thanks to the many contributors to this large and ambitious project. Given the rapid development of social media platforms and their uses, our authors were given a very tight turnaround for their chapters in this collection, and they responded to this challenge with energy and enthusiasm. We are especially pleased to be able to include in this collection a truly international group of experts in their fields, representing all six continents and offering important new perspectives on local developments in an international context.

Similarly, we are very grateful to Routledge, and especially Editorial Assistant Simon Jacobs, for their support for this project. There is in the literature in this field a tendency for studies of the 'usual suspects'—the U.S., UK, and perhaps some other major European countries—to be overrepresented. While many of these studies are valuable and important, the world itself, and the world of social media, is a great deal larger and richer than this focus on leading Western democracies lets on, and it has been a guiding principle of our work in compiling this volume to allow insights from a wider variety of contexts to find an audience. We are delighted by Routledge's strong support for this project—and while no one collection, however large, can claim to offer a comprehensive review of the uses of social media in political communication around the world, we hope that this *Companion* will contribute to putting a broader range of national and regional experiences on the map and may inspire further studies of the fascinating developments which are unfolding in many of these cases.

We are also thankful for the support from the Norwegian Research Council and the research project The Impact of Social Media on Agenda-Setting in Election Campaigns (SAC), based at the University of Oslo, which was responsible for bringing together the editorial team. Additionally, work on this collection was also supported by the Australian Research Council Future Fellowship project Understanding Intermedia Information Flows in the Australian Online Public Sphere.

Finally, our deepest gratitude goes to Nicki Hall, our Project Coordinator at Queensland University of Technology. She took on the difficult task of managing a large and internationally dispersed group of authors (and editors), and completed it with good grace and great efficiency, even as final deadlines loomed. That you now hold this substantial volume in your hands (or are able to access it electronically) is as much due to her hard work as it is to the scholarly excellence of the individual contributors. Thanks, Nicki!

NOTES ON CONTRIBUTORS

Eva Anduiza is Professor of Political Science at Universitat Autonoma de Barcelona. Her main fields of research are political participation, political attitudes, and elections. She has recently edited *Digital Media and Political Engagement around the World: A Comparative Analysis*, with Michael Jensen and Laia Jorba (Cambridge University Press). eva.anduiza@uab.cat

Lemi Baruh is Assistant Professor at the Department of Media and Visual Arts at Koç University, Turkey. His research focuses on new media technologies, social media use, surveillance, and privacy—especially pertaining to the psychology of attitudes about privacy and the culture of voyeurism. lbaruh@ku.edu.tr

Marco T. Bastos is Postdoctoral Researcher at the University of California at Davis. He holds a PhD in Communication Sciences from the University of São Paulo and was previously the NSF EAGER postdoc at Duke University. His research explores the tension between online and onsite networks in the distribution of news, contentious politics, and scholarly work. bastos@ucdavis.edu

Stacy Blasiola is a PhD candidate in the Department of Communication at the University of Illinois at Chicago. Her research interests include social media and politics, legal and policy issues in social media, and online privacy. sblasi2@uic.edu

Marcel Broersma is Professor of Journalism Studies and Media at the University of Groningen. His research focusses on the current and historical transformation of journalism. He has published widely on the use of social media by both journalists and politicians. m.j.broersma@rug.nl

Axel Bruns is an Australian Research Council Future Fellow and Professor in the Digital Media Research Centre at Queensland University of Technology in Brisbane, Australia. He is the author of *Blogs, Wikipedia, Second Life and Beyond: From Production to Produsage* (2008) and *Gatewatching: Collaborative Online News Production* (2005), and a co-editor of *Twitter and Society* (2014), *A Companion to New Media Dynamics* (2012), and *Uses of Blogs* (2006). His research examines the uses of social media in political communication, crisis communication, and other contexts, and he is leading the development of new research methods for large-scale social media analytics. His research Website is at http://snurb.info/, and he tweets at @snurb_dot_info. a.bruns@qut.edu.au

Mercedes Bunz is Senior Lecturer at the University of Westminster, London, where she teaches Digital Media and Journalism. She writes about technology, media, critical theory, and journalism. Her latest book is *The Silent Revolution: How Algorithms*

Changed Knowledge, Work, Journalism, and Politics without Making Too Much Noise (Palgrave Macmillan, 2014). m.bunz@westminster.ac.uk

Andrew Chadwick is Professor of Political Science and Co-Director of the New Political Communication Unit in the Department of Politics and International Relations at Royal Holloway, University of London. www.andrewchadwick.com

Pai-Lin Chen is Associate Professor in the College of Communication at National Chengchi University in Taiwan. His research interests are social media, risk and crisis communication, information gathering and visualization, and journalistic expertise and practice. chen.pailin@gmail.com

Yu-Chung Cheng is Assistant Professor in the Department of Mass Communication at the Hsuan Chuang University in Taiwan. Her research interests are social media, risk and crisis communication, science communication, and technology culture studies. colisa@gmail.com

Christian Christensen is Professor of Journalism at Stockholm University. His research examines the relationships between technology, politics and journalism. christian.christensen@ims.su.se

Camilo Cristancho is a Postdoctoral Researcher in Political Science at Universitat Autònoma de Barcelona. He has published on contentious politics, online social networks and protest, and political use of the Internet on electoral campaigns. His current research deals with the potential of social media for political equality, attitudes and effects of exposure to disagreement, and attitudes towards protest in social media. Camilo.Cristancho@uab.cat

James Dennis is a PhD candidate and Research Assistant in the New Political Communication Unit in the Department of Politics and International Relations at Royal Holloway, University of London. His research focuses on the effect of social media on citizenship and political engagement in Britain. jameswilldennis.com

Gunn Enli is Professor of Media Studies at the Department of Media and Communication, University of Oslo. Enli is the project leader of 'Social Media and Election Campaigns', an international research project examining cross-media and cross-national effects of social media on election campaigns. Her research interests include political communication, social media, media history, and media policy. Enli has published widely in high-ranked international journals and has published five books. Her latest books are *Mediated Authenticity: How the Media Constructs Reality* (Peter Lang, 2015), and *The Media Welfare State: Nordic Media in the Digital Age* (Michigan University Press, 2014). gunn.enli@media.uio.no

Jean-Marc Francony is Senior Lecturer at the Department of Humanities and Social Sciences and an active member of PACTE Laboratory (University of Grenoble Alpes, France). He is currently working on issues related to large-scale Web usage and data mining. His research focusses on how to capture data as well as what methodological and ethical issues are involved with tracking and using the Web in this context. His aim is to establish behavioural profiles and to identify the roles, dynamics, and social interactions of various actors on the Web and on social media. jeanmarc.francony@umrpacte.fr

Debbie Goh is Assistant Professor in the Division of Journalism and Publishing at Nanyang Technological University's Wee Kim Wee School of Communication and Information. Her research focusses on digital inequalities and the processes that influence how marginalized communities engage with new media technologies. DebbieGoh@ntu.edu.sg

Todd Graham is Assistant Professor in Journalism and Political Communication at the Groningen Centre for Media and Journalism Studies, University of Groningen. His main research interests are the use of new media in representative democracies, the intersections between popular culture and formal politics, online election campaigns, online deliberation and political talk, and online civic engagement. t.s.graham@rug.nl

Farid Guliyev is an independent researcher currently based in Baku, Azerbaijan. He holds a PhD in Political Science from Jacobs University in Bremen, Germany (2014), and an MA from Central European University in Budapest (2004). His work has been published in *Democratization*, *Demokratizatsiya*, *Energy Policy*, and as a book chapter in *Challenges of the Caspian Resource Boom* (Palgrave Macmillan, 2012). His current research focusses on comparative regime studies and natural resource management in developing countries. fareedaz@gmail.com

Sharon Haleva-Amir is Adjunct Professor at Tel Aviv University and Beit Berl College and Research Fellow at the Haifa Center of Law and Technology (HCLT), University of Haifa. Her research interests relate to the broader spectrum of Israeli e-Politics, mainly during incumbency. Current research focusses on the 2015 electoral campaigns. sharon@trebcon.com

Rongbin Han is Assistant Professor at the Department of International Affairs, University of Georgia. His research interests centre on regime transition, state–society relations, media politics, and social activism in authoritarian regimes, with an area focus on China. hanr@uga.edu

Tim Highfield is Vice-Chancellor's Research Fellow in Digital Media at Queensland University of Technology, where his fellowship project is 'Visual Cultures of Social Media'. His first book, *Social Media and Everyday Politics*, is due in late 2015. t.highfield@qut.edu.au

Thomas Ingebretsen is a Market Analyst in Omnicom Media Group. He has trained as a media scholar and has written his master thesis with and also worked as a Research Assistant with the Social Media and Election Campaign Project at the Department of Media and Communication, University of Oslo. thomas.ingebretsen@gmail.com

Dan Jackson is Principal Lecturer in Media and Communication at Bournemouth University. His research broadly explores the intersection of media and democracy, including news coverage of politics, the construction of news, political communication, and political talk in online environments. JacksonD@bournemouth.ac.uk

Nigel Jackson is Reader in Persuasion and Communication in the Faculty of Business, Plymouth University, England. He is interested in how political actors such as parties, candidates and representatives use communication and marketing to encourage behavioural change through persuasive messages. He has particularly focussed on online political communication. nigel.jackson@plymouth.ac.uk

Jakob Linaa Jensen is Head of Research for Social Media at the Danish School of Media and Journalism. He has been Associate Professor of Media Studies at Aarhus University for nine years. He is a board member of Center for Internet Studies, Aarhus University. He has also headed a European task force on social media methods. He has published three monographs, three edited volumes, and more than 30 international journal articles. His research interests include political communication, the public sphere, social media, Internet politics, the sociology of the Internet, and the cognitive affordances of new media. jlj@dmjx.dk

Gholam Khiabany teaches in the Department of Media and Communications, Goldsmiths, University of London. He is the author of *Iranian Media: The Paradox of Modernity* (Routledge, 2010), and co-author of *Blogistan: The Internet and Politics in Iran*, with Annabelle Sreberny (I. B. Tauris, 2010). g.khiabany@gold.ac.uk

Ulrike Klinger is Senior Research and Teaching Assistant at IPMZ—Institute for Mass Communication and Media Research, University of Zurich, Switzerland. Her current research focusses on political online communication and digital public spheres. u.klinger@ipmz.uzh.ch

Karolina Koc-Michalska is Assistant Professor at Audencia School of Management (France) and an Associate Researcher at Sciences-Po Paris. Her research focusses on political communication, the role of social networks, and their impact on political engagement. She studies the campaigning effects, media influence on election outcomes, and original methods to study the online public spheres. kkocmichalska@audencia.com

Rajesh Kumar is Associate Professor with the School of Communication, Doon University, Dehradun, India. His teaching and research interests include communication for development, mass media and society, the political economy of communication, and communication programmes and campaigns. rkdoon@gmail.com

Anders Olof Larsson was until recently Postdoctoral Fellow at the Department of Media and Communication at the University of Oslo. From November 2015, he is Associate Professor at Westerdals Oslo School of Arts, Communication and Technology. His research interests include the use of online interactivity and social media by societal institutions and their audiences, online political communication, and methodology, especially quantitative methods. andersoloflarsson@gmail.com

Darren G. Lilleker is Associate Professor in Political Communication in the Faculty of Media and Communication, Bournemouth University. Lilleker's expertise is in the professionalization and marketization of politics and its impact on citizens, on which he has published widely. dlilleker@bournemouth.ac.uk

Stine Lomborg is Associate Professor in Communication and IT at the University of Copenhagen. Her research centres on social media users and methods. She is the author of *Social Media—Social Genres: Making Sense of the Ordinary* (Routledge) and co-editor of *The Ubiquitous Internet: User and Industry Perspectives* (Routledge, with Anja Bechmann). slomborg@hum.ku.dk

Young Min is Professor of Media & Communication at Korea University, Seoul, South Korea. Her research interests concern the roles of political media and interpersonal communication in elections and other political contexts. ymin@korea.ac.kr

Hallvard Moe is Professor of Media Studies at the University of Bergen. He has published widely on the use of media for public debate and issues of media policy. His latest book is *The Media Welfare State: Nordic Media in the Digital Era* (University of Michigan Press, 2014, co-authored with Trine Syvertsen, Gunn Enli, and Ole J. Mjøs). Hallvard. Moe@infomedia.uib.no

Karine Nahon is Associate Professor at the Information School, University of Washington, and the Government School at the Interdisciplinary Center Herzliya (IDC). Her research focus is on the politics of information. More specifically, she studies questions which relate to information flows and virality, network gatekeeping, and power. She has authored one book and over 50 peer-reviewed publications. Her book *Going Viral* (with Jeff Hemsley) won the Best Information Science Book Award and the Outstanding Academic Title Award. Her research Website is at http://eKarine.org/, and she tweets at @karineb. karineb@uw.edu

Anja Aaheim Naper is currently completing a PhD on immigration journalism at Oslo and Akershus University College. She was previously a Research Assistant on the 'Social Media and Agenda-Setting in Election Campaigns' project at the University of Oslo, where she examined the U.S. presidential election campaign on Twitter. anjanaper@gmail.com

Martin Nkosi Ndlela is Associate Professor at Hedmark University College in Norway. His research interests include issues of media and democracy in Africa, in particular, how new information and communication technologies can be harnessed for citizen engagement, participation and empowerment. nkosi.ndlela@hihm.no

Julia Neubarth is Research Assistant and doctoral student at the Department of Communication Studies and Media Research (IfKW) at Ludwig-Maximilians-University Munich. Her research interests include social media, network analysis, finance blogs, and the transnational public sphere. julia.neubarth@ifkw.lmu.de

Christoph Neuberger is a full Professor at the Department of Communication Studies and Media Research (IfKW) at Ludwig-Maximilians-University Munich. His research interests include media change, online journalism, activities of press and broadcasting on the Internet, social media, journalism theory, and media quality. christoph. neuberger@ifkw.lmu.de

Christina Neumayer is Assistant Professor in the Culture and Communication research group at the IT University of Copenhagen, with an interest in digital

media, radical politics, activism, social movements, and civic engagement. chne@
itu.dk

Teke Ngomba is Assistant Professor of Media Studies at the School of Communication and Culture at Aarhus University, Denmark. His research in the fields of political
communication, communication and social change, and journalism and media studies
has been published in several international peer-reviewed journals. imvjnt@dac.au.dk

Christian Nuernbergk is Assistant Professor at the Department of Communication
Studies and Media Research (IfKW) at Ludwig-Maximilians-University Munich. His
research interests include political communication, digital journalism, social media,
networked publics, and network analysis. christian.nuernbergk@ifkw.lmu.de

Mario Orefice is Postdoctoral Research Fellow at University of Urbino–Department of
Media Studies and Humanities. His research areas range from communication and social
media study to alternative forms of political participation performed by political parties,
civic groups, or social movements, online as well as offline. mario.orefice@uniurb.it

Jacob Ørmen is a PhD Fellow at the Department of Media, Cognition and Communication, University of Copenhagen. His primary fields of research are people's engagement and disengagement with the news, and research methods—in particular, digital
methods. dcs499@hum.ku.dk

Natalie Pang is Assistant Professor in the Wee Kim Wee School of Communication and
Information at Singapore's Nanyang Technological University (NTU). Her research
focusses on social media use and information behaviour, specifically in contexts of
uncertainty and risks (e.g. crises and social movements). NLSPANG@ntu.edu.sg

Françoise Papa is Senior Lecturer at the Institute of Communication and Media and
a member of PACTE Laboratory (University of Grenoble Alpes, France). She is con-
ducting research on global communication, media events and social uses of ICTs. She
is studying the evolution of communication paradigms in various configurations, such
as media coverage of global sport events like the Olympic Games, or political elections
and public communication campaigns. Her research focusses on social media uses and
their impacts on the process of information. francoise.papa@u-grenoble3.fr

Zizi Papacharissi is Professor and Head of Communication at the University of
Illinois–Chicago. She is Editor of the Journal of Broadcasting and Electronic Media
and the open access and free journal Social Media and Society. She has published 4
books and over 50 articles and book chapters on the social and political consequences
of newer media. Her latest book is *Affective Publics: Sentiment, Technology and Politics*
(Oxford University Press). zizi@uic.edu

Se Jung Park is a PhD Candidate in the Department of Communication at Georgia
State University. Current research includes information diffusion, social network analysis, environmental communication, and Online PR. spark74@gsu.edu

Katy E. Pearce is Assistant Professor in the Department of Communication at the
University of Washington and holds an affiliation with the Ellison Center for Russian,

East European and Central Asian Studies. Her research focusses on social and political uses of technologies and digital content in the transitioning democracies and semi-authoritarian states of the South Caucasus and Central Asia, but primarily Armenia and Azerbaijan. Kepearce@uw.edu

Stephen Quinlan is Senior Researcher and Manager of Operations of the Comparative Studies of Electoral Systems (CSES) project, GESIS Leibniz Institute for the Social Sciences, Mannheim. His research focusses on electoral behaviour and public opinion, including voter turnout, elections, political parties, referendums, and examining the impact of social media on politics. His research has been published in *Electoral Studies* and *Irish Political Studies*. Stephen.Quinlan@gesis.org

Andrew Quodling is a Doctoral Candidate at Queensland University of Technology. His research focusses on social and political conflict on social media platforms. He examines the ways that users and operators of social media services negotiate political conflict and the ways in which their interactions in these conflicts influence the governance of social media platforms and other online spaces. a.quodling@qut.edu.au

Raquel Recuero is a Professor and researcher at Universidade Católica de Pelotas. She received a PhD and an MSc in Communication and Information Sciences from Universidade Federal do Rio Grande do Sul (UFRGS). raquel.recuero@ucpel.edu.br

Luca Rossi is Assistant Professor at the Communication and Culture research group of IT University of Copenhagen. He is active in the field of digital research methods for social sciences and social network analysis techniques for social media studies. lucr@itu.dk

Mark Shephard is Senior Lecturer in Politics at the Department of Government, University of Strathclyde, and was principal investigator on the ESRC/AQMeN Future of the United Kingdom and Scotland research project focussing on the impact of social media on the Scottish Independence referendum. His works have been published in a number of journals, including *Electoral Studies*, *Political Studies*, *The Journal of Legislative Studies*, *The Journal of Elections*, *Public Opinion and Parties*, *British Politics*, *Parliamentary Affairs*, and the British Journal of Politics and International Relations. mark.shephard@strath.ac.uk

Eli Skogerbø is Professor in Media Studies and Head of the Political Communication Research Group (with Øyvind Ihlen), University of Oslo. Her current research includes social media as tools for journalism, political communication, and minority media. eli.skogerbo@media.uio.no

Morten Skovsgaard is Associate Professor at the Center for Journalism, University of Southern Denmark. His research interests include journalists' professional values and ethics, journalistic routines, and news coverage of politics. skh@sam.sdu.dk

Amy P. Smith is a PhD candidate and Research Assistant in the New Political Communication Unit in the Department of Politics and International Relations at Royal Holloway, University of London. Amy.Smith.2011@live.rhul.ac.uk

Jakob Svensson is Associate Professor in Media and Communication Studies at Uppsala University. Svensson directs the MA program in Digital Media and Society.

His research focusses on two main areas: political participation on digital media platforms and mobile communication in developing regions. jakob.svensson@im.uu.se

Yannis Theocharis is Research Fellow at the Mannheim Centre for European Social Research (MZES), University of Mannheim, a former Alexander von Humboldt Fellow, and Co-Director of the MZES-based project 'Social Media Networks and the Relationships between Citizens and Politics'. His research interests are in political communication and comparative political behaviour, and more specifically, in political participation, new media, protest politics, and social capital. Yannis.Theocharis@uni-mannheim.de

Arjen van Dalen is Associate Professor at the Center for Journalism, University of Southern Denmark. His research interests include the relation between journalists and politicians, political journalism, comparative research, algorithmic journalism, and economic news. avd@sam.sdu.dk

Maurice Vergeer is Media Researcher at the Department Communication Science of the Behavioral Science Institute, Radboud University, in the Netherlands. His interests in Internet research cover political communication, journalism, and people's social capital. His methodological interests cover quantitative research, network analysis, and cross-national comparative research. m.vergeer@maw.ru.nl

Hayley Watson is Senior Research Analyst at Trilateral Research & Consulting, London, UK. Her main area of expertise includes the role of technology in relation to security, the development of citizen journalism, and the role of social media in crisis management. hayley.watson@trilateralresearch.com

Lars Willnat is Professor of Journalism at Indiana University–Bloomington. His research interests include comparative survey research, theoretical aspects of public opinion formation, and journalism studies. He is author and co-editor of four books: *Social Media, Culture and Politics* (Peter Lang 2014); *The Global Journalist in the 21st Century* (Routledge 2012)' *Political Communication in Asia* (Routledge 2009); and *Empirical Political Analysis: Research Methods in Political Science* (Pearson 2008). lwillnat@indiana.edu

Jennifer Wladarsch is a Research Assistant and doctoral student at the Department of Communication Studies and Media Research (IfKW) at Ludwig-Maximilians–University Munich. Her research interests include social media, online journalism and political communication. jennifer.wladarsch@ifkw.lmu.de

Scott Wright is Senior Lecturer in Political Communication, University of Melbourne. His research focusses on everyday political talk in non-political online third spaces; e-democracy; e-petitions; online deliberation; and journalism. He has published in leading international journals, including *New Media & Society*, *Journal of Computer-Mediated Communication*, *European Journal of Communication* and *Political Communication*. scott.wright@unimelb.edu.au

Gabriela Zago is Professor at Universidade Federal de Pelotas (UFPel), in Pelotas, Brazil. She received a PhD and an MSc in Communication and Information Sciences from Universidade Federal do Rio Grande do Sul (UFRGS). gabrielaz@gmail.com

INTRODUCTION

*Axel Bruns, Gunn Enli, Eli Skogerbø,
Anders Olof Larsson, and
Christian Christensen*

Politics and the media have always been closely interrelated. The very dawn of democratic structures, in Ancient Greece, is inextricably linked to the gradual development of effective systems for the mediation of ideas between political leaders and the public. The formalisation of rhetorical strategies, the establishment of functional environments for public speech, and the creation of accountable systems for expressing the will of the *demos*, even if at the time that term encompassed only free, male members of the local *polis*, are all early manifestations of an interdependency between politics and the media.

The subsequent 2,500 years have seen the—halting and unsteady, but in the long term, unstoppable—development of ever more sophisticated frameworks and technologies for political communication, including the printing press, broadcast media, and the Internet, in its various forms and formats. Indeed, the past century is marked by a notable increase in the frequency of the successive waves of such inventions, and thus by an acceleration of the processes of political change: if the fundamental structure of political systems in many countries had remained comparatively static over previous centuries, a person born in Europe at the dawn of the 20th century might have had the misfortune to live through the transition from feudal rule through fledgling democracy to fascist dictatorship before even reaching middle age (not to mention the small matter of two world wars, covered by, and at times, also fought through the media). And the emergent media technologies of the day—newsprint and radio—would have played a crucial role in these political revolutions.

In their own ways, political science and media and communication studies—and allied disciplines beyond—have recognised this interdependency of politics and the media. In a number of cases, they have identified the catalyst moments that document a shifting of the balance between existing and emerging media forms: Franklin D. Roosevelt's 'fireside chats' to a nationwide radio audience, for example, which enabled him to speak directly to the American people and thus bypass editing and interpretation by newspaper journalists, or the first televised presidential debate between Richard M. Nixon and John F. Kennedy, which introduced a focus on the body language and personal demeanour of the candidates in addition to their spoken words. More recently, of course, Barack Obama's 2008 presidential campaign was widely highlighted as the breakthrough moment for the use of contemporary social media platforms in political campaigning—and in doing so also spawned a rapidly growing field of research that investigates exactly how social media intersect with the broader political and electoral process.

Yet, these examples also point to a considerable, persisting limitation of much of the work that examines the nexus of politics and the media, historically as well as—especially—in the present moment: there remains in the literature an overrepresentation of studies that examine these phenomena in the United States, and (already to a lesser extent) in other large nations of the developed world. While excellent work has been done on the situation elsewhere, to be sure, it has failed to generate the same impact as the research emerging from more hegemonic contexts. Attempts to translate the insights gleaned from the US, UK, and other leading Western nations to local contexts elsewhere are all too often frustrated by the significant idiosyncrasies of the respective political and media systems: the convoluted US primary and presidential election system, for example, is without equal anywhere else in the world, and our understanding of how media are being used for campaigning there is, consequently, only of rather limited value for the analysis of media campaigning in elections in Scandinavia or sub-Saharan Africa.

Such imbalances in the literature on media and politics appear to be even more pronounced when we shift our attention exclusively to contemporary social media platforms, such as Facebook and Twitter, as the latest wave of innovation in political communication. Created and first broadly adopted in the United States, these platforms are now used in many countries around the globe, although with widely varying levels of market penetration amongst different user demographics. These considerable localised variations, combined with important differences in political systems, make it even more difficult to translate, say, observations from the Obama 2008 campaign to another country context. What is necessary instead is a broad-based, cross-national investigation of social media use in political communication and campaigning that allows for a charting of the similarities and differences in social media adoption and application against the backdrop of specific national (and indeed, given the rapid ongoing development of social media platforms, temporal) contexts.

Introducing the *Companion*

With this collection, we hope to make a constructive contribution to this continuing project. In compiling the chapters we present here, we have deliberately sought to avoid an overrepresentation of the United States and other global hegemons in the adoption of social media for political purposes; instead, we hope that this *Companion* provides a valuable overview of the no less important and fascinating ideas and innovations for the use of social media in political communication that are emerging from other corners of the globe as well. The energy and enthusiasm with which our host of contributors have taken up the challenge of reporting on developments in their countries and regions, and have made these observations accessible and meaningful for an international audience, has been inspiring.

The *Companion* opens, however, with a selection of keystone chapters in Part I that provide an overview of current and emerging theory on the intersections of social media and politics. Our contributors in this section revisit existing and established theories, from agenda-setting to the public sphere, and explore emerging frameworks for understanding the impact of online and social media on journalism, authenticity, mediation, and the political process. They present concepts such as hybrid media and third spaces as means to conceptualise the continuing transformations in the contemporary media ecology, and examine the impact of networked media logic on existing systems of political communication.

Part II moves to a close examination of the political uses of social media by movements around the world. Some of the studies collected here are concerned with specific events and actions, from the revolutionary protests in Egypt to the emergence of anti-austerity movements in Spain or Greece; others examine more broadly the various developments in their specific countries of interest, from the long history of civic movements in South Korea to the emergent opposition against Azerbaijan's authoritarian regime. While each of these chapters in itself has a fascinating story to tell about how the adoption of social media for political communication is flavoured both by a view towards international trends and a need to cater to local traditions and preferences, we particularly encourage a reading across these chapters, to explore the sometimes surprising inspirations and interconnections that emerge as activists look to learn from social media experiences elsewhere in the world.

Part III, finally, explores in detail the gradually increasing adoption and adaptation of social media for political campaigning, across a range of national and regional elections and referenda. This section of the *Companion* is organised broadly chronologically, opening with two longitudinal studies of campaigning in Swedish and UK elections and closing with a number of snapshots of social media uses in very recent campaigns, including the Brazilian presidential election, the Danish elections for the European parliament, and the Scottish independence referendum, all in 2014. Again, reading across these chapters with an eye towards chronological developments as well as national differences is supremely rewarding: at a general level, it reveals the growing sophistication of social media-based political campaigning approaches, but from case study to case study, it also highlights the reinvention of wheels, the missteps and the dead ends that appear to also be an inescapable aspect of this continuing process.

A collection of this size is not designed to be read cover to cover in one sitting, of course, and so each individual chapter stands on its own to tell a compelling story. For those readers who are interested simply in finding out more about the role of social media in the political debates amongst Indian civil society, or the use of Twitter and Facebook in recent Israeli election campaigns, those chapters will offer valuable new insights. But we encourage you to trace the interconnections, the similarities and differences, the influences and inspirations that connect the many cases collected in Parts II and III, and to return to the theoretical frameworks outlined in Part I which underpin and enrich the empirical analyses. There is no right or wrong way to approach this collection: explore whichever way you prefer, and in doing so uncover the network of connections and complexities that exist at the nexus of social media and politics.

Part I

THEORIES OF SOCIAL MEDIA AND POLITICS

Part I

THEORIES OF SOCIAL MEDIA AND POLITICS

1

POLITICS IN THE AGE OF HYBRID MEDIA

Power, Systems, and Media Logics

Andrew Chadwick, James Dennis, and Amy P. Smith

In a mass, (1) far fewer people express opinions than receive them; for the community of publics becomes an abstract collection of individuals who receive impressions from the mass media. (2) The communications that prevail are so organized that it is difficult or impossible for the individual to answer back immediately or with any effect. (3) The realization of opinion in action is controlled by authorities who organize and control the channels of such action. (4) The mass has no autonomy from institutions; on the contrary, agents of authorized institutions penetrate this mass, reducing any autonomy it may have in the formation of opinion by discussion. (C. Wright Mills, *The Power Elite*, 1956: pp. 303–4, quoted, approvingly, in the closing pages of Jürgen Habermas' *The Structural Transformation of the Public Sphere*, 1962, transl. 1989: p. 249)

Our opening quotation records a happy meeting of minds, just as the broadcast media era was getting into full flow, of two of the most influential social scientists of the last hundred years: C. Wright Mills and Jürgen Habermas. But this quotation inevitably begs a huge question that has been at the heart of the research on media and politics for two decades: to what extent is it an adequate account of how things work in the early 21st century? Political communication is journeying through a chaotic transition period induced by the rise of digital media. But how do we explain how power works amid the chaos? To what extent can the Western media systems of the present post-broadcast era be characterised as more inclusive and democratic than those so acutely analysed by Habermas and Mills?

Consider the following:

* Denver, Colorado, July 2008: Barack Obama's acceptance speech in front of 80,000 supporters at the Democratic National Convention at Denver Football Stadium is an event that symbolises the integration of television, physical space, and digital media—to spectacular effect.

- London, October 2011: British data from reputable polling organisation YouGov shows that some 55 per cent of the British public under the age of 55 years old use social media to engage in real-time commentary about television shows as they watch.
- Boston, April 2013: the confluence of television and social media shapes the reporting of the Boston bombings, as CNN television news reporters routinely check their Twitter feeds for leads, even while reporting on camera to their television audience.
- And, in necessarily undisclosed locations, June 2013: *The Guardian* conducts a live Web chat with fugitive U.S. National Security Agency (NSA) whistle-blower, Edward Snowden, as the 192-year-old news organisation flexes its professional investigative muscle while simultaneously engaging with online social media networks to give the NSA story powerful impact.

The argument of this chapter is that these and many other similar phenomena are episodes in the ongoing construction of a hybrid media system. We discuss how the hybrid media system approach sheds light on recent developments in three centrally important fields of political communication: news and journalism, election campaigning, and engagement and mobilisation. We briefly set out some key themes and empirical developments in these three areas. We then review a range of examples from the emerging body of research that draws upon the hybrid media system approach to make sense of today's increasingly dynamic and volatile political communication environment.

The Hybrid Media System Approach: Power, Systems, and Media Logics

As Carolyn Marvin (1988) has argued, 'old' and 'new' are relative terms. We can reinforce that point by using the terms 'older' and 'newer' media. This chapter argues that that there is a need to integrate the study of older and newer media in politics, and to develop holistic approaches that help us map where the distinctions between older and newer matter, and where those distinctions are dissolving. There is also a need to examine *renewed* media—older media that adapt and integrate the logics of newer media. This requires a systemic perspective, but one rooted in specific illustrations of forces *in flow*, and not abstract structural prejudgments and statistical snapshots. The key here is a conceptual understanding of power, but one that can be illustrated empirically.

The hybrid media system is built upon interactions among older and newer media logics—where logics are defined as bundles of technologies, genres, norms, behaviours, and organisational forms—in the reflexively connected social fields of media and politics. Actors in this system are articulated by complex and ever-evolving relationships based upon adaptation and interdependence and concentrations and diffusions of power. Actors create, tap, or steer information flows in ways that suit their goals and in ways that modify, enable, or disable others' agency, across and between a range of older and newer media settings (Chadwick 2013: 4).

We can study this systemic hybridity in flow—in information consumption and production patterns, in news making, in parties and election campaigns, in activism, and in government communication. A mix of methods can be used: conceptual work, historical analysis, documentary analysis, real-time 'live' online research, and insider ethnography.

The foundation of the approach is an ontology of hybridity. Across the social sciences, hybridity has long been an organising principle for a wide range of research: in political science (hybrid regimes), communication, cultural, and media studies (hybrid cultures and genres), organisation studies (hybrid organisational norms and structures), and science and technology studies (actor-network theory's hybrid networks of human and technological agents, or 'actants', as Bruno Latour, 2005, calls them). Understandably, scholarly research on media technologies has typically paid much attention to newness, even though newer media always exhibit substantial continuities with older media. Hybrid thinking rejects simple dichotomies, nudging us away from 'either/or' patterns of thought and toward 'not only, but also' patterns of thought. It emphasises how older media logics are renewed and ultimately evolve as they interact with newer media logics. It offers a powerful way of thinking about politics and society because it foregrounds complexity, interdependence, and transition. It draws attention to boundaries, to flux, to 'in-betweenness', and it concerns how practices intermesh and coevolve. This basic ontology informs three further theoretical pillars of the hybrid media system approach. First, power. Second, the idea of a system. And third, media logics.

The concepts of power and system have both been absolutely central to the social sciences, and it would take multiple volumes to even rehearse the debates, let alone critically interrogate them. But in basic terms, understanding power involves examining the relations between social actors. Less obviously, we also need to examine the relations between social actors and media technologies. By exploring exchanges among social actors, and how media are used in and come to shape those exchanges, we can get inside power relationships, empirically.

We can take this a stage further and say that these many and diverse interactions aggregate to constitute *systems*. Systems are often flexible and adaptable. They may exhibit hierarchy, fixity, and asymmetrical power relations, but they may also exhibit horizontality, fluidity, and symmetrical power relations. Following Brian McNair's (2006) recent work on media and cultural chaos, we can assume that systems have varying degrees of complexity, instability, and messiness. Systems often undergo long and chaotic periods of change.

A further point about systems is that they are based on competition and conflict, but there is also a great deal of interdependence among actors (Easton 1965; Keohane and Nye 1989). Even the most powerful must cooperate with those who are less powerful, in the pursuit of collective goals. And, as the pluralist tradition in political science has established, those who are powerful in one field may not be powerful across all fields (Dahl 1961). These aspects of systems sometimes give those who appear to have few obvious resources the power to act in ways that force adaptation among those who might have looked like they had greater resources before specific social interactions began. So, building upon what Manuel Castells' (2007, 2009) work has recently reminded us, power is relational and becomes a matter for detailed empirical investigation.

Systems are also based on divisions of labour that emerge among actors in the pursuit of goals, especially in important large-scale societal projects, like politics and media, because these projects cannot be undertaken without some embedded, regularised structures for managing cooperation over time (Grewal 2008). These structures might be formal bureaucratic organisations but increasingly they are not (Bennett and Segerberg 2013). Because digital media are both forms of communication *and* organisation, today the structures for cooperation in civic life may be relatively loose, *ad hoc*, and spontaneous; they are continually adapted according to the goals being pursued. In this sense, they may be understood as *assemblages*.

Assemblage theory, which originates in the social theory of Gilles Deleuze and Félix Guattari (2004), suggests that there are permeable boundaries between different modular units of a collective endeavour, and the meaning and force of any individual modular unit—whether it is a person, a group, a technology, a frame, even a building, and so on—can only be understood in terms of its interactive and interdependent relations with other modular units. The hybrid media system approach shows, for example, that political news making is now carried out in such assemblages, as digital technologies enable individuals and collectivities to plug themselves into the news making process, often in real time, and strategically, across and between older and newer media settings (Chadwick 2011a, 2011b).

Two final points about power and systems. First: the importance of time. Embedding norms through acting with regularity are important parts of exercising power in a system. But so, too, is acting with *timeliness*, which is something different. The mastery of temporal rhythms is an important but surprisingly underresearched force in political communication. Yet, the ability to create and act on information in a timely manner, especially in real time, is key to exercising power. Political and media actors try to master time: they often shock and surprise to get ahead of the game, or they deliberately delay, or drag information from the archives and give it new life. The important point is that this temporal power is now enabled and constrained in different ways by different media, as digital and broadcast media increasingly interact. The second point about power and systems concerns how systems must be enacted and continuously re-enacted, often with incremental changes, by social actors. And this process of enactment and re-enactment is also how power is exercised, as actors come to shape the very systemic conditions under which they may then exercise power over others.

Identifying how older and newer media shape politics also requires that we think about how media interact with the political field. A useful concept here is 'media logic'. First introduced in the late 1970s by sociologists David Altheide and Robert Snow (1979), this approach showed how the norms and practices of mass media have come to penetrate other areas of life. As Altheide and Snow memorably put it: "today all social institutions are media institutions" (1991: ix). More recently, Peter Dahlgren has provided a helpful definition of media logic as "the imperatives that shape the particular attributes and ways of doing things within given media . . . the procedures of selection, form, tempo, informational density, aesthetics, contents, modes of address, and production schedules" (Dahlgren 2009: 52).

The media logic approach suggests that we try to understand the norms that emerge in the daily practice of those in the fields of media and politics—the ongoing decisions about 'what goes where'. So it opens up useful avenues for in-depth qualitative work. However, the media logic approach also has some limitations. It was first developed in the era of mass communication, when mass broadcast media were more obviously dominant than they are today. It also assigned great power to formal media organisations and a singular media logic that was said to pervade social life. Today, the media environment is more polycentric. This calls for a more expansive idea of hybrid media *logics*, in the plural. With this, we can focus on how the norms that determine the character of mediation evolve across and between different media. The hybrid media system constantly requires judgements from actors about which medium or combination of media is most appropriate for shaping a political event or process. Over the last two decades, disruptive media logics have emerged from online networks, and these have created rival sources of authenticity and familiarity for audiences, many of whom themselves become hybrid producers and consumers of media content (Bruns 2008). Yet, these must also be set in the context of older elite media's ongoing prestige, access, expertise, influence, and, of course, their ability to adapt and integrate newer media logics.

Election Campaigning in the Hybrid Media System

No event in recent memory has fuelled as much commentary about digital media and politics as Barack Obama's famous 2008 presidential campaign. But the campaign's significance in building a new model for successful presidential campaigning lay not in its use of the Internet per se, but in how it so ruthlessly integrated online, broadcast, and real space, grassroots activism and elite control, and older and newer media logics. Obama for America displayed a keen and largely neglected awareness of the continuing power of older media in election campaigns, but this also integrated with its newer media strategy.

Consider just one statistic: the 2008 Obama campaign raised 750 million dollars, and 500 million of this was raised online. It spent 407 million dollars on advertising, but just 17 million dollars of this (4 per cent) was spent on online ads (Chadwick 2013: ch. 6).

In U.S. presidential campaigns more broadly, the real-space spectacles of candidate appearances continue to generate the important television coverage that remains crucial for projecting the power of a candidate and for conveying enthusiasm, authenticity, and common purpose to both activists and non-activists alike. Yet these television-fuelled moments now also integrate with newer media logics of data gathering, online fundraising, tracking, monitoring, and managed volunteerism (Kreiss 2012).

Campaign teams can no longer assume that they will reach audiences en masse. They now create content targeted at different audience segments, and they disseminate this content across different media. For example, the Obama campaign was the first to create 'press ads' solely for the campaign website and YouTube. This provided the campaign with a way to target different demographic groups online, including, most importantly, journalists themselves, but also bypass traditional media and their historical gatekeeping role.

Election campaigns are characterised by the growing systemic integration of the Internet and television. We saw this in the 2008 U.S. presidential campaign, for example, with the jointly hosted YouTube–CNN debates and the scandal around Obama's former pastor, Reverend Jeremiah Wright, and his online video sermons. Wright's controversial, racially charged videos that attacked sections of the white population in the United States actually started their mainstream life in an investigative report on ABC TV News, but they were remediated through YouTube. And then there was Obama's 'more perfect union' speech in response to the criticism focused on Jeremiah Wright. The speech was delivered for television, in a small room, but came to have network power through YouTube. Similarly, the pro-Obama 'Yes We Can' video was a viral sensation, but it is often forgotten that it was first broadcast on NBC television and, of course, had a well-connected celebrity cast of musicians and Hollywood actors (Chadwick 2013: ch. 7).

Online tools now also give a campaign team direct access to the public, through campaign websites and social media, and this fosters reciprocity and virality. Citizens can respond to campaigns through the same media formats, create and upload their own content, comment on debates as they are happening, or make candidates' debate or speech gaffes viral. Much of the campaign content discussed online is hybrid, initially beginning life on television or in the press and then travelling across online media through campaign promotion and/or citizen discussion. While election campaigns now exhibit plenty of content from speeches, interviews, debates, and advertisements that appears only online, most of the important campaign events are first mediated by television, before being remediated by online media. And at the same time, television news coverage now frequently displays viewer commentary that has been supplied via email, text message, Twitter, or webcam, as part of a digital montage approach to the representation of politics.

Campaigns can use hybrid strategies to both capture citizen input and mobilise citizens for the campaign, but citizens can also subvert campaign messages using digital media. The fact that the Internet has allowed campaigns to harvest massive amounts of behavioral and demographic data about supporters and other citizens gives campaign teams new sources of power. Campaigns' new media divisions are now much more tightly integrated with field operations and with the campaign war-room elite than has previously been the case. Online activity augments and encourages offline activity, and vice versa. Action taken online inspires supporters to take up more traditional forms of campaigning, such as donating or canvassing, but it also facilitates action in face-to-face settings, such as meet-ups and work on the 'ground war' of door knocking and organised phone canvassing in meeting rooms (Nielsen 2012).

At the same time, traditional elite newspaper organisations still play very important roles in election campaigns, even when they appear not to. We can see this in action in newspaper journalists' framing of the failed 2008 Republican vice presidential candidate Sarah Palin. While much commentary has focused on the reputational damage to Palin caused by the online viral circulation of satirical video footage from the *Saturday Night Live* comedian Tina Fey, in fact it was teams of investigative reporters at the *Washington Post* and the *New York Times* that were equally important in framing the Republican as allegedly not fit for public office (Becker et al. 2008; Dionne 2008). With their repeated front page investigative stories, painstakingly gathered from Palin's state of Alaska, the elite journalists gave Fey and the *Saturday Night Live* entertainers license to criticise. The hybrid media system can shape electoral outcomes by providing new power resources for campaigns that can both create and master the system's modalities—and severe penalties for those who cannot.

New Analyses

Scholars have started to apply the hybrid media system approach to the analysis of election campaigns across a range of countries. Here we briefly discuss examples of studies from Germany, Norway, and the United States.

In a study of the 2009 German federal election campaign, Andreas Jungherr begins from the hypothesis that "the volume of comments on Twitter should rise when the volume of traditional news media coverage of political actors rises" (Jungherr 2014: 242).

Through an analysis of the most retweeted messages during the day of the German televised election debates, he considers whether Twitter follows its own logic or the logic of broadcast coverage finds that the most popular retweets mentioning the debates reveal a hybrid logic of Twitter and broadcast media. In other words, Twitter emerges as a space for political discourse that integrates thematically with the broadcast event but also deviates from it in important respects (Jungherr 2014: 243–253).

In a similar vein, Eli Skogerbø and Arne Krumsvik (2015) examine what they term 'intermedial agenda setting' in the relationship between social media and traditional news producers in Norwegian election campaigns. Their analysis of the social media output of local party candidates finds that Facebook, Twitter, and YouTube are only rarely used by professional journalists as source material for campaign stories (Skogerbø and Krumsvik: 8). They also find that the larger Norwegian parties are adept at generating news stories in local and regional newspapers by creating a ready supply of local media events, such as visits by party leaders or well-known politicians with preestablished celebrity status and 'media capital'. Their conclusion is that in Norwegian campaigns, social media are increasingly used by politicians but journalists still mobilise older news logics associated with newspaper media.

The importance of celebrity in politics is also obvious in Geoffrey Baym's (2014) U.S.-based study exploring *The Rumble*—an online-only, crowdfunded, pay-per-view political debate staged during the 2012 U.S. presidential election campaign and featuring the two most well-known U.S. 'political-entertainment' celebrities of the last decade: Jon Stewart and Bill O'Reilly. Baym discusses the systemic hybridity of the debate, from the simultaneity of watching and commenting in real time in social media environments to the news stories which travelled across various media platforms during and after the event. Baym argues that, as the two main political-entertainment celebrities associated with conservatism and liberalism, O'Reilly and Stewart are "not simply surrogates for the candidates, but representatives of distinct politico-cultural identities" and that they exercise cultural and political power as a result (Baym 2014: 78). Baym's dissection of both the textual hybridity of the debate, and the hybrid role of its protagonists, shows how the hybrid media system creates new ways for elite broadcast media to shape how political discourse reaches and influences audiences that are increasingly fragmented and scattered across different media.

Baym's findings are complemented and extended by Deen Freelon and David Karpf's (2015) interpretation of Twitter discourse during the most significant of the televised U.S. presidential candidate debates of 2012, featuring Barack Obama and Republican challenger Mitt Romney. Freelon and Karpf show that some celebrities from the field of entertainment are able to use Twitter to intervene in real time during the debates in order to influence journalists' and citizens' interpretive frames. They achieve this by circulating their own interpretations of the event to large numbers of followers. Celebrities can become 'bridging elites': individuals without formal political or journalistic identities but whom nevertheless are able to be meaningful political actors through their strategic use of satire in social media (Freelon and Karpf 2015: 4).

Journalism and the Construction of News

The hybrid media system has significant implications for the construction of news. Three key points are discussed here: the blurring of boundaries between the roles, identities, and norms of news production that derive from older and newer media; changes to the organisational structures of news production; and changes to the workings of the news cycles that surround important and fast-moving political news.

Professional journalists increasingly integrate the logics of digital media into their daily practice. However, this process also works in the opposite direction: amateur journalists and bloggers increasingly integrate the logics of professional journalists. At the same time, some of the more successful bloggers have become semi-professionalised. They act as consultants to campaigns, interest groups, government agencies, and older media. The blog and other interactive Internet genres are no longer the radical departure they once were in the mid-2000s; they have been appropriated by all elite sectors of public communication in the advanced democracies, from politicians and agency officials to professional journalists to television and radio presenters. Moving in the direction of something like a model of a professional news organisation, there are (former) group blogs like the *Huffington Post*. Founded in 2005 by Arianna Huffington, a former columnist, California gubernatorial candidate, and wife of a U.S. congressman, the *Post* soon attracted venture capital funding and evolved into a hybrid of group blog and professional news organisation (for her prescient vision, see Huffington 2007). It combined articles from well-known public figures with commentary pieces by academics, and even investigative pieces. It enjoyed the low overheads that derive from online-only publication, not to mention an army of several hundred unpaid volunteer writers. By the time it was acquired by AOL in 2011 for 315 million dollars, the *Post*, with more monthly visitors than the *New York Times* website (Economist 2012), was a world away from the cliché of the plucky independent blog running on a shoestring budget.

As roles and identities have begun to modulate, so too have the organisational structures of news production. Some of the journalists interviewed by Chadwick (2013) pointed out that, online, media producers often move from gatekeeping to curatorial roles. Indeed, this description accurately reflects how many online journalists see themselves when gathering and sharing information, linking to sources through social media, and promoting their work across platforms. The business models of elite media organisations have evolved. *The Guardian*, for example, has successfully integrated social media content produced by its readers into its online presence but it also uses those same social media to project its own power (Chadwick and Collister 2014). Real-time social media also enable former print-only news organisations to release important news before their 20th-century arch rivals—broadcast journalists.

Finally, and most significantly, there have been important changes in the way breaking news is created—particularly fast-moving news of emergencies, political crises, and scandals. These episodes acutely reveal the hybrid nature of political news production. But to see it requires that we look beyond the organisational settings that have typically been portrayed as where news making happens. These are not news cycles as we might traditionally understand them, but are more accurately termed political information cycles (Chadwick 2011a, 2011b, 2013).

Political information cycles are complex assemblages in which the logics of newer online media are hybridized with those of older broadcast and print media. Power relations among actors in these assemblages affect the flows and meanings of news. They comprise multiple, loosely coupled individuals, groups, sites, and media technologies: instances of interaction involving diverse yet highly interdependent news creators that plug and unplug themselves from the news-making process, often in real time. Political information cycles involve greater numbers and a more diverse range of actors and interactions than news cycles as traditionally understood. They contain many non-elite participants, most of whom now interact exclusively online in order to advance or contest news frames in real-time exchanges but also during the subsequent stages of the cycle of news that follows a major event or the breaking of a story.

What makes this work is cross-media iteration and recursion. This loosens the grip of journalistic and political elites through the creation of fluid opportunity structures enabling timely intervention by online citizen activists. However, broadcasters and newspapers themselves increasingly integrate non-elite actions and information from the online realm into their own production practices and routines. They seek to outperform each other and the newer media actors in incessant, micro-level, power struggles. Much of this now takes place in public or semi-public online environments. And elite politicians and their staff are also able to participate directly in social media environments.

New Analyses

In their rich qualitative study of how online journalists view their professional identities, Sheetal Agarwal and Michael Barthel (2015) find that the new generations of U.S. digital news workers enshrine the established norms of traditional professional journalism in their daily practice. At the same time, however, newer norms, adapted from the practices of blogging, have emerged. These emphasise the importance of 'transparency, individualism, and risk taking' and are becoming core features of a new, post-digital culture of journalistic practice. Similarly, Mike Ananny and Kate Crawford's (2015) study of news app design finds evidence for the emergence of a 'liminal press': groups of workers whose daily practice oscillates in a space between journalism and technologist roles, 'embedded within logics of software design, algorithmic personalisation, and dot-com entrepreneurship.' Matters are further complicated if we integrate the important curatorial work of non-elites into our understanding of news, as Kjerstin Thorson convincingly argues (Thorson, forthcoming).

Ulrike Klinger and Jakob Svensson (2014) apply the hybrid media system approach as part of their reconceptualization of news production norms and practices. Focusing on three practices—production, distribution, and use—they argue that social media are now implicated in all three areas, but mass media logic prevails, not least because so much social media content is a response to broadcast media content (Klinger and Svensson 2014: 12). They argue that social media come to play a greater role in the *distribution* of news and in audience consumption patterns than in the everyday *production* of news content.

Similarly, as part of their cross-country comparative study of news, Rasmus Kleis Nielsen and Kim Christian Schrøder (2014) look for survey evidence of the political information cycle, based on the hypothesis that "ordinary people can use social media and other new Internet tools to actively engage in commenting on, sharing, and producing news in a more interactive and decentered environment" (Nielsen and Schrøder 2014: 474). They find that television remains the most significant source for news, even in countries with the highest Internet penetration and even among those who use social media most frequently.

Engagement and Mobilisation

The hybrid media system features conditions that empower or disempower, depending on the context. In the organisational field of politics, the interplay of older and newer media logics has created new repertoires of engagement that change established orthodoxies about what counts as political participation. Empirical analysis of how hybrid media logics are used in engagement and mobilisation allows us to identify and explain the circumstances in which power is successfully enacted or contested. Digital media may be used to reinforce or subvert other mediated and face-to-face modes of engagement.

New hybrid mobilisation movements like 38 Degrees, Avaaz, MoveOn, and GetUp! cannily switch between older and newer media logics in their attempts to mobilise supporters and influence policy (Chadwick 2013: ch. 8). They use a division of labour between older and newer media to structure the 'actions' that serve as their organisational basis, but as David Karpf has argued in the U.S. context, this is not "organizing without organizations" but "organizing *with different* organizations" (Karpf 2012: 3). The leaderships of these movements engage in constant monitoring of the views of their members through a variety of sophisticated digital tools. They use the knowledge gained from these processes to prepare for the launch of campaigns when an issue is prominent in broadcast and newspaper media. These movements are also obliged to react extraordinarily quickly to issues that rise to prominence in the 'mainstream'. Responsiveness produces and reproduces identity and solidarity because it meets expectations of authenticity and connectedness that are embedded as cultural values among activists online. Still, the actions that hybrid mobilisation movement leaderships ask their networks of supporters to perform, such as donating money for ads in newspapers and commissioning opinion polls, are often far from online activism. Indeed, they capitalize on an acceptance of broadcast and newspaper media's enduring roles. These new democratic forms of politics are carved out of the hybrid interstitial spaces between older and newer media, and the historical protest repertoires of embodied interactions.

New Analyses

The hybrid media system approach to engagement and mobilisation has been applied in a range of contexts. For example, James Sloam (2014) explores the role of digital media across two European protest movements: the Spanish *indignados* (outraged) or M15M movement in Spain, and the *Geração à Rasca* (desperate generation) or M12M movement in Portugal, as well as two atypical hybrid movement parties: Beppe Grillo's 5SM in Italy and the German Pirate Party (*Piratenpartei*). Linking these four case studies is the use of digital networks as a core structural foundation and the rejection of ideological unity in favour of issue-based platforms (Sloam 2014: 220). As a rebuttal to those who claim that there is widespread youth disillusionment with politics, Sloam argues that an alternative civic culture is emerging among the relatively affluent and well-educated youth in these countries. Young people are engaging with politics by mobilising around issues and causes that have relevance to their own lives and in ways that display a savvy awareness of the strengths and vulnerabilities of both broadcast *and* digital media, but also of embodied protest.

Sloam uses the hybrid media system approach in two ways. First, he shows that the semi-spontaneous real-space 'occupation' protests are enabled by the organisational capacities embedded in social media. Second, he explains how hybridity offers opportunities for activist groups to shape and disrupt information flows that were traditionally controlled by broadcast media—though the influence of this strategy differs according to the intensity of systemic hybridity in each country. Activists can challenge established actors within these new environments, because, in stark contrast with the broadcast era, parties, professional media elites, and citizen activists now compete with each other within the same variegated but increasingly integrated hybrid system. In order to compete with resourceful elite actors, citizen activists innovate by amalgamating and switching media logics, using online petitions, Facebook 'like' buttons, viral 'selfie' images, and video to interrupt the flow of professionalised communication and, occasionally, position ordinary citizens' voices at the centre of policy debates (Chadwick and Dennis 2014; Dennis 2015).

A growing number of empirical studies have focused on hybrid-mediated forms of political engagement that could not have existed before the integration of digital and broadcast media (Dennis 2014). A good example is the increasingly popular practice of dual screening: using an Internet-connected device such as a laptop, tablet, or smartphone to access social media and find out about and discuss live, televised events. Over the last five years, dual screening has become popular across a wide range of television genres, but it is most significant during what Daniel Dayan and Elihu Katz (1992) termed 'media events': live broadcasts of culturally resonant, ritualistic, defining moments in the evolution of a national or transnational community.

In the UK context, dual screening of political media events can be traced to 2009, when Nick Griffin, the leader of the far-right British National Party (BNP) made an unprecedented appearance on the BBC's political discussion show, *Question Time*. Dual screening using the Twitter hashtag #bbcqt had emerged organically in the months leading up to Griffin's appearance. As Nick Anstead and Ben O'Loughlin show, it reached a new intensity during the live broadcast itself. Twitter users contributed to a parallel discussion that both meshed with *and* deviated from the thematic content of the television broadcast (Anstead and O'Loughlin 2010, 2011). The importance of dual screening was quickly recognised by media and political organisations, some of whom developed strategies to engage supporters and publics in commenting during the 2010 UK general election campaign (Chadwick 2013: ch. 9).

The 2010 UK general election revealed the public's appetite for important political television (Coleman 2011) and this was also the first in which large numbers of people dual screened. Twitter emerged as particularly important (Chadwick 2011a: 77; O'Loughlin 2010). Moreover, there was close temporal integration between the broadcast media event and social media discussion. Research led by Ben O'Loughlin unearthed three main findings. First, there were identifiable communities of Twitter discourse around the thematic rhythms of a political broadcast media event. Second, members of the public used social media to explain quite technical points about opinion polling and policy to those with less knowledge than themselves. Third, citizen activists valued intervening in real time to shape narrative frames that they wanted journalists to use to mediate the event and fellow citizens to adopt when learning about the campaign and formulating their opinions (O'Loughlin 2010). In political communication terms, this resonates with the recent revival of Katz and Lazarsfeld's classic two-step flow model of communication, as social media may often enable the informal propagation of politically-useful information from what Katz and Lazarsfeld termed 'opinion leaders' to less motivated and informed citizens (Chadwick 2009, 2012; Norris and Curtice 2008).

In a similar vein, Anders Olof Larsson and Hallvard Moe (2012) found that political tweeting increases substantially around televised political media events, while Larsson's (2013) study of Twitter interaction around a Swedish talk show revealed the relative significance of journalists' tweets in the structural networks forged by political tweeters. Fabio Giglietto and Donatella Silva's (2014) analysis of a large dataset of tweets related to Italian television political talk shows reveals the relationships between the different subgenres in the television text and the levels and styles of Twitter engagement among dual screeners. Yu-Ru Lin and colleagues' (2014) study of an even larger (290 million tweet) dataset collected during the 2012 U.S. presidential campaign found that big political media events seemed to have an identifiable impact on the routine communicative structure of Twitter. The unusual conditions of 'shared attention' created by these events were associated with reduced levels of interpersonal communication on Twitter. Individuals tended to switch their attention to replying to, and retweeting, elite Twitter users with large followings. Finally, Gil de Zúñiga and colleagues (2014) explore dual screening largely as a dependent variable explained by demographics, motivations, and individuals' other media usage patterns. People tend to dual screen to seek further information and engage in discussion about the news. Dual screening is a positive predictor of online political participation after controlling for demographic factors and a number of other previously demonstrated correlates of online political participation, such as discussion network size, trust in media, partisanship strength, and news consumption. In this account, dual screening emerges as an important step on the mediated pathway to political engagement.

This draws attention to a key point: the hybrid media system does not always imply a more inclusive form of democracy. Hybridity presents opportunities for non-elites to exert power, but media and political elites can, and do, adapt to these new environments. Traditional elites, such as political parties, advocacy groups, and broadcast media, often attempt to reinforce their position by boundary drawing, sealing off aspects of their mediated practices from outside influences. However, as media systems become more hybrid, the power of elite organisational actors has generally weakened.

A good example of these processes at work can be found in Matthew Powers' (2014) account of the role of humanitarian nongovernmental organisations (NGOs) in producing news content for global news media. Drawing upon in-depth interviews with NGO professionals, Powers (2014: 96) argues that media hybridity can empower NGOs by offering an interconnected environment in which messages can cross-fertilise and become unavoidable for even very large audiences (Powers 2014: 102). However, directing information flows across and between newer and older media platforms can prove difficult. The intermeshing of diverse audiences and information flows in digital media networks may result in NGOs losing the power to shape their messages. A notorious example is the Invisible Children's *Kony2012* campaign video aimed at publicising the war crimes of Ugandan rebel leader Joseph Kony. After clocking up more than 100 million views in just six days on YouTube, the video suffered widespread criticism from NGO leaders for what they perceived as Invisible Children's factual omissions and simplistic solutions. Powers (2014: 103) argues that this was the result of the *Kony 2012* video reaching an audience far beyond young college students in the United States, the intended target group. Powers' study shows that the successful management of a campaign message depends on an actor's ability to shape communication flows across different media and at different points.

Conclusion

Participation does not equate to power. Disruptive power is not equally distributed. Those who have the resources and expertise to intervene in the hybrid flows of political information are more able to be powerful. As the process of hybridisation develops and adapts in unpredictable ways, the agency of elites and non-elites remains in flux. There is a need to focus on the specific conditions under which hybridity empowers or disempowers.

Yet we *can* draw some conclusions about the hybrid media system. Debates about the political value of digital media have often been framed in terms of dichotomies: either they will cure the democratic malaise by empowering ordinary citizens or they will usher in a dystopian future by empowering political elites; either digital media are entirely displacing older media or they are entirely negated and absorbed by older media. Such dichotomies are unhelpful if we want to explain the significance of the great changes that are occurring in the field of political communication. The big story of our tumultuous times is not the simple displacement of older media by newer media in politics, but the interaction, adaptation, and coevolution of older and newer media logics.

Today, we might ask whether the average citizen interested in influencing politics should join a party campaign or use their social media accounts to start plugging into news making assemblages where they can try to influence journalists, political elites, and other citizens. Hundreds of millions worldwide seems to have already made their choice to do so. Then again, this, too, is missing an important part of the picture, because even what seem on the surface to be 'pure' newer media activist networks do not in fact rely on newer media: they *combine* older and newer media in effective new ways.

It is primarily activists and the politically interested who are making a difference with inventive combinations of media. Overall, though, political communication is now more polycentric than during the period of mass communication that dominated the 20th century. The opportunities for citizens to *use* and *inhabit* media as a means of influencing the form and content of public discourse are, on balance, greater than they were during the duopoly of mass broadcasting and newspapers. Many of the shifts in political life that have occurred since the mid-20th century were based upon an acceptance of the power of this duopoly. This hardened into an increasing self-confidence and self-awareness among political and media actors that these media, particularly television, were self-evidently important. But the duopoly's power is being partly reshaped, and partly undermined.

With caveats on board, we now have arrangements for the conduct of politics that are, on balance, more expansive, inclusive, and democratic than at any time in the past 60 years. So, we return to where we began this chapter—Jürgen Habermas approvingly quoting C. Wright Mills on the nature of mass media and the public sphere. Our conclusion is that, today, things only *partly* work like that.

References

Agarwal, S. D. and Barthel, M. L. (2015) "The friendly barbarians: Professional norms and work routines of online journalists in the United States," *Journalism* 16(3), pp. 376–391.

Altheide, D. L. and Snow, R. P. (1979) *Media logic*, London: Sage.

—— (1991) *Media worlds in the postjournalism era*, New York: Aldine de Gruyter.

Ananny, M. and Crawford, K. (2015) "A liminal press," *Digital Journalism*, 3(2), pp. 192–208.

Anstead, N. and O'Loughlin, B. (2010) *The emerging viewertariat: Explaining Twitter responses to Nick Griffin's appearance in BBC Question Time* (PSI Working Paper Series), Norwich: University of East Anglia. Available from www.uea.ac.uk/polopoly_fs/1.147340!Anstead_OLoughlin_BBCQT_Twitter_Final.pdf.

—— (2011) "The emerging viewertariat and BBC Question Time: Television debate and real-time commenting online." *The International Journal of Press/Politics*, 16(4), pp. 440–462.

Baym, G. (2014) "Stewart, O'Reilly, and The Rumble 2012: Alternative political debate in the age of hybridity," *Popular Communication: The International Journal of Media and Culture*, 12(2), pp. 75–88.

Becker, J., Goodman, P. S. and Powell, M. (2008) "Once elected, Palin hired friends and lashed Foes," *New York Times Website*, September 13. Available from www.nytimes.com/2008/09/14/us/politics/14palin.html?pagewanted=all.

Bennett, W. L. and Segerberg, A. (2013) *The logic of connective action: Digital media and the personalization of contentious politics*, New York: Cambridge University Press.

Bruns, A. (2008) *Blogs, Wikipedia, Second Life, and beyond: From production to produsage*, New York: Peter Lang.

Castells, M. (2007) "Communication, power and counter-power in the network society," *International Journal of Communication*, 1, pp. 238–266.

—— (2009). *Communication power*, Oxford: Oxford University Press.

Chadwick, A. (2009) "Web 2.0: New challenges for the study of e-democracy in an era of informational exuberance," *I/S: Journal of Law and Policy for the Information Society*, 5(1), pp. 9–41.

—— (2011a) "Britain's first live televised party leaders' debate: From the news cycle to the political information cycle," *Parliamentary Affairs*, 64(1), pp. 24–44.

—— (2011b) "The political information cycle in a hybrid news system: The British prime minister and the "Bullygate" affair," *The International Journal of Press/Politics*, 16(1), pp. 3–29.

—— (2012) Recent shifts in the relationship between the Internet and democratic engagement in Britain and the United States: Granularity, informational exuberance, and political learning, in E. Anduiza, M. Jensen and L. Jorba (eds.), *Digital media and political engagement worldwide: A comparative study*, Cambridge: Cambridge University Press, pp. 39–55.

—— (2013) *The hybrid media system: Politics and power*, Oxford: Oxford University Press.

Chadwick, A. and Collister, S. (2014) "Boundary-drawing power and the renewal of professional news organizations: the case of the *Guardian* and the Edward Snowden NSA leak." *International Journal of Communication*, 8, pp. 2420–2441.

Chadwick, A. and Dennis, J. (2014) *"People. Power. Change.": 38 Degrees and democratic engagement in the hybrid media system.* Paper presented to the American Political Science Association Annual Meeting, Washington, DC, August 27–31.

Coleman, S. (ed.) (2011) *Leaders in the living room: The prime ministerial debates of 2010: Evidence, evaluation and some recommendations*, Oxford: Reuters Institute for the Study of Journalism.

Dahl, R. (1961) *Who governs? Democracy and power in an American city*, London: Yale University Press.

Dahlgren, P. (2009) *Media and political engagement: Citizens, communication, and democracy*, New York: Cambridge University Press.

Dayan, D. and Katz, E. (1992) *Media events: The live broadcasting of history*, Cambridge, MA: Harvard University Press.

Deleuze, G. and Guattari, F. (2004) *A thousand plateaus: Capitalism and schizophrenia* (B. Massumi, Trans. New ed.), London: Continuum.

Easton, D. (1965) *A systems analysis of political life*, London: University of Chicago Press.

Dennis, J. (2014) *All hail the keyboard radical? A new research agenda for political participation and social media.* Paper presented to the Political Studies Association Annual Conference, Manchester, April 14–16.

—— (2015) "38 Degrees," in E. Gordon and P. Mihailidis (eds.), *Civic media project*, Cambridge, MA: MIT Press.

Dionne E. J., Jr. (2008) "Pulling the curtain on Palin," *Washington Post Website*, September 9. Available from www.washingtonpost.com/wp-dyn/content/article/2008/09/08/AR2008090801907.html.

Economist. (2012) "Online newspapers: News of the world," *The Economist Website*, March 17. Available from www.economist.com/node/21550262.

Freelon, D. and Karpf, D. (2015) "Of big birds and bayonets: Hybrid Twitter interactivity in the 2012 presidential debates," *Information, Communication & Society*, 18(4), pp. 390–406.

Giglietto, F. and Silva, D. (2014) Second screen and participation: A content analysis on a full season dataset of tweets," *Journal of Communication*, 64(2), pp. 260–277.

Gil de Zúñiga, H., McGregor, S. and García, V. (2014) *Social TV and democracy: How Second Screening during news relates to political participation*. Paper presented to the Association for Education in Journalism and Mass Communication Annual Conference, Montreal, Canada, August 6–9.

Grewal, D. S. (2008) *Network power: The social dynamics of globalization*, New Haven, CT: Yale University Press.

Habermas, J. (1989) *The structural transformation of the public sphere*, Cambridge, MA: MIT Press.

Huffington, A. (2007) News 2.0: The hybrid future is kicking down the door," *Huffington Post Website*, March 28. Available from www.huffingtonpost.com/arianna-huffington/news-20-the-hybrid-future_b_44401.html.

Jungherr, A. (2014) "The Logic of Political Coverage on Twitter: Temporal dynamics and content," *Journal of Communication*, 64, pp. 239–254.

Karpf, D. (2012) *The MoveOn effect: The unexpected transformation of American political advocacy*, New York: Oxford University Press.

Keohane, R. and Nye, J. (1989) *Power and interdependence: World politics in transition* (Second ed.), London: Scott, Foresman.

Klinger, U. and Svensson, J. (2014) "The emergence of network media logic in political communication: A theoretical approach," *New Media and Society*, Advance online publication, doi: 10.1177/1461444814522952.

Kreiss, D. (2012) *Taking our country back: The crafting of networked politics from Howard Dean to Barack Obama*, Oxford: Oxford University Press.

Larsson, A. O. (2013) "Tweeting the viewer—use of Twitter in a talk show context," *Journal of Broadcasting and Electronic Media*, 57(2), pp. 135–152.

Larsson, A. O. and Moe, H. (2012) "Studying political microblogging: Twitter users in the 2010 Swedish election campaign." *New Media and Society* 14(5): pp. 729–747.

Latour, B. (2005) *Reassembling the social: An introduction to actor network theory*, Oxford: Oxford University Press.

Lin, Y-R, Keegan, B., Margolin, D. and Lazer, D. (2014) "Rising tides or rising stars?: Dynamics of shared attention on Twitter during media events," *PLoS ONE* 9(5). Available from www.plosone.org/article/info%3Adoi%2F10.1371%2Fjournal.pone.0094093.

Marvin, C. (1988) *When old technologies were new*, New York: Oxford University Press.

McNair, B. (2006) *Cultural chaos: Journalism, news and power in a globalized world*, London: Routledge.

Nielsen, R. K. (2012) *Ground wars: Personalized communication in political campaigns*, Princeton, NJ: Princeton University Press.

Nielsen, R. K. and Schrøder, K. C. (2014) "The relative importance of social media for accessing, finding, and engaging with news," *Digital Journalism*, 2(4), pp. 472–489.

Norris, P. and Curtice, J. (2008) "Getting the message out: A two-step model of the role of the Internet in campaign communication flows during the 2005 British general election," *Journal of Information Technology and Politics*, 4(4), pp. 3–13.

O'Loughlin, B. (2010) "TV debate: Initial Twitter analysis shows level of support for party leaders and winners by topic," *New Political Communication Unit Website*, April 20. Available from http://newpolcom.rhul.ac.uk/npcu-blog/2010/4/20/tv-debate-initial-twitter-analysis-shows-level-of-support-fo.html.

Powers, M. (2014) "The structural organization of NGO publicity work: Explaining divergent public-ity strategies at humanitarian and human rights organizations," *International Journal of Communication*, 8, pp. 90–107.

Skogerbø, E. and Krumsvik, A. H. (2015) "Newspapers, Facebook and Twitter," *Journalism Practice* 9(3), pp. 350–366.

Sloam, J. (2014) "The "outraged young": Young Europeans, civic engagement and the new media in a time of crisis," *Information, Communication and Society*, 17(2), pp. 217–231.

Thorson, K. (Forthcoming) "Curated flows: A framework for mapping media exposure in the digital age," *Communication Theory*.

2

NETWORK MEDIA LOGIC

Some Conceptual Considerations

Ulrike Klinger and Jakob Svensson[1]

Introduction

Researchers have long been interested in the interplay between media and politics. Depictions of journalists as watchdogs and of the media as a fourth estate illustrate the strong links between media and democracy.[2] Ideas on media logics even question whether it is possible to regard the two as different domains (Street 1997). Indeed, politics has always dealt with communication, even to the extent that it has been argued that politics *is* communication (Esser 2013). Many studies have discussed how politics and political actors adapt to the rules and formats of news media. For example, Kepplinger (2002) concluded that, while the quantity of information-related activities in the German Parliament increased sharply following the rise of modern mass media, the quantity of decision-making activities remained fairly constant. Studies have also shown that politicians have adapted to the dramatisation style used in media discourses, the increasing prominence of short sound bites, and the visual and entertainment formats used to obtain media coverage (Altheide 2004). In his study on personalisation and polarisation, Asp (1986) demonstrated that politicians phrase their statements so that they have a better chance of media coverage. Indeed, researchers have used the media logic concept as an analytical tool to discuss the interdependence between media and other social institutions. Nowadays it is argued that politicians express themselves in short "tweetable" phrases, such as former Swedish Minister of Finance Anders Borg's comment on the 'wolf pack behaviour on the market' which went viral instantly. This is even acknowledged by mass media outlets, for example, in CNN's statement that right-wing U.S. politician Sarah Palin "represented a brand of conservative politics that was Twitterable [*sic*]" (Granderson 2011: para. 3).

This leads us to the changing landscapes of media and communication. The rise, increasing use and perceived importance of social media has sparked an impressive amount of research in the area of political communication (Jungherr 2014; Larsson & Svensson 2014). Social media is, however, a contested term because it implies that traditional media do not encompass a social dimension. Discussions of social media often refer to online communication platforms, in which the *social* aspect seems to refer to users' ability to influence and *interact* with the content and each other in one way or another. While an elaboration on the definitions of social media (for this, see, e.g. O'Reilly 2005; Ellison & boyd 2007) is beyond the scope of this chapter, we find it important to underline the interactive and networking affordances of social media platforms without downplaying their broadcasting possibilities. Early studies highlighted their interactive, participatory potential to provide many-to-many communication, but more recent empirical studies have largely found that political actors and political organisations tend to 'under-exploit' (Cardenal 2011) this potential and to largely use social media platforms for conventional broadcasting, that is, as one-way information channels (Jungherr 2014; Vergeer & Hermans 2013; Enli & Skogerbø 2013: 770; Grant et al. 2010: 587; Graham et al. 2013; Klinger 2013). Broadcasting thus continues to be central to political social media practices, especially with regard to how some politicians spread messages on platforms like Twitter (see Svensson 2011). In this chapter, we use the term *social media platforms* to refer to online loci in which users can contribute, inform, be informed, and network with others (such as blogs, YouTube, Facebook, and Twitter).

The recent focus on social media platforms within the field of political communication indicates a belief that something is changing when bringing politics to this online realm. However, more deterministic analyses (either conceiving of social media as bringing about positive effects for democracy, or that offline power structures are merely mirrored online) have not fully succeeded in accounting for how political communication changes on social media platforms. Therefore we return to theories of media logics. By conceiving of social media platforms as loci of different media logic, we may move beyond framings of social media platforms as inherently good or bad, while simultaneously avoiding resorting to an argument that they are neutral. We subsequently return to our concept of network media logic (see Klinger & Svensson 2015 for an in-depth definition), comparing it to other approaches to logics within the fields of mass media and politics. But before discussing network media logic we will first provide an overview over discussions of media logic and political logic.

Media Logic and Political Logic

Departing from an understanding of media as a social force in society, Altheide and Snow's (1979) original account sought to understand the role of media as constituting and recognising social reality. According to them, "media logic functions as a form through which events and ideas are interpreted and acted upon" (p. 240). The authors further refer to *formats* as ways to select and organise material, the style of presentation, the focus, emphasis, and the "grammar of media communication" (p. 10). According to Strömbäck and Esser (2014: 381), logic should be understood as appropriate behaviour that is consistent and reasonable within the rules and norms of the institutional context. Many scholars understand logic as *specific rules* that govern a domain. For example, in journalism, logic determines how news is selected, interpreted, and constructed (Esser 2013: 160; Lundby 2014: 28). If, say, conflict has important news value when journalists produce news content, then clearly outlining an enemy becomes part of the rules of the game for a politician who is seeking visibility in news media.

News about politics often results from a co-production between news media and political actors who try to influence the media (Strömbäck & Esser 2014: 392). In other words, it is the tension and interaction between media and other institutions with their different logics that drive social and cultural change (Lundby 2014: 27). Hence, we are not only looking at a one-way relationship in which politicians and political organisations succumb to the rules of the media. Political institutions are strategic organisations that seek to get their messages out in order to influence people to vote for their candidates in election campaigns or to reach other strategic goals. Media out-lets thus expand the action repertoires of politicians and political organisations (Esser 2013: 156).

The concept of media logic has been contested. Couldry (2008), for example, criti-cised what he claimed to be a tendency to identify a "single type of media-based logic that supersedes older logics" (p. 378) and that social transformations were "too het-erogeneous to be reduced to a single media logic" (Couldry 2008). Similarly, Krotz (2009: 26) argued that media logic was a misleading concept, because it does not exist independently of sociocultural contexts or history. Moreover, Lundby (2009: 104–110) criticised media logic for its singularity, its linearity, being fixed to rules and formats rather than to processes and forms of social interactions. We agree that different logics, both in the media and in the political realm, coexist and may have different weight depending on the situation, actors, and other circumstances, and that they are not fixed. In other words, we cannot discuss network media logic without accounting for logics of politics and political organisations if aiming to understand the interplay between them.

Another contestation of diverging media logics in traditional mass media and social media platforms is the argument that contemporary media systems have transformed into hybrid phenomena that include online and offline tools and channels. This notion, while based on Chadwick's (2013) suggestion to overcome the dichotomy of online versus offline media, often misunderstands Chadwick's concept. Understanding media systems as *hybrid* does not dissolve the different norms and processes—the rules of the game—between traditional mass media (which can also be found online, e.g. on news-paper portals) and social media platforms. Chadwick himself acknowledges and dis-cusses media logics as central aspects of this concept in the introduction to *The Hybrid Media System*: "How political and media actors shape and are shaped by older and newer media logics, and the extent to which they mobilize, traverse, and integrate these logics to exercise power, is what this book is about" (Chadwick 2013: 22). In fact, the idea of hybridity relies on at least two definable components that either converge into a hybrid form (such as a *melting pot*) or constitute the poles between gradually diverging hybrid forms. An example is *hybrid regimes* in democratisation studies, that is, political systems that are neither democracies nor dictatorships, but something in between, containing elements of both to different degrees (e.g. Diamond 2002). Similar to components of *democracy* and *dictatorship* in this example, we can only define hybrid forms of media if we can distinguish between the ideal types of mass media and network media even though they often overlap in the real world.

While media and communication scholars have elaborated on media logic, the con-cept of political logic has remained rather vague and multi-faceted. Political logic has been claimed and described in various contexts: Bawn (1993) explored the logic of gov-ernment coalitions and their relationship with ideology, while Day (2004) used the term to trace what holds new social movements together. He argued that recent movements, such as the anti-globalisation movement, have adopted a *logic of affinity*, replacing the social movement *logic of hegemony* that was still prevalent in the 1960s and 1970s:

> The goal is not to create a new power around a hegemonic centre, but to chal-lenge, disrupt and disorient the processes of global hegemony, to refuse, rather than rearticulate those forces that are tending towards the universalization of the liberal-capitalist ecumene. (Day 2004: 730)

Other authors have connected political logic with phenomena as diverse as labour market reforms (Larsen 2008), political violence (Besley & Persson 2011), or the political survival of leaders (de Mesquita et al. 2005). The latter phenomenon claims that maintaining their *winning coalition* is the central political logic behind the old question why corrupt leaders remain in office. Moreover, political logic is not only said to be at odds with media logic, but also with economic logic (e.g. McKay 2005; Pempel 2006).

None of the cases mentioned above refer to political logic as a methodological approach of applying formal logic, as, for instance, Zinnes (2004) does when describing the construction of political logic in the *democratic peace puzzle*: that is, his explanation of why democratic states wage war against non-democracies, but not against each other. Resonating with our understanding of logic as the 'rules of the game', logic is used as a metaphor for the internal workings of politics, as well as the inherent norms, rules, and processes that guide political behaviour. This is similar to what Breiner (1995) describes as *a logic of modernity* in Max Weber's works:

> A logic in which different spheres of life conduct—the economic, the ethical, the scientific, the artistic, the political—represent different and competing values to which we might commit ourselves and demand a variety of conflicting logics of action. (Breiner 1995:41)

Despite such varying accounts of political logic, it has remained unclear how political logic and media logic intersect and/or collide. After all, media societies (Jarren & Donges 2006) manifest themselves in different political systems; and those political systems remain quite stable despite the increased importance and changing landscapes of the media: Electoral systems, party systems, majoritarian versus consociational settings, and one or two-chamber parliaments set the structural context in which political actors develop strategies and in which political logics emerge.

To close this gap, Esser (2013) differentiates between media logic and political logic by referring to the three well-established political dimensions—policy, politics, and polity—underlining the difference between the *production of politics* (making binding decisions) and the *self-presentation of politics* (see also Strömbäck & Esser 2014: 383). Policy logic concerns the production side of politics, such as policy-making and policy implementation. As policy logic is confined to the (backstage) negotiation of policies, it is often not in the centre of the media strategy of politicians and political institutions. Political logic, on the contrary, concerns the presentational side of politics and concerns gaining and remaining in power. Evidently, politicians and political institutions depend more on favourable media coverage and thus have to adapt to the rules of the media to a larger extent, especially during election campaigns (Strömbäck & Esser 2014: 394). Polity logic concerns the institutional side of politics. Here, media are more prone to adapt their coverage to the logic of the political system, since the formal structures, such as the constitution, are likely to remain unchanged regardless of changes in the media landscape. In Sweden, for example, a political party needs 4 per cent of the vote to gain seats in Parliament. This threshold influences how mass media cover elections. Switzerland is another case. From 1959 to 2003, the Swiss Parliament elected the government (*Bundesrat*) according to the principles of consociational democracy: The three strongest parties in parliament could staff two positions, while the fourth strongest staffs one position. In the UK, by contrast, the winner takes all in a constituency, usually resulting in single-party governments. Hence, even among liberal democracies, political systems vary considerably—this in turn influences how media cover elections and day-to-day political processes.

Therefore, the argument we wish to put forward here is that media logic and political logic coexist and inform each other. Altheide and Snow (1979) also clearly stated that media logic should not be understood as "media dictating terms to the rest of society, but [as] an interaction between organized institutional behavior and media" (Altheide and Snow 1979: 15). Having accounted for different logics within the media and politics, we now elaborate on the concept of network media logic, which only recently emerged from social media platforms.

Network Media Logic Reconsidered

In a prior article (Klinger & Svensson 2015) we discussed how social media platforms differ from mass media, and outlined the emergence of network media logic. In this chapter, we provide a condensed, general and non-platform-specific version of this discussion. In previous work, we departed from a delineation of how production, distribution, and media use on social media platforms differ from those of traditional mass media. We know that production, distribution, and media use are not easy to separate, especially on social media platforms. However, for analytical purposes, we continue to distinguish between these processes when comparing network media to mass media logic. In this section, we further develop the concept of network media logic by connecting it to three aspects of news mass media logic: (1) ideals, (2) commercial imperatives, and (3) technology (Esser 2013). Ideals, in our argument, refer to common perceptions about how content should be produced, distributed and how media should be used—as an ideal type and with regard to public communication. *Commercial imperatives* mean the economic contexts and opportunity structures within which media content is produced, distributed and within which media is used. *Technology* refers to the specific affordances that influence how media content is produced, distributed, and how people make use of media.

Esser (2013) and Strömbäck & Esser (2014: 382) argued that professional ideals (1) in news production follow journalistic norms and criteria, that is, news values. As independent and supposedly autonomous professionals, journalists are governed by certain ideals as a distinct set of norms and values. What becomes interesting to discuss here is how such ideals differ on social media platforms compared to mass media. Can we discern distinct *ideals*—in terms of not only how political news is produced but also how it is distributed and used online?

Most mass media are also set in commercial contexts (2) that influence the ways in which information is produced, distributed, and used. Media platforms have to compete for attention, subscriptions, and advertising while keeping the costs of production and dissemination low in order to generate profits. Historically, the commercial pressures of mass media corporations have often been seen as being in opposition to professional ideals. With the rise of neo-liberalism, the commercial imperatives have become even more salient, which has given political news a distinct flavour of entertainment, speculation, and personalisation (Esser 2013:171). This raises the question of what kinds of *commercial imperatives* can be discerned on social media platforms.

Moreover, technology (3) shapes the processes of producing, finding, and reproducing news. The medium is the message, as McLuhan (1964) famously argued—or in the words of Hjarvard (2013), each media technology has inherent characteristics that

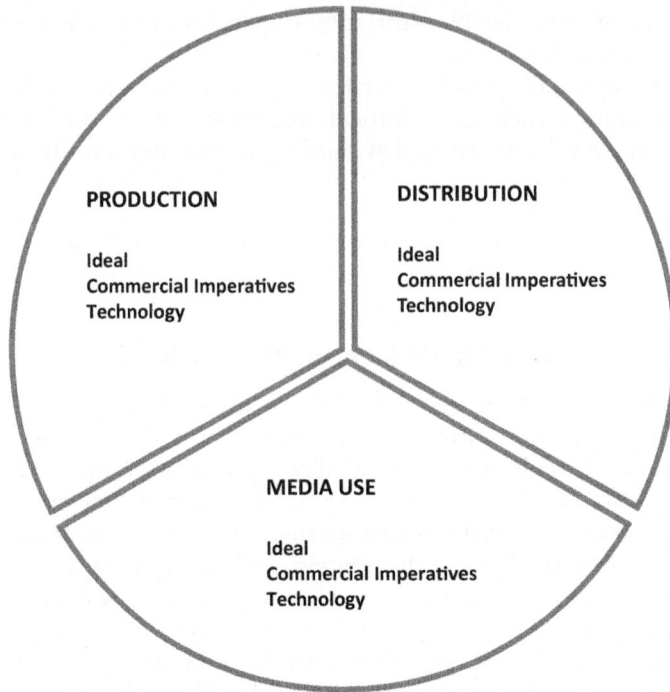

PRODUCTION

Ideal
Commercial Imperatives
Technology

DISTRIBUTION

Ideal
Commercial Imperatives
Technology

MEDIA USE

Ideal
Commercial Imperatives
Technology

Figure 2.1 Dimensions of Media Logic

both enable and restrict news media in their production, processing, and presentation of content. Television, for example, affords more linear, visual, and affective formats than print platforms (Esser 2013: 173). This raises the question of how the *technology* of social media formats affect news practices online.

In Esser's framework, it is apparent that these three aspects—professionalism (ideals), commercialism, and technology—refer only to the process of content production. Limiting media logic to content production has, however, not been particularly helpful in illustrating the transformative shift towards a hybrid media system over the past decade. Hence, and in line with our previous delineation of a network media logic, we now apply these aspects to all three dimensions of media logic: production, distribution, and media use (see Figure 2.1). Do note that our following argument applies only to political, public communication. On social media platforms we also find a large amount of personal, phatic communication taking place within closed circles of friends who do not intend their exchanges to be public, and even less viral.

Production: Ideals, Commercial Imperatives, and Technology

Most of what people know about the world stems from media, because relevant events tend to take place beyond the horizon of personal experiences and encounters. However, only small parts of the endless stream of daily events occurring in the world become news. The processes through which such relevant events are selected, processed, interpreted and transformed into news differ between mass media and social media platforms. Living in an era of information abundance, the challenge is to filter, attribute relevance, and contextualise information.

There is a difference between the professional *ideals* of mass media (the journalistic profession as a gatekeeper of traditional mass media), and the ideals of produsage on social media platforms (converging amateur content producers' and content consumers' roles; see Bruns & Highfield 2012). We have summarised the differences in production in Table 2.1. Although a large part of social media content originates from mass media in the form of, for example, retweeted or shared links to newspaper articles or radio shows (Neuberger & Lobigs 2010), the production ideal is shared personalised content. While a news item becomes relevant in mass media because it has been selected by trained staff who considered it important enough to be brought to the attention of the audience, the personalised selection on social media platforms seldom attributes relevance outside the personal network of the user. In fact, most content on social media platforms could be considered highly irrelevant from a news value point of view (O'Meara 2009). Users thus experience a logic in which content is produced reflexively with regard to personalisation and attention maximisation rather than professional codes, such as news values.

In many occasions, network media logic and mass media logic overlap. Often, users share content from mass media, such as online newspaper articles or TV videos, in their networks. In these cases, users have selected the content according to their personal tastes and interests and at the same time reproduced the selection criteria of journalists. When network and mass media ideals overlap and inform each other, this can lead to role conflicts. Norms and practices change and bend when professional mass media journalists apply their own norms and practices to blogs and social media platforms, while the inherent production logic of networked media on their part penetrates professional news organisations. Bloggers with a professional background as journalists are reported to *normalise* blogs by "sticking to their traditional gatekeeper role" (Singer 2005: 192), while simultaneously moving away from a neutral, non-partisan presentation of information. Mass media journalists have become more personal and reflexive in their addresses. In Sweden (and probably other countries as well) we can find numerous recent examples of news journalists crying openly when reporting natural disasters or refugee catastrophes. There are even indications "that journalism norms are bending

Table 2.1 Dimensions of Media Logics: Production

	Mass Media Logic	*Network Media Logic*
Ideal	Traditional journalism: autonomous, following ideals of news values in the service of what is referred to as public interest	User-generated content: based on ideals of produsage, reflexivity, and personalisation
Commercial Imperatives	High organisational costs privileging business models around infotainment	Low organisational costs privileging business models around personal revelations
Technology	Affordance for a single public sphere	Affordance for fragmented publics

as professional practices adapt to social media tools such as micro-blogging" (Hermida 2010: 300). This exemplifies how mass and network media logics coexist in increasingly hybrid settings as professional journalists and mass media corporations attribute more importance to social media platforms.

Concerning *commercial imperatives*, content production on social media platforms has low organisational cost: Amateur content produsers using ordinary consumer equipment and the sharing of already produced journalistic content involve little to no costs. Providing information on social media platforms is in fact so inexpensive that the commercial logic of mass media is reversed. Woodly (2008: 118) has pointed out that most bloggers are independent of revenue from advertisement, because of low production costs. The few bloggers popular enough to earn a small income from advertisements illustrate this reversed imperative: Usually, the ads reflect the blogger's interests, not the blogger's content or the interests of the corporations advertising there. Updating one's image, life story, and interests becomes a never-ending practice, a necessity that is pushed by social media conglomerates, largely because they capitalise on the information shared on social media platforms (van Dijck 2013; Fuchs 2014). Hence, social media platforms have a commercial incentive to get users to disclose as much personal information as possible. In contrast, content production in mass media comes at a high organisational cost: professional journalists, offices, access to data and resources, to name but a few, must all be funded. However, hybridity is at work also here with increasing mobile journalists using network media to fulfil their journalistic tasks. Several studies have also shown (e.g. Schulz & Zeh 2005; Gerth et al. 2009) that demanding business models exert additional external pressure and that this affects content production, acting as a catalyst for phenomena such as the personalisation, spectacularisation, and dramatisation of the news (also referred to as a shift towards infotainment).

Production practices are also linked to *technology*. Esser (2013: 173) argued that television affords more visual, affective, and less cognitively complex information than print. Social media platforms afford user interaction and participation to a larger extent than mass media. We can thus argue that the technologies of mass media in general afford time-consuming information, produced by professional journalists for an audience of subscribers or a statistically mapped broadcast audience. Social media platforms, on the other hand, afford the quick, lay production of information for friends and like-minded others. This information production is based on reflexivity, since social media platforms afford immediate, more horizontal, interactive, and highly individualised communication. A stable, single public sphere is replaced by multiple and quickly fading spheres (see Rauchfleisch & Schaefer 2014 and the chapter by Bruns and Highfield in the present volume) to the extent that some scholars argued that citizens no longer share the same picture of a common sociopolitical reality (Pariser 2011; Sunstein 2002). Citizens choose the stories that resonate with them the most, and are not necessarily confronted by alternative narratives. In this sense, social media platforms have a tendency to afford filter bubbles and in-group polarisation to a larger extent than news mass media, which address a more heterogeneous audience and hence have to adapt their reports accordingly. With regard to the overlapping of network and mass media logic, we can see how mass media logic is at work on social media platforms when, for example, politicians use social media platforms as if they were tools for broadcasting political statements in an unidirectional way, non-responsive to comments.

Distribution: Ideals, Commercial Imperatives, Technology

Information reaching a large crowd on social media platforms has most likely followed the *ideal* of virality. Virality can be defined as "network-enhanced word of mouth" (Nahon et al. 2011: 1). If information posted on social media platforms does not have the viral quality that induces users to pass it on to like-minded others, it will not reach beyond a very limited circle (Bennett & Segerberg 2012: 8). In Table 2.2 we have summarised the differences between mass media and network media logic regarding the distribution of content.

While professionals working for traditional mass media outlets usually know that their information will reach a certain number of subscribers or broadcast audience, the same information on social media platforms first has to be found and thereafter distributed by and among networks of supposedly like-minded people. As a result, most information on social media platforms does not go viral. Virality, as a "social information flow process" (Nahon & Hemsley 2013:16), is usually an information distribution ideal rather than a reality in networked media. Information on social media platforms is distributed from users to users, like a chain letter in peer networks. We therefore argue that in political communication the logic of virality (that information should spread) is one ideal of network media. We underline that this aspect relates to public communication, while personal or phatic communication posted in peer networks is in most cases supposed to remain within this circle of friends—and only goes viral by 'accident' (e.g. unintended masses at Facebook parties).

This arguably differs from mass dissemination to a broadcast audience or paying subscriber base in traditional mass media. These logics do intersect in hybrid ways, for example in the party press, which distributes information to like-minded recipients but also to other subscribers. Indeed, a broadcast audience or the subscribers to a newspaper are not necessarily heterogeneous, but the ideals of information distribution are fundamentally different from the viral spreading ideal on social media platforms. This being said, as most mass media have online presence today, both distribution ideals intersect. We have the example of singer Susan Boyle's first appearance on the BBC broadcast *Britain's Got Talent*, distributed to broadcast audience mainly in the UK—as well as being catapulted into world fame by connected individuals who deemed the fairytale-like clip of the plain women with a surprisingly beautiful voice worthy of attention, appreciation and passing on.

Table 2.2 Dimensions of Media Logics: Distribution

	Mass Media Logic	*Network Media Logic*
Ideal	Mass dissemination to subscribers	Viral distribution to like-minded others
Commercial Imperatives	Business models depend on centralised distribution by professional journalists	Business models depend on principles of connectivity and popularity
Technology	Affordance for broadcasting	Affordance for updating in peer networks

Besides advertising revenues, mass media, especially print media and cable TV, *commercially* depend on a base of subscribers paying for professional information curation. The relevance of information on networked media does not stem from professional selection and content production, but rather from like-minded individuals' viral distribution of information. This is also the case when users link to content from mass media, because they attribute relevance to online newspaper articles or broadcast clips by re-tweeting or sharing it. Information on social media platforms mostly reach a number of self-selected, like-minded others, but often not the general public. In fact, only very little information on social media platforms receives much attention, most remains unnoticed. Virality implies that the asymmetry of the information distribution is based on both popularity (as with the Susan Boyle example) and like-mindedness in the sense that social media platforms enhance the domination of popular information and popular produsers. Certain users and their postings gain more visibility than others. Elite and top general-bloggers facilitate swift information dissemination (Nahon et al. 2011). Hence, distribution on social media platforms depends partly on like-minded and popular online intermediaries who serve as catalysts. In some cases these intermediaries overlap with mass media professionals in hybrid ways, but often they are not the professional gatekeepers we find in mass media. One noteworthy example is Swedish computer game commentator and YouTube celebrity PewDiePie (Felix Kjellberg), who has launched campaigns for threatened animals, save the children, and clean water to name a few via his YouTube fans (30 million).

Distribution online has been discussed as a *connective culture* (van Dijck 2013); a culture that thrives on social media platforms and that is supported by the business models of today's social media conglomerates. Van Dijck (2013: 13, 62) talks about a *popularity principle* underpinning what she refers to as an attention economy in social media. This is also reflected in the commercial imperatives of social media platforms. Revenue depends on popularity (measured, for example, by the Klout Score) and viral distribution within algorithmically determined target groups. When PewDiePie uploads a new video clip, this upload is likely to spread faster than if a regular user would provide the same video. Indeed, there is an increasing incentive for users to network and connect with many well-connected others in order to spread their information and thereby to sustain an infrastructure of virality for their own information to spread.

Information distribution online is based on reflexivity, since network media *technology*, to a large extent, affords immediate, interactive, and individualised communication. In other words, social media platforms afford peer-to-peer-communication, while news mass media instead afford a traditional top-down broadcasting model of distribution. Sometimes these logics intersect. PewDiePie's fans, for example, *subscribe* to his YouTube channel, signalling how the mass media logic of a subscription as well as top-down broadcasting has made its way to social media platforms. However, on social media platforms users may connect among each other in ways impossible for mass media audiences. It thus becomes important to keep each other updated online (Svensson 2012). Social media platforms thus adopt the technological rules often associated with the Web 2.0 concept (O'Reilly 2005), affording peer-to-peer distribution by means of updating practices in self-selected networks.

Media Use: Ideals, Commercial Imperatives, and Technology

Today, users navigate media landscapes that are characterised by an abundance of information. Users thus constantly need to discern which information is relevant to them, which is why content sharing and suggestions from popular and like-minded others within their social networks become influential. The basic tenets of this third and last dimension of media logics, detailing aspects of media use, are outlined in Table 2.3.

Networks inform users about the variety of choices before them, while also providing cues regarding how their peers have acted in similar situations with similar choices (Anderson 2006: 108, 174; Manovich 2001: 35). This sharing of (personal) information is an online ideal, which involves reflexively confessing and spreading information and minute-to-minute updates on thoughts, feelings, whereabouts, opinions, and like-minded others' doings. Castells (2008) refers to this personalised information use as mass self-communication. This idealisation of the self, in tandem with idealising peers and like-minded others, when using network media differs from mass media use which instead is based on *ideals* of a rather passive consumption of professionally selected, framed, and interpreted news items (this is not to deny the notion of a cognitively active audience that unconsciously makes sense of the messages conveyed to it). These ideals may overlap in, for example, how mass media outlets invite subscribers to share their thoughts and feelings on a news topic via, for the occasion created hashtag, on Twitter or on their Facebook page.

The constant and reflexive sharing of information online also taps into the *commercial imperatives* on network media. When connecting to like-minded others and peers on social media platforms, users indirectly tailor what information will reach them. In other words, users increasingly construct and organise their social realities through their online social networks. News feeds displaying the online behaviours of selected others enable users to anticipate their future needs and wants based on actions undertaken by their peers, as well as on their own, aggregated past choices (Anderson 2006). It has become apparent that the capitalist logic of platforms owners, capitalising on the information their users share, informs social media practices. Time spent online contributes to the economic value of social media companies (van Dijck 2013; Fuchs 2014: 114). By spending time online and updating their social media profiles, users allow capitalist companies to exploit their information—knowingly or not. Social media companies accumulate capital through data mining of displayed personal information, which they sell to commercial actors or other organisations interested in targeting users with information. The logic of updating thus fits neatly into the

Table 2.3 Dimensions of Media Logics: Media Use

	Mass Media Logic	*Network Media Logic*
Ideal	Consumption of professionally selected and framed information	Sharing reflexive and personal information among peers and like-minded others
Commercial Imperatives	Business models depend on advertisements and subscriptions	Business models depend on data mining, target advertising, and surveillance
Technology	Affordance for passive use along geographically defined boundaries	Affordance for interactive use in peer and interest-based networks

logic of capital accumulation and the business models of such companies. In contrast, mass media corporations' income largely depends on their audience's belief that they provide quality content—only then will they pay or accept advertising breaks. While broadcasting companies marketise the attention of viewers or listeners during their use of the program, social media platform owners sell the data of their users; even collecting profitable data when users have left the social network sites (e.g. about their online shopping routines).

As discussed previously, social media platform's *technology* affords reflexive updating in more fragmented peer networks. Social media platforms thus allow for broader repertoires of media use rather than only for the consumption of professionally produced, reframed, and redistributed news broadcasts. Social media content may be manipulated by discerning, assembling, adding, or removing information (Manovich 2001: 27–30). Programming and manipulating media is easier in the network environment, and ordinary network media users are capable of doing so. Thus, news and information are constantly being produced and are endlessly variable (Manovich 2001). Social media platforms allow for a more interactive use of media content than traditional mass media and are bound to communities of peers and like-minded others to a larger extent than mass media (even though this started to change already with satellite and cable television). And as we have exemplified throughout, it is not as easy any longer to separate mass media from social media content. Most mass media corporations do have an online presence, often with similar content and the added feature of user comments, opportunities to share and like the professionally produced content, and closely monitor these activities (as shown by their ranking of most shared/most read article online).

Conclusion

Network media logic differs from traditional mass media logic in three different but interrelated dimensions: the production of media content, the distribution patterns of information, and the way people use media. Within these three dimensions, we can further delineate the underlying ideals, commercial imperatives, and technology that distinguish mass media from network media, although the two logics overlap. The remaining question is: How does this connect with politics and political logic?

As mentioned above, political logic is highly context sensitive. The political strategies in election campaigns, for instance, strongly depend on the specific political structures in which political parties and candidates compete for votes. Are they running in a two-party or multi-party competition? Does the *winner takes all* principle apply, or is it possible to form a multi-party coalition government? Are votes cast for parties or for candidates—or for both? As political systems and media systems tend to remain stable over time, the potentials and effects of social media platforms depend on this structural background. Social media platforms cannot per se *revolutionise* election campaigns or other political processes, because it is first and foremost the design of political institutions that determines whether, and in what way, social media platforms can be meaningfully employed in political communication. It is against this background that mass media logic and network media logic resonate with the strategic communication efforts of political actors and political organisations.

In electoral campaigns as well as in routine situations, political actors and organisations seek visibility for their heads and ideas. Their communication strategies and media repertoires should reflect the different ways in which information is produced, distributed, and used in mass media and on social media platforms. The distribution patterns of social media platforms, for instance, promote personalisation: In self-selected and reflexive networks, private information about a candidate or representative will spread more easily than information about a new parliamentary initiative (see, e.g. Bennett 2012 on the personalisation of politics). On the other hand, journalists (despite the trend towards more personalisation in mass media) might find the parliamentary initiative more interesting, because, when put in context, it may constitute an even better story.

The objective of visibility is also closely connected to the different audiences of mass media and on social media platforms. When dealing with journalists, political actors know who the recipients of the shared information will be: The readers of a high-quality newspaper or the viewers of a late-night talk show on TV. They can also estimate the number of recipients that will be reached. When posting information on social media platforms, on the contrary, it remains unclear if and how far this information will spread. The number of followers on Twitter or friends on Facebook are only weak predictors of visibility, because they indicate to how many people the post will be broadcast, but not if and how it will travel from there via re-tweets and other means of sharing. This means that social media platforms cannot reliably and transparently deliver political information and create visibility for politicians or political organisations. It thus comes as no surprise that politicians continue to rely heavily on journalists and mass media when they seek to get their messages out (i.e. broadcasting information). What social media can do is provide data about friends and followers, enabling micro-targeting techniques in election campaigns—a feature that is increasingly used and might in the future change the strategies of political actors in election campaigns (Cookson 2015).

Network media logic poses a variety of challenges to political actors and organisations, not least because they have adapted to the rules of the game of news mass media and now struggle with the potentials and problems when communicating outside a well-rehearsed *broadcasting mode*. One of those challenges, for example, is the coherence of party politics and individual politicians. How can political parties ensure that the self-presentation of candidates, parliamentarians, and other politicians in their organisation is in line with the party manifesto and the strategic communication of the party? Traditionally, party communication was organised in a centralised way, by communications departments and heads of strategic communication. While this is still the case, individual politicians now have the opportunity to use social media platforms to portray themselves more personally and as a platform for sharing diverging views— views that could be more in line with their constituents' opinions than those of the party (see Svensson 2011).

This brief discussion of the consequences of emerging network media logic is, of course, far from complete. Social media platforms change political communication, but they do not substitute journalistic mass media. Moreover, they do not change political communication in a deterministic way based on their technology but can resonate only within the bounds of institutional design and contexts. Media logic is not external from society but results from the ideals, commercial imperatives, and technological aspects of media production, distribution, and use. They way media logic can unfold in political communication, then, depends on the political logic that shapes the communication strategies of political actors and organisations.

Notes

1 Both authors have contributed equally to this chapter.
2 Parts of this chapter are based on Klinger and Svensson (2015).

References

Altheide, D. L. (2004) "Media logic and political communication." *Political Communication* 21(3): pp. 293–296.

Altheide, D. L. & Snow R. P. (1979) *Media logic*, Beverly Hills, CA: SAGE.

Anderson, C. (2006) *The long tail—How endless choice is creating unlimited demand*, London: Random House Business Books.

Asp, K. (1986) *Mäktiga massmedier: Studier om politisk opinionsbildning* [Powerful Mass Media: Studies of Political Opinion Formation], Stockholm: Akademilitteratur.

Bawn, K. (1993) "The logic of institutional preferences: German electoral law as a social choice outcome," *American Journal of Political Science*, 37, pp. 965–989.

Bennett, W. L. (2012) "The personalization of politics political identity, social media, and changing patterns of participation," *The Annals of the American Academy of Political and Social Science*, 644(1), pp. 20–39.

Bennett, W. L. & Segerberg, A (2012) "The logic of connective action," *Information, Communication & Society*," 15(5), pp. 739–768.

Besley, T. & Persson, T. (2011) "The logic of political violence," *The Quarterly Journal of Economics*, 10.1093/qje/qjr025.

Breiner, P. (1995) "The political logic of economics and the economic logic of modernity in Max Weber," *Political Theory*, 23(1), pp. 25–47.

Bruns, A. & Highfield, T. (2012) "Blogs, Twitter, and Breaking News: The produsage of citizen journalism," in R.A. Lind (ed.), *Produsing theory in a digital world: The intersection of audiences and production*, New York: Peter Lang, pp. 15–32.

Cardenal, A. S. (2011) "Why mobilize support online? The paradox of party behaviour online," *Party Politics*, 19(1): 83–103.

Castells, M. (2008) "The new public sphere: Global civil society, communication networks, and global governance," *ANNALS of the American Academy of Political and Social Science*, 616(1), pp. 78–93.

Chadwick, A. (2013) *The hybrid media system: Politics and power*, Oxford University Press.

Cookson, R. (2015) "Parties make it personal with tailored messages in election battle," *Financial Times*, February 17, 2015. http://www.ft.com/intl/cms/s/0/ad97068e-b062–11e4–92b6–00144feab7de.html?siteedition=uk#axzz3Sr96mNi3

Couldry, N. (2008) "Mediatization or mediation? Alternative understandings of the emergent space of digital storytelling." *New Media & Society* 10(3): pp. 373–391.

Day, R.J.F. (2004) "From hegemony to affinity: The political logic of the newest social movements." *Cultural Studies* 18(5): pp. 716–748.

de Mesquita B., Smith, A., Siverson, R. M. & Morrow, J. D. (2005) *The logic of political survival*, Cambridge: MIT Press.

Diamond, L.J. (2002) "Thinking about hybrid regimes," *Journal of Democracy*, 13(2), pp. 21–35.

Ellison, N. & boyd, d. (2007) "Social Network Sites: Definition, history and scholarship," *Computer-Mediated Communication*, 13(1), pp. 210–230.

Enli, G.S. & Skogerbø, E. (2013) "Personalized campaigns in party-centered politics: Twitter and Facebook as arenas for political communication," *Information, Communication & Society*, 16(5), pp. 757–774.

Esser, F. (2013) "Mediatization as a challenge: Media logic versus political logic," in H. Kriesi et al. (eds.) *Democracy in the age of globalization and mediatization*, Basingstoke: Palgrave Macmillan, pp. 155–176.

Fuchs, C. (2014) *Social media. A critical introduction*, London: Sage.

Gerth, M., Rademacher, P., Pühringer, K., Dahinden, U. & Siegert, G. (2009) "Challenges to political campaigns in the media: Commercialization, framing, and personalization," *Studies in Communication Sciences*, 9(1), pp. 149–169.

Graham, T., Broersma, M., Hazelhoff, K. & van´t Haar, G. (2013) "Between broadcasting political messages and interacting with voters. The use of Twitter during the 2010 UK general election," *Information, Communication & Society*, 16(5), pp. 692–716.

Granderson, L. Z. (2011) "Sarah Palin proves she's no fool." http://edition.cnn.com/2011/10/06/opinion/granderson-palin-presidency/

Grant, W.J., Moon, B. and Busby Grant, J. (2010) "Digital dialogue? Australian politicians' use of the social network tool Twitter," *Australian Journal of Political Science*, 45(4), pp. 579–604.

Hermida, A. (2010) "Twittering the news: The emergence of ambient journalism," *Journalism Practice*, 4(3), pp. 297–308. DOI:10.1080/17512781003640703

Hjarvard, S. (2013) *The mediatization of culture and society*, London: Routledge.

Jarren, O. & Donges, P. (2006) *Politische Kommunikation in der Mediengesellschaft* [Political communication in media society], Wiesbaden: Verlag für Sozialwissenschaften.

Jungherr, A. (2014, February 7) *Twitter in politics: A comprehensive literature review* (Working Paper). Retrieved from Social Science Research Network (SSRN): http://papers.ssrn.com/sol3/papers.cfm?abstract_id=2402443

Kepplinger, H. M. (2002) "Mediatization of politics: Theory and data," *Journal of Communication*, 52(4), pp. 972–986.

Klinger, U. (2013) "Mastering the art of social media: Swiss parties, the 2011 national election and digital challenges," *Information, Communication & Society*, 16(5), pp. 717–736.

Klinger, U. & Svensson, J. (2015) "The emergence of network media logic in political communication: A theoretical approach," *New Media & Society*, 17(8), pp. 1241–1257.

Krotz, F. (2009) "Mediatization: A concept with which to grasp media and social change," in K. Lundby (ed.) *Mediatization: Concept, changes, consequences*, New York: Peter Lang, pp. 21–40.

Larsen, C. A. (2008) "The political logic of labour market reforms and popular images of target groups," *Journal of European Social Policy*, 18(1), pp. 50–63.

Larsson, A. O. & Svensson, J. (2014) "Politicians online—Identifying current research opportunities," *First Monday*, 19(4). Published online 7 April http://firstmonday.org/ojs/index.php/fm/article/view/4897

Lundby, K. (2009) "Media logic: Looking for social interaction," in K. Lundby (ed.) *Mediatization: Concept, changes, consequences*, New York: Peter Lang, pp. 101–119.

Lundby, K. (2014) "Mediatization of Communication," in K. Lundby (ed.) *Mediatization of Communication*, Berlin: De Gruyter Mouton, pp.1–38.

Manovich, L. (2001) *The language of new media*, Cambridge, MA: The MIT Press.

McKay, D. (2005) "Economic logic or political logic? Economic theory, federal theory and EMU 1," *Journal of European Public Policy*, 12(3), pp. 528–544.

McLuhan, M. (1964) *Understanding media: The extensions of man*, New York: McGraw Hill.

Nahon, K., Hemsley, J., Walker S., et al. (2011) "Fifteen minutes of fame: The power of blogs in the lifecycle of viral political information," *Policy & Internet*, 3(1), pp. 6–33.

Nahon, K., & Hemsley, J. (2013) *Going viral*, Cambridge: Polity Press.

Neuberger, C. & Lobigs, F. (2010) *Die Bedeutung des Internets im Rahmen der Vielfaltssicherung. Gutachten für die Kommission zur Ermittlung der Konzentration im Medienbereich (KEK) (The significance of the internet for the protection of pluralism. Report for the Commission on Concentration in the Media KEK)*, Berlin: Vistas.

O'Meara, R. (2009) "Do cats know they rule YouTube? Surveillance and the pleasures of cat videos," *M/C Journal*, 17(2).

O'Reilly, T. (2005) "What is Web 2.0: Design patterns and business models for the next generation of software." http://oreilly.com/web2/archive/what-is-web-20.html

Pariser, E. (2011) *The filter bubble: What the Internet is hiding from you*, New York: Penguin.

Pempel, T. J. (2006) "A decade of political torpor: When political logic trumps economic rationality," in Peter J. Katzenstein, Takashi Shiraishi (eds.): *Beyond Japan: The dynamics of East Asian regionalism*, Ithaca: Cornell University Press, pp. 37–61.

Rauchfleisch, A. & Schaefer, M. S. (2014) "Multiple public spheres of Weibo: A typology of forms and potentials of online public spheres in China," *Information, Communication & Society*, 18(2), pp. 139–155.

Schulz, W. & Zeh, R. (2005) "The changing election coverage of German television: A content analysis: 1990–2002," *Communications: The European Journal of Communication Research*, 30(4), pp. 385–407.

Singer, J. B. (2005) "The political j-blogger 'normalizing' a new media form to fit old norms and practices," *Journalism*, 6(2), pp. 174–198.

Street, J. (1997) "Remote control? Politics, technology and 'electronic democracy'," *European Journal of Communication*, 12(1), pp. 27–42.

Strömbäck, J. & Esser, F. (2014) "Mediatization of politics: Transforming democracies and reshaping politics," in K. Lundby (ed.) *Mediatization of Communication*, Berlin: De Gruyter Mouton, pp. 374–404.

Sunstein, C. R. (2002) *Republic.com*, Princeton: Princeton University Press.

Svensson, J. (2011) "Nina on the Net—A study of a politician campaigning on social networking sites," *The Central European Journal of Communication*, 2(8), pp. 190–206.

Svensson, J. (2012). "Social media and the disciplining of visibility: Activist participation and relations of power in network societies," *European Journal of E-Practice*, 16 (June/July), pp. 16–28.

van Dijck, J. (2013) *The culture of connectivity: A critical history of social media*, Oxford: Oxford University Press.

Vergeer, M. & Hermans, L. (2013) "Campaigning on Twitter: Micro-blogging and online social networking as campaign tools in the 2010 general elections in the Netherlands," *Journal of Computer-Mediated Communication*, 18(4), 399–419.

Woodly, D. (2008) "New competencies in democratic communication? Blogs, agenda setting and political participation," *Public Choice*, 134(1–2), pp. 109–123.

Zinnes, D. A. (2004) "Constructing political logic: The democratic peace puzzle," *Journal of Conflict Resolution*, 48(3), pp. 430–454.

3

WHERE THERE IS SOCIAL MEDIA THERE IS POLITICS

Karine Nahon

Introduction

The recent general elections in Israel, held on 17 March 2015, were won by the right. When examining empirically the content created by politicians on social media, it was clear that right-wing politicians exhibited higher levels of activity in terms of the number of posts, likes, and shares. However, users who were supporters of the centre or left-wing parties would subsequently complain that they had been certain of a centre-left victory, as indicated by their Facebook feeds. It was full of posts, videos, and images attacking the incumbent right-wing Prime Minister Benjamin Netanyahu, who eventually won, and supporting the idea of replacing the government.

The Facebook algorithm was largely responsible for the gap between their hopes and illusions and the electoral reality. Facebook presents users with only a small fraction of the information flows created by their friends (Constine, 2014). If I had 100 friends on Facebook, and they all posted at the same time, Facebook would show me only a few and I would not even know that the remainder posted as well. This reduced feed is even more bounded as Facebook prioritizes homophilous contents and those articles with which one is more likely to agree (Pariser, 2012). These two practices of the Facebook platform are an example of how the self-selection power of users can be skewed. This gap between electoral preferences as reflected in social media and the actual preferences of Israeli society, in this case, is a distinct product of social media politics.

"No idea is more provocative in controversies about technology and society than the notion that technical things have political qualities. At issue is the claim that the machines . . . can embody specific forms of power and authority" (Winner, 1996, 19). Politics of social media refers to the power interplays among actors on social media platforms, as they attempt to promote their interests and values. The concept of social media politics remains elusive despite the recent wealth of empirical case studies on related topics, such as on the bias of algorithms (Gillespie, 2010, 2014); power law of networks (Barabási, 2003; Nahon, Hemsley, Walker, & Hussain, 2011); mediators' control of information flows (Barzilai-Nahon, 2008; Lievrouw, 2009; Shaw & Hill, 2014) and user attention (Wihbey, 2014); agenda-setting in networks (Wallsten, 2007; Woodly, 2008); and the politics of protocols (Elmer, 2010), search engines (Halavais, 2008; Segev, 2010), and technology in general (Introna, 2006; Tufekci, 2014). These diverse topics have something in common: they are all different manifestations of the politics of social media.

Social media are the collection of Web- and mobile-based platforms where individuals and groups interact. They include blogs such as Wordpress, update streams such as Twitter, general social networks such as Facebook, image-sharing platforms such as Flickr, location platforms such as Swarm, social news forums such as Reddit, business networks such as LinkedIn, and curation platform such as Pinterest. Given its unique affordances and rules, each platform is conducive to particular power dynamics.

The politics of social media may have the power to affect the behaviours, preferences and value systems of individuals and groups according to the intentions of those operating social media platforms. This may have significant consequences for the sort of information people receive, potentially shifting the gravity centres of meaning-making power. Researchers have observed some of these changes, for example, through the skews and biases of information flows. However, they largely remain obscure. The scope of this concept is broad, and this chapter does not pretend to provide a comprehensive typology. Rather, it represents an interdisciplinary attempt to enrich the conversation in the field while suggesting, defining, and classifying a number of ways to better understand the building blocks of the politics of social media.

This chapter makes the normative claim that social media cannot exist without some kind of political involvement or bias. In social media, neutrality is the exception rather than the rule. This is followed by a description of the different manifestations of social media politics, a review of empirical evidence, and discussion of several examples of this powerful phenomenon. As the literature on these topics is scattered, this chapter attempts to classify and organize the different types of political manifestations of social media.

The Neutrality Myth Shattered: Power Modes in Social Media

Information technologies and social media in particular are not neutral artefacts but significantly political and social spaces. Power relations are fundamental to any society, whether mediated offline or online. Wherever there are people and social relationships there are power relationships (Castells, 2009). Politics does not reside in a vacuum, but in a social locus where actors (potentially) exercise their power. The first question we need to ask therefore is, are social media social? If so, to what extent? Trottier and Fuchs (2014) answer the first question in the affirmative and identify three forms of sociality which determine the extent to which social media are social: cognition, communication, and cooperation or coproduction. Individuals have certain cognitive features that they use to interact with others, "so that shared spaces of interaction are created. In some cases, these spaces are used not just for communication but also for the coproduction of novel qualities of overall social systems and for community building" (Trottier & Fuchs, 2014, p. 6).

The special appeal of social media resides in their ability to not only host but also facilitate and enhance social interactions. This is the source of their impact but at the same time also of their flux and complexity, as so many groups have a stake in them. Every decision about how technology is designed, how information is produced, shared, distributed or accessed, involves various stakeholders jostling for different normative positions. This dynamic, political process leads perforce to a struggle over the hegemony of certain actors (individuals, institutions, groups, or networks) over others, influencing their values and behaviours. How these issues are resolved will, thus, determine which people, under what circumstances, can do what on Facebook, Twitter, or WhatsApp. The politics of social media, like any other technology, produces, reproduces, reinforces, and shifts power and privilege among designers and users, but also—increasingly—among non-users. Just like in the Roman forum, the outcomes of the politics of social media promote the interests and values of the powerful.

True enough, social media have empowered users (especially non-professionals) with ready-made tools that enable them to share and distribute information, create viral events, enrich content through metadata, locate people with similar interests, develop applications, collaborate to produce knowledge, and build on others' work and donations to create new things much more easily than before. This empowerment was accompanied by the illusion of social media being neutral, egalitarian, objective and democratic. In fact, the basic elements of social media—their architecture (platforms and network structure) and dynamics (network structure,[1] information flows, and curated flows)—are political, non-neutral and non-democratic in design, practices, and policies. These elements are inherently biased by the values of particular stakeholders, which in and through social media regulate others' behaviour in line with those values.

Since politics is the exercise of power in the resolution of issues—which for our purposes may arise in or be addressed through social media—we need to define power in social media. I have discussed the notion of power in networks in depth in some of my earlier writings (Barzilai-Nahon, 2008; Nahon, 2011), and since this is not the main focus of this chapter, I will briefly present the three main power modes critical to the understanding of the phenomenon in question, and will later use them to inform some of its instances.[2]

The first power mode has to do with the capacity to influence the decisions of other social actors. This is aligned with the ideas of political scientists in the 1950s and 1960s, such as Robert Dahl (1957) and Nelson Polsby (1963), who argued that decision-making analysis would be the best way to determine which individuals and groups have more power in social life, and that decisions involve direct, that is actual and observable, conflict. For example, in the context of social media, Liu et al. (2011) found in a qualitative study that 36 per cent of content remained shared with the default Facebook privacy settings. They also found that in the majority of cases there was a gap between the desirable privacy settings and the actual controls users decided to apply. In most cases, users exposed content to more users than expected, aligned with the Facebook's vested interest to exercise power over its users, or more precisely influence their decisions regarding what content to expose, and to whom, in service of its business model.

The second major mode of power is the shaping of and control over the political agenda, which determines how social media are designed and operate and how potential issues are kept out of the political process and public sphere. The conceptualisation of the second mode of power is informed by political scientists of the 1960s, 1970s, and 1980s, such as Peter Bachrach and Morton Baratz (1962). Any satisfactory analysis of power thus involves not only examining social media's influence on decisions (the first mode of power), but also examining *non*-decisions (suppressing challenges to the status quo or adding new issues to the agenda) as decisions. For example, Twitter restricts tweets to 140 characters. This design has had major ramifications on the content flowing across the service. When users are limited to 140 characters, their posts must be short, laconic, and simplistic, if not outright blunt. It is no coincidence that Twitter is mainly used for live event updates. It has been purposely structured this way by its designers, imitating SMS practices and consequently appropriating this user behaviour as a tool for sharing activities in the immediate present (Sagolla, 2009). By constraining the agenda (to 140 characters), Twitter has privileged a particular type of content (real-time posts) over other content, such as complex and nuanced arguments.

The third mode of power focuses on actions and inactions aimed at shaping and influencing one's perceptions, cognitions, and preferences (latent or manifest). This is done, for example, by securing acceptance of the status quo since no alternatives appear to exist, or because it is seen (but actually shaped) as 'natural', unchangeable, or favourable. This conceptualisation is well aligned with Lukes (2005) and to some extent also with Foucault (1978, 1990) who argued that power is the ability to shape the mind and construct meaning for phenomena. While this mode of power is difficult to observe, it has the strongest impact among the three, as the changes occur *within* the social actor (person or group) affected by it. It involves a profound transformation of value systems, making Social Actor A believe and choose to act in a way that reinforces the system's bias, thereby promoting the interests of Actor B at A's own expense, usually in the form of compliance. For example, Bond et al. (2012) studied the effect of the iVote button added by Facebook in order to encourage voting in the 2010 U.S. congressional elections on the actual behaviour of 61 million users. The study showed that the button directly influenced the "political self-expression, information seeking and real world voting behavior of millions of people. Furthermore, the messages not only influenced the users who received them but also the users' friends, and friends of friends" (Bond et al., 2012, p. 295). Critical voices raised the concern that the use of the iVote button by Facebook was not transparent, and could be exploited to create social pressure on particular groups and exclude others (e.g. by providing the iVote button only to people identified by Facebook as Democrat supporters). Be that as it may, this study exemplified the ability of social media politics to change the preferences of people who were reluctant to vote, and mobilize them to vote.

One way to enrich the debate on the spectrum of social media politics is by classifying it into social media *architecture* and the *dynamics* (see Figure 3.1). The three modes

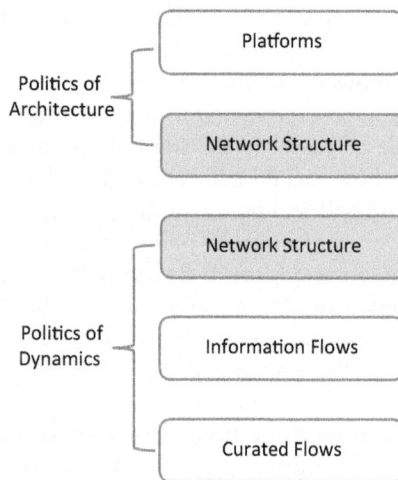

Figure 3.1 Politics of Social Media: Dimensions

of power are exercised in each one of these dimensions by influencing decisions, setting the agenda, or shaping stakeholder preferences. The overlap between the dimensions is minimal, as the politics of dynamics focuses directly on content, while the politics of architecture focuses on technology and only indirectly on content. Both, however, aim at changing people's behaviour, preferences, and values.

Politics of Architecture

The architecture of social media—the design of the actual components that make up social media (hardware, software, operating, and network systems) and their interrelations—is ultimately based on code written by developers. This code is constructed hierarchically: similarly to any other human language, where words come together to form a sentence, and many sentences form a text that expresses an idea. The lines of code form the algorithm, or set of rules for making the technology 'do something'. The algorithm is at the heart of any automated or semi-automated technological process in social media: from making the hardware react to users pressing a button to unfriending someone with a click. More important for our current purposes, the architecting of social media is a conscious, deliberate, non-neutral act by various stakeholders, usually designers or developers, but also users. The struggle over who gets to architect the platforms and affordances, and how they are architected, is one of the key manifestations of the power struggles and political arrangements in social media.

Technocrats tend to argue that because technology is based on algorithms devoid of human interference, it is able to construct consistently neutral and non-discriminatory processes. However, by the very fact that humans design it, every technology is inherently political, involving values and interests cast in the image of its architects and subsequently shaped by its users. Architecting social media is a conscious act of exercising power in its three modes: influencing decisions, setting the agenda, and shaping preferences of stakeholders around questions of affordances and use. Through the design of infrastructure architects influence the decisions of users regarding their privacy, what to share, how to write, and how to behave on that platform. Through the design of infrastructure architects determine the rules and boundaries of users' speech, and their behaviour on their platforms: what to write, what types of photos to upload or not, what types of videos to share. And through the design of infrastructure architects not only change the decisions and boundaries of behaviour, but also shape the preferences and values of users according to their own interests.

One example of controversy manifesting a power struggle between users and the platform is the issue of nude photos. Facebook has a policy of removing such photos. However, users have complained that this policy also censors breastfeeding, nudes in art, naked mannequins, and kisses between same-sex individuals. In January 2015, a group of mothers protested online by uploading breastfeeding images. Consequently, in March 2015 Facebook announced it would no longer remove such images, as they did not violate its rules on nudity. The updated policy states that:

> we restrict the display of nudity because some audiences within our global community may be sensitive to this type of content. . . . In order to treat people fairly and respond to reports quickly, it is essential that we have policies in place that our global teams can apply uniformly and easily when reviewing content. . . . We remove photographs of people displaying genitals or focusing

in on fully exposed buttocks. We also restrict some images of female breasts if they include the nipple, but we always allow photos of women actively engaged in breastfeeding or showing breasts with post-mastectomy scarring. We also allow photographs of paintings, sculptures, and other art that depicts nude figures. ('Facebook: Community Standard Page', n.d.)

Studies on how the architect's role introduces valence into technology, and social media in particular, have flourished in the last decade. These include analyses of censorship policies of Facebook and YouTube, their changes over time, and their impact on user behaviours (Gillespie, 2010, 2014); as well as studies on biases in Google content provision and ranking for different localities (Halavais, 2008; Segev, 2010). Gillespie (2014) articulates six dimensions of the political valence of algorithms, which he uses as a heuristic for considering the scope of the 'politics of algorithm': (1) the choices (of those who architect the algorithms) behind the platforms' inclusion/exclusion rules; (2) the collection of information not necessary for the algorithm to operate; (3) the level of obscurity of what is relevant; (4) the way the algorithm's technical character is positioned as an assurance of impartiality; (5) the technology's appropriation for purposes of political contest; and (6) how the algorithmic presentation shapes the public's sense of itself. Gillespie argues that the algorithm's outputs, presented as the objective results of queries, shape users' practices and serve as a legitimization apparatus for the production of biased knowledge.

While it is important to focus on the platforms' architects as those who determine the values of social media affordances, as Gillespie suggests, the power struggles ecosystem involves more than just a unilateral, omnipotent type of actor. It involves many other actors: users and non-user individuals, groups, and ephemeral networks of people and institutions. Each of these stakeholders seeks hegemony by pushing their own value sets and interests in the context of the various debates arising in or addressed by social media. Winner suggests that one way for an artefact to contain political properties are "instances in which the invention, design, or arrangement of a specific technical device or system becomes a way of settling an issue in the affairs of a particular community" (Winner, 1996, p. 2). How these issues are resolved and by whom will determine the extent to which social media will reproduce power structures and biases, or enforce new structures of power in an attempt to regulate user behaviour.

When social media users appropriate (or attempt to appropriate) a technology by altering the algorithm to their purposes or by using the same algorithm for purposes other than intended—this is a political act. This is when latent power struggles occur between the original architects and the users. Nevertheless, platforms and architects have an inherent power advantage when it comes to determining affordances on their platforms. They can decide to change the design unilaterally, arbitrarily and again—non-neutrally. Users can invoke a power struggle, but in a manner somewhat reminiscent of labour struggles, this would require them to unite in order to create a critical mass that can counter the values imposed by the architects.

Two examples illustrate this politics of platforms: one has to do with the decisions of several leading platforms to censor any explicit illustrations of the beheadings carried out by ISIS. These guidelines came after the beheading of American journalist James Foley in August 2014. On 20 August the CEO of Twitter, Dick Costolo, tweeted: "We have been and are actively suspending accounts as we discover them related to this graphic imagery" (Costolo, 2014). Subsequently, Twitter changed its policies to allow family members to request the removal of content depicting a deceased user. Unlike Twitter, YouTube did not feel compelled to make any specific changes, as its community guidelines already included specific rules against content that incites violence or depicts violence with the intent of causing shock. This example shows, however, that platforms do not hesitate to dictate their values on critical questions such as the boundaries of freedom of expression.

Another example of the politics of social media is when Facebook introduced the "Year in Review" app at the end of 2014. This application invited members to watch and share the important moments of their life over the past year with the default caption 'It's been a great year! Thanks for being a part of it'. Soon users began complaining on the inadvertent algorithmic cruelty (Meyer, 2014), which reminded them of events they did *not* want to remember, such as death and divorce. Here, Facebook exemplified the third power mode by proactively impacting on the memories and awareness of people, sometimes against their choice.

Network Structure: Between Politics of Architecture and Politics of Dynamics

The structure of networks encompasses two main aspects. First, a conceptualization derived from the social sciences denoting the rules, practices and arrangements through which the behaviour of people is regulated in networks (Bourdieu, 1977; Durkheim, 1982; Foucault, 1978, 1990; Giddens, 1986; Weber, 1946). These rules can be social rules determined by a group of people but can also be created by algorithms. Both interpretations refer to regulating users' behaviour in networks, and both are related to particular manifestations of politics. For example, McKelvey (2010) studied the conflict around two types of algorithms: quality-of-service and end-to-end algorithms. Each type offers a different solution for the network neutrality issue: the former prioritizes preventing network congestion while the latter focuses on providing equality between communication modalities. Accordingly, each promotes different values, and the dynamics of promoting these values is a manifestation of the politics inherent in the networks' structure.

A second aspect of the network structure refers to "the typology of interconnected nodes" (Castells, 2009), identified by "the observed set of ties linking the members of a population" (Watts, 2004, p. 48) in their social networks. This definition complicates our discussion of politics, as social media offer different types of structures. Bruns and Moe (2014) classify these structures on Twitter into three types: macro (hashtagged exchanges), meso (follower–followee networks), and micro (@reply conversations). More generally, there are two important types of network structures relevant to our discussions. The first is a more permanent and stable model of network structure directly related to the platform's architecture—for example, the network of Twitter followers or Facebook friends of a single social media account. While their number changes, it is a slow change and the boundaries of the network are clearly identified. There is little room for power dynamics here as the network structure is determined to a large extent by the platform designers. An example for the politics of network structure at the architecture level is the Internet backbone, which serves as the physical basis for the social media operation and refers to the core routers that connect large networks, including network access points that control traffic between countries. The competition for joining the exclusive group of backbone network providers is a political, not just a business one, as it affects the scope of control these institutions have.

Ephemeral types of network structures are the shapes and patterns we see in the links connecting people in social networks as information flows on topical issues (e.g. a conversation around a particular hashtag). Network structures like that are constituted dynamically around a topic, and their boundaries and members are also dynamic. Importantly, hashtags were not originally a Twitter design feature. Norms around their use emerged out of the collective practices of users. The use of hashtags later spread to other platforms, and they are now commonplace. The hashtag is part of the network structure in that it functions as a classifier that allows other people to follow specific conversations or topics. It evolves as information flows and dissolves as that flow fades. Politics of network structure with an ephemeral nature should be classified as politics of dynamics. In summer 2014, for example, Israel launched a military operation in the Gaza Strip against the Hamas Rule, called Operation Protective Edge. The event was tweeted about by Israeli and Palestinian users under different hashtags, such as #IsraelUnderFire and #GazaUnderAttack, representing competing narratives. This exemplifies the dynamic politics of topical network structure, as both sides attempt to capture the attention of users around the world and influence their awareness and evaluation of the conflict.

Politics of Dynamics

Most of the literature on the politics of social media focuses on instances in which algorithm writers and platform providers introduce values into social media components, or on the way architects shape policies and standards. However, the politics of social media is not just about the architecture. It is also about the forms of power which operate as the dynamics of interactions between social actors evolve. These relationship dynamics are revealed to us, as researchers, through the information as it flows or is curated in social media.

Politics of Information Flows

In the information age, the ability to control the flows of information is a significant source of power. The politics of information flows refers mainly to the conflict around how information, the most critical resource in social media, is shared and distributed among users. Studies have repeatedly demonstrated the formation of skewed information flows in social media, which result in unequal distribution of attention, and unequal impact on behaviour and preferences (see, e.g. Nahon & Hemsley, 2013; Wihbey, 2014).

Not every skewed information flow is a result of a political intervention. For example, homophilous patterns of users found in conversations in social media platforms may form independently of any intervention by platforms. However, collective patterns of behaviour (manifested by the clustering of information flows) rarely evolve without any political intervention, let alone political implications. In this section, I focus solely on patterns that are driven or exploited by social actors, which I consider as political dynamics. A systematic review of the politics of information flows should include a discussion of (1) *mediators*, or gatekeepers, the actors who control of information flows and (2) *clustering effects* that are the product of information flow politics.

Mediators

Network gatekeepers have a tremendous impact on information flows: by choosing which information can or cannot pass, by connecting networks or clusters to one another, or more generally by regulating the movement of information as it flows. They can impact the chances of one video getting millions of views, while millions of other videos will receive only few. Network gatekeepers (people, collectives, or institutions) are those with the discretion to control information as it flows in and among networks. However, their power is not absolute and their impact depends to a large extent on the gated—those subjected to their gatekeeping—and on the power dynamics with other network gatekeepers (Barzilai-Nahon, 2008, 2009; Nahon, 2011).

Network gatekeepers are social actors that control information as it flows, so by definition they exercise power and are therefore political actors.

> Actors in this system are articulated by complex and evolving power relations based upon adaptation and interdependence. They create, tap, or steer information flows in ways that suit their goals and in ways that modify, enable, or disable others' agency, across and between a range of older and newer media settings. (Chadwick, 2013, p. 157)

Therefore, a major power struggle in social media is over the number and identity of gatekeepers or mediators. Technological improvements have immensely enhanced the individual user's ability to both produce and disseminate data. Despite this ability, however, true control of information flows still lies in the hands of a small number of mediators. The huge amount of information produced every second, as well as the need to create, share, and read content, require the user to rely on their services. They help users in all their activities in social media, from filtering excess information through connectivity with others to producing new content. We rely on Google to find what we are looking for, on social media opinion leaders to keep us posted, or on Facebook and Twitter to show us the posts uploaded by our friends. Facebook, for example, does not show us all of our friends' posts, but only those it selects. In return for this service, it gets to control the agenda of the information transferred from one subscriber to another. The struggle over the number and identity of gatekeepers or mediators is a struggle for controlling the agenda of the information conveyed and transferred from one person to another.

While traditional gatekeeping focuses mainly on selection (e.g. by newspaper editors), network gatekeepers have many additional information control mechanisms. The power of network gatekeepers does not necessarily reside in their ability to stop or filter information as it is transferred. On the contrary, it is concealed in their ability to link networks together, allowing information to travel far and fast, and to connect people to information and ideas. Attracting users' attention is the name of the game for network gatekeepers (Wihbey, 2014). Content will spread if people know it is available to be spread, and mediators bring content to the attention of those who follow them. This is their main source of being network power hubs.

Clustering Effects

Skewed clustered information flows can occur for a number of collective behaviour effects, including power-law and follow-the-herd tendencies, homophilous tendencies and polarization. Research has demonstrated that linking entities in social networks follows a power-law distribution, where a few elites receive the attention of many and thus have a disproportionate amount of influence (Adamic & Glance, 2005; Drezner & Farrell, 2008; Karpf, 2008; Nahon et al., 2011; Wallsten, 2011). Scientists have shown that the structure of networks plays an important role in how, and to what degree, information spreads. For example, Barabási uses mathematical models to show that many social networks are scale-free, which means that the number of connections between individuals follows a power-law distribution (a few nodes have many connections while most have relatively few), supporting the idea that the attention of the masses is concentrated on a few influential actors. It turns out that a power-law distribution of attention or linking is a fairly normal social pattern evident both online and offline. Of course, capturing the attention of others may later translate into the ability to influence them (Nahon & Hemsley, 2013).

Figure 3.2 illustrates this increasingly uneven distribution through the growing market share of the top four search engines from 2002 to 2015. From 2010 they have captured the attention of more than 98 per cent of users. While the identity of the four top has changed with time (AOL and MSN were replaced by Baidu and Bing after 2010), the main question we need to address is what this implies in terms of the variety and value bias of the information we consume daily. These leading search engines exercise all three forms of power. Through their responses to billions of queries they control the personal agendas of every one of us: from how to find a particular plumber to what type of news to read. What information to exclude or include and with what priority are clearly manifestations of power over information flows and political decisions. The power-law tendency is also evident in other types of social media: in the blogosphere with dominant blogs such as *Huffington Post*, in micro-blogging with Twitter,

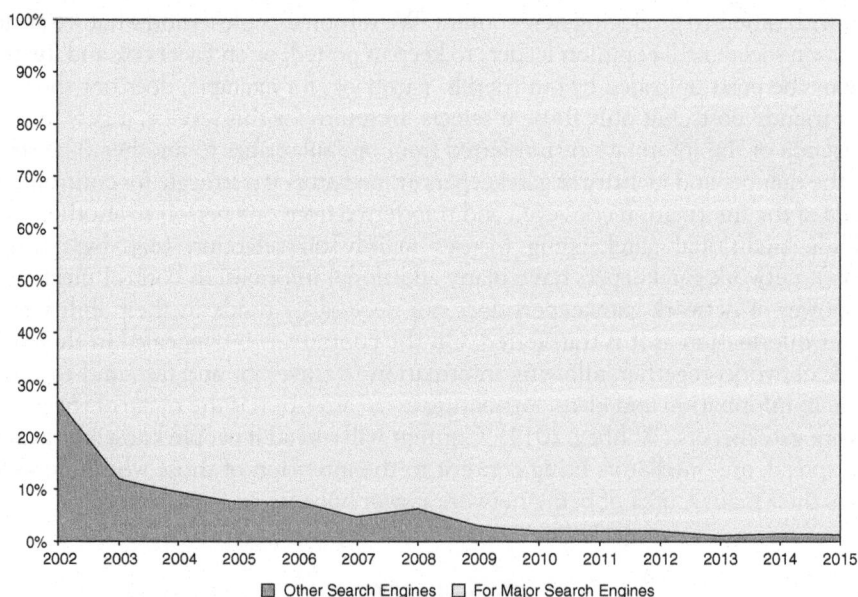

Figure 3.2 Four Top Search Engines' Market Share
Sources: Alexa, Netmarketshare, Search Engine Watch

or in general social media with the dominance of Facebook—making the social media landscape significantly political.

The power law is just one dominant information flow tendency with political implications in social media. Empirical studies have also demonstrated that social networks also introduce homophily, fragmentation, and polarization (Benkler, 2006; Sunstein, 2009). In particular, homophily, the tendency of people with similar attributes to associate with each other more frequently than they associate with others (Lazarsfeld & Merton, 1954; McPherson, Smith-Lovin, & Cook, 2001), has long been recognized as a factor in linking behaviour. More recently, it has been shown to be statistically confounded with influence (Shalizi & Thomas, 2011), meaning that statistics cannot be used to differentiate between similar behaviour due to homophilous linking or due to the influence of Actor A over B. Scholars who have attempted to quantitatively distinguish homophily from personal influence (e.g. Aral, Muchnik, & Sundararajan, 2009; Centola, González-Avella, Eguíluz, & San Miguel, 2007) have been refuted by prominent statisticians who show that the two processes are generically confounded (Shalizi & Thomas, 2011).

Thus, a complex relationship exists between homophily and influence. Homophilous links in social media arise because people interact with similar others. As they interact over time, they co-influence each other and become more similar. Thus, over time, homophily changes the group structure, in a process indistinguishable from social influence (Centola et al., 2007). Homophily is fundamentally a mechanism of selection, but at the same time it is also a mechanism of (albeit latent) influence at the individual and group levels. It is induced by social structure and, in turn, influences those structures in what Centola et al. (2007) refer to as a *co-evolutionary model*. Going back to our example at the beginning of the chapter on the Israeli elections, users' homophilous tendencies were exploited and intensified by Facebook, resulting in a more skewed clustering of information flows, and ultimately in an illusory electoral reality.

Politics of Curated Flows

> Data and data sets are not objective; they are creations of human design. We give numbers their voice, draw inferences from them, and define their meaning through our interpretations. Hidden biases in both the collection and analysis stages present considerable risks. (Crawford, 2013: para. 2)

The vastness of information in social media is created and shared by users, not the platforms themselves, and continues to explode on a daily basis. These big data are the basis of social media platforms' business models. Many stakeholders engage with this information: users, platforms, third-party companies, governments, researchers, and more. Politics also occurs *after* information flows, at the curation phase.

> To curate, historically, has meant to take charge of or organize, to pull together, sift through, select for presentation, to heal and to preserve. Traditionally reserved for those who worked with physical materials in museum or library settings, curation today has evolved to apply to what we are all doing online. (Mihailidis & Cohen, 2013: p. 3)

For the purposes of the current discussion, I would like to borrow the term 'curated flows' from Thorson and Wells (2015), which refers to curation in the broadest sense: to select and organize, to filter abundance into a collection of manageable size, to search, reframe and remix, or in short manage information flows after they have flowed in, particularly, social media.

Being a participatory space, social media empower users to perform functions previously reserved to professional curators, such as archiving, annotating, appropriating, and recirculating real-time information (Jenkins, Purushotma, Weigel, Clinton, & Robison, 2009). In the social media and big data era, there are suddenly many stakeholders who curate content, raising many different information issues: What is the most appropriate way to harvest information flows? What are the ethical considerations regarding privacy that need to be addressed when archiving public data? Who is responsible if a post is taken out of context? Who can access this data? The resolution of these and other emerging issues is a political act, given that interpretations and behaviours that rely on curated flows are inherently biased as they depend on how we collect information flows, how we clean the noise, how we understand the data, and most importantly, what our power motivations are.

For example, interpreting the impact politicians have on social media will depend on multiple decisions: the hashtags or keywords we collect, the languages, the platforms, the technical constraints (such as the API), and the way we understand the context. These are *political* decisions, no matter whether they are manually or automatically operated. Someone behind the scenes has to decide about how to curate flows, and this decision will have an impact on others. Politicization of curation occurs in small amounts of data and all the more so in big data. Expecting the curation of flows to be a neutral, objective and accurate process in big data because they are too big for humans to handle them directly is a myth (boyd & Crawford, 2012).

In another key example, Crawford and Gillespie (2014) show how the flagging mechanism for reporting offensive content on social media platforms "serves both as a solution to the problem of curating massive collections of user-generated content and as a rhetorical justification for platform owners when they decide to remove content". In practice, it is a political mechanism of negotiating contentious public issues between users, groups, moderators and platforms which attempt to promote certain values by reconciling "their ability to directly know or quantify community values with their practical and rhetorical value" (Crawford & Gillespie, 2014, p. 3).

Power struggles in Wikipedia will serve as our final example for a political struggle around curated flows. Wikipedia's stated mission is to provide a free encyclopaedia that people all over the world can use and contribute to. However, multiple studies have shown that it is rife with struggles around determining why and how content is included that have, for the most part, taken place behind the scenes and far from the public eye. These dynamics occur among editors who represent different value systems. In January 2006, a Wikipedia entry item was created to document the controversy surrounding the publication of a cartoon depicting the prophet Muhammad by Danish broadsheet *Jyllands-Posten*, which in return sparked a controversy around whether the original cartoons should be published or made available via thumbnails or links. When editors involved in the article's initial creation decided to republish a large thumbnail version of the original cartoons at the top of the article, many Wikipedia readers and editors objected to this as unnecessarily inflammatory. After a power struggle among editor groups, those in favour of keeping the images on the top won the day, claiming that a consensus decision had been reached (Morgan, Mason, & Nahon, 2011).

Conclusion

This chapter discussed and demonstrated the pervasiveness of the role played by politics in social media. Social media politics represents conscious and frequent acts whereby multiple actors exercise power to as they grapple with issues relevant to the governance and use of social media themselves, but also engage with issues with political ramifications outside of the social media realm.

Lately there has been growing discourse raising concerns that most decisions related to social media algorithms are not only non-neutral but heavily biased politically, leading to the conclusion that "cyberspace never was—and never could be—independent from the governing institutions, economic structures, and culture and social worlds that gave rise to it" (Kreiss, 2014, p. 133). This chapter has attempted to add a further refinement to this discourse by deconstructing the general and opaque notion of *algorithm* and focusing on the locus of the political process: whether it occurs while information flows are curated, or while the basic elements of a social media platform are architected (see Figure 3.3). Manifestations of politics can be identified in social media *architecture* (on the platform and network structure levels) and *dynamics* (on the network structure, information flow, and curated flow levels). In all instances, the product is the same: a continuing attempt to regulate human practices and norms, and, moreover, to transform or reinforce the behaviour, preferences, and values of individuals and groups according to the worldview and interests of those in power.

The politics of platform architecture is different from the dynamic politics of information flows. Whereas the former mainly involves infrastructure as a mechanism to regulate behaviour, the latter mainly involves the content of information flows. The legitimacy of the information that flows is derived mainly from users who share the

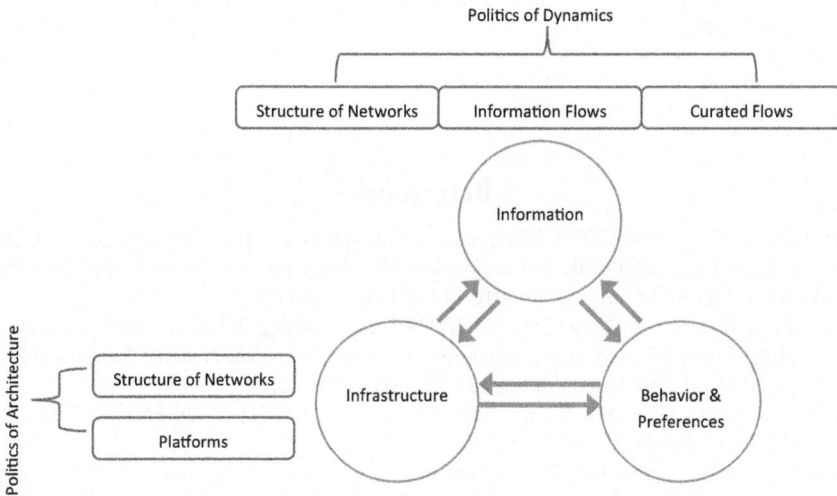

Figure 3.3 Politics of Social Media: Relationships

content. In contrast, platforms receive their operational legitimacy from the false belief in procedural justice, the myth that platforms are neutral.

For example, there is a difference between the politics of allowing users to post nude photos on a particular platform and that of making it go viral or preventing it from being shared at all. It is a subtle but important difference. The politics of information flows entails a greater number of stakeholders and is more inclusive in terms of the power at play since it usually does not reside in a single platform. Deconstructing the politics of social media also allows the discourse to move from examining specific dominant actors such as platforms and governments to a more nuanced evaluation of interrelations that also involve users and non-users.

Identifying the political manifestations is only a small fraction of the story. Most of the political processes occur without any serious public discussion about the values at stake. Questions about the right to be forgotten by Google, about what governments may collect about me on social media, or about whether nude photos should be censored inevitably receive different answers from different people. What holds for one community does not hold for another community in the same network. This messy ecosystem creates a political vacuum in which platforms get to play the police (sometimes against their will) while users look for creative solutions to circumvent policing. Political struggles and actions are determined without thorough scrutiny by *all* relevant stakeholders, rather than just the powerful. Where there is social media there is politics.

Acknowledgments

I would like to express deep gratitude to Ami Asher for helping me with the language editing of this chapter. Also, I thank Shawn Walker and Alison Wohlers for providing comments on earlier drafts of the chapter.

Notes

1 As elaborated further below, the politics of network structure can occur both on the architecture level and on the dynamics level.
2 For an extensive discussion of social power in general, see Lukes (2005). For a discussion of power in networks, see Castells (2009), and a special volume dedicated to network theory and power in the *International Journal of Communications* (Vol. 5, 2011).

References

Adamic, L. A., & Glance, N. (2005). The political blogosphere and the 2004 U.S. election: Divided they blog. In *Proceedings of the 3rd International Workshop on Link Discovery* (pp. 36–43). New York, NY, USA: ACM. http://doi.org/10.1145/1134271.1134277

Aral, S., Muchnik, L., & Sundararajan, A. (2009). Distinguishing influence-based contagion from homophily-driven diffusion in dynamic networks. *Proceedings of the National Academy of Sciences*, 106(51), 21544–21549. http://doi.org/10.1073/pnas.0908800106

Bachrach, P., & Baratz, M. S. (1962). Two Faces of Power. *The American Political Science Review*, 56(4), 947–952. http://doi.org/10.2307/1952796

Barabási, A. L. (2003). *Linked*. New York: Plume.

Barzilai-Nahon, K. (2008). Toward a theory of network gatekeeping: A framework for exploring information control. *Journal of the American Society for Information Science and Technology*, 59(9), 1493–1512.

Barzilai-Nahon, K. (2009). Gatekeeping: A critical review. *Annual Review of Information Science and Technology (ARIST)*, 43, 433–479.

Benkler, Y. (2006). *The wealth of networks: How social production transforms markets and freedom*. New Haven: Yale University Press.

Bond, R.M., Fariss, C.J., Jones, J.J., Kramer, A.D.I., Marlow, C., Settle, J.E., & Fowler, J.H. (2012). A 61-million-person experiment in social influence and political mobilization. *Nature*, 489(7415), 295–298. http://doi.org/10.1038/nature11421

Bourdieu, P. (1977). *Outline of a theory of practice*. (R. Nice, Trans.). New York: Cambridge University Press.

boyd, danah, & Crawford, K. (2012). Critical questions for big data. *Information, Communication & Society*, 15(5), 662–679. http://doi.org/10.1080/1369118X.2012.678878

Bruns, A., & Moe, H. (2014). Structural layers of communication on Twitter. In K. Weller, A. Bruns, J. Burgess, M. Mahrt, & C. Puschmann (Eds.), *Twitter and Society* (Vol. 89, pp. 15–28). New York: Peter Lang. Retrieved from http://eprints.qut.edu.au/66324/

Castells, M. (2009). *Communication power*. Oxford University Press, USA.

Centola, D., González-Avella, J.C., Eguíluz, V.M., & San Miguel, M. (2007). Homophily, cultural drift, and the co-evolution of cultural groups. *Journal of Conflict Resolution*, 51(6), 905–929. http://doi.org/10.1177/0022002707307632

Chadwick, A. (2013). *The hybrid media system: Politics and power*. Oxford University Press.

Constine, J. (2014). *Why is Facebook page reach decreasing? More competition and limited attention*. Retrieved from http://social.techcrunch.com/2014/04/03/the-filtered-feed-problem/

Costolo, D. (2014, August 20). *We have been and are actively suspending accounts as we discover them related to this graphic imagery*. Retrieved from https://twitter.com/dickc/status/502005459067625473

Crawford, K. (2013, April). The hidden biases in big data. *Harvard Business Review*. Retrieved from https://hbr.org/2013/04/the-hidden-biases-in-big-data

Crawford, K., & Gillespie, T. (2014). What is a flag for? Social media reporting tools and the vocabulary of complaint. *New Media & Society*. http://doi.org/10.1177/1461444814543163

Dahl, R.A. (1957). The concept of power. *Behavioral Science*, 2(3), 201–215. http://doi.org/10.1002/bs.3830020303

Drezner, D., & Farrell, H. (2008). The power and politics of blogs. *Public Choice*, 134(1–2), 15–30. http://doi.org/10.1007/s11127–007–9198–1

Durkheim, E. (1982). *Rules of Sociological Method*. New York: Free Press.

Elmer, G. (2010). Exclusionary rules? The politics of protocols. In A. Chadwick & P.N. Howard (Eds.), *Routledge handbook of Internet politics* (pp. 376–384). London: Taylor & Francis.

Facebook: Community Standard Page. (n.d.). Retrieved from http://www.facebook.com/community standards

Foucault, M. (1978). *Discipline & punish: The birth of the prison* (2nd Edition). New York: Vintage.

Foucault, M. (1990). *The history of sexuality* (R. Hurley, Trans., Fifth or Later Edition). New York: Vintage.

Giddens, A. (1986). *The constitution of society: Outline of the theory of structuration*. Oakland: University of California Press.

Gillespie, T. (2010). The politics of "platforms." *New Media & Society*, 12(3), 347–364. http://doi.org/10.1177/1461444809342738

Gillespie, T. (2014). The relevance of algorithms. In T. Gillespie, P. Boczkowski, & K. Foot (Eds.), *Media technologies* (pp. 167–194). Cambridge, MA: MIT Press. Retrieved from http://www.academia.edu/2257984/The_Relevance_of_Algorithms

Halavais, A. (2008). *Search engine society*. Cambridge: Polity.

Introna, L.D. (2006). Maintaining the reversibility of foldings: Making the ethics (politics) of information technology visible. *Ethics and Information Technology*, 9(1), 11–25. http://doi.org/10.1007/s10676–006–9133-z

Jenkins, H., Purushotma, R., Weigel, M., Clinton, K., & Robison, A.J. (2009). *Confronting the challenges of participatory culture: Media education for the 21st century*. Cambridge, MA: The MIT Press.

Karpf, D. (2008). *Measuring Influence in the political blogosphere: Who is winning and how can we tell?* George Washington University's Institute for Politics, Democracy and the Internet. Retrieved from http://www.the4dgroup.com/BAI/articles/PoliTechArticle.pdf

Kreiss, D. (2014). A vision of and for the networked world: John Perry Barlow's *A Declaration of the Independence of Cyberspace* at twenty. In J. Bennett & N. Strange (Eds.), *Media independence: Working with freedom or working for free?* (pp. 117–138). London: Routledge.

Lazarsfeld, P., & Merton, R. (1954). Friendship as a social process: A substantive and methodological analysis. In M. Berger (Ed.), *Freedom and control in modern societies* (Vol. 18, pp. 18–66). New York: Van Nostrand.

Lievrouw, L. A. (2009). New media, mediation, and communication study. *Information, Communication & Society, 12*(3), 303–325. http://doi.org/10.1080/13691180802660651

Liu, Y., Gummadi, K. P., Krishnamurthy, B., & Mislove, A. (2011). Analyzing Facebook privacy settings: User expectations vs. reality. In *Proceedings of the 2011 ACM SIGCOMM Conference on Internet Measurement Conference* (pp. 61–70). New York, NY, USA: ACM. http://doi.org/10.1145/2068816.2068823

Lukes, S. (2005). *Power: A radical view* (2nd ed.). London: Palgrave Macmillan.

McKelvey, F. (2010). Ends and ways: The algorithmic politics of network neutrality. *Global Media Journal, 3*(1), 51–73.

McPherson, M., Smith-Lovin, L., & Cook, J. M. (2001). Birds of a feather: Homophily in social networks. *Annual Review of Sociology, 27*, 415–444.

Meyer, E. (2014, December 24). *Inadvertent algorithmic cruelty.* Retrieved from http://meyerweb.com/eric/thoughts/2014/12/24/inadvertent-algorithmic-cruelty/

Mihailidis, P., & Cohen, J. N. (2013). Exploring curation as a core competency in digital and media literacy education. *Journal of Interactive Media in Education, 2013*(1), Art–2.

Morgan, J. T., Mason, R. M., & Nahon, K. (2011). Lifting the veil: The expression of values in online communities. In *Proceedings of the 2011 iConference* (pp. 8–15). ACM. Retrieved from http://dl.acm.org/citation.cfm?id=1940763

Nahon, K. (2011). Fuzziness of inclusion/exclusion in networks. *International Journal of Communication, 5*(17), 756–772. Retrieved from http://ijoc.org/index.php/ijoc/article/view/1119/552

Nahon, K., & Hemsley, J. (2013). *Going viral* (1 edition). Cambridge: Polity.

Nahon, K., Hemsley, J., Walker, S., & Hussain, M. (2011). Fifteen minutes of fame: The power of blogs in the lifecycle of viral political information. *Policy & Internet, 3*(1), 6–33. http://doi.org/10.2202/1944-2866.1108

Pariser, E. (2012). *The filter bubble: How the New Personalized Web is changing what we read and how we think* (Reprint edition). New York: Penguin Books.

Polsby, N. W. (1963). *Community power and political theory.* New Haven, CT: Yale University Press.

Sagolla, D. (2009). *140 Characters: A style guide for the short form* (1st ed.). Hoboken, NJ: Wiley.

Segev, E. (2010). *Google and the digital divide: The bias of online knowledge* (1st edition). Oxford: Chandos.

Shalizi, C. R., & Thomas, A. C. (2011). Homophily and contagion are generically confounded in observational social network studies. *Sociological Methods & Research, 40*(2), 211.

Shaw, A., & Hill, B. M. (2014). Laboratories of oligarchy? How the iron law extends to peer production. *Journal of Communication, 64*(2), 215–238. http://doi.org/10.1111/jcom.12082

Sunstein, C. R. (2009). *Republic.com 2.0.* Princeton, NJ: Princeton University Press.

Thorson, K., & Wells, C. (2015). How gatekeeping still matters: understanding media effects in an era of curated flows. In P. V. Tim & H. Froncois (Eds.), *Gatekeeping in transition* (pp. 25–44). Retrieved from https://wordery.com/gatekeeping-in-transition-tim-p-vos-9780415731614

Trottier, D., & Fuchs, C. (2014). Theorising social media, politics and the state. In *Social media, politics and the state* (pp. 3–38). New York: Routledge. Retrieved from http://www.bokus.com/bok/9780415749091/social-media-politics-and-the-state/

Tufekci, Z. (2014). Engineering the public: Big data, surveillance and computational politics. *First Monday, 19*(7). Retrieved from http://www.firstmonday.dk/ojs/index.php/fm/article/view/4901

Wallsten, K. (2007). Agenda setting and the blogosphere: An analysis of the relationship between mainstream media and political blogs. *Review of Policy Research, 24*(6), 567–587. http://doi.org/10.1111/j.1541-1338.2007.00300.x

Wallsten, K. (2011). Beyond agenda setting: The role of political blogs as sources in newspaper coverage of government. In *2011 44th Hawaii International Conference on System Sciences* (HICSS; pp. 1–10). http://doi.org/10.1109/HICSS.2011.80

Watts, D. J. (2004). *Six degrees: The science of a connected age.* New York: W. W. Norton & Company.

Weber, M. (1946). *From Max Weber: Essays in sociology* (H. H. Gerth & C. W. Mills, Eds. & Trans.). New York: Oxford University Press.

Wihbey, J. P. (2014). The challenges of democratizing news and information: Examining data on social media, viral patterns and digital influence. *Shorenstein Center on Media, Politics and Public Policy Discussion Paper Series.* Retrieved from http://dash.harvard.edu/handle/1/12872220

Winner, L. (1996). Who will we be in cyberspace? *The Information Society, 12*(1), 63–72.

Woodly, D. (2008). New competencies in democratic communication? Blogs, agenda setting and political participation. *Public Choice, 134*(1), 109–123.

4

IS HABERMAS ON TWITTER?

Social Media and the Public Sphere

Axel Bruns and Tim Highfield

Introduction

The concept of the public sphere, first introduced by Jürgen Habermas in his seminal book *Strukturwandel der Öffentlichkeit* (1962), translated into English as *The Structural Transformation of the Public Sphere* (1989), has proven to be an influential model for our understanding of media and communication processes, especially in the political arena. Habermas described a significant structural transformation—the *Strukturwandel* of the German title—which led to the replacement of the rational-critical public sphere of 18th-century coffeehouses and civic societies with a much more heavily mediatised public sphere at the dawn of the 20th century, as a result of the arrival of mass-circulation daily newspapers and the growing popularity of radio. This largely transitioned political and societal deliberation to this mediatised realm, where it was now carried out by a range of state, civic, and commercial actors on behalf of the public, removing more direct forms of participation on such debate and deliberation from the public.

Habermas thus conceived of his *Öffentlichkeit*—the public sphere—as a space that is framed and structured by the operations of the mass media (primarily print and broadcast), and where "mediated political communication" is thus "carried on by an elite" (Habermas 2006: 416) composed of journalists themselves as well as of those public actors whom journalism affords an opportunity to speak; by contrast, ordinary people—the public—are cast in the role of audience members who for the most part are merely able to watch the events unfolding on this "virtual stage of mediated communication" (2006: 415).

In following this highly hierarchical, top-down model, the public sphere concept betrays its origins in the 1950s and 1960s, at the height of the mass media age when a small number of mainstream media organisations—in Habermas's native Germany and elsewhere in Western Europe, chiefly also including a handful of dominant public service broadcasters—were indeed positioned as highly influential, agenda-setting and opinion-leading institutions. The leading newspapers and broadcast news bulletins of the day could rightly claim to provide a 'virtual stage' on which the daily drama of national and international politics was played out in front of a nationwide audience, creating a shared attention space that at least came close to the ideal public sphere described by Habermas. But the model thus also presupposes the existence of a media sector that adheres to a strong public service ethic even amongst commercial media organisations, which are driven as much by their social and societal responsibilities as by their profit motives, and it assumes the presence of a politically engaged, rationally deliberating public.

Considering such implied preconditions, it is apparent that if critiques of the public sphere concept could be raised during the mass media age, then today there are even more significant challenges to our conceptualisation of the public sphere. Not least, the model's explicit focus on societal elites instead of ordinary citizens is not necessarily well-aligned with contemporary contexts. The processes of *Strukturwandel* which Habermas identified in the transition from the coffee houses to mass media did not stop there but continued further beyond the mass media age, and the contemporary media ecology is thus considerably different from that of the 1960s: the dominance of a small number of public as well as commercial media organisations has declined substantially in most developed nations, while a range of readily available alternative media forms and platforms have emerged at local, national, and transnational levels. Television audiences have dispersed across a growing range of broadcast and cable options, and are now increasingly also making use of streaming and on-demand online options: 2013 and 2014 data from the U.S., for example, points to an average 10 per cent drop in year-on-year viewer numbers for conventional TV (Evans, 2015). Newspaper readership is similarly declining in many media markets: in the UK, for instance, 2014 figures show an average annual decrease of circulation figures of some 8 per cent (Greenslade, 2014). While some of this shift away from traditional broadcast and print and towards online content constitutes a simple change of technologies, with viewers remaining loyal to established media organisations, many other users also end up exploring the wider variety of content options now available to them. This necessarily reduces the dominance which leading media organisations enjoyed in a pre-digital era, when receiving broadcast or print content from outside of one's own geographical area was often prohibitively difficult.

Such changes have been driven to a significant degree by the emergence of the Internet and the World Wide Web as leading channels for the dissemination of news, amongst their many other functions. Since the 1990s, the Web has gained a substantial share of the news market, to the detriment of print and broadcast news and to the point that such conventional news organisations are now themselves using the Web as a key channel for the dissemination of the news; even more importantly, the instant global connectivity provided by the Web has fundamentally disrupted local news markets and forced regional and domestic news organisations to compete on an international level for audience attention. The more recent emergence of social media as even more connected, even more rapid, even more diverse spaces for the dissemination and discussion of news and public affairs, and for mediatising everyday life, has only served to increase the complexity of the contemporary media environment. This has further blended and merged the individual national public spheres that may exist into an increasingly global network of information flows.

News and public affairs reporting as it presents itself to the everyday user has thus transformed from a largely oligopolistic media environment, dominated by a few major public and commercial media organisations providing mass market news products for general consumption by a domestic audience, to a diverse, complex and even confusing media ecology. Here, mass and niche news services from all over the world compete for increasingly specific audience segments that are defined more by shared interests rather than by shared geographic origins or national identities. The concept of a unified domestic public sphere, then, must necessarily be questioned. In the present environment, even the leading mainstream media outlets no longer command a truly 'mass' audience: the 'virtual stage' that each organisation continues to present is now watched by an ever shrinking subset of 'the public', while the total number of 'virtual stages' available to these increasingly niche audiences has multiplied beyond counting.

Indeed, such trends towards a fragmentation of the national 'public', posited as the audience observing and reacting to the processes unfolding in the public sphere, may have accelerated since the emergence of the Web as a mass medium. However, critics of the idea of 'the' public sphere have long pointed out that the assumed unified nature of the public sphere as an all-encompassing space of public debate is an "explicitly idealist concept" (Webster 2013: 25) at any rate: even at the height of the mass media age, the public's attention to public matters was never uniform, as individual audience members exercised their own agency in selecting issues of interest from all of the themes and topics covered by the media. As Hartley and Green (2006) bluntly put it, "'the' public sphere is a convenient fantasy" (347).

If today the existing cracks in the idea of 'the' public sphere have merely become more obviously visible, and if the public sphere concept in its original Habermasian formulation no longer appears to be able to fully represent the complexities of the contemporary global media ecology, then we are facing the question of how the public sphere concept may be adjusted to better describe present experiences, or in fact of whether the 'public sphere' as an idea is still relevant at all. As Webster (2013) suggests, perhaps we are "reaching a time when we need . . . to consider abandoning the concept" (Webster 2013: 25)? This chapter explores these questions by examining some of the extensions and alternatives to 'the' public sphere that have been proposed in recent years, and by examining the evidence for the existence of such alternative structures which may be established through empirical research especially on social media platforms such as Facebook and Twitter. It suggests that there may be a need to augment or even replace the Habermasian public sphere in its most orthodox formulation by embracing a more complex, dynamic, and multifaceted model that allows for connections and overlaps between a multitude of coexisting public spheres. In the second half of this chapter, we apply such conceptualisations to the extended network of Australian Twitter users (the Australian 'Twittersphere'): this examination of social media connections and publics, with a view to developing an alternative or adapted public sphere model, also acts as an example of how to trace and identify such aggregations, their overlaps, divisions, and interactions.

Calls for a critical reassessment of the public sphere idea, or even for its replacement by a model that inherently allows for multiple coexisting and competing public spheres at the same time, are not new, even if they appear to have grown more insistent as a result of the increasing importance of global and digital media spaces. Fenton and Downey, for example, point to "the rise of counter-publicity," resulting in multiple "counter-public spheres" (2003: 16). In doing so, they build on a rich tradition of research that examines the tactics of resistance by groups and communities that are marginalised in the predominantly bourgeois public sphere which Habermas describes. But as Calhoun (1992) notes in *Habermas and the Public Sphere*, a major collection of critical responses to Habermas's work that marked its translation into English, if such critiques are accurate, how do we understand the more complex structures we must now describe? He warns that to say that there are many public spheres . . . will leaves us groping for a new term to describe the communicative relationships among them. It might be productive rather to think of the public sphere as involving a field of discursive connections. (Calhoun 1992: 37)

The Continued Structural Transformation of the Public Sphere

A reappraisal of the public sphere concept has always been a possibility: after all, Habermas's original work explicitly describes the structural transformation (*Strukturwandel*) of the public sphere towards its then-current state rather than a stable, static, unchanging system. If the rise of the mass media saw a transformation towards a universal, nationwide public sphere—'the' public sphere, as Hartley and Green (2006) describe it—then its subsequent decline simply signals a further period of transformation that may or may not result in a new, stable, but temporary equilibrium model.

It is important to state here that the point of this discussion, at least for our present purposes in the context of this volume, is not so much the continuation of Habermasian theoretical frameworks as such, as if they are somehow inherently more valuable than other, different models. Much contemporary media theory makes only very passing reference to Habermas's frameworks, even when it explicitly uses the term 'public sphere' itself; Fraser (1992) has lamented that such research "involves the use of the very same expression 'public sphere' but in a sense that is less precise and less useful than Habermas's" (1992: 110). Alternatively, a more positive perspective on this proliferation of the term, detached from its Habermasian origins, in media and communication studies is that 'public sphere' itself has proven so productive an idea that it has given rise to a wide variety of competing conceptualisations, in the same manner as terms like 'society', 'culture', or 'community', for example. Some of these variations on the Habermasian theme may be just as useful as the original public sphere model, even if they have relatively little in common with it. In the face of this divergence of streams of thought and theory on 'the' public sphere, which utilise Habermas's own work as a point of departure to a greater or lesser extent, then, this chapter seeks to review a number of the key contributions to reimagining public sphere concepts—including, indeed, some of Habermas's own recent work.

It seems obvious that the central feature of such a new model must be the fragmentation of the unified public sphere into a range of diverging yet potentially overlapping publics. In Habermas's Germany, mainstream media managed to attract truly mass audiences, and thus constructed what can genuinely be described as a unified, nationwide public sphere: in the 1960s, the prime-time public service television news bulletin *Tagesschau* regularly attracted more than 50 per cent of the total television audience (Launer 1981), and major newspapers achieved comparable mass circulation throughout the country. But the gradual diversification of media channels and audiences, combined with fundamental technological and lifestyle changes (as on-demand access to news online has replaced the daily ritual of morning newspaper and evening TV news), has caused an irreversible decline in audience sizes: the growing number of news sources and media channels may still be able to attract their own publics, but these no longer join together to form a unified public sphere in the way that existing theory had imagined it.

Such publics may be defined at different levels of resolution, and it is useful to explore the diverse constructs of publics (and indeed, public spheres) that have been proposed by various scholars in recent years before we attempt to find any empirical evidence for them in social media spaces. First, at the most general level, a number of scholars envisage a separation of the public sphere into broad domain publics: Dahlgren (2009) and Webster (2013) both refer to the 'political public sphere', while Hartley and Green (2006) also describe a 'cultural public sphere'—and a range of other potential candidates for such subordinate spheres (the business public sphere, the sporting public sphere, and so on) readily come to mind.

Cutting across such broad domain publics are more technologically driven public spheres, defined by their chief medium of communication—Benkler (2006), for example, develops the idea of a 'networked public sphere' that draws centrally on online communication platforms, and analogous partial public spheres defined by print, radio, or television may also be imagined; indeed, the existence of individual platform-specific public spheres is at least implied in terms such as the blogosphere and Twittersphere, encompassing all users of specific social media platforms as well as their public communicative activities.

However, given the considerable overlap and interweaving between such different media channels, such technocentric definitions of specific public spheres may not be particularly productive. There may still be significant generational differences in media usage practices which result in somewhat divergent dynamics within newspaper and online publics, for example, but few everyday citizens will engage exclusively only in one or another of these technologically defined public spheres. Indeed, even users continuing to favour conventional mass media channels such as newspapers and television will increasingly access these news sources through Internet technologies, given the continuing shift towards on-demand and mobile access to content and the decline in subscription rates and live viewing. As the Internet becomes the chief backbone for any kind of media distribution, distinctions between networked and non-networked public spheres are increasingly meaningless.

A similar argument also applies, in fact, to the broad domain public spheres we encountered above: few participants are likely to be interested only in politics but not in culture, or only in business but not in sports; few news stories are clearly one or the other, rather than playing into a number of these domains. News about economic policy, for example, is clearly part of both the political and the business public sphere, while articles about sports fandom address both culture and sports. Thinking through a combination of domain- and technology-specific public spheres makes it especially clear that these deceptively simple models are anything but straightforward: a TV news report about a new government policy initiative may originate in the television and politics public spheres, for example, but be disseminated across the networked public sphere via social media, leading to discussions about its economic and social implications on online news sites and blogs (and thus entering those respective domain-specific public spheres) and in face-to-face conversations, thus once again transitioning from the online to the offline public sphere. These technology- and domain-specific public spheres merely constitute different overlapping sectors within the overall Habermasian public sphere, without substantially departing from the idea; most centrally, they also continue to assume that a society-wide conduct of current public debates is possible and even likely.

A second, alternative perspective emerges not from the segmentation of 'the' public sphere into a small number of relatively broad domain- or technology-based subsets, but from a much more specific and fine-grained observation of the temporary publics that emerge around particular themes. This is where a number of scholars situate 'public sphericules' (Gitlin 1998; Cunningham 2001; Bruns 2008), described as "social fragments that do not have critical mass [but] share many of the characteristics of the classically conceived public sphere" (Cunningham 2001: 135). Such public sphericules no longer claim to reflect public discourse within entire domains back to society at large; rather, they address particular thematic debates within and across the broader domains, and in doing so draw on a smaller subset of participants with a specific interest in these themes. This reduction in size and reach may indeed improve the quality of the deliberation which takes place in such public sphericules, as a certain level of shared interest and knowledge amongst participants may be assumed. Given enough popular interest, such debates may come to transcend their public sphericules and reach a wider, less directly engaged audience, but even where they fail to do so they are still likely to involve a narrow but inherently interested public.

Third, an even more specific and bespoke form of public debate may be conducted in the "issue publics" already envisaged by Habermas (e.g. 2006: 422) and explored in more detail by a range of other scholars. Such issue publics no longer serve as a 'virtual stage' for the mass public, but in keeping with the metaphor instead represent studio spaces where specific debates between stakeholders are rehearsed amongst a smaller, self-selecting company of interested actors. Issue publics form especially around shorter-lived topics and events and are thus considerably more temporary and dynamic than some of the other formations we have already encountered—they "emerge, exist for varying durations, and then eventually dissolve" (Dahlgren 2009: 74) as public debate moves on. Issue publics are themselves thus related to, and arguably form subsets of, the wider public sphericules that exist around specific themes—but while a sphericule may address, for example, the overall longer-term challenge of anthropogenic climate change, the issue publics it contains would form around specific research reports, policy initiatives, and other short-term aspects that drive public debate on the topic. Nonetheless, public "attitudes are influenced by everyday talk in the informal settings or episodic publics of everyday society at least as much as they are by paying attention to print or electronic media" (Habermas 2006: 416).

The increasing specificity of debates which we are likely to encounter as we progress from broad domain-based public spheres through thematic public sphericules to narrow topical issue publics is likely to be reflected also in the range of media outlets that such subsets of 'the' public sphere draw on. Where the conventional public sphere model is largely predicated on the hegemonic role of dominant mass media institutions, the lower-order publics are likely to be increasingly more reliant on specialist and niche media, in keeping with their own much more narrowly defined interests. This is also a transition from broadcast to interactive communication structures, and from mainstream to alternative and amateur media outlets, then: in this second and third tier of 'the' public sphere, trusted non-mainstream voices engaging in what Castells (2009) describes as 'mass self-publication' can, potentially, gain as much influence as professional journalists.

Finally, a further extension of conventional public sphere concepts must ultimately also challenge the very boundaries of what it means to be public. In many ways, issue publics may really be best described as issue communities, and today are most likely to gather in the spaces provided by online community platforms—including, centrally, social media sites, such as Facebook and Twitter. Here, in particular, everyday social interaction between peers and public participation in issue publics overlap and are often inextricably intertwined, as users move seamlessly between interpersonal and public topics and registers of expression from one Facebook post to the next, and from one tweet to another: within the Australian Twittersphere, as will be seen later in this chapter, users cluster together in highly connected (but loosely thematic) groups around shared interests, with issue- and event-focussed discussions crossing over these overlapping assemblages as they are taken up by an audience beyond the specific context of the topic in question.

Indeed, Schmidt (2011, 2014) explicitly describes even the egocentric networks—the collections of Facebook 'friends' or Twitter 'followers'—which exist around each social media profile as 'personal publics'; similar such personal publics also exist in offline, face-to-face contexts, of course, and the complete personal public of any one individual thus encompasses the totality of their personal connections across any and all such communications platforms and media. The multitude of personal publics—overlapping with each other as friendship connections are shared between individual users and thus enable flows of information that are determined by common sociodemographic identities, topical interests, and communication practices amongst users—in combination constitutes a global patchwork of interconnected micro-publics, tying together social media, face-to-face, and other communication forms and channels, that may be seen as the lowermost foundation of the overall public sphere.

Alternatively or simultaneously, the patchwork of personal publics also serves as a point of transition into what Papacharissi (2010) describes as the "private sphere": a liminal space where social media participants are afforded the opportunity to engage in "privately public" conversations that are neither conducted entirely behind closed doors nor inherently exist in full view of the public. As she describes it, "operating from a civically *privé* environment, the citizen enters the public spectrum by negotiating aspects of his/her privacy as necessary, depending on the urgency and relevance of particular situations" (2010, 131–132). What emerges from these observations is a considerable challenge to the very idea of a *public* sphere, then: although what is public and what is private has never been entirely clear, the fuzzy boundary between the two is being exposed as problematic even more strikingly by the current generation of social media platforms. These platforms actively reconfigure the criteria by which we distinguish public from private, and/or offer their users the tools to develop an individual and idiosyncratic range of transitional steps between 'fully public' and 'fully private'. Even if communication amongst friends on Facebook is not fully public, for example (in the sense of 'visible to an outside observer'), its dissemination across the patchwork of overlapping personal micro-publics may nonetheless come to have widespread effects on public debate if it achieves sufficient reach and impact.

In more recent work, Habermas (2006) acknowledges the importance of this patchwork of publics as a foundation for 'the' public sphere at least in passing, in an update to his framework: he notes that "the public sphere is rooted in networks for the wild flows of messages—news, reports, commentaries, talks, scenes and images" (415). It is unfortunate that conventional public sphere theory, with its persistent focus on the mass media, only rarely acknowledges and investigates the network structures that enable this 'wild flow' of information beyond the mainstream, which in the contemporary media ecology chiefly include the leading social media platforms: the impact of such many-to-many communications media as amplifiers of or correctives to the mass media, and the structures of public communication which they enable and support, thus remain comparatively under-theorised— at least from a public sphere perspective.

If we do take seriously the various public spaces which now emerge as successors to 'the' public sphere, then rather than as a unified, mass-mediated space through which public debate is conducted, the public sphere is thus revealed as a complex combination of multiple interlocking elements that sometimes counteract, sometimes amplify each other, and that each possess their own specific dynamics; the contemporary public sphere is "comprised of a vast array of interactional constellations, some relatively more permanent, others more fleeting" (Dahlgren 2009: 74). What becomes all the more important, then, is to study the operation of these individual elements, and to develop a better understanding of just how they interact with each other. As we will see, online and especially social media spaces provide a particularly useful environment for the empirical analysis of such processes.

An investigation of the various interlocking parts that constitute this new multifaceted public sphere may also serve as a useful antidote to fears of a fragmentation of public debate and deliberation in the wake of the decline of the deceptively simple and stable model of the mass-mediated public sphere. The abundance of publics in the contemporary environment, from elite discourse in leading mainstream media through niche debates in more or less short-lived issue publics to everyday interpersonal exchanges in face-to-face and online contexts, could be seen as lending support to dystopian scenarios of a multitude of 'filter bubbles' (Pariser 2011) that are each caught in their own feedback loops of self-reinforcing 'groupthink' and actively defend against the intrusion of alternative, oppositional points of view. But while the 'filter bubble' metaphor suggests that such bubbles are each hermetically sealed from one another, observable reality appears to point to a much greater degree of interpenetration through shared connections and information flows; our brief discussion of the horizontal patchwork of personal micro-publics, as well as of the vertically layered nature of issue publics within public sphericules within domain-based publics, already points to this perspective, and later in this chapter we further explore the extent to which such filter bubbles can persist, by examining the structural characteristics of an entire national Twittersphere. Indeed, Habermas (2006) himself suggests that as "a larger number of people tend to take an interest in a larger number of issues, the overlap of issue publics may even serve to counter trends of fragmentation" (2006: 422).

The 'wild flows' of information that are enabled especially by the patchwork of personal publics may play a particularly important role in this context. Personal publics, in their relative disconnection from very specific themes and topics, can be seen as the conduits which provide for a—perhaps random and unintentional, but nonetheless real and important—exchange of information and ideas across issue publics and public sphericules. A focus on these crucial if liminal spaces of communication and dissemination also substantially broadens the range of actors which are seen as contributing to public debate and deliberation, since personal publics in both offline and online forms present considerably lower barriers to entry for a larger number of participants. This, then, moves beyond the temporary restrictions, both in visible participation and in scholarly attention to such participation, that were common at the height of the mass media age, and once again moves to consider the public sphere (or its diverse constituent elements) as a space that a wide range of citizens engage in, rather than as something that is played out for them by elite actors on a 'virtual stage'.

As a comprehensive analysis of these liminal spaces in the offline world remains difficult, a focus on contemporary mass social media platforms such as Twitter and Facebook as imperfect reflections of wider patterns of participation is valuable and instructive for the further exploration of the changing internal structures and dynamics of the wider public sphere—not least also because, as Papacharissi (2010) suggests, "social network sites expand the number and range of individuals who may enter the privately public space of the private sphere" (2010: 140). Similarly, social media encourage different ways of engaging with or participating within public, civic communication, with 'affective publics' (Papacharissi, 2015) bringing highly individual interpretations and framing to discussions, providing another dimension to ideas of 'personal' publics (Schmidt, 2014). Within these platforms, then, as well as across the range of private and public forms of communication they enable, it is possible to find evidence for the various post-public sphere constructs we have encountered so far.

Social Media Communication Structures as Reflections of Public Sphere Constructs

As widely adopted, versatile and global communication platforms, social media such as Facebook and Twitter enable an observation of the dynamics of many of the extensions and alternatives to conventional public sphere constructs that we have encountered so far. This is possible most of all because these platforms offer Application Programming Interfaces that provide access to unprecedentedly large datasets on the public communicative interactions of their hundreds of millions of users—so-called 'big social data' (Manovich 2012) that constitute an in-depth and second-by-second trace of individual users' activities. Further, contrary to other research approaches, such data-driven observations of social media activities can be made without influencing user behaviours themselves: users remain unaware of the presence of the researcher, and communicative processes are unaffected by the data being gathered on them.

This also raises significant ethical and privacy concerns, however, which have been outlined in detail in recent scholarly literature (see, e.g. boyd & Crawford's 2012 critique of 'big data' research in the humanities), and in the following discussion we are therefore refer only to aggregate and non-identifiable user activity patterns which relate to clearly *public* (rather than private or semi-private) forms of communication. For the same reason, we are also focussing on Twitter rather than on Facebook in the examples we discuss. The simple distinction between globally public and individually protected (private) accounts which Twitter has instituted, compared to Facebook's considerably more complex system of graduated (and frequently changing) privacy options, allows us to assume that, in general, the decision by 95 per cent of the global Twitter user base to set their account visibility is set to 'public' demonstrates an awareness of the consequences of that choice.

For both Twitter and Facebook, however, it is possible to map the various layers and structures of public communication which we have outlined above onto specific communicative processes and functions enabled by the social media platforms themselves. We explore this here with particular focus on Twitter, drawing on a framework developed by Bruns and Moe (2014) that identifies a number of communicative layers on the platform that are enabled by its technological features and sustained by the unwritten communicative conventions developed over time by the Twitter user base itself.

Central to both platforms are the profiles of individual users, of course, around which Schmidt's (2014) 'personal publics' emerge; these self-selecting (and in the case of Facebook, reciprocal) networks of 'friends' or 'followers' serve in the first place as an audience for the account around which they have formed, and the account owner is likely to be at least vaguely aware of the make-up and interests of that audience. Furthermore, the personal publics of various individual accounts will also overlap to a certain extent, creating the loose networks of egocentric publics that we have described as part of the patchwork of micro-publics which exists at the very foundation of the overall public sphere framework. These personal publics around each Twitter and Facebook account also complement and spill over into the personal publics that each individual draws on or performs to by using other media channels and platforms; in combination, the Twitter, Facebook, face-to-face, and other channel-specific personal publics thus form the complete personal publics for the individual behind the account.

Additionally, social media users are also able to bring into existence a narrower, more exclusive, temporary personal public by directly addressing other users—on Twitter for example by making a public @mention of other users' account names. This brings the @mentioning tweet to the attention of the addressee(s), and—if the tweet begins with '@user . . .'—is only visible to the sender and receiver as well as any other users who follow them both; it thus constitutes a more bespoke, dyadic personal public that is created *ad hoc* by the first user and persists only as long as both sides continue the conversation. By contrast, tweets which contain @mentions anywhere else in their text are visible to all followers of the sender; contrary to the first model, which creates a common personal public that incorporates only the active participants and a shared subset of all of their followers, then, this second form of @reply conversation in essence encompasses the union of both their follower bases. Already, it is evident that such casual, *ad hoc* connections between the personal publics of individual users hold the potential to facilitate a wide range of liminal information flows at the very edges of 'the' public sphere.

A second form of social media communication that is particularly prevalent on Twitter transcends this liminality and moves further into outright and deliberately public communication. Drawing on the hashtag, a technological feature that makes it easy to advertise specific topics for participation by other users by prepending the hash symbol '#' to a thematic keyword (Halavais, 2014), any Twitter user can attempt to kickstart a discussion about the themes that interest them, while others can use Twitter search functionality to find and follow all tweets that contain the same hashtag. This is supported by apps and third-party software, such as Tweetdeck, which enable users to follow keyword and hashtag discussions as specific channels in addition to users' individual following feeds. Such hashtags have been shown to be crucial to Twitter's response especially to breaking news events (Bruns *et al.* 2012), but also enable users to come together around common topics of interest or to engage in shared audience activities (Highfield, Harrington, & Bruns 2013; Page 2012).

The groups of users which gather around and engage in shared hashtags can be seen as a form of *ad hoc* public (Bruns & Burgess 2011; 2015), and especially where they relate to specific events and topics should be understood as the Twitter subset of the wider issue topics that accompany such phenomena. The lifecycles of hashtags as they are observable on Twitter provide important insights into the dynamics of issue publics more generally, and it may be possible to distinguish a wide range of dynamics that relate to the characteristics of the issues around which such publics have formed: in the context of breaking news, in which Twitter has been observed to act as an 'ambient news network' (Hermida, 2010; Burns, 2010) can form very rapidly, peak at high levels of activity, and may dissolve just as quickly once the breaking news issue is resolved, while longer-term issues may result in less active, but longer-lived engagement. Indeed, very long-term hashtag communities may in fact be better understood as constituting the kernels for the formation of public sphericules rather than representing issue publics. In either case, it is important to stress again that such hashtag communities do not constitute *entire* issue publics of public sphericules, but only that subset of such publics which exists on Twitter, and which is connected with corresponding subsets in other communication channels through cross-platform interlinkages.

Evidence for the existence of public sphericules around broader themes within public debate can also be found by returning to the level of personal publics, but considering the network of such micro-publics in its totality rather than focussing only on the egocentric networks around each individual user. As we have already noted, these individual networks interweave and overlap with each other, both within specific platforms such as Twitter and Facebook and from one platform to another, and as the creation of friend or follower links is likely to be based at least in part on shared backgrounds, attitudes, or interests, such overlapping personal publics may then also serve as an early stage in the formation of public sphericules: networks of like-minded friends in social media environments that group together to discuss certain themes that are of mutual interest. Commonplace processes of structuration in social networks, such as preferential attachment to the identified lead users, over time lead to the formation of network clusters around such shared themes which constitute an increasingly solid basis for the operation of such sphericules, and the network structures which thus emerge come to influence and structure the flow of information and communication across the network, facilitated on Twitter for example through the retweeting of messages from one account to another. Retweets enable users to pass on public messages that were posted by one of the accounts they follow to their own network of followers, verbatim or with added commentary, and in many cases constitute an implicit endorsement of the retweeted message as relevant and important to the personal public of the retweeting user (this does not always signal agreement, however: messages may also be passed on to encourage critical responses, for example). It is likely that the choice to retweet a message is usually influenced by the retweeting user's picture of their imagined audience—that is, by the network clusters they feel they belong to; retweets and other messages are thus ultimately more likely to be directed at and widely disseminated through closely connected clusters of users than to bridge the gap to other, more remote parts of the network.

Through the use of additional communication features offered by social media platforms—such as Facebook groups and pages and Twitter hashtags—the public interactions sustained by such broader networks may also articulate at times to the issue public level, especially as specific events and topics trigger a phase of more intensive involvement, and in doing so attract a different subset of the overall public sphericule network; at the conclusion of the issue public's lifecycle, users may then once again return to more general participation in thematic discussions relation to their public sphericule. Once again, the existence of such structural formations within social networks should not be seen as inherently supporting the idea of a 'filter bubble' (Pariser 2011); instead, the vertical interrelationships between hashtag-supported issue publics and follower network-based public sphericules on the one hand, and the horizontal overlaps between individual hashtag publics or network clusters on the other, both make it less and not more likely that information will travel between and across these formations. Only if the analysis of empirical evidence truly shows there to be practically no active connections whatsoever between individual hashtag communities or network clusters is it possible that 'filter bubbles' might exist on Twitter—and even then it would still be likely that outside information could reach those bubbles through cross-platform links which are not evident from the Twitter data alone.

Reviewing the Evidence: Public Sphere Structures on Twitter

A brief exploration of public communication structures as they can be identified on Twitter illustrates the observations we have made here. For this, we draw on the results of a long-term study that has focussed in the first place on determining the follower/ followee network structure of the Australian Twittersphere (for more details, see Bruns et al. 2014), and by September 2013 had identified a total of 2.8 million Australian-based Twitter accounts. By using the force-directed Force Atlas 2 algorithm (Jacomy et al. 2012) to map the network connections of the 140,000 most networked accounts in this overall user base—identified as those accounts whose combined number of followers and followees amounted to 1,000 connections or more—it becomes possible to discern a number of obvious clusters of highly mutually interconnected accounts within this overall network, and to determine the degrees of interconnection between these individual clusters; additionally, a qualitative review of the most central accounts in each of the clusters also enables us to identify the key themes and topics around which each such cluster has formed.

The overall clusters emerging from this map (see Figure 4.1) can thus be understood as the Twitter components of broader public sphericules existing within Australian public debate, relating *inter alia* for example to politics, sports, and teen culture, while within these clusters a number of narrower subsets that may relate to temporary issue publics, or form the kernels of emerging public sphericules in their own right, can also be identified. The map also demonstrates the fact that few such clusters would fit the description of filter bubbles which are far removed and difficult to reach from the remainder of the network; it is perhaps unsurprising that the large teen culture cluster appears to be the most inward-looking and least interconnected of all significant clusters within the network, but even it is linked to the rest of the network by a common interest in popular and celebrity culture. Furthermore, a comparison of this map with previous iterations produced by our project (e.g. Bruns et al. 2014) also shows the comparative stability of the overall structure of these network clusters and the thematic interests represented by them: while they may wax and wane in relative size (the teen culture cluster has emerged only since 2012, for example, and high turnover in the user base and in the identities of relevant cultural icons within a teen-oriented cluster would be expected in future mappings of the network), the public sphericules they reflect appear to be consistent.

While this overall network depicts the general structure of the patchwork of personal publics that exists in the Australian Twittersphere, which we have already argued is representative of the distribution of shared interests across the user base, and by extension also of the public sphericules likely to exist in wider Australian society, it is also important to explore the day-to-day activities of Australian Twitter users as they relate to specific issues, topics, and themes, manifested for example in their participation of specific hashtags. For the purposes of illustration, we turn here to a dataset containing accounts which participated in the #qanda hashtag accompanying the popular political television talk show *Q&A*, broadcast by the Australian Broadcasting Corporation, over a period of several weeks in 2014, and indicate within the underlying network map the location of the most active accounts participating within the hashtag (see Figure 4.2).

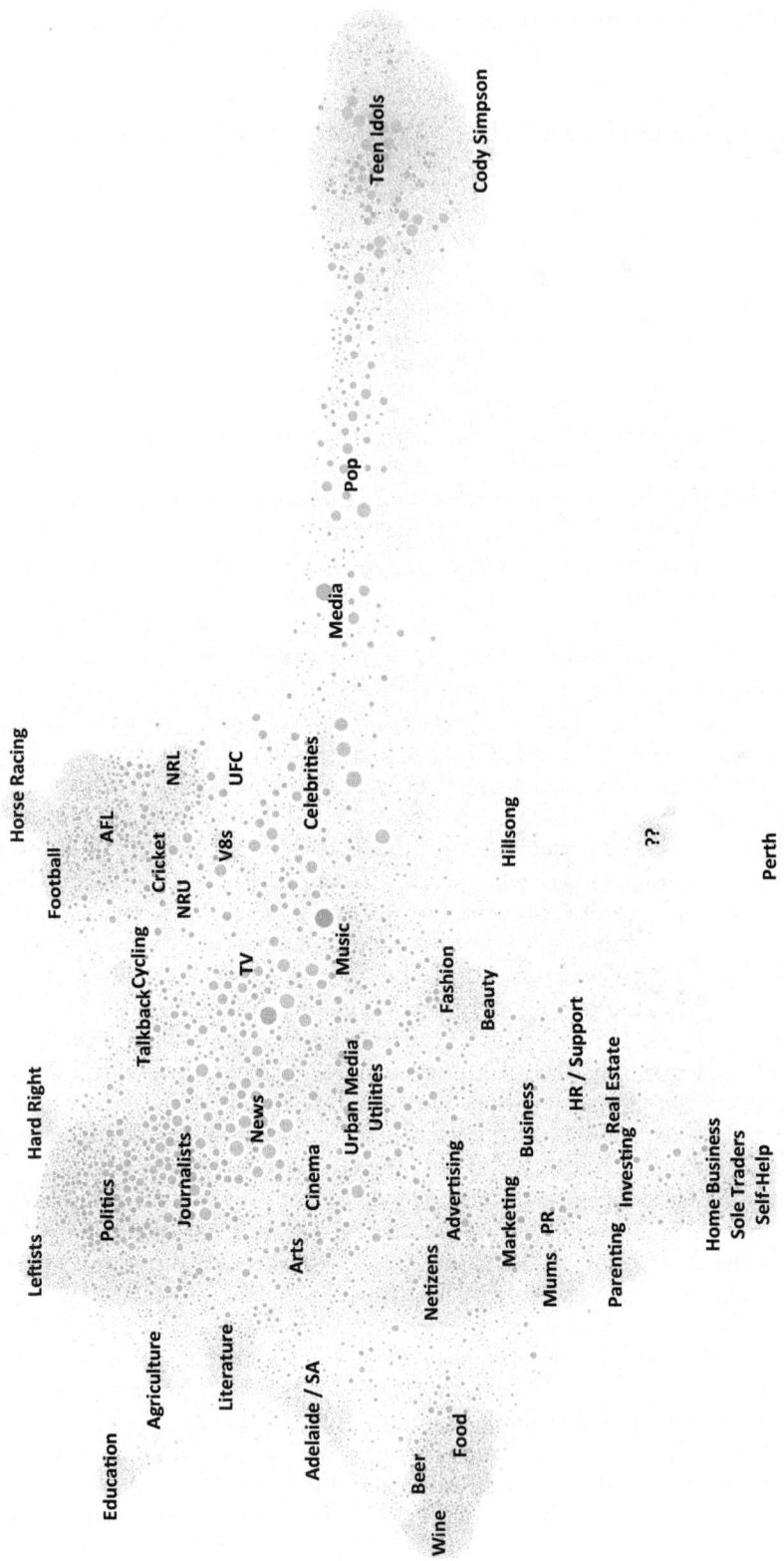

Figure. 4.1 The Australian Twittersphere (data current to Sep. 2013)

Figure 4.2 #qanda Hashtag Participants over Several Weeks in 2014

Given the specific thematic focus of each episode, the *Q&A* audience can be considered to be the subset of *ad hoc* issue public forming around the topics addressed by the shared television text during each week's broadcast; the #qanda hashtag community constitutes a related and similarly *ad hoc* public whose composition overlaps with the television public to significant extent. Such activity is encouraged by the broadcaster, too, as ABC editors integrate and highlight tagged tweets on screen during each episode of *Q&A* (see also Given & Radywyl, 2013). The #qanda public and the television public are not entirely homologous, though: anecdotal evidence points to the presence of a number of Twitter users who respond only to the Twitter debate each week, *without* also viewing the television broadcast, while of course there will also be TV viewers who do not participate in the Twitter debate. In addition, we may also postulate the existence of other members of the public who are interested in and vocal (through other media channels) about the themes addressed by *Q&A* and #qanda, but participate in neither of these media texts. In combination, then, the *Q&A* audience, the #qanda users, and this third group of other non-present participants can be regarded as the complete issue public which exists around the topics discussed by *Q&A*.

Furthermore, the subset of this issue public that is active on Twitter relates in interesting ways to the wider public sphericule around Australian politics. This is reflected in the structure of our overall Twittersphere map: while #qanda recruits its participants largely from the larger politics cluster within this map, it does so preferentially from certain sectors of the cluster (in the present case, mainly from that part of the cluster which represents more progressive political views, though this may be an artefact of the specific topics addressed by *Q&A* during the time we gathered our data). The layered nature of issue publics and public sphericules is apparent here, with the former constituting, at least to some extent, a smaller and more temporary outgrowth of the latter. At the same time, the #qanda hashtag also attracts involvement from users who are not usually an integral part of the politics cluster within the Australian

Twittersphere: this, in turn, supports the view that issue publics are not simply a subset of wider public sphericules, but that their more specific topical focus may also enable them to attract participants whose day-to-day interests are more strongly focussed on the themes addressed by an alternative public sphericule. Issue publics may then also serve as bridges between public sphericules.

Even this description is necessarily overly simplistic, of course. Individuals are rarely simply part of one public sphericule, or just one issue public. These constructs are not mutually exclusive, and the accounts found in the Australian Twittersphere are similarly allocated to one cluster or another by our algorithm because of their predominant network attachments, but may address a wide variety of themes in their day-to-day tweeting practices, similarly reflecting different motivations to participate. But such *caveats* also simply serve to underline the point that the structure of the public sphere, or of the various public spaces which have come to replace it as a result of the continuing structural transformations of 'the' public sphere following the decline of the mass media's hegemony, is today highly complex, dynamic, and changeable—more so than orthodox Habermasian public sphere theory can account for. As Dahlgren (2009) points out, "traditional perspectives on the public sphere do not help us understand how publics 'come alive,' . . . what their sociocultural dynamics look like" (74).

Conclusion

Revisiting the Habermasian concept of the public sphere for a media ecology featuring many-to-many channels including social media platforms, it appears that the idea of structural transformation can—and should—be extended beyond the public sphere as singular: a more complex system of distinct and diverse, yet inter-connected and overlapping, publics can be identified which represent different topics and approaches to mediated communication (from the explicitly political to the tangential and otherwise). The threat of 'cyberbalkanisation' (Sunstein, 2008), wherein voices of a particular ideological viewpoint would cluster together and never become exposed to, or communicate with, opposing views, was used to criticise online discourse through the possibility of fragmented discussions; the multiple publics model, though, suggests that fragmentation does not necessarily beget isolation or complete separation. Publics exist at various levels, for different lifespans, from the long-standing topical clusters identified in the Australian Twittersphere in Figure 4.1 through egocentric personal publics to more *ad hoc* assemblages and issue publics developing in response to particular stimuli, which, while relevant to specific topical publics, are not restricted in their scope to these groups.

As this chapter has argued, moving beyond the orthodox model of the public sphere to a more dynamic and complex system provides the opportunity to more clearly recognise the varying forms public communication can take online. Unpacking the traditional public sphere into a series of public sphericules and micro-publics, none of which are mutually exclusive but which coexist, intersecting and overlapping in multiple forms, is one approach to understanding the ongoing structural transformation of the public sphere. It is also important to note that these publics may follow their own logics and norms, making use of affordances of social media platforms for their own purposes, which may differ from established practices. The various publics, whether issue or personal, might operate in combination, providing further prominence or activity for each other, but they might also work in opposition, counteracting one another. Similarly, participation in one public is neither a pre-requisite nor an implication that participating in another will result. The publics identified here both represent and bridge the macro-, meso-, and micro-levels of public communication on social media, as introduced by Bruns and Moe (2014), but participation remains a choice on the part of the individual. At the same time, it remains noteworthy that the sheer availability of this choice is a relative novelty within the mass-mediated public sphere model.

The transformation from public sphere to public spheres—and the spread of political and public debate across multiple actors, platforms, and publics—remains an ongoing process. This chapter has outlined a contemporary conceptualisation of the public sphere based especially on our extensive research into public communication on Twitter. The current mainstream and social media ecology, though, is not fixed; new platforms will arise and become adopted for public communication in different forms, providing a further fuzziness around ideas of public, semi-public, and private discussions. It is worth remembering, too, that the traditional leaders and featured actors within public debate and the bourgeois public sphere (journalists, the traditional media, and politicians) are often slower to officially adopt newer channels for discussion, from the Internet in general to specific platforms such as blogs, YouTube, or Twitter. If and when new social media platforms emerge and are adopted by ordinary citizens for public debate, including as 'third spaces' (Wright, 2012) where political discussion is not the focus but develops alongside and from within other topics of conversation, further disruptions to the public sphere model may follow. Additional disjunctures between new and old, between different approaches to publics, are part of the process of an evolving social media ecology and the mediasphere; while further enabling debate and discussion, in different forms and with different affordances, they continue to complicate and challenge our conceptualisation of a 'public' sphere—whether in the singular or plural.

References

Benkler, Yochai. (2006) *The Wealth of Networks: How Social Production Transforms Markets and Freedom.* New Haven: Yale UP.

boyd, danah, and Kate Crawford. (2012) "Critical Questions for Big Data: Provocations for a Cultural, Technological, and Scholarly Phenomenon." *Information, Communication & Society* 15.5: 662–679. DOI: 10.1080/1369118X.2012.678878.

Bruns, Axel. (2008) "Life beyond the Public Sphere: Towards a Networked Model for Political Deliberation." *Information Polity* 13(1–2): 65–79.

———, and Hallvard Moe. (2014) "Structural Layers of Communication on Twitter." In Katrin Weller, Axel Bruns, Jean Burgess, Merja Mahrt, and Cornelius Puschmann, eds., *Twitter and Society.* New York: Peter Lang, 15–28.

———, and Jean Burgess. (2011) "The Use of Twitter Hashtags in the Formation of *Ad Hoc* Publics." Paper presented at the European Consortium for Political Research conference, Reykjavik, 25–27 Aug. 2011. http://eprints.qut.edu.au/46515/

———, and Jean Burgess. (2015, forthcoming) "Twitter Hashtags from Ad Hoc to Calculated Publics: The Power and Politics of Networked Discourse Communities." In Nathan Rambukkana, ed., *Hashtag Publics.* New York: Peter Lang.

———, Jean Burgess, and Tim Highfield. (2014) "A 'Big Data' Approach to Mapping the Australian Twittersphere." In Paul Arthur and Katherine Bode, eds., *Repurposing the Digital Humanities.* Basingstoke: Palgrave Macmillan.

———, Jean Burgess, Kate Crawford, and Frances Shaw. (2012) "#qldfloods and @QPSMedia: Crisis Communication on Twitter in the 2011 South East Queensland Floods." Brisbane: ARC Centre of Excellence for Creative Industries and Innovation. http://cci.edu.au/floodsreport.pdf

Burns, Alex. (2010) "Oblique Strategies for Ambient Journalism." *M/C Journal* 13(2). http://journal. media-culture.org.au/index.php/mcjournal/article/view/230

Calhoun, Craig. (1992) "Introduction: Habermas and the Public Sphere." In Craig Calhoun, ed., *Habermas and the Public Sphere*. Cambridge, MA: MIT Press, 1–50.

Castells, Manuel. (2009) *Communication Power*. Oxford: Oxford UP.

Cunningham, Stuart. (2001) "Popular Media as Public 'Sphericules' for Diasporic Communities." *International Journal of Cultural Studies* 4(2): 131–47.

Dahlgren, Peter. (2009) *Media and Political Engagement: Citizens, Communication, and Democracy*. Cambridge: Cambridge UP.

Evans, Pete. (2015) "Nielsen Ratings Data Shows Big TV Decline due to Streaming Video." *CBC News*, 4 Feb. 2015. http://www.cbc.ca/news/business/nielsen-ratings-data-shows-big-tv-decline-due-to-streaming-video-1.2944432

Fenton, Natalie, and John Downey. (2003) "Counter Public Spheres and Global Modernity." *Javnost—The Public* 10(1): 15–32.

Fraser, Nancy. (1992) "Rethinking the Public Sphere: A Contribution to the Critique of Actually Existing Democracy." In Craig Calhoun, ed., *Habermas and the Public Sphere*. Cambridge, Mass.: MIT Press, 109–142.

Gitlin, Todd. (1998) "Public Sphere or Public Sphericules?" In T. Liebes and J. Curran, eds. *Media, Ritual and Identity*. London: Routledge, 175–202.

Given, Jock, and Natalia Radywyl. (2013) "Questions & Answers & Tweets." *Communication, Politics & Culture* 46: 1–21.

Greenslade, Roy. (2014) "Latest ABCs Show Newspaper Market Decline Running at 8% a Year." *The Guardian*, 11 July 2014. http://www.theguardian.com/media/greenslade/2014/jul/11/abcs-national-newspapers

Habermas, Jürgen. (1962) *Strukturwandel der Öffentlichkeit: Untersuchungen zu einer Kategorie der bürgerlichen Öffentlichkeit*. Neuwied: Hermann Luchterhand Verlag.

———. (1989) *The Structural Transformation of the Public Sphere: An Inquiry into a Category of Bourgeois Society*. Cambridge: Polity.

———. (2006) "Political Communication in Media Society: Does Democracy Still Enjoy an Epistemic Dimension? The Impact of Normative Theory on Empirical Research." *Communication Theory* 16(4): 411–26.

Halavais, Alexander. (2014) "Structure of Twitter: Social and Technical." In Katrin Weller, Axel Bruns, Jean Burgess, Cornelius Puschmann, and Merja Mahrt, eds., *Twitter & Society*. New York: Peter Lang, 29–42.

Hartley, John, and Joshua Green. (2006) "The Public Sphere on the Beach." *European Journal of Cultural Studies* 9(3): 341–362.

Hermida, Alfred. (2010) "From TV to Twitter: How Ambient News Became Ambient Journalism." *M/C Journal* 13(2). http://journal.media- culture.org.au/index.php/mcjournal/article/view/220

Highfield, Tim, Stephen Harrington, and Axel Bruns. (2013) "Twitter as a Technology for Audiencing and Fandom: The #Eurovision Phenomenon." *Information, Communication & Society* 16(3): 315–39. DOI: 10.1080/1369118X.2012.756053.

Jacomy, Mathieu, Sebastien Heymann, Tommaso Venturini, and Mathieu Bastian. (2012) "ForceAtlas2, a Continuous Graph Layout Algorithm for Handy Network Visualization." Working paper. http://www.medialab.sciences-po.fr/publications/Jacomy_Heymann_Venturini-Force_Atlas2.pdf

Launer, Ekkehard. (1981) "Produktionsbedingungen und Qualität von Fernsehnachrichten." In Jörg Aufermann, Wilfried Scharf, and Otto Schlie, eds., *Fernsehen und Hörfunk für die Demokratie: Ein Handbuch über den Rundfunk in der Bundesrepublik Deutschland*. Wiesbaden: Springer Fachmedien, 287–300.

Manovich, Lev. (2012) "Trending: The Promises and the Challenges of Big Social Data." In Matthew K. Gold, ed., *Debates in the Digital Humanities*. Minneapolis: University of Minnesota Press, 460–475.

Page, Ruth. (2012) "The Linguistics of Self-Branding and Micro-Celebrity in Twitter: The role of hashtags." *Discourse & Communication* 6(2): 181–201.

Papacharissi, Zizi A. (2010) *A Private Sphere: Democracy in a Digital Age*. Cambridge: Polity.

———. (2015) *Affective Publics*. Oxford: Oxford University Press.

Pariser, Eli. (2011) *The Filter Bubble: What The Internet Is Hiding from You*. London: Penguin.

Schmidt, Jan-Hinrik. (2011) *Das neue Netz: Merkmale, Praktiken und Folgen des Web 2.0*. 2nd ed. Konstanz: UVK.

———. (2014) "Twitter and the Rise of Personal Publics." In Katrin Weller, Axel Bruns, Jean Burgess, Cornelius Puschmann, and Merja Mahrt, eds., *Twitter & Society*. New York: Peter Lang, 3–14.

Sunstein, Cass. (2008) "Neither Hayek nor Habermas." *Public Choice* 134(1–2): 87–95.

Webster, Frank. (2013) "What's the Use of the Public Sphere in the Age of the Internet?" In Francis L.F. Lee, Louis Leung, Jack Linchuan Qiu, and Donna S.C. Chu, eds., *Frontiers in New Media Research*. New York: Routledge, 19–38.

Wright, Scott. (2012) "Politics as Usual? Revolution, Normalization and a New Agenda for Online Deliberation." *New Media & Society* 14(2): 244–261.

5

THIRD SPACE, SOCIAL MEDIA, AND EVERYDAY POLITICAL TALK

Scott Wright, Todd Graham, and Dan Jackson

Introduction

Thanks to its ubiquity, social media is increasingly being used by governments, politicians, activists, and citizens for political purposes. As such, the dynamics of political communication and civic engagement in these communicative spaces and networks have become a central nub of concern for scholars across a range of disciplines. As will be shown in more detail below, much scholarly attention in this sphere focuses on the activities of political elites in their attempts to communicate with the masses, or on how activists and social movements utilize social media to pursue their goals. The focus is therefore on the dynamics of communication and engagement on social media in clearly political settings and often involving explicitly political actors. While much of this research has emphasized the potential of online spaces and networks for political knowledge-sharing, interpersonal deliberation and coordinated collective action, we maintain that it ignores the 'everydayness' of political communication and engagement and the networks where such talk emerges. We argue for the adoption of a more expansive notion of political talk: one that embraces the vernacular, expressive, and porous characteristics of everyday public speech.

This chapter steps back from the domain of formal politics and develops a theoretically informed argument for research that focuses on citizens' informal political talk in everyday online spaces. We define political talk as something that (a) emerges in the process of everyday talk, often interweaved with conversations that do not have a political character; (b) includes mundane reflections upon power, its uses and ramifications; and (c) possesses qualities that enable it to contribute to meaningful public action.

We are also concerned with where such talk occurs online, particularly in everyday, formally non-political, online 'third spaces': public spaces beyond the home (first space) or work (second space) where people can meet and interact informally and where political talk, organizing, and action can occur. We are especially interested in the array of online communities dedicated to lifestyle issues, such as personal finance, parenting/childcare, popular culture, sports, and hobbies. Such spaces foster a connection between the personal and political and can potentially help bridge the gap between the everyday lives of participants and formal politics. Our initial investigations of such spaces/communities suggest that much of the talk that takes place in these fora constitutes political talk that is reciprocal, reflexive, and (often) deliberative. In turn, this talk could inform self-representation and potentially activate people to mobilize and organize political action (Graham 2010, 2012; Graham and Harju 2011; Graham and Wright 2014; Graham et al. 2015).

In the following section, we provide a brief overview of the field of online deliberation research. Second, we establish the importance of everyday political talk as both an expression of political participation and as an essential lubricant to other forms of engagement. Third, we discuss the concept of third space, and set out the existing research in this area. Fourth, third space has been primarily associated with, and analysed through, discussion forum-based communities. Here, we discuss and consider whether social media such as Facebook and Twitter constitute third spaces. Finally, we argue that everyday political talk—particularly in third spaces—has the potential to overcome many of the identified issues with online deliberation, including political polarisation and the avoidance of political talk.

The Internet, Social Media, and Online Deliberation

The nature of political deliberation online has been studied for decades. We can identify four distinct phases within this research, characterized by attempts to keep pace with technological developments and interrelated changes in the sites and practice of online deliberation. In the earliest phase, there was little if any empirical research; scholars tended to put forward hypotheses about what political debate would look like. For example, there was extensive debate about whether the perceived anonymity of online communication would lead people to talk more freely about politics, and often polarized debates about whether the Internet would be positively revolutionize deliberation or be its death knell (Rheingold 1993). In response to this period of hype, there was an empirical turn in the literature—often described as the cyber-realist school because the evidence largely disproved the earlier hype. Scholars such as Davis (1999) and Wilhelm (2000), for example, operationalized Habermas-inspired definitions of deliberation to analyse political debate on Usenet discussion forums, finding that talk online was largely not deliberative but marked by polarization and flaming. Moreover, as the use and understanding of the Internet as a space for political debate expanded, this was accompanied by more refined theorizing of the Internet as a public sphere and space for deliberation (see, e.g. Papacharissi 2004; Dahlberg 2001). The third phase of the research acknowledged that the nature of deliberation online depended on a range of factors, including the design of the website interface (e.g., Wright and Street 2007), the nature of the moderation and facilitation (e.g. Wright 2006), and how existing comments shape interaction (e.g. Sukumaran et al. 2011). It was also marked by a focus on the websites of formal politics, such as governments (e.g. Wright 2006, 2007; Coleman and Blumler 2009), legislatures/parliaments (e.g. Lusoli et al. 2006), political parties (e.g. Jackson and Lilleker 2009a), and elected representatives (e.g. Jackson and Lilleker 2009b; Gibson et al. 2003).

More recently, studies on the political uses of social media platforms such as Facebook, Twitter, and YouTube have emerged and a small sub-stream of this has analysed key aspects of the debates in these spaces. Often this follows similar themes to earlier research, such as how technical affordances and moderation shape deliberation—while there also remains a significant focus on formal political actors and events. For example, Halpern and Gibbs (2013) have analysed interactions on the Facebook and YouTube channels of the White House, finding that the greater anonymity of YouTube debates leads to more flaming and impoliteness than Facebook. Other studies have focused solely on Facebook, examining deliberative norms in newspaper Facebook pages (e.g. Stroud et al. 2014), pages set up to discuss public matters (e.g. Es et al. 2014), and political parties' use of Facebook pages to facilitate citizen dialogue (e.g. Steenkamp and Hyde-Clarke 2014).

Research into the nature of political debate on Twitter has been more voluminous, and we give only a brief summary here of some key points and arguments (much of this literature is discussed elsewhere in this volume). Boynton et al. (2014) have analysed tweets mentioning the word 'Obama', capturing around 200,000 messages a day. Comparing their findings with previous research, they conclude that "political communication on Twitter is a domain that is differentiable from the main Twitter stream [. . . , with] much greater use of hashtags, retweets, and URLs in the political domain than what is true for the total stream of Twitter messages" (Boynton et al. 2014: 14). This points to Bruns and Burgess's (2011b) earlier findings that *ad hoc* publics sometimes formed around hashtags. Second, research has shown that political debates on Twitter tend to be highly polarized, though topic, norms and the predilection of users affect this within the communication structure of Twitter (Colleoni et al. 2014; Himelboim et al. 2013). Third, numerous studies have identified often highly active super-participants (Graham and Wright 2014) in political debates on Twitter; these people often hold important positions in discussion networks; and they tend to come from the political classes (Larsson and Moe 2012; Bruns and Burgess 2011a).

While much has been learned, there are, however, some important limitations in the literature on political debate and social media—that repeat patterns identified in earlier phases (Wright 2012a). First, there are surprisingly few studies that analyse whether political debate in spaces such as Facebook and Twitter is deliberative—and related debates over what models of talk, discussion or deliberation should be used to assess this. Surprisingly, there has been very little focus on the extent to which such platforms foster discursive reciprocal exchange: the extent to which participants are actually *reading* and *replying* to each other's posts; and the level of continuity—*extended reciprocal exchange* on a particular issue so that (normatively speaking) deeper levels of understanding can be achieved such as reflexivity and (communicative) empathy. Yet, words such as 'conversation', 'discussion', and 'debate' are routinely used. Second, there has been a disproportionate focus on formal political actors (e.g. elected representatives, candidates, activists, journalists), institutions (e.g. political parties, campaign organizations) and external political events (elections, consultations, TV debates) in these spaces. Research—be it for methodological reasons or choice—has often *not* focused on the very aspects of social media that are marked out for it being so important: the facilitation of informal political talk amongst everyday citizens. While focusing on political hashtags, actors, and events might by expedient in terms of research manageability, the danger is that this largely captures the usual political suspects—ignoring the vast amount of everyday political talk in such spaces. Let us unpack this analysis of social media and deliberation further by outlining exactly why everyday political talk is worthy of our attention.

Everyday Political Talk: Why Is It Important?

Everyday political talk is considered an important aspect of democratic citizenship. It performs a key educative role in terms of citizenship; it is where public opinion can form and "in every conversation in which private individuals assemble to form a public body" it constitutes "a portion of the public sphere" (Habermas, Lennox, and Lennox, 1974, p. 49). Everyday conversations have been shown to change people's political attitudes (Huckfeldt et al. 2004). Political talk can be considered a "fundamental underpinning of deliberative democracy" because, for Kim and Kim (2008: 51) "through everyday political talk, citizens construct their identities, achieve mutual understanding, produce public reason, form considered opinions, and produce rules and resources for deliberative democracy." Similarly, Mansbridge (1999) argues that everyday political talk is a key aspect of the deliberative system. She conceives deliberation as a broader process, spread throughout time and space. It is the web of everyday political talk, which takes place over time and across different discursive spaces that prepare citizens, the public sphere, and the political system at large for political action. While Mansbridge (1999: 212) notes that everyday talk is not always deliberative because it can lack considered, critical reflection—she argues that "theorists of deliberation ought to pay as much attention to citizens' everyday talk as to formal deliberation in public arenas," not least because if people do not understand how to talk and listen, formal public deliberations can fail.

Dahlgren argues that discussion is one of six prerequisites for participatory democracy (alongside knowledge, values, experience, identities, and affinity). In this sense, everyday political talk can be pre/proto-political; latent or standby; and 'potentially political'—important to the "microdynamics of democracy" (Dahlgren 2006: 282). Such latent forms of participation can thus be "a good gateway toward the stirrings of a broader social consciousness" (Howe 2012), creating a sense of public empowerment and voice (Coleman 2013: 219–220). Finally, some scholars (e.g. Barber 1984; Fearson 1998) argue that political talk encourages shared perspective building, or what McAfee (2000: 134–135) calls complementary agency: intersubjective processes whereby people link their personal ideas, issues, and actions with one another, cultivating political agency, solidarity and community. Many scholars recognize and argue for the importance of everyday political talk to democracy. However, what it should look like is a highly contested normative debate, and it is to this debate we now turn.

The Nature of Everyday Political Talk

Normative debates about the nature of everyday political talk have generally occurred in response to criticisms that using formal, typically Habermas-inspired models of deliberation is unrealistic and unfair. First, such an account ignores the nature of political talk, which tends to be fragmented, anecdotal, messy, incomplete, and less formally deliberative. Dahlgren (2006: 278–279; see also Van Zoonen 2005), for example, cautions against "clinging too rigidly to formal deliberation" because this

> risks losing sight of everyday talk and its potential relevance for democracy. There remains an awful lot of discussion which can have political relevance but which has no status in a strict deliberative perspective [. . .] It is via meandering and unpredictable talk that the political can be generated, that the links between the personal and the political can be established.

Second, privileging reasoning by means of argumentation as the only relevant communicative form also ignores the plurality and differences within modern Western societies. As Eckersley (2001: 25–26) argues, deliberation based solely of rationality privileges a "gentlemen's club": it is "too dispassionate, rationalist, disembodied, masculine, and Western/Eurocentric in its orientation in insisting only on certain modes of rational, critical argument in political discourse." Similarly, Warren (2006: 171) states, "Those on the outside must often shout in order to enter the conversation, and when they shout, they do so with accents, mannerisms, and ways of making points that don't fit with the dominant model of deliberation."

This has led some scholars to call for the adoption of a more expansive notion of political talk: one that embraces the vernacular, expressive, and porous characteristics of everyday public speech rather than strictly instrumental or institution-bound conceptions. Within the context of deliberation and the public sphere, we have seen, for example, an emphasis on the performative (Kohn 2000); on the importance of rhetoric (Mayhew 1997); on the role of humour (Basu 1999); and other communicative forms such as storytelling, the use of narratives and greeting (e.g. Dryzek 2000). The role of emotions in deliberation and political talk has also been a key area of debate. Rosenberg (2004), for example, maintains that productive deliberation requires emotional connections between participants. Such connections, for example, fuel a participant's effort to understand other positions and arguments.

Regarding online political talk, much of the empirical-based research has adopted very rational, Habermasian inspired models of deliberation (see Graham and Witschge 2003; Kies 2010), focusing on for example the level of rational-critical debate, reciprocity, discursive equality, and excluding most, if not all, of the other communicative forms and styles of political talk discussed above (some exceptions include: Polletta and Lee 2006; Graham 2009, 2010, 2012). Graham's (2009) comparison of political talk between the (political) *Guardian Talkboard* (which closed in 2011) and two forums dedicated to fans of reality TV, for example, found that expressives (humour, emotional comments, acknowledgements) were a common ingredient, accounting for a third or more of the posts in each case. Moreover, expressives tended to impede political talk in the Guardian while facilitate it in the formally non-political forums of reality TV. Graham attributes it to two factors (156–161): the topic and nature of political talk. His findings suggest that online political forums dedicated to traditional politics, like the *Guardian's Talkboard*, tend to foster a communicative environment centered on 'winning' the debate. In an atmosphere in which they were not ignored or discouraged, expressives were used in a very strategic way (e.g. humour as an ad hominem attack against other participants). While in the forums dedicated to reality TV, expressives seemed to play an important role in enhancing and facilitating political talk by fostering deeper levels of understanding and solidarity. This was due to the nature of the forum (Graham 2009: 168):

> [they were communicative spaces] where the mixing of the private and public was the norm, [spaces] where participants took personal experiences and life lessons and bridged them to society at large, fostering a more personal and lifestyle-based form of politics. All of this seemed to foster a communicative environment that was about learning rather than winning or convincing. It was an environment that seemed to promote solidarity rather than polarization among participants.

The nature of political talk in everyday online communities dedicated to lifestyle issues, topics and needs (e.g. TV/Films, parenting, personal finance) tend to be deeply rooted in the personal (see also Graham and Wright 2014; Graham et al. 2015; Van Zoonen 2007). As researchers, they provide us a glimpse, at the micro-level, of the blurring between private and public, personal and political. We move on now to discuss the concept of third space where this type of talk is occurring.

'Third Space' and Everyday Political Talk

While many researchers have made a compelling case for the importance of everyday political talk, the problem, as Mansbridge noted, is that such talk is rarely analysed. For Hay (2002: 4–5), "we need political analysis which refuses to restrict its analytical attentions to obviously political variables and processes," while Saward (2003: 166) concurs: "An extraordinary feature of the literature on deliberative democracy has been its unwillingness to take an encompassing view of democratic sites, institutions and procedures." Building on Bauman's (2005) concept of liquid modernity, Papacharissi (2010) argues that in an era of convergence "the political becomes more elusive, as there exist no longer sites that are anchored to politics, confirming what Arendt termed an emptiness of political space" (Papacharissi 2010: 77). This does not mean that the context does not matter, or that we can apply some kind of random, scattergun approach as Dahlgren maintains (2006: 279),

> If we accept that all forms of talk are of potential relevant for civic discussion, that politics can materialise even in unexpected contexts of daily conversation, this does not mean we would want to study any and all contexts of verbal interaction. Obviously, we would have to be selective about where we aim our analytical searchlights, trying to glean that which is beginning to percolate politically.

This leads us to the importance of the spaces wherein political talk emerges, and we now turn to concepts of third space.

The concept of third space is built on a critique of Ray Oldenburg's concept of the third place. A third place, for Oldenburg, is a public space beyond the home or workplace where people can meet and interact informally. As the name suggests, they are place based spaces; the common denominator is the location of the participants and that community can thrive: "The third place is a generic designation for a great variety of public spaces that host the regular, voluntary, informal, and happily anticipated gatherings of individuals' and is a core setting of informal public life" (Oldenburg 1989: 16). Oldenburg argues that third places perform a crucial role in the development of societies and communities, helping to strengthen citizenship and thus are "central to the political processes of a democracy" (Oldenburg 1989: 67). Oldenburg cites numerous examples of third places from the traditional English pub to a Parisian cafe. It should be noted that, for Oldenburg, it is not that certain types of venue constitute a third place; rather they exist when venues and participants exhibit certain characteristics: they are place-based arenas beyond home and work with easy access, and a home away from home feel that is neutral and typically has a group of regulars that set the tone. In other words, not all pubs are third places: they are constructed through specific social and environmental characteristics. Mirroring de Tocqueville, Oldenburg argues that in third places decency is more highly regarded than wealth, status or education. For Lasch (1996: 122) such "considerations make it appropriate to argue that third place sociability, in a modest way, encourages virtues more properly associated with political life than with the 'civil society' made up of voluntary associations." Lasch (1996: 123) also confers upon third place and the everyday political talk an important "protopolitical" status and questions whether "the decline of participatory democracy may be directly related to the disappearance of third places."

Oldenburg was highly critical of the idea of virtual communities and the network society, which he feared isolated people in their homes (Oldenburg 1989: 77) and so "atomized the citizenry that the term 'society' may no longer be appropriate" (Oldenburg 1989: 204). Nevertheless, scholars of virtual community have considered whether they might be equivalent to a third place. Rheingold (1993: 10) for example, suggested that while online communities "might not be the same kind of place that Oldenburg had in mind [but] many of his descriptions of third places could also describe the WELL [online community]. Perhaps cyberspace is one of the informal public places where people can rebuild the aspects of community that were lost when the malt shop became a mall." This analysis was broadly supported by Steinkuehler and Williams's (2006: 903) empirical study of whether online gaming platforms can be considered third places, which they concluded were "new (albeit virtual) 'third places' for informal sociability."

Wright (2012b) has argued for a re-theorization of the concept of third place, based on an argument that we should not privilege place-based communities over issue (or other) communities that often exist on- and offline and that while there are barriers to participation in third spaces, there are also numerous barriers to third places. Following Oldenburg, third spaces can be commercial environments and are formally non-political, but political talk emerges within them through everyday conversation. A third space is, thus, a formally non-political online discussion space where political talk can emerge (see Wright 2012b for more details).

The analysis of online third spaces is emerging, and we therefore have significantly more knowledge about the nature of political talk in such spaces—particularly within discussion forum-based lifestyle communities. First, it is worth noting that there *is* a significant amount of political talk in third spaces. Drawing on a representative national sample, Wojcieszak and Mutz (2009: 45) found that the most frequently visited types of online (discussion forum-based) communities—those revolving around e.g. hobbies—were in essence political with 53 per cent of American participants engaging in political talk within such spaces. Focusing on the nature and quality of debate, a growing body of case studies have shown that political talk not only emerges in lifestyle communities, but it can be deliberative (as discussed above), and that it is typically deeply rooted in the personal, the everyday (Graham 2010, 2012; Graham and Harju 2011; Graham and Wright 2014; Van Zoonen 2007), and can lead to political actions or calls to action (Graham et al. 2015).

Much of the research done on third spaces focuses primarily on discussion forums, but there is less knowledge about social media platforms. Some of the research discussed in this chapter, show that there is a lot of formal and everyday political comments (and perhaps debate) on social media. However, it remains unclear whether Facebook and Twitter—or different parts of these social media—meet the criteria of a third space. It is to this question that we now turn.

Twitter and Facebook: Third Spaces?

The social media platforms Facebook and Twitter include political areas, for example presentations of political parties or elected representatives, or political hashtags linking tweets to specific political public spheres. In a sense, such areas might not be considered as third spaces because they are explicitly political. However, in a similar vein to Habermas' revised model of the public sphere, there are constellations of public, private, and potentially third spaces within social media. Put simply, the question is not whether social media platforms represent a third space, but whether there are specific areas (pages, profiles, and hashtags) that constitute a third space. While political Twitter hashtags might not formally meet the criteria of a third space, the problem—as with the broader definitions of politics and the political—is that what constitutes a political hashtag has what might be called soft edges. Thus, there is an element of judgment involved in making such distinctions. Because researchers often use explicitly political hashtags (when not focusing on political actors or events) to create an initial corpus of political tweets, there has been relatively little research into the potential for third spaces to form on social networking sites (SNS). There are several ways to overcome this limitation, such as to select clearly non-political hashtags. However, our concerns do not stop here.

The design of public space affects the nature of deliberation that occurs, be it "rooms, buildings, streets, squares, parks, etc." (Drucker and Gumpert 1996: 280) or the nature of website interfaces and the norms and structures of communication (Wright and Street 2007). We are concerned that the interface design and discursive structure in Twitter and on Facebook groups, pages, and profiles might serve to undermine the potential for third spaces to form. To explain our concerns, we will focus on Twitter. In theory, a hashtag could constitute a third space, including having a group of 'regulars' and the structure of a discursive community (see Bruns and Burgess 2011b). However, it remains unclear whether hashtags might be so fluid and lacking in a sense of a group identity amongst the regulars that they do not form a third space. Put simply, the discursive formations in social media such as Twitter might lack the requisite sense of identity that contributes to third space, and thus they are at best weak examples of third space. Second, the structural form of communication on Twitter, and to a lesser extent Facebook groups/pages, does not facilitate deliberation (as argued above regarding reciprocity). In particular, the lack of threading and often more broadcast (as opposed to discursive) form on Twitter makes meaningful reciprocal and reflexive interaction harder, thus potentially hindering the development of deeper relationships, a sense of community.

Recent research on everyday political talk on Twitter supports such an analysis; according to Brooker et al. (2015), Twitter discussion of a controversial British TV documentary on people receiving state welfare (*Benefits Street*) tended to be more kneejerk, one-off (as opposed to discursive) comments in the broadcast form. However, 'off peak' participants (i.e. the debates that continued after the broadcast) tended to have more depth, bringing in their own experiences and perspectives to counter or support narratives from the documentary, and to broaden the debate to broader social issues that would be indicative of a third space. Semaan et al.'s (2014) qualitative analysis of social media use amongst 21 U.S. citizens found that participants used a range of political and non-political spaces, routinely switching between platforms to meet their needs and that they went out of their way to seek out a diverse range of information and discussants. Put simply, participants noted that each medium had different characteristics (e.g. Twitter is a broadcast medium, their Facebook profile is more private) and shaped their interactions accordingly. This suggests that to understand third space online, we might need to move beyond focusing on individual platforms in isolation (Wright 2012a), and to study the interactions on *and* between these platforms in hybrid forms (Chadwick 2013).

Political Polarization and the Avoidance of Politics

One of the most prominent debates, to date, has been whether the Internet will become polarized, with like-minded people flocking together, enabling them to ignore alternative viewpoints. This is problematic because "the benefits of deliberation depend on disagreement, which is defined in terms of interaction among citizens who hold divergent viewpoints and perspectives regarding politics" (Huckfeldt et al 2004: 11). Surveys, for example, show that Americans regularly talk about politics in their everyday lives, but that this is amongst like-minded people (Mutz, 2006). Often associated with Sunstein's (2001) *Daily Me*, the fear is that online debate could exacerbate this problem: "discussions via the Internet are more likely to be as narrow or perhaps even narrower than those across the backyard fence. Those with differing views gravitate to their own discussion groups" (Davis and Owen 1998: 124). For Van Alstyne and Brynjolfsson (1997: 3–4), this is because "if IT provides a lubricant that allows for the satisfaction of preferences against the friction of geography," such as communicating with like-minded people, the Internet might lead to apparently "local heterogeneity" to "give way to virtual homogeneity as communities coalesce across geographic boundaries."

The potential for homophily are explicitly embedded into the architecture of much social and digital media. Search technologies and the increasing personalization of the Internet experience can facilitate this, using past actions and choices to filter 'your' Internet. For example, we can choose to add and remove Facebook friends, which has a filtering effect, but this is exacerbated by the Edgerank filter which attempts to sort the information presented to people potentially without the user even realizing (Pariser 2011). While this can be seen as a helpful way to cope with data overload, and can in theory improve the user experience, there are concerns that it can remove alternative political views from people's feeds.

Empirical research has often found that politics online is polarized. For example, Gilbert et al.'s (2009: 2) study of blogs found that they were echo chambers, with agreement outnumbering disagreement in comments by over 3:1, and this rose to 9:1 for political blogs. Bloggers are often found to be segregated along political boundaries (Adamic and Glance 2005; Lawrence et al. 2010). Social network analysis has identified similar trends in Twitter topic networks (Himelboim et al. 2013) and on political debates on Twitter more broadly (e.g. Smith et al. 2014). Content analysis of political, and particularly partisan-framed online groups, has also found polarization (e.g. Davis 1999; Wilhelm 2000). News and broader political information consumption online has a polarized structure that leads to the reinforcement rather than challenging of existing views (e.g. Smith 2011).

The picture is not completely straightforward though. A large-scale, broader study by Gentzkow and Shapiro (2011: 24) found that "ideological segregation on the Internet is low in absolute terms" and there is evidence that people at least claim to want to hear alternative voices (Stromer-Galley 2003). Of course, people may still attempt to avoid people or threads where they experience or perceive cross cutting debate. As

Mutz (2006: 12) argues: "The level of heterogeneity in a person's political *network* is not necessarily the same as the heterogeneity of the social *context* he or she inhabits. One can certainly influence the other, but hearing the other side takes place at the level of discussants within a network rather than within some larger, aggregate social context." In other words, we need to analyse not just macro-heterogeneity but also actual interactions at the micro-level, and this speaks to the danger that people can simply choose to avoid talking about politics online: that there is not just a left-right polarization but also a polarization between those that do, and do not, talk about politics online.

The notion of avoiding politics is perhaps most strongly associated with Nina Eliasoph's seminal ethnographic analysis of political talk in (offline) arenas like social clubs in America. Eliasoph (1998) observed that when political issues were mentioned, people avoided talking about the issue because they did not want to show disagreement or ignorance. Both Mutz and Martin (2001) and Noelle-Neumann (1984) have reported what can be seen as related findings: the spiral of silence theory suggests that if people feel that they belong to a majority it encourages political talk. Having set out these challenges, how might third spaces provide an environment that can limit them?

We argue, following Brundidge (2011) and Wojcieszak and Mutz (2009) that political talk in *third spaces* is less likely to be polarized and quite simply it is harder to 'avoid'. Why might this be so? First, to polarize would require that people had, and understood, ideologically informed views that they could gather around, which is not necessarily true outside of the political classes in countries such as the UK, where there has been a shift to the centre and more fluid political identity (Wright 2012b). Second, whether this be a discussion forum, Facebook group, or Twitter hashtags, people normally 'visit' third spaces because of some kind of shared tie, be it that they have an interest in cooking, fashion, football, or parenthood. Crucially, though, the tie is *not* political and thus while people might have similarity in background, it is more likely that people will inadvertently (Brundidge, 2011) come across people with divergent political views as social boundaries appear to be weakened online. Third, while we argue that third spaces are a *form* of virtual community—many people have a strong sense of community identity with strong ties—third spaces have a fluidity that facilitates a wide range of weak ties too. If Mutz (2006: 54) is correct to argue that "the solution [to political polarization] resides in part in more political conversations among 'weak ties', that is those who are not intimate friends or family members," we believe that third spaces facilitate this. Subsequent, work by Wojcieszak and Mutz (2009) tested their hypothesis: the dominant form of political interaction online was found to be homogenous, as would be expected given their earlier research. However, their representative survey data found that non-political forums were less polarized than explicitly political ones. Thus, we argue: "[. . .] fragmentation theory makes little sense once we move beyond the politically oriented communicative landscape" (Graham and Harju 2011: 29). While there may be polarization *within* forums around specific topics or sub-forums, this is rarely about politics, and similarly some people might avoid 'political' sub-forums, but such talk emerges across a wide range of threads, sub-forums and topics (Graham et al. 2015; Graham and Wright 2014).

Conclusion

Social media represents part of an ongoing convergence between media, audiences, and publics. Here, convergence melds and blurs traditional boundaries among media and audiences; citizens and consumers; and producers and consumers (Papacharissi 2010). There is an important opportunity here, then, to see social media as occupying the ambiguous territory of everyday public space, where the personal and even the private can quite comfortably overlap with the political. As our chapter has shown, across a range of social media platforms, everyday political talk is present, and in some cases thriving. For us, this makes understanding the dynamics of these everyday encounters of pressing concern for researchers.

This chapter has put forward a research agenda on everyday political talk and third spaces with the aim to better understand the interwoven nature of politics and everyday life. Moreover, whilst the vast majority of conversations in such spaces are nonpolitical, when conversations do turn political we are discovering how it can overcome some of the problems traditionally found in online discussion in political spaces. We should not be nonchalant about such findings: they contradict many early theoretical and empirical studies, and should prompt us to ask further questions about what is happening in such spaces. Here, more work should examine the relationship between talk in everyday spaces and political action. Our own work has begun to unpack this, but many questions remain, not least the flows of conversations and political actions between online and offline environments, and between different social media platforms.

Understanding the dynamics of everyday political talk and participation matters, as these are key issues in the context of ongoing reflections on the health of civic life in many Western democracies. As Papacharissi (2010: 78) argues, "it is possible that our quest for civic behaviors has not produced the desired results because we have not been looking at places that civic behaviors now inhabit: spaces that are friendlier to the development of contemporary civic behaviors." If we look in the right places, and ask the right questions, we might be able to identify some of the new repertoires emerging through social media.

Here, we see numerous fruitful avenues for future research on third spaces. The first is the relationship between some third spaces and governments and politicians. Whilst they are first and foremost 'non-political' everyday spaces devoted to various lifestyle issues, forums such as Netmums and MoneySavingExpert in the UK have attracted the attention of government officials, who are tapping into the online communities for policy consultation purposes (see Graham et al. 2015). Further research into the nature and impact of these relationships is important.

Another area in need of further research is the views of participants in the forums. This could include interviews with key actors, such as people identified as having made calls to political action and forum administrators and owners. The former could explore whether actions were actually taken and what role the forum played, while the latter could help us to better understand how owners conceive the political role (if any) of their forum, and whether/how they go about facilitating this. Alongside interviews, focus groups or surveys with a broader range of participants could explore people's views of political talk, their degree of involvement, and also the demographics of the politically active.

References

Adamic, L. and Glance, N. (2005) "The Political Blogosphere and the 2004 US Election: Divided They Blog," Paper Presented at the *WWW 2005 2nd Annual Workshop on the Weblogging Ecosystem*, Chiba, Japan, May.

Barber, B. R. (1984) *Strong Democracy: Participatory Politics for a New Age*, Berkeley: University of California Press.

Basu, S. (1999) "Dialogic Ethics and the Virtue of Humor," *The Journal of Political Philosophy*, 7(4), pp. 378–403.

Bauman, Z. (2005) *Liquid Modernity*, Cambridge: Polity.

Boynton, G.W., Cook, J., Daniels, K., Dawkins, M., Kopish, J., Makar, M., McDavid, W., Murphy, M., Osmundson, J., Steenblock, T., Sudarmawan, A., Wiese, P., and Zora, A. (2014) "The Political Domain Goes to Twitter: Hashtags, Retweets and URLs," *Open Journal of Political Science*, 4(1), pp. 8–15.

Brooker, P., Vines, J., Sutton, S., Barnett, J., Feltwell, T., and Lawson, S. (2015, 15–18 April) *Debating Poverty Porn on Twitter: Social Media as a Place for Everyday Socio-Political Talk*, in Proceedings of the 2015 ACM SIGCHI Conference on Human Factors in Computing Systems, Seoul, South Korea.

Brundidge, J. (2011) "Encountering 'Difference' in the Contemporary Public Sphere: The Contribution of the Internet to the Heterogeneity of Political Discussion Networks," *Journal of Communication*, 60(4), pp. 680–700.

Bruns, A. and Burgess, J.E. (2011a) "#ausvotes: How Twitter covered the 2010 Australian Federal Election," *Communication, Politics & Culture*, 44(2), pp. 37–56.

Bruns, A. and Burgess, J. E. (2011b) "The Use of Twitter Hashtags in the Formation of Ad Hoc Publics." Retrieved from: http://snurb.info/files/2011/The%20Use%20of%20Twitter%20 Hashtags%20in%20the%20Formation%20of%20Ad%20Hoc%20Publics%20(final).pdf

Chadwick, A. (2013) *The Hybrid Media System: Politics and Power*, Oxford: Oxford University Press.

Coleman, S. (2013) *How Voters Feel*, Cambridge: Cambridge University Press.

Coleman, S. and Blumler, J.G. (2009) *The Internet and Democratic Citizenship: Theory, Practice and Policy*, Cambridge: Cambridge University Press.

Colleoni, E., Rozza, A., and Arvidsson, A. (2014) "Echo Chamber or Public Sphere? Predicting Political Orientation and Measuring Political Homophily in Twitter Using Big Data," *Journal of Communication*, 64(2), pp. 317–332.

Dahlberg, L. (2001) "Computer-Mediated Communication and The Public Sphere: A Critical Analysis," *Journal of Computer-Mediated Communication*, 7(1). Retrieved from http://onlinelibrary. wiley.com/doi/10.1111/j.1083-6101.2001.tb00137.x/full

Dahlgren, P. (2006) "Doing Citizenship: The Cultural Origins of Civic Agency in the Public Sphere," *European Journal of Cultural Studies*, 9(3), pp. 267–286.

Davis, R. (1999) *The Web of Politics: The Internet's Impact on the American Political System*, Oxford: Oxford University Press.

Davis, R. and Owen, D. (1998) *New Media and American Politics*, Oxford: Oxford University Press.

Drucker, S. J. and Gumpert, G. (1996) "The Regulation of Public Social Life: Communication Law Revisited," *Communication Quarterly*, 44(3), 280–296.

Dryzek, J.S. (2000) *Deliberative Democracy and Beyond: Liberals, Critics, Contestations*, Oxford: Oxford University Press

Eckersley, R. (2001) "Ecofeminism and Environmental Democracy: Exploring the Connections," *Women & Environments International Magazine*, pp. 23–26. Retrieved from http://sks.sirs.bdt.orc. scoolaid.net

Eliasoph, N. (1998) *Avoiding Politics*, Cambridge: Cambridge University Press.

Es, K., van Geenen, D., and Boeschoten, T. (2014) "Mediating the Black Pete Discussion on Facebook: Slacktivism, Flaming Wars, and Deliberation," *First Monday*, 19(12). Retrieved from: http://firstmonday.org/ojs/index.php/fm/article/view/5570/4180.

Fearson, J.D. (1998) "Deliberation as Discussion," in J. Elster (ed.) *Deliberative Democracy*, Cambridge: Cambridge University Press, pp. 44–68.

Gentzkow, M. and Shapiro, J. (2011) "Ideological Segregation Online and Offline," *The Quarterly Journal of Economics*, 126(4), pp. 1799–1839.

Gibson, R. K., Margolis, M., Resnick, D., and Ward, S. J. (2003) "Election Campaigning on the WWW in the US and the UK: A Comparative Analysis," *Party Politics*, 9(1), pp. 47–76.

Gilbert, E., Bergstrom, T., and Karahalios, K. (2009). "Blogs are Echo Chambers: Blogs are Echo Chambers," in *Proceedings of the 42nd Hawaii International Conference on System Sciences*. IEEE, pp. 1–10.

Graham, T. (2009) *What's Wife Swap Got to Do with It? Talking Politics in the Net-Based Public Sphere*, doctoral dissertation, University of Amsterdam: http://dare.uva.nl/record/314852

Graham, T. (2010) "Talking Politics Online within Spaces of Popular Culture: The Case of the Big Brother Forum," *Javnost—The Public*, 17(4), pp. 25–42.

Graham, T. (2012) "Beyond 'Political' Communicative Spaces: Talking Politics on the Wife Swap Discussion Forum," *Journal of Information Technology and Politics*, 9(1), pp. 31–45.

Graham T. and Harju, A. (2011) "Reality TV as a Trigger of Everyday Political Talk in the Net-Based Public Sphere," *European Journal of Communication*, 26(1), pp. 18–32.

Graham, T. and Witschge, T. (2003) "In Search of Online Deliberation: Towards a New Method for Examining the Quality of Online Discussions," *Communications: The European Journal of Communication Research*, 28(2), pp. 173–204.

Graham, T. and Wright, S. (2014) "Discursive Equality and Everyday Political Talk: The Impact of Super-Participants," *Journal of Computer-Mediated Communication*, 19(3), pp. 625–642.

Graham, T., Jackson, D., and Wright, S. (2015/in press) "From Everyday Conversation to Political Action," *European Journal of Communication*.

Habermas, J., Lennox, S., and Lennox, F. (1974 [1964]) "The Public Sphere: An Encyclopedia Article (1964)," *New German Critique*, 3, pp. 49–55.

Halpern, D. and Gibbs, J. (2013) "Social Media as a Catalyst for Online Deliberation? Exploring the Affordances of Facebook and YouTube for Political Expression," *Computers in Human Behavior*, 29, pp. 1159–1168.

Hay, C. (2002) *Political Analysis: A Critical Introduction*, Basingstoke: Palgrave.

Himelboim, I., McCreery, S., and Smith, M. (2013) "Birds of a Feather Tweet Together: Integrating Network and Content Analyses to Examine Cross-Ideology Exposure on Twitter," *Journal of Computer-Mediated Communication*, 18(2), pp. 40–60.

Howe, J. P. (2012) "Slacktivism: A Gateway, and Only a Gateway, to Truly Changing Lives," *Huffington Post*. Retrieved from http://www.huffingtonpost.com/john-p-howe-iii-md/slacktivism-a-gateway-and_b_1422388.html

Huckfeldt, R., Mendez, J. M., and Osborn, T. L. (2004) "Disagreement, Ambivalence, and Engagement: The Political Consequences of Heterogeneous Networks," *Political Psychology*, 25(1), pp. 65–95.

Jackson, N. and Lilleker, D. (2009a) "Building an Architecture of Participation? Political Parties and Web 2.0 in Britain," *Journal of Information Technology & Politics*, 6(3/4), pp. 232–250.

Jackson, N. and Lilleker, D. (2009b) "MPs and E-representation: Me, MySpace and I," *British Politics*, 4, pp. 236–264.

Kies, R. (2010) *Promises and Limits of Web-deliberation*, Basingstoke: Palgrave.

Kim, J. and Kim, E.J. (2008) "Theorizing Dialogic Deliberation: Everyday Political Talk as Communicative Action and Dialogue," *Communication Theory*, 18(1), pp. 51–70.

Kohn, M. (2000) "Language, Power, and Persuasion: Towards a Critique of Deliberative Democracy," *Constellations*, 7, pp. 408–429

Larsson, A. O. and Moe, H. (2012) "Studying Political Microblogging: Twitter Users in the 2010 Swedish Election Campaign," *New Media & Society*, 14(5), pp. 729–747.

Lasch, C. (1996) *The Revolt of the Elites and the Betrayal of Democracy*, New York, NY: W. W. Norton.

Lawrence, E., Sides, J., and Farrell, H. (2010) "Self-Segregation or Deliberation? Blog Readership, Participation, and Polarization in American Politics," *Perspectives on Politics*, 8(1), pp. 141–157.

Lusoli, W., Ward, S., and Gibson, R. (2006) "(Re)connecting Politics? Parliament, the Public and the Internet," *Parliamentary Affairs*, 59(1), pp. 24–42.

Mansbridge, J. (1999) "Everyday Talk in the Deliberative System," in S. Macedo (ed.) *Deliberative Politics: Essays on Democracy and Disagreement*, Oxford: Oxford University Press, 211–239.

Mayhew, L. (1997) *The New Public*, Cambridge: Cambridge University Press.

McAfee, N. (2000) *Habermas, Kristeva, and Citizenship*, Ithaca, NY: Cornell University Press.

Mutz, D. C. (2006) *Hearing the Other Side: Deliberative versus Participatory Democracy*, New York: Cambridge University Press.

Mutz, D. C. and Martin, P. S. (2001) "Facilitating Communication Across Lines of Political Difference: The Role of Mass Media," *American Political Science Review*, 95, pp. 97–114.

Noelle-Neumann, E. (1984) *The Spiral of Silence: Public Opinion, Our Social Skin*, Chicago: University of Chicago Press.

Oldenburg, R. (1989) *The Great Good Place: Cafes, Coffee Shops, Community Centers, Beauty Parlours, General Stores, Bars, Hangouts, and How They Get You through the Day*, New York: Paragon House.

Papacharissi, Z. (2004) "Democracy On-line: Civility, Politeness, and the Democratic Potential of On-line Political Discussion Groups," *New Media & Society*, 6(2), pp. 259–284.

Papacharissi, Z. (2010) *A Private Sphere: Democracy in a Digital Age*, Malden, MA: Polity Press.

Pariser, E. (2011) *The Filter Bubble: What the Internet Is Hiding From You*, New York: Penguin Press.

Polletta, F. and Lee, J. (2006) "Is Telling Stories Good for Democracy? Rhetoric in Public Deliberation after 9/11," *American Sociological Review*, 71, pp. 699–723.

Rheingold, H. (1993) *The Virtual Community: Homesteading on the Electronic Frontier*, Reading, MA: Addison-Wesley.

Rosenberg, S. W. (2004) *Reconstructing the Concept of Democratic Deliberation*. Retrieved from: http://repositories.cdlib.org/csd/04–02

Saward, M. (2003) "Enacting Democracy," *Political Studies*, 51(1), pp. 161–179.

Semaan, B. C., Robertson, S. P., Douglas, S., and Maruyama, M. (2014) "Social Media Supporting Political Deliberation Across Multiple Public Spheres: Towards Depolarization," in Proceedings of the 17th ACM Conference on Computer Supported Cooperative Work & Social Computing (CSCW '14). New York, pp. 1409–1421.

Smith, A. (2011) *The Internet and Campaign 2010*, Pew Research Internet Project. Retrieved from: http://www.pewinternet.org/2011/03/17/the-internet-and-campaign-2010/

Smith, M. A., Rainie, L., Shneiderman, B., and Himelboim, I. (2014) *Mapping Twitter Topic Networks: From Polarized Crowds to Community Clusters*, Pew Research Internet Project. Retrieved from: http://www.pewinternet.org/2014/02/20/mapping-twitter-topic-networks-from-polarized-crowds-to-community-clusters/

Steenkamp, M. and Hyde-Clarke, N. (2014) "The Use of Facebook for Political Commentary in South Africa," *Telematics and Informatics*, 31, pp. 91–97.

Steinkuehler, C. and Williams, F. (2006) "Where Everybody Knows Your (Screen) Name: Online Games as 'Third Places,'" *Journal of Computer Mediated Communication*, 11(4), pp. 885–909.

Stromer-Galley, J. (2003) "Diversity of Political Conversation on the Internet: Users' Perspectives," *Journal of Computer-mediated Communication*, 8(3).

Stroud, N. J., Scacco, J. M., Muddiman, A., and Curry, A. L. (2014) "Changing Deliberative Norms on News Organizations' Facebook Sites," *Journal of Computer-Mediated Communication*, 20(2), pp. 188–203.

Sukumaran, A., Vezich, S., McHugh, M., and Nass, C. (2011) "Normative Influences on Thoughtful Online Participation," in *Proceedings of the 2011 Annual Conference on Human Factors in Computing Systems—CHI '11*, New York: ACM Press, pp. 3401–3410.

Sunstein, C. (2001) *Republic.com*, Princeton, NJ: Princeton University Press.

Van Alstyne, M. and Brynjolfsson, E. (1997) *Electronic Communities: Global Village or Cyberbalkans?* Retrieved from: http://web.mit.edu/marshall/www/papers/CyberBalkans.pdf

Van Zoonen, L. (2005) *Entertaining the Citizen: When Politics and Popular Culture Converge*, Lanham, MD: Rowman & Littlefield.

Van Zoonen, L. (2007) "Audience Reactions to Hollywood Politics," *Media, Culture & Society*, 29(4), pp. 531–547.

Warren, M. E. (2006) "What Can and Cannot Be Said: Deliberating Sensitive Issues," *Journal of Social Philosophy*, 37(2), pp. 163–181.

Wilhelm, A. G. (2000) *Democracy in the Digital Age: Challenges to Political Life in Cyberspace*, London: Routledge.

Wojcieszak, M., and Mutz, D. (2009) "Online Groups and Political Discourse: Do Online Discussion Spaces Facilitate Exposure to Political Disagreement?," *Journal of Communication*, 59(1), pp. 40–56.

Wright, S. (2006) "Government-run Online Discussion Fora: Moderation, Censorship and the Shadow of Control," *British Journal of Politics and International Relations*, 8(4), pp. 550–568.

Wright, S. (2007) "A Virtual European Public Sphere? The Futurum Discussion Forum," *Journal of European Public Policy*, 14(8), pp. 1167–1185.

Wright, S. (2012a) "Politics as Usual? Revolution, Normalization and a New Agenda for Online Deliberation," *New Media & Society*, 14(2), pp. 244–261.

Wright, S. (2012b) "From 'Third Place' to 'Third Space': Everyday Political Talk in Non-Political Online Spaces," *Javnost—The Public*, 19(3), pp. 5–20.

Wright, S. and Street, J. (2007) "Democracy, Deliberation and Design: The Case of Online Discussion Forums," *New Media & Society*, 9(5), pp. 849–869.

6

TIPPING THE BALANCE OF POWER

Social Media and the Transformation of Political Journalism

Marcel Broersma and Todd Graham

Introduction

When, during a campaign visit to Rochester, a small town in Kent, Emily Thornberry tweeted a photo of a house covered with St. George's flags and a white van in front of it, she didn't imagine this swift and impulsive act would cause a scandal. "It was just trying to give, to the people who follow me on Twitter, a kind of picture of what the Rochester by-election is like," the British Labour MP and shadow attorney-general explained somewhat disconcertedly to the *Guardian* in November 2014. Her political opponents, ranging from UKIP leader Nigel Farage to Tory MPs and fellow Labour politicians, quickly responded on Twitter to disqualify her tweet as snobbish. Because the English flag and the 'white van man' are considered emblematic for the British working classes, they argued that it showed how elitist and disconnected with the man in the street the Labour party is. 'Derogatory', 'dismissive' and 'disgraceful', they called it, while Farage even suggested that the post let Labour leader Ed "Milliband's mask slip" (Mason 2014: para. 4). While Thornberry's tweet went viral on Twitter, it was only a question of minutes until what would now become an affair was picked up by political journalists. Articles based on the postings from Twitter appeared on websites and somewhat later in the newspapers and broadcast news. The general sentiment was that the tweet "cemented the impression that Thornberry, who lives in a £3 million house in Islington, was part of the insufferable quinoa-munching metropolitan elite" (Wallop 2015: para. 21). That same evening, Emily Thornberry resigned from the shadow cabinet and was demoted to the back benches in Westminster.

This political gaffe might in itself seem insignificant, but it illustrates well how the advent of social media has changed the dynamics between politicians and political reporters. In the era of mass communication, they had different aims but shared interests. Politicians needed entry to the news media to get their message out to the citizenry, while news outlets needed politicians as sources for the kind of news that is considered essential to citizens and key to legitimize a news outlet's role in democracy. To a large extent, this interdependence based on information distribution monopolies stabilized the press–politics power relationship and consequently the democratic sys-tem. The immediacy of social media, however, has made visible what used to remain hidden when instant publication by everyone was not an option. In the era of mass media, both journalists and politicians had the third player in the triangle of political communication—the audience, also known as the electorate—in the back of their mind when doing their job. But although the public's perceived wishes and needs influenced (strategic) behaviour, this relationship remained somewhat of an unconsummated love. Both political and media elites were to a large extent shielded from citizens and were able to negotiate the political and public agenda merely among themselves (cf. Brants and Voltmer 2011).

With the rise of the Internet and social media, the relationship between politics, journalism, and the public changed into an actual *ménage à trois*. Reporters and politi-cians are very aware of the opportunities and challenges networked communication offers them in both relating to each other and reaching out to the public. This has become more important now that political parties have lost their relatively stable grassroots support and voters have become increasingly volatile. To make up their minds, these floating voters—who have become harder to reach through institutional channels—base their opinions on information from a diverse set of sources presented in mass media, the Internet, and now, on social media. A hybrid media system is taking shape where a mass media logic and a networked logic interact, and the various agents in the triangle of political communication "create, tap, or steer information flows in ways that suit their goals and in ways that modify, enable, or disable others' agency, across and between a range of older and newer media settings" (Chadwick 2013: 4; cf. Klinger and Svensson 2014; see also the chapters by Chadwick et al. and Klinger and Svensson in this volume). The hybridization that occurs can create significant changes to established working practices. For politicians, impression management is thus increasingly important to win voters (see Enli in this volume). At the same time, journalists cope with the issue of how to attract the attention of this fragmented audi-ence and how to profile their brand in a hybrid communication paradigm.

The possibility of direct and open communication with and to citizens, even when it is unidirectional, has changed the power structures in political communication for bet-ter and for worse, as becomes clear from the Twitter gaffe of Emily Thornberry, an avid tweep. However, to what extent and how the communicative space of politics will be transformed is still up for debate because the use of various social media platforms and their functions in an evolving hybrid media system are still very much in flux. Initially, in scholarship and public discourse high expectations reigned of the empowerment of citizens and a direct and vivid exchange of arguments between voters and their repre-sentatives (see Coleman and Blumler 2009). This would enrich the quality of public debate. The promise of direct communication with voters prompted the *Guardian* even to label the 2010 elections in the UK as 'the first social media election' (Arthur 2010).

However, it has become clear that Twitter, just as other social media, is only partly about deliberation. The majority of politicians' tweets broadcast opinions, updates about what they are doing, or messages to mobilize their base. At the other end, most users use the platform to get informed without feeling the necessity to get in touch with politicians or enter a debate. This seems to suit the affordances of the platform (Gra-ham, Jackson, and Broersma 2014). Gradually, Twitter has developed from primarily a social networking and messaging site with status updates by a relatively small circle of 'friends' into first and foremost a news and information platform for a broad audience.

The company has successfully redirected the focus of use from tweeps' personal lives to the world around them. Since 2009, the Twitter interface no longer asks "What are you doing?," which encourages personal status updates and chatter, but "What's happening?," which encourages sharing of eyewitness observations, opinions, and other information. In this new networked space where various types of agents are connected, user patterns seem to be dominated by posting, referring and reading, and to a lesser extent by interaction, engagement and discussion. This behaviour is preordained and thus shaped by the economic interests and programmed affordances of the platform. Twitter's business model has been increasingly focused towards 'datafication' and acquiring as much meaningful information as possible by persuading its users to post enriched information about questions of the day (van Dijck 2013). Journalists and news organizations are thus important to have on board, which was publicly acknowledged in a series of tweets by founder Jack Dorsey on Twitter's ninth birthday: "Journalists were a big part of why we grew so quickly and still a big reason why people use Twitter: news. It's a natural fit. . . . We wouldn't be here without you" (@jack, 21 Mar. 2015).

For established news outlets the rise of social media is both an opportunity and a threat (Anderson, Bell, and Shirky 2012; Broersma and Peters 2013). The network logic of social media sites erodes the information monopolies of news companies even more than relatively static publishing platforms such as websites and blogs do. The sharing of news on Twitter and Facebook challenges their role as society's gatekeepers for information on current affairs, which is part and parcel of journalism but also harms their business model. The upside of a hybrid system is that they can brand themselves, distribute their news on social media, and in this way direct many news consumers to their platforms. Especially Facebook, and to a lesser extent Twitter and Instagram, now generate a large part of the traffic to news outlets' homepages (Pew 2014). Moreover, journalists gain instant and convenient access to a potentially unlimited amount of sources and information through social networks. Because of its affordances, focus on current information, and users, Twitter is particularly important in this respect (Cision 2013b). Social media have therefore been integrated quickly into daily routines and have become increasingly important to news outlets.

The main question, however, is whether and to what extent social media fundamentally change political communication. Initially, a utopian discourse prevailed (Arceneaux and Schmitz Weiss 2010). Especially journalists who were early adapters of social media were enthusiastic about the opportunities these platforms offered to journalism. One senior *Guardian* journalist, for example, called Twitter a "revolution" that is "redefining everything that the industry does and how it behaves" (personal interview). When journalists grasp the opportunities, she argued, Twitter "can act like a wire service, a fact checking service, a propaganda vehicle, an advertising vehicle—everything that you could possibly want from the Internet is boiled down in Twitter—into one very, very simple service". Although her opinion touches upon important features of social media, these kinds of utterances might be emblematic for the discourse that comes with the introduction of every new medium. Conversely, other journalists have argued that social media do not change journalism fundamentally. They contend that existing norms, routines and practices are simply migrated to an online context. These viewpoints are reflected in academic discourses around journalism and social media.

This chapter argues that the rise of social media has extended and simultaneously changed the playing field for political reporting. Although many practices that journalists are familiar with in the offline world of national parliaments, state houses, and town halls at first sight seem to stay in place, social media have extended their spatial and temporal dimensions. We argue that a distinctive repertoire of social media practices, grounded in the logic and affordances of networked media, is evolving. This functions according to a very different logic than the mass media logic that still partly underlies political reporting in the current hybrid media system. The pace of political communication processes has increased substantially now that it is easier to connect with sources and information flows, and possible to post information instantly. Moreover, networked communication has blurred the distinctive but interdependent roles of journalists and politicians now that they can both broadcast information. The normalization thesis (Lasorsa et al. 2012; Hedman 2015) which contends that new media challenge traditional practices and routines, but that these are merely adapted to fit online and are not essentially changed, thus misses the point. We argue that the power balance between journalists and sources is fundamentally changing. To ground our argument we will focus on Twitter because it has developed into a daily and almost inevitable service to journalists. While Facebook is mainly used to distribute and promote news stories and—to a lesser extent—engage with readers, Twitter's affordances make it tremendously useful for reporting.

Twitter as a Beat for Political Reporting

The easy availability of potentially interesting sources, information and opinions has turned Twitter into a convenient and increasingly important beat for reporters (Broersma and Graham 2012, 2013). To ensure steady and reliable news flows, reporters are traditionally assigned to beats which cover a specific topic, ranging from politics to crime, science and showbiz. Beats have both spatial and social dimensions. They usually include a specific geographic place (such as parliament, town hall, or a court of law) where reporters go on a regular basis to gather, share, and negotiate information with sources. Similarly, for many reporters Twitter has become a space to go, find information, and talk with others on a daily basis. It offers a convenient way to build and develop online social networks which mirror and expand beats beyond geographical borders (Broersma and Graham 2013).

The platform has become indispensable for general reporting or foreign reporting in which journalists have to cope with sudden news events such as disasters, incidents, and political uprisings (Bruno 2011). Twitter then becomes a one-off news beat. In many cases reporters are not on the ground (yet) and thus have to rely upon the information that others put online. Moreover, they do not have a network in place that supplies them with reliable information. Through Twitter they can easily get in touch with people who are not well known yet but who are suddenly interesting in the light of a certain news topic. This can extend the diversity of voices in the news beyond the usual elite sources. However, for other reporters, the use of the platform by many typical elite sources, such as politicians and celebrities, is a major attraction. In areas such as entertainment and sports, sources are not very easy to approach. Social media can compensate for this lack of sources by providing reporters access to selected aspects of the daily lives, thoughts, and emotions of celebrities and athletes (Broersma and Graham 2013; Paulussen and Harder 2014).

Since its start in 2006, Twitter has applied a deliberate strategy to encourage as many politicians, journalists, and celebrities as possible to join. Because these groups attract other users and add valuable information to the network, the company has established teams that help them to set up and manage their accounts (O'Leary 2012). Accordingly, one of the main assets of Twitter is that it has succeeded in connecting ordinary people to the popular, powerful, and rich. In addition to that, it has increasingly developed into a network in which professionals meet each other and exchange information. The fabric of the platform in which, contrary, for example, to Facebook and LinkedIn, reciprocity is not necessary to follow or to be followed, makes Twitter an easily accessible and valuable beat for journalists looking for information or contacts (Broersma and Graham 2013).

A vast body of survey research and a growing number of qualitative studies confirm that social network sites are nowadays part and parcel of the daily work routines of journalists around the globe. In 2013, 96 per cent of 589 surveyed British journalists indicated that they used social media on a daily basis for reporting. Twitter was the most popular platform and used almost exclusively for professional reasons, as opposed to Facebook, Pinterest, or Instagram which also have more private purposes. While 70 per cent of journalists used it for work-related reasons in 2011, this number rose to 92 per cent in 2013. "Social media was an add-on originally, a little something extra you used to do," said one of the interviewed journalists. "Now it's intrinsic to everyday life, it's completely woven into the newsroom" (Cision 2013a). Whether and how social media are embedded in the institutional structures of newsrooms differs between news outlets. Some have strict social media policies while others leave it up to individual journalists to use platforms as they like.

There are notable differences between various national contexts. The UK (92 per cent) ranks highest when it comes to the daily use of Twitter for reporting, with France (91 per cent), Canada (89 per cent), the Netherland (88 per cent), Australia (85 per cent), the U.S. (79 per cent), and Sweden (77 per cent) in its slipstream. In Finland (61 per cent) and Germany (59 per cent), daily use is consistently lower (Cision 2013b). However, the percentages in these countries have more than doubled since 2011, suggesting that they are quickly catching up. Results from other parts of the world, notably South America and Asia, suggest that the numbers here are between 40 and 70 per cent, and also on the rise (Schmitz Weiss 2015). As an Indian journalist states: "These days I see more journalists and editors go to social media in response to a major event. You have to use social media because the conversation online is way ahead of what's in the paper" (Bélair-Gagnon et al. 2014: 1068). In 2011, Twitter for Newsrooms was started, including an online resource and a team offering support to reporters and news outlets.

For political reporters the presence of a large number of politicians has been an important asset attracting them to the platform. As a Dutch journalist reveals:

> I resisted it for a long time, until I noticed it had become inevitable. I did not want to follow the 2012 elections without Twitter, risking that colleagues anticipate things they already know, while I don't because I'm too stubborn to be on Twitter. (Brands 2014: 76)

Indeed, after the successful Obama campaign of 2008, which fully embraced the use of social media, joining Twitter has been seen as a major asset during elections for both politicians and political reporters. The company, too, actively promotes and supports the use of the platform in politics, for example, by launching a Twitter Government and Elections Handbook (2014). It emphasizes that tweeting offers politicians the opportunity for a virtual "handshake" and direct conversation with voters. It advertises the platform as a virtual town hall meeting, easily accessible to all voters. But it also points to the value of the platform for developing contacts with journalists, for example, by encouraging politicians to 'engage with the reporter on Twitter' after an interview.

Nowadays, social media strategies have become firmly integrated into political prac-tice and the PR policies of politicians (Graham et al. 2014). In 2013, about 60 per cent of French, British, Swedish, and Norwegian MPs were active on Twitter, while around one fifth to a quarter of the latter had a Facebook page. In the Netherlands, 93 per cent of the MPs were active tweeps, while in the U.S., 90 per cent of Congress members had active accounts. Of the Dutch MPs, 86 per cent indicated that they considered Twitter as the most important social network, while only 9 per cent mentioned Face-book (Frame and Brachotte 2014; Larsson and Kalsnes 2014; Weber Shandwick 2014). Politicians use Twitter during elections and on a day-to-day basis to reach out directly to voters. However, they use it even more to put issues on the public agenda through legacy media (also see the chapter by Skogerbø et al. in this volume). "Sometimes one tweet gets things going," Dutch MP Pieter Omzigt states. He was reading documents about a new tax policy which were just sent by the government to parliament while waiting for departure in an aeroplane. "I thought: this has an impact on five million citizens, so I quickly launched a tweet. I could not believe my eyes when I switched my telephone back on after the one hour flight" (Korteweg 2014: para. 15). The over-whelming public response that the information on Twitter provoked and was picked up in news outlets firmly put the issue on the political agenda.

Dominant Reporting Practices and Routines on Twitter

For political reporters, Twitter is not so much a replacement of personal contact, but provides them with a spatial and temporal extension of their geographical beat. For large parts of the week they are physically present in and around parliament and the various departments, and immersed fully in the social network that constitutes the political beat. Usually they are in close contact with politicians, spokespersons, staff members, and civil servants, and have developed long-term relationships based on mutual trust. This sense of closeness and mutual interdependence promotes the exchange of tips for news stories, comments, and information and facilitates the verification of information. Although there are differences in the frequency and patterns of use between reporters (Revers 2014; Hedman and Djerf-Pierre 2013; Engesser and Humprecht 2014; Rogstad 2014), social media have been widely adopted as a tool that enhances existing practices and routines. What is often neglected, however, is the fact that social media simultane-ously change these practices.

Based on a meta-analysis of Twitter research, we have developed a cross-national typology of seven dominant reporting practices and routines of political journalists on Twitter: monitoring, networking, engaging, sourcing, publishing, promoting, and branding. Together these patterns of online behavior have developed into a new and consistent repertoire of how reporters use Twitter. Although they build upon estab-lished practices and routines, this repertoire has been shaped over time according to the affordances of Twitter; user behavior is to a large extent inscribed in the design of the platform. Features such as retweets, @mentions, hashtags, lists, and embedded links and content are closely connected to the professional roles political journalists adhere to on social platforms. While some research (Engesser and Humprecht 2014) has argued that journalists use Twitter frequently but not in a skilful way, we argue that many have developed a coherent repertoire and have adapted to the logic of Twitter very well over the past years.

Monitoring

Twitter is a very fruitful and relevant place to go for journalists because it provides them with an efficient tool for monitoring key debates and tendencies in society. Twitter has become an awareness system that facilitates 'ambient journalism' in which journalists monitor public opinion, the sources they follow, and the instant unfolding of news events through small snippets of only implicitly related information (Hermida 2010). Reporters indicate that monitoring is an important reason for using social media; between 81 (Australia) and 66 (Germany) per cent of the surveyed journalists in nine Western countries use Twitter for this reason (Cision 2013b). Political journalists describe Twitter as a thermometer that allows them to know the mind of the people. The frequency of tweeting about a parliamentary debate or a political topic, including Twitter's trending topic function, is factored in when deciding whether a topic is newsworthy and whether to spend time covering it.

There are different ways to monitor the political realm on Twitter. First, political reporters follow topics and debates through hashtags or by searching for keywords. Second, they follow a mix of politicians, other journalists, and media outlets as well as others in the political domain, such as civil servants, interest groups, and PR people. Third, they make lists based on topics or distinctive groups, such as political parties, which allows them to quickly scan for valuable tweets. Twitter offers a convenient and quick way to get a sense of what is going on in parliament and not miss out on current developments. An American political reporter compares it to a cocktail party 2.0: "you can listen to *all* the conversations you want to, that you are physically capable of following, you can participate in all of them at the same time and you don't have to overcome any shyness" (Revers 2015: 9).

Reporters use Twitter to find news and generate ideas for new stories. "The best part is any inside information that comes out or when a politician like Sarah Palin or someone else makes news with their comments," an American reporter says (Parmelee 2014: 438). "As a journalist, that's what I look for in tweets: nuggets of interesting, new and exclusive information." Tweets also give them a sense of what competitors are working on, so they will not miss out on important news. It generates story ideas and enables them to decide quickly if they want to pick up on issues in the news coverage. What are the topics on the political agenda and how are representatives of various parties thinking about pressing issues? When a topic breaks, using Twitter is much faster to develop an impression of what is going on (and gauging politicians' opinions) than making phone calls or even following the wires. "It is my first and last stop online every day," an American political reporter said (Parmelee 2013: 299).

Networking

A second function of social media is that they are used to build and maintain professional networks. Journalists compare it to a rolodex, an old-fashioned address book, or call it "the modern equivalent of the phone book" (Heravi, Harrower, and Boran 2014: 25). Political journalists indicate that they consider Twitter to be an important means for following their beat. "It is our job to closely follow politicians," a Dutch reporter argues. "Part of their public life takes place on Twitter, so a parliamentary journalist who takes himself seriously can't do without it anymore" (Brands 2014: 75–76). The platform offers journalists a convenient way to get an impression of politicians' daily activities, opinions and experiences, without giving them the feeling that they have to sacrifice their independence or get too close to their sources. An American political reporter put it like this: "I'm comfortable 'following' a source [on Twitter] but not comfortable 'friending' one [on Facebook] because of perceptions that go along with being 'friends' with someone I cover" (Parmelee 2014: 442).

The direct messaging function of Twitter is a key affordance of the platform for journalists who want to establish exclusive relationships with sources. It is much quicker and more direct than email and in daily practice it often functions as chat tool. Reporters can easily approach MPs for direct comments, also when they want to circumvent spokepersons, even if they are in parliamentary meetings. A Dutch political commentator relates that he sometimes watches the live broadcast of a debate from home and then can see on his television when an MP gets his message and is typing a response (private interview). A large extent of political communication thus takes place behind the scenes and is not evident to other users. Reporters often indicate that they are reluctant to communicate openly with politicians and other sources because they are well aware that their competitors are watching them closely on Twitter. As a senior political correspondent at the *Guardian* reveals: "People often address things to me via Twitter openly, but I usually reply by the direct message that only they can see—just 'cause I think most people are not really interested in our exchange, and it's probably better done just between me and that person" (private interview). This refers both to the fact that sources might be more willing to share detailed information in private, and to reporters' needs to get a preferred position and publish exclusive news.

Interacting

Social media offer political journalists an opportunity to engage with readers and sources in a public forum. Whether they actually do so is very much dependent on their personal stance towards social media. Some journalists, mainly at legacy media organisations, feel they should remain objective and detached on social media and thus not personally engage with readers and sources. Others, especially at 'born digital' news outlets, feel they have to develop personal bonds on Twitter to engage readers in news production, but also to become a 'hub' in the network and thus attract news consumers to their work and platforms (Zeller and Hermida 2015; Rogstad 2014). Retweets offer an opportunity to distribute interesting news and simultaneously engage with the sender of the original tweet, whose message gains more credibility and a wider circulation. This is done passively by simply retweeting or adding a comment to the original post. A more active way of interacting is entering into a dialogue with other users. Political reporters indeed get in touch with the audience to ask for their imput and to discuss political events such as election debates (Reis Mourão 2014).

Political journalists indicate that they interact relatively little with politicians via public tweets (Revers 2014). They say they do not have the time to get into discussion and emphasize that they, unlike citizens, can speak to MPs personally. Moreover, they want to avoid communication via tweets because their competitors from other media watch them closely and they do not want to show openly what they are working on. Research that analyses the interaction patterns of political journalists on Twitter specifically is still lacking. However, from analysing political candidates' tweets during general elections we know that they do 'talk' on Twitter. During campaigns, politicians interact mainly with members of the public (between 60 and 65 per cent of the interactions during the 2010 Dutch and UK, and 2012 Dutch general elections) and fellow politicians (between 16 and 22 per cent). However, journalists follow in their slipstream. In the 2010 campaigns, 10 per cent of politicians' online interactions in the British and 12 per cent in the Dutch case were with journalists, dropping to 7 per cent during the 2012 Dutch elections. In tweets directed at reporters, candidates mainly talked about their political views, critiqued or acknowledged journalists' articles, or gave updates from the campaign trail. Interestingly, about 15 per cent of the exchanges were of a personal nature, suggesting close and friendly relations between politicians and reporters (Graham et al. 2014; Graham et al. 2015).

Sourcing

Survey research indicates that between 93 (France) and 79 (Germany) per cent of journalists use Twitter for sourcing the news; between 78 (Australia) and 60 (Germany) per cent use it to verify information (Cision 2013b; see also the chapter by Skogerbø et al. in this volume). Political reporters often state that although Twitter can be a useful start for a story, whenever possible, journalists have to talk to politicians in person. "I always use Twitter as the start of something," a Dutch reporters states. "Just to see what somebody has already said, so you can refer to it when you call them. Sometimes they'll tell me: I already tweeted about it" (Brands 2014: 77). For MPs, a tweet often replaces a press release. It provides a convenient way to convey information or a political viewpoint, in the hope that it will be picked up by legacy news outlets. Media say they are reluctant to use tweets, however, because information is not 'exclusive' when it is published on Twitter. Basing a story on a tweet is broadly considered a last resort if time runs short or a politician does not pick up the phone. And when a tweet is used in news coverage, whether as a primary source that started off a story or as an illustrative quote, it is not always attributed. Some political reporters consider it redundant to mention Twitter as the source because they believe that it does not matter where a politician said something. Only when it is relevant to understand the context of a story, they argue, the platform should be mentioned (Parmelee 2014; Brands 2014).

But in spite of professional rhetoric, using tweets as quotes in news reporting has become a widely used textual convention. Tweets themselves can trigger news stories, as becomes clear from Thornberry's inappropriate tweet. Not only gaffes are newsworthy. Especially information posted on Twitter that is not available in another way, because the source cannot be contacted directly or refuses to answer questions, is able to trigger stories. This provides opportunities for sources to set the media agenda, to promote themselves and their work, and to influence public opinion. Dutch right-wing politician Geert Wilders, for example, is very medium-savvy in this respect. He tends to avoid talking to journalists and instead sends out opinionated tweets that he knows will be controversial. When these are picked up by reporters and political opponents comment on them, his take on the particular issue takes centre stage. In 2011, for example, 52 of his 333 tweets were published in Dutch newspapers (Nederlandse Nieuwsmonitor 2011). In most cases, however, tweets are quoted to illustrate broader news developments. They add flavour to a story because they convey personal impressions and experiences, or *couleur locale*. In other cases, tweets are presented as 'stand-alone'. Many newspapers now include 'tweets-of-the-day' columns that collect remarkable, witty, or funny tweets. For journalists, Twitter thus offers a sea of potentially interesting information that can be remixed into news stories. Journalists do not have to 'get out on the streets' any more to find information. The world is on hand from behind the desk (Broersma and Graham 2013; cf. Paulussen and Harder 2014).

Publishing

Due to its limitation to 140 characters per message, Twitter is not the most suitable platform for publishing news stories. The vast majority of political reporters therefore do not use it in this way. They indicate that they object against 'instant sharing' and save 'exclusives' for more substantial stories on their 'mother' platforms. Snippets of information which are interesting in themselves, but do not immediately trigger coverage, are posted on Twitter, however. Moreover, reporters publish by curating information on Twitter. By retweeting, mentioning and linking to the content posted by others, they present remarkable opinions, humorous posts and source material about the news of the day (Molyneux 2014). As a U.S. political reporter reveals:

> There is no quicker way to get a piece of news to an audience of that size. And it's very organic—you send it out there and then it gets retweeted. It's like an echo and each time it echoes it reaches another audience. And if they see your name pop up two or three times they start following you; it kind of builds on itself. (Revers 2014: 8)

Some journalists cover parliamentary debates, briefings or other meetings by live-tweeting them (Artwick 2013). Their tweets can be followed through the use of hashtags but are usually also gathered in feeds on a news outlet's website. Twitter offers convenient widgets for this. The move to digital-first publishing might foster this trend further. Andrew Sparrow, the *Guardian*'s political correspondent, writes a daily political blog with 'rolling coverage' about the political events in Westminster. Sparrow, who has almost 40,000 followers, not only integrates many tweets of politicians into his blog, and directs readers to it via Twitter but also uses the platform to distribute snippets of news from parliament. "If journalism is the first draft of history," Sparrow argued after the 2010 UK elections, "live blogging is the first draft of journalism" (Newman 2010: 17). Social media enhance the opportunities to publish evolving news on a rolling basis instead of presenting complete stories.

Promoting

Social media are not only new publishing platforms but also new distribution channels. Promoting stories on social media is more and more important now that news consumption has become increasingly social. Currently, the majority of users do not come directly to the homepage of a news outlet but access its site through links shared on social media. This is important for legacy media, but even more so for online-only media, such as *MediaPart* in France. These outlets all have institutional Twitter accounts, or even multiple accounts for different beats, which distribute headlines, teasers, and links during the day. Typically these accounts are automated, using tweet bots that send tweets as soon as news stories appear online. Due to the mechanic 'feel' of these accounts, more substantial news outlets, especially in the US and the UK, have hired social media editors or even teams to manage news distribution on social platforms. But individual reporters also actively promote their stories on Twitter to build an audience, and sometimes this is even a result of editorial policy. Studies have shown that if journalists retweet or include links, these mainly refer to content from their own news organization (Artwick 2013).

Branding

While promoting is about directing readers to distinct news stories, branding relates to the opportunity social media offer to freelance and staff journalists to brand themselves and develop a more personal relation with their audience. When done successfully, this does not only increase reader loyalty but also helps to strengthen the profile and market value of the journalist. Now that journalism is in flux and employment opportunities are getting precarious, it is increasingly important to be 'visible' online and to become a 'hub' in online networks where people go to be informed. As one political reporter says: "If you are looking at a beat or a job in 5 years you don't want to lose out because the other guy has 10,000 Twitter followers and you abstained from that" (Revers 2014: 9). Acquiring authority is one strategy that journalists apply. It helps when their posts are retweeted while they retweet users who provide comments on their work. Preferably, positive remarks are retweeted, but reporters increasingly understand that they also benefit from redistributing tweets that are critical of their work (Molyneux 2014; Hedman and Djerf-Pierre 2013). Most political journalists are hesitant, however, to include personal information in their tweets.

Normalization or Shifting Power Relations?

Research on how Twitter has changed journalism often implicitly or explicitly argues that social media are *normalized* to fit established professional practices and routines. The normalization thesis thus links up with journalists' discourse in which Twitter is commonly referred to as a new 'tool' in journalism's 'toolkit', too. It would first and foremost allow reporters to do what they have always done when working their (political) beat, but more effectively and in an online environment. In other words, Twitter is for 21st-century journalists what the telephone was for 20th-century reporters: a helpful tool to make news production easier and quicker (Lasorsa, Lewis and Holton 2012; Reis Mourão 2014). In contrast, results from a content analysis of tweets suggest that professional norms might change because journalists, or at least some of them, are experimenting with 'what works' on Twitter. Although there is no clear trend at this stage, reporters might become more transparent and responsive, more humorous, opinionated and personal on social media. However, scholars usually conclude that reporters will try to align these new features and behavioral patterns with the norms of impartiality and objectivity that guided journalism in the era of mass communication—which brings us back to normalization theory (Lasorsa 2012; Lasorsa, Lewis and Holton 2012; Parmelee 2013; Lawrence et al. 2014; Hedman 2015; Molyneux 2014).

We argue that normalization theory as a conceptual framework sells short the fact that coherent and distinct social media repertoires have emerged in the past decade. These follow from the affordances of social media platforms and, more broadly, from a networked logic that fundamentally differs from the industrial mass media logic which underpins legacy journalism (Broersma and Peters 2013; see also Klinger and Svensson in this volume). The way in which information becomes news and resonates among users does not depend on the power to monopolize and control distribution channels here. It depends on the ability to push information through the network by persuading other users to share, like, remix, and annotate data. In other words, in the industrial logic news derives its credibility and authority from the platform and the institutional context in which it is produced, but in a networked form of communication it does so from the users who push it through the network. This implies that the social media practices and routines as described above have a function and character that is fundamentally different from their counterparts in mass communication. Although they might look alike on the outside, they are not being *normalized*. They are essentially different categories of diverging but interlinked repertoires.

In the current hybrid system agents partly capitalize upon the legitimacy and authority acquired in offline environments (like parliament) and mass communication (news outlets). Simultaneously, their social, cultural, and economic capital is increasingly dependent on the way in which they succeed in converting their institutional assets to these new interwoven social media networks. In the classic triangle of political communication the three groups of agents (politicians, journalists, and citizens) are sharply distinguished categories with distinctive aims, characteristics, and behavioral patterns. Conversely, in a network these agents, as hubs or nodes, are essentially similar. The diminished significance of institutional structures and authority forces both journalists and politicans to position themselves, by means of newly developed social media repertoires, in relation to others in the network, and thus to anticipate a quickly transforming and fundamentally unstable environment.

Systematic studies of how politicians integrate social media into their daily political practice are still quite scarce (cf. Svensson 2011). Much of the research here tends to build on network analysis and the analysis of the content of tweets that are posted during elections or other political events, often through event-related hashtags. But, interestingly, what the literature here does suggest is that the use of Twitter by politicians tends to mimic that of journalists. They have developed a repertoire of practices and routines that is similar to that of the journalists. Politicians monitor; they indicate that they use the platform to get a sense of the important issues of the day. In an environment in which it is incredibly important to quickly anticipate new information and in which one does not want to be surprised by the critical questions of reporters, social media offer a far faster way than traditional media to obtain news, and they provide politicians with a way to gauge public opinion. "On Twitter everybody is watching the timeline in real-time," Dutch Christian-Democratic MP Pieter Omtzigt states (Weber Shandwick 2014). Politicians network with reporters, and they interact with citizens and journalists. They utilise social media to harvest the stories and experiences of citizens to use in parliamentary debates. They publish information about the viewpoints of their political party and promote their activities and websites not just during election time but also increasingly in their regular political work. Finally, they use social media to brand themselves and to acquire a more prominent position in the party–political pecking order (Frame and Brachotte 2014).

Politicians who are less prominent and receive little journalistic coverage have a pronounced interest in social media because it allows them to relate to voters directly and because it can position their message on the radar of reporters. Their lack of media experience, combined with the desire to become newsworthy, does bear the risk of gaffes. Especially, more centrally directed parties on the far left and far right therefore have strict social media policies that prohibit overly active tweeting by politicians who are not part of the inner party circles (Skovsgaard and van Dalen 2013; Graham et al. 2014). For influential politicians, such as party leaders or members of government, who attract a lot of attention from the established news media and already have a strong position in social media networks, social media allow them to either place issues on the public agenda or to communicate with voters directly, both in the form of broadcast messages and through actual interaction.

Politicians thus use social media to bypass and manipulate journalists, communicate their message, and set the public agenda themselves. When social media are used effectively, politicians gain more control over whether and when they get a voice in public, which topics are addressed, and how public issues are framed. When they 'publish' strategically, either by broadcasting their own stances or by attacking opponents, and their message attracts attention in social networks, journalists usually will follow and pick up on the trending topic. When a news outlet distributes the message, both a broad audience and authority are guaranteed. Similarly, political reporters use the emerging social media repertoires to critically approach politicians, political parties, and the government. They aim to gain the upper hand in the reconfigured power structure to serve both their democratic and commercial aims. The democratic system is thus slowly moving away from the interdependence between political reporters and politicians that has stabilized it for over a century. While the basis of political communication largely remains the same, power relations change fundamentally because of emerging social media repertoires.

References

Anderson, C., Bell, E. and Shirky, C. (2012) *Post-Industrial Journalism: Adapting to the Present.* Available at: http://towcenter.org/research/post-industrial-journalism-adapting-to-the-present-2

Arceneaux, N. and Schmitz Weiss, A. (2010) "Seems Stupid Until You Try It: Press Coverage of Twitter, 2006–9," *New Media & Society*, 12(8), pp. 1262–1279.

Arthur, C. (2010) "2010: The First Social Media Election," *The Guardian*, 3 May.

Artwick, C. G. (2013) "Reporters on Twitter. Product or Service?," *Digital Journalism*, 1(2), pp. 212–228.

Belair-Gagnon, V., Mishra, S. and Agur, C. (2014) "Reconstructing the Indian Public Sphere. Newswork and Social Media in the Delhi Gang Rape Case," *Journalism*, 15(8), pp. 1059–1075.

Brands, B.J. (2014) *Social Media Sourcing. The Usage of Tweets in Newspaper Coverage of Dutch Politics*, unpublished MA thesis, University of Groningen. Available at: http://scripties.let.eldoc.ub.rug.nl/root/Master/DoorstroomMasters/Journalistiek/2014/BrandsE.H.J.

Brants, K. and Voltmer, K. (2011) "Introduction: Mediatization and De-centralization of Political Communication," in K. Brants and K. Voltmer (eds) *Political Communication in Postmodern Democracy: Challenging the Primacy of Politics*, Basingstoke: Palgrave Macmillan, pp. 1–16.

Broersma, M. and Graham, T. (2012) "Social Media as Beat: Tweets as News Source during the 2010 British and Dutch Elections," *Journalism Practice*, 6(3), pp. 403–419.

Broersma, M. and Graham, T. (2013) "Twitter as a News Source. How Dutch and British Newspapers Use Tweets in Their News Coverage, 2007–2011," *Journalism Practice*, 7(4), pp. 403–419.

Broersma, M. and Peters, C. (2013) "Rethinking Journalism: The Structural Transformation of a Public Good," in M. Broersma and C. Peters (eds.) *Rethinking Journalism. Trust and Participation in a Transformed Media Landscape*, London: Routledge, pp. 1–12.

Bruno, N. 2011. *Tweet First, Verify Later? How Real-time Information Is Changing the Coverage of Worldwide Crisis Events*, Oxford: Reuters Institute for the Study of Journalism.

Chadwick, A. (2013) *The Hybrid Media System: Politics and Power*, Oxford: Oxford University Press.

Cision (2013a) *Social Journalism Study 2013: United Kingdom*, http://www.cision.com/uk/wp-content/uploads/2014/05/Social-Journalism-Study-2013.pdf

Cision (2013b) *2013 Social Journalism Study: How Journalists View and Use Social Media and Their Relationship with PR*, http://us.cision.com/thought-leadership/2013-social-journalism/

Coleman, S. and Blumler, J.G. (2009) *The Internet and Democratic Citizenship: Theory, Practice and Policy*, Cambridge: Cambridge University Press.

Engesser, S. and Humprecht, E. (2014) "Frequency or Skillfulness: How Professional News Media Use Twitter in Five Western Countries," *Journalism Studies*, online first, DOI:10.1080/1461670X.2014.939849.

Frame, A. and Brachotte, G. (2014) "Le Tweet Stratégique: Use of Twitter as a PR Tool by French Politicians," *Public Relations Review*, online first, DOI:10.1016/j.pubrev.2014.11.005.

Graham, T., Broersma, M., Basile, V., & Nijzink, W. (2015). "Social Networking and the Cultivation of Online Campaigning: A Comparative Study of Dutch Politicians' Use of Twitter during the 2010 and 2012 General Election Campaigns." Paper presented at ECREA Political Communication Conference 2015: Changing Political Communication, Changing Europe? Odense, Denmark, 27/28 August 2015.

Graham, T., Jackson, D. and Broersma, M. (2014) "New Platforms, Old Habits? Candidates' Use of Twitter during the 2010 British and Dutch General Election Campaigns," *New Media & Society*, online first, DOI: 10.1177/1461444814546728.

Hedman, U. (2015) "J-Tweeters. Pointing Towards a New Set of Professional Practices and Norms in Journalism," *Digital Journalism*, 3(2), pp. 279–297.

Hedman, U. and Djerf-Pierre, M. (2013) "The Social Journalist. Embracing the Social Media Life or Creating a New Digital Divide?," *Digital Journalism*, 1(3), pp. 368–385.

Heravi, B. R., Harrower, N. and Boran, M. (2014) *Social Journalism Survey: First National Study on Irish Journalists' Use of Social Media*, HuJo, Insight Centre for Data Analytics, National University of Ireland, Galway.

Hermida, A. (2010) "Twittering the News. The Emergence of Ambient Journalism," *Journalism Practice*, 4(3), pp. 297–308.

Klinger, U. and Svensson, J. (2014) "The Emergence of Network Media Logic in Political Communication. A Theoretical Approach," *New Media & Society*, online first, DOI: 10.1177/1461444814522952.

Korteweg, A. (2014) "Wat Kunnen Kamerleden Leren van Pieter Omtzigt?," *de Volkskrant*, 11 December.

Larsson, A.O. and Kalsnes, B. (2014) "'Of Course We Are on Facebook': Use and Non-use of Social Media among Swedish and Norwegian Politicians," *European Journal of Communication*, 29(6), pp. 653–667.

Lasorsa, D. (2012) "Transparency and Other Journalistic Norms on Twitter," *Journalism Studies*, 13(3), pp. 402–417.

Lasorsa, D., Lewis, S. and Holton, A. (2012) "Normalizing Twitter," *Journalism Studies*, 13 (1), pp. 19–36.

Lawrence, R. G., Molyneux, L., Coddington, M. and Holton, A. (2014) "Tweeting Conventions: Political Journalists' Use of Twitter to Cover the 2012 Presidential Campaign," *Journalism Studies* 15(6), pp. 789–806.

Mason, R. (2014) "Ed Milliband Takes MP to Task over Rochester Flag Tweet," *The Guardian Online*, 20 November, http://www.theguardian.com/politics/2014/nov/20/labour-mp-rochester-tweet-emily-thornberry

Molyneux, L. (2014) "What Journalists Retweet: Opinion, Humor, and Brand Development on Twitter," *Journalism*, online first, DOI:10.1177/1464884914550135.

Nederlandse Nieuwsmonitor (2011) "Politiek 2.0: Debatteren in 140 Tekens. Een Analyse van Geert Wilders' Tweets in Nederlandse Dagbladen," http://www.socialmediasocialmedia.nl/downloads/76702662-Wilders-Tweets.pdf

Newman, N. (2010) *#UKelection2010, Mainstream Media and the Role of the Internet: How Social and Digital Media Affected the Business of Politics and Journalism*, Oxford: Reuters Institute for the Study of Journalism. Available at: https://reutersinstitute.politics.ox.ac.uk/sites/default/files/UKelection2010,%20mainstream%20media%20and%20the%20role%20of%20the%20internet.pdf

O'Leary, A. (2012) "Twitter Dynamos, Offering Word of God's Love," *New York Times*, 2 June.

Parmelee, J. (2013) "Political Journalists and Twitter: Influences on Norms and Practices," *Journal of Media Practice*, 14(4), pp. 291–305.

Parmelee, J. (2014) "The Agenda-building Function of Political Tweets," *New Media & Society*, 16(3), pp. 434–450.

Paulussen, S. and Harder, R.A. (2014) "Social Media References in Newspapers," *Journalism Practice*, 8(5), pp. 542–551.

Pew Research Center. (2014). *Social, Search & Direct. Pathways to Digital News*, http://www.journalism.org/files/2014/03/SocialSearchandDirect_PathwaystoDigitalNews.pdf

Reis Mourão, R. (2014) "The Boys on the Timeline. Political Journalists' Use of Twitter for Building Interpretive Communities," *Journalism*, online first, DOI:10.1177/1464884914552268.

Revers, M. (2014) "The Twitterization of News Making. Transparency and Journalistic Professionalism," *Journal of Communication*, online first, DOI:10.1111/jcom.12111.

Revers, M. (2015) "The Augmented Newsbeat: Spatial Structuring in a Twitterized News Ecosystem," *Media, Culture & Society*, 37(1), pp. 3–18.

Rogstad, I. D. (2014) "Political News Journalists in Social Media. Transforming Political Reporters into Political Pundits?," *Journalism Practice*, 8(6), pp. 688–703.

Schmitz Weiss, A. (2015) "The Digital and Social Media Journalist: A Comparative Analysis of Journalists in Argentina, Brazil, Colombia, Mexico, and Peru," *International Communication Gazette*, online first, DOI:10.1177/1748048514556985.

Skovsgaard, M. and van Dalen, A. (2013) "Dodging the Gatekeepers? Social Media in the Campaign Mix during the 2011 Danish Elections," *Information, Communication & Society*, online first, DOI: 10.1080/1369118X.2013.783876.

Svensson, J. (2011) "Nina on the Net: A Study of a Politician Campaigning on Social Networking Sites," *Central European Journal of Communication*, 2(7), pp. 195–208.

Twitter Government and Elections Handbook (2014), San Francisco: Twitter.

van Dijck, J. (2013) *The Culture of Connectivity: A Critical History of Social Media*, Oxford and New York: Oxford University Press.

Wallop, H. (2015) "8 Rules to Ensure Twitter Doesn't Get You Sacked," *The Telegraph*, 7 January.

Weber Shandwick (2014) *Twitter en de Tweede Kamer*, http://webershandwick.nl/wp-content/uploads/2015/01/WS-TWeTWK-def-2-2.pdf

Zeller, F. and Hermida, A. (2015) "When Tradition Meets Immediacy and Interaction. The Integration of Social Media in Journalists' Everyday Practices," *Sur le journalisme, About journalism, Sobre jornalismo*, 4 (1), pp. 106–117.

7

AGENDA-SETTING REVISITED

Social Media and Sourcing in Mainstream Journalism

Eli Skogerbø, Axel Bruns, Andrew Quodling, and Thomas Ingebretsen

Introduction

Who sets the media agenda? is a particularly vital question in agenda-setting studies, argues Maxwell McCombs (2014). He points to three key elements: major and powerful sources, other news organisations, and journalistic norms. We address the question of how social media, in this case Twitter, contribute to media agenda-building and agenda-setting by looking at how tweets are sourced in election campaign coverage in three different countries: Australia, Norway, and Sweden.

In political journalism, the battle over agenda-setting between journalists and their sources has been described using many metaphors and concepts (Davis 2009). Herbert Gans, for instance, saw it as a dance where the two parties competed for leadership, arguing that sources usually got the lead (Gans 1980). Norwegian sociologist Gudmund Hernes (1978) took the opposite view when he referred to the 'media twisting' of political news, arguing that journalistic practices almost inevitably provided journalists with the power to interpret and frame stories. Over the past decades, the continuous tug of war between journalists and their sources for the power to define and frame news has been described in terms of institutional practices, such as media logics (Altheide 2013) and mediatisation (Hjarvard 2013, Mazzoleni and Schulz 1999). However, the relationship is currently being renegotiated because of the entrance of digital and social media that change the practices of journalism as well as of their sources.

For journalists, social media have become news beats for picking up stories, contacting and getting access to sources informally or formally (Broersma and Graham 2013). For sources, in our case defined as political actors such as parties, politicians, and the like, social media have become alternative channels both for addressing and talking to citizens directly and for 'dodging the gatekeepers' of mainstream media by publishing stories and material that can be picked up by journalists or citizens (Skovsgaard and van

Dalen 2013). Social media are potentially yet another channel for sources to influence journalism, as they allow sources to control staging and content, and thereby a means to influence the agenda-building and agenda-setting processes of the news media. For both sides, digitisation has increased the amount of potentially accessible information sources immensely. This situation, on the one hand, may have led to a devaluation of source power, as the sheer ubiquity means that each source has little exclusive control of information. Similar pieces of information may be accessible to journalists through more than one channel, thereby weakening source power. On the other hand, digitisation has increased the number of platforms where stories break and flow. Online and social media have added to the number of potential outlets that sources can use to get their stories out, thereby reducing the value of access to journalists and mainstream news media channels, and increasing source power. Either way, the integration of social media and journalism may alter the power of sources and journalists to set the agenda for the news media, other political actors, or voters.

In this chapter, we discuss whether and how the agenda-setting hypothesis is transferred to an online, hybrid media environment, where social media increasingly constitute tools for both journalists and their sources. In the first section we provide an overview of literature addressing the development of agenda-setting studies, and explore how the hypothesis can be applied in a journalistic environment characterised by 24/7 news production, increased citizen journalism, and news breaking interchangeably in mainstream and social media (Bruns 2011; Chadwick 2011, 2013). In the second section, we draw on and present recent studies of the extent to which mainstream media are sourcing information from Twitter, illustrating how media content travels across platforms. Our examples include comparative analyses of political news sourcing and intermedia agenda-setting practices during election campaign periods in three different political settings: Australia, Norway, and Sweden.

The Agenda-Setting Hypothesis

Agenda-setting is defined as "the successful transfer of salience from the media agenda to the public agenda" (M. McCombs 2014: Kindle Location 2530). The concept was coined in the late 1960s by Maxwell McCombs and Donald Shaw, and their first seminal article on the topic was published in the early 1970s (McCombs and Shaw 1972). The theory in its original form was an extension of effects studies. For decades, research had shown that it was difficult to prove direct media influence on voters' opinions or actions. By the 1960s, it was well established that the media had less direct than indirect influence on the public's minds (Lazarsfeld, Berelson, and Gaudet 1948; Merton 1949), and the development of the agenda-setting hypothesis filled a theoretical and empirical gap on how the media influenced politics and voters. The findings from the early studies of McCombs and Shaw suggested that the main effect of the media coverage of election campaigns was to draw voters' attention to and increase the salience of issues, rather than to influence voters on what candidate or party to vote for. Accordingly, agenda-setting as a hypothesis not only updated ideas about media effects; it also added a theory that was able to account for media effects not only on individuals but also on institutions, processes and systems.

Over the years, agenda-setting as theory and a field of research has been expanded and refined into several new sub-topics and research areas. David Weaver (2014) recently described the field of research as being expanded from work concerning topic agenda-setting effects, via studies of attribute agenda-setting and of the contingent conditions, to investigations into the consequences of agenda-setting. A recent development is the Network Agenda-Setting model that suggests that news media not only tell us what to think about and how to think, but also what issues are connected (Guo 2014). Concerning the fact that citizens now live with a variety of media platforms, Shaw and Weaver have suggested that the mixing of agenda objects and attributes from a variety of media to construct a picture of the world should be termed *agenda-melding*:

> Agenda-melding is the way we balance agendas of civic community and our valued reference communities with our own views and experiences to create a satisfying picture of the world. Agenda-melding does not replace media agenda-setting, but rather seeks to explain why the strength of media agenda-setting varies between different media, groups and individuals. (Shaw and Weaver 2014: Kindle Locations 4562–4563)

Methodologically, agenda-setting research has moved from simple techniques of ranking issue salience to advanced statistics and time-series analyses, as well as to being researched by qualitative methods (McCombs 2014; McCombs and Shaw 1993). In her review of agenda-setting research, Tai makes a slightly different distinction, drawing on Dearing and Rogers (1996) who pinpointed three major research traditions: *the media agenda-setting tradition, the public agenda-setting tradition*, and *the policy agenda-setting tradition* (Tai 2009). The present study places itself clearly in the media agenda-setting category, and even more precisely, following Wallsten (2015b: 24), we are concerned with "agenda building—the process by which news outlets determine what to cover".

While the opening phases of agenda-setting research concentrated on the question "Who sets the public agenda—and under what conditions?," the focus shifted to the question "Who sets the media agenda?" from the early 1980s onwards. That question has linked agenda-setting research to a number of social science, communication, and journalism subfields, and increasingly to online and digital media (Johnson 2014; McCombs 2014; McCombs, Shaw, and Weaver 1997). For instance, Tran (2014) argues that while Internet-related developments have not fundamentally altered the traditional understanding of agenda-setting theory, they change the complicated relationships through which the media agenda is built. In the political sphere, citizen-created blogs reconfigure the traditional power structures between media and citizens by influencing the media agenda and rising in prominence as both sources and topics of the news. Source-created content outside the traditional media has resulted in a more bidirectional stream of influences on the media agenda, although the traditional media have retained most of their influence on the public agenda (Meraz 2014; Meraz and Papacharissi 2013; Wallsten 2007). It can be argued, as Meraz does, that "traditional media is no longer capable of leveraging complete media agenda-setting influence" (Meraz 2014: Kindle Location 556). Nevertheless, the agenda-setting hypothesis seems to remain robust and productive in an online environment.

Here, we limit our discussion to three elements of online agenda-setting. First, how social media contribute to setting the agenda in mainstream media: this addresses the *agenda-building* capacities of the transfer of social media contents to news media, and explores whether the influx of news items from social media also allows for a larger diversity of sources. The findings of previous studies are contradictory. Some studies conclude that social media, in particular Twitter, make up just another arena for opinion leaders and political elites, thereby reinforcing their power (Karlsen 2015; Meraz 2009). Other suggest that social media may not necessarily diminish the power of elite sources, but that "Twitter has the capacity to increase the diversity of voices in the news by including both unknown and well-known sources that are not available—or at least not easily accessible—other than on social media" (Paulussen and Harder 2014: 549).

Second, we place ourselves in the field of *intermedia agenda-setting*, discussing how items and issues travel from one media platform to another. In this respect, particularly the relationship between social media and mainstream media is interesting: intermedia agenda-setting by the inclusion of social media items in news production. Several studies have established that social media have become tools for both journalists and their sources (Meraz 2014), yet the degree to which they influence the agenda-building in mainstream media is less evident and seem to vary between contexts (Bruns 2012; Burgess and Bruns 2012; Hermida 2013).

Third, in the realm of politics, the relationship between journalists and political actors can, as noted previously, be characterised as interdependent and as an ongoing struggle for control over the agenda. For decades, debates over whether media logics influence decisions, voter behaviour, issue formation, and the way politics is carried out have been a favourite subject for political analysis. From this perspective, the entrance of online and—particularly—social media, providing easy access to voters and journalists, is another challenge to the power balance between journalists and their sources.

Political Campaigning and Intermedia Agenda-Setting

Political actors, whether they represent parties, organisations, or NGOs, often state that one main reason for seeking media attention is to set the agenda for the media, the public and, in times of elections, for the campaigns. Studies of election campaign communication in Western democracies show that from the mid-1990s, websites and other online channels were included among campaigning tools, expanding to encompass a large number of other web-based communication strategies, such as candidate blogs, campaign websites, and online political advertisements. Politicians and parties have continuously adapted and specialised their techniques and messages—from press releases to strategic leaks—to contemporary journalism and media formats. This adaptation, or mediatisation, of politics also includes parties' and politicians' use of websites, blogs, Facebook, Twitter, and numerous other social media platforms (Bruns and Burgess 2011; Karlsen 2011; Kiousis, Soo-Yeon, McDevitt, and Ostrowski 2009; Martin 2014; Skogerbø and Karlsen 2014; Tedesco 2005; Tran 2014; Xenos 2005).

While some of these studies indicate that the adaptation to media formats, as well as adoption of techniques to bypass the gatekeepers, for example of social media, give sources the upper hand in setting the agenda of political journalism, others find that the processes of influence are more difficult to nail down. In line with Gans's original assertion that sources 'lead the dance', Broersma and Graham (2013) argue that the entrance of online and social media has shifted the balance of power in the sources' favour. By using social media as channels for direct communication with the public, sources can publish or withhold information on any platform and within any period that they prefer. Previous studies have also supported this view: Meraz concluded that political blogs represented new arenas for mainstream media actors, in fact favouring established sources (Meraz 2009). Wallsten, on the other hand, suggests that the agenda-setting powers of social media sources and mainstream media are less obvious.

He sees political blogs as "a high-speed, two-way street rather than a slow-moving, one-way road leading from media coverage to blog discussion or vice versa" (Wallsten 2007: 567). Taking a more cautious view on the importance of social media to news production, Wallsten follows up the same point in his study of how Twitter was used as a source by leading U.S. newspapers during the 2012 presidential election campaign, arguing that social media are important but not taking over as agenda-setting sources (Wallsten 2015b). Chadwick describes a cyclical relationship between mainstream and social media in the breaking of news stories: news break, are commented on and added to, on social media as well as on news media platforms (Chadwick 2011). In Norway, studies of the way that content travels from political candidates' social media accounts to newspapers show a rather moderate transfer of items and issues (Ingebretsen 2014; Skogerbø and Krumsvik 2014).

The Impact of Culture and Politics on Agenda-Setting

So far, there exist few comparative studies of the role of social media in agenda-setting processes. McCombs indicates that cultural frames may impact on agenda-setting (M. McCombs 2014), and recent findings suggest that the sourcing of news varies considerably between countries (Tiffen et al. 2013). We therefore assume that the sourcing of content from social media and the transfer of news items from one platform to another may vary across different media systems and political systems. In order to illustrate these systemic differences, we now turn to discuss findings from two different but related studies that examine four different national media and political systems.

Our approach to this comparative analysis builds on Kevin Wallsten's study of the social media sourcing practices of leading U.S. news media during the 2012 presidential election, from January to November 2012. Wallsten studied the coverage of the presidential election campaign in the *New York Times*, the *Washington Post*, *USA Today*, the *Los Angeles Times*, and Associated Press, and tracked the sourcing of information from Twitter in election news. This study found clear evidence that Twitter had influenced the way newspapers sourced election coverage. Tweets were cited in 289 newspaper articles out of approximately 5,000 pieces of election coverage in these five news channels, suggesting that Twitter "seems to have had a noticeable, but relatively minor, impact on election reporting" (Wallsten 2015b: 33).

Although the newspapers in Wallsten's study quoted tweets on a nearly daily basis during the pre-election period in 2012, there was substantial variation in their propensity to cite Twitter over time. The number of articles mentioning Twitter fluctuated considerably between January and November. Specifically, journalists were likely to supplement their election coverage with tweets in the immediate lead-up to and aftermath of major campaign and media events, e.g. the Super Tuesday primaries, the presidential debates, and the Republican and Democratic National Conventions.

Furthermore, Wallsten found that the American journalists were concerned primarily with the tweets of political elites. His findings also provided evidence that there are important cross-national differences in how 'old media' are responding to social media. Broersma and Graham (2012) found that British newspapers were more likely to quote the tweets of non-elite actors than the tweets of political leaders, and that most of the cited tweets were opinionated arguments. Dutch papers, by contrast, largely eschewed non-elite and opinionated tweets in favour of factual statements made by tweeting politicians. Wallsten's findings suggest that American newspapers were travelling a different path compared to their British and Dutch counterparts. Specifically, U.S. newspapers were mimicking the Dutch media's dependence on elites while also following the British media's tendency to cite opinionated tweets. These findings provide a compelling reminder of how important cross-national differences can be in shaping the impact of social media on news coverage (Wallsten 2015b).

Intermedia Agenda-Setting in Different Settings: Australia, Norway, and Sweden

Our aim in the following discussion is to extend Wallsten's research by complementing it with further analysis of similar data drawn from three media environments outside the United States. For this, we are using data on the social media sourcing practices of major news organisations in Australia, Norway, and Sweden. Although located in opposite parts of the globe, these countries have a number of common characteristics. They are all, in global terms, small states in terms of population, if not in territorial size, and are highly industrialised welfare states that, on average, score highly also on social and economic indices.

They are also constitutional monarchies organised as multi-party parliamentary democracies with public service broadcasting systems. The public broadcasters in each country play major roles both in news production and in providing citizens with a full range of programming. Their market positions against commercial competitors vary somewhat across the three national media systems; however, they are key producers of nation-wide political and election news, and important sources of information for voters, as are the local, regional, and nationwide newspapers (and their respective websites). In addition to the news media, online, mobile and social media are ubiquitous in all three countries. Social media, such as Facebook, Twitter, YouTube, blogs and other platforms, are in all three cases employed by parties, politicians and journalists, as well as by citizens.

However, there are also significant differences. Australia is a federal state with some 23 million citizens, with a bicameral federal parliament. Elections to the lower house, the House of Representatives, take place every three years and follow the Westminster model, where only one candidate is elected from each constituency in a 'first-past-the-post' system. The Westminster system results in a strong focus on a two-party system dominated by the Australian Labor Party and the (essentially permanent) Coalition between the conservative Liberal and National Parties. Australia's preferential voting system adds further complexity to the electoral system. This trait distinguishes Australia markedly from Scandinavia, as does the fact that Australia is one of a very few countries in the world where voting is mandatory and failure to vote can incur fines; this results in a substantially higher voter turnout in each election, compared to most other nations.

By contrast, Norway and Sweden have some five and 10 million citizens, respectively. Both have parliamentary governments, stable multiparty systems and well-organised membership parties. The electoral systems include direct elections and proportional representation. The systems are somewhat different in Norway and Sweden, to the effect that the Swedish system benefits smaller parties less than the Norwegian one. Political power shifts between the Non-Socialist and the Socialist party blocs pending election results. Formations of coalition governments have been the normal practice on the Non-Socialist side of the political spectrum since the 1960s; however, there is a shorter history of coalition formation on the Socialist side. Minority governments and minority coalitions are quite common in both countries.

In Norway and Sweden, the regional party organisations nominate the candidates. In other words, the election systems are party-centric, not candidate-centric; in effect, this means that once the nominations are made, voters are left with a choice between the parties' lists as a whole, not between individual candidates. Further, in both countries the parties lay out the communicative strategies in election campaigns. Accordingly, this closed-list, proportional representation system is highly different from the Australian one, which allows voters, not only party members, to actually influence the success of individual of candidates.

There are also some important differences in the shapes of the media landscapes across the three countries. Australia has two public broadcasters: the mainstream Australian Broadcasting Corporation (ABC) and the minority Special Broadcasting Corporation (SBS); of these, the ABC has the stronger positioning in the television and radio broadcast market, where it also competes with a small number of popular commercial stations. The ABC also has a significant online presence, with its website ranking in the top six Australian news sites in terms of total site visits and the top two in terms of news links being shared on Twitter (Bruns forthcoming). The Australian newspaper market is similarly limited, and dominated by the Murdoch-controlled News Corporation (which publishes the only national broadsheet, *The Australian*, as well as a number of regional and local middle-brow and tabloid papers) and the Fairfax company (which publishes the broadsheets *Sydney Morning Herald* and *The Age*, in Melbourne, as well as the specialist daily *Australian Financial Review*), amongst other titles. Both corporations also operate extensive websites for their leading titles and engage in considerable content syndication across their respective stables of titles. Overall, a number of wire services, led by the Australian Associated Press (AAP), also support the news organisations.

The Norwegian Broadcasting Corporation (NRK), the public broadcaster, provides a wide range of programmes on TV and radio channels, including nationwide and regional news services in several languages, as well as one of the most popular online sites, nrk.no. Our data are collected from the news site. Newspaper readership in Norway is high, although declining for print formats, and all 229 newspapers also have online editions. The newspaper market is quite concentrated and dominated by two large ownership groups, Schibsted and Amedia, and a few smaller competitors. Schibsted controls the two largest newspaper titles in Norway, *Aftenposten* and *Verdens Gang* (VG), both included in our study. The largest business newspaper, *Dagens Næringsliv*, belongs to a smaller group. Internet and mobile services are used by almost the entire population; to a degree that online and mobile readership of newspapers is higher than reading in print.

Sweden has a system quite similar to the Norwegian, although the public broadcaster is organised differently. While the NRK is an integrated corporation, public broadcasting in Sweden is organised in several companies. Sveriges Television (SVT) runs a number of television services, as well as a popular online site, *svt.se*, which was selected for our data collection. Among Sweden's 164 newspapers (as of 2013), *Dagens Nyheter*, owned by Bonnier, and *Svenska Dagbladet*, controlled by Schibsted, are studied here; both of them are quality newspapers with rather different editorial platforms. The popular tabloid *Aftonbladet* is Sweden's largest newspaper, also owned by *Schibsted*, and it is included. It is quite similar to the Norwegian VG both in its online and print strategies.

Methods and Data

Following the lead of Broersma and Graham (2013) and Wallsten (2015b), our study was designed to study intermedia agenda-setting and agenda-building processes in three different countries with different political and media systems. We included the major news organisations in each country. In Australia, we selected the newspapers *The Australian*, *Sydney Morning Herald* (and its Sunday version, the *Sun Herald*), and *Australian Financial Review*, the online content of public broadcaster ABC, and the wire service AAP. The Norwegian newspapers are *VG*, *Aftenposten*, and *Dagens Næringsliv*, combined with the online content of the NRK, and the NTB wire service. In Sweden, our study included the newspapers *Dagens Nyheter*, *Svenska Dagbladet*, and *Aftonbladet*, the online content of public broadcaster SVT, and the wire service TT.

For each country and news outlet, we used electronic databases (LexusNexis and Retriever) to collect articles that included references to Twitter as a source, by searching for any articles containing twit* or tweet*. The collection period was 10 weeks prior to the election day in the most recent national elections, which in Australia were held on 9 September 2013, in Norway on 12 September 2013, and in Sweden on 14 September 2014. Articles were manually filtered, so that only those news items which related clearly to the national election campaign in each country, and which directly cited one or more tweets (as opposed to more generally discussing the role of Twitter and other social media platforms in the campaign), were included. This resulted in 214 relevant articles from Australian news outlets, 69 from Norwegian outlets and 76 from Swedish outlets.

Articles were then manually coded for content: here, we coded for the type of actor whose tweet was cited (including politicians, journalists, celebrities, experts, and ordinary users); for the function of the original tweet (providing facts, opinion, calls to action, jokes, or other content); for the role of the cited tweet in the news article (supporting a larger story, or serving as the centre of the story itself); and for whether the tweet was used verbatim, or paraphrased by the journalist. Additionally, we also recorded the authors of the news articles (to the extent that such information was provided in by-lines), and the names of specific key Twitter users whose tweets were being cited. The coding process was piloted, tried out on parts of the material and adjusted by coders in Australia and Scandinavia before being finalised, in order to secure reliability and validity of the data.

Findings

The results of our analysis show that the social media sourcing practices, and thus the potential for social media content to set the media agenda, vary widely across the different news outlets in each country, and across the different countries. For Australia, we found that broadsheets *The Australian* and *Sydney Morning Herald*, as well as wire service AAP, cited tweets considerably more frequently than the *Australian Financial Review* and the public broadcaster ABC. However, the figures for the broadsheets are also considerably inflated by their respective recurring 'media diary' or 'political diary' columns that offer an irreverent or snarky look at politics and media, and which frequently build their commentary and gossip around snippets from tweets. Close to 60 per cent of all tweets cited by *The Australian* were cited by its diarists writing such columns (see Figure 7.1a). When these were removed from the count, wire service AAP emerges as the leading user of tweets in its articles. It is also evident that the status of the journalistic author appears to affect the role that cited tweets play in an article. Generally, and with the exception of the *Sydney Morning Herald*, the diarists are more likely to build their pieces around a given tweet, while journalists whose names are used in an article's by-line cite tweets mainly in support of a story, not as its central element. Unattributed articles were comparatively rare in most Australian outlets, and usually used tweets only to support their stories; the one exception from this rule is again the *Sydney Morning Herald*, where tweets are considerably more likely to be at the centre of unattributed articles than they are to be central to by-lined articles (see Figure 7.1b).

In the following discussion, we thus exclude the diarists from our analysis, as their journalistic roles and activities differ considerably from those of other journalists; this reduces the total number of Australian articles we are considering from 214 to 155. Strikingly, in most outlets, the group of actors whose tweets were cited most frequently were politicians, followed at some distance by journalists. Only the ABC did not cite any tweets from journalists during the time of our study, but instead cited politicians' tweets almost exclusively, suggesting that the agenda-setting power of political sources is indeed noticeable. Named or unnamed ordinary users were the third most frequently cited group; unnamed users being cited also included references to the general mood within common hashtags such as #auspol (cf. Sauter and Bruns 2015) and #ausvotes, and such references were especially prominent in the *Sydney Morning Herald*, while they remained entirely absent from ABC News articles. Domain experts were cited in some 7 to 14 per cent of all articles across most outlets, although only one expert tweet was cited in the *Sydney Morning Herald*. That paper was the only outlet to cite celebrities, however. Finally, with four such tweets cited across all five news outlets, citing tweets by relatives of politicians remained the least prominent category (see Figure 7.2a).

Furthermore, the tweets cited across all news outlets were predominantly presenting the tweet author's opinion; the next most prominent categories were facts (a tweet category which was absent in ABC content, and most prominent in the wire stories of the Australian Associated Press) and calls to action (absent from *Australian Financial*

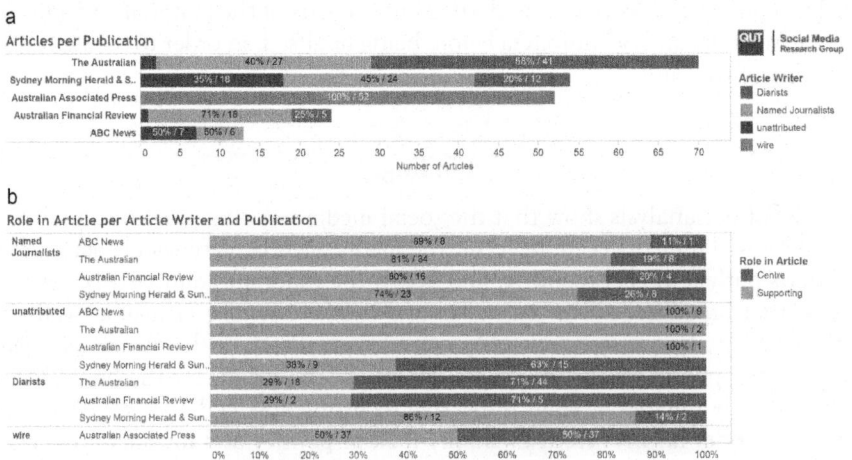

Figure 7.1 Twitter Citations in Election Coverage over the 10 Weeks Prior to the 2013 Australian General Election

Review articles). Jokes were especially prevalent in the *Sydney Morning Herald*, while surprisingly the self-declared highbrow papers *The Australian* and *Australian Financial Review* featured the highest percentage of selfies and other photo tweets in their coverage. This may be related to the posting of a number of widely retweeted selfies by then-Prime Minister Kevin Rudd in the lead-up to the election (see Figure 2.b).

For Norway, we found similar variations between the different media outlets, but different patterns from those observed in Australia. VG, the popular tabloid newspaper, cited tweets in more than three times as many articles as the public broadcaster did, and accordingly VG was the only outlet for which we found extensive usage of tweets in the election coverage (see Figure 7.3a). However, similar to *The Australian* and the *Sydney Morning Herald* in the Australian case, much of its tweet citations stem from its regular column 'Sagt', which cites tweets but does not include them in an article context. We classified such ritual use of tweets under the 'media diary' category and excluded these articles from our further analysis.

When these 30 'Sagt' quotations were eliminated from the overall analysis, then, NRK emerged as the most prolific user of tweets, if still at a comparatively low level: it cited tweets in 12 articles over the period examined here, while the remaining news outlets published fewer than 10 articles each that cited tweets during the same period. All outlets, with the exception of wire service NTB and VG's 'Sagt' column, predominantly included tweets in articles by named journalists. Overall, the very low total number of articles citing tweets in the Norwegian media environment already indicates a very limited agenda-setting role for social media (or at least for Twitter) here.

Furthermore, the role of tweets in articles is clearly related to whether articles are attributed to a named journalist. Of the 62 tweets cited in articles by named journalists, only nine form the centre of articles; conversely, five of the nine tweets cited in unattributed articles are at the centre of these articles (see Figure 7.3b).

The Norwegian media varied quite substantially concerning their quoting practices (see Figure 7.4a). In all media outlets except for specialist financial paper *Dagens Næringsliv*, which generally only cited a very small number of tweets, tweets by politicians still constituted an important category but failed to represent the majority of all tweets; indeed, named ordinary users emerged as a comparable or more prominent presence in VG, *Aftenposten* and NRK (but were absent from *Dagens Næringsliv* and

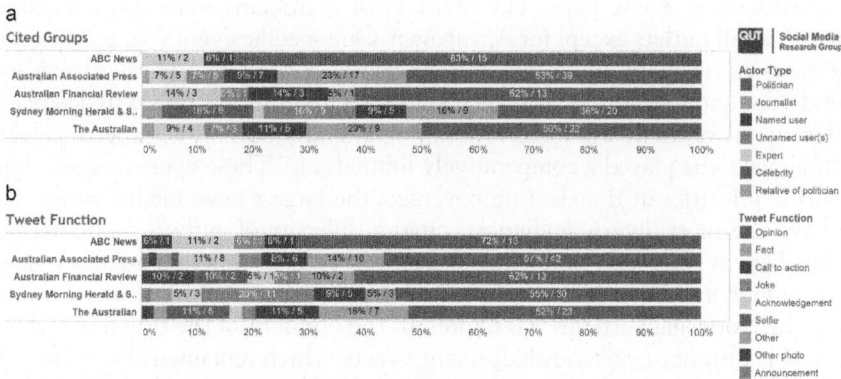

Figure 7.2 Tweet Citations and Functions in Articles in the 2013 Election Coverage in Australia (Excluding 'Media Diary' Sections)

a

Articles per Publication

b

Role in Article per Article Writer and Publication

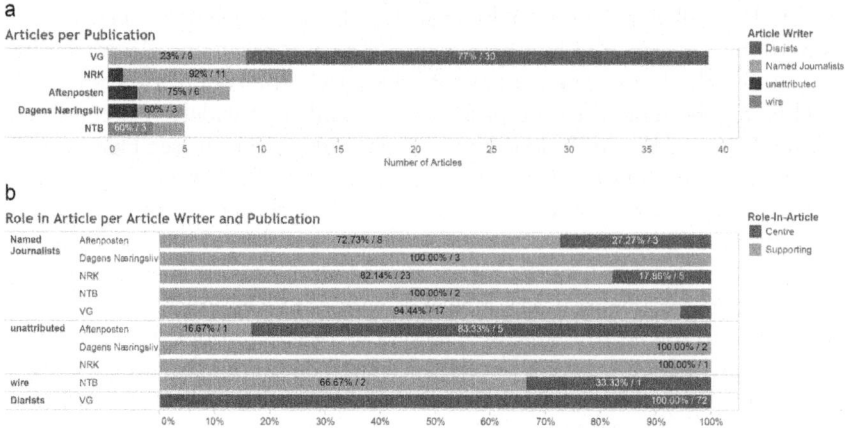

Figure 7.3 Twitter Citations in Election Coverage over the 10 Weeks Prior to the 2013 General Election in Norway

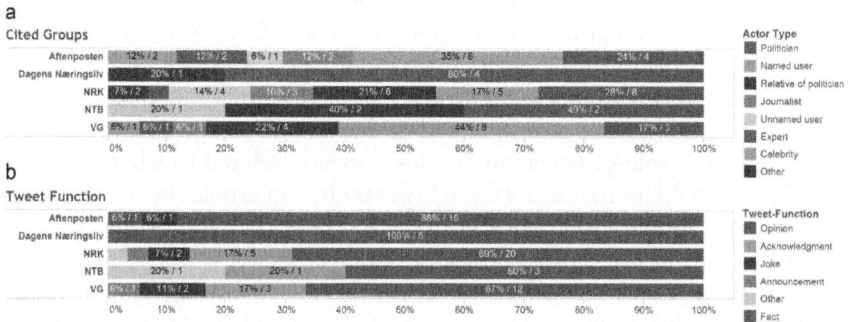

a

Cited Groups

b

Tweet Function

Figure 7.4 Tweet Citations and Functions in Articles in the 2013 Election Coverage in Norway (Excluding VG's 'Sagt' Section)

wire service NTB), indicating widely diverging approaches to the use of Twitter as an alternative source of vox pops. The relatives of politicians were also comparatively prominent in all outlets except for *Aftenposten*. One specific event resulted in a number of the news stories containing tweets from relatives: the Conservative Party leader's husband was quoted extensively and across media outlets for his tweets in defence of his wife during one of the television election programmes. Journalists, experts, celebrities, and unnamed users played a comparatively limited role. These figures suggest different journalistic priorities in the election coverage: the largest news media, which accordingly have the most diverse audiences, cited a diversity of authors on Twitter, while specialist *Dagens Næringsliv* and wire service NTB cater to different audience needs.

Even more comprehensively so than in Australia, the main function of the tweets cited in the Norwegian articles was to present the opinions of the tweeters, followed at considerable distance by acknowledgement tweets, which remained absent from *Aftenposten* and *Dagens Næringsliv* (see Figure 7.4b). Other categories (jokes, announcements, factual tweets) were rarely cited by the Norwegian media, and selfies and photographs remained entirely absent from the coverage.

Unlike Norway, and closer to the findings for Australia, the five Swedish news media had rather similar distributions of tweet citations. The broadsheet *Svenska Dagbladet* cited tweets in twenty articles over the examined period, followed by fellow broadsheet *Dagens Nyheter*, public broadcaster SVT and the other outlets with 13 to 15 articles each (see Figure 7.5a). Most of the articles citing tweets were attributed to named journalists; the obvious exception to this pattern was the wire service TT, most of whose articles were unattributed.

In Sweden, too, there was a clear relationship between journalistic authorship and the role of tweets in articles (see Figure 7.5b). In articles by-lined by journalists, tweet citations mainly played a supporting role, exclusively so in *Svenska Dagbladet*. Only the public broadcaster SVT had a substantial number of authored news pieces where tweet citations were at the centre of the election coverage. In many of these pieces, Twitter citations seemed to substitute for interviews presenting alternative opinions, an indication of a journalistic use that was more prevalent in Sweden than in Norway. In the unattributed and wire service articles, tweet citations were at the centre of all stories in *Dagens Nyheter* and *Svenska Dagbladet*, as well as of half of the stories from TT and SVT.

The citation patterns across different groups of actors in Sweden largely matched those observed for Australia: politicians and journalists clearly constituted the most frequently cited groups across all five publications (see Figure 7.6a). A third major group, unnamed users, were especially prominent in the Swedish case, however, and point to the use of Twitter citations as an alternative to conventional vox pops across all outlets. While this group is least prominent in *Dagens Nyheter*, that publication cites the largest number of named ordinary users, indicative, perhaps, of a different attribution policy for tweets in that news organisation. Experts were also prominent, though mainly in the articles of the wire service TT, while celebrity tweets were comparatively absent.

Tweet functions in the Swedish data were highly divergent from the Australian picture, however: while opinion tweets were prominent (see Figure 7.6b), there was also a significant presence of joke tweets and announcement tweets amongst the tweets cited in news articles (with announcements especially strong in SVT and TT articles). Selfies and other photos were absent from the Swedish data, by contrast—this suggests that the focus on such content during the election campaign may have been a purely Australian phenomenon during the elections studied here.

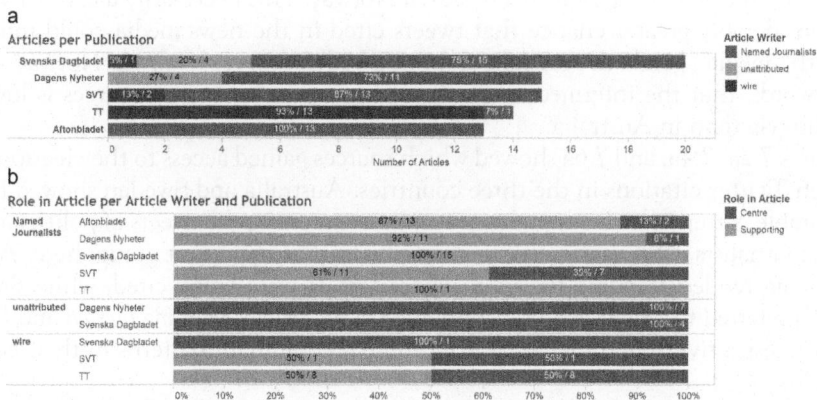

Figure 7.5 Twitter Citations in Election Coverage 10 Weeks Prior to the 2014 General Election in Sweden

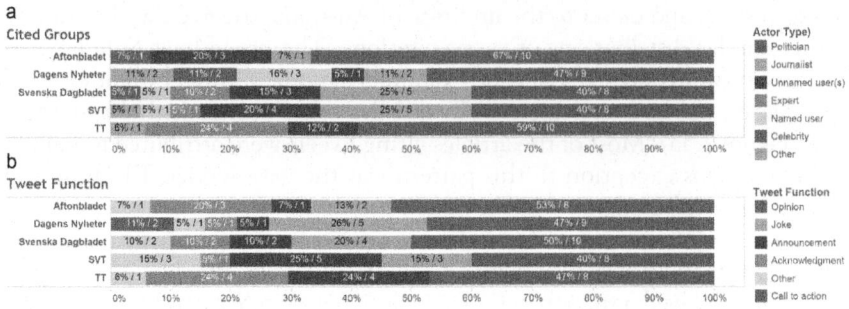

Figure 7.6 Tweet Citations and Functions in Articles in the 2014 Election Coverage in Sweden

Comparing the Role of Tweets

In the analysis above, *The Australian* and Norway's *VG* respectively stand out for using a much larger number of tweets in election coverage articles than their competitors (see Figures 7.1a, 7.3a, and 7.5a). This is largely due to their practice of building a large number of small articles specifically around tweets from well-known people in sport, politics, or culture, in 'media diary' or similar sections offering 'colour commentary' on the political process or seemingly catching the buzz of the day. Such editorial priorities point to the use of Twitter as a cheap source of material, but we suggest that tweets cited in such articles are unlikely to contribute in any significant way to either agenda-building or agenda-setting processes in the news media. However, these practices demonstrate that content travels from social to news media and that some sources—mainly elites and celebrities—further increase their public visibility plainly by being present on Twitter.

Even if we exclude this inflated number of tweets from our analysis, however, Australian media still stand out as citing tweets in election-related news articles considerably more frequently than their Scandinavian counterparts. The five Australian media outlets cited tweets in some 155 articles during the period examined here, compared to 77 articles in Sweden and only 39 articles in Norway. This necessarily means that there is a considerably greater chance that tweets cited in the news media could influence or set the media agenda in Australia than in Sweden and especially in Norway—or in other words, that the intermedia agenda-setting power of Twitter sources is lower in Scandinavia than in Australia.

Figures 7.2a, 7.4a, and 7.6a showed which sources gained access to the election news through Twitter citations in the three countries. Australia and Sweden showed largely comparable patterns, with a significant emphasis on citing the tweets of politicians and fellow journalists. Ordinary users constituted a further important group; here, Australian media tended to name the users whose tweets were being cited, while Swedish outlets preferred to leave such users unnamed. The *Sydney Morning Herald* and *Dagens Nyheter*, respectively, both departed from these predominant patterns in their country of origin.

Norwegian media, on the other hand, devoted considerably less space to the tweets of political actors or journalists, and instead presented a broader range of tweeters, with named ordinary users and the relatives of politicians emerging as especially prominent categories. Considering the generally low number of cited tweets in Norwegian news articles, however, specific campaign incidents in the material, as noted above, may have inflated these categories. Furthermore, this may also point to a more marginal role for tweets in news articles: they may merely be added to colour the articles, and given such very limited importance, journalists were prepared to give voice to actors that are more marginal by citing their tweets.

Concerning the way that tweets were integrated into journalism (see Figures 7.2b, 7.4b, and 7.6b), they were mainly cited as expressions of opinions. This was common to all three countries but was especially dominant in the Norwegian media. Jokes and announcements were particularly prominent in Sweden, whereas tweets presenting facts were almost exclusively found in Australian news articles and acknowledgments most strongly in Norwegian publications. Australian media generally used Twitter citations in more diverse ways than the Scandinavian media, with the reproduction of self-ies and other photos emerging as a uniquely Australian practice.

Discussion and Conclusion

The research question we have addressed in this chapter is how Twitter contributes to media agenda-building and agenda-setting. Our analysis has so far shown that Twitter is established as a source of political journalism and election campaign coverage in news media in the three countries included in our study. As such, our findings concur with previous studies that content on Twitter travels to the news media and contributes to intermedia agenda-setting and agenda-building. However, both the amount of articles and the way that Twitter citations were integrated into journalistic coverage varied substantially across political settings and media systems. In line with Broersma and Graham (2013) and Wallsten (2015a, 2015b), we find general traits and national specifics. The dominance of elite political sources is a common characteristic across all countries and media. It seems clear from this that sourcing material from Twitter reinforces the power of the political elites to set the agenda of the news media—they are indeed 'still leading the dance'. The political elites were sourced more often than other groups everywhere, and Twitter content travels to the news media in many different forms: as opinions, comments, announcements, factual statements, and photos.

Still, there are variations that must be explained both by reference to the different political and cultural characteristics of the three countries, as well as by the available resources and journalistic profiles of each media outlet. First, when comparing Australia and Scandinavia, our findings suggest that the sheer difference in the number of tweets quoted in the news media shows that Twitter contributes more often to agenda-setting and agenda-building in Australia than in Scandinavia. Tweets were included into the election coverage regularly in Australia, while Norwegian and Swedish news media included them less often but were somewhat more open to citing non-elite sources, named and unnamed. The diversity of sources quoted was thus larger in Scandinavia than in Australia. Both population size and electoral system may be drawn on for explaining these differences: the focus on individual politicians may be larger in Australia where voters can influence these individual candidates' chances to be elected, and this may be conducive to including their tweets in news coverage.

The relationship between political journalists and their sources also depends on actual and perceived distance, and this may be smaller in Scandinavia. The differences in citing practices may reflect such differences: Norwegian political journalists report that they regard an interview with a top politician as more credible and valuable than citing social media, and studies of Norwegian political journalism indicate that journalists have few problems in getting access to top politicians and parties, inside and outside government (Allern 2011). The Swedish data, however, indicated that tweets sometimes substituted for interviews. Studies from both Norway and Sweden show that there is rather little interaction between the top politicians and journalists on Twitter, and that journalistic norms of distance and objectivity prevail among journalists (Hedman and Djerf-Pierre 2013; Rogstad 2013; Skogerbø and Moe forthcoming). In Australia, journalistic access to politicians may be comparatively more difficult to obtain, resulting in a greater reliance on tweets as a substitute.

Twitter is thus clearly a source of intermedia agenda-setting in political news production. Our study nevertheless shows that national differences exist. In Australia, the sourcing of material from Twitter for political news coverage seems to have generated some degree of journalistic innovation, resulting in practices that were not discernible in the election news from Norway and Sweden. The Scandinavian media draw on a larger diversity of sources on Twitter, but there was less integration into journalistic coverage, and accordingly a lower likelihood of substantial intermedia agenda-setting.

References

Allern, S. (2011) *Fjernsynsvalgkampen: Program, deltakere og maktkamp 1961–2009*, Oslo: Pax.

Altheide, D.L. (2013) "Media Logic, Social Control, and Fear," *Communication Theory*, 23(3), pp. 223–238.

Broersma, M., and Graham, T. (2012) "Social Media as Beat," *Journalism Practice*, 6(3), pp. 403–419.

—— (2013) "Twitter as a News Source," *Journalism Practice*, 7(4), pp. 446–464.

Bruns, A. (2011) "News Produsage in a Pro-Am Mediasphere: Why Citizen Journalism Matters," in G. Meikle and G. Redden (eds.), *News Online: Transformations and Continuities*. Basingstokes: Palgrave Macmillan.

—— (2012) "Journalists and Twitter: How Australian News Organisations Adapt to a New Medium," *Media International Australia incorporating Culture and Policy*, 142, pp. 97–107.

Bruns, A. (forthcoming) "Making Audience Engagement Visible: Publics for Journalism on Social Media Platforms," in B. Franklin and S. A. Eldridge II (eds.), *The Routledge Companion to Digital Journalism Studies*, New York: Routledge.

Bruns, A., and Burgess, J. (2011) "#ausvotes: How Twitter Covered the 2010 Australian Federal election," *Communication, Politics and Culture*, 44(2), pp. 37–57

Burgess, J., and Bruns, A. (2012) "(Not) The Twitter Election," *Journalism Practice*, 6(3), pp. 384–402.

Chadwick, A. (2011) "The Political Information Cycle in a Hybrid News System: The British Prime Minister and the 'Bullygate' Affair," *The International Journal of Press/Politics*, 16(1), pp. 3–29.

—— (2013). *The Hybrid Media System: Politics and Power*, Oxford: Oxford University Press.

Davis, A. (2009) "Journalist–Source Relations, Mediated Reflexivity and the Politics of Politics," *Journalism Studies*, 10(2), pp. 204–219.

Dearing, J. W., and Rogers, E. (1996) *Agenda-Setting*, Thousand Oaks, CA: Sage.

Gans, H. (1980) *Deciding What's News*, London: Constable.

Guo, L. (2014) "Toward the Third Level of Agenda-setting Theory: A Network Agenda Setting Model," in T.J. Johnson (ed.) *Agenda Setting in a 2.0 World: New Agendas in Communication* (Kindle edition), New York: Routledge, Taylor and Francis.

Hedman, U., and Djerf-Pierre, M. (2013) "The Social Journalist," *Digital Journalism*, 1(3), pp. 368–385.

Hermida, A. (2013) "#Journalism," *Digital Journalism*, 1(3), pp. 295–313.

Hernes, G. (1978) "Det medievridde samfunn," in G. Hernes (ed.) *Forhandlingsøkonomi og blandingsadministrasjon*, Oslo: Universitetsforlaget.

Hjarvard, S. (2013) *The Mediatization of Culture and Society*. Milton Park: Routledge.

Ingebretsen, T. (2014) *Nye medier, gammel portvokter? En analyse av den intermediale dagsordensettingen fra politikere i sosiale medier til redaksjonelle i valgkampen 2013*. (Master), Oslo: Universitetet i Oslo.

Johnson, T.J. (ed.) (2014) *Agenda Setting in a 2.0 World: New Agendas in Communication: New Agendas in Communication* (Kindle edition), New York: Routledge, Taylor and Francis.

Karlsen, R. (2011) "Still Broadcasting the Campaign: On the Internet and the Fragmentation of Political Communication with Evidence from Norwegian Electoral Politics," *Journal of Information Technology and Politics*, 8(2), pp. 146–162.

—— (2015) "Followers Are Opinion Leaders: The Flow of Political Communication and Beyond Social Networking Sites," *European Journal of Communication*, first published on April 15, 2015, doi:10.1177/0267323115577305.

Kiousis, S., Soo-Yeon, K., McDevitt, M., and Ostrowski, A. (2009) "Competing for Attention: Information Subsidy Influence in Agenda Building during Election Campaigns," *Journalism and Mass Communication Quarterly*, 86, pp. 545–562.

Lazarsfeld, P.F., Berelson, B., and Gaudet, H. (1948). *The People's Choice: How the Voter Makes up His Mind in a Presidential Campaign* (Second edition), New York: Columbia University Press.

Martin, J.A. (2014) "Agenda Setting, Election and the Impact of Information Technology," in T.J. Johnson (ed.) *Agenda Setting in a 2.0 World: New Agendas in Communication* (Kindle edition), New York: Routledge, Taylor and Francis.

Mazzoleni, G., and Schulz, W. (1999) "'Mediatization' of Politics: A Challenge for Democracy?," *Political Communication*, 16(3), pp. 247–261.

McCombs, M. (2014) *Setting the Agenda: The Mass Media and Public Opinion* (Second edition, Kindle edition), Cambridge: Polity Press.

McCombs, M.E., and Shaw, D.L. (1972) "The Agenda-setting Function of Mass Media," *Public Opinion Quarterly*, 36(2), pp. 176–187.

—— (1993) "The Evolution of Agenda-Setting Research: Twenty-Five Years in the Marketplace of Ideas," *Journal of Communication*, 43(2), pp. 58–67.

McCombs, M.E., Shaw, D.L., and Weaver, D.H. (1997) *Communication and Democracy: Exploring the Intellectual Frontiers in Agenda-setting Theory*. Mahwah, NJ: Erlbaum.

Meraz, S. (2009) "Is There an Elite Hold? Traditional Media to Social Media Agenda Setting Influence in Blog Networks," *Journal of Computer-Mediated Communication*, 14(3), pp. 682–707.

—— (2014) "Media Agenda Setting in a Competitive and Hostile Environment: The Role of Sources in Setting Versus Supporting Topical Discussant Agendas in the Tea Party Patriots' Facebook Group," in T.J. Johnson (ed.) *Agenda Setting in a 2.0 World: New Agendas in Communication* (Kindle edition), New York: Routledge, Taylor and Francis Group.

Meraz, S., and Papacharissi, Z. (2013) "Networked Gatekeeping and Networked Framing on #Egypt," *The International Journal of Press/Politics*, 18(2), pp. 138–166.

Merton, R.K. (1949) "Patterns of Influence: A Study of Interpersonal Influence and of Communications Behaviour in a Local Community," in P. Lazarsfeld and F. Stanton (eds.), *Communications Research 1948–1949*, New York: Harper and Brothers.

Paulussen, S., and Harder, R.A. (2014) "Social Media References in Newspapers," *Journalism Practice*, 8(5), pp. 542–551.

Rogstad, I.D. (2013) "Political News Journalists in Social Media," *Journalism Practice* 8(6), pp. 688–703.

Sauter, T., and Bruns, A. (2015) "#auspol: The Hashtag as Community, Event, and Material Object for Engaging with Australian Politics," in N. Rambukkana (ed.) *Hashtag Publics: The Power and Politics of Discursive Networks*, New York: Peter Lang, pp. 47–60.

Shaw, D.L., and Weaver, D.H. (2014) "Epilogue Media Agenda-Setting and Audience Agenda-Melding," in M. McCombs *Setting the Agenda: Mass Media and Public Opinion* (Kindle edition), Cambridge: Polity.

Skogerbø, E., and Karlsen, R. (2014) "Mediatisation and Regional Campaigning in a Party-Centred System: How and Why Parliamentary Candidates Seek Visibility," *Javnost—The Public*, 21(2), pp. 5–22.

Skogerbø, E., and Krumsvik, A.H. (2014) "Newspapers, Facebook and Twitter," *Journalism Practice* 9(3), pp. 350–366.

Skogerbø, E., and Moe, H. (Forthcoming) "Twitter på tvers—koblinger mellom journalister og politikere," *Norsk medietidsskrift*.

Skovsgaard, M., and van Dalen, A.V. (2013) "Dodging the Gatekeepers?," *Information, Communication and Society* 16(5), pp. 737–756.

Tai, Z. (2009) "The Structure of Knowledge and Dynamics of Scholarly Communication in Agenda Setting Research, 1996–2005," *Journal of Communication*, 59(3), pp. 481–513.

Tedesco, J.C. (2005) "Issue and Strategy Agenda Setting in the 2004 Presidential Election: Exploring the Candidate-Journalist Relationship," *Journalism Studies*, 6(2), pp. 187–201.

Tiffen, R., Jones, P.K., Rowe, D., Aalberg, T., Coen, S., Curran, J., and Soroka, S. (2013) "Sources in the News," *Journalism Studies*, 15(4), pp. 374–391.

Tran, H. (2014) "Online Agenda Setting: A New Frontier for Theory Development," in T.J. Johnson (ed.) *Agenda Setting in a 2.0 World: New Agendas in Communication* (Kindle edition), New York: Routledge, Taylor and Francis.

Wallsten, K. (2007) "Agenda Setting and the Blogosphere: An Analysis of the Relationship between Mainstream Media and Political Blogs," *Review of Policy Research*, 24(6), pp. 567–587.

Wallsten, K. (2015a) "Microblogging and the News: Political Elites and the Ultimate Retweet," in A.M.G. Solo (ed.), *Political Campaigning in the Information Age*, Hershey, PA: IGI Global.

Wallsten, K. (2015b) "Non-Elite Twitter Sources Rarely Cited in Coverage," *Newspaper Research Journal*, 36(1), pp. 24–41.

Weaver, D.H. (2014) "Agenda Setting in a 2.0 World," in T.J. Johnson (ed.) *Agenda Setting in a 2.0 World: New Agendas in Communication* (Kindle edition), New York: Routledge, Taylor and Francis.

Xenos, M.K.A.F. (2005) "Politics as Usual, or Politics as Unusual? Position Taking and Dialogue on Campaign Websites in 2002 U.S. Elections," *Journal Communication*, 55(1), pp. 169–185.

8

"TRUST ME, I AM AUTHENTIC!"

Authenticity Illusions in Social Media Politics

Gunn Enli

Introduction

The most crucial element of a politician's image building is the construction of trust; in a media-centred democracy, nothing is more important for a politician than being regarded as authentic, genuine, and real. If a politician is considered trustworthy, voters might disagree on certain political issues, but they will believe that he or she is guided by an integrity and a personal motivation that ensures a degree of reason; and, conversely, if a politician is considered untrustworthy and fake, it does not matter much if the voters agree with him or her in certain political matters.

Although it definitely helps not to be caught lying or misleading people, trust is not solely earned as a direct result of being an honest politician but is also gained through various kinds of image-building strategies. In this chapter, I will investigate one such image-building strategy, namely, the use of social media and online campaign videos to construct an image of the politician as authentic.

In social media, content with an appeal as authentic, often portraying ordinary people in seemingly unscripted moments, has been proven to be exceptionally spreadable, as it tends to connect emotionally with the users who make it into a viral phenomenon (Enli 2009). This chapter will explore what has been termed 'the paradox of mediated authenticity', referring to the fact that "although we base nearly all our knowledge about the world and the society in which we live on mediated representations, we remain well aware that the media is constructed, manipulated, and even faked" (Enli 2015a: 1). Mediated authenticity is a social construction but claims legitimacy as a representation of raw and unscripted reality.

Mediated authenticity is constructed by *illusions of authenticity*; these illusions take place in mainstream media through various degrees of scripting of the performances of ordinary people. Through various production techniques, raw material is manipulated in order to be compatible with media logics and format criteria (Ytreberg 2004; Enli 2015a). This chapter investigates authenticity illusions in political communication in social media, with emphasis on online campaign videos and the visual representations of political candidates. Based on insights from the analysis, the chapter discusses the possible effects of an increased focus on authenticity illusions in political communication, in terms of both imposing changes on the mediated representations of politicians and thereby also representing a new arena for negotiations of politicians' trustworthiness.

In this study, I will draw on a textual analysis of two political campaign videos: the Buzzfeed video featuring U.S. president Barack Obama, titled 'Things Everybody Does But Doesn't Talk About'[1], and the online video with the Norwegian prime minister Jens Stoltenberg, referred to as 'The Secret Cab Driver' or 'Norway's Prime Minister Turns Taxi Driver'[2]. These videos were made, respectively, to promote a U.S. healthcare program and a re-election campaign for the Norwegian Labour Party. There are three main rationales for selecting these particular campaign videos. First, they are both examples of *personalised campaign videos* in the sense that they focus on the politician, even though the aim of the campaign videos is to promote health reform or a political party. Second, they represent two *different political cultures*, as U.S. politics is highly candidate-centred while Norwegian politics is party-centred (see Enli and Skogerbø 2013). Third, the videos originate in very *different media systems*, as commercial companies dominate the U.S. media system and political TV advertising is a central element in political campaigns, while public service companies are more central in the Norwegian media system and political TV advertisements are a marginal phenomenon as a result of political regulation.

This chapter has four main parts, following this introduction. The first part presents a theoretical discussion of authenticity illusions and their role in the self-presentation of politicians in social media. The second part analyses authenticity in social media, with an emphasis on U.S. president Barack Obama and the former Prime Minister of Norway, Jens Stoltenberg, and discusses key authenticity markers in social media. The third part presents a comparative analysis of authenticity illusions in the two selected political campaign videos for Obama and Stoltenberg. The fourth part discusses to what degree authenticity illusions under-communicate power relations in politics, and to what degree illusions of authenticity might contribute to restoring public trust in politicians.

Authenticity Illusions

The obsession with authenticity, and its expressions in concepts of 'the real', 'the genuine', 'the intimate', and 'the inner self', dominates contemporary culture (Dovey 2000; Guignon 2004; Baudrillard 2008). A prominent reason why the fascination with genuine, real, and unstaged moments has intensified is that the media have become increasingly unreal, staged, and manipulated, not least as a result of new technologies. As a counterweight to phenomena such as virtual reality, video games, and advanced special effects, the seemingly unproduced and unprocessed has become appealing in the context of popular culture.

While we in our role as customers are approached by the authenticity argument in the form of, for example, 'genuine coffee', 'original blue jeans', and 'authentic tourism', we are approached in our role as citizens with arguments in the form of an 'authentic politician', a 'trustworthy candidate', and a 'genuine political leader'. Following from this, authenticity has become a currency in the branding of politicians, and the use of authenticity illusions therefore flourishes in contemporary political communication, not at least fuelled by the rhetorical potential of social media.

Social media have established certain conventions for authenticity illusions, partly based on genre conventions from traditional media, such as the observational fly-on-the-wall documentary and reality TV productions. Authenticity illusions are, for the most part, accepted by audiences. Television viewers, for example, understand that canned laughter is a technique for enhancing the comedy show and not a precisely timed outburst of a real audience.

This tacit understanding or agreement between producers and audiences might be defined as 'the authenticity contract': a social construction where both parties agree on a set of conventions and techniques (Enli 2015a: 2). However, occasionally, the audience realises that what they believed was an authentic story or unscripted reality was, in fact, produced and constructed. One recent example is the 'First Kiss' (2014)[3] video, in which 20 strangers were filmed when they kiss for the first time, with the intention to capture moments of authentic intimate encounters. Tatiana Pilieva was credited as having made the film, and it was soon revealed that the purpose of the film was to market her new clothing line, and that the 'ordinary people' kissing were, in fact, actors, models, and artists who were paid to participate. Even though the encounters between the couples caught on camera were authentic in the sense that they had never met before, and that the embarrassment and awkwardness in the scenes was genuine, they were also cast and the authenticity was constructed. When these authenticity illusions became publicly known, the reactions from the 'Internet hordes' were infused with disappointment and feelings of betrayal, according to a comment in the newspaper *The Globe and Mail*:

> The "strangers" were in fact models, actors, indie musicians and even a member of the Hemingway clan, all thrown together for staged passion.
> Once again, the Internet hordes complained, another corporate gimmick disguised as authentic moment proffered by the Web. (Bielski 2014: paras. 2–3)

As we shall see in the analysis, similar disappointment is found in the reactions against political campaign videos using a similar set of authenticity illusions, such as the use of casting, or street casting, rather than randomly picked participants. The appeal of the seemingly emotional rawness and the unrehearsed meetings in front of a camera seems to be partly devalued as it becomes known that the media content is actually produced.

'First Kiss' can be classified as a post-modern marketing stunt, as "the whole thing was an ad shilling clothing for a hip, Los Angeles-based retailer named Wren" (Bielski 2014: para. 2). Highly influenced by tools from commercial marketing, political communication has been quick to include authenticity narratives into its storytelling. Image building in politics is closely related to contemporary branding and advertising culture, the practices of which influence not only consumer markets but also political communication (Maarek 2011; Banet-Wiser 2012). Recent branding studies argue that Barack Obama is *the* U.S. president who, more than any previous president, is promoted as a brand in line with 'Nike, Starbucks and Apple', and that authenticity is a prominent aspect of the brand (Klein 2010; Scott 2011).

From an historical perspective, authenticity is a fairly recent tendency and has gradually become more important in political communication and other realms of communication since the emergence of modernism and self-reflexivity. The rhetoric of authenticity was, for example, not a virtue of any significance in ancient Greece and its ideals for political speeches. Rather, the opposite: speeches were supposed to seem natural, but it was considerably more important to seem prepared, systematic, and competent in politics than to seem authentic and genuine. Consequently, a claim to authenticity is not an inherent quality of political rhetoric but rather related to technological, political, and cultural changes.

With the introduction of every new media technology, politicians have adjusted their rhetoric and communicative styles and, moreover, the understanding of what is authentic and genuine changes. In politics, innovations such as the microphone and audio-visual broadcasting have reduced the distance between politicians and their audiences, and as a consequence political rhetoric has changed quite quickly. The new political rhetoric was characteristically more personal, open, and conversational, and, in turn, the ideals of the 'authentic' and the 'sincere' politician became more dominant (Jamieson 1988; Jamieson and Waldman 2003).

Performing the Role of an Authentic Politician

A key criterion for being elected as a politician in most media-centred democracies is to come across to voters as a trustworthy and honest person, who has genuine and positive intentions. However, for voters, their knowledge about a politician is primarily, if not exclusively, derived from the media: how they perform in the media, how they are portrayed in news media and other media genres, and how they are promoted in various forms of advertisements (Thompson 2000; Jamieson and Waldman 2003; Trent et al. 2011; Sides and Vavreck 2013).

Being an honest politician is about speaking the truth and never telling lies to improve one's social status or to avoid uncomfortable situations. However, being an authentic politician is about *performing*. According to the philosopher Lionel Thrilling (1972), there is a distinction between being genuine and being authentic; while the former is about being true to others, the latter is about being true to your inner self (Thrilling 1972).

'Authenticity' is a complex term and relates not only to psychological dimensions, behaviourism, or ethical dilemmas but also to sociological dimensions. The main theorist in the field of performance and self-presentation in everyday life is sociologist Erving Goffman (1959; 1967), who argues that human interactions always involve a degree of performance and that people adjust their behaviour according to social norms and expectations. Goffman (1959) is well-known for developing the dual terms 'front stage' and 'back stage', referring to, on the one hand, the arenas where a formal or official performance is required, and on the other hand, the arenas where an informal and relaxed performance is allowed.

A couple of decades later, Joshua Meyrowitz (1985) suggested the term 'middle-region behaviour' as a description of the arenas where the distinction between 'front region behaviour' and 'back region behaviour' becomes blurred. The main example of the 'middle region' in Meyrowitz's theory was television, the audio-visual broadcast medium which was, and still is, used by politicians to come across as personalities and to demonstrate their character to the voters.

Elite politicians are often competent performers, either trained by PR consultants or more naturally gifted, and they often gain popularity from their appeal in the 'middle region'. Former U.S. president Ronald Reagan, who was a movie actor before he entered politics, exemplifies this point, and he is famously quoted to have answered 'How can a president *not* be an actor?' when asked how an actor can be president.

Likewise, in Norway, and in spite of a fairly different political culture, Carl I. Hagen, a former party leader who is among the nation's most visible politicians, is quoted to have said: "Every politician is an actor. When the famous former Norwegian Prime Minister Einar Gerhardsen gave a speech at the actors' association, he started off with 'honourable colleagues' (author's translation) (Juul 2015).

Yet, 'middle region behaviour' is also associated with risk and might be a threatening arena if politicians fail to communicate authenticity, or come across as dishonest or shady. One politician who suffered from television's merciless close-ups was former U.S. presidential candidate Al Gore, who was regarded as inauthentic by commentators and viewers because he wore too much makeup in a TV debate and also seemed scripted and cautious (Jamieson and Waldman 2003: 29). Moreover, when shifting from avoiding environmental issues to promoting these issues heavily, Al Gore failed to come across as consistent, which is key in performed authenticity; consistency in mediated appearances will make politicians seem more grounded and predictable. In contrast, Al Gore's opponent in the 2000 U.S. presidential election, George W. Bush, was called 'Mr. Consistency' because he was consistent to the degree that he repeated himself like a parrot throughout the campaign (Johansen, 2002, 75). In the context of the logics of 'middle region behaviour' and with authenticity as a key to the public's trust, George W. Bush might have compensated for seeming less knowledgeable by seeking to appear trustworthy. Since then, however, the rapid spread of social media as tools for both mundane and political communication has imposed changes, and added new dimensions, to the rhetoric of authenticity.

Authenticity in Social Media Politics

In social media politics, defined broadly as political communication in social media, the notion of authenticity is essential. First, social media are associated with *symbolic authenticity*, as user-generated content is framed as more authentic than mainstream media content simply by being produced and posted by individuals rather than media companies. Although political communication in social media is no less commercial and professional than in mainstream media, particularly when produced by top staffers, social media are associated with authenticity. The effect of this symbolic authenticity is that it builds an image of the politician as willing and able to adapt to contemporary culture's emphasis on networked communication, sharing, and participation.

A second aspect of authenticity in social media politics is related to *self-presentation*, meaning that politicians themselves—in collaboration with their campaign staff—decide how to present themselves rather than the presentation being a result of journalistic gatekeeping and decision making. According to previous studies, most elite politicians rarely or never update their social media statuses themselves, and to the degree that they do, the politicians' posts are presented as authentic by the use of a signature (such as '–bo' in the case of Barack Obama). They do so to fend off criticism, as the press were eager to announce the news that 'Obama Is Actually Writing His Own Tweets Now' (Ho 2011). Still, during the 2012 election campaign, these initials were used in only a fraction—about 1 per cent—of the total tweets posted to the @Barack Obama account (also see the chapter 26 in this volume).

A key strategy against criticisms of inauthenticity is transparency, and for that reason the @BarackObama account bio has since January 2013 informed Twitter users that "This account is run by Organizing for Action staff. Tweets from the President are signed –bo". These lines indicate that once Obama's second term started, a non-profit, non-partisan entity called Organizing for Action (OFA) was given control over major parts of the campaign, including the social media accounts, the website, and the email list. Previously, the account had been managed by the campaign Obama for America, run by staffers but under the ultimate direction of the president. Even though the account is verified as official (with a blue badge), the account is not really an account related to the president or his political team but is completely outsourced.

In a critical article in *The Atlantic*, political commentator Philip Bump questions whether this manoeuvre is ethical, or even legal, and makes the comparison that "the President, mid-conversation, handed over his phone to a telemarketer who does a great Obama impression" (Bump 2013: 2). The legal grey area here is, according to Bump, that the OFA as a non-profit organisation is allowed to raise money but not advocate for a political candidate. The ethical dilemma is that Twitter users are not sufficiently informed that they are, in fact, following not Barack Obama but the OFA, and that this could be made clear through a name change and a change of profile images.

The need for President Obama to make his Twitter use more authentic led the way to the launch of a new account with the Twitter username @POTUS on 18 May 2015. The profile was a hybrid of the intimate: "Dad, husband, and 44th President of the United States," and the formal: "Tweets may be archived: http://wh.gov/privacy". The message is mixed, and it seems clear that the new Twitter account is an attempt to handle the challenge of living up to the official statement from the White House to create an "unprecedented level of openness" in government, and to "ensure the public trust and establish a system of transparency, public participation, and collaboration."[4] Obamas first Tweet from the @POTUS account was: "Hello, Twitter! It's Barack. Really! Six years in, they're finally giving me my own account."[5] The following six tweets were also more or less in the same tone, and play on a combination of humour and symbolic interaction.

In smaller nations, such as the Nordic region, it is more common that elite politicians update their own social media accounts and even engage in Twitter debates with selected users. In research interviews with Norwegian party leaders, I found that they were indeed concerned with being recognised as authentic, and even the sitting Prime Minister, Jens Stoltenberg, claimed that

> I do almost everything on social media myself. That is important to me, because it has to be real. I would never be on Facebook or Twitter if my social media presence were based on an advisor who sat there and pretended to be me. I think people would see through that. (Stoltenberg, e-mail interview, 3 September 2013, my translation)

Such statements by Nordic elite politicians must, however, not be interpreted as an indication of total authenticity in social media but rather of a partial authenticity in which politicians delegate some of the updates while managing others themselves. Moreover, they should be read as intending to come across as authentic and 'real', an aim that is rooted in Nordic political culture where consensus and egalitarianism are key values (Syvertsen et al. 2014). Still, elite Norwegian politicians are not as authentic and accessible in social media as they claim to be in interviews regarding the democratic potential of social media. In practice, they rarely engage in extensive conversations with ordinary people (Skogerbø and Moe 2015; Enli and Skogerbø 2013).

Self-presentation in social media is not dependent only on a genuine author but might also be a result of a negotiation between the politicians and their consultants. The element of self-presentation is key in social media, and the construction of online personas in profiles and updates has been proven to generate more engagement than, for example, the presence of a political party or an organisation (Bruns and Highfield 2013; Enli and Skogerbø 2013). Consequently, the rhetoric and communicative modes of social media invite the personalisation of politics—for politicians and their teams, social media first and foremost represent an opportunity to communicate a more personal, and even intimate, side of the politician, compared to more formal presentations of politicians. Certainly, these images of 'the genuine politician' are also pre-planned and staged, but they are manufactured to come across as authentic backstage versions of the politicians, drawing extensively on illusions of authenticity.

Third, a technique to construct authenticity in social media is to seemingly display an unrehearsed 'backstage' by performing *spontaneity*. A key advantage of politicians' seeming spontaneity is that they can come across as innocent and honest, or at least less cynical and dishonest than if they seem scripted at all times. A typical way to construct the image of a trustworthy politician is to post images and quotes from the private arena, seemingly spontaneous and heartfelt.

This illusion of authenticity is found in the social media presences of both U.S. President Barack Obama and Norwegian Prime Minister Jens Stoltenberg, but the seemingly spontaneous moments selected for exposure are highly different. In the U.S. case, the intimate images of Barack Obama tend to show him playing with his children, traveling on a bus, or hugging his wife. A characteristic of these images is a documentary aesthetic—a fly-on-the-wall style—when the politician is not posing or looking into the camera but seems unaware of the photographer and is busy doing something else. The 'Michelle and Barack hug' image (see Figure 8.1) was posted on Obama's

Figure 8.1 Barack and Michelle Obama Hugging on the Campaign Trail in Iowa
Posted on Twitter and Facebook 06 Nov. 2012. Photographer: Scout Tufankjian. Permission holder: Polaris Images[6]. Reprinted by permission.

social media accounts on election night in 2012 to announce his victory, with the three words: 'Four more years'. The tweet became the (at that point) most retweeted post in history and has received nearly 4.5 million likes on Facebook.

This image was inauthentic in the sense that it was *not* taken in the moment when President Barack Obama and his wife had finally realised that they had succeeded in their campaigning and expressed their happiness with a long, intimate hug. Rather, the image was previously posted on the account and re-used for the purpose of the victory tweet. Even the photographer was surprised that this image was posted as the first victory statement from the President (Nanos, 2012). The choice of using social media before the news media and the traditional press conference to announce the election victory might be motivated by social media's potential to spread content more quickly and more engagingly. Through their engagement with the post, social media users did the job of spreading the message and added a portion of authenticity by sharing it directly through their networks rather than via the mass media.

In the Norwegian case, the spontaneous images of Jens Stoltenberg tend to show him engaging in the national sport, cross-country skiing, or as a cyclist, being ordinary and sensible by using a helmet. Some of the images seem spontaneous because they are amateurish while others give a glimpse of privacy and intimacy that seems authentic, such as the hug with his father (see Figure 8.2). This image was followed by a message about his transfer to Brussels in the role as Secretary-General of NATO: "Goodbye. Ready for new missions and to live in Brussels" (Jens Stoltenberg Facebook page: 29

Figure 8.2 Photo of Jens Stoltenberg Hugging His Father Thorvald Stoltenberg
Posted on Facebook 29 Sep. 2014. Photo: Daniel Sannum Lauten[7]. Reprinted by permission.

September 2014). The image of father and son resonated well with followers, both because it seemed like an authentic goodbye hug, given that the public knew that Stoltenberg was leaving for the NATO job in Brussels, and also given that they were familiar with the father–son relationship from previous media stories, as the father is also a well-known politician.

This post was well received, with 40,405 likes, 242 shares, and nearly 200 comments, and among the most liked user comments was: "The best Prime Minister ever!" In comparison, a photo of Stoltenberg with the Danish Prime Minister (20 April 2015) was 'liked' 6,129 times, and a photo of Stoltenberg and Obama (26 May 2015) 16,444 times[8]. This demonstrates that intimate and private family photos appear to connect better with users than photos of official meetings between state leaders.

Comparing the authenticity illusions in the Obama hug photo and the Stoltenberg hug photo, there are similarities in the motive; a hug between two celebrities who are also intimately related. This implies that there is a generic way of communicating intimacy and spontaneity among Western state leaders. Nevertheless, the two images are indeed also very different: first, the U.S. version portrays the President and the First Lady as a team and a couple, while the wife of a Norwegian Prime Minister would be a more distant public figure, and less associated with the political leadership than in America. The second difference is that the U.S. version is more cinematic and glamorous and that the Nordic image is more naturalistic and melancholic.

Political Campaign Videos and Authenticity Illusions

In addition to intimate images, short videos presenting the candidates have been an increasing trend in online political communication in recent years. There is support in research for the argument that videos elicit a high level of trust, ahead of audio, photos, and text (Riegelsberger, Sasse, and McCarthy 2005).

The length of these videos is a factor that influences the chances of becoming a viral phenomenon through massive sharing. According to a recent survey, users are more likely to watch and share videos that are shorter than 30 seconds, and the risk that users stop watching increases gradually and significantly for every additional 30 seconds the video lasts. In general, the shorter the video, the more likely users are to watch the entire message (Ruedlinger 2012).

In this section, I analyse two selected political campaign videos, made for marketing purposes, within two different political cultures: North American candidate-centred politics and Norwegian party-centred politics. First, I briefly present the two videos separately, and thereafter I compare them to identify authenticity illusions in the videos and discuss the rhetoric of authenticity utilised here.

Obama Video: 'Things Everybody Does But Doesn't Talk About' (2015)

'Things Everybody Does But Doesn't Talk About" (2015) is a video featuring US President Barack Obama, published by the online news site BuzzFeed in February 2015. The video (which also aired on national TV stations and was covered in mainstream media) is 1:58 minutes long, and as of 10 April 2015 had reached 51,367,464 views. The title promises a glimpse of authenticity, meaning moments in the powerful politician's life which are commonly not addressed in public because of their personal, intimate, and embarrassing character. The video's title insinuated that viewers could meet one of the world's elite politicians 'backstage', meaning that he would be performing in line with this arena's requirements for informality and spontaneity.

In contrast, elite politicians such as Barack Obama are most commonly seen in various types of 'front-stage' performances, such as public speeches, press briefings, and televised interviews. Among the manifold expectations of social media was that they would provide a new arena of networked communication with more authentic political communication, less infused with PR consultants and political spin. In recent decades, elite politicians' 'front-stage behaviour' had become predictable and dictated by the formulas of media logic, and so when social media entered politics from the mid-2000s, they represented a timely turn towards 'backstage behaviour'. Social media tapped into participatory culture and had an aura of authenticity, which connected well with key trends in society.

The campaign video was produced to promote the U.S. government's health-care program, and to encourage citizens to enrol in the program. The infotainment video thus had a clear message, but this was not in any way explicitly addressed. Rather, it was communicated implicitly as a hidden message, with the main narrative of the video being that of Obama preparing for a meeting with the press to inform them about the health-care program. In this process of preparing, Obama is portrayed as having a private moment; and, as the title indicates, he does 'things everybody does but doesn't talk about' such as trying to look cool in front of a mirror.

The Obama BuzzFeed video is presented almost as a fiction movie, with Obama introduced as if he were an actor rather than a politician. The secondary title of the video is 'Featuring President Obama', as in a movie trailer (such as, 'Featuring Meryl Streep'). Moreover, the video includes much-used features from fiction movies, such as the cross-cutting between two main characters who meet in the last sequence, and a funny scene when the young journalist steps on a brick and spills his take-away coffee on the sidewalk.

The main criticism of the video came from the President's political opponents, in particular the conservative press, who argued that the informal language and use of the selfie stick totally undermined his political authority. The blog Media Matters for America has collected these reactions from conservative journalists and politicians: 'At Some Point, We Stopped Having a Fire Sale on Presidential Dignity', 'What President Says YOLO?', and 'America's Commander-in-Chief Is Goofing Off . . . While the World Burns' (Power and Rogers 2015). The message seems to be that the president should have better and more important issues to deal with than to communicate his coolness and easy-going attitude in a marketing stunt.

Stoltenberg Video: 'The Secret Cab Driver' (2013)

"The Secret Cab Driver" (2013) was an election campaign video produced by the largest political party in Norway, the Labour Party, and was launched by the party through social media in August 2013, about a month before the upcoming election. In the video, the incumbent Norwegian Prime Minister Jens Stoltenberg, is presenting himself before the camera and explains that he usually spends his days in formal meetings, but that this is going to be an extraordinary day, as he will dress in a uniform and take on a role as a cab driver, in order to meet everyday people and get a better understanding of what politics the country needs.

The video went viral and reached a high number of social media users as well as achieving broad coverage in the Norwegian and international press. The video was shared in spite of its length, which, at 3:41 minutes, was almost two minutes longer than the Obama video discussed above. This might be explained by two factors: first, that Norwegians might be more tolerant of lengthy clips as they are not regularly exposed to audio-visual political advertisements (which are prohibited under existing broadcast TV regulations). Second, that the two years between these videos might have had some impact on the length, as campaign strategists might have become more aware of the impatient logics of social media use during this period.

Among the criticisms towards the secret cab driver video was that the Prime Minister was a bad and even dangerous driver, and that it requires a specific license to serve as a cab driver in Norway, and that Stoltenberg thus broke the law. This criticism was quickly dismissed as irrelevant because he did not earn money as a cab driver, and none of the passengers paid for their journeys. A much more serious criticism was that the video was inauthentic as it became publicly known that some of the passengers in the back seat were cast, and not random customers waiting for a cab. This criticism pinpoints how expectations of authenticity are communicated by the audience, as they connect with the films because of the authenticity in the human reactions and therefore feel betrayed when the authenticity illusions are uncovered. In the next section, I will compare the use of authenticity illusions in the two videos.

Authenticity Illusions in the Campaign Videos

In the book *Mediated Authenticity* (Enli 2015a), I distinguish between seven types of authenticity illusions, of which four are particularly evident in the campaign videos studied in this chapter. First, *predictability* is an essential element in rhetoric intended to seem authentic. In the BuzzFeed video, for example, Barack Obama plays basketball and draws Michelle Obama on a piece of paper. Viewers will already know that he likes to play basketball and that he is married to Michelle. Likewise, they will already know that Jens Stoltenberg had been in office as Prime Minister for eight years when he drove the taxi and that this explained his bad driving, as he himself also mentioned in apologising to a passenger for a sudden stop.

A second authenticity illusion in the social media videos is *spontaneity*, or more precisely, pre-planned spontaneity. Barack Obama, for example, suddenly starts to play with a selfie-stick and improvises seemingly spontaneously with various angles and shots, and also suddenly starts to play air-basketball at a time when he should be ready for meeting the press. In the taxi, the spontaneous responses from the very astonished and surprised passengers in the backseat once they recognise the prime minister behind the wheel are adding an essential layer of authenticity to the Stoltenberg video.

Although the reactions from all the passengers seemed authentic, some of them—five out of fourteen—had been 'street cast', meaning that they were recruited on the street, offered a small remuneration, and informed that they would partake in an election campaign video (but without knowing that the they would meet the Prime Minister). The rest of the passengers were real passengers entering a regular cab and did not have any reason to expect that the cab ride should be included in a produced event (Johnsen 2013). Their spontaneous reactions indeed constituted much of the appeal in the video, and created scenes of humour, humanity, and authenticity.

The third authenticity illusion is *ordinariness*, which is a well-known and much-used rhetorical mode in political communication. A trustworthy politician needs to come across as an ordinary person, who can relate to everyday life and the issues regular people struggle with. In the Obama BuzzFeed video, the main narrative is precisely built around a portrayal of the president as an ordinary person, just like everyone else. Presented through the parallel storylines, the video portrays two persons of different status—the U.S. president and a young journalist—preparing for the same press meeting. In spite of their different roles, the two men prepare for the meeting with fairly backstage behaviour: they both make faces and try to look cool in front of a mirror, they both rehearse their pronunciation of common words (such as 'February' and 'Wednesday'), they both take funny selfies, they both make practical mistakes, they both make amateur drawings, and they both play air basketball. Moreover, the last scene explicitly demonstrates Obama's ordinariness by having the journalist enter the room while the president is still in his play mode. Surprised by seeing the president in such an informal and unexpected mode, the journalist exclaims: "Mr. President?!," and Obama answers with arms wide open, and a question: "Can I live?" and later to a laughing, but invisible crowd, "Yolo, man" (referring to the phrase 'you only live once'). The message to users is that Obama is just like everyone else, and that he also likes to have fun and does not just spend his life as a formal and uptight politician.

Similarly, when Norway's Prime Minister talks to ordinary people in the taxi video, the message to the voters is that he is not ignoring the concerns of everyday people but rather engages in their problems and effortlessly discusses their concerns and responds to their problems. In the video's introduction, Prime Minister Stoltenberg speaks directly to the camera and explains with a pedagogic tone his motives for taking on the role as a taxi driver: "In my job as the prime minister it is essential to know people's *true opinions*, and if there is one place people really speak their mind, it is in the taxi."

Another shared feature in both the Obama video and the Stoltenberg video is the message that political leaders have limited power and should not be blamed for everything. In the Obama video, the ironic phrase: "Thank you, Obama!" is declared both by the reporter and by Obama himself when they face practical challenges, and the message is that they unfairly blame the president because there is nobody else to blame. Transferred to real politics, the message is that Obama is not to be blamed for everything that is wrong and unfair in society. Likewise, the taxi video includes an elderly woman's complaints about the high salaries of top-level managers: "They should not have all this money!," to which Stoltenberg explains that this is difficult to regulate even for a Prime Minister, because, as he says: "I do not have the power to decide the salaries in these companies."

A fourth authenticity illusion in the two videos is *imperfection*. In the Obama video, elements of imperfection are included to communicate realism, such as the dirty spots on the mirror Obama is performing in front of, and the untidiness in the bookshelf behind Obama when he plays with the selfie stick. Moreover, the President struggles with pronouncing the word 'February' correctly, and thus demonstrates that he is not perfect. Likewise, the secret cab driver video exposes Stoltenberg as a bad driver when he abruptly steps on the brakes, so that the passenger is pulled out of her seat and screams before the situation normalises. Moreover, when one of the passengers expresses scepticism against the taxi driver, Prime Minister Jens Stoltenberg, and his political party, it adds trustworthiness to the video by including also non-supportive arguments. The inclusion of the passenger's statement "I did not vote for you" served to make the video more authentic than a more polished campaign video where the producers would make sure to cast supporters rather than attackers.

Authenticity Illusions in Social Media Under-Communicate Power Relations

The above analysis identified a set of authenticity illusions in the campaign videos, and how these were used to communicate a 'backstage' image, as if users were given personal access directly to the politicians. Yet the rhetoric of authenticity might be a disguise for highly staged, pre-planned and expensive productions, and a way to make politicians seem like harmless and likeable everyday people 'like you and me' rather than powerful politicians with control over economic resources and influence over our lives. As such, politicians' use of social media and self-presentations in informal settings (as in the role of a cab driver or a playful slacker) might be a way to under-communicate the real power relations between politicians and voters.

Portrayals of celebrity politicians in the role of an ordinary person are nevertheless also appealing, and bring an element of ordinariness and recognition into politics, which might help voters to identify and relate more to those politicians. Moreover, as in the 'First Kiss' video, there are authentic elements in the political campaign videos which cannot be dismissed as entirely staged and faked, as they provide glimpses of authentic encounters between people (as in the secret cab driver video) and of a president who allows the camera to film him in awkward settings (as with the selfie stick or air basketball scenes).

The current relationship between politicians and citizens has been characterised as a 'Wall of Suspicion', meaning that both parties mistrust the other and that the media are adding fuel to the fire by running stories about politicians who fail to deliver as promised (Coleman and Wright 2008). However, the media might also offer a kind of remedy for mistrust: political communication might also construct an image of politicians as trustworthy, authentic and likeable. Authentic talk has even been characterised as a 'guarantee of truth' (Montgomery 2001). Following this line of thought, Margaretten and Gaber (2012: 3) argue that authentic communication is both a goal and a requirement for trust in politicians: "without the perception of authenticity, trust cannot be established." In politics, trustworthiness is of key importance, and, quite paradoxically, the search for authentic moments has increased as a result of the professionalisation and commercialisation of political communication. Voters want to believe that they are told the truth, "without the spin and manipulation all too common in political communication" (Margaretten and Gaber 2012: 3).

In theory, politicians acquire their mandate as a result of the authenticity, sincerity, and consistency they display (Coleman 2006). Yet, being authentic in a mediated context is not directly related to being honest or sincere in their actions and decision making, but rather to coming across to voters as authentic. Therefore, being authentic has become a strategy in its own right, and Hillary Clinton, for example, is quoted to have said: "I believe in being as authentic as possible" (Rosenbloom 2011: para. 6), and Michele Bachmann told ABC News that "I am authentic" (Rosenbloom 2011: para. 1). Being authentic has thus turned into a slogan that politicians can use to promote themselves, and social media are perhaps the most accessible tools to communicate authenticity in contemporary politics.

In this chapter, I have analysed how elite politicians in two Western democracies of differing size, system, and political culture have emphasised symbolic authenticity in their social media strategies. Research has suggested that authentic talk from politicians might reduce mistrust in politicians and that if voters feel less distance between themselves and the politicians, trust might be regained (Margaretten and Gaber 2012).

Thus, social media were expected by some to provide precisely for this kind of authentic expression, without interference from media producers, political journalists, or the political spin apparatus. However, as demonstrated in this analysis, politicians are staged as authentic in social media, and political advisors calculate that by making the politicians' self-representations seem real and authentic, voters will come to trust them, and, in turn, vote for them. Voters do not however gain access to the genuine politician, but to an image, partly staged as authentic and partly based on elements of the real politician.

The implications of this increased focus on authenticity in political communication require further research, but based on the findings of this study I will point to three possible implications. First, mediated politics becomes increasingly personalised, both in candidate-centred and in party-centred countries. In turn, voters will be increasingly concerned about candidate's seeming authenticity and trustworthiness, compared, for example, to their skills in leadership and knowledge about the society. Second, the role of media and communication advisors, and especially social media experts, might be strengthened in relation to the political party organisation. Third, and related, the use of social media as an image-building strategy will probably be professionalised over the next decade, and the production of mediated authenticity and strategies to make highly manipulated material seem authentic will expand. Paradoxically, authenticity will require advanced production techniques, a point which can be related to a famous quote by Dolly Parton: "It costs a lot of money to look this cheap."

Notes

1 www.buzzfeed.com/andrewgauthier/the-president-uses-a-selfie-stick#.nyEdDRW3r
2 www.youtube.com/watch?v=uqsoWbQewIo
3 www.youtube.com/watch?v=IpbDHxCV29A
4 www.whitehouse.gov/the_press_office/TransparencyandOpenGovernment/
5 www.npr.org/sections/thetwo-way/2015/05/18/407721123/president-gets-his-own-twitter-account-its-barack-really
6 https://twitter.com/BarackObama/status/266031293945503744
7 www.facebook.com/jensstoltenberg/photos/pb.21646763580.2207520000.1432045286./10152415368468581/?type=3&theater
8 Likes/shares/comments numbers are per 28 May 2015.

References

Banet-Weiser, S. (2012). *Authentic TM: The Politics of Ambivalence in a Brand Culture*. New York: New York University Press.

Baudrillard, J. (2008). *Radical Alterity*. Los Angeles, CA.: Semiotext(e)/Foreign Agents Series.

Bielski, Z. (2014). The fake, viral First Kiss video: What's "Real" on the Internet, and How Real Do We Actually Want It?," *The Globe and Mail*, 13 March 2014. Retrieved from www.theglobeandmail.com/life/relationships/the-fake-viral-first-kiss-video-whats-real-on-the-internet-and-how-real-do-we-actually-want-it/article17487129/

Bruns, A. and T. Highfield (2013). May the Best Tweeter Win: The Twitter Strategies of Key Campaign Accounts in the 2012 US Election. In Bieber and Kamps (eds.) *The United States Presidential Election 2012: Perspectives from Election Studies, Political and Communication Sciences*. Wiesbaden: VS Verlag.

Bump, P. (2013). You're Not Really Following @BarackObama on Twitter. *The Atlantic*, 8 April 2013. Retrieved from www.theatlantic.com/politics/archive/2013/04/youre-not-following-barack obama-twitter/316523/

Chadwick, A. (2013): *The Hybrid Media System: Politics and Power*. Oxford: Oxford University Press.

Coleman, S. (2006) "Parliamentary communication in an age of digital interactivity," *ASLIB PROC*, 58 (5): 371–388.

Coleman, S. and S. Wright (2008). "Political Blogs and Representative Democracy," *Information Policy: The International Journal of Government & Democracy in the Information Age*, 13 (1–5).

Dovey, J. (2000). *Freakshow: First Person Media and Factual Television*. London: Pluto Press.

Ekman; M. and A. Widholm (2014). "Politicians as Media Producers: Current Trajectories in the Relation between Journalists And Politicians in the Age of Social Media," *Journalism Practice*, 9 (1): 78–91.

Enli, G. (2009). "Mass Communication Tapping into Participatory Culture: Exploring Strictly Come Dancing and Britain's Got Talent," *European Journal of Communication*, 24 (4): 481–493

Enli, G. (2015a). *Mediated Authenticity. How the Media Constructs Reality*. New York: Peter Lang.

Enli, G. (2015b). Politisk logikk eller Medielogikk: Norske Partilederes strategier i sosiale medier [Political logic or media logic: Norwegian party leaders strategies in social media]. *Norsk medietidsskrift*, Autumn 2015.

Enli, G. and H. Moe (2013). "Social Media and Election Campaigns—Key Tendencies and Ways Forward," *Information, Communication & Society*, 16 5: 637–645.

Enli, G. and E. Skogerbø (2013). "Personalized Campaigns in Party-Centred Politics: Twitter and Facebook as Arenas for Political Communication," *Information, Communication & Society*, 16, 5: 757–774.

Guignon, C. B. (2004). *On Being Authentic: Thinking in Action*. London: Routledge.

Goffman, E. (1959). *The Presentation of Self in Everyday Life*. New York: Doubleday.

Goffman, E. (1967). *Interaction ritual: Essays on face–to–face behavior*. Garden City, NY: Anchor.

Ho, E. (2011). Obama Is Actually Writing His Own Tweets Now, *Time*, 20 June 2011. Retrieved from http://techland.time.com/2011/06/20/obama-is-actually-writing-his-own-tweets-now

Howard, P. N. (2006): *New Media Campaigns and the Managed Citizen*. New York: Cambridge University Press.

Jamieson, K. H. (1988). *Eloquence in an Electronic Age: The Transformation of Political Speechmaking*. Oxford: Oxford University Press.

Jamieson, K. H. (2000). *Everything You Think You Know About Politics . . . : And Why You're Wrong*. New York: Basic Books.

Jamieson, K. H. and P. Waldman (2003). *The Press Effect: Politicians, Journalists, and the Stories that Shape the Political World*. Oxford: Oxford University Press.

Johansen, A. (2002). *Talerens troverdighet. Tekniske og kulturelle betingelser for politisk retorikk* [*The speaker's credibility. Technical and cultural conditions for political rhetoric*]. Oslo: Universitetsforlaget.

Johnsen, N. (2013). "Fem av passasjerene fra Aps taxifilm med Jens Stoltenberg var hentet inn via casting, og visste at de skulle være med på en valgkampfilm," *VG Nett* 12.08.2013. Retrieved from www.vg.no/nyheter/innenriks/arbeiderpartiet/fikk-betalt-for-tur-med-taxi-jens/a/10119280/

Juul, K. (2015). "Jeg har ingen venner—Hagen angrer ikke på at han var ikke var for partnerskapsloven," *Vårt Land*, 24. April 2015. Retrieved from www.vl.no/jeg-har-ingen-venner-1.353254

Klein, N. (2010). *No logo. 10th Anniversary Edition*. London: Picador.

Kleis Nielsen, R. (2012): *Ground Wars: Personalized Communication in Political Campaigns*. Princeton: Princeton University Press.

Larsson, A. (2015): "Pandering, Protesting, Engaging. Norwegian Party Leaders on Facebook during the 2013 'Short Campaign'," *Information, Communication & Society*, 8 (4): 459–473.

Larsson, A. O. and B. Kalsnes (2014). "'Of Course We Are On Facebook'—Social Media Adoption in Swedish and Norwegian Parliaments:, *European Journal of Communication*, 18 (4): 459–473.

Larsson, A.O. and H. Moe (2013). Twitter in Politics and Elections—Insights from Scandinavia. In A. Bruns, J. Burgess, K. Weller, C. Puschmann and M. Mahrt (Eds.), *Twitter and Society*. New York: Peter Lang.

Lomborg, S. and A. Bechmann. (2013). "Mapping Actor Roles in Social Media: Different Perspectives on Value Creation in Theories of User Participation," *New Media & Society*, 15 (5): 765–781.

Maarek, P.J. (2011). *Campaign Communication & Political Marketing*. London: Wiley-Blackwell.

Margaretten, M. and I. Gaber (2012). "The Crisis in Public Communication and the Pursuit of Authenticity: An Analysis of the Twitter Feeds of Scottish MPs 2008–2010," in *Parliamentary Affairs* 67 (2): 328–350.

Meyrowitz, J. (1985): *No Sense of Place: The Impact of Electronic Media on Social Behaviour*. New York: Oxford University Press.

Montgomery, M. (2001). "The Uses of Authenticity: 'Speaking from Experience' in a U.K. Election Broadcast," *The Communication Review*, 4 (4): 447–462.

Nanos, J. (2012). "How a Campaign Photographer Captured the Most Liked and Most Tweeted Photo Ever," *The Boston Daily*, 8 November 2012. Retrieved from www.bostonmagazine.com/news/blog/2012/11/08/obama-hug/

Power, L. and N. Rogers (2015). "Cue Conservative Media Outrage Over Obama's Selfie, Use Of 'YOLO' in BuzzFeed Video," *Media Matters For America* February 13 2015. Retrieved from http://mediamatters.org/research/2015/02/13/cue-conservative-media-outrage-over-obamas-self/202531

Rosenbloom, S. (2011). "Authentic? Get Real," *The New York Times*. Published Sept 9 2011.

Riegelsberger, J., A. M. Sasse and J. D. McCarthy (2005). "Do People Trust Their Eyes More than Their Ears? Media Bias While Seeking Expert Advice," Poster at *CHI 2005*, Portland, Oregon, USA.

Ruedlinger, B. (2012). "Does Length Matter?," *Wistia*, 7 May 2012. Retrieved from http://wistia.com/blog/does-length-matter-it-does-for-video-2k12-edition

Scott, D.M. (2011). *The New Rules of Marketing and PR: How to Use Social Media, Online Video, Mobile Applications, Blogs, News Releases, and Viral Marketing to Reach Buyers Directly*. Hoboken, NJ: John Wiley and Sons.

Sides, J. and L. Vavreck (2013). *The Gamble: Choice and Chance in the 2012 Presidential Election*. Princeton, NJ: Princeton University Press.

Skogerbø, E. and H. Moe (2015). "Twitter på tvers: koblinger mellom journalister og politikere" [Twitter Twist: How Politicians and Journalists Interact]. *Norsk medietidsskrift*, Autumn 2015.

Stayner, J. (2013): *Intimate Politics: Publicity, Privacy, and the Personal Lives of Politicians in Media-Saturated Democracies*. Cambridge: Polity Press.

Syvertsen, T., G. Enli, O. J. Mjøs and H. Moe (2014). *The Media Welfare State: Nordic Media in the Digital Era*. Ann Arbor: University of Michigan Press.

Thompson, J. B. (2000). *Political Scandal: Power and Visibility in the Media Age*. Oxford: Bl.

Trent, J.S., R. V. Friedenberg and R. E. Denton (2011). *Political Campaign Communication: Principles and Practices* (7th ed.). Lanham: Rowman & Littlefield.

Trilling, L. (1972). *Sincerity and Authenticity*. Boston: Harvard University Press.

Ytreberg, E. (2004). "Formatting Participation in Broadcast Media Production," *Media, Culture & Society*, 26 (5), 677–692.

9

HOW TO SPEAK THE TRUTH ON SOCIAL MEDIA

An Inquiry into Post-Dialectical Information Environments

Mercedes Bunz

Introduction

This chapter will look into the use of digital media in the context of political activism and will describe and analyse the oppositional use of media in regard to two different platforms: the global participatory platform Indymedia, created to cover political and social issues underreported by mainstream news; and the use of Twitter to report and oppose the brutal and fatal treatment of black people by U.S. police during the Ferguson unrest after the shooting of teenager Michael Brown, underreported by mainstream news.

The purpose of this chapter is thereby not to describe the organisational changes of oppositional activity due to media use, but to study conceptual changes in their ethical argument. Instead of looking at the hegemony of opinions, we will observe the establishment of "truths" following Foucault's take of it: truth not as an "objectivity" but as a "regime" that emerges to penetrate preceding ones (Foucault 1995: 19). Focusing on truth instead of opinion allows one to study the role of digital media from the following perspective: What is the role of digital media in a public argument, and does it change?

How do counterpublics, as oppositional media, claim to speak a different truth? This is a question that has become important to ask, as there seems to be a recent shift within our discourse. If we zoom out of our contemporary media discourse to look at it from the perspective of discourse analysis—as if we were a drone flying curiously over our discursive landscape—we notice an interesting pattern. A range of traditional oppositions, like private/public, work/play, global/local, virtual/real, online/offline, and nature/culture, to name but a few, seem to have changed their interrelationships. Media researchers and public intellectuals have discussed the change. The complex conflation of 'public/private' has been shown by Zizi Papacharissi (2010), among many others, and explained to a broader public by Jeff Jarvis (2011). Wendy Chun (2008) has looked into 'control/freedom' and described how the praise of the Internet as a medium spreading democratic freedom goes along with the fact that it also accelerates the potential for control and global surveillance. The merger of 'work/play' has been studied in management organisations by Niels Åkerstrøm Andersen (2009), but the spreading of game mechanics to non-game contexts has also troubled game researchers, who have named this 'gamification' (Fuchs et al. 2014). Finally, yet importantly, the overcoming of the 'nature/culture' opposition has come into view, triggered by man-made climate change and discussed in the humanities as the rise of a new geological epoch, the Anthropocene, in which our human activity has become the most important impact to the earth's ecosystem (Parikka 2014, but also Diederichsen & Franke 2013). All these examples share the same discursive pattern: a breakdown of oppositions. Once antithetical, the conceptual relation of the terms in each pair does not seem to be essentially oppositional anymore, although there are still differences and a dialectical tension remains. In the context of this chapter, this relation will therefore be described as 'post-dialectical' and can be defined as follows: post-dialectical is when an opposition has changed from antagonism to a relationship that could be described more as the flip side of the other: '/' instead of 'vs'. What effect does this shift have on a counterpublic?

On what grounds can an opposing political position now claim to speak a different truth, as there is no essential otherness in its base? And can a public truth be spoken on a personal account that is using a social media service such as Twitter? To answer those questions it is necessary to understand the role of a counterpublic first. So what is a counterpublic?

On Theories of Counterpublics and Indymedia

As explained above, a counterpublic tends to emerge when the public sphere, instead of being open to all, is suppressing a social or political conflict and thereby creating a motivation for a marginalised group to form their own public. Oskar Negt and Alexander Kluge (1972/1993) coined the term in order to complement the theorisation of the public sphere by Jürgen Habermas (1962/1991, 1964) from a Marxist perspective. It was later adapted and developed further by Nancy Fraser (1990) and Seyla Benhabib (1992) from a feminist perspective, and discussed by Michael Warner from a queer perspective, whose book introduced categories useful in the age of social media. Habermas himself had already flagged the problem that manipulative corporate interests might endanger an open public conversation and with it, the public sphere. Negt and Kluge took his doubt further. They disputed that the public was a sphere, which (a) concerned the people as a whole and (b) was free of corporate interest at all (Negt & Kluge 1972/1993: 9). Habermas—in following Kant—they said, had made a conceptual mistake, which was evident to all Marxists: the public sphere rests on a material base. One cannot ignore that news organisations belong to an owner influencing the information. In an ideal world, the public sphere would be open to all. In the factual world, the public sphere is owned by a few: "the construction of the public sphere derives its entire substance from the existence of owners of private property" (Kluge & Negt 1972/1993: 10). The media are subordinate to ownership, a theme that I will return to throughout the chapter. Instead of critically controlling power, the media are manipulating the public according to the owners' interest. Opposition within the public sphere seemed fundamentally flawed, as the media owners manipulate information according to their opinions. More than 25 years later, this theoretical critique is still relevant. With the rise of digital media it can be addressed with reference to a new form of media praxis: the open journalism introduced by Indymedia. The example of Indymedia sheds light on the ownership issue: when digital media entered the public sphere, at first the participatory potential seemed to offer a solution to the problem of ownership; however, not for very long.

Indymedia as Counterpublic

Indymedia, also referred to as Independent Media Center, or IMC, was founded in November 1999 in anticipation of the Seattle anti–World Trade Organization protests. During the WTO summit, grassroots journalists, anti-globalisation organisers, and international tech activists printed a daily newsletter called *The Blind Spot* and ran a website using an "open publishing system" for user-generated content (Platon & Deuze 2003: 338). For this they had set up two locations in which video-editing facilities, networked computers, faxes, and telephones were made available for around 400 volunteers (Downey & Fenton 2003: 197). The strategy of producing 'alternative news' was successful: the website received 1.5 million hits in the week of the summit. It had been widely linked to on the Web, and traditional mainstream media picked up its news. Spurred by this success, the idea of Independent Media Centers spread rapidly. Indymedia started to become a network that loosely connected regional activists' struggles throughout the world. By 2002, there were 89 Indymedia websites covering 31 countries. By 2006, there were 150 local centres on six continents (Wolfson 2012: 149).

As a strong global counterpublic, however, Indymedia managed to stay in effect only for a limited period. On a technical level, the sites could not keep up with the pace in fast-developing commercial digital platforms (Giraud 2014). Digital technology, which in the beginning had allowed spontaneous freedom, began to become a problem. On a political level, the tension between democratic decision making and local autonomy reportedly weakened the network (Wolfson 2013). The number of active IMCs declined. By 2014, only 22 functioning centres were left (Giraud 2014: 435). After the peak of its influence, the project's legacy lived on in movements such as 'Occupy'.

This rise and fall of Indymedia has been extensively researched, and not all of the relevant studies can be named here. The following ones have been especially relevant in the course of this argument: Platon and Deuze's (2003) discussion of Indymedia's 'open publishing'; Bruns's (2005: 81–107) detailed analysis of the journalistic elements in its opinionated approach ; Downey and Fenton's (2003) take on its 'counter publicity' and Milioni's (2009) analysis of online counterpublic space; Pickard's (2006) and Wolfson's (2014) specific focus on the technological means of Indymedia; Lovink and Rossiter's (2009) short and Wolfson's (2012) more extended critique on Indymedia's lack of general impact as it failed to reach out beyond its own 'radical ghetto'; and Giraud (2014) who gives an excellent overview over its current status and legacy.

These studies agreed that Indymedia was more than an organisation of anti-globalist activists: it was a counterpublic that evolved through *participatory journalism*. Indymedia was "welcoming people to publish more than just the facts" and "to tell their tale as they witnessed it" (Indymedia 2003: 228). As such, it followed two tracks: as much as publishing the activists' information, its strategy was to be open to everyone. 'Don't Hate the Media. Be the Media! We are everywhere' was the claim stated on @indymedia's Twitter profile. Instead of telling the whole story, corporate media focused on statistics and numbers. The mainstream media's technical truth—'the facts'—concealed what was really going on. Thus, Indymedia was set up *against* the "corporate media's monopoly on information" (Indymedia 2003: 228) and its power.

In their organisation, corporate hierarchies should be replaced by direct democracy and consensus-based decision making. This is what made Indymedia essentially different: it was *open to all*.

In line with the argument of Kluge and Negt, Indymedia understood the close relation between ownership and production of the news as a problem. However, the rise of digital media seemed to offer a way to escape the subjection to ownership: free, open source software enabled Indymedia to produce news differently, based on code that could be freely used, changed, and shared.

> Open source is based on the notion that ideas should be shared without copyright (also known as 'copyleft'), so that all interested parties can work with it and cooperatively improve the product, preferably without commercial interests. Open-source journalism, made possible by online communities, applies these principles to news stories. (Platon & Deuze 2003: 341)

Early on, Indymedia discovered the significance of free software, analysed in detail by Christopher Kelty (2008). In fact, for Indymedia free software would be so important that it became part of Indymedia's so-called Principles of Unity, 10 rules that guide the self-organised, autonomous IMCs across the globe:

> 9. All IMC's [sic] shall be committed to the use of free source code, whenever possible, in order to develop the digital infrastructure, and to increase the independence of the network by not relying on proprietary software. (Indymedia 2015a)

Using open-source technology, Indymedia started to build an 'open publishing platform' (Bruns 2005: 65), with two important outcomes: instead of being subject to ownership, the reporting was owned by the citizen journalists and it was open for everyone to contribute, at least in theory.

However, let us take a step back. If we analyse Indymedia as a counterpublic with regard to its production of its different public truth, there is a range of noticeable aspects. First, Indymedia claims an 'essential otherness' for its media production that is based on digital technology. Its material base—its media—is made of open source technology and not defined by corporate ownership. Its internal organisation is bound to consensus-based decision-making processes and not defined by corporate hierarchies, and this coordination is made possible by using email mailing lists, such as IMC Communication. Finally, its readers are invited to participate directly using its digital open-publishing platform instead of passive reception. In short, its essential otherness is facilitated by a new technological situation, which supports Indymedia's claim to speak the truth, a truth that had been concealed before by the 'fact-focused' reporting of corporate journalism. Here, digital media is not levelling oppositions, on the contrary. Only because of its usage can Indymedia claim to be in possession of a bigger truth. Owing to digital media, Indymedia functioned as an open and thus essentially different media space. However, it would not last long before digital media introduced the flip side of this openness.

Indymedia did not find itself in an exclusive role of crashing the gates of the information hegemony for long. The participatory power potential was also observable in social media (Gillmor 2006). Despite being essentially different from mainstream media in terms of participatory potentials, social media cannot claim the position of essential otherness. While Twitter and other social media platforms have certainly been used to create 'counterpublic moments' (and this chapter will turn to concrete examples further below), their platforms are not. The next section describes social media in general and Twitter in particular against the backdrop of Indymedia in order to make the different ethical logics of both platforms apparent.

On the Post-Dialectical Concept of Parrhesia and the Ambience of Social Media Services

Social media have been the focus of many academic studies. Apparently not very different from Indymedia, their roles as social phenomena have been discussed in great depths: their contribution to political activism, from 'clicktivism' to 'Twitter revolutions', has been both acknowledged and criticised (e.g. Morozov 2009; Fuchs 2012, 2013). Their complex positions as media introducing opportunities for more free speech, but also more surveillance, have been critically analysed (e.g. Chun 2008; Trottier 2012; Tunick 2014). Their effect on journalism and the public sphere has been both hailed and problematised (e.g. Gillmor 2006; Dean 2010).

When comparing Indymedia and social media from an ethical perspective, however, one should notice first that both ground their existence on the same technology. Both can be described using the digital media concept of the 'platform', even though digital platforms are quite individual, as Tarleton Gillespie (2010) has pointed out. All platforms have their specific computational, architectural, and political notions; answer differently to users, advertisers, clients, and shareholders; follow a policy, and have 'edges' from which you can fall off when their algorithms have been programmed to make your content not appear (Gillespie 2010: 59). The counterpublic of Indymedia and the public spaces of social media are certainly very different, even though both platforms are part of the public sphere. Indymedia grounds its otherness on a participatory openness brought about by digital media. As we see below, with social media this openness seems to have a very different effect. So what is their difference in detail?

The first noticeable difference between social media and Indymedia regards the question of ownership. Indymedia builds its claim to speak a different truth on the fact that it is not owned by anyone and therefore has no hidden agenda. Surely, this cannot be claimed in the same way for social media. From Facebook to Google+ to Twitter and others, all successful current social media platforms are owned by thriving new media companies with economic interests, not very different from traditional media. But is its content as controlled as traditional media? The following three aspects show that the answer needs to be a complex, post-dialectical one:

1. Platform ownership: In social media, the link between the platform owner and the content is rather weak. The owners of social media companies do not identify with their content; one could even speak of disinterest. Their approach towards content is purely from a conceptual perspective. In traditional media, this role is somewhat different; Rupert Murdoch is not the only owner known to have strongly influenced his editorial managers (Evans 2009).

2. Labour ownership: On the other hand, no wage ties the producers of content to the platform owner. Here, the aspect of "free labour" that has been problematised elsewhere (and rightly so; see Terranova 2004; Scholz 2012) has the interesting effect of ensuring the freedom of the writer/publisher—a social media contributor does not care if he writes against the interests of a platform owner.
3. Content ownership: Social media users are not responsible for other content on the platform. By contrast, within news organisations, advocated positions can be furiously debated in editorial meetings, as journalists very much care about the content published by their institution. Interestingly, this was also the case with Indymedia (Wolfson 2013).

Compared to traditional media, one can conclude that social media users are somewhat freer in what they publish on a platform, although they remain dependent on the benevolence of platform owners. The platforms' terms of service set the rules, the companies can decide to delete material, redirect information and news feeds to make certain publications less visible, or completely cease to exist. However, their publishing is not as dependent as the traditional journalists is of their employer (Oborne 2015). Here we encounter a post-dialectical condition that seems to confront us frequently in our digital realities. Social media are not an independent platform that marks an essentially different position to the mainstream media; however, that does not mean it can be of no use to promote an oppositional public truth. Being partly independent is a substantial change for its ethical position; however, there is another one: the role their platforms have in creating a public.

Indymedia was created as a platform to actively take part in the public discourse, "a democratic media outlet for the creation of radical, accurate, and passionate telling of truth," as the website states (Indymedia 2015b). Twitter defines itself as a tool to 'to connect with people, express yourself and discover what's happening' (Twitter 2015), not as a tool to address the public sphere. Public speech works in a different way: as Michael Warner (2005: 76) notices, its address needs to be both personal and impersonal. That something is relevant to all of us and of common concern is indeed an essential aspect. Hannah Arendt points out,

> the term "public" signifies two closely interrelated but not altogether identical phenomena: It means, first, that everything that appears in public can be seen and heard by everybody. [. . .] Second, the term "public" signifies the world itself, in so far as it is common to all of us. (Arendt 1958/1998: 50–52)

While many social media postings are openly accessible, they are not "common to all of us" but feature content only interesting for a "personal public" of friends (Schmidt 2014). This form of usage can be described as 'ambient', a term introduced by Alfred Hermida (2014) to indicate how easily available the service is. His notion of ambient also helps us to understand the different potentials: Indymedia is a media outlet with a very specific aim, the 'passionate telling of truth'. Compared to this, one can say that social media are open publishing for their users because what is to be published does not need to be specific or relevant for all: ambient usage. Nevertheless, this ambient usage has a flip side. In the continuous stream of open information, important facts, or voices becomes hard to spot. As equal access causes an erosion of differences, the rise of information abundance creates the danger that reports that are relevant to all of us could be overlooked. Or can the ambient noise be disturbed? How can something appear as 'essentially other' in a post-dialectical environment such as Twitter? To answer this question, we will take a short detour to the research of the late Foucault before turning to the two practical examples that mark the last part of this chapter.

Foucault's interest in the Greek concept of parrhesia evolved from his rereading of ancient philosophy. This means, of course, that his important texts (Foucault 2001, 2010, 2011) were written before social media came into existence. However, Foucault did not study Greek philosophy to explore Greek history. As he states himself, he was not interested in "past people's behavior," "nor ideas" (Foucault 2001: 171). Foucault's interest in parrhesia should be read as a continuation of his analysis of the relation of power and truth to which parrhesia was introducing a new perspective (Ross 2008; see also Bech Dyrberg 2015). Seen from this angle, his research inspires the answer to the main question of this chapter: "How to speak the truth on social media?" Foucault's research on parrhesia has also found its entry into media studies earlier, in the foreword of "Censored 2014" (Huff & Roth 2013). So what does parrhesia stand for?

In the ancient world, parrhesia meant, literally, "to say everything" or "to speak freely" (Foucault 2001: 12). Foucault distinguished between two types of free speech; one seems to be the flip side of the other. Most of the time, "to say everything" had the positive meaning of "to tell the truth" (Foucault 2001: 13) in a specific way. Foucault explains it as follows: A grammar teacher who tells the truth to the children he teaches would not be a "parrhesiastes" (Foucault 2001: 16). But if he or she would tell a friend to act wrongly, thereby risking the friendship, or if he or she would take part in a political debate and risk becoming unpopular because his or her opinions were contrary to the one of the majority, he or she would use parrhesia: "It demands courage to speak the truth in spite of danger. And in its extreme form, telling the truth takes place in the 'game' of life and death" (Foucault 2001: 16). In short, parrhesia in its positive meaning denotes a form of truth gained from speaking out boldly (Foucault 2011: 26). In this case, not very different from today's counterpublics, parrhesia is likely to "provoke negative reactions, irritation, and anger," and might expose its speakers "to vengeance or punishment" (Foucault 2001: 37). I will return to Foucault's interest in the connection between taking a risk and speaking the truth later in the chapter. For now, Foucault describes parrhesia in a way fitting the post-dialectical conditions: next to its positive meaning, there is also a pejorative sense of the word. Here, "to say everything" needs to be read in a very different direction: as the opposite of truth, to speak freely in a way not very far from "chatting" but "saying anything or everything one has in mind without qualifications" (Foucault 2001: 13). Similar to the openness discussed above for social media and Twitter, the parrhesiastic freedom that could be found in Greek democracies gives scope for everyone to express their opinions and say what is

> in this parrhesiastic freedom, understood as freedom of speech given to everybody and anybody (to both good and bad orators, to those pursuing their own interest as well as those devoted to the city), true and false discourses, useful as well as bad or harmful opinions, all become mixed up and intermingled in the fame of democracy. (Foucault 2001: 36)

As this quote shows, Foucault's take on parrhesia is two-sided: parrhesia allows for speaking the truth, but it has a flip side. The concept is not simply useful or dangerous; it is useful and can be dangerous at the same time—which is precisely the case with Twitter's openness. However, if the term 'parrhesia' and the openness of Twitter share a conceptual similarity, can the truth be spoken on Twitter in a way that parrhesia addresses it?

As Foucault points out, truth speaking necessarily involves "an essential position of otherness" (Foucault 2011: 340). Indymedia could claim this otherness: its authentic voice, uncompromised by economic interests, allowed it to reinstate a truth that had been concealed by corporate media. As discussed above, the ownership of social media platforms is different and complex, but surely current social media cannot be understood as independent media. Owned by corporations, their counter-conceptual moment cannot rise from their media base. Thus, their otherness need to work in a different way. Voices on social media cannot claim an essential otherness just because of the media they use, and reinstating a truth that had been concealed before must therefore necessarily feed on something else. How can truth be spoken on social media? Moreover, can it work in a similar way as the speaking freely of parrhesia? In the last part of this chapter, this question will be explored by analysing the Twitter feed of Antonio French and the use of Twitter to cover and comment the events after the killing of Michael Brown in Ferguson, Missouri.

Counterpublics on Social Media: #Ferguson and @AntonioFrench

Antonio French had been tweeting regularly about crime rates and the social issues at stake in the St. Louis, Missouri, suburb of Ferguson, USA, although not a lot. A typical day for the Democratic alderman, re-elected in 2013, would mean five to eight tweets. This would change with the death of Michael Brown, who was killed unarmed by the police in Ferguson on 9 August 2014. Darren Wilson, 28, a white police officer, fatally shot the 18-year-old black teenager. The circumstances of the shooting and the way the incident was handled by the police resulted in protests and civil unrest.

From the start, French covered the vigils and their subsequent escalation on Twitter. His tweets included pictures and videos, he reported what was happening, and right from the start, he covered the investigations and reactions of the police after the killing in real time. While the crime scene was still roped off, he sent a picture of a bulletproof, blast-resistant 'Bearcat" vehicle for armoured rescue with the text "Police have brought out the large gear in #Ferguson" (French 2014, Aug 9, 6:25 p.m.). Shortly after, one could see a picture showing a group of about 60 men and women, some of them with their kids, gathering peacefully on a street: "People marching to the #Ferguson Police Dept headquarters following the killing of a 17-year-old boy" (French 2014, Aug 9, 7:18 p.m.). Then, he reported that the highly charged atmosphere would not calm down: "Ferguson Police have dogs and shotguns. The unarmed crowd is raising their hands. https://vine.co/v/MVTjXW5tXwa" (French 2014, Aug 9, 8:48 p.m.). Later, he would comment on the use of police dogs as "at the very least, culturally and historically insensitive" (French 2014, Aug 9, 10:32 p.m.). In the evening, the police finally left the crime scene, a black neighbourhood: "People are angry, frustrated but peaceful tonight in #Ferguson. The police department's heavy handed approach made things worse. Leaving [of the police] was good" (French 2014, Aug 9, 9.34 p.m.). However, as his Twitter feed documented later on, it would end with the police dispersing the angry but mostly peaceful crowd with tear gas. The protests would turn violent.

Over the next days and weeks, French continued to tweet material about the protests, covering the aggressive actions of the police but also of protestors on Twitter, always filming and calming down people on both sides but also sharing anecdotes of people travelling to St. Louis to join demonstrations. As much as writing his own tweets, he retweeted and distributed the opinions, experiences, and insights of others, the coverage of news organisations, and the appeal of politicians or the police. French made very specific use of social media: he did not publish his account of things, but reported. This one aspect made @AntonioFrench stand out from the Twitter crowd. He followed a journalistic ethic of accuracy, supported his claims with images and videos, and republished a plurality of opinions. At the height of the crisis between 12 and 18 August, he would produce more than 300 tweets each day (Mandaro 2014).

Another important aspect of his usage of social media: @AntonioFrench was a Twitter account one could follow to be *up to date* with the crisis of Ferguson *in real time*. As I have shown elsewhere (Bunz 2014: 90–92), it is important that Twitter embeds temporal and (optionally) spatial specificity in a tweet. This meta-information provides an account of the exact moment a tweet was sent and, sometimes, also about the location it was sent from. A tweet has fixed coordinates in time and space, emphasising the immediacy of information: real time. Real-time coverage, however, creates an interesting aspect of truthfulness: authenticity. An aspect that Wendy Chun has described in more detail:

> If before visual indexicality guaranteed authenticity (a photograph was real because it indexed something out there), now real time does so, for real time points elsewhere—to "real world" events, to the user's captured actions. That is, real time introduces indexicality (. . .), an indexicality felt most acutely in moments of crisis, which enable connection and demand response. (Chun 2011: 96–97)

Antonio French's real-time usage added an original voice that gave first accounts from the ground, and this made him a real alternative to the media crowd that by now had gathered. But it did not make him a voice of 'essential otherness', at least not yet—not until the night of Wednesday, 13 August. On this day, something interesting happened: At 23:57 his wife @senka reported on her Twitter feed that Antonio was arrested for 'unlawful assembly', a tweet reposted 973 times. French was imprisoned while reporting on Twitter what was going on. He was released the day after, but his imprisonment had triggered an interesting development. Overnight, about 30,000 people subscribed to his feed, doubling his follower numbers to more than 60,000 (Hunn 2014). This steep rise in followers cannot be fully explained by the news coverage of his arrest alone, which was reported on local television's *Fox2Now St. Louis* as well as on the webpages of national newspapers like *USA Today* and *The Washington Post*. However, Antonio French had given interviews to *The New York Times* and other media outlets before. The steep growth of his Twitter followers on that specific day while he was in custody indicates that in the moment of this arrest something else was happening. The arrest had turned the alderman from an authentic voice in the suburb into a public persona who practiced parrhesia. It was the moment of his arrest, in which he became a parrhesiastes.

Here, we encounter the side of parrhesia discussed above: free speech "provoke(s) negative reactions, irritation, and anger," and exposes a speaker "to vengeance or punishment" (Foucault 2011: 37). As we have heard, to qualify as parrhesia, opposition must be voiced in the face of danger for the individual, "who, for noble reasons, wishes to oppose the will of the others" (Foucault 2011: 37). In French's case, this danger manifests itself in the moment of his arrest. Of course, Antonio French had been speaking up before in the name of all. Moreover, he was speaking both personally and impersonally as it is essential for addressing a public (Warner 2005: 79). However, the arrest changed his public speaking into a parrhesiatic moment of truth speaking and triggered the rise of an *ad hoc* counterpublic.

Counterpublics on Social Media: #Ferguson and #IfTheyGunnedMeDown

Counterpublic moments on social media, however, are not only reduced to individuals. Much as newspapers, which produce a crowd that "does not have to assemble" (Canetti 1960/2000: 52), hashtags assist users who wish to take part in a wider communicative process. The use of keywords preceded by the hash symbol '#' are commonly used on Twitter to mark a specific topic and make it discoverable to other users. Axel Bruns and Hallvard Moe describe this as an *ad hoc* 'hashtag public', which forms as rapidly as it dissolves (Bruns & Moe 2014). In the context of Ferguson, such an *ad hoc* hashtag public was formed. On 10 August 2014, the day after Michael Brown was killed, the hashtag #IfTheyGunnedMeDown appeared on Twitter. Within 24 hours, over 100,000 people had used it, and for the next days this figure would rise further. Portraits of African Americans using the hashtag started to fill social media channels, and a Tumblr blog aggregating those pictures was created. The double portraits showed different stereotypes of one and the same person side-by-side, one time as a role model and the other time as a criminal, accompanied by the question, "Which photo does the media use if the police shot me down?"

The creation of this hashtag needs to be understood in the context of a series of public violence against African Americans, some of them with fatal outcomes. As a quick look at the early summer of 2014 makes apparent, several encounters of black men with police or security had ended deadly. Trayvon Martin and Eric Garner were killed in encounters with police or security, and soon after Brown's shooting, 12-year-old Tamir Rice would be shot by a police officer while playing with a gun replica in a park. Other forms of police violence against black people had also been reported (Parham 2014). On 20 May 2014, Ersula Ore was stopped when crossing a road and questioned by an Arizona State University police officer, who arrested the professor of the English Department without explanations; the arrest ended in physical conflict. On 23 July, Jahmil-El Cuffee was stopped in Brooklyn by the NYPD for smoking a joint and subdued on suspicion of marijuana possession, after which an officer stomped on the black man's head while he was lying on the ground. On 1 July, a California Highway Patrol officer kneeled on Marlene Pinnock, a 51-year-old black homeless woman, and, as shown in a video, punched her repeatedly in the head. On 26 July, NYPD used what looked like a chokehold on a seven-months-pregnant black woman who had cooked a barbecue on the sidewalk in front of her home; just a few days earlier, Eric Garner had died under similar circumstances, when a police officer put him in a grappling hold. On 27 July, Minneapolis police officers punched black community activist Al Flowers 30 to 40 times during an arrest at his home. Media reported those incidents, but failed to start a public campaign fighting this racist pattern. To negotiate a black public space (Brown

Barkley 1994; Black Public Sphere 1995), African Americans turned to Twitter to create a series of counterpublic moments—#iftheygunnedmedown, #blacklivesmatter, #sobu (state of the black union).

These campaigns started out as a response to the way that mainstream media had portrayed the teenager. While a few media outlets had used a picture of Brown that showed him graduating from high school in cap and gown, the portrait more widely used showed him in sportswear with the fingers of his right hand extended in what some considered a gang sign and others a peace sign. It was from his Facebook page, where it was his profile but not the only picture to be found: on the same page was a photo he took of himself when looking after a younger child. Most news organisations, however, chose to depict the young black man stereotypically as a rapper and bad boy, perpetuating the underlying suggestion that black people in conflict with the police had asked for it. How Brown was depicted in the news, however, illustrates that not only the police tended to view black people with suspicion, but also the media. Troubled by this development in the public sphere, defence lawyer C. J. Lawrence turned to Twitter to express his concern and posted: "Yes let's do that: Which photo does the media use if the police shot me down? #IfTheyGunnedMeDown" (Lawrence 2014, Aug 10, 12.34 p.m.). In the tweet, he embedded two pictures of himself. One shows the lawyer alongside guest speaker Bill Clinton at his university graduation, the other from Halloween, where he wore the costume of a rapper. Posting those pictures, he started a campaign that brought an *ad hoc* 'hashtag public' together to show a suppressed public truth.

In comparison with the Antonio French's case, the danger and courage necessary to bring forth the parrhesiatic moment of creating a different public truth functions slightly different. While the courage of Antonio French was brought forth when he was threatened individually, the collective courage that is asked from every black person in the U.S. became apparent in those flip-side-pictures. In the public sphere of the U.S., being black was stereotyped in a dangerous and even fatal way. The stereotype raised suspicion against blacks, and this suspicion had an effect: it perversely turned attacking a black person into self-defence. It turned the victim into an attacker and the police attacker into a victim. Here, the violence a post-dialectical concept can unfold becomes apparent, which shows that one needs to be aware of its perfidious logic.

Conclusion

Social media have often been suspected of depoliticisation. By analysing two cases in which social media has been used to create a counterpublic moment that interfered in the public discourse, however, this inquiry has found that they have political potential. Surely, they are not political, per se. However, their ambient usage creates a broad public. Moreover, the access to this social media public is an essential part for a counterpublic claiming a different truth. In other words, when parrhesia happens and a different truth is told, social media helps to establish and broaden its force. While social media are not per se counterpublic, they are essentially assisting in creating a counterpublic moment and thus are of political usage. If that is the case, however, one needs to think about the following: As our discursive conditions, show up differently in the context of digital media—post-dialectical—suspecting social media of depoliticisation might itself depoliticise them.

References

ABC News (2014, Dec 7) "'This Week' Transcript: Mayor Bill de Blasio". http://abcnews.go.com/ThisWeek/week-transcript-mayor-bill-de-blasio/story?id=27369383&singlePage=true.

Allan, S., and Thorsen, E. (eds.) (2009) *Citizen Journalism: Global Perspectives* (Vol. 1), New York: Peter Lang.

Andersen, N. Åkerstrøm (2009) *Power at Play: The Relationships Between Play, Work and Governance*, Basingstoke: Palgrave Macmillan.

Arendt, Hannah ([1958] 1998) *The Human Condition*, Chicago, University of Chicago.

Bech Dyrberg, T. (2015) *Foucault on the Politics of Parrhesia*, Basingstoke: Palgrave Macmillan.

Benhabib, S. (1992) "Models of Public Space," in Calhoun, C. (ed.), *Habermas and the Public Sphere*, Cambridge, MA: MIT Press, pp. 73–98.

Black Public Sphere (ed.) (1995) *The Black Public Sphere*, Chicago: University of Chicago Press.

Brown Barkley, E. (1994) "Negotiating and Transforming the Public Sphere: African American Political Life in the Transition from Slavery to Freedom," *Public Culture* 7.1, pp. 107–146.

Bruns, A. (2005) *Gatewatching: Collaborative Online News Production.* New York: Peter Lang.

Bruns, A., and Moe, H. (2014) "Structural Layers of Communication on Twitter," in K. Weller, A. Bruns et al. (eds.), *Twitter and Society.* New York: Peter Lang, pp. 15–28.

Bunz, M. (2014). *The Silent Revolution: How Digitalization Transforms Knowledge, Work, Journalism and Politics Without Making Too Much Noise.* Basingstoke: Palgrave Macmillan.

Canetti, E. ([1960] 2000) *Crowds and Power*, London: Phoenix Press.

Chun, W.H.K. (2008). *Control and Freedom: Power and Paranoia in the Age of Fiber Optics*, Cambridge, MA: MIT Press.

Chun, W.H.K. (2011) "Crisis, Crisis, Crisis, or Sovereignty and Networks," *Theory, Culture & Society*, 28(6), pp. 91–112.

Dean J. (2010) *Blog Theory*, Cambridge, UK: Polity.

Diederichsen, D. and Franke, A. (2013) *The Whole Earth: California and the Disappearance of the Outside*, Berlin: Sternberg Press.

Downey, J., and Fenton, N. (2003) "New Media, Counter Publicity and the Public Sphere," *New Media & Society*, 5(2), pp. 185–202.

Evans, H. (2009) *My Paper Chase: True Stories of Vanished Times.* London: Abacus.

Foucault, M. (1995) *Discipline and Punish: The Birth of the Prison*, New York: Vintage.

Foucault, M. (2001) *Fearless Speech*, Los Angeles: Semiotext(e).

Foucault, M. (2010) *The Government of Self and Others: Lectures at the College de France, 1982–1983* (Vol. 7), Basingstoke: Palgrave Macmillan.

Foucault, M. (2011) *The Courage of Truth (The Government of Self and Others II). Lectures at the Collège de France, 1983–1984.* Basingstoke: Palgrave Macmillan.

Fraser, N. (1990) "Rethinking the Public Sphere: A Contribution to the Critique of Actually Existing Democracy," *Social Text* (Duke University Press), 25(26), pp. 56–80.

French, A. [AntonioFrench] (2014, Aug 9, 6:25 p.m.) *Police have brought out the large gear in #Ferguson.* [Tweet, photograph] https://twitter.com/AntonioFrench/status/498248648699150336.

French, A. [AntonioFrench] (2014, Aug 9, 7:18 p.m.) *People marching to the #Ferguson Police Dept headquarters following the killing of a 17-year-old boy.* [Tweet, photograph] https://twitter.com/AntonioFrench/status/498262106937237504.

French, A. [AntonioFrench] (2014, Aug 9, 8:48 p.m.) *Ferguson Police have dogs and shotguns. The unarmed crowd is raising their hands.* [Tweet, video] https://twitter.com/AntonioFrench/status/498283364672348160.

French, A. [AntonioFrench] (2014, Aug 9, 9:34 p.m.) *People are angry, frustrated but peaceful tonight in #Ferguson. The police dept's heavy handed approach made things worse. Leaving was good.* [Tweet] https://twitter.com/AntonioFrench/status/498296205777326080.

French, A. [AntonioFrench] (2014, Aug 9, 10:32 p.m.) *The presence of police dogs in #Ferguson is, at the very least, culturally and historically insensitive.* [Tweet] https://twitter.com/AntonioFrench/status/498492003903356928.

French, A. (2014, August 16, 2014–10:54 a.m.) [Twitter verification] https://twitter.com/Antonio French/status/500671515558309888.

Fuchs, C. (2012, Oct) *"Behind the news:* Social Media, Riots, and Revolutions," *Capital & Class,* 36(3), pp. 383–391.

Fuchs, C. (2013). *Social Media: A Critical Introduction,* London: Sage.

Fuchs, M., Fizek, S., Ruffino, P., and Schrape, N. (eds.) (2014) *Rethinking Gamification.* Lüneburg: meson press by Hybrid Publishing Lab.

Gillespie, T. (2010) "The Politics of 'Platforms'," *New Media & Society, 12*(3), pp. 347–364.

Gillmor, D. (2006) *We the Media: Grassroots Journalism by the People, for the People.* Sebastopol, CA: O'Reilly Media.

Giraud, E. (2014) "Has Radical Participatory Online Media Really 'Failed'? Indymedia and Its Legacies," *Convergence: The International Journal of Research into New Media Technologies,* 20(11), pp. 419–437.

Habermas, J. (1991 [1962]). *The Structural Transformation of the Public Sphere: An Inquiry into a Category of Bourgeois Society.* Cambridge, MA: MIT Press.

Habermas, J. (1974 [1964]): "The Public Sphere: An Encyclopedia Article (1964)," *New German Critique,* 3, pp. 49–55.

Hermida, A. (2014) "Twitter as an Ambient News Network," in K. Weller, A. Bruns, et al. (eds.), *Twitter and Society,* New York: Peter Lang, pp. 359–372.

Huff, M., and Roth, A. L (2013) *Censored 2014: Fearless Speech in Fateful Times. The Top Censored Stories and Media Analysis of 2012–13,* New York: Seven Stories Press.

Hunn, D. (2014, Aug 14) "Frontline Activism Boosts Antonio French's Profile," *St. Louis Post-Dispatch,* http://www.stltoday.com/news/local/govt-and-politics/frontline-activism-boosts-antonio-french-s-profile/article_eb47c8cc-d451–50dd-9bf2–4801769c45b7.html.

Indymedia (2003) "Don't Hate the Media, Be the Media!" in Credland, T., Chesters, G., Jordan, J., Ainger, K. (eds.), *We Are Everywhere: The Irresistible Rise of Global Anti-Capitalism,* London: Verso.

Indymedia (2015a) "Documentation Project," retrieved from http://docs.indymedia.org/view/Global/PrinciplesOfUnity.

Indymedia (2015b) "Independent Media Center," retrieved from http://www.indymedia.org/.

Jarvis, J. (2011) *Public Parts: How Sharing in the Digital Age Improves the Way We Work and Live,* New York: Simon and Schuster.

Kelty, C. M. (2008) *Two Bits: The Cultural Significance of Free Software,* Durham: Duke University Press.

Lawrence, C. J. (2014, Aug 10, 12:34 p.m.) "Yes let's do that: Which photo does the media use if the police shot me down? #IfTheyGunnedMeDown". [Tweet] https://twitter.com/CJ_musick_lawya/status/498537843170353152).

Lovink G., and Rossiter N. (2009) "The Digital Given: 10 web 2.0 Theses," *Fibreculture,* 14, http://fourteen.fibreculturejournal.org/fcj-096-the-digital-given-10-web-2-0-theses.

Mandaro, L. (2014, Aug 26) "300 Ferguson tweets: A day's work for Antonio French," *USA Today,* http://www.usatoday.com/story/news/nation-now/2014/08/25/antonio-french-twitter-ferguson/14457633/.

Milioni, D. L. (2009) "Probing the Online Counterpublic Sphere: The Case of Indymedia Athens," *Media, Culture & Society, 31*(3), pp. 409–431.

Morozov, E. (2009) "Iran: Downside to the Twitter Revolution," *Dissent,* 56(4), pp. 10–14.

Negt, O., and Kluge, A. ([1972] 1993) *Public Sphere and Experience: Toward an Analysis of the Bourgeois and Proletarian Public Sphere.* Minneapolis: University of Minnesota Press.

Oborne, P. (2015, Feb 17) "Why I have resigned from the Telegraph," *openDemocracy,* http://www.opendemocracy.net/ourkingdom/peter-oborne/why-i-have-resigned-from-telegraph.

Papacharissi, Z. (2010) *A Private Sphere: Democracy in a Digital Age,* Cambridge: Polity.

Parham, J. (2014, Aug 4) "It Is Time We Treat Police Brutality as a National Crisis," http://gawker.com/it-is-time-we-treat-police-brutality-as-a-national-cris-1613935053.

Parikka, J. (2014) *The Anthrobscene*, Minneapolis: University of Minnesota Press.

Pickard, V. W. (2006) "Assessing the Radical Democracy of Indymedia: Discursive, Technical, and Institutional Constructions," *Critical Studies in Media Communication*, 23(01), pp. 19–38.

Platon, S., and Deuze, M. (2003) "Indymedia Journalism: A Radical Way of Making, Selecting and Sharing News?, *Journalism*, 4(3), pp. 336–355.

Ross, A. (2008). "Why is 'Speaking the Truth' Fearless? 'Danger' and 'Truth' in Foucault's Discussion of Parrhesia," *Parrhesia: A Journal of Critical Philosophy*, 4, pp. 62–75.

Rusbridger, A. (2012, Feb 29.) 'Journalists are not the only experts in the world'—video. *The Guardian*, http://www.theguardian.com/media/video/2012/feb/29/alan-rusbridger-open-journalism-guardian-video.xxx.

Schmidt, Jan-Hinrik (2014) "Twitter and the Rise of Personal Publics" in K. Weller, A. Bruns, et al. (eds.), *Twitter and Society*, New York: Peter Lang, pp. 3–14.

Scholz, T. (ed.) (2012) *Digital Labor: The Internet as Playground and Factory*, Oxford: Routledge.

Shirky, Clay (2008) *Here Comes Everybody: The Power of Organizing Without Organizations*, London: Penguin, 2008.

Terranova, T. (2004) *Network Culture: Politics for the Information Age*, London: Pluto Press.

Trottier, D. (2012) *Social Media as Surveillance*, Farnham: Ashgate.

Tunick, M. (2014) *Balancing Privacy and Free Speech: Unwanted Attention in the Age of Social Media*, Oxford: Routledge.

Twitter (2015) "About," https://about.twitter.com/.

Warner M. (2005) *Publics and Counterpublics*, New York: Zone Books.

Wolfson, T. (2012) "From the Zapatistas to Indymedia: Dialectics and Orthodoxy in Contemporary Social Movements," *Communication, Culture & Critique* 5, pp. 149–170.

Wolfson, T. (2013) "Democracy or Autonomy? Indymedia and the Contradictions of Global Social Movement Networks," *Global Networks*, 13(3), pp. 410–424.

Wolfson, T. (2014) *Digital Rebellion: The Birth of the Cyber Left*, Champaign: University of Illinois Press.

Part II

POLITICAL MOVEMENTS

10

ALL POLITICS IS LOCAL

Anonymous and the Steubenville/ Maryville Rape Cases

Christian Christensen

Introduction

The phrase 'all politics is local' is attributed to the former United States Speaker of the House of Representatives, Democrat Tip O'Neill. What O'Neill was attempting to convey was that while the popular understanding of politics is one in which politicians deal with large-scale, grand ideas, what voters *actually* care about is what happens to them at the everyday, local level. In other words, if politicians want to appeal to their base, and thus get votes and remain in office, they must both understand these local concerns, and act on them. In addition to contextualising politics, the phrase is also a reminder to researchers that while large-scale national and global political events (such as wars or elections) are important and worthy of attention, we should not forget how events at the lesser-covered regional or local levels usually encapsulate fundamental social and political issues. In turn, how these regional and/or local events are, for example, covered in the news media or impacted by social media use is also becomes extremely important.

An excellent example of the local as a microcosm of the global was the 2014 shooting death of the African American teenager Michael Brown by the white police officer Darren Wilson in Ferguson, Missouri, and the importance of social media (particularly Twitter) in raising national awareness in the U.S. about the case. The shooting death was a 'local' event, yet after a relative paucity of national coverage, intense social media activity by a number of dedicated activists and local citizens turned Ferguson into a large-scale story. Once the story reached national attention, what we saw was that the shooting of one teenager by police on the outskirts of St. Louis resonated with citizens throughout the U.S., precisely because it involved the widely recognised themes of racism, police violence, local governance, judicial impartiality, and media underperformance. In other words, it was about politics writ large. Clearly, for a local story to gain traction on social media, it must involve themes or tropes that 'click' with users beyond a small geographical zone, and the killing of Michael Brown in Ferguson was just such a case.

Taking the case of Ferguson—and the relationship between the local, social media and the national—as a conceptual point of departure, I would like to use other 'local' cases from the U.S. as a springboard for discussing the relationship between social media and politics using the involvement of the online 'hacktivist' group Anonymous in two particular events: rapes that took place in the small towns of Steubenville, Ohio, in 2012, and Maryville, Missouri, in 2013. Of course, it is important to note that this chapter deals with two specific Anonymous actions that took place in the U.S. Thus, the discussion and analysis presented here should be understood as being within the context of U.S. media and politics (although the implications outside of the U.S. will be addressed in the concluding section). With this caveat in mind, I would like to consider how scholars have conceived of Anonymous as a political entity and also to address how localised activist engagements in the U.S. on issues as specific as individual rape cases spill over into activism and information about local politics and power that has relevance well beyond the city limits of the small towns at the centre of the events. Rather than a detailed empirical analysis, this chapter is intended as a springboard for considering the actions of Anonymous in these cases within the context of social media and (local) politics.

Before delving into the specifics of the two cases, I would like to begin with a brief description of Anonymous, followed by an outline of some of relevant writing on the politics and political actions of the loosely coordinated group.

Anonymous

Anonymous is a group that many have heard of, but few can actually define or explain. An exception to this is anthropologist Gabriella Coleman (2011, 2013a, 2013b, 2014), who has been seminal in providing researchers with a clearer understanding of the group and its origins. Anonymous, according to Coleman, is usually misunderstood:

> Relying on a fairly predictable script, most commentators—including journalists and academics alike—usually introduce Anonymous as an evasive and shadowy group of hackers. This description distorts sociological reality. Although Anonymous is certainly a home to hackers, a great many Anons are neither hackers nor difficult to find. (Coleman 2013a: 12)

There are no technical barriers to participation in Anonymous, and while it is best known as a 'hacking' collective, Coleman is quick to note that the majority of 'Anons' are, in fact, not hackers but rather 'geeks' who possess a variety of skills. Importantly, "no single group or individual can dictate the use of the name or iconography of Anonymous, much less claim legal ownership of its names, icons and actions" (Coleman 2013a: 12), and while Anonymous actions often appear to be random, they are usually instigated in response to specific events. In terms of actions, the group has a variety of tools at its disposal:

> Anonymous tactics range from simple DDoS and botnet attacks["Distributed Denial of Service" attacks where systems are overloaded and shut down], website defacement, and social engineering (tricking people into revealing security details), through to sophisticated hacking, locating, and exploiting security vulnerabilities and breaching large organizations' information technology

networks. Tactics are commonly mixed within particular "Ops." DDoS attacks work on scale: large numbers of people (requiring few technical skills) use simple software to overwhelm a site with traffic. (Goode 2015: 77)

The 'birth' of Anonymous is usually traced back to a website called 4chan (created in 2003) and a specific section of 4chan known as the '/b/board'. As Norton (2011: paras. 33–34) notes:

At some moment lost in its unrecorded history, /b/ and Anonymous reached an inflection point, and the id spilled into the rest of the net in the form of "ultra-coordinated motherfuckery," as one anon described it to Coleman. This was the ability to use the technological tools of social coordination so quickly and well that anons working together could collectively attack targets for any perceived slight, or just for fun, without those targets ever having a chance to see it coming or defend themselves. These came to be called "raids."

These early years, from 2003 until around 2008, were marked be a heavy dose of 'trolling' on 4chan, which Coleman (2011: para. 5) described as a combination of, for example, "telephone pranking, having many unpaid pizzas sent to the target's home, DDoSing, and most especially, splattering personal information, preferably humiliating, all over the Internet". According to Coleman (2011), a shift came in 2008 when Anonymous began a trolling campaign against the Church of Scientology, which was followed by a split within the group between those more interested in trolling for entertainment and those who wished to pursue more clearly defined political goals.

A great deal of the Anonymous focus upon Scientology remained until 2010, at which point the group began to diversify. In 2010, Anonymous ran 'Operation Payback', which began by targeting the Motion Picture Association of America (MPAA) but evolved to also target the websites of companies such as PayPal, MasterCard and Amazon: organisations that had withdrawn their services to WikiLeaks following their release of a number of U.S. diplomatic cables and what was understood to be U.S. state pressure. In 2011, Anonymous ran 'OpTunisia', supporting anti-government protesters in that country by, for example, providing 'care packets' containing information of how to avoid government surveillance, as well as helping to distribute videos demonstrating state violence. As Coleman (2011: para. 15) wrote, while previous actions usually focused on Internet-based issues (such as censorship), the OpTunisia operation, "moved squarely into human rights activism as it converged with an existing social movement (para. 16". The movement toward more 'traditional' activism continued after Tunisia, as Anonymous "also led attacks in Italy as Silvio Berlusconi faced accusations of sleeping with an underage prostitute, and in Wisconsin to protest a law that seeks to shred collective bargaining rights of public unions" (Coleman 2011: para. 16).

The 'Politics' of Anonymous

The post-2008 shift of certain members of Anonymous toward more overt political action should lead us to consider the relationship between them and what we might

CHRISTIAN CHRISTENSEN

define as mainstream politics—in addition to considering their role as activists, hack-tivists, vigilantes, and bandits. For Woods (2014), Anonymous is an important subject for analysis as it demonstrates, "that the Internet is not just a tool for communication, it is increasingly a location of conflict, contestation, and community formation" (Woods 2014: 345). While few would argue with the contention that the group is provocative, exactly *how* we should consider or define Anonymous (structurally and politically) is a more open question. Wong and Brown (2013: 1015) offer a good starting point when they ask of groups such as Anonymous and WikiLeaks:

> Are they freedom-of-speech fighters or tech-savvy terrorists? Non-governmental organizations (NGOs), social movements, or a new international criminal? We argue that WikiLeaks, Anonymous, and other groups engaged in what has become described as hacktivism are "extraordinary bandits" (e-bandits), adapting Hobsbawm's iconic "social bandit" for the challenges of politics in the digital age.

Wong and Brown (2013: 1021) contend that groups such as Anonymous are contem-porary versions of the feudal bandits who have "occupied the space between lords, states, and the peasantry throughout history by challenging the status quo". Exam-ples of such bandits include 'noble robbers', individuals who (1) rectify injustice by taking from the rich and giving to the poor, (2) feel they are in the right as they are seeking a rebalance of justice though honourable tactics, and (3) emerge from (and have the support of) a clearly-defined community (Wong and Brown 2013: 1021). This Robin Hood-esque image is one echoed in the recent work of Coleman (2013a, 2014), who coined the term 'weapons of the geek' to describe the actions of Anons, in deliberate contrast to the term 'weapons of the weak' created by James Scott (1985) to describe "the unique, clandestine nature of peasant politics" (Coleman 2013a: 14). For Coleman, while peasant dissent was marked by the actions of "disen-franchised, economically marginalized populations" engaging in "small-scale illicit acts," the actions of groups such as Anonymous, "is a modality of politics exercised by a class of privileged and visible actors who often lie at the centre of economic life" (Coleman, 2013a: 14).

So, can we then speak of an Anonymous 'politics'? Given the nebulous nature of the group, it would appear to be difficult. Goode (2015) defines the Anonymous roots as 'prepolitical' and as a sub-culture dedicated primarily to amusement and fun (Goode makes sure to note, however, that this was *prepolitical* rather than *apolitical*). As noted, after the period between 2003 and 2008, the group took a more serious turn, with actions targeting larger corporate and state actors. In particular, the support given by Anonymous to WikiLeaks in 2010 was a clue as to the political/ideological leanings of the group:

> Since Anonymous actively supports Wikileaks [sic], one can presume that their ideologies overlap. Anonymous' ideology must include some form of the radi-cal transparency for institutions paired with strong privacy for individuals that is at the core of Wikileaks' ideology. The radical transparency advocated by Wikileaks is conceptually not far from the mantra of the hacker ethic: 'Infor-mation wants to be Free'. (Serracino-Inglott 2013: 224)

This alliance with WikiLeaks has led many to assume that Anonymous are 'cyberlibertarians': a term that "reflects the prevailing philosophy of the hackers and technology entrepreneurs responsible for developing the internet and for defending it from government regulation" (Goode 2015: 77). For cyberlibertarians, their faith in technology is matched by their mistrust of state power and regulation. In addition—and linking them to conventional libertarians—there is also a belief in the importance and utility of the free market. For Goode, however, this is a simplistic understanding of the group that "could lead to a view that Anonymous has little to contribute and may even be anathema to a progressive politics founded on positive as well as negative freedoms" (Goode 2015: 83). Goode accepts that libertarian values may be the "most pronounced" within Anonymous, but notes that "the contradictory nature of the Anonymous ethos also signals space for a progressive political agenda" (Goode 2015: 84).

The deep mistrust of the state suggested by the cyberlibertarian label, in addition to the chaotic, lawless imagery evoked by notions such as 'bandits' or 'vigilantes', combines to suggest an organisation committed to working outside of the boundaries of the state. On this issue Serracino-Inglott (2013: 222) admits that "Anons are general antagonistic to states" and that the organisation "is not willingly accountable to any state". In addition, Anons are more than willing to break laws they consider to be barriers to the service of justice. However, "as Anonymous becomes more clearly political it is condemning the existing apparatus of state as defective much more explicitly" (Serracino-Inglott (2013: 222), and, in this condemnation, while making their displeasure at the failure of the state clear, Anons do not demand 'street justice' but rather 'effective state-served justice'. Thus, "not all Anons are opposed to the idea of the state *per se*. So, one must not fall into the temptation of declaring the state passe, an irrelevant concept to be overcome in the information age" (Serracino-Inglott (2013: 222). Thus, when considering actions such as those taken on/in Steubenville and Maryville, it is worth remembering that this is an organisation advocating the use of formalised political structures to rectify what it considers to be injustice. In this way, and perhaps at odds with popular perceptions of the group, there are "significant indications that the ideological frameworks of Anonymous and the citizens of liberal democracies are on converging paths of evolution" (Serracino-Inglott 2013: 238). In order to place some flesh on these conceptual bones, I would now like to discuss the two cases, and the Anonymous involvement.

The Steubenville Rape Case

On the night of 11 August 2012, in the town of Steubenville, Ohio, a 16-year-old high school girl was sexually assaulted by members of the local high school football team. The girl, who had attended a series of parties and had been drinking heavily, was incapacitated and/or unconscious at the time of the assaults. The accused (and a number of witnesses) took pictures and videos on their mobile phones before, during, and after the assaults, and these images were spread via text message, Facebook, Twitter, YouTube, and Instagram. The most damning evidence was a 12-minute video posted to YouTube showing another student (not one of the convicted rapists) discussing the girl and what had been done to her. In March of 2013, two students (who were aged 16 at the time of the crime) were convicted of the rape of a minor, while three other students were found guilty of obstructing the rape investigation.

This simple synopsis of the case hides a much more complicated and political story. First, while the crime was in no way unusual, the capture of video and still images by those convicted, and their spread via social media, marked (at least in popular terms) a new phase in the collection of evidence. Thus, in the Steubenville case, technology and social media played a central role. As reported in the *New York Times* in late 2012 (Macur & Schweber 2012: para. 10):

> It is a sexual assault accusation in the age of social media, when teenagers are capturing much of their lives on their camera phones—even repugnant, possibly criminal behavior, as they did in Steubenville in August—and then posting it on the Web, like a graphic, public diary.

The second significant aspect is the role that politics played in the way in which the case was handled by local authorities. Interestingly, even though the story was covered in September of 2012 by the Cleveland Plain Dealer (Dissell 2012), it was not until the *New York Times* article, cited above, that a sea-change took place in how the case was handled in Steubenville: a change that would have a profound impact upon local politics. The change was not due to simple mainstream media attention but to the involvement of Anonymous.

In the aftermath of the *New York Times* article, on 24 December 2012, an offshoot of Anonymous, known as KnightSec, hacked the website of the Steubenville high school football team (www.rollredroll.com) and posted a video in which a masked Anon (with a signature, digitally simulated voice) issued a warning that unless all involved in the rape came out with a public apology by 1 January 2013, the group would release personal information on members of the football team, the coaching staff, and their families (including addresses and Social Security Numbers). This was the start of what came to be called #OpRollRedRoll (named after the nickname of the Steubenville football team). When no confessions or apologies emerged, KnightSec followed through with their threat, releasing an incriminating video showing Steubenville students who dubbed themselves the 'rape crew' discussing the assault. In addition to the video and the release of names and personal information, Anonymous (via social media) promoted a series of 'Occupy Steubenville' protests in late 2012 and early 2013 (Abad-Santos 2013a, 2013b). Attendance at these protests was lower than hoped, but they garnered media attention, and the embattled Sherriff of Steubenville attended a 5 January 2013 protest and fielded a small number of questions from attendees (Simpson 2013).

The Maryville Rape Case

In 2013 a strikingly similar case to the one in Steubenville took place in the small town of Maryville, Missouri. In January of 2012, a 14-year-old girl left her house at 1 a.m. (together with a 13-year-old friend) to meet with a 17-year-old Maryville high school student with whom she had been texting. The girls had been drinking, and they continued to drink after they met up with the older boys. After passing out from the alcohol, the victim was driven home in the early hours of the morning, where her mother would find her, three hours later, scratching at the front door in sub-freezing temperatures, wearing nothing but a T-shirt and sweatpants. The victim had no memory of what had happened, and her mother immediately contacted the police. Upon testing, it was shown that, seven hours after she had stopped drinking, the girl still had a blood-alcohol level of 0.13 (Bazelon 2013; Elgion 2013).

While there were striking overlaps with the Steubenville case, one key difference was that the accused 17-year-old never denied having had sex with the victim, nor did he deny that he left her outside of her house in sub-freezing temperatures. The accused claimed that while the victim had been drinking, and that he had supplied alcohol, she was coherent at the time had given consent for sex to take place. The accused was immediately arrested and charged with sexual assault and endangerment of a child. Despite the evidence, and the confession of the accused, two weeks later the charges were dropped. A virulent online hate campaign started against the victim and her family who were subsequently forced to leave Maryville. Six months later, in April of 2013, the victim's house was burnt to the ground in what were described as 'suspicious' circumstances.

It was at this point that Anonymous took up the story. After the *Kansas City Star* ran a piece in October of 2013 questioning the handling of the case (Arnett 2013), Anonymous members released the following statement on #OpMaryville:

Greetings, World

We are #OpMaryville

Two young girls have been raped in the town of Maryville, Missouri. Another high school football star, the grandson of a Missouri state official, has walked free. The people of Maryville turned their backs on these victims and one family has been forced to flee the town. Their house was later burned to the ground.

(...)

We demand an immediate investigation into the handling by local authorities of Daisy's case. Why was a suspect, who confessed to a crime, released with no charges? How was video and medical evidence not enough to put one of these football players inside a court room? What is the connection of these prosecutors, if any, to Rep. Rex Barnett? Most of all, We are wondering, how do the residents of Maryville sleep at night? (Anonymous: http://pastebin.com/3rq0ZSrY)

The tactic employed by Anonymous was a 'Twitterstorm' scheduled to start at precisely 5 p.m. on October 15, 2013:

#OpMaryville Twitterstorm Package!

OBJECTIVE:

Raise Awareness in social media, put pressure on Attorney General Chris Koster to launch an investigation into the lack of charges against Matthew Barnett (despite a confession and evidence of his guilt), and promote that on Tuesday, October 22, 2013, at 10:00am we will meet at the Nodaway County Courthouse in Maryville, Missouri with daisies in our hands for a peaceful protest in support of Daisy Coleman.

Date & Time: Tuesday, October 15, 2013, 5PM EST / 2PM PST

INSTRUCTIONS:

Copy + Paste these tweets. Do not retweet, the hashtag will not trend.

If you are writing your own tweets, make sure to include the #opMaryville hashtag!

You do not need to post more than once every five minutes, especially to avoid suspension of your account. (Anonymous: http://pastebin.com/G0ahgG6Q)

While impossible to gauge the specific impact that the involvement of Anonymous had upon the police and the judicial system in Maryville, the case was almost immediately re-opened. After further investigation, no rape charges were filed, and in January of 2014 (two years after the event), the accused pled guilty to a single count of child endangerment (a misdemeanour charge) and was sentenced to two years' probation and a suspended four-month jail term (Dockterman 2014).

The response of the part of Anonymous to reports of two sexual assaults quickly evolved into interesting case studies on the interaction between social media, activism, and politics. As noted in multiple newspaper stories on the Steubenville and Maryville cases, social media played a central role in both cases, not only because these platforms were used by Anonymous, but also because a great deal of the evidence surrounding both assaults was captured on cell phones and distributed via social media. The presence of this material on social media, in turn, supplied Anonymous with the opportunity to attempt to obtain these images, videos and texts (through targeted hacks) and then use those same platforms to expose those they considered to be guilty (or guilty of the obstruction of justice).

This social media activism also linked both sexual assaults to local politics. In the case of Steubenville, there were widespread accusations that the two high school football players were given preferential treatment, and the case downplayed, as a result of a close relationship between local law enforcement, politicians, legal structures, and the football team. In the case of Maryville, the political connections were even closer, as one of the accused was the grandson of a former four-term member of the Missouri House of Representatives (and 32-year member of the Missouri Highway patrol), and there were concrete accusations that strings had been pulled in order to have the initial charges dropped (Arnett 2013).

The rapid increase in the visibility of the two cases following the involvement of Anonymous, the release of the names and personal information of several local students and calls to action including the Maryville 'Twitterstorm' and the three 'Occupy Steubenville' protests (also coordinated online and via social media) also focused a considerable degree of attention upon the (supposedly) politically incestuous nature of small-town politics. Yet, media coverage of the case, while extensive, was far from uniform in support of what Anonymous (and the blogger Alexandria Goddard) had done, including their use of social media for activism. In a number of high-profile articles in the *New Yorker, The Guardian, Washington Post* and *Jezebel*, the 'vigilantism' of Anonymous, while generally accepted to have been in good faith, not only misrepresented the towns of Steubenville and Maryville (and overstated the level of political nepotism) but also inflicted personal damage by 'outing' individuals who were not involved in the attacks, as well as (in the case of Steubenville) spreading potentially traumatic images of the victim across social media (Levy 2013; Filipovic 2013; Baker 2013; Reese 2013).

Discussion

In discussing the role of social media in contemporary politics, how should we then consider groups such as Anonymous and actions such as those that took place in Ohio and Missouri? As discussed above, one of the components of both the Steubenville and Maryville cases that enabled Anonymous to gain a foothold was the fact that much of the material was digital—and, thus, potentially 'hackable.' Coleman (2013a: 15) noted the relationship between this type of environment and hacktivism:

> Since Anonymous' forte is publicity, it can create a PR nightmare for its targets. This reflects an important aspect of the contemporary media and information environment: the reputations of institutions or individuals are now more vulnerable to credible critiques and leaks, as well as false smear campaigns. Even if information is not featured on the evening news, it may still spread like wildfire if enough individuals circulate it on social media.

The notion of individual and institutional vulnerability in conjunction with the possibility of both credible and/or slanderous critique is critical. The use of social media for the purposes of information and disinformation by political activists is a matter of fact, but what separates Anonymous from other more traditional activist groups is that, via hacking, they also tap into a well of information that is hidden from the general public. Such information can be both illuminating and problematic. The release of the infamous Steubenville video showing a student discussing the alleged sexual assault was powerful (and the views on YouTube have reached the millions), yet Anonymous have also released the names, addresses, and personal details of individuals who have been shown to be innocent of any crimes. Coleman's second point—about the ability to bypass mainstream media—is also important, but it also brings us back to the issue of the potential dangers of the spread of de-contextualised, raw information.

What we saw in in both Steubenville and Maryville was how attacks upon individuals morphed into attacks on broader political institutions. Both the local police and judicial systems in the United States are highly politicised: County Sheriffs, for example, are elected, as are judges and, in some states, District Attorneys. The intertwining of social and political issues meant that Steubenville and Maryville were as much about politics as they were about sexual assault, in much the same way that Ferguson was just as much about local and state politics as it was about police violence.

As their combination of online and offline activism illustrated, conceptions of Anonymous as a 'online-only' group are misplaced. During the cases discussed in this chapter, their actions followed the definition of 'hacktivism' discussed by Li (2013: 305):

> Although "hacktivism" is a loaded term that elicits mixed responses to its legitimacy, hacktivism can be broadly defined as the "combination of grassroots political protest with computer hacking" through the "nonviolent use of illegal or legally ambiguous digital tools [to pursue] political ends."

Linking this to Serracino-Inglott's (2013) discussion on the relationship between Anonymous and the state, it is worth asking not only what type of 'political ends' Anonymous seek as a result of their actions, but also the tools used to achieve those ends. Looking at the Steubenville and Maryville cases, we can see varying levels of trust in the efficacy of the state on the part of Anonymous, as well as varying forms of action.

In what many (at least in popular terms) would consider to be the quintessential Anonymous *modus operandi*, we have the obtaining and leaking of personal information on individuals suspected of criminal activity (or the obstruction of justice) and threats to expose (via social media such as YouTube or Twitter) these individuals unless they confess and/or take action. These methods are closest to the form of extra-judicial vigilantism with which Anonymous is usually associated. Here, the law and politics are seen to have failed, and, thus, action is needed in order to rectify such failure, with the specialist knowledge possessed by Anons—the 'weapons of the Geek', as defined by Coleman—utilised to obtain the information required to apply pressure. This can be seen as the 'first phase' of political action.

In order to expand pressure, however, the participation of interested parties outside of the Anonymous group is required. Thus, Anonymous used 'Twitterstorms' and organised rallies in order galvanise interest surrounding the two cases. Here, we see a far more 'traditional' implementation of political action, with goals more firmly rooted in what we might consider 'conventional' politics. While hacks and the spreading of personal information in order to intimidate targets can both strain and break the borders of legality, online message sending and physical rallies in front of courthouses or police stations are far more accepted, and can have greater impact. In this 'second phase' of political action (after the specialised hacks), the goal was a resolution of the two cases via conventional legal and political avenues (trials or official censure). Thus, one could argue that Anonymous' actions in relation to Steubenville and Maryville are a contradictory combination of anti-statist libertarian vigilantism (fuelled by specialist technical knowledge) and more conventional political dissent with an aim toward state-centred resolutions.

Of course, no discussion of online (or offline) activism would be complete without a consideration of impact. As I have noted, this chapter is not an empirically based study on Anonymous and the two rape cases but rather a reflection upon what these two events should lead us to consider in relation to this type of 'hacktivism'. Nevertheless, the analysis of Woods (2014) is worth considering:

> Although virality can initially amplify a campaign's message and energize would-be supporters, visibility and interest can be difficult to maintain long-term. #OPRollRedRoll and #OccupySteubenville, for instance, gained widespread exposure in the weeks and months after Doe's sexual assault, retaining some visibility (albeit in a less intense form) in 2013 as the case went to trial (. . .) The campaign quietly resurfaced in autumn 2014 alongside news that one of the convicted men was rejoining the Steubenville football team. By this time, however, many Anons and their followers had directed their attention elsewhere. (Woods 2014: 1097)

This critique from Woods is reminiscent of a great deal of research on, and analysis of, the longer-term impact of social media use for the purposes of online activism and political change. An excessive focus on 'virality', one could argue, ignores the offline activities and participation Anonymous (and others) attempted to foster in the two towns, and the longer-term impact (upon the participants) such activism could engender. Similarly, while Anons may have indeed moved on to other issues, the fact remains that a great deal of public discourse on sexual assault, social norms. and the U.S. legal system had been stimulated.

Conclusions

As noted at the start of this chapter, the focus in this analysis of Anonymous has been in relation to events that have taken place in the U.S. While the U.S. media and legal systems—in addition to U.S. sociopolitical structures—clearly played a large role in shaping how both Steubenville and Maryville evolved, these two cases (in conjunction with the consideration about the 'politics' of Anonymous) raise questions relevant beyond the U.S. border. The somewhat paradoxical combination of unfettered (and occasionally misguided) releases of information with calls for injustices to be rectified via established political or legal structures is one which only has relevance if political and/or legal structures maintain some level of legitimacy. Although critical of these structures in the U.S. context, Anonymous does not dismiss them as irrelevant or utterly corrupt. This raises the question of how similar political actions by hacktivist groups would function in countries where trust in the political and legal systems had dissolved. In the U.S., Anonymous provide an interesting example of the interplay between legal (protests, calls for arrests, petitions) and extra-legal (hacking of private or classified information) activity. Future research should pay attention to how nation-specific levels of trust in policing, legal, and political systems impact the efficacy and tactics of groups engaged in similar activities beyond U.S. borders.

References

Abad-Santos, A. (2013a) "Everything You Need to Know About Steubenville High's Football 'Rape Crew'." http://www.thewire.com/national/2013/01/steubenville-high-football-rape-crew/60554/

Abad-Santos, A. (2013b) "Inside the Anonymous Hacking File on the Steubenville 'Rape Crew'." http://www.thewire.com/national/2013/01/inside-anonymous-hacking-file-steubenville-rape-crew/60502/

Arnett, D. (2013) "Nightmare in Maryville: Teens' Sexual Encounter Ignites a Firestorm against Family," *Kansas City Star*, 24 October 2013. http://www.kansascity.com/2013/10/12/4549775/nightmare-in-maryville-teens-sexual.html

Baker, K. (2013) "'A Town Destroyed for What Two People Did': Dispatch from Steubenville." http://jezebel.com/a-town-destroyed-for-what-two-people-did-dispatch-fr-1298509440

Bazelon, E. (2013). "Horrifying Maryville Rape Case Follows Familiar Pattern: Why Does This Keep Happening?" *Slate*, 14 Oct. 2013. http://www.slate.com/blogs/xx_factor/2013/10/14/maryville_rape_case_the_horrifying_details_of_what_happened_to_daisy_coleman.html

Coleman, G. (2011) Anonymous: From the Lulz to Collective Action. *The New Everyday: A Media Commons Project*, 6. http://mediacommons.futureofthebook.org/tne/pieces/anonymous-lulz-collective-action

—— (2013a) *Anonymous in Context: The Politics and Power Behind the Mask*. Waterloo, CA: The Centre for International Governance Innovation. http://www.cigionline.org/sites/default/files/no3_8.pdf

—— (2013b) *Coding Freedom: The Ethics and Aesthetics of Hacking*. Princeton: Princeton University Press.

—— (2014) *Hacker, Hoaxer, Whistleblower, Spy: The Many Faces of Anonymous*. New York: Verso Books.

Dissell. R. (2012) "Rape Charges Against High School Players Divide Football Town of Steubenville, Ohio." http://www.cleveland.com/metro/index.ssf/2012/09/rape_charges_divide_football_t.html

Dockterman, E (2014) "Suspect in Maryville Rape Case Pleads Guilty to Misdemeanor Charge." http://nation.time.com/2014/01/09/suspect-in-maryville-rape-case-pleads-guilty-to-misdemeanor-charge/

Elgion, J. (2013) "High School Sexual Assault Case Is Revisited, Haunting Missouri Town," *The New York Times*, 19 October 2013. http://www.nytimes.com/2013/10/20/us/high-schoolsexual-assault-case-is-reopened-haunting-missouri-town.html

Filipovic, J. (2013) "In Maryville, Anonymous Must Beware the Risk of Vigilantism." *The Guardian*, October 18. http://www.theguardian.com/commentisfree/2013/oct/18/maryville-anonymous-beware-risk-vigilantism

Goode, L. (2015) Anonymous and the Political Ethos of Hacktivism. *Popular Communication, 13*(1), 74–86.

Levy, A. (2013) Trial by Twitter. *The New Yorker*, 5 August 2013.

Li, X. (2013) Hacktivism and the First Amendment: Drawing the Line Between Cyber Protests and Crime. *Harv. J. Law & Tec, 27*, 301–587.

Macur, J., & Schweber, N. (2012) "Rape Case Unfolds on Web and Splits City." *New York Times*, 16 December 2012.

Norton, Q. (2011) "Anonymous 101: Introduction to the Lulz." *Wired*, 8 November 2011. http://www.wired.com/threatlevel/2011/11/anonymous-101/2

Reese, D. (2013) @Maryville, Mo. Attacked in Social Media Response to Daisy Coleman Rape Case. http://www.washingtonpost.com/blogs/she-the-people/wp/2013/10/24/maryville-mo-attacked-in-social-media-response-to-daisy-coleman-rape-case/

Scott, J. C. (1985) *Weapons of the Weak: Everyday Forms of Peasant Resistance*. New Haven, CT: Yale University Press.

Serracino-Inglott, P. (2013) "Is it OK to be an Anonymous?" *Ethics & Global Politics*, 6(4).

Simpson, C. (2013) "Occupy Steubenville: Anonymous vs. The Sheriff." http://www.thewire.com/national/2013/01/occupy-steubenville-anonymous-vs-sheriff/60637/

Wong, W. H., & Brown, P. A. (2013) E-bandits in global activism: WikiLeaks, anonymous, and the politics of no one. *Perspectives on Politics, 11*(04), 1015–1033.

Woods, H. S. (2014) "Anonymous, Steubenville, and the Politics of Visibility: Questions of Virality and Exposure in the Case of #OPRollRedRoll and #OccupySteubenville," *Feminist Media Studies, 14*(6), pp. 1096–1098.

11

SOCIAL MEDIA ACCOUNTS OF THE SPANISH INDIGNADOS

Camilo Cristancho and Eva Anduiza

Introduction

The role of organisations in social networks has been traditionally identified as a decisive factor in inspiring and motivating political action, from de Tocqueville (1840/1969) to the 'resource mobilization' approach (Edwards and McCarthy 2004; della Porta and Diani 2009). In these accounts, organisations as leaders, and organisational involvement in itself, provide opportunities for joint accomplishments by aggregating and articulating collective demands. More recently, social media use has consistently raised questions about the possibility to bypass organisations in the processes of involving like-minded people and translating shared identities, emotions, and motivations into collective action offline. The potential for social media in political mobilization has consequently received scholarly attention, especially after the Arab Spring uprisings in 2010 and the following worldwide wave of protest (Earl and Kimport 2011).

Contentious responses all over the world have followed fairly similar mobilization dynamics, with a diffuse leadership and a broad notion of membership, as in the case of the *Indignados* and of Occupy in many countries. The *Indignados* (the 'outraged') is an emergent social movement in Spain which first appeared following massive demonstrations in response to austerity policies and calling for 'real democracy now' in the spring of 2011. They have become a prototypical movement in the line of the Greek Aganaktismenoi, the Occupy movement in the U.S. or the Portuguese Geração à Rasca (Theocharis et al. 2015). Unlike the protest events mobilized by formal organisations, the *Indignados* mobilizations involved informal linkages and decentralized coordination for action. As such, they shifted away from organisational hierarchies towards leaderless networks.

Social media have provided an opportunity for organisational processes in which crowd-enabled networks are activated, structured, and maintained in the absence of recognised leaders, common goals, or conventional organisation structures (Bennett et al. 2014). However, the processes involved in this type of organisation, and how they lead to collective action, are very much still a black box, especially regarding the cognitive processes that underlie mobilisation from a framing perspective. A dynamic analysis of the activity on Twitter regarding the 15 May 2011 event (the demonstration that kicked off the *Indignados* movement) has shown that the platforms staging the event succeeded in their mobilisation because their decentralised structure was based on coalitions of smaller organisations. This enabled the activation of a core of users who contributed to the growth of the movement by generating cascades of messages that triggered new activations (González-Bailón et al. 2011).

Following on from this analysis of the recruitment patterns in social media mobilisation to protest, this chapter examines the contents of these information flows, and how their contents relate to the cognitive processes that have been argued to spark action—namely movement frames. We are thus interested in tracing the framing dynamics of the mobilisation processes in order to shed light on the role of the organisations staging the events. To analyse framing patterns, we investigate the three main *Indignados* demonstrations that took place on 15 May 2011, 12 May 2012, and 12 May 2013. We undertake a two-fold comparison between the Twitter accounts of the organisations staging the *Indignados* events and those of other organisations that have also been involved in anti-austerity protests and have been traditionally close to social contestation on economic and political issues (leftist parties, unions), as well as the Twitter accounts of ordinary users (who do not have an explicit organisational affiliation).

Using Twitter records from the *Indignados* demonstrations we question to what extent organisations staging the first events 'pass down' their leadership to different types of actors in the dynamic structures of social media networks—or alternatively, to what degree emerging organisations, ordinary users, or the more formal and traditional organisations take over the control of meaning generation processes. This involves the need to explore how framing processes change over time and how users differ in their framing practices according to their network position and their initiative for leading or following in the use of movement frames.

Our approach to framing processes in the communication dynamics of social media contributes to the literature in two ways: first, it advances the research on the discursive mechanisms that drive collective action by studying framing processes in unstructured conversations in social media. Research on social media contents has focused on inferring meaning (i.e. latent topics) from tweets (Barberá et al. 2014) or has been limited to aggregated content by studying hashtags (Borge-Holthoefer et al. 2011; Aragón et al. 2013). We follow on from the scarce research that brings discursive processes into these types of analyses (Fabrega and Sajuria 2013), and focus on movement frames in order to capture discursive processes that respond to a substantive interest rather than following trending topics or the most prominent content. This approach allows us to categorize contents according to their theoretically intended purposes. It is thus an innovative way to leverage Twitter conversations for the study of mobilisation processes, as it connects social media contents to actual movement discourses and combines structural and text analyses.

Secondly, our dynamic analysis enlightens current understandings on framing processes, especially regarding the questions on organisation leadership in frame diffusion and alignment (Ketelaars et al. 2014) and the processes underlying personalization (Bennett and Segerberg 2013; Cristancho and Anduiza 2014). This approach provides unprecedented evidence for the study of framing processes in the context of social media and unstructured organisational patterns.

This chapter presents a brief review of the framing approach in the social movement literature and proposes how it can be integrated into a study of social networks and organisational leadership. It then moves on to the *Indignados* case, introducing the data and methods used in the analysis of framing in dynamic networks in social media.

We discuss the implications of our findings on the role of organisations in framing processes in the mobilisation to protest in online social media.

Framing in Emergent Organisational Forms

Framing has been regarded as a central factor in explaining collective action in contentious politics as frames underlie grievance and identity formation mechanisms that link individual interests, values, and beliefs (Benford and Snow 2000; Gamson 1988). To understand how people make sense of common grievances and whether they adapt these views and share them with social movement organisations (SMOs) is the central aim of the framing approach to explaining collective action (Snow et al. 1986). Framing implies selecting a particular definition for an issue, establishing a causal interpretation, a moral evaluation, and possible actions to influence change (Entman 1993). In this sense, SMOs use frames for diagnosing a social problem, attributing political responsibility for it, proposing a course of action towards desired solutions or expected outcomes, and providing motivations for action by referring to shared values and reasons (Snow and Benford 1988). Moreover, these functions have socialisation effects that affect collective identity formation by establishing group boundaries (Melucci 1995).

Framing processes involve the actions taken to diffuse frames across movements, cultures, and time (Snow and Benford 2000: 622). This involves three types of framing processes: discursive processes, aimed at shaping frames through their articulation and amplification; strategic processes, for adapting them to the context by bridging, amplifying, extending, and transforming movement frames; and contestation processes, for competing with alternative frames for attention and legitimation of the particular way in which the movement understands contested issues.

These cognitive processes have been traditionally attributed to SMOs as central agents in collective action. However, the assumption of organisational leadership has been revised in the last ten years in light of the progressive transformation in social organisation patterns and its implication for collective action. The centrality of formal and established organisations in providing structure and incentives for collective action has decreased as social interactions in online media tend toward more loosely coupled and informal organisation patterns (Benkler 2006; Bimber et al. 2005; Bimber et al. 2012; Shirky 2008). In a longer timeframe, decreasing associational linkages have generated great concerns over their potential effects on civic engagement, at least since Putnam's (2000) foresight of the collapse of the American community. However, alternative forms of social interaction that do not rely on organisational membership seem to have taken over three social network mechanisms that explain collective action: namely, socialization and identity formation, structural processes that connect individuals to mobilisation opportunities, and conversational processes in which meaning is shared and decisions are taken (Passy and Monsch 2014). These alternative forms of social interaction seem to adapt better to a style of democratic engagement which is "increasingly . . . an expression of personal hopes, lifestyle values, and the promise of individual opportunity that further eroded group memberships and loyalties to parties and political institutions" (Bennett and Segerberg 2013: 23).

This individualization of political action emphasizes the importance of networks for the cognitive resources of collective action. The understanding of social networks as 'islands of meaning' (White 1992) is especially relevant to make sense of how movement frames are used in the re-creation of contents in social media. Furthermore, this perspective can illuminate as well how networks are generated through the use of movement frames; interactions in social media (network ties) reflect common understandings, conflicts, or narratives where identities emerge in a particular political context. In that sense, a network tie becomes constituted by a particular frame, which defines a common social time by its narrative of ties (White 1992). In this chapter we analyse these structural and meaning-generating processes dynamically, and determine the extent to which they depend on each other.

We are specifically interested in how framing processes evolve over time, and how different actors take part in these processes. A first relevant question is how framing processes change over time with the progression of demonstrations and changing online publics. As social media use by SMOs implies relinquishing control over the production and transformation of content, the strategic perspective of frame alignment is transferred to a fluid corpus of online publics. We thus expect that organisations delegate their leadership to social media publics who take over a process of co-creating meaning as an alternative to frame adoption or contestation. This opens up new questions regarding which publics take over, or at least assume the leading role in these meaning-generation processes enabled by social media.

Hierarchical Networks and Social Movements

Digital media have changed collective action by allowing organisation in a decentralised and more flexible manner. However, the fact that organisations leading political action do not take over information processes in a centralised manner, or design top-down strategies, does not imply that the social networks underlying collective action online become more horizontal; even more,

> online networks . . . form uneven structures where some nodes are much better connected than others. It is this unequal connectivity that allows online social networks to be more efficient in the spread of information; it is also the reason why everybody in the network is at a short distance—or a few links away— from each other. (González-Bailón 2013: 1)

Consequently, it is crucial to characterize social networks in terms of their underlying structure and their change over time. This enables an understanding of the role of different types of actors in the continuous development of network structures, and of their function in the diffusion of movement frames and discursive alignment between staging organisations and other types of Twitter users. We thus question how the account hierarchy as observed in retweet networks is related to the use of movement frames. In other words, we are interested in the potential differences between central and peripheral accounts in their use of movement frames.

Leaders in Collective Action and Headless Organisations

Structural analysis provides insights into the role of actors in framing processes in social media; nonetheless, we are also interested in exploring potential changes in roles. This entails exploring the ways in which organisational patterns emerge within the fluid networks of social media interactions. We examine networks composed of multiple Twitter accounts which involve diverse types of organisations and individuals, and how they interact as hybrid organisations (Chadwick 2007). Actor types are a continuum of organisational types ranging from those with a defined structure, clear membership criteria, and an established organisational identity to those with looser, more informal methods of coordination that rely on personal ties and informal interaction (della Porta and Diani 2009). Staging organisations for the *Indignados* are mostly of the latter type (Anduiza et al. 2014), and the more traditional leftist and labour union organisations which have usually advocated for socio-economic issues would be on the former end of the continuum. Our aim is to compare these organisational types with each other, and with Twitter accounts who do not report any organisational affiliation. More concretely, we question to what extent staging organisations 'pass down' their leading role regarding framing processes to other types of organisations and ordinary users— or, alternatively, we ask whether these other actors take over control of meaning-generation processes.

In summary, we address the following research questions:

1. How do framing processes change with the progression of demonstrations and the movement over time?
2. To what extent does hierarchy in retweet networks affect the use of movement frames? Do central and peripheral accounts differ in their use of movement frames?
3. To what extent do staging organisations 'pass down' their leading role regarding framing processes to other types of organisations and ordinary users? Or alternatively, to what degree do these other actors take over control of meaning-generation processes?

Data

In order to explore framing processes in the *Indignados* mobilisation, we collected and stored a large sample of public tweets for the three major demonstrations in Spain, filtering the Twitter API by search queries on major trending topics (see Table 11.1). We take accounts as our unit of analysis ($N \approx 376,000$) and focus on retweets ($N \approx 1,100,000$), as this guarantees that we capture the most salient content, considering that they have been validated (for topic relevance) and signalled as having content that is worthy enough to endorse by retweeting. The three protest events from the *Indignados* movement in Spain had substantial activity on Twitter.[1] The kick-off event (15M) included 50 simultaneous demonstrations and encampments in public plazas all over Spain from 15 May to 12 June 2011. Those protests were promoted by *ad hoc* platforms that operated mainly through online social media under the overall motto Real Democracy Now. More than 400 organisations were involved, calling for a reform of the Spanish political system and the adoption of measures to foster transparency, accountability and participation (Anduiza et al. 2014). They awakened strong public support among Spanish citizens since the beginning of the movement and sustained it for several consecutive years.[2] The *Indignados* took to the streets one year later, on 12 May 2012, to celebrate the second anniversary of the movement in the 12M15M protests with 20 simultaneous demonstrations in different Spanish cities. Another year later, in 2013, country-wide demonstrations followed important direct action such as *escraches*, resulting from a citizen initiative to change eviction laws, and the occupation of bank offices. These events took place on 12 May 2013, focusing again on anti-austerity measures.

Table 11.1 Twitter Samples for *Indignados* Events

Event	Identifier	Event dates	Search strings	Period of analysis		Retweets	Frames
Kick-off demo + encampments	15M	15 May to 12 June 2011	15M OR *Indignados* OR acampadas OR 'El 15-M' OR 'Democracia real ya' OR '15-M' OR 'Movimiento 15-M'	2011–05–01 2011–12–01	19 days 3 weeks	729,060	47,194
1st anniversary	12M15M 2012	12 May 2012	'15-M' OR 'Movimiento 15-M'	2012–05–01 2012–05–31	31 days 4 weeks	317,322	41,504
2nd anniversary	12M15M 2013	12 May 2013	15M OR *Indignados* OR acampadas OR 'El 15-M' OR 'Democracia real ya' OR '15-M' OR 'Movimiento 15-M' OR (manifestacion AND('segundo aniversario' AND '15M')) OR (manifestacion AND('primer aniversario' AND '15M'))	2013–05–13 2013–05–17	11 days 2 weeks	69,349	5,918

The distribution of our sample varied considerably between events as the demonstrations in each year evolved differently and this resulted in divergent attention cycles. In 2011, social media attention peaked four to six days after the 15 May kick-off demonstration (accounting for almost 40 per cent of the 2011 sample), when the occupation of the squares all over the country came as an unexpected demonstration of popular discontent. For the first anniversary demonstration, attention peaked on the day of the demonstrations, with 23 per cent of the tweets on 12 May 2012 and further steady activity until 15 May (with 30 per cent more of the 2012 sample occurring from 13 to 15 May). For 2013, the highest peaks took place during the 12 May demonstration and the actual anniversary day of 15 May (19 per cent and 36 per cent of the 2013 sample, respectively).

We use dynamic social network data by considering weekly periods in order to study temporal change in account involvement and framing practices. However, only one out of every 10,000 accounts in our sample tweeted about matters related to the *Indignados* in every week of the three events, and 87 per cent tweeted in fewer than four of the weeks covered by our sample. This limits our possibilities for dynamic analysis. However, identifying the endurance of accounts on Twitter is a useful proxy for considering their closeness with the *Indignados*.

The Indignados on Twitter

The organisations staging the 15 May 2011 demonstrations established the Coordination Platform for Citizen Mobilisation Groups (*Plataforma de coordinación de grupos pro-movilización ciudadana*) with the now famous slogan Real Democracy NOW! (*Democracia Real YA!*). They created a Facebook group on 20 February 2011, which brought together various organisations such as ADESORG (*Asociación Nacional de Desempleados*, National Association for the unemployed), *Juventud en Acción* (Youth in Action), *Estado del malestar* (Ill-fare State), *No les Votes* (Do not vote for them), and *Ponte en Pie* (Get on your feet). Later on, other established organisations joined the movement and led the mobilisation processes. These included *Juventud Sin Futuro* (Youth with no future), Anonymous, X.net, and some local groups of the international ATTAC movement. We identified the Twitter accounts for these organisations, and categorized them as 'staging organisations'.

We are interested as well in the organisations that emerged from the interaction between these organisations and other individuals and groups taking part in the events. The organisational Twitter accounts were mostly established during the 2011 occupation of the squares, or emerged as belonging to local organisations in charge of the logistics of the demonstrations and encampments. Some others emerged later on, representing local assemblies and particular groups, such as the *yayoflautas*—the elderly *Indignados*. We grouped all of these types of accounts under the broad category 'Indignados organisations', which includes *Asambleas* (assemblies), *Acampadas* (encampments), *Yayoflautas* (elderly *Indignados*) and the *Plataforma de Afectados por la Hipoteca*—PAH (People affected by evictions) accounts. Our 15M categories of 'staging organisations' and 'Indignados organisations' also have an empirical base as they have been identified as independent communities in previous studies using community detection algorithms for Twitter networks (Borge-Holthoefer et al. 2011).

Twitter accounts for political parties and labour unions are not central communities in the networks for any of the events, but we are interested in identifying their marginal roles in the mobilisation processes, considering their substantive importance in anti-austerity contestation. Twitter accounts which were not identified as belonging to any of the organisation categories were bundled into an 'ordinary users' category. This includes highly central accounts such as social movement organisations on other issues, respected activists, broadcast media, and celebrities.

Methods

In order to identify social movement frames in retweets, we used dictionary coding techniques to find keywords and phrases in each tweet (Matthes and Kohring 2008). We identified social movement frames from event manifestos as provided by staging organisations and used the central concepts in their wording in order to build keyword and phrase dictionaries. This process allowed for the automatic identification of frames in social media content (Casas et al. 2015). This type of coding provides a loose approximation of frame usage in tweets. A similar method was used for coding actor types, by mining keywords from the account names and profiles.[3]

We use social network analysis in order to study social movement frames on Twitter by analysing retweets as a diffusion network (Ratkiewicz et al. 2011). Retweets are direct interactions between tweeters which are used as a form of endorsement as they allow individuals to rebroadcast content generated by other accounts, thus raising the content's visibility (Honeycutt and Herring 2009). Analysing retweet networks enables characterising accounts by establishing their hierarchy and thus their diffusion potential. The position of actors in the network is crucial to understanding their role in framing processes as the structure of communication networks explains how frames propagate through the Twittersphere.

Retweeting movement frames can have any framing process as its purpose. Staging organisations may be interested in strategic purposes such as bridging, amplifying, or extending the use of movement frames, while the accounts of unions or parties will most probably be interested in contesting or shaping movement frames. We focus on the interactions of accounts using movement frames without analysing their purpose (as this would imply coding the contents of tweets), in order to establish their relative importance in the meaning-generation process that is shared in Twitter interactions. This implies the need for a structural analysis of interactions in retweet networks.

Previous research has dealt with clusters (Aragón et al. 2013) and hashtags (Yang et al. 2012) in order to focus on community structures with high levels of interaction, or interactions based on similar topics. We follow other studies that integrate these approaches by analysing core-periphery structures in order to distinguish nodes in densely connected cores from those in sparsely connected peripheries (Conover et al. 2012; González-Bailón et al. 2011). Core analysis is a structural approach to hierarchy in retweet networks, intended to analyse meso-scale network structures. To identify the core and the periphery of the network we use the k-shell (k-core) decomposition of the network. This allows us to discover organisational patterns in framing processes that might not be apparent either at the local level of actors or at the global level of summary statistics of the social media activity relating to the *Indignados* movement. Prior research has established that the topology of the network plays an independent role from node connectivity in diffusion processes. This means that a well-connected node at the periphery of a network will have a minimal impact on the diffusion process through the core of the network, whereas a less connected node in the core of the network will have a diffusion potential that could reach a large fraction of the network (Kitsak et al. 2010).

In order to describe the dynamic perspective of framing processes, we study retweets as streams of messages. These streams can be viewed as sequences of decisions (i.e. whether to use a certain frame or not), with later participants watching the frame adoption of earlier participants. Therefore, users are influenced by the decisions to adopt or contest movement frames that are taken by others. Using movement frames is thus a matter of social influence. This means that the actions of one user can induce others to behave in a similar way; in this case, influence appears explicitly when someone 'retweets' someone else (Guille et al. 2013).

Results

Movement frames are only used by 17% of the accounts in our sample. This could reveal that most of the social media conversations do not deal with framing as a meaning-generation process, or that they do so without engaging with the particular language proposed by the pioneering organisations of the movement. However, this small proportion of accounts provides useful evidence on how different types of movement frames evolve in time, and, most importantly, how Twitter accounts from multiple organisations and unaffiliated users interact in framing processes. Ordinary users account for the largest part of the use of movement frames (98 per cent), but they are mostly peripheral users. They are followed by the accounts of the *Indignados* organisations and the 15M/staging organisations (41 per cent and 35 per cent. respectively), which use frames in a similar proportion to labour union accounts (33 per cent). Parties fall behind considerably, with less than 9 per cent of their accounts tweeting movement frames.

Regarding the types of frames, motivational frames mostly based on the idea of success in changing the current situation ('podemos' and 'sí se puede'—yes we can) played a marginal role in all events (see Figure 11.1). However, they followed the same temporal patterns as other types of frames, with the higher peaks occurring shortly after each event. The only exception to this pattern were prognosis frames; this signals the difficulty in finding common aspirations amongst the heterogeneous groups of followers of a fledgling movement that aimed first to build a common identity and expressed

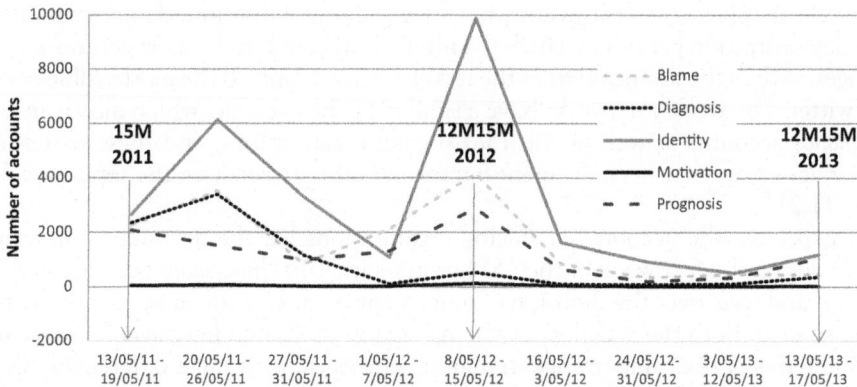

Figure 11.1 Volume of Movement Frames in Retweets

despair rather than proposing future alternatives. This is clearly evidenced by the relative distancing of identity, blame attribution, and diagnosis frames during the week of the 15M kick-off event and a few days beyond, when the squares were occupied and the movement received its highest public visibility in broadcast media.

Framing patterns changed in the first anniversary demonstrations in 2012. The reaffirmation of a broad and inclusive identity and the will to carry on was central to the movement, as signalled by the most prominent frames during the three events. There was a growth of blame attribution that peaked after the 2012 demo, while diagnosis frames, such as those focused on the inequality, corruption, unresponsiveness, and obsolescence of the system, plummeted. Prognosis frames also received the most attention across the entire timeframe, probably as a response to generalized critiques and concerns about the pointless nature of a movement with no clear claims. By 2013, the greatest attention on Twitter was devoted to identity and prognosis frames, with a similar growing tendency and a slight difference over diagnostics frames. However, the overall volume of tweets relating to the *Indignados* anniversary protests was well down compared to the previous years.

We have described the relative volume of retweets that contain movement frames. However, we are also interested in the relative involvement of accounts in retweeting movement frames. We calculated the weekly distributions of retweets containing frames by the number of accounts involved. These resulted in fat-tailed distributions, indicating how weekly retweet networks are scale free and highly hierarchical (power law distributions). We also found important differences between weeks and in user activity. This evidence provides a first description of the influence of network hierarchy over the prominence of frame types, but the volume of retweets and the number of retweets per account do not provide a complete picture of framing processes, as these depend on the interactions between accounts.

Table 11.2 presents the results of the structural analysis by indicating the network position of accounts and their role in framing processes. Accounts have a weekly indicator of their relative placement in the network, with higher 'coreness' values in the retweet networks represented by darker shades. Accounts with higher coreness values have greater diffusion potential in the network, and are consequently more important in framing processes. This implies that they have retweeted or have been retweeted by equally important users, but not necessarily by those with a higher number of retweets.

We can see important differences between accounts both between and within events. Each year involves different events, but they share mobilisation, demonstration, and post-demonstration periods in which the interaction between the most central accounts changes, as does the attention from the less central accounts to the most visible content on Twitter. The weekly networks have a similarly cohesive core, which mostly involves *Indignados* accounts as well as the 15M/staging organisations, and these patterns are similar across tweets with movement frames and other tweets (see the topmost cells in Table 11.2).

As expected, the accounts of staging organisations led the diffusion of movement frames during the first week of the 15M protests in 2011. *Indignados* accounts followed early on and took over the diffusion of movement frames for the most part of the timeframe studied. Both the accounts of staging organisations and *Indignados* played similar roles in terms of their importance in framing processes, with small differences. Staging organisations played a leading role regarding identity frames, and to a lesser extent on prognosis frames. If we interpret this as non-adoption of the central movement frames

Table 11.2 Framing Patterns in Tweets By Centrality and Type of Actor (K-Core Values Per Week)

			May 2011			May 2012				May 2013	
			13–19	20–26	27–31	1–7	8–15	16–23	24–31	3–12	13–17
			%								
No frames N= 314,817	Ordinary users	83.7	2.65	2.64	2.19	1.69	1.92	1.54	1.44	1.58	1.46
	Unions	70.3	2.44	2.84	2.09	2.19	2.92	2.21	1.45	2.05	1.82
	Indignados	70.1	8.67	11.34	9.54	7.14	9.02	3.90	3.18	4.26	3.11
	15M Staging orgs.	66.3	8.00	7.22	7.35	5.00	5.90	3.60	2.48	3.29	8.56
	Leftist parties	85.7	3.33	2.50	1.11	3.63	1.64	2.25	1.20	1.00	2.22
	Socialist parties	80.6	5.67	5.53	3.15	1.41	3.72	1.94	1.27	2.57	1.67
Blame N= 15,041	Ordinary users	3.98	6.77	6.26	5.27	2.83	4.28	2.67	3.60	2.38	3.02
	Unions	11.5	6.50	11.00	5.00	2.78	5.29	4.00	6.33	1.00	2.44
	Indignados	6.61		21.00	11.00	11.20	19.40	5.38	5.25	10.50	6.00
	15M Staging orgs.	5.71	15.50	27.33	8.50	9.00	12.56	3.67	7.25	7.00	5.00
	Leftist parties	2.52				2.00	1.00			1.00	
	Socialist parties	3.95	9.00	27.00		2.67	3.67				6.00
Diagnosis N = 8,049	Ordinary users	2.14	7.58	7.50	5.37	5.97	4.75	3.54	5.36	2.52	2.86
	Unions	0.85	24.00	12.00					12.00		1.00
	Indignados	3.19	11.00	18.14	24.00	17.00	20.00	5.67	8.00	11.50	11.00
	15M Staging orgs.	2.1	12.00	10.30	19.00			2.00			4.00
	Leftist parties	2.52	1.50					3.00			
	Socialist parties	2.37	11.00		5.00	9.00					2.00
Identity N = 27,288	Ordinary users	7.21	11.44	10.98	8.74	6.07	7.38	3.75	2.27	3.67	2.80
	Unions	9.62	19.75	20.56	19.20	7.71	11.85	5.25	1.33		3.20
	Indignados	16.9	17.00	27.87	17.00	19.13	31.85	9.50	7.50	8.83	3.50
	15M Staging orgs.	20.8	41.38	28.24	27.22	19.15	34.58	12.42	7.92	9.20	23.50
	Leftist parties	5.04		4.00			23.00	6.00			
	Socialist parties	4.35	10.00	19.50	15.00	2.00	13.75		1.00		
Motivation N = 262	Ordinary users	0.07	4.84	7.58	14.00	4.00	2.08	1.04	2.20	4.11	1.71
	Socialist parties	0.79					7.00				4.00
Prognosis N = 10869	Ordinary users	2.87	8.68	8.12	5.76	4.58	5.14	3.53	3.56	3.32	1.78
	Unions	7.69	8.00			4.92	10.54	1.67	6.00	1.00	
	Indignados	3.19	15.00	37.00	18.00	14.75	25.60	7.13	9.33		5.33
	15M Staging orgs.	5.14	24.00	20.50	19.67	8.33	28.33	11.00	14.00		10.00
	Leftist parties	4.2					7.67				18.50
	Socialist parties	7.91	14.00		12.00	3.50	5.63			3.00	1.00
	Accounts per week		66,074	90,343	63,475	17,396	72,055	16,108	17,260	10,400	23,215

Darker shades represent higher k-cores in weekly retweet networks (most central users)
The % column shows the percentage of tweets using frames for each type of actor

by other actors, it seems reasonable that identity and prognosis frames were more sus-ceptible to be personalized in the encampments and assemblies during the period where most interaction between actors took place.

Political parties have a minor involvement with movement frames, except for blame attribution and identity. There are few differences between the accounts of leftist and socialist parties. Nevertheless, accounts close to the incumbent Socialist Party (PSOE) were quite active during the 2011 event, as the party was directly blamed for demo-cratic deficits by using a particular blame attribution frame: 'PPSOE', which claimed that there was no difference between the conservative PP and the socialist PSOE. The central role of accounts from to the Socialist Party in identity framing processes during 2011 could indicate their interest in regional elections and the potential influence of the 15M on the results of these elections. Leftist parties were important in identity and prognosis framing processes only in 2012 and 2013, when they associated more closely with the *Indignados* movement. The role of Alberto Garzón, an MP from the leftist party Izquierda Unida who was acknowledged as the Indignados' representative in par-liament (and who is also an influential Twitter user), was crucial for the involvement of the leftist parties in the Indignados' discursive space on Twitter.

Labour unions engaged from the beginning of the Indignados in blame attribution frames, but their major role was mostly with identity frames. These interactions prob-ably had bridging and alignment purposes, considering their interest in establishing commonalities with their constituencies and with the people involved in contesting austerity measures under their leadership in previous years. The role of unions could also reflect efforts to reshape frames, aimed at changing the prevailing perception of unions as institutionalized actors close to government decisions that was part of the Indignados discourse.

Discussion

This chapter set out to explore the changing role of organisations in the mobilisation to protest in social media. Our approach to the increasing scholarly attention to this matter was to investigate framing processes in order to shed light on the interactions between the formal SMOs which have traditionally driven mobilisation processes, as well as labour unions or political parties, and fluid organisations, such as the ones that make up the *Indignados* movement. Our results provide an indication of the extent to which the accounts of multiple types of organisations interact with each other, and consequently take control of the framing processes that used to be led by staging organisations.

Our description of the prominence of the accounts tweeting movement frames reveals that framing varies considerably over time, and that changes in framing occur in parallel with a fluctuating involvement of users. This signals the dynamic nature of meaning-generation processes, and the importance of studying the extent to which dif-ferent actors get involved in framing processes. We addressed this with the structural analysis of account 'coreness' in order to describe framing patterns.

The organisations staging the 15M and those that emerged from the occupation of the squares and the assemblies (referred to as Indignados organisations) have a large number of Twitter users in highly influential positions (with high-order k-cores). This means that they enjoy structural advantages for diffusing their particular choices and perspectives of movement frames. Their dominant position signals their potential for effectively spreading information through these networks. These results corroborate the findings of existing research which indicates that highly connected actors are the most effective spreaders of information (Fabrega and Sajuria 2013). The accounts of *Indignados* organisations are more likely than others to be connected with the retweet network, and this enables them to facilitate the diffusion of movement frames on their own terms. These results point to Indignados organisations taking a leading role in the cognitive processes of mobilisation to protest, through a socially engaged and densely interconnected population of Twitter users who have outperformed more traditional actors and forms of organisation such as parties and unions, and to some extent, the organisations staging the 15M demonstration.

These findings raise intriguing questions regarding the nature and extent of mobilisation through online media, as they confirm the changing role of organisations by describing their involvement in the framing processes and the importance of the hierarchical structures of fluid networks. This confirms that what distinguishes contemporary movements is not the *absence* of organisation, but a particular *mode* of organisation that can be described in its own right (Agarwal et al. 2014; Nunes 2014). We can thus rest assured that there is no such thing as a headless movement that will come back to search for its lost head.

Notes

1 A detailed description of the Twitter activity of the Indignados is available from the original source: the T-Hoarder project (www.t-hoarder.com). We thank Mariluz Congosto for granting us access to these data.

2 Sympathy towards the Indignados reached 77.1 per cent on 23 May 2011, dropped to 66 per cent on 1 June 2011, and further to 51 per cent on 10 May 2012, according to the Metroscopia polls data in *El Pais*. A similar pattern was registered by Simple Lógica polls, with 73.3 per cent approval of the 15M demonstrations on 6 June 2011, 64.4 per cent approval on 15 June 2012, and 75.9 per cent approval on 8 April 2013.

3 Frame and actor dictionaries are presented in Appendix 1. Casas et al. 2015 report accuracy levels of 95.51 per cent using similar dictionaries and media sources with the same dictionary coding technique.

References

Agarwal, S.D., Bennett, W.L., Johnson, C.N., & Walker, S. (2014). A Model of Crowd Enabled Organization: Theory and Methods for Understanding the Role of Twitter in the Occupy Protests. *International Journal of Communication*, 8, 27.

Anduiza, E., Cristancho, C., & Sabucedo, J. M. (2014). Mobilization through Online Social Networks: The Political Protest of the *Indignados* in Spain. *Information, Communication & Society*, pp.1–15. doi: 10.1080/1369118X.2013.808360

Aragón, P., Kappler, K., Kaltenbrunner, A., Laniado, D., & Volkovich Y. (2013). 'Communication Dynamics in Twitter During Political Campaigns: The Case of the 2011 Spanish National Election'. *Policy & Internet*, 5(2), 49–69

Barberá, P., Bonneau, R., Egan, P., Jost, J. T., Nagler, J., & Tucker, J. (2014, August). *Leaders or Followers? Measuring Political Responsiveness in the US Congress Using Social Media Data*. Prepared for the 2014 Annual Meeting of the American Political Science Association, Washington, DC.

Benford, R. D., & Snow, D. A. (2000). Framing Processes and Social Movements: An Overview and Assessment. *Annual Review of Sociology*, 26, 611–639.

Benkler, Y. (2006). *The Wealth of Networks: How Social Production Transforms Markets and Freedom.* New Haven, CT: Yale University Press.

Bennett, W. L., & Segerberg, A. (2013). *The Logic of Connective Action: Digital Media and the Personalization of Contentious Politics.* New York: Cambridge University Press.

Bennett, W. L., Segerberg, A., & Walker, S. (2014). Organization in the Crowd: Peer Production in Large-Scale Networked Protests. *Information, Communication & Society*, 17(2), 232–260. doi:10.1080/1369118X.2013.870379

Bimber, B., Flanagin, A., & Sthol, C. (2005). Reconceptualizing Collective Action in the Contemporary Media Environment. *Communication Theory*, 15(4), 365–388

Bimber, B., Flanagin, A., & Stohl, C. (2012). *Collective Action in Organisations: Interaction and Engagement in an Era of Technological Change.* Cambridge: Cambridge University Press.

Borge-Holthoefer, J., Rivero, A., García, I., Cauhé, E., Ferrer, A., et al. (2011). Structural and Dynamical Patterns on Online Social Networks: The Spanish May 15th Movement as a Case Study. *PLoS ONE*, 6(8): e23883. doi:10.1371/journal.pone.0023883

Casas, A., Davesa, F., & Congosto, M. L. (2015). *Protesta multitudinaria ¿Mensaje caótico? La interacción entre el 15-M y los medios de comunicación.* Working paper. Retrieved from http://students.washington.edu/acasas2/casas_davesa_congosto_Feb_2015.pdf

Chadwick, A. (2007). Digital Network Repertoires and Organizational Hybridity. *Political Communication*, 24(3), 283–301.

Conover, M. D., Gonçalves, B., Flammini, A., & Menczer, F. (2012). Partisan Asymmetries in Online Political Activity. *EPJ Data Science*, 1(1), 1–19.

Cristancho, C., & Anduiza, E. (2014). Digitally Networked Action in European Mass Protest. In *APSA 2014 Annual Meeting Paper*. Retrieved from http://ssrn.com/abstract=2454304

Della Porta, D., & Diani, M. (2009) Social Movements and Organizations. Chapter 6 in *Social Movements: An Introduction.* New York: John Wiley & Sons.

Earl, J., & Kimport, K. (2011). *Digitally Enabled Social Change: Activism in the Internet Age.* Cambridge, MA: MIT.

Edwards, B., & McCarthy, J. D. (2004). Resources and Social Movement Mobilization. In D. A. Snow, S. A. Soule, & H Kriesi (Eds.), *The Blackwell Companion to Social Movements* (pp. 116–152). London: Blackwell,

Entman, R. M. (1993). Framing: Toward Clarification of a Fractured Paradigm. *Journal of Communication*, 43(4), 51–58.

Fabrega, J., & Sajuria, J. (2013). The Emergence of Political Discourse on Digital Networks: The Case of the Occupy Movement. *arXiv Preprint arXiv:1308.1176.* Retrieved from http://arxiv.org/abs/1308.1176

Gamson, W. A. (1988). Political Discourse and Collective Action. *International Social Movement Research*, 1(2), 219–244.

González-Bailón, S. (2013). Online Social Networks and Bottom-up Politics. In W. H. Dutton & M. Graham (Eds.), *Society and the Internet: How Information and Social Networks are Changing our Lives* (pp. 1–14). Oxford: Oxford University Press. Retrieved from http://papers.ssrn.com/sol3/papers.cfm?abstract_id=2246663

González-Bailón, S., Borge-Holthoefer, J., Rivero, A., & Moreno, Y. (2011). 'The Dynamics of Protest Recruitment through an Online Network.' *Scientific Reports*, 1(0), 197. doi:10.1038/srep00197

Guille, A., Hacid, H., & Favre, C. (2013). Predicting the Temporal Dynamics of Information Diffusion in Social Networks. *arXiv preprint arXiv:1302.5235.* Retrieved from http://arxiv.org/abs/1302.5235

Honeycutt, C., & Herring, S. C. (2009, January). Beyond Microblogging: Conversation and Collaboration via Twitter. In *42nd Hawaii International Conference on System Sciences, 2009. HICSS'09*, (pp. 1–10). New York: IEEE.

Ketelaars, P., Walgrave, S., & Wouters, R. (2014). Degrees of Frame Alignment: Comparing Organisers' and Participants' Frames in 29 Demonstrations in Three Countries. *International Sociology*. doi:10.1177/0268580914548286

Kitsak, M., Gallos, L.K., Havlin, S., Liljeros, F., Muchnik, L., Stanley, H.E., & Makse, H.A. (2010). Identification of Influential Spreaders in Complex Networks. *Nature Physics*, 6(11), 888–893.

Matthes, J., & Kohring, M. (2008). The Content Analysis of Media Frames: Toward Improving Reliability and Validity. *Journal of Communication*, 58(2), 258–279. doi:10.1111/j.1460–2466.2008.00384.x

Melucci, A. (1995). The Process of Collective Identity. *Social Movements and Culture*, 4, 41–63.

Nunes, R. (2014). *Organisation of the Organisationless: The Question of Organisation After Networks*. Berlin: PML Books

Passy, F., & Monsch, G.A. (2014). Do Social Networks Really Matter in Contentious Politics? *Social Movement Studies*, 13(1), 22–47. doi:10.1080/14742837.2013.863146

Putnam, R. D. (2000).*Bowling Alone: The Collapse and Revival of American Community*. New York: Simon & Schuster

Ratkiewicz, J., Conover, M., Meiss, M., Gonçalves, B., Patil, S., Flammini, A., & Menczer, F. (2011, March). Truthy: Mapping the Spread of Astroturf in Microblog Streams. In *Proceedings of the 20th International Conference Companion on World Wide Web* (pp. 249–252). New York: ACM.

Shirky, C. (2008). Here Comes Everybody: The Power of Organizing without Organisations. New York: Allen Lane.

Snow, D.A., & Benford, R.D. (1988). Ideology, Frame Resonance and Participants Mobilization. *International Social Movement Research*, 1, 197–219.

Snow, D.A., Rochford, E., Worden, S., & Benford. R. (1986). Frame Alignment Processes, Micromobilization, and Movement Participation. *American Sociological Review*, 51(4), 464–481.

Theocharis, Y., Lowe, W., van Deth, J.W., & García-Albacete, G. (2015). Using Twitter to Mobilize Protest Action: Online Mobilization Patterns and Action Repertoires in the Occupy Wall Street, Indignados, and Aganaktismenoi Movements. *Information, Communication & Society*, 18(2), 202–220.

Tocqueville A. (1840/1969). *Democracy in America*. New York: Ancho

White, H.C. (1992). *Identity and Control*. Princeton, NJ: Princeton University Press.

Yang, L., Sun, T., Zhang, M., & Mei, Q. (2012, April). We Know What @You #Tag: Does the Dual Role Affect Hashtag Adoption? In *Proceedings of the 21st International Conference on World Wide Web* (pp. 261–270). New York: ACM.

Appendix 1—Coding

Frames

Motivation	
felicidad	
situacion	economi*
panorama	social
podemos cambiar	si todos nos unimos
	todos unidos
en movimiento	
echar a andar	

Blame	
PPSOE	
partito	
tecno	cracia
dictadura	
ppsoe	
partido	culpa

179

Motivation	
hora de construir	entre tod*
sociedad mejor	
llevar nuestra voz	
procura	grueso de la sociedad
	movemos el mundo
puedo	cambiar
	ayudar
unidos podemos	
sal con nosotr*	
es tu derecho	

Prognosis	
derecho	básico
	vivienda
	trabajo
	cultura
	salud
	educación
	participación
libre desarrollo	
bienes necesarios	vida sana y feliz
democracia	pueblo
gobierno	
demos	cracia
cauces directos	
participación	ciudadan

Identity	
más progresistas	más conservadores
derechas	izquierdas
unos creyentes, otros no	
ideologías	apolíticos
preocupados	político
ciudadano de a pie	
ni pp	ni psoe
somos	anónimos
	personas
	productos del mercado
	lo que compro
indignado	

Diagnosis

empresarios	
	banqueros
estado del malestar	
prioridades	sociedad avanzada
desarrollo	
bienestar	soci*
sistema económico	no atiende
beneficio	desigualdad
modelo económico	obsoleto
	antinatural
enriquec*	unos pocos
	minoria
sumi*	pobreza
	escasez
	colapso
sufrimos	carencias
acumula	dinero
despilfarr*	recursos
destru*	planeta
desempleo	
consumidores infelices	
rentabilidad	
dinero por encima	ser humano
corrupción	políticos
indefensión	
igualdad	
progreso	
solidaridad	
partidos	
sistema gubernamental	obstáculo
clase política	escucha
enriqu*	a nuestra costa
poderes económicos	atendi*

Diagnosis

	atiend*
poder	aferra*
	acumula*
	ansi*
	crispación
	injusticia
	violencia
bloquea	maquinaria social
no fiar	futuro
beneficio de la mayoría	
revolución ética	
la situación	daño a todos
libre acceso a la cultura	
sostenibilidad ecológica	
engranaje	
eliminar los abusos	

Actors

Unions	ccoo
	ugt
	cgt
	sat
	rosatristan
	jasmusatl85
	sindical
	sindicaestudian
	cnt
Indignados	asamblea
	acampada
	yayoflautas
	iaioflautas
	pah

Actors

15m Staging organizations	adesorg
	dry
	democraciareal
	juventud_accion
	nolesvotes
	ponte_en_pie
	anonymous
	juventudsin
Leftist parties	iunida
	iu_
	llamazares
	agarzon
	cayo_lara
	revillamiguela
	syriza_es
	equo
	comunista
	pce
Socialist parties	socialista
	psoe
	psc
	psv

12

EVERY CRISIS IS A DIGITAL OPPORTUNITY

The Aganaktismenoi Movement's Use of Social Media and the Emergence of Networked Solidarity in Greece

Yannis Theocharis

Introduction

In late 2009, many of the most widely read international news outlets dedicated their cover page to news and commentary about the unfolding 'Greek tragedy.' Many analysts voiced the concern that Greece's economic crisis could spread into other heavily indebted countries, which would ignite a European sovereign debt crisis. After widely criticised policy manoeuvres (and in exchange for multi-billion euro bailouts) the Greek government signed a series of memoranda with the European Commission, the European Central Bank, and the International Monetary Fund (the so-called troika), which committed it to tough austerity measures that quickly started tearing the country's social fabric apart. The public's response was immediate and strong: massive, and often violent, social unrest, including mass demonstrations, strikes, riots, and occupations of public institutions.

In May 2011, with Greece's two-party system near collapse, the Aganaktismenoi (or 'indignant citizens') movement emerged. It was a bottom-up anti-austerity initiative that was not only incited by, but was also closely affiliated to and resembled, the Spanish 15M movement (named after the beginning of the Madrid protests on 15 May 2011), also known as *Indignados*. The Aganaktismenoi sought to serve as a new political voice representing a new generation of protesters, which would be radically different from the left-wing labour union activists that have been filling the capital's streets over the last several decades. The Aganaktismenoi also claimed to be non-partisan and non-violent, and to support greater citizen intervention in politics through direct democratic practices. While some members of the public supported the movement's aims and saw it as a first and productive effort to increase the citizens' voice in policy making, others rejected it as an immature, politically uninformed, and aimless gathering of disillusioned and outraged citizens that would achieve nothing and quickly be forgotten.

Regardless of how one evaluates the overall impact of Aganaktismenoi, their extensive use of social media sets it apart from previous mobilisations in the country. The movement's mobilisation took place entirely via social networking sites and microblogs (Ekathimerini 2012), which conforms to recent observations elsewhere in Europe suggesting that protesters have been recruited in recent years using more open mobilisation channels (Verhulst & Walgrave 2009; Klandermans et al. 2014), especially digital media (Bennett et al. 2008). Most importantly, this mobilisation is in striking contrast to the organisation-based protests that have taken place in the country for many decades, which were mainly organised—and brought to the streets—by the 'usual suspects', such as labour union and political party activists (Rüdig & Karyotis 2013a). Indeed, the protesters who filled Syntagma (Constitution) Square in Athens during the Aganaktismenoi mobilisations displayed a rather unusual profile.

Although the movement's formal institutional outcomes were not significant (Sotiropoulos 2014), it had important and visible ramifications for Greek civil society, in large part due to the extensive and innovative use of social media. In this chapter I argue that social media have presented Greek citizens with five unique opportunities. *First*, to self-organise and coordinate their opposition to the government's unpopular measures without the support of traditional political organisations. *Second*, to establish solidarity ties and extend their voice well beyond Greece through cooperation with similar anti-austerity movements elsewhere in Europe. *Third*, to mobilise a different segment of the population than in previous protests in Greece. *Fourth*, to create a loosely connected online network of individuals that would maintain ties long after the end of the mobilisations and which could be immediately activated when needed, helping bottom-up solidarity initiatives relying on social media to find an audience and recruit volunteers. *Finally*, and perhaps most importantly, to give Greek citizens the opportunity to strengthen civil society by creatively implementing social media-based civic innovations.

The chapter is organized as follows. First, it introduces some theoretical considerations about the impact of social media on collective action organisation and provides some contextual information about the use of these tools for protest organisation in Greece. Focusing on Twitter, it then discusses the structure of the Aganaktismenoi network. It documents some of the key aspects of its operation and suggests that there are indications that the Aganaktismenoi mobilisations represented a crowd-enabled connective action mobilisation. Before concluding with a discussion of the consequences of social media use during the Aganaktismenoi mobilisations on Greek civil society, the chapter shows how networks established during the mobilisations were subsequently used to support bottom-up solidarity initiatives.

Social Media, Political Action, and Organisational Change: Theoretical Considerations

In the past decade, much of the scholarship focusing on the transformative effect of information and communication technologies has investigated the Internet's role in political mobilisation. The strengthening of the communication strategies of advocacy groups and social movements, and the addition of Internet-enabled and Internet-supported action repertoires, have been among the many changes brought about by the Internet (Merry 2012; Van Laer & Van Aelst 2010; Chadwick 2007; Vegh 2003).

Some of the best-documented outcomes of these changes are the empowerment of campaign practices like fundraising and the facilitation of activist network collaboration and coalition building among organisations (Bennett 2003; Kahn & Kellner 2004; Juris 2005; Postmes & Brunsting 2002). Although the adoption of the Internet seems to have forever altered the mobilisation strategies of social movements and activist groups, the extent to which these changes have fundamentally affected (rather than simply magnified) the underlying processes that bring people to the streets remains a contentious topic.

The emergence of more collaborative and social networking-oriented Web 2.0 tools has reignited the debate about how central a role information and communication technologies play in the organisation of collective action. Over the last five years, millions of people across the globe, from Cairo and New York to Madrid and Hong Kong, have used platforms such as Facebook and Twitter—and their mobile versions—to become more informed about the heated social and political issues facing their countries (Castells 2012). In the process, they have become (often accidentally) more connected with others who happen to share their frustrations, values and aspirations; have taken advantage of numerous social media-enabled opportunities to encourage their networks to support specific causes; and have been invited (and persuaded) by friends or acquaintances to take to the streets (Gerbaudo 2012; Tufekci & Wilson 2012). Adding a score of highly customisable and cheap ways to engage with political and social issues—such as creating groups, organising events, sharing hashtags, and uploading videos—social media are considered to be agents of change in the field of collective action (Bennett & Segerberg 2013; Earl & Kimport 2011; Tufekci 2014).

A central question in the field, however, is whether social media have fundamentally changed the dynamics of political mobilisation. Two theoretical approaches address this question. The first argues that social media have not altered the fundamental dynamics of participation; rather, participation levels and the diversity of participatory forms have increased to the point that they are 'supersized' (Earl & Kimport 2011, p. 71). The second approach argues that the emergence and widespread use of Web 2.0 platforms (see Bruns 2008) is creating a new model of mobilisation. This type of mobilisation has three key elements (for an in-depth discussion, see Bimber et al. 2012; Bennett & Segerberg 2013). First, Web 2.0 platforms such as Facebook and Twitter have the capacity to dramatically reduce the costs of organising and participating in collective action through embedded features, such as group and event creation (and many others). A second element is that user-generated political content can be easily personalised and adapted to one's values, identity, and self-expressive inclinations. The third element is that such content can be easily communicated across social networks of friends, acquaintances or simple 'followers', facilitating organisation without the need for, or the support of, formal organisations or other traditional mobilising agents. By assuming that social media is the central organising agent, this protest organisation logic—which some argue renders organisations' long-established resource mobilising role (see McCarthy & Zald 1977) less relevant (Tufekci 2014)—has been understood as one of 'connective action' (Bennett & Segerberg 2013). In its ideal form, the logic of connective action helps crowds organise protest acts using digital media communication as the primary organisational agent; the brokering functions of formal organisations are not needed. One of the core consequences of this model change is that a new type of protester may be emerging (Earl 2014; Earl et al. 2013; Earl & Kimport 2011;

Chadwick 2012): the skilful young social media user who is occasionally (and ephem-erally) mobilised by calls for action in her news feed, is not affiliated with any formal organisations (but contributes information from the demonstration using the protest event's official hashtag), has not previously been politically involved, and is more prone to participating in a one-off mobilisation or protest event that expresses her values and identity preferences.

Mobilisation in the Aganaktismenoi Movement

Greece adopted Internet technologies later than other countries in the region and is still at the low end of European Internet penetration rates (68 per cent). Thus, it was not among the first countries to see a popularisation of social media use (and hence their extensive use during protest events). In 2011, only around 30,000 Internet users had a Twitter account, and less than half of the country's six million Internet users were on Facebook (Internet World Stats 2014; Communication Effect 2011). Yet, there has been a radical rise in the number of Facebook and Twitter users over the last five years. An estimated 4.5 million Greeks have a Facebook account, which, in terms of propor-tion of Facebook users, is almost equal to rates in Spain and Italy but much lower than in the UK, Sweden, and Norway (Kemp 2014). Most of those (nearly three million) access social media on their mobile devices (Kemp 2014). Although Twitter users are substantially fewer—around 370,000 at the time of writing—Twitter it is the preferred tool for actively following the latest developments and its users believe it has fairly trustworthy information (Monitor 2014; ELTRUN 2013).

The Aganaktismenoi movement, the most visible public reaction to the crisis, was predominantly a movement of citizens completely disillusioned with the party system and with any notion of 'left' and 'right', who were devoid of any trust in the estab-lished political elite, the labour unions and the media (Sotiropoulos 2014). Much of the movement's rhetoric emphasised the lack of avenues for political expression and representation, and the high levels of corruption among politicians (To Vima 2012). They criticised the media particularly strongly—especially traditional media chan-nels, which they asserted were highly corrupt and accountable for the lack of credible political reporting (and reporting about the movement). Facebook and Twitter were alleged to be the main organising platforms of the Aganaktismenoi protest events, especially the major mobilisation of May 25 (Ekathimerini 2012; Ethnos 2011). The calls for participation through the Aganaktismenoi's Facebook page and the hashtag #greekrevolution encouraged citizens to meet at Athens' Syntagma Square and in other Greek cities to protest peacefully without party banners. Although the number of protesters is difficult to determine, the most commonly accepted estimate is 140,000 at the movement's peak (Sotiropoulos 2014, p.22). Inspired by Madrid's 'acampadas' (encampments) during the 15M protests, some protesters also occupied Syntagma Square and held regular daily meetings and general assemblies until the protests gradu-ally faded out in July.

Since organisations—especially labour unions—have played a crucial role in Greece's protest culture over the last 50 years (Rüdig & Karyotis 2013b), the Aganak-tismenoi protesters' mobilisation via social media was a novel feature (To Vima 2012). Although such platforms were used to organise past protests (see, for example, Tsaliki 2010), the response to this call to action was far greater than that of any previous social media-enabled (or social media-supported) protest event. The size of the mobilisation thus raises a number of stimulating questions with regards to the organisational role of these platforms: How were social media used for mobilisation purposes? Is there any evidence that this mobilisation was close to the ideal type of crowd-enabled connective action, or did organisations play a role (albeit a subtle one) simply by providing personalised action frames (Bennett & Segerberg 2013)? If this was indeed a case of connective action, how did the Aganaktismenoi build their network of support, and what did that network look like? Was the mobilised crowd composed of a 'new' type of protester? Finally, since the movement produced little policy impact, did the mobilisations nevertheless have other social or political repercussions? And what role did social media play in them?

An Example of Connective Action?

There is very little research on the use of social media during the Aganaktismenoi mobilisations, and even less empirical evidence from the protests on the ground (but see the comparative studies by Theocharis et al. 2015; Lu et al. 2012). Yet, the Aganaktismenoi, who emerged a few days after Spanish protesters in Madrid raised a poster with the sentence 'Be quiet, the Greeks are sleeping,' shared many characteristics with the 15M movement that make them closely comparable, including the intensive use of social media for organisational purposes. Insightful studies by Anduiza and colleagues and others (Anduiza et al. 2014; see also González-Bailón et al. 2011; Bennett & Segerberg 2013; also see the chapter by Anduiza and Cristancho in this volume) demonstrate that the 15M mobilisation was one of the most empirically robust examples of connective action. That is, traditional mobilising agents played no significant role in organising the protests and digital media channels were the predominant organisational and recruitment agents. There are indications that social media may have played a comparably mobilising role in the Aganaktismenoi mobilisations (Theocharis et al. 2015).

Figure 12.1 uses Twitter data collected using Discovertext's (discovertext.com) social media crawler. It analyses the structure of the Aganaktismenoi network from 31 May 2011 to 25 June 2011 using the open-source social network analysis software Gephi (see Bruns 2012, on the generation of conversation networks on Twitter); an in-depth exploration of the tweets' content was beyond the scope of this chapter. The network was generated from 17,866 tweets posted under the two most widely used hashtags during the period: #greekrevolution and #25Mgr. Despite the absence of data during the grand protest event of 25 May, as the mobilisations remained vibrant for more than a month, the data cover the peak of the Aganaktismenoi mobilisations and provide a sufficient source for observing Twitter's role as a mobilising agent. In order to better understand how extensively information was distributed on Twitter (and by whom), the network includes both tweets and retweets. Basic network analysis measures reveal a good deal about the network's organisation. Traditional political organisations (such as parties, labour unions or other coalitions) played no organisational role on social media. None of the 500 most-active Twitter accounts (which, put together, generated or re-generated most of the distributed content) belonged to a traditional political organisation.[1]

As other studies have shown (Gruzd et al. 2011; Theocharis 2013), most of the content (re)production was (unexpectedly) carried out by well-established and popular

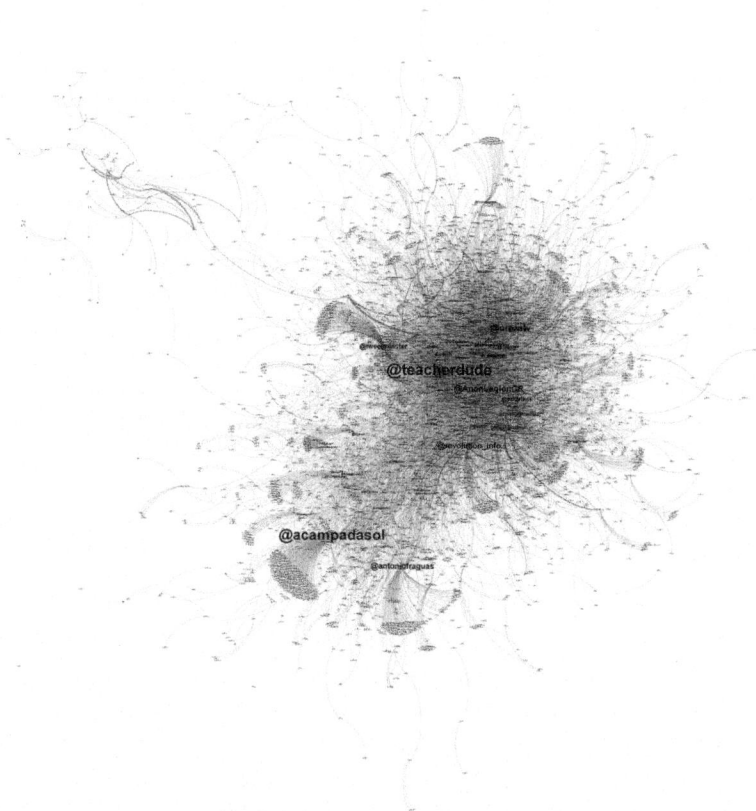

Figure 12.1 Conversation Network Based on 17,866 Tweets Posted under #greekrevolution, #25Mgr, 31 May–25 June 2011

Twitter users (for example, only one of the top 10 most popular Twitter users had fewer than 1,000 followers, while most had more than 5,000). The accounts of alternative media channels and influential blogs (such as @radiobubblenews, @thepressproject, and @prezatv) and the Greek branch of the hacktivist network Anonymous (@AnonLegionGR) also played a major role in (re)producing content. Considering that Twitter use in Greece by that time amounted to a little more than 30,000 users—and that the top five most popular Greeks tweeting under #greekrevolution alone had more than 50,000 followers combined—it is fair to assume that the vast majority of Greek Twitter users saw in their feed at least some information related to the activities of the movement on a daily basis. Given that Twitter is the most prominent "stitching mechanism used to coordinate . . . actors and platforms within the wider protest ecology" (Bennett et al. 2014, p. 272), it is likely that much of this information was also widely shared on Facebook, reaching a substantially broader audience.

A striking feature of the network is the support and co-production of content by Twitter accounts that also included the main hashtags of the 15M mobilisation

(#15M, #spanishrevolution), which was peaking around the same time. Using Gephi's modularity statistic that attempts to find clusters in the graph by identifying highly interconnected components, two clearly distinct communities can be discerned. Going through the Twitter handles of the 100 most influential Twitter users of the first community, it is evident that the upper part of the network—in dark grey—consists of Greek Twitter users using mainly the #greekrevolution hashtag. By contrast, the lower one, in light grey, consists exclusively of Spanish Twitter users who, along with spreading information in solidarity with the Aganaktismenoi movement using the official hashtag #greekrevolution, bring the two causes together by also using the 15M hashtag. That the two movements were showing solidarity and closely supporting each other online is evident not only from the integration of these two communities but also from the fact that many of the top 10 most influential Twitter users of the #greekrevolution network were Spanish (e.g. the account established by the occupants of the Puerta del Sol Square in Spain (@acampadasol), accounts of other encampments in Spain (@acampadaPalma, @acampadabcn), popular bloggers and journalists (@antoniofraguas), and various self-organised platforms (@democraciareal, @juventudsin).

It is clear that the protests were, as far as online mobilisation using Twitter was concerned, indeed carried out without the involvement of traditional political organisations. Internet-based alternative news channels, bloggers, and the wider Twitter public within and outside Greece were responsible for the (co)production and circulation of content about the events. In this respect, combining these insights with evidence from other studies demonstrating that the Aganaktismenoi demonstrators heard about the events though social media (*To Vima* 2012)[2], we can cautiously argue that the mobilisations conformed to two important aspects of the crowd-enabled type of connective action: that the prevalent mobilisation channels indeed heavily involved the use of social media, and that no traditional political organisations were involved in organising the events through these avenues.

A final important aspect of crowd-enabled connective action protests that distinguishes them from protests that are organised—or at least supported to some extent—by traditional political organisations is the composition of the protest public. Did the widespread circulation of the Aganaktismenoi movement's activities on social media result in the mobilisation of a different crowd? Recent research shows that non-partisan mobilisation (a rare occurrence in Greek protests which have always been dominated by part factions) preceded the involvement of political parties in protests against successive austerity packages—although after the end of the Aganaktismenoi mobilisations, as the crisis evolved, demonstrations organised by parties of the opposition grew significantly (Koussis & Kanellopoulos 2013; Sotiropoulos 2014, p.10). Furthermore, findings from a unique study on the demonstrators' composition during the anti-austerity protests in Greece (Rüdig & Karyotis 2013a) suggests a contrast between traditional vs. new protesters. Rüdig and Karyotis (2013b) concluded that, once protest experience is taken into account,[3] new protesters who took part in anti-austerity demonstrations and strikes in 2010 did not conform to the typical well-educated protester profile, and were less likely to be members of traditional political organisations or associated with left-wing ideology. Although the mobilisations examined in their study preceded the rise of the Aganaktismenoi by five months (and thus the question of whether social media played a major role in mobilising such a different crowd should be subjected to further empirical investigation), evidence from interviews with Aganaktismenoi protesters in Syntagma Square shows that the events drew in a similar crowd (*To Vima* 2012). In all, although the causal role of social media mobilisation remains the subject of empirical scrutiny, extant evidence shows that these self-organised protests may have also produced (or contributed to) one of the most important consequences of connective action protests: the mobilisation of a new type of protest participant.[4]

Connective Action and Beyond: The Emergence of Networked Solidarity

The Aganaktismenoi encampment lasted approximately one month (from late May to mid-July 2011), after which the protests died out (Sotiropoulos 2014). One of the most interesting questions that emerges from these events, is whether the utility of these mobilisation channels and networks extended beyond the end of the pro-test events. This question has become very relevant, especially after the mainstream international media documented bottom-up solidarity initiatives that emerged after the end of the Aganaktismenoi mobilisations (by people who participated in those mobilisations) (Henley 2012a, 2012b, 2012c). These were largely loosely organised and informal citizen groups that were focusing on, among other things, exchanges of food, clothes and services, provision of health care, community and educational work (a rough overview of such initiatives can be found in Sotiropoulos 2014). The formation and volunteer base of many of these bottom-up initiatives can be traced back to the Syntagma Square protests (Demertzian 2014). Their rise and supportive role to existing civil society organisations is an important consequence of the Aga-naktismenoi movement, especially given the dire condition of Greek civil society over the last several years (Sotiropoulos & Karamagioli 2006). Yet, perhaps even more interesting, due to their formation in the virtual space, are the spontaneous, social media-based and social media-*enabled* networked solidarity initiatives. These initiatives were built upon connective action networks established during the Aga-naktismenoi mobilisations (both online and offline), and were maintained long after that period.

A prominent example of such initiatives is #tutorpool, which began with a tweet on 12 December 2011. Following vibrant discussions with a good number of Twitter users from all over Greece, Twitter user @doltsevito, a statistician and teacher, voiced the idea for a networked solidarity initiative focused on the voluntary teaching of children whose parents were in financial difficulties.[5] The plan was to use online social networks to distribute calls for volunteers who could provide children in their area with free one-on-one lessons. Google Maps would help pinpoint the location of the children so that nearby volunteers would know where support was needed. If no one could provide support locally, teachers with the relevant expertise could arrange Skype lessons. In agreement that many schoolchildren whose families had been hit hard by the crisis were losing out, many qualified Twitter users immediately offered to help, and those who were not qualified spread the word with retweets or contributed in other ways (e.g. computer specialists built a website or configured the maps). Three months later, more than 300 families had registered with #tutorpool, which had more than 500 volunteer tutors across Greece (and beyond).

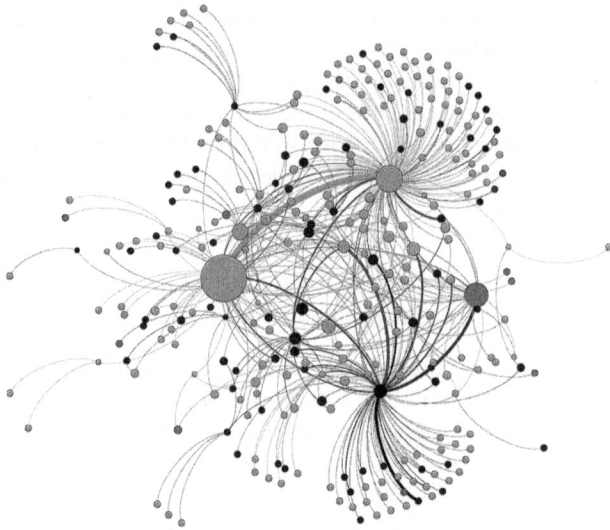

Figure 12.2 Conversation Network Based on 1,100 Tweets Posted under #tutorpool, 11 and 17 November 2012

There is little doubt that many of the people who played an important role in organising the Aganaktismenoi movement by distributing information on Twitter helped #tutorpool reach a large audience and, as a consequence, an unexpectedly large base of volunteers. Although this cannot be substantiated with Twitter data from the days of #tutorpool's beginnings, data from #tutorpool's activity one year later were available to the author. Figure 12.2 uses tweets posted under #tutorpool to depict the Twitter network's activity between 11 and 17 November 2012. Node size is set to out-degree, aiming to capture the most active users in terms of content (re)production. Twitter accounts that were found to have produced content in the #greekrevolution dataset are coloured in black (Twitter account names have been removed for better graph clarity).

The message is fairly clear. More than one third of the 293 Twitter accounts that engaged in activities related to #tutorpool (most of them call for, or redistribute messages about, teachers needed in certain areas) during the given timeframe were also involved in content distribution for the Aganaktismenoi movement. Most importantly, some of them ranked in the top 10 content producers in both datasets. Indeed, as the black nodes on Figure 12.2 demonstrate, very substantial support to, and solidarity with, #tutorpool's endeavour came from pre-existing networks of Twitter users that had been active in organising the Aganaktismenoi more than 18 months earlier. This solidarity network was invaluable for #tutorpool's effort to reach a large audience, build a considerable base of volunteers, and even receive coverage from national and international mainstream media, such as *The Guardian* (Henley 2012a).

Looking Ahead: A Digital Opportunity for Strengthening Greek Civil Society

This chapter discussed the use of social media, specifically Twitter, by the Aganaktismenoi movement. Such tools set this movement apart from all other previous mobilisations in Greece. In line with at least the main aspects of what Bennett and Segerberg (2013) call the logic of connective action, social media were the prevalent mobilising channels, leading to one of the biggest and probably most diverse—in terms of protester characteristics—protest events in years. This was achieved largely through the use of platforms such as Facebook and Twitter, which gave citizens the opportunity to create groups quickly and easily, and distribute personalisable content[6] about the events across social networks. Much of the personalised political content was co-distributed and co-produced by Spanish Twitter users, which created a strong link and sense of solidarity with the 15M movement.

Although the Aganaktismenoi will be remembered as a peaceful and innovative protest movement, the abrupt end of the mobilisation and the lack of follow-up resulted in a lot of negative coverage and in the supposed vindication of many who, from its beginning, condemned the movement as aimless, apolitical, and immature. Although assessing the movement's impact is beyond the scope of this chapter, it is worth stressing that despite the lack of visible political outcomes (contrary to 15M, which morphed into Podemos, currently a rising political power in Spain—see Fominaya, 2014), the Aganaktismenoi may have had more subtle, but nevertheless significant, ramifications.

Many of the innovative citizen-initiated groups that played a vital role in shoring up (and strengthening) Greece's notoriously weak civil society trace their origins to the Syntagma public meetings (Demertzian 2014). Many of the people who later became organisers of solidarity initiatives and leaders of civic innovations visited the protests and met like-minded people with whom they kept in touch via social media. These communication channels gave them the opportunity to discuss their ideas publicly, find an audience using networks of friends or unknown others with whom they created loose online ties during the Aganaktismenoi mobilisations, and build new solidarity networks.

Importantly, what this chapter reveals is that connective action networks offer a flexibility that may, on certain occasions, have long-lasting consequences and utility for those involved in the self-organisation of protest action—but also for those who were not and got in touch with those networks later on. Once formed, such networks can remain active—albeit on a sort of 'standby mode'—long after the particular mobilisation they were shaped for, and be quickly re-activated to support other mobilisations or smaller initiatives. Highly successful examples such as #tutorpool indicate that social media, especially Twitter, can act as what Putnam calls a 'social glue' that leads to—or at least lays the groundwork for—some sort of social capital generation (for some preliminary evidence that such processes may be at work see Sajuria et al. 2015).

Although much more research is needed in order to understand the precise mechanisms, the type of participants, and the impact of social media-enabled initiatives such as #tutorpool, it is clear that such digital technologies can give creative and willing citizens opportunities to strengthen civil society through self-organised networked solidarity initiatives. Since such initiatives are easily transferable to different political contexts via online interpersonal networks, weak civil societies in particular can benefit greatly from the opportunities offered by digital technology.

Notes

1 Level of activity (in terms of tweeting or retweeting information) was calculated using the accounts' out-degree centrality, which represents the number of ties that the node directs to others—in this context, when addressing or retweeting another user. It needs to be added that the notion of 'betweenness' centrality is crucial to understanding information distribution (and thus organization) on a Twitter network. The node with the highest betweenness centrality in a network lies in the shortest path between every other pair of nodes. Thus, from an organizational point of view, nodes with high betweenness centrality have a large influence on the network due to their awareness of the information circulating the network and their ability (and influence) to act as information gatekeepers. A calculation of the 500 most influential nodes based on betweenness centrality did not, however, yield different results (compared to out-degree centrality) as to the presence of organizations.
2 A summary of the study by Georgiadou and colleagues can be found in a report by the Greek newspaper *To Vima* (2012).
3 This is particularly important, given that participation in protests and strikes was a regular feature of Greek life well before the anti-austerity protests. See Rüdig & Karyotis (2013b, p. 492) and Pappas & O'Malley (2014, p. 1597).
4 Parallels with the 15M movement can be drawn here too. As Anduiza and colleagues have shown, Spain had never before experienced street demonstrations of that scale without the involvement of traditional organizations or significant coverage from the mainstream media, while the sociopolitical composition of the demonstrators was also significantly different from the typical very politically active, organizationally affiliated protesters (Anduiza et al. 2014, pp. 751, 762).
5 It is (still) broadly accepted that the teaching provided by Greece's high school system is insufficient preparation for a place at university. As a result, private tuition—which often places a very substantial economic burden on Greek families—has, for decades, been necessary for almost anyone planning to enter higher education.
6 Personalization included slogans about 'Real Democracy Now!' adapted by the Spanish 15M movement, as well as a lot of creative—and often humorous—content depicting people's common frustration with the governing elites. Photos with thousands of indignant people outside the Greek Parliament with their hands raised in a demeaning gesture common in Greece became one of the symbols of the demonstrations.

References

Anduiza, E., Cristancho, C., & Sabucedo, J. M. (2014) "Mobilization through Online Social Networks: The Political Protest of the Indignados in Spain". *Information, Communication & Society*, 17(6), pp.750–764.
Bennett, L. W. (2003) "Communicating Global Activism". *Information, Communication & Society*, 6(2), pp.143–168.
Bennett, L. W., Breunig, C., & Givens, T. (2008) "Communication and Political Mobilization: Digital Media and the Organization of Anti-Iraq War Demonstrations in the U.S." *Political Communication*, 25(3), pp. 269–289.
Bennett, L. W., & Segerberg, A. (2013) *The Logic of Connective Action: Digital Media and the Personalization of Contentious Politics*, Cambridge: Cambridge University Press.
Bennett, L. W., Segerberg, A., & Walker, S. (2014) "Organization in the Crowd—Looking Ahead". *Information, Communication & Society*, 17(2), pp. 272–275.
Bimber, B., Flanagin, A. J., & Stohl, C. (2012) *Collective Action in Organizations: Interaction and Engagement in an Era of Technological Change*, Cambridge: Cambridge University Press.
Bruns, A. (2008) *Blogs, Wikipedia, Second Life and Beyond: From Production to Produsage*, New York: Peter Lang.

—— (2012) "How Long is a Tweet? Mapping Dynamic Conversation Networks on Twitter Using Gawk and Gephi". *Information, Communication & Society*, 15(9), pp.1323–1351.

Castells, M. (2012) *Networks of Outrage and Hope: Social Movements in the Internet Age*, Cambridge: Polity Press.

Chadwick, A. (2007) "Digital Network Repertoires and Organizational Hybridity". *Political Communication*, 24(3), pp.283–301.

Chadwick, A. (2012) "Recent Shifts in the Relationship Between the Internet and Democratic Engagement in Britain and the United States: Granularity, Informational Exuberance, and Political Learning". In E. Anduiza, J.M. Jensen, & L. Jorba, (eds.) *Digital Media and Political Engagement Worldwide: A Comparative Study*, Cambridge: Cambridge University Press, pp.39–55.

Communication Effect (2011) "Twitter in Greece". Available at: http://communicationeffect.com/twitter-in-greece/.

Demertzian, M. (2014) "Αναζητώντας τους Αγανακτισμένους της πλατείας σήμερα . . . ". *Huffington Post* (GR). Available at: http://www.huffingtonpost.gr/2014/11/19/story_n_6177356.html.

Earl, J. (2014) "Something Old and Something New: A Comment on 'New Media, New Civics'". *Policy & Internet*, 6(2), pp.169–175.

Earl, J., & Kimport, K. (2011). *Digitally Enabled Social Change: Activism in the Internet Age*, Cambridge: MIT Press.

Earl, J., McKee-Hurwitz, H., Mesinas, A.M., Tolan, M., Arlotti, A. (2013) "This Protest will be Tweeted: Twitter and Protest Policing During the Pittsburgh G20". *Information, Communication & Society*, 16(4), pp.459–478.

Ekathimerini (2012) "In Syntagma Square, some see the dawn of a new politics". Available at: http://www.ekathimerini.com/4dcgi/_w_articles_wsite3_1_26/06/2011_396010.

ELTRUN (2013) "Annual Study of Greek Social Media Users". Available at: http://www.eltrun.gr/wp-content/uploads/2013/10/EthsiaEreynaKoinonikhsDiktyoshs2013-4.pdf.

Ethnos (2011) "Ο Μάης του Facebook και με ομπρέλες". *Ethnos*. Available at: http://www.ethnos.gr/article.asp?catid=22768&subid=2&pubid=63092999.

Fominaya, C. F. (2014) "'Spain is Different': Podemos and 15-M". *Opendemocracy*. Available at: http://www.opendemocracy.net/can-europe-make-it/cristina-flesher-fominaya/"spain-is-different"-podemos-and-15m.

Gerbaudo, P. (2012) *Tweets and the Streets: Social Media and Contemporary Activism*, New York: Pluto Press.

González-Bailón, S., Borge-Holthoefer, J., Rivero, A., & Moreno, Y. (2011) "The Dynamics of Protest Recruitment through an Online Network". *Nature*, 1(197).

Gruzd, A., Wellman, B., & Takhteyev, Y. (2011) "Imagining Twitter as an Imagined Community". *American Behavioral Scientist*, 55(10), pp.1294–1318.

Henley, J. (2012a) "Greece on the Breadline: Pooling Resources to Provide an Education". *The Guardian*. Available at: http://www.theguardian.com/world/blog/2012/mar/14/greece-breadline-pooling-education-resources.

Henley, J. (2012b) "Greece on the Breadline: 'Potato Movement' Links Shoppers and Farmers". *The Guardian*. Available at: http://www.theguardian.com/world/blog/2012/mar/18/greece-breadline-potato-movement-farmers.

Henley, J. (2012c) "Greece on the Breadline: Volunteer GPs Help Those with Nowhere Else to Go". *The Guardian*. Available at: http://www.theguardian.com/world/blog/2012/mar/18/greece-on-breadline-volunteer-medics.

Internet World Stats (2014) "Internet World Stats: Usage and Population Statistics". Available at: http://www.internetworldstats.com/stats4.htm.

Juris, J. S. (2005) "The New Digital Media and Activist Networking within Anti–Corporate Globalization Movements". *The Annals of the American Academy of Political and Social Science*, 597(1), pp.189–208.

Kahn, R., & Kellner, D. (2004) "New Media and Internet Activism: From the 'Battle of Seattle' to Blogging". *New Media & Society*, 6(1), pp.87–95.

Kemp, S. (2014) *European Digital Landscape 2014*, London. Available at: http://wearesocial.net/blog/2014/02/social-digital-mobile-europe-2014/.

Klandermans, B., van Stekelenburg, J., Damen, M-L., van Troost, D., & van Leeuwen, A. (2014) "Mobilization Without Organization: The Case of Unaffiliated Demonstrators". *European Sociological Review*, 30(6), pp.702–716.

Koussis, M., & Kanellopoulos, C. (2013) "Large Scale Mobilizations against Austerity Policies and the Memoranda, 2010–2012," paper presented at the *Crisis in Greece* Conference, Athens, 14–15 January.

Lu, X., Cheliotis, G., Cao, X., Song, Y., & Bressan, S. (2012) "The Configuration of Networked Publics on the Web: Evidence from the Greek Indignados Movement". In *WebSci '12 Proceedings of the 4th Annual ACM Web Science Conference*, New York: ACM, p.1850194. Available at: http://dl.acm.org/citation.cfm?id=2380742.

McCarthy, J. D., & Zald, M. N. (1977) "Resource Mobilization and Social Movements: A Partial Theory". *American Journal of Sociology*, 82(6), pp.1212–1241.

Merry, M. K. (2012) "Environmental Groups' Communication Strategies in Multiple Media". *Environmental Politics*, 21(1), pp.49–69.

Monitor (2014) "Social Media Monitoring. Social Media Monitoring". Available at: http://monitor.sidebar.gr/.

Pappas, T. S,. & O'Malley, E. (2014) "Civil Compliance and 'Political Luddism' Explaining Variance in Social Unrest During Crisis in Ireland and Greece". *American Behavioral Scientist*, 58(12), pp. 1592–1613.

Postmes, T., & Brunsting, S. (2002) "Collective Action in the Age of the Internet: Mass Communication and Online Mobilization". *Social Science Computer Review*, 20(3), pp.290–301.

Rüdig, W., & Karyotis, G. (2013a) "Beyond the Usual Suspects? New Participants in Anti-austerity Protests in Greece". *Mobilization*, 18(3), pp.313–330.

Rüdig, W., & Karyotis, G. (2013b) "Who protests in Greece? Mass opposition to austerity". *British Journal of Political Science*, 44(3), pp.487–513.

Sajuria, J., vanHeerde-Hudson, J., Hudson, D., Dasandi, N., & Theocharis, Y. (2015) "Tweeting Alone? An Analysis of Bridging and Bonding Social Capital in Online Networks". *American Politics Research*, 43(4), 708–738.

Sotiropoulos, D. (2014) *Civil Society in Greece in the Wake of the Economic Crisis*. Available at: http://www.eliamep.gr/wp-content/uploads/2014/05/kas.pdf.

Sotiropoulos, D., & Karamagioli, E. (2006) *The Greek Civil Society: The Road to Maturity*. Available at: http://www.civicus.org/media/CSI_Greece_Executive_Summary.pdf.

Theocharis, Y. (2013) "The Wealth of (Occupation) Networks? Communication Patterns and Information Distribution in a Twitter Protest Network". *Journal of Information Technology & Politics*, 10(1), pp.35–56.

Theocharis, Y., Lowe, W., van Deth, J. W., & Garcia-Albacete, G. (2015) "Using Twitter to Mobilize Protest Action: Online Mobilization Patterns and Action Repertoires in the Occupy Wall Street, Indignados, and Aganaktismenoi movements". *Information, Communication & Society*, 18(22), pp.202–220.

To Vima (2012) Η πλατεία ήταν γεμάτη . . . αγανακτισμένους. *To Vima*. Available at: http://www.tovima.gr/society/article/?aid=467898.

Tsaliki, L. (2010) "Technologies of Political Mobilization and Civil Society in Greece: The Wildfires of Summer 2007". *Convergence*, 16(2), pp.151–161.

Tufekci, Z. (2014) "The Medium and the Movement: Digital Tools, Social Movement Politics, and the End of the Free Rider Problem". *Policy & Internet*, 6(2), pp.202–208.

Tufekci, Z., & Wilson, C. (2012) "Social Media and the Decision to Participate in Political Protest: Observations From Tahrir Square". *Journal of Communication*, 62(2), pp.363–379.

Van Laer, J., & Van Aelst, P. (2010) "Internet and Social Movement Action Repertoires". *Information, Communication & Society*, 13(8), pp.1146–1171.

Vegh, S. (2003) "Classifying Forms of Online Activism: The Case of Cyberprotests against the World Bank". In M. McCaughey and M. D. Ayers (eds.) *Cyberactivism: Online Activism in Theory and Practice*. New York: Routledge.

Verhulst, J., & Walgrave, S. (2009) "The First Time is the Hardest? A Cross-National and Cross-Issue Comparison of First-Time Protest Participants". *Political Behavior*, 31(3), pp.455–484.

13

SOCIAL MEDIA USE DURING POLITICAL CRISES

The Case of the Gezi Protests in Turkey

Lemi Baruh and Hayley Watson

Introduction

The widespread adoption of social media within the past two decades has led to an increased interest in how social media may transform the nature of communication during political crises. Researchers have investigated a number of questions related to how activists use social media for coordination purposes, such as social media's potential as a source of information and a platform giving voice to citizens (e.g. Allagui and Kuebler 2011; Allan 2009; Andén -Papadopoulos 2013; Castells 2012; Hänska-Ahy and Shapour 2013; Johnson 2011). Nevertheless, little attention has been paid to how social media users may exhibit different usage patterns during times of crises. This chapter aims to fill this void by providing findings from two studies that examined how individuals used social media during the 2013 Gezi protests in Turkey.

In Turkey, particularly since the 1990s, the consolidation of media has led to a significant decrease in the availability of diverse news/information sources. Since the current ruling party (AK Parti) came to power in the 2002, national elections, press freedom, and media bias have become heavily debated issues. Critics have frequently argued that during AK Parti's tenure, political pressure on the press has increased and the mainstream media have been quickly (re)configured to create what critics named *yandaş* media (a derogatory term for describing uncritical partisanship in favour of the ruling AK Parti; see Çarkoğlu, Baruh and Yıldırım 2014).

Within a context where homogenisation of content in mainstream media is increasing, the use of social media during the Gezi protests emerges as a key case study for understanding the roles that these media can play in political crises. The unrest started in Istanbul at the end of May 2013, when a small group of protesters against the removal of trees for the new redevelopment project in the Taksim square area was violently evicted by police. Following the police action, the protests spread around Turkey. The agenda of the protestors quickly evolved to include not only the redevelopment project in Taksim, but also related issues such as the increasing encroachment of the ruling party into the private lives of citizens and threats to freedom of speech. Protestors and their supporters were highly vocal in their criticism of the lack of and bias in the news media coverage of the protests, resulting in an increase in the use of social media. For example, Topsy Labs (2013) reported about 10 million tweets containing hashtags related to the protests between 30 May and the 4 June 2013.

This chapter gives a brief overview of current research on social media during political crises. Moreover, as an addition to this area of research, we will summarise findings from two studies of social media use during the Gezi Park protests. First, findings from a survey on Twitter use during the protests and, second, results from a content analysis of blogs that citizens produced in order to share information and opinion about the protests. Both studies shed light on social media use in times of political crises.

Citizens and the Use of Social Media in a Crisis

Numerous studies have shown the potential value of social media in aiding communication efforts and enhancing situational awareness in a crisis (e.g., Starbird and Palen 2010; Watson and Wadhwa 2014). In the midst of a political crisis, new media technologies enhance individuals' abilities to network and offer new opportunities for citizens to organise, engage, and coordinate action as social activists. With the help of online networks, activists can locally and globally push grassroots ideas, organise and coordinate action (such as during the Occupy movements), and, crucially, through acts of citizen journalism, get their voices heard by the wider public (Anduiza et al. 2014; Castells 2012). Significantly, the use of network technologies have the potential to transform the organisational structures of activist networks in ways that may have long-term implications for the future of political organisations and participatory politics (Castells 2012; Juris 2005).

Social media have brought about new means through which citizens can produce, share, and gain access to information. This information includes, but is not limited to, information produced and shared by fellow citizens, and information shared by activists and organisations using social media platforms (Watson and Wadhwa 2014). The growth of social media platforms means that individuals are no longer merely consumers of information; rather, they can actively participate in the production, distribution, curation, and verification of information. As argued by Allan (2009: 18), citizens are able to 'bear witness' to unfolding events, thereby providing an additional lens to crisis reporting.

By participating in the construction of news, and moreover, consuming news produced and published by other citizens, individuals may be able to bypass the traditional gatekeepers, such as mainstream news media sources. User-generated content provides an alternative voice to mainstream media, thereby contributing to the democratisation of the news (Reese and Dai 2009; Young 2009). The increased role that citizens play in production and dissemination of information not only create new opportunities but also pose new challenges. For example, while citizen engagement may help dissemination of information and democratisation of access, it may also exacerbate problems related to distribution of misinformation (Andén-Papadopoulos 2013; Kuhn 2007; Watson and Wadhwa 2014).

A useful framework for understanding the interactions of citizens with news and information through social media is the uses and gratification theory (UGT), which holds that media users have an active, rather than passive, relationship with the media

(Newbold et al. 2002). As such, media users actively seek, or indeed create, content that will satisfy their needs.

In the last two decades, increased use of the Internet has led to a surge in the application of functional approaches in media studies, such as the UGT, for understanding users' interaction with interactive media, including, but not limited to, social networking sites (Chen 2011). Examples of such studies include why people use the Web for accessing political information (e.g. Kaye and Johnson 2002); individuals' motivations for using social media (e.g. Bazarova and Choi 2014; Joinson 2008; Nadkarni and Hofmann 2012); and how social media use contributes to enhancing social capital (e.g. Ellison, Steinfield and Lampe 2007).

With respect to Twitter, Chen (2011) conducted a study using UGT to understand how Twitter was perceived to have satisfied the need for connecting with others. The findings from this study indicated that the more time individuals spent on Twitter over a longer period (months), the more they fulfilled their need for connecting with others. In addition, actively participating in a conversation played a significant role in satisfying the need for connectivity. More recently, Hughes et al. (2012) utilised UGT to investigate the differences between uses of Facebook and Twitter. They found that those who used Twitter for gathering information did so for its "utilitarian value and cognitive stimulation" (Hughes et al. 2012: 567).

While UGT has provided important insights as to how and why people use social media, less attention has been paid to the use of social media during political crises. Until recently, studies that examined social media use in a crisis mostly focused on crises relating to *natural* disasters (e.g. a study of social media use following the Haiti earthquake by Yates and Paquette 2011). Lately, however, a number of studies have investigated the use of social media during political crises such as the Arab Spring and the Occupy movements (e.g. Anduiza et al. 2014; Juris 2012; Tüfekçi and Wilson 2012). For example, Tüfekçi and Wilson (2012) examined the role social media played in informing individuals of the protests as well as enabling them to participate in the demonstrations in the Tahrir Square in the Egyptian capital Cairo in 2011. Other studies, such as those by Castells (2012) and Garrett (2006), focused on how online media facilitated formation and organisation of new social movements.

Yet, given the potential of social media applications to allow users to not only seek information but also produce and disseminate information, a more comprehensive understanding of the role of social media during crises would require that we investigate a wider range of uses of social media in the context of political crises. As such, our study seeks to understand different patterns of social media usage in a political crisis, moreover, how user motivations may influence behaviour. The next two sections will aim to accomplish this goal by first summarising results from a survey that mapped Twitter usage types during Gezi protests. Then, we will summarise results from a brief content analysis of citizen-generated content during the protests.

Study 1: Use of Twitter during the Gezi Protests

Participants and Method

The survey was administered online between 10 and 29 June 2013. Respondents (adults older than 18) were recruited using a snowball sample through invitations sent via email, blogs, Facebook, Twitter, and LinkedIn. As such, the results of the survey are not statistically generalisable to the larger population, but provide a picture of how users gained information about the Gezi protests.

Out of 890 respondents who started the survey, 240 completed it. On average, the survey took about 20 minutes. Two-thirds of the respondents were women, and their mean age was 28 years. Approximately half of the respondents indicated that they were students at a higher education institution (undergraduate or graduate). On average, the respondents reported using the Internet for about four hours per day for purposes other than school or work. More than half of them reported visiting news websites (69 per cent), instant messaging (60 per cent), visiting video sharing sites (58 per cent), and using Facebook (77 per cent) at least once a day. A considerably smaller percentage of respondents reported using the Internet at least once a day for writing blogs (13 per cent).

Results

Almost all the respondents were Twitter users before the Gezi Park protests. During the protests, respondents on average spent approximately two and a half hours per day on Twitter and logged into their accounts about eight times per day. Slightly more than half of the respondents used their smart phones to access Twitter during the protests, whereas about a third used personal computers and a few accessed social media by tablets (10 per cent).

In terms of uses and gratifications of Twitter in general, we measured four types of uses of social media (e.g. Ellison, Steinfield, and Lampe 2007; Chen 2011). First, using Twitter for surveillance (e.g. 'To be up to date about news'), second, for relationship maintenance (e.g., 'To stay connected with people I know'), third, for connectivity (e.g., 'To expand my social circle') and, fourth, for self-expression (e.g., 'To make others understand me better'). Overall, respondents had significantly higher scores for using Twitter to fulfil surveillance needs than for self-expression needs, relationship maintenance needs, and connectivity needs.

Respondents also completed an open-ended question regarding why they used Twitter during the protests. Their answers were initially analysed via a grounded theory approach, using an open (substantive) coding of the responses (Corbin and Strauss 2008). Following the open coding, the 10 most frequently occurring categories of responses were formalised into a content analytic coding scheme. The ensuing coding scheme measured the absence/presence of each of the categories in the open-ended responses (each response could potentially be coded for all relevant categories). Two coders (the first author and a graduate student) coded each response independently from each other. With the exception of 'feeling of comradery' and 'wanted to gauge public opinion' categories, the intercoder reliabilities for the categories were higher than Krippendorff's $\alpha = 0.67$, the minimum acceptable level according to Krippendorff (2004). In cases when there were disagreements about the codes assigned to a given response, the differences were resolved through discussion between the two coders.

Accordingly, respondents predominantly indicated that Twitter was useful for getting up to date information (see Figure 13.1). In addition, 10 per cent of respondents reported that they were able to get first-hand information from peers who were actively participating in the protest via social media. For example, one respondent indicated that "the only way to attain true information was to get it first hand from people" and at many times, social media, despite issues regarding reliability of information, "were the only sources of information." Relatedly, close to 40 per cent of the respondents

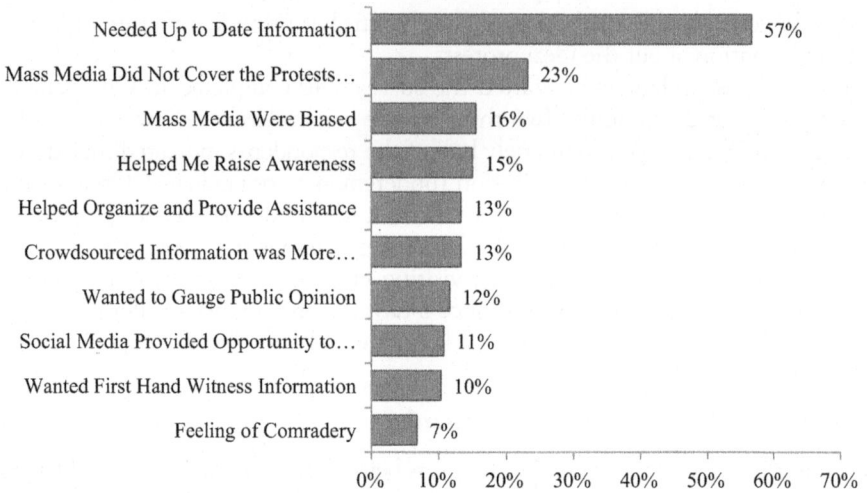

Figure 13.1 Reasons for Using Twitter during the Gezi Protests, by Percentage, 2013, N = 233

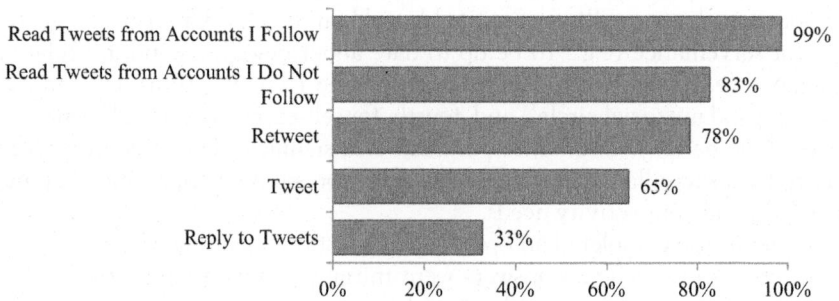

Figure 13.2 Activities Performed on Twitter during Gezi Protests by Respondents for at Least Half the Time They Logged on to Twitter, by Percentage, 2013, N = 239

indicated that they did not trust the mainstream mass media because they found coverage inadequate (23 per cent) or biased (16 per cent).

Using a 5-point scale that ranged between 'almost every time I log onto Twitter' to 'never' respondents also reported the extent to which they engaged in other activities such as tweeting about the protests, reading tweets published by other people, or retweeting or replying to others' tweets (see Figure 13.2). In line with the reasons of use reported above, respondents were more likely to use Twitter for information or opinion seeking than for sharing purposes.

We used an open-ended question to investigate the ways in which respondents verified information they received from Twitter: the most frequent method of information verification was direct contact with friends who were in the protest zone (see Figure 13.3).

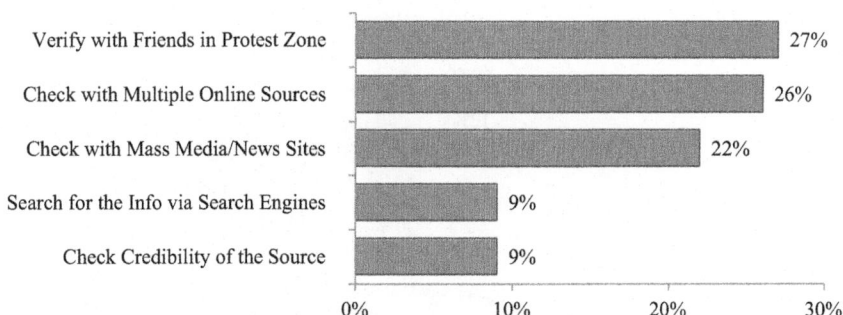

Figure 13.3 Activities Performed on Twitter during Gezi Protests by Respondents for at Least Half the Time They Logged on to Twitter, by Percentage, 2013, N = 239

Gezi Protests and Comparison of Twitter Usage Segments

For the segmentation analysis, respondents were asked to complete two questions (using a 9-point scale) to indicate the extent to which they would categorise their use of Twitter during Gezi Protests as oriented towards:

1. 'voicing your opinions' (1) . . . (9) 'share news/updates'
2. 'sharing updates/opinions' (1) . . . (9) 'following updates/news from others'

For both questions, approximately 30 per cent of the respondents categorised themselves as being in-between the two extremes. In line with the previous results, twice as many respondents were likely to categorise themselves as using Twitter to learn about opinions and updates from other people (46 per cent) than sharing their own opinions about the protests (23 per cent).

To segment the respondents in terms of Twitter utilisation orientations, a two-step cluster analysis using the Schwarz's Bayesian information criterion (BIC) was performed on the responses to these two questions. The results of this cluster analysis revealed four segments of Twitter users (see Figure 13.4):

- *Update seekers:* This segment comprised users who overwhelmingly reported using Twitter for news and updates and for learning about what others have shared.
- *Update hubs:* Close to half of the respondents in this segment were oriented towards news and updates rather than opinions. The majority of respondents reported maintaining a balance between sharing and learning about what others have shared.
- *Opinion seekers:* A large majority in this segment reported that for them Twitter was useful for learning about what others have shared.
- *Voice makers:* All members of this segment reported that they used Twitter for sharing their own opinions.

We observed no statistically significant differences between the segments in terms of using Twitter to fulfil surveillance (information seeking), self-expression, and relationship maintenance needs. However, the voice makers were more likely to use Twitter to expand their networks than members of other segments, i.e. the update hubs, update seekers, and opinion seekers members.

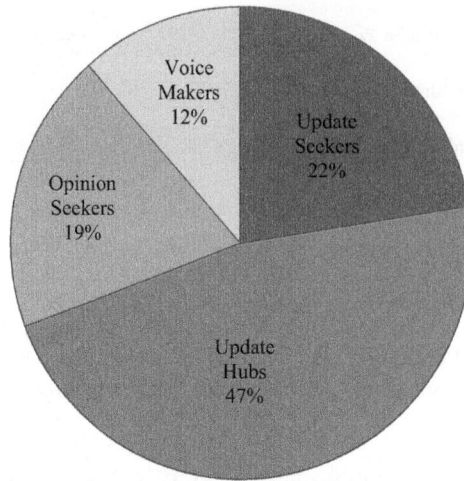

Figure 13.4 Twitter Usage Segments, 2013, N = 218

Table 13.1 summarises the comparison of the segments in terms of Twitter-related activities. The percentages reflect the shares of the respondents who indicated that they engaged in the activity in question at least half of the time that they logged onto Twitter. Update hubs and voice makers tended to write tweets and retweet others' tweets more than the other segments. The results show that close to half of the respondents in the voice makers segment replied to tweets at least half of the times they logged on Twitter compared to a third of the respondents who belonged to other segments.

Table 13.1 Comparison of Usage Segments in Terms of Activities on Twitter during the Gezi Protests, 2013, by Percentage, N = 217

	Update seekers	Update hubs	Opinion seekers	Voice makers	χ^2
Read tweets from accounts I follow	98	100	95	100	5.444
Read tweets from accounts I don't follow	90	81	81	80	2.241
Retweet others' tweets	69	86	69	80	8.112*
Write tweets	50	74	59	68	8.836*
Reply to others' tweets	33	30	29	48	3.328

Notes. N = 217, *p < .05, **p < .01, ***p < .001 (two-tailed).

Table 13.2 summarises the extent to which different segments utilised the most common three information verification techniques. First, opinion seekers were least likely to directly contact people from the protest zone and verify information (7 per cent). Second, update hubs (35 per cent) were more likely than other segments to cross-check information with multiple sources.

Table 13.2 Comparison of Usage Segments in Terms of Information Verification Techniques, by Percentage, N = 217

	Update seekers	Update hubs	Opinion seekers	Voice makers	χ^2
Verify with friends in protest zone	34	31	7	39	8.765*
Check with multiple online sources	21	35	29	4	9.162*
Check with mass media/news sites	18	15	29	30	3.674

Notes. *$p < .05$, **$p < .01$, ***$p < .001$ (two-tailed).

Study 2: Blogging and Content of Citizen-Generated News

As discussed above, particularly during political crises, social media can help provide alternative spaces for individuals to bypass mainstream media as gatekeepers of information. The data that we collected about Twitter usage indicate how general mistrust of mainstream media may have contributed to the use of social media as a source of information. Our data demonstrate that in the case of the Gezi protests, users were more likely to use Twitter for receiving and forwarding information and opinions rather than to generating news. Our second study took this as a starting point and focused on how citizens utilised blogs to generate and share information about the protests.

Method

We carried out a content analysis on citizen-journalism articles that were retrieved online from blogs of individuals. Entries in five blogs, altogether 25 blog articles, were analysed. We used 'paragraphs' as a unit of analysis. This resulted in 289 units (paragraphs) that were coded by three independent coders who were trained for this purpose. The content analysis focused on the following variables: Types of news sources utilised (e.g. mainstream media, wire services, identified news sources); quotations and citations of news sources; use of audio-visuals; the balance between information vs. commentary; utilisation of episodic vs. thematic frames; targets and sources of criticism (i.e. who voices criticism about whom). The intercoder reliability of the items were higher than Krippendorff's $\alpha = 0.67$. Disagreements about the codes were resolved through discussion between the coders and the first author.

Results

As discussed above, an important potential benefit of citizen-generated content is its ability to democratise access by providing voice to alternative sources of information. As such, one of the key variables that the content analysis focused on was the extent to which various news sources (including the blogger as a witness of the events) were utilised by the five bloggers. Figure 13.5 summarises the distribution of news sources. Accordingly, blog entries frequently referred to either confidential news sources or did not identify the source of the information. Also frequently, more than a third of the blog entries provided first-hand updates about events that were in progress. This is

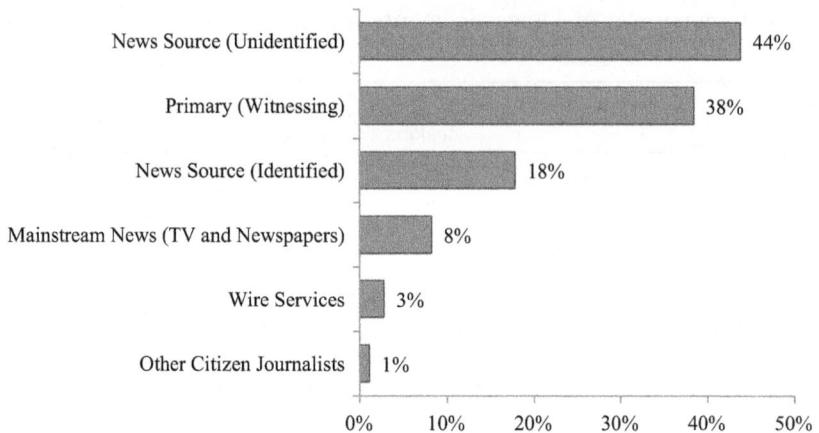

Figure 13.5 Information Sources, 2013, N = 281

indicative of the prevalence of 'witnessing' as an element of citizen journalism during emergencies. Third, news sources such as citizens, government sources, experts, were referred to in a fifth of the units analysed. In contrast, and importantly, mainstream media sources, such as television channels, news sites, or wire services, were rarely sourced by the bloggers.

Next, we will discuss the types of news sources that are included in the category 'news source—identified'. As can be seen from Figure 13.6, while government sources, as is the case in mainstream media, are frequently quoted, bloggers tend to give considerably more standing (voice) to citizens as protestors and eyewitnesses. Unlike mainstream media, who frequently quotes elite sources and experts, citizens seems to be given a voice in their capacities of being participants in the Gezi park-events.

Related to witnessing is the use of citizen-generated audio-visuals to substantiate a claim. The sources of such audio-visuals may include other citizens, mainstream media, or, increasingly, audio-visuals recorded by citizens themselves. Audio-visuals were highly prominent in the bloggers' coverage of the Gezi protests: More than three quarters of articles on witness accounts contained audio-visual evidence. Although we did not do a systematic analysis of the images, we observed that many of these audio-visuals (including photographs) supported what can be named as a 'sousveillance' function (ordinary citizens doing the watching, particularly to engage in inverse oversight of those in power; Mann 2009). They contained content that was to substantiate claims about police violence during the protests (e.g. injured citizens, police aiming gas canisters directly at protestors).

As the analysis has shown, social media can be a key outlet for the dissemination of opinions, or more precisely, alternative ways of making sense of events. Citizens engaging in reporting will be less likely to be constrained by commercial imperatives or editorial pressure that may limit the choice of frames, and, connected to that, an important question concerns whether this relative freedom will translate into their use of alternative and oppositional news frames that open for other ways of making sense of the Gezi events. Particularly, as Iyengar (1991) notes, use of thematic frames, which focus on the context and not just the incident, may help readers make sense of factors

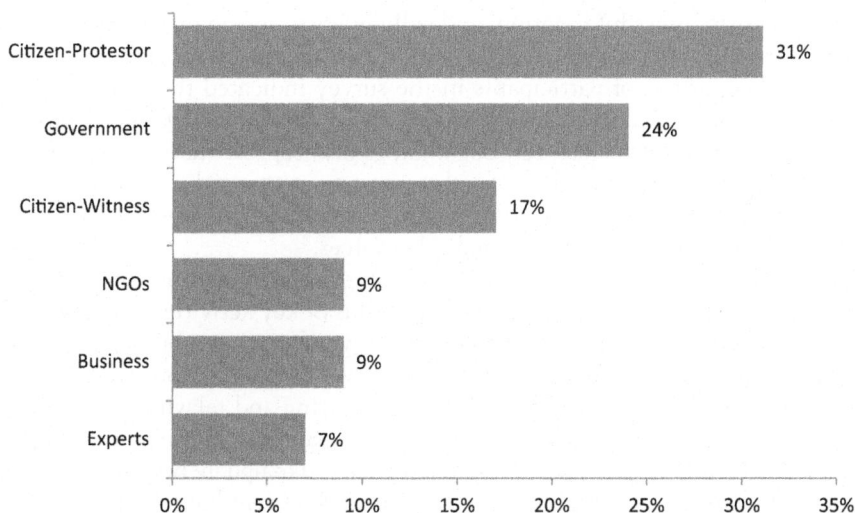

Figure 13.6 Distribution of Sources Quoted for 'News Sources—Identified' Category, N = 54

that may have contributed to an incident. Conversely, use of episodic frames, defined as those focusing on concrete, isolated events, would be considered more in line with a detached 'just the facts' approach that is often adopted by commercial news outlets (Tiegreen and Newman 2008).

Our analyses indicate that during the Gezi protests, bloggers were much more likely to have provided commentaries (63 per cent) rather than straight news and information (37 per cent). Likewise, a large majority of the units analysed adopted a thematic frame rather than an episodic frame while describing the protests. Related, a considerable proportion of the content generated by bloggers contained criticism of various institutions. Namely, close to half of the units contained some form of criticism targeting government and about one fifth of the units criticised commercial media companies. The most common form of criticism that was present consisted of criticisms raised by politicians, followed by bloggers' own statements (46 per cent), and criticism voiced by citizens.

Conclusion

The increased penetration of social media applications into citizens' daily lives may present important opportunities for communicating in a crisis. One such opportunity concerns the incorporation of citizens into the communication mix, both as consumers of information, and as potential producers and disseminators of information via social media. As such, this chapter has aimed to provide a summary of how individuals utilised social media during a political crisis: the 2013 Gezi protests in Turkey.

The chapter reported findings form two separate studies. First, we summarised findings from a survey conducted on a convenience sample of Internet users that focused on how individuals utilised Twitter during the Gezi protests to get access to information, share information and opinions and verify information. The findings from this study suggest that particularly in the case of this political crisis, mistrust in mainstream media, desire for access to direct information, and willingness to spread information and voice opinions were the main factors that led to increased reliance on social media. Indeed, a significant proportion of participants in the survey indicated that one of the main reasons why they utilised Twitter (and social media in general) was their mistrust of conventional sources of media. Yet, our findings also suggest that this preference for using Twitter did not necessarily mean that users trusted social media as a source of information. Consequently, they utilised different methods for verifying information and crosschecked information across multiple sources.

The segmentation analysis performed on Twitter users underlines the existence of four segments of Twitter users who differed in terms of key activities engaged on Twitter (and motivations for them) and information verification techniques. In terms of motivation, we observe that while all segments were equally motivated by "getting information," the update hubs, who valued both getting and relaying the information (by retweets and tweets), were also motivated by expanding their own networks. This may explain why acting as a hub was useful for them. Like update hubs, members of the voice makers segment were highly likely to tweet and retweet but (possibly) since they were oriented towards sharing opinions rather than information they were much less likely than the other segments to crosscheck information with multiple sources.

Our study supports the findings of others, such as Yates and Paquette (2011), who found that in times of crisis, one key use of social media is for information gathering. In addition, our study shows that, crucially, users are also (albeit to a lesser extent) using Twitter as a means for having a voice. Our findings emphasise the need to investigate the possibility that the complementarity of roles (e.g. sharer, acknowledger, reader) factor into the sustainability of networks on Twitter and other online social networks. Finally, the findings from the first study imply that functional approaches to understanding Twitter users' motivations and gratifications (e.g. Chen 2011; Johnson and Yang 2009) would benefit from further refinement based on usage types.

While producing information did not stand out as a major driver of Twitter use in our first study, social media, as noted by a number of researchers (e.g. Allan 2009), present opportunities for individuals to challenge the control that mainstream media have over gatekeeping and sense-making functions. As such, the second study entailed a content analysis of blogs produced by individuals during the protests.

The results of the content analysis underlined a number of key points that are indicative of the potential of social media as a platform for dissemination of alternative voices. First, the findings suggested that citizens reporting about the events were more likely to report what they witnessed rather than recycling content from mainstream media. Second, an indication of what may be considered as a 'democratisation' of access was the extent to which citizens were cited or quoted as information sources by bloggers. Third, as discussed in the preceding sections, freedom from commercial concerns and editorial constraints can potentially enable citizens to adopt writing styles that are less likely to be present in mainstream news outlets. To some extent the use of news frames by bloggers reflected this potential. Namely, we observed that bloggers often utilised 'thematic' frames, which provided contextual information that can help readers understand the context of the event.

When considered in conjunction with each other, the findings from the survey and the content analysis are indicative of how users utilised online forms of communication to fill what they perceived as a void in mainstream media during a political crisis like

Gezi protests. For Twitter users, the platform provided an opportunity to get up to date information at a time when mass media coverage (or lack thereof it) were considered as a symptom, if not a factor leading to, a democratic deficit. In many respects, by collecting and passing information to others, the largest segment of Twitter users (i.e. update hubs) were seeking to act as an information filter. Likewise, the findings from the content analysis that bloggers predominantly gave voice to other citizens and employed thematic frames underline how a sense of disillusionment with the coverage in the mainstream media may have contributed to the content of blogs.

Acknowledgments

The chapter is based on research emanating from the Contribution of Social Media In Crisis management (COSMIC) project. This project has received funding from the European Union's Seventh Framework Programmed for research, technological development and demonstration under grant agreement no. 312737). The views in this chapter are those of the authors alone and are in no way intended to reflect those of the European Union.

Parts of the findings summarised in this chapter were previously published in the 2014 European Conference on Social Media (ECSM; Baruh and Watson 2014).

References

Allagui, I. and Kuebler, J. (2011) "The Arab Spring and the Role of ICTs," *International Journal of Communication*, 5, pp. 1435–1442.

Allan, S. (2009) "Histories of Citizen Journalism," in S. Allan and E. Thorsen (eds.) *Citizen Journalism: Global Perspectives, Volume 1*, Oxford: Peter Lang, pp. 17–31.

Andén -Papadopoulos, K. (2013) "Citizen Camera-Witnessing: Embodied Political Dissent in the Age of 'Mediated Mass Self-Communication,'" *New Media & Society*, 16(5), pp. 753–769.

Anduiza, E., Cristancho, C., and Sabucedo, J.M. (2014) "Mobilization through Online Social Networks: The Political Protest of the Indignados in Spain," *Information, Communication & Society*, 17(6), pp. 750–764.

Baruh, L. and Watson, H. (2014) "Using Twitter for What? A Segmentation Study of Twitter Usage During Gezi Protests," in A. Rospigliosi and S. Green (eds.) *Proceedings of the European Conference on Social Media (ECSM)*, pp. 33–41. Bristol, UK.

Bazarova, N.N. and Choi, Y.H. (2014) "Self-Disclosure in Social Media: Extending the Functional Approach to Disclosure Motivations and Characteristics on Social Network Sites," *Journal of Communication*, 64(4), pp. 635–657.

Çarkoğlu, A., Baruh, L., and Yıldırım, K. (2014) "Press-Party Parallelism and Polarization of News Media during an Election Campaign: The Case of the 2011 Turkish Elections," *The International Journal of Press/Politics*, 19(3), pp. 295–317.

Castells, M. (2012) *Networks of Outrage and Hope*, Cambridge: Polity Press.

Chen, G.M. (2011) "Tweet This: A Uses and Gratifications Perspective on How Active Twitter Use Gratifies a Need to Connect with Others," *Computers in Human Behavior*, 27(2), pp. 755–762.

Corbin, J. and Strauss, A. (2008) *Basics of Qualitative Research: Grounded Theory Procedures and Techniques*, London: Sage.

Ellison, N.B., Steinfield, C., and Lampe, C. (2007) "The Benefits of Facebook 'Friends': Social Capital and College Students' Use of Online Social Network Sites," *Journal of Computer-Mediated Communication*, 12(4), pp. 1143–1168.

Garrett, R.K. (2006) "Protest in an Information Society: A Review of Literature on Social Movements and New ICTs," *Information, Communication and Society*, 9(2), pp. 202–224.

Hänska-Ahy, M. T. and Shapour, R. (2013) "Who's Reporting the Protests?: Converging Practices of Citizen Journalists and Two BBC World Service Newsrooms, from Iran's Election Protests to the Arab Uprisings," *Journalism Studies*, 14(1), pp. 1–17.

Hughes, D. J., Rowe, M., Batey, M., and Lee, A. (2012) "A Tale of Two Sites: Twitter vs. Facebook and the Personality Predictors of Social Media Usage," *Computers in Human Behavior*, 28(2), pp. 561–569.

Iyengar, S. (1991) *Is Anyone Responsible? How Television Frames Political Issues*, Chicago: University of Chicago Press.

Johnson, P. R. and Yang, S-U. (2009) "Uses and Gratifications of Twitter: An Examination of User Motives and Satisfaction of Twitter Use," paper presented at the annual meeting of the *Association for Education in Journalism and Mass Communication*. Boston, Massachusetts. Available at: http://www.researchgate.net/publication/228959109_Uses_and_gratifications.

Johnson, T. J. (2011) "Overthrowing the Protest Paradigm ? How the *New York Times*, Global Voices and Twitter Covered the Egyptian Revolution," *International Journal of Communication*, 5, pp. 1359–1374.

Joinson, A. N. (2008) "'Looking at', 'Looking up' or 'Keeping up with' People? Motives and Uses of Facebook," in *Proceedings of the SIGCHI Conference on Human Factors in Computing Systems (CHI '08)*, New York: ACM Press, pp. 1027–1036.

Juris, J. S. (2005) "The New Digital Media and Activist Networking within Anti-Corporate Globalization Movements," *Annals of the American Academy of Political and Social Science*, 597, pp. 189–208.

Juris, J. S. (2012) "Reflections on #Occupy Everywhere: Social Media, Public Space, and Emerging Logics of Aggregation," *American Ethnologist*, 39(2), pp. 259–279.

Kaye, B. K. and Johnson, T. J. (2002) "Online and in the Know: Uses and Gratifications of the Web for Political Information," *Journal of Broadcasting & Electronic Media*, 46(1), pp. 54–71.

Krippendorff, K., (2004) *Content Analysis: An Introduction to its Methodology*, Thousand Oaks: Sage.

Kuhn, M. (2007) "Interactivity and Prioritizing the Human: A Code of Blogging Ethics," *Journal of Mass Media Ethics*, 22(1), pp.18–36.

Mann, S. (2009) "Sousveillance: Wearable Computing and Citizen 'Undersight,'" *Humanity+ Magazine*. Available at: http://hplusmagazine.com/2009/07/10/sousveillance-wearable-computing-and-citizen-undersight/.

Nadkarni, A. and Hofmann, S. G. (2012) "Why Do People Use Facebook?," *Personality and Individual Differences*, 52(3), pp.243–249.

Newbold, C., Boyd-Barrett, O., and Van den Bulck, H. (2002) *The Media Book*, London: Arnold.

Reese, S. D. and Dai, J. (2009) "Citizen Journalism in the Global News Arena: China's New Media Critics," in S. Allan and E. Thorsen (eds.) *Citizen Journalism: Global Perspectives, Volume 1*, Oxford: Peter Lang, pp. 221–231.

Starbird, K. and Palen, L. (2010) "Pass It On? Retweeting in Mass Emergency," in *Proceedings of the 7th International ISCRAM Conference*, pp. 1–10.

Tiegreen, S. and Newman, E. (2008) "How News is 'Framed'." Available at: http://dartcenter.org/content/how-news-is-framed.

Topsy Labs, Inc. (2013) Available at: http://topsy.com/activity.

Tüfekçi, Z. and Wilson, C. (2012) "Social Media and the Decision to Participate in Political Protest: Observations from Tahrir Square," *Journal of Communication*, 62(2), pp. 363–379.

Watson, H. and Wadhwa, K. (2014) "The Evolution of Citizen Journalism in Crises: From Reporting to Crisis Management," in E. Thorsen & S. Allan (eds.) *Citizen Journalism: Global Perspectives, Volume 2*, New York: Peter Lang, pp. 321–332.

Young, C. W. (2009) "OhmyNews: Citizen Journalism in South Korea," in S. Allan and E. Thorsen (eds.) *Citizen Journalism: Global Perspectives, Volume 1*, Oxford: Peter Lang, pp. 143–152.

Yates, D. and Paquette, S. (2011) "Emergency Knowledge Management and Social Media Technologies: A Case Study of the 2010 Haitian Earthquake," *International Journal of Information Management*, 31(1), pp. 6–13.

14

STRUCTURES OF FEELING, STORYTELLING, AND SOCIAL MEDIA

The Case of #Egypt

Zizi Papacharissi and Stacy Blasiola

Introduction

Every movement has its own story and every era is historicised via its own storytelling tools. For our era, social media platforms provide a variety of ways with which to tell, share and feel our way into developing stories. When we think about the meaning of social media for developing movements of a political, sociocultural, economic, or all-those-things-together nature, we must understand that what these platforms chiefly do is permit movements to frame their story in their own terms. In fact, they go one step beyond that: They permit each individual involved, affiliated, or interested in a movement to become a storyteller, contributing to the collaborative narrative woven online and offline about the movement itself.

Much has been written about the role of social media in uprisings in the Middle East and North Africa (MENA) region, with particular emphasis on uprisings in Egypt that led first to reversal of the Mubarak regime and then to the downfall of the Morsi government. Some dismiss or downplay the existence of a causal relationship between use of social media and subsequent protests. People protested and brought down governments long before social media existed; Facebook and Twitter are simply places where revolutionaries congregate online (Gladwell 2011; Morozov 2011). Others maintain that use of social media accelerated the development of social movements in those countries in ways similar to those in which the printing press and other media facilitated revolutions in the past (Tufekci 2011; Ingram 2011). It is important to not lose sight of the fact that these are *human* revolutions, ultimately enabled by human cost and sacrifice, that had been accumulating and culminating over time (York 2011; Zuckerman 2011). Our own perspective suggests that these platforms do not make or break revolutions but rather, through their storytelling capabilities, afford movements voice and visibility that amplifies both the potential of the movement *but also the expectations associated with a given movement.*

Without a doubt, context matters. Moreover, whether these reprises will historically be claimed as revolutions can only be determined by long-term democratic outcomes. In the meantime, asking whether social media *caused* these uprisings misses the point. It also mischaracterises the nature of the media employed in the context of these upheavals. This chapter provides an overview of relevant research on how social media were utilised in recent Egyptian politics, by key political movements. In doing so, we synthesise research findings toward presenting propositions on the meaning, role, and impact of social media platforms in the context of recent Egyptian politics. The chapter is organised around what we know thus far, that is, what research has shown, and what questions remain unanswered.

#Egypt

Although the wave of protests and uprisings that swept through the Middle East and North Africa in late 2010 and into 2011 became largely known as the 'Arab Spring', it is important to recall that "there has been no single Arab uprising, but rather a series of different uprisings, which have each taken a different course according the intersection of domestic politic" (El-Hibri 2014: 841). Thus, we take to the current task with the intention of focusing on the events that occurred in Egypt in the 18-day span of protests between January 25 and February 11, the day that marked the removal of the 30-year-long regime of President Hosni Mubarak, who had long kept the country under dictatorial rule. The Egyptian uprising became known to Westerners as 'The Facebook Revolution', and even in Egypt, "The politicized, Internet-savvy generation that organized the initial events is known as 'The Facebook kids'" (Lindsey 2012: 54). That social media played a role in the events of the Egyptian uprising is clear enough, but numerous scholars have sought to understand the extent to which social media were used, by whom, and how. Needless to say, every movement possesses its own character, and to the extent that it adopts digital pathways to expression, its own digital footprint. Our focus on #Egypt highlights the unique and multiple textures of expression and connection of that movement, digital and non-digital. Our goal is to infer some broader conclusions about modalities of expression movements acquire online, but also to dispel the myths that all movements develop in identical ways that make or break revolutions online.

We do know from general research on the use of Twitter that addressivity and conversational markers shape the direction of information flows via Twitter. Networked publics are further textually rendered through the use of hashtags that define a topic or a direction for information sharing. Research generally indicates that content in select hashtags follows a power-law distribution in terms of popularity, time, and geo-location (Singh and Jain 2010). Locality further shapes the tone and tenor of flows organised by hashtags. Local tags may display denser social connectivity between posting users (Yardi and boyd 2010a). In conversations around controversial topics, replies between like-minded individuals tend to strengthen group identity, whereas replies between different minded individuals reinforce in-group and out-group affiliation (Yardi and boyd 2010b). For emerging movements, locality and homophily effects may play a part in accelerating the formation of network ties that enhance the spreadability of information.

Further research underscores the connection between shared geo-locality and communal bonds strengthened via Twitter posts, permitting forms of "peripheral awareness and ambient community" (Erickson 2010: 1194). The practice of following opinion leaders on Twitter has been likened to emerging disciplines of listening in social media, characterised by background listening, reciprocal listening, and delegated listening (Crawford, 2009). In this manner, the practice of listening may strengthen connectedness with others (Henneburg et al. 2009), resemble the practices of conversation (Honeycutt and Herring 2009; Steiner 2009), and add elements of physicality to web design (Hohl 2009). For burgeoning and ongoing movements, Twitter may serve as an always-on social environment that sustains conversations between homophilic and discordant publics, and these conversations frequently become more intense and spreadable when further sustained by a local connection or other shared interest.

During protests, uprisings, or periods of political instability, Twitter is frequently used to call networked publics into being and action. Understandably, the homophily encouraged by Twitter lends itself to calls for solidarity among publics, imagined or actual, that share a common set of goals. The enhanced connectivity experienced between Twitter users with shared geo-locations may further help activate and deepen ties during uprisings. Ultimately, the ambient nature of this social awareness environment lends itself to providing an always-on, interconnected web of information that mobilised actors might utilise, serving as more efficient and "electronic word of mouth" (Jansen et al. 2009: 2169). At the same time, it permits individuals to change the dynamics of conflict coverage and shape how events are covered, and possibly, how history is written (Hamdy 2010).

Under these circumstances, platforms like Twitter force a radical pluralisation of news dissemination and democratic processes (Dahlberg 2009). In regimes or during times when media are controlled, inaccessible, or not trusted, platforms like Twitter permit individuals to bypass traditional gatekeepers and contribute directly to the news process. News streams generated through the organic use of hashtags combine input from a variety of actors in ways that introduce *hybridity* into the news system. They encourage accidental or coordinated collaborations between journalists and citizens tracking the same story that further blur boundaries between information, news, and entertainment and introduce hybridity in the balance of power that shapes news production (Chadwick 2013). Moreover, the "broad, asynchronous, light-weight and always-on" aspect of platforms like Twitter afford individuals "an awareness system [with] diverse means to collect, communicate, share and display news and information, serving diverse purposes . . . on different levels of engagement" (Hermida 2010: 301). The ambience, homophily, and strengthening of bonds between those sharing a geo-local connection are essential in understanding the sociotechnical texture of Twitter, especially in situations that call for individuals to mobilise and show solidarity. They provide an always-on, ambient storytelling infrastructure that enables networked agents to presence their own takes on events ongoing and of the past. They thus shape the *storytelling infrastructure* of the platform.

Thus, given what we know about movements and the dynamic of Twitter, we turn our attention to current research to examine what findings have shown specifically about social media and the Egyptian uprising, and to shed light on questions yet to be answered.

The Role of Social Media in #Egypt

Previous scholarship reflects a range of opinions concerning the level of influence that social media played in the Egyptian uprising. Western mainstream media were fairly quick to attribute much of the success in mobilising masses to the organising efforts made on Facebook and Twitter. Scholarship on the area, however, paints a different, more cautious picture. Some warn that over-emphasising the role of social media is the result of focusing too intently on digital traces that may not be representative of the overall efforts of protestors (Aday et al. 2012), and that may only capture the role of affluent Egyptians (Nunns and Idle 2011). Others have argued that efforts made by the longstanding and frequent use of blogs by Egyptian activists paved the way for the 2011 uprising (el-Nawawy and Khamis 2014) and those efforts were simply extended to social media spaces such as Facebook and Twitter (Howard and Hussain 2011). Tufekci and Wilson (2012) argue that social media should be treated as one component of an evolving system of political communication in the Middle East and North Africa. In Egypt in particular, the influx of uncensored satellite television, privately owned print and online newspapers, and the growth of Internet accessibility—and ultimately the rise of social networks—all contributed to a shift from the monopolistic, state-controlled news environment to a pluralistic media environment that enabled oppositional viewpoints to spread (Khamis 2011). McGarty and colleagues (2014) succinctly state what the majority of scholars who investigated this topic have concluded or argued: As with all protests, the efforts made on the ground are what overthrow regimes, and so the Egyptian revolution was not a product of social media, but rather social media were one of several new technologies that enabled and facilitated social change.

Bolstering the position that social media should not be overly credited with the revolution's success are the modest Egyptian social media adoption numbers that preceded the uprising. Only an "infinitesimal proportion of the Egyptian population (.001%)" were Twitter users (Wilson and Dunn 2011: 1250), and only 4.7 million Egyptians had Facebook profiles. Despite these figures, social media acquired a starring role in Western perceptions of the Egyptian revolution, and its use among Egyptians may have taken a more significant role as local, state controlled media were restricted from accurately reporting on events on the ground (Arif 2014; Nunns and Idle 2011). Additionally, after the primary protests on January 25, Facebook in particular saw a jump in the number of Egyptian users (Aouragh and Alexander 2011). To understand how social media were utilised in the Egyptian uprising and to gauge its importance in motivating Egyptians to offline action, scholars have taken a number of methodological approaches from surveys and interviews of people on the ground, to content and network analyses of tweets, videos, and blogs. Questions have addressed who was using social media, what types of content were shared, and which messengers rose to prominence.

Observers and Participants: The People of #Egypt

Because any Twitter user is capable of using a hashtag and few users attach geo-location to their tweets, simply counting the number of tweets tells little about who was participating. Thus, researchers sought to gain a better idea of who was contributing and where those users were located. Twitter conversations about the Egyptian uprising circulated via two prominent hashtags: #Egypt and #jan25 (Wilson and Dunn 2011). Using the profile information collected from users who tweeted #Egypt, Howard and colleagues (2011) discovered that early on, most tweets were generated outside the region, but after January 25 and as Mubarak's resignation loomed, outsiders' participation dropped and those in the region began to account for the majority of tweets. Analysis of the dominant languages used in prominent hashtags support Howard and colleagues' (2011) findings. Several studies indicate that the majority of tweets in #Egypt and #jan25 were Latin based (Papacharissi and de Fatima Oliveira 2011; Meraz and Papacharissi 2013; Wilson and Dunn 2011). Expanding on this, Bruns, High-field, and Burgess (2013) examined #Egypt tweets over time and found that early on, although Latin based languages dominated, a few weeks after Mubarak resigned, non-Latin based languages became dominant. These findings support Lotan et al.'s (2011) research, which determined that early tweets were written in English to help spread protestors' messages to external, mainstream media outlets.

In addition to media outlets, external non-Arabic speaking observers became partici-pants in the Twitter discussions when they chimed in or showed support. Papacharissi and de Fatima Oliveira (2012) attribute the influx of non-local participants to the blending of news, opinion, and drama that created an affective news stream of tweets and encouraged commentary from participants and non-participants alike. Bruns and colleagues (2013) argue that the subsequent and significant shift in language also reflected a shift in attention as English-speaking countries turned their consideration elsewhere, and users of the hashtag became primarily Arabic speaking.

Affective News Streams: The Content of #Egypt

Analyses that examined the content of social media messages in relation to the Egyp-tian uprising conclude that in addition to using social media to communicate infor-mation about the protests, participants and observers bonded over an abundance of sentiment expression. These tweets, mixing sentiment, opinion, and live reports of events on the street created an affectively fuelled news stream that sustained an online home for the movement, even when there was little news to report about the move-ment itself. Specifically, #Egypt sustained an ambient, always-on news stream for the movement with a pulse of its own, working alongside events within and outside Egypt and affectively supporting the movement's growth (Papacharissi and de Fatima Oliveira 2012). To this point, in their content analysis of #Egypt tweets, Meraz and Papacharissi (2013) discovered that

> most tweets were not just news or opinion, but typically a blend of emotionally charged opinions on news or news updates to the point where it was difficult to distinguish news from opinion and from emotion, and doing so missed the point. (Meraz and Papacharissi 2013: 18)

In a visual content analysis of the most viewed YouTube videos, Arif (2014: 157) found that the image of Khaled Said's beaten face was used as an "icon of outrage" to gen-erate emotional responses that inclined viewers to the notion "if it can happen to Khaled Said, it can happen to me". This sentiment was also reflected in the title of the Facebook page 'We Are All Khaled Said', which was created by blogger, activist, and Google executive Wael Ghoneim (Vargas 2012). This Facebook page was used throughout as an organisational tool for protestors and as a space for individuals to express their 'virtual dissidence' (Allam 2014). According to Lim (2012: 241–242), the page created a "schemata of interpretation" for individuals in that "the story and images of the torture of Khaled Said personified the injustice and brutalities of the Mubarak regime and thus intensified the emotion of the oppositional movement". In conjunc-tion with messages of dissidence, participants included emotional appeals to national-ity in tweets and posts through the use of songs and slogans that reflected national pride (Eltantawy and Wiest 2011).

In their survey of Tahrir Square protestors, Tufekci and Wilson (2012) found that of those who had a Facebook profile—about half the sample—nearly all of them used their profile to communicate about the protests. Those messages included confirmation that one would participate, and in some cases, information about where and when protests would occur. However, fearing that security forces were actively monitoring social media sites Facebook and Twitter (Lindsey 2012), organisers sometimes used social media to spread disinformation about the specifics of protests (El-Hibri 2014), turning to more private communication methods such as email, SMS, and word-of-mouth to acquire and share the accurate locations and times of the protests (El-Hibri 2014; Tufekci and Wilson 2012).

In addition to their organising role, social media were also used to document and record protestors' experiences. Facebook posts were a place for participants to disseminate their own photos and videos of the protests (Howard and Hussain 2011; Tufekci and Wilson 2012). In some instances, personal Facebook videos were then pushed to YouTube where they attained widespread diffusion. This was the case for popular activist Asmaa Mafouz who posted Facebook videos in which she explained to friends and family her decision to protest and how others could participate (Wall and Zahed 2011). Once videos were posted to YouTube, they were viewed by outsiders and in some cases ended up appearing on mainstream news (Wall and Zahed 2011).

Just as messages in one social media space were often connected to or shared through other social media, protests in Egypt were connected to events elsewhere in the region. Egyptian activists posted words of support to Tunisian activists in the days preceding the Egyptian revolt and those words were echoed back by Tunisians who then lent their support to Egyptians (Eltantawy and Wiest 2011). Additionally, on Twitter, hashtags for the Egyptian protests were used in conjunction with hashtags related to neighbouring events, such as those in Tunisia, Libya, and Bahrain, in a manner that connected participants (Meraz and Papacharissi 2013).

Creating the News: Citizen and Journalist Use of #Egypt

Throughout the revolution, broadcast and online media outlets appeared to rely heavily on the use of material that was sourced from various social media sites. Tweets appeared on the scrolls of major news organisations' broadcasts, and videos pulled from YouTube were featured in news coverage. In Egypt, state-controlled media were prohibited from airing the protests and local Al Jazeera operations were suspended by the Egyptian government. Despite these efforts to curtail reporting, a number of media outlets provided thorough coverage of the events (Hermida et al. 2014). These circumstances led researchers to examine how traditional and social media worked together to shape the presentation of the revolution in the news. Researchers have questioned how social media influenced journalistic practices, and how individual citizens and activists rose to prominence.

At the time of the uprising, the use of social media by journalists was a relatively nascent development in the organisational routines of news work. In interviews with BBC workers who covered the Egyptian protests and the larger Arab Spring, Ahy (2014) describes a previously tumultuous relationship between news workers and social media. That relationship improved as a result of revamped work flows, whereby professional outlets leveraged their ability to acquire information via online tools and formalised processes to verify news reported by citizens through social media (Ahy 2014). Previous work on journalistic practices revealed that news sources are a function of news values in that journalists are pushed by the demands of the profession to find sources that are trustworthy and authoritative, so they often turn to people in positions of power (Gans 1979). This workflow typically limits the ability of ordinary citizens or those operating outside of recognised institutions to influence the news. In their larger study of Arab Spring, Harlow and Johnson (2011) found that in the case of the Tahrir Square protests, the *New York Times* adhered to news norms by relying on established sources, a finding bolstered by Al Maskati (2012) in his study of six mainstream newspapers and their coverage of the Egyptian uprising. However, Harlow and Johnson (2011) showed that non-traditional media spaces such as the citizen journalist website Global Voices and the Twitter feed of *New York Times* reporter Nick Kristof were more likely to position protestors as legitimate sources. Similarly, a case study of tweets by NPR reporter Andy Carvin found that he favoured alternative voices in both @mentions and Retweets (Hermida et al. 2014). In their work on #Egypt, Papacharissi and de Fatima Oliveira (2011) found that in addition to media elites, who rose to prominence often as a function of their place in Twitter's overall network, citizen leaders were crowdsourced to prominence via retweets, mentions, and follows. Collectively these studies describe a networked system that links protestors, observers, and journalists alike.

Lotan and colleagues (2011) identified and analysed information flows related to #Egypt and #jan25 on Twitter. They found that tweets operated as an important bridge that helped connect news of events from within the region to outside areas, as mainstream media used Twitter to learn of developments. This bridging aspect feeds into what Meraz and Papacharissi (2013) describe as *networked gatekeeping*: "the process through which actors are crowdsourced to prominence through the use of conversational, social practices that symbiotically connect elite and crowd in the determination of information relevancy" (Meraz and Papacharissi 2013: 21). In other words, Twitter, in particular, provided a means for marginalised voices to gain visibility and generate alternate narratives (Hamdy and Gomaa 2012). As traditional media faced limitations in their ability to cover on-the-ground events, Twitter users worked together to push particular frames and individuals to prominence (Meraz and Papacharissi 2013), thus giving non-elites more control in what was considered newsworthy and how those events were framed. Similarly, YouTube was used to amplify the message of protestors, particularly when broadcast media were prevented from reporting on the protests (Arif 2014). As a result, social media afforded bloggers, protestors, and activists the opportunity to co-construct news alongside professional journalists (Lotan et al. 2011). These tendencies can be understood as a form of *networked framing*, that is, processes through which a particular problem definition, causal interpretation, moral evaluation, and/or treatment recommendation attain prominence through crowdsourcing practices (Meraz and Papacharissi 2013; Papacharissi 2014; Papacharissi and Meraz 2012).

What We Know

There are three things then we can learn, from research on how social media were used in a series of unfolding mobilisations that preceded and followed the downfall of the Mubarak regime. First, that a variety of socially oriented platforms serve as connective conduits. These facilitate avenues for coordination and planning, and burgeoning movements employ these platforms much like they have utilised media in the past, including radio, print material, zines, songs, and prose. Each movement differs in its use of social media, so what we learn from #Egypt is relatable and comparable to other movements, but certainly not translatable and identical. Social media afford connective and expressive means.

As a second point, these platforms amplify and affectively drive a movement in a manner much grander, versatile, and diverse than previous media permitted, but typically in tandem with some form of offline mobilisation and always subject to context. Perhaps this is where we run the risk of overestimating the ability of social media to determine the outcome of mobilisation; it is not only voice and visibility for a movement that are augmented, but our own expectations that are amplified. To this point, it is worth noting that, even though each movement carries its own digital footprint— meaning that it makes use of online and digital means in ways that support its objectives and connect its publics—there is little sense in distinguishing between online and offline mobilisation. All forms of mobilisation are enabled by people, convening in a variety of spaces and taking action through a variety of means, none less or more real, or impactful than the other. Impact is generative, additive, and the result of combined efforts.

Therefore, and as a third point, our attention must turn elsewhere: These platforms, each in its own way, change the process through which a movement tells its own story. They transform the ways in which journalists and citizens experience and cover events collaboratively, they pluralise the manner in which movements are framed and thus, they inform how a movement is perceived and eventually historicised. These are the conclusions we can draw from the events we have observed take place in Egypt and the corresponding research on #Egypt. We can then extrapolate and compare those findings to our general understanding of mobilisation and participatory politics in contemporary societies. Given these conclusions, we turn next to unknowns, the interesting questions that have emerged in the process of studying #Egypt that are worth of further research.

What We Can Learn

As we consider the progression of political mobilisation in Egypt alongside the use of social media to network and presence the movement for change, three important directions for future research emerge. First, as media scholars know, there are events, and there are the stories that we tell about events that we have experienced or that we cannot experience directly. Lippmann (1922) famously referred to this distinction as the world outside and the pictures in our heads. Yet, every medium provides a different way for telling a story. Some scholars have referenced this distinction between the storytelling affordances of each medium by drawing a comparison between the concepts of mediatisation and mediation, and suggesting that the latter provides more "flexibility for thinking about the open-ended and dialectical social transformations . . . articulated new [forms] of digital storytelling" (Couldry 2008) and recognising how hybrid and new forms of storytelling may bridge formerly disconnected spheres of inquiry (Chouliaraki 2008; Livingstone 2009). Alongside those concepts, we could consider that the discursive mediality of each platform imprints each event with its own unique storytelling texture. We may in fact distinguish between different *events*, some rendered on the streets, others rendered textually via Twitter, and yet others mediated through TV and mainstream media. Alternatively, we may think of events that possess different forms of mediality and, as a result, offer distinct yet imbricated views of an event. It might be meaningful to consider how affective infrastructures of storytelling turn an event *into* a story, and how these stories may sustain a variety of distinct, yet imbricated, events and perceptions of an event.

Second, given that that mediality of news streams generated about these events via social media tends to be generative, additive, and affective, the story (or stories) prodused about an event are even more so multi-layered, polysemic, and pluralised. Journalists no longer have the privilege of being the first or the only ones to report on events. As their prominence as primary storytellers is renegotiated, what becomes (or should become) important for journalists is not being the first to tell the story but rather being the ones to fully curate and synthesise the multiple voices within the stories, even if that means being the last ones to tell the story itself. However, the intensity, or affect, generated by streams that develop as journalists and citizens collaboratively tell a story, sways both sentiment and expectations about the course of an event. And yet, affect itself is not an event; it is a layer to an event. What is problematic is reporting affect as the event, especially if that leads to drawing emphasis away from other layers of a story.

Finally, it is common during the course of an event, to be caught up in the accelerated pace with which stories are told and spread through social media. Yet, the intensity with which a story spreads is not equivocal to the speed with which institutional change may occur. In other words, virality describes the pace of story sharing, not the rhythm of societal change. Events are instantaneous, revolutions are slow, and change is gradual. This does not mean that platforms built to facilitate connection and expression cannot support mobilisation and change. They present structures of storytelling and as such are meaningful habitats for imagining and, potentially, enacting change. Storytelling (of the self, of everyday events, and of societies) enables sense making, and that is where the impact of these platforms lies. Legislative, economic, and political impact may emerge out how we put these technologies to use, and impact is always subject to context. But for the people telling these stories, and for the societies coming to life as these stories are told, the impact lies elsewhere. For publics that are convened online around affective commonalities, impact is *symbolic*, agency is claimed *discursively* and is of a *semantic* nature, and power accessed is *liminal* (Papacharissi 2014). It may seem like a transient route to transcendence, but it is not. Symbolic impact, semantic redefinition, and liminality have and always will be the precursors of change. In order for institutions to change, they must be reimagined first.

References

Aday, S., Farrell, H., Lynch, M., Sides, J., and Freelon, D. (2012) *New Media and Conflict after the Arab Spring*, Washington DC: United States Institute of Peace.

Ahy, M. H. (2014) "Networked Communication and the Arab Spring: Linking Broadcast and Social Media," *New Media & Society*, DOI: 10.1177/1461444814538634.

Al Maskati, N. (2012) "Newspaper Coverage of the 2011 Protests in Egypt," *International Communication Gazette*, 74(4), pp. 342–366.

Allam, N. (2014) "Arab Revolutions: Breaking Fear: Blesses and Curses: Virtual Dissidence as a Contentious Performance in the Arab Spring's Repertoire of Contention," *International Journal of Communication*, 8, pp. 853–870.

Aouragh, M., and Alexander, A. (2011) "The Egyptian Experience: Sense and Nonsense of the Internet Revolutions," *International Journal of Communication*, 5(1), pp. 1344–1358.

Arif, R. (2014) *Social Movements, YouTube and Political Activism in Authoritarian Countries: A Comparative Analysis of Political Change in Pakistan, Tunisia & Egypt* (Unpublished doctoral dissertation). University of Iowa, Iowa City.

Bruns, A., Highfield, T., and Burgess, J. (2013) "The Arab Spring and Social Media Audiences: English and Arabic Twitter Users and Their Networks," *American Behavioral Scientist*, 57(7), pp. 871–898.

Chadwick, A. (2013) *The Hybrid Media System*, Oxford: Oxford University Press.

Chouliaraki, L. (2008) "The Mediation of Suffering and the Vision of a Cosmopolitan Public," *Television & New Media*, 9(5), pp. 371–391.

Couldry, N. (2008) "Mediatization or Mediation? Alternative Understandings of the Emergent Space of Digital Storytelling," *New Media & Society*, 10(3), pp. 373–391.

Crawford, K. (2009) "Following You: Disciplines of Listening in Social Media," *Continuum: Journal of Media & Cultural Studies*, 23(4), pp. 525–535.

Dahlberg, L. (2009) "Libertarian Cyber-Utopianism and Globalization," in C. El-Ojeili and P. Hayden (eds.), *Utopia and Globalization*, London: Palgrave.

El-Hibri, H. (2014) "Arab Revolutions: Breaking Fear: The Cultural Logic of Visibility in the Arab Uprisings," *International Journal of Communication*, 8(18), pp. 835–852.

El-Nawawy, M., and Khamis, S. (2014) "Arab Revolutions: Breaking Fear: Blogging against Violations of Human Rights in Egypt: An Analysis of Five Political Blogs," *International Journal of Communication*, 8(18), pp. 962–982.

Eltantawy, N., and Wiest, J. B. (2011) "The Arab Spring: Social Media in the Egyptian Revolution: Reconsidering Resource Mobilization Theory," *International Journal of Communication*, 5, pp. 1207–1224.

Erickson, I. (2010) "Geography and Community: New Forms of Interaction Among People and Places," *American Behavioral Scientist*, 53(8), pp. 1194–1207.

Gans, H. J. (1979) *Deciding What's News: A Study of CBS Evening News, NBC Nightly News, Newsweek and TIME*, New York: Pantheon Books.

Gladwell, M. (2011, Feb 2) "Does Egypt Need Twitter?" *The New Yorker*, Retrieved from http://www.newyorker.com/online/blogs/newsdesk/2011/02/does-egypt-need-twitter.html

Hamdy, N. (2010) "Arab Media Adopt Citizen Journalism to Change the Dynamics of Conflict Coverage," *Global Media Journal: Arabian Edition*, 1(1), pp. 3–15.

Hamdy, N., and Gomaa, E. (2012) "Framing the Egyptian Uprising in Arabic language Newspapers and Social Media," *Journal of Communication*, 62(2), pp. 195–211.

Harlow, S., and Johnson, T.J. (2011) "The Arab Spring: Overthrowing the Protest Paradigm? How the New York Times, Global Voices and Twitter Covered the Egyptian Revolution," *International Journal of Communication*, 5, pp. 1359–1374.

Henneburg, S., Scammell, M., and O'Shaughnessy, N. (2009) "Political Marketing Management and Theories of Democracy," *Marketing Theory*, 9(2), pp. 165–188.

Hermida, A. (2010) "Twittering the News," *Journalism Practice*, 4(3), pp. 297–308.

Hermida, A., Lewis, S.C., and Zamith, R. (2014) "Sourcing the Arab Spring: A Case Study of Andy Carvin's Sources on Twitter During the Tunisian and Egyptian Revolutions," *Journal of Computer-Mediated Communication*, 19(3), pp. 479–499.

Hohl, M. (2009) "Beyond the Screen: Visualizing Visits to a Website as an Experience in Physical Space," *Visual Communication*, 8(3), pp. 273–284.

Honeycutt, C., and Herring, S.C. (2009) "Beyond Microblogging: Conversation and Collaboration Via Twitter," in *Proceedings of the Forty–Second Hawaii International Conference on System Sciences*, Retrieved from http://ella.slis.indiana.edu/~herring/honeycutt.herring.2009.pdf

Howard, P.N., Duffy, A., Freelon, D., Hussain, M., Mari, W., and Mazaid, M. (2011) "Opening Closed Regimes: What Was the Role of Social Media During the Arab Spring?, "Seattle: PITPI, Retrieved from http://ictlogy.net/bibliography/reports/projects.php?idp=2170

Howard, P.N., & Hussain, M.M. (2011) "The role of digital media," *Journal of Democracy*, 22(3), 35–48.

Ingram, M. (2011, Jan 14). "Was What happened in Tunisia a Twitter Revolution?" *Gigaom*, Retrieved from http://gigaom.com/2011/01/14/was-what-happened-in-tunisia-a-twitter-revolution

Jansen, B.J., Zhang, M., Sobel, K., and Chowdury, A. (2009) "Twitter Power: Tweets as Electronic Word of Mouth," *Journal of the American Society for Information Science and Technology*, 60(11), pp. 2169–2188.

Khamis, S. (2011) "The Transformative Egyptian Landscape: Changes, Challenges and Comparative Perspectives," *International Journal of Communication*, 5, pp. 1159–1177.

Lim, M. (2012) "Clicks, Cabs, and Coffee Houses: Social Media and Oppositional Movements in Egypt, 2004–2011," *Journal of Communication*, 62(2), pp. 231–248.

Lindsey, U. (2012) "Revolution and Counterrevolution in the Egyptian Media," in J. Sowers and C. Toensing (eds.) *The Journey to Tahrir: Revolution, Protest, and Social Change in Egypt*, New York, NY: Verso.

Lippmann, W. (1922) *Public Opinion*, New York: Free Press.

Livingstone, S. (2009) "On the Mediation of Everything: ICA Presidential Address 2008," *Journal of Communication*, 59(1), pp. 1–18.

Lotan, G., Graeff, E., Ananny, M., Gaffney, D., and Pearce, I. (2011) "The Arab Spring: The Revolutions Were Tweeted: Information Flows During the 2011 Tunisian and Egyptian Revolutions," *International Journal of Communication*, 5, pp. 1375–1405.

McGarty, C., Thomas, E. F., Lala, G., Smith, L. G., and Bliuc, A.M. (2014) "New Technologies, New Identities, and the Growth of Mass Opposition in the Arab Spring," *Political Psychology*, 35(6), pp. 725–740.

Meraz, S., and Papacharissi, Z. (2013) "Networked Gatekeeping and Networked Framing on #Egypt," *The International Journal of Press/Politics*, 18(2), pp. 138–166.

Morozov, E. (2011, March 7) "Facebook and Twitter Are Just Places Revolutionaries Go," *The Guardian*, Retrieved from http://www.guardian.co.uk/commentisfree/2011/mar/07/facebook-twitter-revolutionaries-cyber-utopians

Nunns, A., and Idle, N. (2011) *Tweets From Tahrir: Egypt's Revolution As It Unfolded, in the Words of the People Who Made It*. New York: OR Books.

Papacharissi, Z. (2014) *Affective Publics*, Oxford: Oxford University Press.

Papacharissi, Z., and de Fatima Oliveira, M. (2011, September) "The Rhythms of News Storytelling on Twitter: Coverage of the January 25th Egyptian Uprising on Twitter," in *World Association for Public Opinion Research Conference*, Vol. 312, p. 3188.

Papacharissi, Z., and de Fatima Oliveira, M. (2012) "Affective News and Networked Publics: The Rhythms of News Storytelling on #Egypt," *Journal of Communication*, 62(2), pp. 266–282.

Papacharissi, Z. and Meraz, S. (2012) "The Rhythms of Occupy: Broadcasting and Listening Practices on #ows," *Association of Internet Researchers Conference*, Salford, UK.

Singh, V. K., and Jain, R. (2010) "Structural Analysis of the Emerging Event-Web," *WWW '10: Proceedings of the ACM Conference on Computer Supported Cooperative Work* (pp. 241–250), New York: ACM.

Steiner, H. (2009) "Reference Utility of Social Networking Sites: Options and functionality," *Library Hi Tech News*, 26(5-6), pp. 46.

Tufekci, Z. (2011) "Tunisia, Twitter, Aristotle, Social Media and Final and Efficient causes" [blog post] Technosociology, Retrieved from http://technosociology.org/?p=263

Tufekci, Z., and Wilson, C. (2012) "Social Media and the Decision to Participate in Political Protest: Observations From Tahrir Square," *Journal of Communication*, 62, pp. 363–379.

Vargas, J. (2012, Feb 17) "Spring Awakening: How an Egyptian Revolution Began on Facebook," *The New York Times*, Retrieved from http://www.nytimes.com/2012/02/19/books/review/how-an-egyptian-revolution-began-on-facebook.html?pagewanted=all

Wall, M., and El Zahed, S. (2011) "The Arab Spring: 'I'll be waiting for you guys': A YouTube Call to Action in the Egyptian Revolution," *International Journal of Communication*, 5, pp. 1333–1343.

Wilson, C., and Dunn, A. (2011) "The Arab Spring: Digital Media in the Egyptian Revolution: Descriptive Analysis From the Tahrir Data Set," *International Journal of Communication*, 5, pp. 1248–1272.

Wright, R. (2011) *Rock the Casbah: Rage and Rebellion Across the Islamic World*, New York: Simon & Schuster.

Yardi, S., and boyd, d. (2010a) "Tweeting From the Town Square: Measuring Geographic Local Networks," in *ICWSM '10: Proceedings of the International AAAI Conference on Weblogs and Social Media* (pp. 194–201). New York, NY: AAAI.

Yardi, S., and boyd, d. (2010b) "Dynamic Debates: An Analysis of Group Polarization over Time on Twitter," *Bulletin of Science, Technology and Society*, 30(5), pp. 316–327.

York, J.C. (2011) "Not Twitter, Not WikiLeaks: A Human Revolution," [blog post]. *Jilliancyork. com*, Retrieved from http://jilliancyork.com/2011/01/14/not-twitter-not-wikileaks-a-human-revolution/

Zuckerman, E. (2011) "The First Twitter revolution?" *Foreign Policy*, Retrieved from http://www.foreignpolicy.com/articles/2011/01/14/the_first_twitter_revolution?page=full

15

THE IMPORTANCE OF 'SOCIAL' IN SOCIAL MEDIA

Lessons from Iran

Gholam Khiabany

Introduction

Since the financial crisis in 2008, the popular uprisings in Iran in 2009, the revolutions in several Arab countries at the beginning of 2011, and the occupy movements in the U.S. and elsewhere in the global north have indicated a growing resistance to dictatorships and decades of neo-liberal globalisation. From the streets of Tehran to Tahir Square, Syntagma Square, Puerta del Sol, and Zuccotti Park, we have witnessed a new wave of resistance to a system that has failed to generate wealth and freedom for all. The past decade has also provided some of the most evocative moments when power met its opposite; in some cases, in decisive and surprising ways. Technology, again and again, has emerged as one of the main explanations for this new wave of revolts.

The very use of a wide range of media and communicative platforms, the innovative use of image, sound, and music to inform, organise and mobilise dissent and demonstrations, and in particular the circulation of information via Facebook, Twitter, and other platforms has prompted many commentators to suggest that it is impossible to comprehend the political nature of the existing protests in Iran, the Arab World, and elsewhere, without recognising the centrality of the new technologies (Giroux, 2009). Manuel Castells has also argued that the Internet has contributed to the eruptions of such popular power because, he argues, "the more interactive and self-configurable communication is, the less hierarchical is the organisation and the more participatory is the movement. . . . This is why the networked social movements of the digital age represent a new species of social movement" (Castells, 2012: 15). But others have criticised celebratory accounts of the role of new media for neglecting or putting less emphasis on the importance of organisation. For example, Gladwell (2010) has stressed that such claims fail to consider the strong organisational ties that are crucial for any social movement. The debate, somehow, has been reduced to a false binary of 'believers' and 'non-believers'. The continuing use of the Internet to mount challenges against injustice, repression, and discrimination on the one hand, and the effective use of social media by the terrifying Islamic State (ISIS) on the other, has shown that there is nothing inevitable about the use of these tools and that they are the direct outcome of broader social and economic policy and as such are subject to alteration and direction.

In addition, treating social movements' effective use of, and reliance upon, communication technologies as a sociological novelty ignores significant historical precedents of importance and relevance of communications of various kinds to protests, revolts, and revolutions. What is novel, perhaps, is identifying the new waves of struggle not with the cause but with the tools of these movements. There are nevertheless two important points that should be highlighted. If the impact of social media in this conjuncture has been rather overstated and exaggerated, there is very little doubt that the media (social and otherwise) has been crucial in recording the events and the courage of thousands and millions of citizens who have managed to reclaim real public spaces and make them their own. One Egyptian demonstrator reminded us of this reality in a simple and yet powerful way: "Before, I was watching television; now it is television that's watching me" (cited in Badiou, 2012:110). Second, and without a doubt, social movements and significant events not only use media but also make them and put them on the map. In the same way that war and turmoil made the likes of CNN and Aljazeera into internationally recognised 'brands', social movements have given the likes of Facebook, Twitter, and YouTube a much-needed political and social legitimacy. The 'Facebook generation' is no longer a negative or pejorative term used to lament the younger generation's detachment from and indifference towards politics. Political activism in Iran certainly has contributed a great deal in converting technologies that were initially considered banal and irrelevant to politics into respectable and highly prized platforms. As Andy Greenberg (2009) suggested in *Forbes*: Iranian protests are good for Twitter's business.

However, even if we limit our focus to the significant and visible boiling points of social movements and ignore daily, protracted, and not highly visible digital activities, we are confronted with the how and why of the outcomes of such social awakening. The failure of the Iranian uprising, the breathlessness of the Arab revolutions, and the collapse of the Occupy movements demonstrate that while such movements have shaken, at least in some instances, the foundations of the system, they have failed to form a coherent and sustainable opposition. If it is really true that we cannot begin to comprehend the revolts and political activism in Iran and elsewhere without understanding the new realities of screen culture, then what does the failure of such movements reveal about the myths of new media? This chapter examines aspects of digital activism with particular reference to and examples from Iran, where cyberspace came to be seen as a unified, unproblematic and un-segmented site of resistance (Sreberny and Khiabany, 2010). By looking at a specific example of a hugely successful Facebook campaign (My Stealthy Freedom; www.facebook.com/StealthyFreedom), this chapter highlights the importance of concrete analysis of concrete situations and pays particular attention to what can/cannot be achieved through digital activism and participation.

Unveiling Threats in Iran

The Iranian Revolution of 1979 remains problematic, both theoretically and politically, and the 'trans-class' and 'religious' nature of the revolution has been the main source of confusion over the precise nature of the state which replaced the monarchy. Gilbert Achcar (2004: 57) has described the Iranian revolution as a 'permanent revolution in reverse', something that started with such emancipatory potential and something that could have grown over into a socialist transformation but instead produced a strange polity and state. The revolution, without a doubt, had an emancipatory character, but elements of counter-revolution were clearly visible from early on. The tension between the revolution and the counter-revolution, and the existence of multiple sovereignty, aspiration and power contentions, urges an analytical distinction between the Iranian revolution and the Islamic Republic (Moghadam, 1989:75).

The contestation of the result of the June 2009 presidential election in Iran was a significant indication of the continuing tensions and contradictions within Iran, and above all, of the failure of the Islamic state to impose its monopoly over the legitimate use of symbolic violence and its continuing struggle to manufacture consent to its rule. That electoral coup triggered unprecedented and impassioned involvement inside Iran and brought many simmering dissatisfactions—about the lack of rights and freedoms, inflation and growing inequality—to the surface. In 2009, as has been the case in the past 36 years, the condition of women in Iran was one of the major source of dissatisfaction.

The Islamic Republic of Iran does not recognise the equality of both sexes; indeed, it denies women equal rights. The constitution of the Islamic Republic itself was (and is) part of a wholehearted attack on women's rights and an important aspect of overall policy of exclusion of women from public life. In the first few years of the Islamic Republic, many of the rights that women had gained under the Pahlavi dictatorship were taken back. The segregation of the sexes in public spaces; overt gender discrimination; compulsory hijab (which was one of the first official policy of the new state); the exclusion of women from a number of professions; reinforcing patriarchal policies in terms of divorce, guardianship of children, and lowering the age of marriage for girls were among measures used to 'purify' women and society and bringing back the 'glorious' tradition of what was perceived to be the true Islam (Tohidi, 2002). The 'women's question' remains the most significant and visible sign of the Iranian state's contempt for political and cultural rights and democracy. And it is also no accident that the most popular digital campaign in recent years has focused on this very issue. This campaign, which has received wide international and national coverage, is My Stealthy Freedom (www.facebook.com/StealthyFreedom).

On 5 May 2014, Iranian journalist and activist Massih Alinejad set up a Facebook page named Stealthy Freedom (Azadiye Yawaschaki). This page is dedicated to posting images of women with hijab removed. In a few days, the page had received over 100,000 likes, and at the time of writing (less than a year after the launch of the campaign), the page had over 760,000 followers: a much bigger following than the winner of 2009 presidential election, Mir-Hossein Musavi's, Facebook page at the peak of 2009 Iranian uprising (Christensen, 2009). So far, hundreds of women have submitted their pictures without hijab. Pictures are taken in various locations in Iran: parks, beaches, markets, streets, and elsewhere. Alinejad states that the campaign began rather simply:

> Once I posted pictures of [myself] in London, free, without a scarf. I received messages from Iranian women saying: "Don't publish these pictures because we envy you." Soon after I published another picture of myself driving in my hometown in Iran, again without a scarf. And I said to Iranian women: "I bet you can do the same." Many of them started to send me their photos without hijab, so I created a page called "My Stealthy Freedom." . . . If I were in Iran this website wouldn't exist. From far away those voiceless women can express themselves for the first time [in] more than 30 years. (Kowalska, 2014: paras. 17–19)

A post on the Stealthy Freedom Facebook page states:

> This page does not belong to any political group and the initiative reflects the concerns of Iranian women, who face legal and social restrictions. All of the photos and captions posted have been sent by women from all over Iran and this is a site dedicated to Iranian women inside the country who want to share their "stealthily" taken photos without the veil.

Indeed, Alinejad, in an interview with BBC, insisted that women who have sent their pictures "are not women activists, but just ordinary women talking from their hearts" (BBC, 2014: para. 5).

Many of the amazing pictures are accompanied by captions: some short, some longer, some in a poetic language, and others are mischievous or defiant. One caption reads: "I just want to have the right to CHOOSE! Maybe I would have even chosen to wear a scarf if I'd had options to choose from. But it hurts me so much when others make decisions for ME instead of myself."

Another says:

> "I'm free
> I'm a woman from a country with the least respect for human rights.
> I was born in a country where religion, tradition, and Islamic Regime has destroyed the beauty.
> I can see the freedom I will have gained soon.
> And I'll enjoy the feeling of belonging to myself.
> I'll enjoy my rights as a citizen.
> I'll enjoy human rights.
> I'll enjoy having freedom of choice."

In some pictures women are holding their scarves behind them, while the wind blows them like a flag. One of these scarves is green, and the caption reminds everyone, with a reference to the colour of Musavi's campaign, that "once the colour of green was forbidden." In one picture we see three women, of three generations, side by side, in the street. The caption is simple and powerful: "Three generations in one frame. And we beget freedom for ourselves at a corner of the street. Grandmother, mother, and daughter. Hoping for the day this new generation can achieve their simplest right before their hair turns grey." Another picture is accompanied by a caption which, in a simple and yet powerful way, expresses the sense of freedom, the beauty and pleasure, of wind blowing through the hair: "This is Iran. . . . The feeling of the wind blowing through every strand of hair is a girl's biggest dream."

Others go beyond articulating the very basic (and denied) feeling and pleasure of sensing the wind. Many insist on the fundamental rights of citizens, of the right to choose, on the importance of solidarity, and express the hope:

> We are saying "no" to the compulsory hijab with all our force and conviction. As someone belonging to the new generation of this country with my mother firmly defending one of the most basic human rights. We have the best judgement ourselves and we do not need anyone to guide us on our behalf. I hope

that one day we will achieve freedom and equality for every single citizen of our beloved Iran that we will proudly call our homeland.

Not all submitted pictures are images of *veil-less* women. The campaign has also moved beyond a simple show of defiance to bold statements highlighting the brutal force of the state's 'morality'. In one post there is a sequence of images, showing a couple being harassed by the police in a park. The caption reads:

> "Islamic Republic" of Iran; where a compassionate touch is a sin and the act of sympathizing is a crime. I would like my motherland back. In fact, we will take it back, it may not be tomorrow or next year, but it will happen.

The campaign increasingly—and perhaps inevitably—includes videos, critical assessments of events in Iran, as well as the international coverage of the campaign and expression of international solidarity. Solo singing by women has been officially banned since 1979, and after yet another pronouncement by state officials that women's solo singing must be forbidden, Masih Alinejad launched #myforbiddensong as the new campaign for #mystealthyfreedom. The controversy began after the release of an album entitled *Love You, Oh Ancient Land*. The album, which was released on 27 January 2015, is a compilation of traditional Iranian music that includes a vocal solo by a woman artist. Some conservative officials used this as an opportunity to warn against 'moral decay' and 'corruption' in Iran. On 9 February 2015, Masih Alinejad posted a video of herself singing on the platform of the Temple underground station in London. This is how she explains her reasoning:

> After starting a Facebook page where women could post pictures of themselves without their hijab, the state launched a violent smear campaign against me: I was raped by three men in London. Under the influence of mind-altering drugs, I had removed items of clothing, and the men raped me in front of my son. That is what the Iran state TV reported in a short news segment about me. For the record, I was never assaulted or raped or took any mind-altering drugs. But my real revenge is to use what the hardliners are most petrified of: a video of myself singing in a London subway station, without a veil.

Alinejad also launched #myforbiddensong as part of My Stealthy Freedom campaign, and encouraged others to do the same and send the videos to the Facebook page. One of the significant outcomes of the myth of the role of social media in the Iranian uprising was to confuse, or perhaps even substitute, media for the movement. 'You are the media' was one of the claims of the so-called Green Movement. Yet at the same time that activists were being confined to the realm of small media, many well-known figures appeared on mainstream media as the voice of the movement. The same people who appeared in the mainstream media also controlled the organised networks, including the Facebook pages of the 'Green movement'. In a post in March 2015, Alinejad revived the slogan of 'You are all media.' In her post she said:

> Suggestion: Every woman a media. A veiled woman appears on Iranian state television to say compulsory hijab is the demand of all women. You, every single one of you, can be a media, and if you agree, take a film of yourself as

Iranian women, wherever in the world you are, and say in one minute, why you are against compulsory hijab, or describe what problems compulsory hijab has created for you.

The Not So Stealthy Reactions to the Campaign

The popularity of this online campaign is unprecedented in Iran. No other digital campaign has generated such a level of participation and interest in terms of 'likes', comments, shared pictures, and international coverage. Yet the very success of this campaign itself raises a very interesting question: Why have pictures of women with dishevelled hair, many in romantic poses, many smiling, looking dreamy, or defiant, received such a level of support and coverage? After all, these are the types of pictures that are very common for Facebook profiles. My argument is that this campaign and the fantastic and wide range of images, text, and music that have appeared on this Facebook page are not just about social media. The answer to the aforementioned question, as well as the reason for the campaign itself, can be found not in the Facebook page but in the very specific social context in Iran. The condition of each social group in this wider context goes a long way in explaining the reaction and the interest they generate. How strongly different groups feel, and more importantly, how strongly and vigorously they could, want, and be willing to fight is also more than about social media. The women's question, as I have already indicated, has been and remains a political volcano under the feet of the Islamic Republic. Let us start with the reaction of the state.

Despite the massive support for the 'Stealthy Freedom' campaign, it has also generated different forms of backlash and criticism. Two weeks after the launch of the original campaign, a Facebook page entitled 'Men's Stealthy Freedom' (www.facebook.com/menstealthysfreedom) appeared and began to publish pictures of men covering their head or body with sheets and scarves. This attempt to ridicule the original campaign, with 100,000 likes, has turned into a familiarly laddish and sexist page containing not only men with scarves and/or make-up but with the type of juvenile jokes, cartoons, videos, and semi-nude pictures that grace similar online/offline publications across the world.

The backlash, however, has also taken a more familiar and aggressive form. One of the most powerful weapons utilised by certain sections of the Iranian state, used to suppress dissent in the online environment, is the colonisation of the Internet. The Iranian state has long recognised the usefulness of the Internet as a tool for propaganda and furthering its policies and aims. In that respect, it has embraced technologies and launched many initiatives and religious/conservative websites (Sreberny and Khiabany, 2010). As such, it came as no surprise that a number of rival Facebook groups were set up to ridicule and challenge the Stealthy Freedom campaign. Among such rivals is the Real Freedom of Iranian Women page (www.facebook.com/RealFreedomOfIranianWomen). This page was launched on 12 May 2014, exactly a week after the launch of the Stealthy Freedom campaign. The offensive began with a message celebrating the veil: 'Beautiful Hijab; My Right, My Choice, My Life'. The second message, posted on the same day, explains the reason for the launch of this Facebook page:

> In recent days it has been observed that the actors of foreign media led by a spy, Masih Alinejad, have called for de-veiling in public places in Iran and

have asked Iranian women to send pictures of de-veiling in public places such as metro, streets, etc. to the Facebook page entitled 'Women Stealthy Freedom in Iran' which Masih Alinejad is managing.

The post claims that Alinejad campaign is set up with the help of "her organisation" [British intelligence organisation MI6], and has received a wide coverage in international media. In response, the rival campaign asked their supporters to help them challenge the Stealthy Freedom campaign by sending pictures, graphics, poems, translations, memories, as well as helping with administrating the page. Insisting that Stealthy Freedom is part of 'soft war' against the Islamic state, this page has published a wide range of images, videos, and texts promoting and propagating support for compulsory hijab. If an important and recognisable aspect of Stealthy Freedom has revolved around generating international coverage and solidarity, the so-called Real Freedom of Iranian Women campaign has also tried to demonstrate its own 'international' appeal by publishing pictures of veiled women elsewhere, including in the West. The purpose of the page, however, is not just to remind women that hijab is compulsory and an Iranian women's 'choice' but to also generate fear. One early post, on 18ᵗ May 2014, warns:

> be careful of your photos in Facebook and Instagram
>> stealing women's photos under the name of "stealthy freedoms"
>> stealing women's private pictures by Masih Alinejad
>> in this short video one of the viewers of Voice of America program says that
> her private pictures were stolen by Masih Alinejad and were put in the stealthy freedoms page without her knowing about it!
>> Mrs. Masih Alinejad! this is the violation of privacy
>> you claim that you are a good person, so why do you steal??
>> any way no one is not expecting more from betrayers and servants of intel-
> ligence service.

Warnings about privacy from a state which brutally intervenes in the most private of affairs is, of course, more than ironic. However, many posts go beyond that and openly threaten women who choose to be seen in public without hijab. Some have tried to identify women who have appeared without hijab on the Stealthy Freedom page. Additional Facebook pages have been launched for that very purpose (against privacy). The Real Freedom of Iranian Women page, however, has less than 10,000 likes, and another rival page, For the Attention of Supporters of Stealthy Freedom, has only received 280 likes.

The backlash is even more aggressive and threatening offline. Just two days after the launch of Stealthy Freedom, hundreds demonstrated in Tehran demanding the immediate arrest of women who ignore and defy the compulsory hijab. At the same time, conservative officials and media have tried their best to attack the Stealthy Freedom campaign and smear it. In the summer of 2014, Iranian state television ran a false story reporting that Masih Alinejad was in a drug-induced, hallucinatory state when she removed her clothing and was raped by three men in front of her son. Also, in June 2014, just over two-thirds of the Islamic Republic's parliamentarians signed a letter urging the President to take measures to enforce and safeguard compulsory hijab. In their letter, 195 out of 295 MPs blamed the foreign media, and in particular satellite television channels, for the defiant attitudes of Iranian women. The MPs suggested that, "one of the main areas of cultural invasion is in trying to change the way of life of Iranians regarding the veil. We ask that you give the necessary orders to enforce the law" (Arab News, 2014: para. 5). Such threats are real. Over the past 36 years, regardless of what has been suspended, the violent enforcement of the particular brand of Iranian state 'moral' policy has remained intact. The constant threats and attacks against Iranian women over the past 30 years, the arrest of a group of Iranian fans who created a tribute to Pharrell Williams's hit song *Happy*, not to mention the horrifying incidents in which many women had acid thrown at their faces, are all clear examples of the denial of the very basic right to life and freedom. The varied reactions to the Stealthy Freedom campaign, the launch of rival pages, and the Iranian state's response to it, also clearly demonstrated that the debate over compulsory hijab is hotly contested and unsettled.

Contradictions and Limits of Digital Activism

The Stealthy Freedom campaign has to be seen as a continuation of the challenges, concerns, and anxieties over hijab in Iran. This concern has been expressed, produced, and reproduced in different forms. Without a doubt, the Stealthy Freedom campaign has to be seen as an innovative and effective idea for highlighting the real concerns over compulsory hijab in particular, and women's personal freedom in general. The campaign also reveals the great potential of civil disobedience against 'moral' concerns of the Iranian state. Yet, the campaign is not free from contradictions and limits. Let us briefly examine some of the limitations of these forms of digital activism.

The first point worth highlighting is the mismatch between local context and concerns (internal) and the framing and reception of these concerns outside the geographical boundaries of the local (external). In contrast to the virtual and real attacks and threats against the Stealthy Freedom campaign by Iranian state officials, media, and supporters, the overwhelming feeling *outside* Iran has been one of support, solidarity, and encouragement. Yet, the positive international coverage and support should not obscure a number of contradictions and dilemmas. There is always a danger, as Zishad Lak (2014) reminds us, that a local struggle might be assimilated into something completely different. For her, the Stealthy Freedom campaign is one of those instances in which "local resistance risks being thrust into obscurity to be protected from colonial interpretations. What we should be wary of is the audience or the interlocutor that is implicit in the message around which the actor organises her actions" (Lak, 2014: para. 7), In every story published in mainstream British or American media, one comes across supporting statements encouraging Iranian women with phrases such as 'Go Girls!', or simply describing participants in this campaign as 'Beautiful, smart, confident, and happy' and welcoming them 'to the 21st century'.

The problem with such expressions of solidarity is not that the information provided about the lack of freedom in Iran is inaccurate but rather, as Haleh Anvari suggested in the *New York Times*, the Western fetish of and obsession with gazing at Iranian women has turned them into "Iran's Eiffel Tower or Big Ben" (Anvari, 2014: para. 4). Such constructions of Muslim women as 'cultural icons', as Leila Abu-Lughod (2013) has demonstrated, not only has been used to simplify the complex realities of the Middle Eastern societies but also have been used as an excuse for military interventions that are partly justified to 'save' Muslim women. Since the 9/11 terrorist attack, these 'cultural icons' have come to represent the dividing line between 'us' and 'them', modern and traditional, civilised and barbaric.

There are two additional points that need to be highlighted. First of all, as the international success of the Stealthy Freedom campaign shows us, new technologies do, indeed, break geographical boundaries and precipitate international sympathy and solidarity. However, these technologies are also born in specific historical societies and social relations. Time and space compression (Harvey, 1990) does not make space irrelevant, and new technologies by themselves cannot bypass assumptions, prejudices, and stereotypes. The Stealthy Freedom Facebook campaign is not immune from such prejudices and stereotypes but also (whether by accident or design) reinforces them.

Furthermore, and again, as Abu-Lughod (2013) passionately reminds us, the problem of gender inequality is not simply a religious matter alone. Neither animosity towards social rights and freedom and popular rule nor the hostility to the idea of gender equality is particular or peculiar to Islam. The idea of gender equality is not a God-given truth divorced from space and time. Let us remember the controversy over *Monty Python's Life of Brian*, or the violent attack against Martin Scorsese's *The Last Temptation of Christ*. Let us also not forget that the level of opposition of Vatican to abortion or women's right to divorce was (and is) such that Pope John Paul II asked victims of rape in Bosnia-Herzegovina not to have abortions. Let us also not forget the controversy over women priests in the Church of England. Indeed, if women bishops are any index of 'development', then the Church of England has only recently stepped 'into the 21st century'!

Second, it is important to note that, as far as Iran is concerned, and in the context of the war on terror,

> the knowledge production about Iran has become a lucrative business for those who provide expertise in different capacities, from testimonials in media, books and human rights reports, to research and collection of information in think tanks, state and private intelligence firms and universities. (Shakhsari, 2011: 7).

The hyper- visibility of some Iranian digital activism in the west cannot be understood outside of this context. Shakhsari describes an Iranian blogger outside of Iran as a figure "that acts as an entrepreneur, who is responsible for his/her own economic well-being and markets him/herself as the source of valuable information" (Shakhsari, 2011: 11).

This is not to ignore the impact of the Stealthy Freedom campaign nor to underplay or underestimate the very aggressive state policy towards Iranian women. Gender discrimination, or to put it more accurately, sexual apartheid, is one of the most visible and key defining features of the Islamic Republic of Iran. And yet, violent measures taken by the Iranian state, from the very beginning, have provoked the persistent opposition of Iranian women who have refused to conform to the moral conceptions of conservative Islamists in the country. For 36 years, Iranian women have used every opportunity to challenge those very 'moral' conceptions, including compulsory hijab. Therefore, Masih Alinejad was wrong to suggest that the Stealthy Freedom website could not exist if she were in Iran, or to suggest that Iranian women can only express themselves 'from far away', or that this is the first time in 30 years that Iranian women have done so. It is not for the first time, since the coming to power of the Islamic Republic, Iranian women have defied the state and have expressed themselves.

Second, the Stealthy Freedom campaign has reinforced the myth of the role of social media in the Iranian context and confuses, or perhaps even substitutes, media for the

movement. 'You are the media' was one of the claims of the so-called Green Movement. Masih Alinejad is still promoting the same idea. Yet, it is worth remembring
that at the time that activists were being confined to the realm of small media, many of
the well-known figures of the Green Movement appeared on mainstream media as the
voice of the movement. What was brushed aside was the historical fact that how individuals are organised as intellectuals is by definition a social process. Who gets noticed,
who gets to speak, and who is allowed to 'represent' the public is never given. In addition, it is rather interesting that in the the current campaign, which has been hailed as
a step towards 'reclaiming individuality' (Azizee, 2014), the only recognised individual
is Masih Alinejad herself. Similar concerns have been raised by Gilda Seddighi who,
in her study of Iranian Mothers of Park Laleh and the organisation of priviledges in
online space, demonstartes how the network of Iranian mothers who were inspired by
the Madres de Plaza de Mayo were excluded from the online activism launched in their
names (Seddighi, 2014).

The third issue to consider is the Stealthy Freedom campaign's narrow focus on hijab.
As Azadeh Davachi (2014) has suggested, the campaign effectively reduces the concerns over gender equality in Iran to compulsory hijab when, in fact, for many Iranian
women the issue is simply not about hijab but rather a whole set of policies of control,
monitoring, and traditions (including hijab) which act as weapons in denying—and
violently suppressing—women's rights. In short, the campaign, by highlighting hijab,
neglects or brushes aside different variables and aspects of women's lack of freedom in
Iran. The campaign's focus on publishing pictures of veil-less Iranian women divides
them into two distinct groups defined only in terms of their attitudes towards hijab.
This false binary might appeal to the international media, as we have seen, but it fails
to provide any concrete and comprehensive model of achieving women's liberation
in Iran.

And finally, it is worth remembering that many such campaigns that highlight a
single issue, or a range of issues, have come and gone without leaving much trace or
establishing a sustained, influential, long-term campaign. No social change is possible
without a sustained and well-established organisation. The 'networks' of this kind cannot possibly mount a significant challenge to repression and injustice if they are not
transformed into a real network of activists. And, we have been here before. The experience of Iran, Tunisia, and Egypt in the aftermath of the uprisings in these countries
clearly indicates what can happen in the absence of real networks and political organisations. Public spaces, such as Tahrir Square (as was the case in Wall Street in New
York, Puerta del Sol in Madrid, Syntagma Square in Athens, and St. Paul's Cathedral
in London) were significant instruments of resistance when other means of struggle had
been denied to the public. As Harvey has suggested, "what Tahrir Square showed to the
world was an obvious truth: that it is bodies on the street and in the squares, not the
babble of sentiment on Twitter or Facebook, that really matter" (Harvey, 2012: 162).

Conclusion

As I have stated, the Stealthy Freedom campaign has been a very innovative initiative.
It has provided many Iranian women with a safe place to protest and has highlighted
the significant concerns over compulsory hijab in Iran. A significant and valid point
made again and again in celebratory accounts of new media is the 'low barrier to entry'
to the digital media field. But, and as we have seen in the case of Iranian uprising of

2009 and the revolts in the Arab World in 2011, this reality does not make the huge obstacles and contradictions in a major challenge against repressive states redundant. What the experiences of Iran, and in particular Syria and Libya, have shown us is that the state can increase the cost of political participation to a terrifying and deadly level. The cost of digital and real participations (at least in dictatorships) is not the same. Therefore, the false binary of believers (Shirky, 2008) versus non-believers (Morozov, 2011) puts aside the idea of the 'social' in 'social media'. Some people (but not everybody) indeed do come and form a public, but they do not simply under the conditions created by digital media. What makes a campaign popular and successful in the first place has nothing to do with digital technologies. Here it is really worth asking if a different campaign focusing on workers struggles, health service, poverty, or the religious minorities in Iran would have received such significant coverage. But, in addition to the question of the extent to which digital media creates new potentials and tools for liberation or domination, perhaps we can also ask what kind of politics are possible in a virtual environment, why, and to what effect? As I have argued, the success of the Stealthy Freedom campaign is impossible to comprehend and even imagine without considering the broader political and social struggle in Iran. It is also clear that even in the so-called 'deterritorialised' media environment, territories and their associated political and cultural histories shape and inform (or misinform) different aspects of digital campaigns.

References

Abu-Lughod, L. (2013) *Do Muslim Women Need Saving?* Cambridge, MA: Harvard University Press.

Achcar, G. (2004) *Eastern Cauldron: Islam, Afghanistan, Palestine and Iraq in a Marxist Mirror*. London: Pluto.

Anvari, H. (2014) "The Fetish of Staring at Iran's Women," available on: http://www.nytimes.com/2014/06/17/opinion/the-fetish-of-staring-at-irans-women.html?_r=0

Arab News (2014) "Iran MPs Demand Stronger Veil Enforcement," available on: http://www.arabnews.com/news/587126

Azizee, N.Z. (2014) "My Stealthy Freedom: The Reclaiming of Individuality," available on: http://alochonaa.com/2014/06/23/my-stealthy-freedom-the-reclaiming-of-individuality/

Badiou, A. (2012) *The Rebirth of History: Times of Riots and Uprisings*. London: Verso.

BBC (2014) "BBC trending: The Women in Iran Taking off the Hijab," available on: http://www.bbc.co.uk/news/blogs-trending-27373368

Castells, M. (2012) *Networks of Outrage and Hope: Social Movements in the Internet Age*. Cambridge: Polity.

Christensen, C. (2009) "Iran: Networked Dissent," *Le Monde Diplomatique*, available on: http://mondediplo.com/blogs/iran-networked-dissent

Davachi, A. (2014) "Stealthy Freedom: The Hidden and Visible Voice of Iranian Women?," available on https://jahanezan.wordpress.com/2014/05/20/12345-2006/

Giroux, H. (2009) "The Iranian Uprisings and the Challenge of the New Media," available on: http://www.counterpunch.org/2009/06/19/the-iranian-uprisings-and-the-challenge-of-the-new-media/

Gladwell, M. (2010) "Small Change: Why the Revolution Will Not Be Tweeted, 'Twitter, Facebook, and Social Activism," *The New Yorker*, October 4.

Greenberg, A. (2009) "Twitter's Activist Initiation," available on: http://www.forbes.com/2009/06/16/twitter-iran-election-markets-equity-dissent.html

Harvey, D. (1990) *The Condition of Postmodernity*. Oxford: Blackwell.

Harvey, D. (2012) *Rebel Cities: From the Right to the City to the Urban Revolution*. London: Verso.

Kowalska, A. (2014) "Project Exile: Out of Iran, a Voice for Human Rights," available on: http://globaljournalist.org/2014/10/project-exile-iran-voice-human-rights/

Lak, Z. (2014) "Stealthy Freedoms and the Colonial Gaze," available on: http://www.feminisms.org/6640/stealthy-freedoms-and-the-colonial-gaze/

Moghadam, V. (1989) "One Revolution or Two? The Iranian Revolution and the Islamic Republic," in R. Miliband, L. Panitch and J. Saville (eds.) *Socialist Register 1989: Revolution Today: Aspirations and Realities*. London: The Merlin Press.

Morozov, E. (2011). *The Net Delusion: The Dark Side of Internet Freedom*. New York: Public Affairs.

Seddighi, G. (2014) "Mothers' Affective Networking and Privileges in Online Space: The Case of Iranian Mothers of Park Laleh," *Feminist Media Studies*, 14(3): 523–527.

Shakhsari, S. (2011) "Weblogistan Goes to War: Representational Practices, Gendered Soldiers and Neoliberal Entrepreneurship in Diaspora," *Feminist Review*, 99: 6–24.

Shirky, C. (2008) *Here Comes Everybody: The Power of Organizing without Organizations*. New York: Penguin Press.

Sreberny, A. and G. Khiabany (2010) *Blogistan: The Internet and Politics in Iran*. London. I. B. Tauris.

Tohidi, N. (2002) "The Global-Local Intersection of Feminism in Muslim Societies: The Cases of Iran and Azerbaijan," *Social Research*, 69(3): 851–887

16

DIGITAL KNIVES ARE STILL KNIVES

The Affordances of Social Media for a Repressed Opposition against an Entrenched Authoritarian Regime in Azerbaijan

Katy E. Pearce and Farid Guliyev

Introduction

Twenty-first century authoritarian regimes manage and deter dissent in less overt forceful ways than in the past, instead using more creative methods for repression of those that oppose them. Some argue that information and communication technologies can provide new opportunities for oppositionists to overcome barriers. This case study of authoritarian Azerbaijan will look at the challenges that regime critics face and how technology and social media can be leveraged to overcome these challenges, especially due to reduced costs of content creation and distribution as well as organising without co-location. We identity six ways that the Azerbaijani opposition is repressed: (1) The opposition cannot be elected or engage with the formal political process; (2) it cannot communicate with citizens because of strict media control; (3) it cannot freely assemble or rent offices; (4) individuals face tremendous harassment; (5) it has internal capacity challenges; and (6), it lacks credibility with the general population. We then address affordances of technology and social media for each of these challenges. Despite the affordances of technology, we find that in Azerbaijan the challenges faced by the opposition remain (and may even be amplified) in the era of social media. Social media are not empowering oppositionists because the increased visibility and surveillance of opinions shared on social media silences rather than empowers, online activities are swiftly and severely punished, and there is greater competition amongst opposition personalities due to social media creating a new space for opposition outside of the traditional parties.

Authoritarianism

Authoritarianism is both an ideological construct and a set of formal and informal institutions that govern access to and exercise of authority. In such environments, authority exclusively rests with a leader or a small group (Linz 2000) and citizens experience great social control, and are commonly excluded from policy making and denied civil liberties (Vaillant 2012). However, in the 21st century, it has become more difficult for authoritarian regimes to maintain control over their citizens for a number of reasons. First, there is no longer a large Soviet patron helping to support broader authoritarianism (Dobson 2012; Levitsky & Way 2010). Second, the democracy promotion community (organisations like the National Endowment for Democracy, National Democratic Institute, and European Endowment for Democracy) provides financial and educational support to opposition movements (Dobson 2012). Third, transnational human rights advocacy groups (like Amnesty International and Human Rights Watch) coordinate campaigns from democratic states that impact politics within authoritarian states (Keck & Sikkink 1998). And finally, fourth, information and communication technologies have provided citizens access to information and means to organise themselves in ways previously unavailable (Dobson 2012), and as a result, authoritarian leaders have had to become more sophisticated, savvy, and nimble (Dobson 2012); appear more democratic (Linz 2000); and avoid using overt force (Schatz & Maltseva 2012). Instead, the means by which authoritarian regimes now maintain control are legitimisation (demonstrating that they have support), repression (actual or threatened physical sanctions), and co-optation/loyalty (tying strategically relevant actors to the regime elite; Gerschewski 2013; Schatz 2009).

Authoritarian Azerbaijan

While Azerbaijan experienced some political liberalisation after the Soviet collapse, the country has developed in increasingly authoritarian ways, especially over the past decade. Today, Azerbaijan is considered to be one of the most authoritarian of the post-Soviet states (Frichova Grono 2011), although it engages in the performance of particular democratic norms (Heinrich 2011). Azerbaijan is a hegemonic electoral authoritarian regime (LaPorte 2014), that is, a type of electoral authoritarianism in which although elections are held regularly and political opposition is legally allowed, the elections are uncompetitive (Howard & Roessler 2006) and "little more than a theatrical setting for the self-representation and self-reproduction of power" (Schedler 2002a: 47). Rather than choosing representatives, elections in these kinds of autocracies serve to gain external legitimacy, even if it is only performative (Wilson 2005), to gather and signal information, to manage intra-elite relations, and to project strength to the population.

Azerbaijan's ruling regime has been in power, essentially, since the collapse of the Soviet Union. With the exception of 15 months of rule by the Azerbaijan Popular Front Party in the early 1990s, post-Soviet Azerbaijan was ruled by a former Soviet-era leader, Heydar Aliyev. Aliyev consolidated a highly personalistic authoritarian regime, with a backbone of a patronage network formed from his former Soviet allies and clan connections (King 2008). After Heydar Aliyev's death in 2003, he was succeeded by his son, Ilham Aliyev, who maintained his father's system of balancing competing patronage networks—although with some differences (International Crisis Group 2010). The regime elite tightened power beginning in the mid-2000s when the oil boom began (Ahmadov 2011; Guliyev 2009; Radnitz 2012). While concentration of economic resources within the governing elite is the primary contributor to the regime's hegemony, wealth also allows the regime to maintain an elaborate patronage system to manage personal loyalty through exchange of material rewards (Guliyev 2012, 2013).

In authoritarian systems, the regime relies on active and passive loyalty of the strategic elites through co-optation and material enticements but also requires the passive support of the population sometimes through coercion (Stepan 1990). Thus, the Azerbaijani regime exerts strong social control on its citizens. Citizens fear the regime (Abbasov 2010; Gahramanova 2009) and assume serious repercussions for not adhering to what the regime wants (Pearce 2015). Many Azerbaijanis are apathetic about the possibility of change (Abbasov 2010). In this environment, Azerbaijanis distrust others and self-censor (Gahramanova 2009; Pearce & Vitak 2015).

Opposition in Azerbaijan

Those who do not adhere to social control and do not passively (or actively) support the regime are considered 'opposition'. Some 'oppositionists' are formally affiliated with oppositional political parties (in Azerbaijan, the Azerbaijan Popular Front Party [APFP] and the Musavat Party). The Azerbaijani opposition groups that emerged out of the turbulent early 1990s, APFP and Musavat, were emasculated, but throughout 1990s and early 2000s they still acted as a 'small constraint on the ruling elite's power' (Ahmadov, 2011: 208), especially during the highly contentious presidential succession in 2003 and parliamentary elections in 2005, where the opposition parties won six of 125 seats (Freedom House 2014). But by the parliamentary elections of 2010, the opposition parties had been so marginalised that they received no seats (Freedom House 2014). But confusingly, the regime also maintains power by co-opting potential opponents through a handful of 'pocket' opposition parties, which are government-created and controlled to mimic an opposition and channel it for regime-supporting directions for the purpose of performing democratic practices and prevent opposition vote coordination (Schedler 2013). But oppositionists not affiliated with a political party have become increasingly common. This is for two reasons. First, the term 'oppositional' is used to label anyone promoting Western-style democracy. This allows the regime to create a sense of *us* and *them* and claim that any pro-democratic thinking is motivated by a desire to come to power (Bedford 2014). Second, the Internet and social media have provided a new space to be oppositional that previously required the scaffolding of an organisation. In this paper we use the term "the opposition" to include both those who are affiliated with a party, and those who are not.

Opposition Repression

While these opposition parties and individuals are tolerated— LaPorte (2014) argues that it would be too difficult and costly to annihilate them completely—Azerbaijan and other authoritarian regimes make life difficult for these individuals and organisations through repression (Gerschewski 2013; Levitsky & Way 2010) which simultaneously harms oppositionists and deters others from considering becoming one. Opposition parties and oppositionally minded individuals in Azerbaijan are repressed in six distinct ways: The opposition cannot be elected or engage with the formal political process; it is not allowed to communicate with citizens because of strict media control; it is not allowed to freely assemble or rent offices; individuals associated with the opposition face tremendous harassment; the opposition has capacity challenges; and it lacks credibility with the general population.

Given the repression faced by regime opponents, some believe that information and communication technologies can allow the opposition to overcome barriers. This case study will examine what information and communication technologies, and especially the Internet and social media, afford for oppositionists in Azerbaijan. For context, it is important to note that not all Azerbaijanis are on the Internet or use social media. Only a third of adults, as of a November 2013 national survey, have *ever* used the Internet, and only 13 per cent of Azerbaijani adults use the Internet daily. Those who use the Internet are likely to be male, urban, and well-educated (Pearce & Rice 2014). And, as of July 2015, according to Facebook, only 16 per cent of Azerbaijanis (ages 14 and over) are on Facebook, although 28 per cent of Azerbaijani men and 11 per cent of Azerbaijani women are on the site.

Cannot be Elected or Engage in the Formal Political Process

Authoritarian regimes vary in the degree to which opposition parties are allowed to engage in the formal political process, ranging from strictly managed participation to being excluded altogether (Lust-Okar 2005). Elections are the primary means for a party to become involved in the political process. Elections in hegemonic authoritarian states, like Azerbaijan, typically serve to enhance regime resilience by providing a veneer of popular legitimacy and more importantly as informational signalling and elite management tools (Schedler 2013). Although the current Azerbaijani regime allows elections to occur, and opposition candidates occasionally get on the ballot, it also ensures that non-pocket opposition candidates cannot be elected by employing electoral manipulation and fraud at all of stages of an election: registration, campaigning, voting, and counts (Bedford 2014; Herron 2011; Sjoberg 2014). Social media do provide an alternative platform for campaigning, and a lot of pre-election activity does occur online in Azerbaijan.

But it is unknown how much support the opposition has, regardless of any campaign efforts. Few are willing to publicly endorse the opposition, and even if opposition votes are registered, manipulation of results gives no sense of reality. Even if individuals support the opposition privately, they hide their views both offline and online because of the risk of being persecuted. The lack of information about the preferences of others—preference falsification—has a serious impact on elections. Voting for the opposition is a 'tipping game' because citizens will only vote for the opposition if they think that others will as well (Kuran 1991).

Social media can have an impact on preference falsification through the process known as *preference revelation*—a mechanism in which individuals make their private preferences known. Social media can make it easier for people to reveal their preferences, sometimes without facing repercussions for preferring something unpopular or undesirable, and for others to learn of different preferences (Lynch 2011). However, unlike Lynch, we argue that in fact support registered digitally may be *riskier* because of greater visibility and the ability to be captured as evidence. Individuals calculate the audience, the likelihood of an audience member will disagree, and the possible repercussions of revealing the preference (Pearce & Vitak 2015). While social media make revelations easier, they also mean that the preference is more visible to a broader audience

(Ellison & Vitak 2015). Given that Azerbaijani society has a norm of (perceived and real) surveillance and punishment for violations from family, peers, and the authorities, social media surveillance also increases the likelihood of repercussions (Pearce 2015; Pearce & Vitak 2015). Azerbaijanis have already seen severe consequences of social media distributed dissent, which results in increased self-censorship (Pearce 2014, 2015; Pearce & Hajizada 2014; Pearce & Kendzior 2012; Pearce et al. 2014).

Some argue that social media can have an impact on elections as a tool for sharing information about fraud (Reuter & Szakonyi 2013), but again, fear of repercussions holds many back. In Azerbaijan, because of the likelihood of repercussions for noting election fraud, especially on social media, it is unlikely that most citizens would share such information. In the 2013 election, although there was documented fraud, few social media users in Azerbaijan were willing to share this information.

Cannot Communicate with People Because of Media Control

Authoritarian regimes repress opposition through careful control of information flow (Schatz 2009; Whitten-Woodring & James 2012). Such regimes do not want citizens to receive information because it can legitimise the opposition (Gamson & Wolfsfeld 1993), bring about critical discussions (Whitten-Woodring & James 2012), and potentially allow oppositionists to broadcast plans for mobilisation (Whitten-Woodring & James 2012). In Azerbaijan, the regime controls all mainstream print and broadcast media, has banned opposition and independent media outlets, and harasses newspaper kiosks and print shops willing to distribute opposition print news (LaPorte 2014). Even during elections, opposition candidates have almost no access to mainstream media (LaPorte 2014). Given such an environment, one of the most powerful effects of the Internet and social media is the potential for alternative information dissemination and deliberation, either between citizens (Leijendekker & Mutsvairo 2014; Reuter & Szakonyi 2013) or from organisations or alternative news outlets (Leijendekker & Mutsvairo 2014).

The mechanism through which alternative information could aid the opposition is through what Bailard (2014) calls *window opening*—exposure to wider information and *mirror holding*—using the new information to create a different evaluation of the political situation. Azerbaijani formal opposition parties, opposition-allied media outlets and organisations with opposition leanings all use social media in order to share information and events. In fact, the Facebook pages of these organisations are much more dynamic than the official websites. But it is important to note that merely liking an opposition organisation or politician has repercussions (Pearce & Vitak 2015), so Facebook 'likes' are no indication of actual popularity among citizens, and with bots and fake accounts, Facebook 'likes' may not even represent actual people with Facebook profiles.

Nonetheless, there is no doubt that social media's role as an information source is the most significant affordance of the Internet for the opposition in Azerbaijan. Some would argue that without the Internet, there would be no alternative media in Azerbaijan today.

Cannot Freely Assemble or Rent Offices

Denying freedom of assembly—the right of individuals to form and participate in peaceable, noncommercial groups, including the ability to dissent (Inazu 2011) and preference signification (Muller et al. 1980)—is another way that authoritarian regimes repress opposition. Thus, unsurprisingly, in Azerbaijan, freedom of assembly and opposition parties' and organisations' ability to assemble in public spaces is severely restricted (Bedford 2014; LaPorte 2014). The regime rarely issues permits for opposition events (rallies or protests), and when it does it is at the last minute and the location is far from the city centre and difficult to find. Once at an event, the police presence is overwhelming. Officers line the walls of the nearest metro system, multiple police vehicles surround the event space, and upon entering, individuals are frisked and bags are searched, and sometimes events turn violent and participants are detained or physically assaulted (Amnesty International 2011). Also pro-regime social media users flood event-related hashtags and pages with mockery and threats. Not only does this intimidate those wanting to attend the event, but it also discourages non-attendees.

Related to the challenges in being able to gather, Azerbaijani opposition parties and oppositional-minded organisations also have serious challenges renting office space (LaPorte, 2014), which makes it difficult for the leadership to meet and conduct routine organisational business. Laptops and Wi-Fi do make it easier for groups to gather and work together, and the Internet does reduce barriers for organising without co-presence and at a reduced cost (Bennett & Segerberg 2013; Earl & Kimport 2011; Lynch 2011). There is evidence that these gathering affordances have led to both offline (Breuer et al. 2014) and online collective action (Bondes & Schucher 2014) in some authoritarian contexts.

In Azerbaijan, oppositionists have also leveraged the affordances of social media to work around the regime's roadblocks to freedom of assembly. First, social media allow for an event's location and time to be distributed much more easily and affordably. Second, the difficulty in finding the location is reduced through Google Maps and longitude/latitude coordinates. Often, the event's Facebook page will include annotated directions on a Google map (see Figure 16.1). Third, if an event turns violent or the location suddenly changes due to violence, attendees use social media to inform others.

Figure 16.1 Annotated Map to a Rally (*Mitinq*) Location Posted on a Facebook Event

However, an additional affordance (or hindrance) of social media for events is the ability for individuals to RSVP with great visibility. Because Azerbaijanis are generally fearful of letting their political preferences be known, clicking 'attending' on an oppostion-organised event has symbolic purposes because of the publicness of the act—one's Facebook followers will see the 'attending' in their newsfeed and anyone viewing the event page will see that individual on the list of attendees. Even if one is not able to attend the event, merely clicking 'attending' demonstrates to that individual's audience that the individual supports the event and may inform a wider audience that the event is taking place. Yet, clicking 'attending' also increases individual risk—family, friends, strangers, or the authorities witness this and there could be repercussions.

Individuals Face Tremendous Harassment

Perhaps the most common and powerful form of opposition repression comes in the form of harassment (Dobson 2012; Schatz 2009). This harassment includes surveillance, physical harassment and intimidation, and denial of career and educational opportunities (Gerschewski 2013). Azerbaijan is no exception to this sort of activity (Gahramanova 2009; LaPorte 2014; Pearce 2015; Radnitz 2012), with oppositionists experiencing blackmail, recording and distribution of intimate relations photos and videos, arbitrary arrests, long prison sentences, beating, torture, kidnapping, and the inability to be hired (Human Rights Watch 2014; U.S. Department of State 2013). Harassment has increased dramatically since 2012, and especially in the second half of 2014, with dozens of journalists, human rights workers, and political activists being arrested and imprisoned on bogus charges (Human Rights Watch 2013). Harassment creates a tremendous challenge for formal or informal opposition groups to recruit members and attract supporters as many Azerbaijanis are, reasonably, deterred from criticising the government.

Yet, technology affords documentation and dissemination of proof of harassment. Taking screenshots of online harassment or photographing assault provides evidence. This is essentially counter-surveillance, which some argue can potentially reduce harm (Wilson & Serisier 2010), especially in the case of dramatic visual images, like severe beatings (Lim 2013). Moreover, social media provides a means to disseminate this information. As highlighted by Howard (2011), social media can aid those experiencing harassment to broadcast their grievances to the outside world and (of particular importance) reach transnational human rights groups and international media outlets. Using social media to broadcast human rights violations allows oppositionists direct and indirect access individuals and organisations that may be able to help (Joseph 2012), which should, hypothetically, raise the cost of harassment for the regime (Lynch 2011). But these authors do not also consider the importance of evidence for domestic audiences as well for awareness-raising and solidarity.

A case of domestic and international attention received because of documentation of graphic images is the brutal August 2014 beating of Azerbaijani human rights advocate and journalist Ilgar Nasibov. Photographs of the results of the beating were released (by his family) to opposition online newspapers a few days later. Because on Facebook a thumbnail photo is used when sharing a photo, the sharing of the news story about Nasibov's beating meant that a user's Facebook newsfeed was filled with gruesome images, making it impossible to ignore the story. Because of the shocking and unintentional viewing of these photographs, it is possible that this story received more

241

attention than other cases of physical violence, both amongst Azerbaijani social media users and the broader international community.

Have Internal Challenges and Capacity Problems

Although the Azerbaijani opposition faces external problems, it also has internal capacity issues. Scholars describe the Azerbaijani opposition parties as personality-driven (LaPorte 2014), internally fractured (LaPorte 2014), divided (Guliyev 2009), "feeble and disorganized" (Radnitz 2012: 61), "completely ineffective" (LaPorte 2014: 1) and unable to organise efficiently (Bedford 2014). We do not claim to be able to untangle these issues or determine their causes, but we will attempt to describe some specific ways that the opposition is challenged internally.

First, the opposition parties do not embody broad values that are an alternative to the current regime. As Przeworski (1991) rightly observes, undermining the source of the regime's legitimacy does not make a difference; what matters is proposing an alternative. The Azerbaijani opposition parties fail to demonstrate clear differences from the regime. Nor do the opposition parties and unaffiliated oppositionists formulate specific alternative policy solutions. Even if they could disseminate information more widely or become a part of the formal political process, the lack of coherent policies does not register confidence in these groups' abilities. New policies for Azerbaijan's poor and deteriorating education and health systems are relevant and low-hanging fruit for opposition parties to pick, yet they do not present alternatives to the population.

Next, most of the traditional opposition parties are organised around particular personalities who are veteran politicians from the 1990s. Some observers argue that these parties thus operate as personalist party machines rather than mature organisations with rules and platforms. If social media afford anything for these capacity problems, it may be in providing a space for experience gaining, learning via cross-national sharing of ideas, and deliberation within the movement, which can all help an opposition movement develop better strategies (Nikolayenko 2011). If social media provides opportunities for oppositionists to learn more effective tools, it could help reduce these internal challenges.

Credibility Problem

Another problem for the opposition is that the general population may not find them credible. Some Azerbaijanis believe the opposition is poorly organised, vulnerable, and dysfunctional (LaPorte 2014; Sultanova 2014). This is a problem that is both external and internal. Externally, because oppositionists cannot participate in the political process, it is difficult for them to demonstrate their capacity or credibility to citizens. This is compounded by the way in which oppositionists are portrayed on state-controlled media. As Schedler (2002b) remarks, authoritarian regimes orchestrate aggressive campaigns to destroy the reputation of opposition candidates and groups. But the opposition's credibility problem is also due to actual capacity issues. Nonetheless, without the ability to convey credibility to citizens, opposition parties and groups have little hope to gain support, much less power. However, just as social media can allow oppositionists to disseminate information and campaign, social media can allow a group to build its reputation and establish political credibility (Housholder & LaMarre 2014).

Conclusion: New Players

Azerbaijanis are using social media to address credibility issues. A number of individuals and some organisations have used social media creatively and wisely to move from lesser-known oppositionists to influential voices within the opposition by growing an audience and sharing their opinions widely. Many of these oppositionists have larger and more dynamic social media followings than the traditional opposition party leaders do. Mixing personal content (such as informal photographs and humorous news articles) with political content, these personalities are much more attractive to the average Azerbaijani social media user than middle-aged professional politicians reposting texts from speeches.

These newer oppositionists are unencumbered by the challenges that a large organisation faces when deciding what messages to deliver and positions to take on issues, and often can draw attention to regime behaviour in a way that the traditional parties cannot. An individual can post an immediate reaction to the news of an arrest of a human rights activist, simultaneously spreading the news and letting it be known how she or he feels about the situation, as well as often sparking a discussion of the arrest. Musavat or the APFP and their leaders must collaborate on a statement, which inevitably means compromise between strong personalities and demonstrations of loyalty to particular personas, cautiously presenting an opinion (likely full of compromises or crafted to not displease certain individuals) and generally take hours, if not days, to react. Meanwhile, the unaffiliated have been discussing the issue at length, deliberation has occurred, organising around a reaction has been discussed, all the while the traditional parties are left in the digital dust.

The newer opposition organisation (seeking party status), the REAL (Republican Alternative) movement is one such case. The organisation uses social media to promote its policies and actively engages with organisational members and interested individuals. Interestingly, it has built its reputation almost entirely through social media, although it engages in many offline activities as well. REAL ran over a dozen candidates in the 2015 Parliamentary election with highly professional digital posters and an organized social media campaign.

Individuals can also build their political reputations via social media in Azerbaijan by being known as information disseminators (such as Hebib Muntezir, arguably one of the most important information sources in Azerbaijan, with over 22,000 followers on Facebook), or promoting their professional journalism online like popular young photojournalist Mehman Huseynov (129,000 Facebook followers), investigative journalist Khadija Ismayilova (18,000 Facebook followers), interesting political commentators (such as journalist Mirza Khazar (10,000 Facebook followers), historian Altay Goyushov (15,000 Facebook followers), or political aspirants like Natiq Jafarli (10,000 Facebook followers), Erkin Gadirli (11,000 Facebook followers), Bakhtiyar Hajiyev (14,000 Facebook followers), and Emin Milli (17,000 Facebook followers). There would be no other way for these individuals to have grown their political influence without social media. But this political influence comes at a cost. These individuals become targets themselves. Some have fled Azerbaijan. Some have lost their jobs. Many have spent time in prison related to their online activities. And Muntezir was allegedly the target of an assassination attempt, while Milli's brother-in-law was imprisoned and Milli received a death threat about his online reporting.

But while these individuals have followings and credibility, it is unlikely that the opposition's overall credibility problem is being alleviated by these individuals in any meaningful way. While it is possible that these individuals' credibility could impact overall attitudes toward the opposition, it seems as if their role is more as a healthy alternative to the traditional parties to those already oppositionally minded. It remains unknown whether this independent type of opposition personality is recruiting new Azerbaijanis to the opposition. And while these new social media oppositionists have inserted new healthy blood of pluralism into the backwater of opposition politics in Azerbaijan, this process, like most opposition politics in Azerbaijan, has been driven by personalities rather than deliberation and institution building. These upstarts' social media presence and discussions are sometimes squabbles and have yet to lead to concrete deliberation. The lack of concrete policy solutions have hurt the traditional opposition parties in the past, and it seems that history may repeat itself with these upstarts, resulting in detrimental consequences for the institutionalisation of the opposition and its capacity to organise and sustain collective action. But time may prove otherwise.

We have documented the ways that the Azerbaijani opposition is repressed and how social media have and may possibly afford opportunities to reduce the challenges faced. Yet, we remain pessimistic about the opposition's ability to leverage social media to fully overcome the challenges it faces. We also suggest that social media may in fact threaten the traditional opposition because it affords greater competition from these independent upstarts. Social media allow for new ways for individuals to participate in and escalate opposition activities besides joining a formal opposition group. In this way, social media are more inclusive and participatory (Lim 2012). But social media also harm the monopoly that the traditional opposition parties have had for years.

This competition may cause greater division within oppositionally minded Azerbaijanis. It appears as if independents are *doing something* because of their social media activity, making the traditional opposition parties look even less capable than believed before social media. Additionally, some of these independent oppositionists are not shy in expressing their disdain for the traditional opposition parties. While some younger oppositionists have allegiances based on family ties, many independents, to differing degrees of politeness, ignore or bash the traditional parties via social media.

In conclusion, even if the opposition leveraged the affordances of social media to address the existing challenges it faces, these new challenges of overcoming social-media enhanced fear and dealing with competition compound the problems faced by the opposition. The small victories via social media do little to contribute to the greater battle that the opposition needs to fight. While perhaps social media may ease some pain (especially if social media can help to decrease harassment), because the regime is firmly entrenched, there is no hope—digital or otherwise—for the Azerbaijani opposition.

References

Abbasov, S. (2010) "Civil Society in Azerbaijan: Under Fire but Still Resisting," *Caucasus Analytical Digest*, 12, available at: http://www.css.ethz.ch/publications/pdfs/CAD-12.pdf.

Ahmadov, A. (2011) *A Conditional Theory of the "Political Resource Curse:" Oil, Autocrats, and Strategic Contexts*, PhD thesis, London School of Economics.

Amnesty International (2011) *Azerbaijan: The Spring that Never Blossomed: Freedoms Suppressed in Azerbaijan*, available at: http://www.amnesty.org/en/library/info/EUR55/011/2011/en.

Bailard, C. S. (2014) *Democracy's Double-Edged Sword: How Internet Use Changes Citizens' Views of Their Government*, Baltimore: Johns Hopkins University Press.

Bedford, S. (2014) "Introduction to the Special Section: Political Mobilization in Azerbaijan—The January 2013 Protests and Beyond," *Demokratizatsiya*, 22(1), pp. 3–14.

Bennett, W. L. and Segerberg, A. (2013) *The Logic of Connective Action: Digital Media and the Personalization of Contentious Politics*, Cambridge, UK: Cambridge University Press.

Bondes, M. and Schucher, G. (2014) "Derailed Emotions: The Transformation of Claims and Targets During the Wenzhou Online Incident," *Information, Communication & Society*, 17(1), pp. 45–65.

Breuer, A., Landman, T., and Farquhar, D. (2014) "Social Media and Protest Mobilization: Evidence from the Tunisian Revolution," *Democratization*, 22(4), pp. 764–792.

Dobson, W. (2012) *The Dictator's Learning Curve: Inside the Global Battle for Democracy*, New York: Doubleday.

Earl, J. and Kimport, K. (2011) *Digitally Enabled Social Change: Activism in the Internet Age*, Cambridge, MA: MIT Press.

Ellison, N. B. and Vitak, J. (2015) "Social Media Affordances and their Relationship to Social Capital Processes," in Sundar, S. (Ed.),*The Handbook of Psychology of Communication Technology*, Boston: Wiley-Blackwell, pp. 205–237.

Freedom House (2014). *Nations in Transit*, available at: http://freedomhouse.org/sites/default/files/NIT14_Azerbaijan_final.pdf.

Frichova Grono, M. (2011) *Nations in Transit: Azerbaijan*, Washington, DC: Freedom House.

Gahramanova, A. (2009) "Internal and External Factors in the Democratization of Azerbaijan," *Democratization*, 16(4), pp. 777–803.

Gamson, W. A. and Wolfsfeld, G. (1993) "Movements and Media as Interacting Systems," *Annals of the American Academy of Political and Social Science*, 528, pp. 114–125.

Gerschewski, J. (2013) "The Three Pillars of Stability: Legitimation, Repression, and Co-optation in Autocratic Regimes," *Democratization*, 20(1), pp. 13–38.

Guliyev, F. (2009) "Oil Wealth, Patrimonialism, and the Failure of Democracy in Azerbaijan," *Caucasus Analytical Digest*, 2, available at: http://www.css.ethz.ch/publications/pdfs/CAD-2.pdf.

Guliyev, F. (2012) "Political Elites in Azerbaijan," in Heinrich, A. and Pleines, H. (Eds.), *Challenges of the Caspian Resource Boom: Domestic Elites and Policy-Making*, Houndmills: Palgrave Macmillan, pp. 117–130.

Guliyev, F. (2013) "Oil and Regime Stability in Azerbaijan," *Demokratizatsiya*, 21(1), pp. 113–147.

Heinrich, A. (2011) "The Formal Political System in Azerbaijan," *Caucasus Analytical Digest*, 4, available at: http://kms1.isn.ethz.ch/serviceengine/Files/ISN/126919/ipublicationdocument_singledocument/07097e04-b140-4fb5-91c7-b40437645b96/en/CaucasusAnalyticalDigest24.pdf.

Herron, E.S. (2011) "Measuring Dissent in Electoral Authoritarian Societies: Lessons from Azerbaijan's 2008 Presidential Election and 2009 Referendum," *Comparative Political Studies*, 44(11), pp. 1557–1583.

Housholder, E. E. and LaMarre, H.L. (2014) "Facebook Politics: Toward a Process Model for Achieving Political Source Credibility through Social Media," *Journal of Information Technology & Politics*, 11(4), pp. 368–382.

Howard, M. M. and Roessler, P.G. (2006) "Liberalizing Electoral Outcomes in Competitive Authoritarian Regimes," *American Journal of Political Science*, 50(2), pp. 365–381.

Howard, P. N. (2011) *The Digital Origins of Dictatorship and Democracy: Information Technology and Political Islam*, New York: Oxford University Press.

Human Rights Watch (2013) *Tightening the Screws: Azerbaijan's Crackdown on Civil Society and Dissent*, available at: http://www.hrw.org/node/118310.

Human Rights Watch (2014) *Country Report: Azerbaijan*, available at: http://www.hrw.org/world-report/2014/country-chapters/azerbaijan.

Inazu, J. D. (2011) *Liberty's Refuge: The Forgotten Freedom of Assembly*, New Haven: Yale University Press.

International Crisis Group (2010) *Azerbaijan: Vulnerable Stability*, available at: http://www.crisisgroup. org/~/media/Files/europe/caucasus/azerbaijan/207 Azerbaijan—Vulnerable Stability.pdf.

Joseph, S. (2012) "Social Media, Political Change, and Human Rights," *Boston College International and Comparative Law Review*, 35(1), pp. 145–188.

Keck, M. E. and Sikkink, K. (1998) *Activists Beyond Borders: Advocacy Networks in International Politics*, Ithaca: Cornell University Press.

King, C. (2008) *The Ghost of Freedom: A History of the Caucasus*, Oxford: Oxford University Press.

Kuran, T. (1991) "Now Out of Never: The Element of Surprise in the East European Revolution of 1989," *World Politics*, 44(1), pp. 7–48.

LaPorte, J. (2014) "Hidden in Plain Sight: Political Opposition and Hegemonic Authoritarianism in Azerbaijan," *Post-Soviet Affairs*, 31(4), pp. 339–366.

Leijendekker, I. and Mutsvairo, B. (2014) "On Digitally Networked Technologies, Hegemony and Regime Durability in Authoritarian Regimes: A Zimbabwean Case Study," *Information, Communication & Society*, 17(8), pp. 1034–1047.

Levitsky, S. and Way, L. A. (2010) *Competitive Authoritarianism: Hybrid Regimes after the Cold War*, Cambridge: Cambridge University Press.

Lim, M. (2012) "Clicks, Cabs, and Coffee Houses: Social Media and Oppositional Movements in Egypt, 2004–2011," *Journal of Communication*, 62(2), pp. 231–248.

Lim, M. (2013) "Framing Bouazizi: 'White Lies', Hybrid Network, and Collective/Connective Action in the 2010–11 Tunisian Uprising," *Journalism*, 14(7), pp. 921–941.

Linz, J. J. (2000) *Totalitarian and Authoritarian Regimes*, Boulder, CO: Lynne Rienner Publishers.

Lust-Okar, E. (2005) *Structuring Conflict*, Cambridge: Cambridge University Press.

Lynch, M. (2011) "After Egypt: The Limits and Promise of Online Challenges to the Authoritarian Arab State," *Perspectives on Politics*, 9(2), pp. 301–310.

Muller, E. N., Pesonen, P., and Jukam, T.O. (1980) "Support for the Freedom of Assembly in Western Democracies," *European Journal of Political Research*, 8(3), pp. 265–288.

Nikolayenko, O. (2011) *Citizens in the Making in Post-Soviet States*, London: Routledge.

Pearce, K. E. (2014) "Two Can Play at That Game: Social Media Opportunities in Azerbaijan for Government and Opposition," *Demokratizatsiya*, 22(1), pp. 39–66.

Pearce, K. E. (2015) "Democratizing Kompromat: The Affordances of Social Media for State-sponsored Harassment," *Information, Communication & Society*, 18(10), pp. 1158–1174.

Pearce, K. E., Freelon, D., and Kendzior, S. (2014) "The Effect of the Internet on Civic Engagement Under Authoritarianism: The Case of Azerbaijan," *First Monday*, 19(6), available at: http://firstmonday.org/ojs/index.php/fm/article/view/5000.

Pearce, K. E. and Hajizada, A. (2014) "No Laughing Matter: Humor as a Means of Dissent in the Digital Era: The Case of Authoritarian Azerbaijan," *Demokratizatsiya*, 22(443), pp. 67–85.

Pearce, K. E. and Kendzior, S. (2012) "Networked Authoritarianism and Social Media in Azerbaijan," *Journal of Communication*, 62(2), pp. 283–298.

Pearce, K. E. and Rice, R. E. (2014) The Language Divide—The Persistence of English Proficiency as a Gateway to the Internet: The Cases of Armenia, Azerbaijan, and Georgia," *International Journal of Communication*, 8, pp. 2834–2859.

Pearce, K. E. & Vitak, J. (2015) "Performing Honor Online: The Affordances of Social Media for Surveillance and Impression Management in an Honor Culture". New Media & Society.

Przeworski, A. (1991) *Democracy and the Market: Political and Economic Reforms in Eastern Europe and Latin America*, Cambridge: Cambridge University Press.

Radnitz, S. (2012) "Oil in the Family: Managing Presidential Succession in Azerbaijan," *Democratization*, 19(1), pp. 60–77.

Reuter, O. J. and Szakonyi, D. (2013) "Online Social Media and Political Awareness in Authoritarian Regimes," *British Journal of Political Science*, pp. 1–23.

Schatz, E. (2009) "The Soft Authoritarian Tool Kit: Agenda-Setting Power in Kazakhstan and Kyrgyzstan," *Comparative Politics*, 41(2), pp. 203–222.

Schatz, E. and Maltseva, E. (2012) "Kazakhstan's Authoritarian 'Persuasion,'" *Post-Soviet Affairs*, 28(1), pp. 45–65.

Schedler, A. (2002a) "The Menu of Manipulation," *Journal of Democracy*, 13(2), pp. 36–50.

Schedler, A. (2002b) "The Nested Game of Democratization by Elections," *International Political Science Review*, 23(1), pp. 103–122.

Schedler, A. (2013) *The Politics of Uncertainty*, Oxford: Oxford University Press.

Sjoberg, F. M. (2014) "Autocratic Adaptation: The Strategic Use of Transparency and the Persistence of Election Fraud," *Electoral Studies*, 33, pp. 233–245.

Stepan, A. C. (1990) "On the Tasks of a Democratic Opposition," *Journal of Democracy*, 1(2), pp. 41–49.

Sultanova, S. (2014) "Challenging the Aliyev Regime: Political Opposition in Azerbaijan," *Demokratizatsiya*, 22(1), pp. 15–37.

U.S. Department of State (2013) *Human Rights Report: Azerbaijan*, available at: http://photos.state.gov/libraries/azerbaijan/749085/hrr/2013_Human_Rights_Report.pdf.

Vaillant, G. G. (2012) "Authoritarian Regimes," in G. Ritzer (ed.), *Wiley-Blackwell Encyclopedia of Globalization*, Oxford, UK: Blackwell.

Whitten-Woodring, J. and James, P. (2012) "Fourth Estate or Mouthpiece? A Formal Model of Media, Protest, and Government Repression," *Political Communication*, 29(2), pp. 113–136.

Wilson, A. (2005) *Virtual Politics: Faking Democracy in the Post-Soviet World*, New Haven: Yale University Press.

Wilson, D. J. and Serisier, T. (2010) "Video Activism and the Ambiguities of Counter-Surveillance," *Surveillance & Society*, 8(2), pp. 166–180.

17

SOCIAL MEDIA AND SOCIAL MOVEMENTS

Weak Publics, the Online Space, Spatial Relations, and Collective Action in Singapore

Natalie Pang and Debbie Goh

Introduction

With the mass adoption of social media, much has been said about the robustness and the inclusiveness of the online space as a sustainable public sphere. This involves a reinvention of political deliberation and participation, reflecting a shift and negotiation of power between the state and citizens, and participants moving back and forth between online and offline media environments. In social media, opinion expression can also be closely followed by political action, and activities in one country can affect similar protests elsewhere. For instance, the mobilisation of people for civic or political causes as in the case of social media and the protest in Tahrir Square (Tufekci & Wilson 2012) can lead to eventual motivation and mobilisation of people to support the White Paper protest in Singapore (Pang & Goh 2014).

In Singapore, the average social media penetration rate is 70 per cent, one of the highest in Asia (Hashmeta 2014), with Facebook being the most popular, followed by Instagram and Twitter. In a recent study comparing 9,417 Internet users in France, Germany, India, Singapore, the U.S., and the UK, Singaporeans were revealed to be the most emotionally connected to the Internet (Tata Communications 2014), with 78 per cent reporting negative emotions when they are without Internet access. Such results have a number of implications: Singaporean users are heavily dependent on the Internet for information; the Internet may have emerged as a space where users interact meaningfully with others and form what they perceive to be substantial relationships; and/or the Internet is such an integral and important part of their everyday lives that they are emotionally affected without it.

With the amount of time Singaporeans spend online, boundaries distinguishing their lives online and offline are increasingly blurred, and online interactions can often lead to deliberate actions and the mobilisation of social and political movements. The mobilisation potential and use of social media is clear enough—but what functions do online chatter serve in social and political movements? In what ways are online communities functioning, and how do they contribute to the dynamics of such movements? This chapter will examine these questions via three case studies conducted in Singapore between 2011 and 2013. Two cases focus on the context of political participation and information seeking during two elections, and the third is concerned with social media use during a protest. The cases are selected as they form part of our case-based investigation into social media use in the sociopolitical context from 2011 to 2013. We begin with the first study in 2011 on social media use during Singapore's general election, move to the by-election in 2012, and end with the study of a protest in 2013.

Social Media and Social Movements in Singapore

The Internet and social media landscape in Singapore should be understood within the context of changing policies on relaxing public and free speech. It was only in 2000 that public speeches were encouraged in Singapore, with the gazetting of a Speakers' Corner in central Singapore to allow citizens to give public speeches without a public entertainment license. The space, however, was rarely used for eight years, until the easing of restrictions to allow public demonstrations and rallies without a police permit, although the privilege was only for Singaporeans and excluded non-citizens residing Singapore. Since then, use of the space has grown, but remained largely focused on civic and social issues such as LGBT rights (Berger 2004).

In 1994, Sintercom (short for the Singapore Internet Community) was founded. Like the U.S.-based WELL (Whole Earth 'Lectronic Link), which has been described as the most influential virtual community born in the 1980s (Rheingold 1993), Sintercom flourished within a short time, with more than 20 editors and 1,200 subscribers on its mailing list at its height (George 2006). The site was shut down in 2001 due to disagreements with the authorities over the introduction of the Class License scheme (Rodan 1998), which asked Internet content providers that discussed religious or political issues to register and to "bear full responsibility for contents on the website and [take] all reasonable steps to ensure that such content comply with the laws of Singapore" (MDA 2010: 6). Two decades later, social media have become instrumental in filling the gaps left behind by Sintercom: growing civic journalism (Kirk 2014), fostering alternative discourse and public deliberation, and providing opportunities for direct engagement.

In May 2013, 17 years after the introduction of the Class Licensing scheme, new plans to govern online discourse were announced: online news sites that report regularly on issues related to Singapore and have significant reach among readers would require an individual license, to be consistent with the requirements imposed on traditional news platforms (MDA 2013). Public exchanges highlighting objections to the new rules, and ambiguity from the media authorities eventually led to a social movement framed as #FreeMyInternet in Singapore, with the first protest held on 8 June 2013 at the Speakers' Corner (Reuters 2013).

The Public Sphere Reloaded

The original conception of the public sphere by Habermas (1962) has received much attention and criticism, largely relating to the structural limitations to participation and the class differences between individuals able to come together for public deliberation (also cf. Chapter 4 by Bruns & Highfield in Part I of this collection). Mass media were also seen critically, in their potential influence on public opinion—thereby reducing the effectiveness and pluralization of the public sphere.

The media environment and communication technologies have changed much since 1962, especially with the introduction of social media into the landscape. The dissemination of information, even via mass media, is rarely one way, and anyone can participate if they want to. The plurality of voices birthed and facilitated by the Internet implies that more can be heard, more issues may be raised, and more people can rally around a common cause.

Such democratizing potential, however, may be limited by different levels of access to the Internet. Marginalized groups who do not have access for reasons such as affordability and digital literacy are unable to participate; but even if they had access, their voices may be undermined because of differences in language, abilities in expressing opinions, and dominance relative to others online.

The online sphere as originally conceptualised by Habermas (1962) also did not include the possibility of other public spheres. With social media bringing about 'new' kinds of spaces in which online discourse about salient issues can flourish, they can function as 'weak publics', which function as spaces of deliberation and discourse, participated in by private individuals and performing discursive checks on the decisions made by the state.

Furthermore, Fraser (1990: 64) suggested that since "a space of zero degree culture, so utterly bereft of any specific ethos" is highly unlikely, having multiple publics is in fact advantageous since it will foster a greater plurality of perspectives and enable less dominant cultural groups to participate.

The Online Space

Findings from many studies have pointed to the fact that people congregate in distinct enclaves online, forming their own social norms and values to guide their behaviour and interactions (Rheingold 1993; Wojcieszak & Rojas 2011). Echo chambers sometimes result from these online enclaves, where information and beliefs are reinforced and amplified.

The small-world concept developed by Chatman (1991) may provide further clues for understanding the function of online enclaves as multiple publics, their use of social media, and their implications for social movements. In small worlds, interactions are guided by what Chatman (1991: 444) described as "first-level lifestyle": people are dependent "either on personal experiences or on hearsay from someone who is accepted as having knowledge of things being discussed" (Chatman 1991: 215). For them, information is sought "from others much like themselves" and rejected especially when such information threatens and challenges their beliefs and norms. Such defensive behaviour is partly due to their worldview as "insiders" and a distrust of anyone who is not part of their intimate small world. These insiders set "boundaries on behavior" (Chatman 1991: 214): they define and redefine what is acceptable and normative within their community. Such small worlds provide a common sense of social reality and the problems associated with it. Members of a small world share beliefs which are reflected in collective action and social movements, aligned with the expectations and reality they believe exist.

Traditional theories of collective action have been challenged in recent years for their relevance and external validity within the changing media environment (Bimber, Flanagin, & Stohl 2005). Bimber et al. (2005) questioned the assumptions of free-riding and central organisation in such theories, expanding the theory to account for other contemporary collective action, especially in online situations when individuals cross their private boundaries into the public to come together for collective discourse and action. Both are key ingredients for social movements, but should also be understood within the small world contexts of how they come about.

The Cases

Social Media and the General Election of 2011

Since Singapore's independence in 1965, it has grown rapidly, rising in prominence through its economic and infrastructural development—an achievement that is often associated with the dominance of its ruling party, the People's Action Party (PAP), since 1959. With the government's control also over the mainstream media platforms in the republic, the growth of the Internet and social media has been seen as positive in assisting with the development of deliberative democracy, as many Singaporeans are taking to these platforms to express their opinions on various issues and to connect with other like-minded citizens.

In 2011, Singapore held its 16th general election, described by both academics and political parties as a 'watershed election' (Lim, 2011). It was a 'watershed' also in the way that social media were at the forefront of the contest between the ruling party and the opposition parties. Opposition parties used social media actively during the elections, and citizens used them to either express their opinions and/or connect with the respective parties or political candidates.

With the goal of understanding how opposition parties and citizens used social media, as well as examining the discourse within these platforms, our project focused on the online content created and used both by political parties and by citizens during the general election. A total of 1,380 Facebook posts, six party websites, and 764 blog posts were analysed (for full details, see Pang & Goh, 2012; Goh & Pang, 2012).

Issues that dominated the online discourse were identified. Some of these issues would later resurface in our subsequent study in the following year, which we discuss below. From the content analysis, we generated two main findings contributing to the theoretical propositions. One of them relates to the generation of issues and agenda setting: whilst there were core issues identified by mainstream media, political parties and citizens were both able to further deliberate and analyse those issues online, and generate different sub-issues and agendas. Certain sites also exhibited more intense and cohesive interactions within the online community, to the point that individuals who diverged from their social norms or introduced new kinds of information were asked to leave.

The By-Election of 2012

Momentum from the 2011 general election was picked up again with a by-election for the constituency of Hougang in 2012, after the dismissal of an elected member of parliament belonging to the opposition camp. Two parties contested this by-election, namely the ruling party (PAP) and the by-now-dominant opposition Workers' Party.

By now, there was interest in the representation of online voices, and our goal was to investigate whether and how opinions and discourse were similar or different online and offline. Issues identified from the earlier study of social media content in the general election in 2011 were incorporated into the coding of online discourse and opinions here (for a detailed discussion, see Goh, Pang, & Ang, 2013).

Our content analysis revealed that there were unresolved, persistent issues since the last general election, and online, there was much dissent and negative sentiments building up towards them. One example was the issue of foreign labour, which led to a protest and social movement at the Speakers' Corner in 2013. Our findings in this case reinforced our proposition that social media were functioning as weak publics that were fluid but also significant in sustaining momentum and dialogue on issues of interest. The discourse generated online was also providing much context for the development of frames to examine the subsequent collective action and protest.

The White Paper Protest: Proximal Groups and the Shaping of Participation

By early 2013, dissatisfactions with certain issues gained much ground online. One issue was the issue of relaxed foreign labour and immigration policies, leading to an increase in the number of foreigners in the small republic. By 2013, Singapore citizens comprised only 62 per cent, or 3.3 million, of the country's population of 5.3 million. Blogs, Facebook pages, and Twitter feeds were filled with growing resentment against foreigners by locals facing growing social fragmentation, overcrowding, high housing prices, depressed wages, and competition for space, jobs, and schools.

In January 2013, a Population White Paper was released, aimed at controlling and calibrating the growth of foreigners to a more steady state. It projected a population growth to 6.9 million by 2030, of which 50 per cent would be foreigners. The Population White Paper, with its best intentions to recalibrate population growth, backfired, with citizens enraged by what they perceived to be a lack of concern about salient problems, the welfare of citizens, and the stubbornness of government in continuing with its liberal foreign labour and immigration policies.

Weeks after the release of the White Paper in early February, Gilbert Goh, the founder of a website providing support services to unemployed Singaporeans, called for a protest against the White Paper. News of the protest went viral on social media and was picked up and disseminated by various sociopolitical blogs. On 16 February 2013 an estimated 4,000 Singaporeans of various ages and races turned up at Singapore's Speakers' Corner for the protest. Although the number of protesters in Singapore may seem small compared to mass protests elsewhere, the protest was highly significant given the country's small population and history of strict laws against public demonstrations. It was also the first mass political demonstration against the PAP government.

Following the success of the first protest, a second protest was quickly announced and held on 1 May 2013. Social media played an integral role in mobilisation, since mainstream media did not cover news of the event. A diverse crowd of participants turned up at the protest, almost equalling the number of participants to the first protest. The social movement was nevertheless short lived. Participation at a third protest in October dropped to around 1,000 people, further decreasing in a fourth protest. The first two protests raise questions about how social media mobilised a politically apathetic population. The failure to sustain the social movement also presents doubts about the efficacy of social media-driven collective action.

Our study, focused on the second protest, consisted of two parts: a content analysis investigating the way social media framed the protest, and a survey done in real time during the protest, seeking to understand protesters' motivations, uses of social media, information behaviours, and exposure to different collective action frames prior to attending the protest (for a full analysis, see Goh & Pang, forthcoming; Pang & Goh, 2014).

Theoretical Propositions

From our work we provide three propositions by which social media shape collective action and social movements. These were derived from our findings but also provide directions for further research.

Proposition 1: Social Media as Weak Publics

As in many societies, there is a cohesive system of social control in Singapore (George 2005), and some demographic groups may be more dominant than others in their access to social media. Dominant voices tend to be younger and have also received higher levels of education. Not everyone has access or chooses to access social media, although barriers to entry are low in Singapore. With the ability to be anonymous that comes with many social media sites, a good plurality of perspectives and issues can be raised. However, the anonymity of discourse does not hold individuals accountable to the discourse, resulting in a questionable quality of deliberation. These factors can result in a weakened democracy.

What is the function of such online discourse? With greater plurality, more issues can be raised—although some of them may not necessarily reflect the interests of the general public, and were raised because of the dominance of certain social groups online. For instance, in our 2011 project we began by coding online content for those issues that mainstream media and the authorities thought to be pertinent issues for the electorate. But we found many more issues raised and discussed online.

But those discourses that also reflect the interests of the general public can evolve into protests and social movements, as we observed between 2011 and 2013. Back in 2011, the issue of foreign labour was recognized as a salient issue by the mainstream media, and it was also widely discussed online. The same issue was raised again in 2012 during the by-election, and by 2013 the dissent and discourse had culminated in a series of protests.

Other issues can also result in social movements. However, they are of a much smaller scale and are not attended by a wide representation of various demographic groups. For instance, a protest against the ruling government's move to regulate the Internet, which happened soon after the White Paper protest, saw participation and attendance at the Speakers' Corner on a much smaller scale compared to the White Paper protest. To date, the #FreeMyInternet movement is still largely driven by a small locus of activists.

In this sense, we can use social movements to answer the question of how online discourse reflects the interests of the larger public. There is no unified model to explain all these dynamics, but what we have observed since 2011 is that if the movements reflect a plurality of people and perspectives, online discourses are quite aligned to the sentiments and opinions of the larger public. But if the movements are composed of a relatively homogenous and focused group of people, it is not likely that the online reflects the offline.

The framing of the collective action also mattered as they reflect a collective aggregate of how individuals interpret the problem and protest (Gamson 1992): most of the frames we found in the White Paper protest were motivational, and used various reasons to motivate participation and promote both individual and collective agency. The second dominant frame (diagnostic) focused on identifying the problem to be solved and the perpetrator of the injustice. The third frame we found related to the prognostic frame, associated with identifying solutions to the problem.

Thus, whilst the online sphere is not *the* public sphere, because of its fragmentation, it serves two purposes as a weak public: (a) it acts as a platform for salient issues to be surfaced, some of which gain momentum enough to evolve into an offline protest and a larger social movement; (b) it acts as a space in which framing around collective action and other activities associated with a social movement is deliberated. Such framing can have effects on actual protest motivations and behaviours. Diagnostic frames which interpret the situation by identifying the injustice, the perpetrators, and the victims were significant in driving purposeful actions at the White Paper protest. People who were exposed to and engaged with this particular frame were more likely to participate in the protest in order to drive change, rather than joining it because of other reasons (such as bandwagon behaviour).

Proposition 2: The Small World Online

Like Wojcieszak and Rojas (2011), we draw the conclusion that online, people function in egocentric publics, and some such egocentric publics are more exclusive than others. It is through the existence and interactions of people in these small publics that social norms, social roles, and worldviews are shaped and lend impetus to civic action and social movements. Whilst social media can act as a tool and mechanism for mobilisation, the tool alone is insufficient. Other scholars such as Putnam (2000) and Hebenstreit (2014) have expressed similar opinions, arguing that there is much fragmentation and clustering of like-minded people who do not easily interact with others online.

Like-mindedness can also evolve into collective defence, described by Chatman (1991) as 'defensive information behavior'. Such individuals are fiercely defensive of the social norms operating within, and reject outside information that may oppose or threaten the beliefs and norms within their communities. Although it is difficult to define the boundaries of online communities since individuals are not limited by physical, spatial borders and can move in and out of multiple communities, such defensive behaviours were observed at various online sites.

In our content analysis of posts during the 2011 general election and 2012 by-election, there were been many instances where an individual posts comments that were contrary to the discourse that was developing within the discussion. The fact that there were outsiders and insiders was apparent: the regulars (the commenters and, in some cases, the people who posted the original messages) responded to outsiders by telling them to, in some cases, 'get out of here' or by 'ganging up' negatively on them.

Through such responses and gatekeeping processes they set boundaries on what is acceptable according to the social norms within the community, regardless of whether or not the new information is useful or relevant. With these boundaries they create a 'worldview' for themselves, along with language, values and symbols that give particular meanings to the problems perceived with the worldview. Chatman (1991) found that, so long as the community is still functioning, such worldviews result in information avoidance or rejection. Hebenstreit (2014) also argued that deliberation on issues in such contexts encourages polarization—and we argue that this provides also the basis for framing collective action and, eventually, social movements.

Especially in situations where an issue is limited to a relatively small group of individuals (not of interest to the general public sphere), such small worlds provide the impetus and momentum for collective action. This offers new perspectives on the concept of the critical mass in collective action theory. Traditional theories of collective action posit that the critical mass—"a relatively small cadre of highly interested and resourceful individuals" (Marwell & Oliver 1993: 2)—is responsible for driving collective action. In the online round, social media not only shape the ways in which these individuals come together; they also remove the social barriers for these individuals, in effect 'persuading' those who have social proximity (even if only perceived) to engage in the same cause and collective action. For instance, in our study of the White Paper protest, those who perceived greater social proximity to the core activists—the critical mass—were also more motivated to attend the protest out of support for the cause.

Proposition 3: Social Media, Space, and Collective Action

The year 2011 saw a widespread increase in social media use by various social movements. Many studies have emerged not only examining the mobilisation role of social media, but also the meanings they convey. As Mason wrote:

> Facebook is used to form groups, covert and overt—in order to establish those strong but flexible connections. Twitter is used for real-time organization and news dissemination, bypassing the cumbersome "newsgathering" operations of the mainstream media. YouTube and Twitter-linked photographic sites— Yfrog, Flickr and Twitpic—are used to provide instant evidence of the claims being made. Link-shorteners like bit.ly are used to disseminate key articles via Twitter. (Mason 2012: 75)

But as Gerbaudo (2012) rightfully pointed out, whilst the mobilisation role of social media is obvious, a pressing question is how we can understand the "spatial relationships" (Gerbaudo 2012: 12) between social media and protest camps (protests and social movements that take place outside the online realm of the Internet). The types of interactions online and at protests are vastly different: online, individuals interact over a distance and retain their individualization (Bauman 2001) while at a protest, interactions are much more intense and there is much pressure to conform to and as a collective. Protesters who used mobile chats in Hong Kong in the Umbrella Movement, for instance, were more likely to engage in frontline activism—that is, to directly participate in the protest (Lee 2014).

It has been argued by many scholars that elements of a Panopticon exist inherently within the structures of the Internet (Brignall 2002; Tang & Yang 2011; Campbell & Carlson 2002). In a Panopticon, 'prisoners' are perpetually exposed to the gaze of watchers. They know they are under surveillance, but do not know exactly when because they are not able to see the watchers or watchtower (Bentham 1843). As a result, they take responsibility for regulating their own behaviour and "a state of conscious and permanent visibility" is induced in them (Foucault 1977: 201). On social media, everything we do is tagged to our identities: the posts, the likes, the links and posts we share, the things we purchase online, the articles we read, our tagging activities, and the things we are tagged in. No one may actually be reading all this, but it is also equally likely that many are watching. Consequently, we are conscious about what we do, and this consciousness is permanent, and the only people who are exempt from this effect are those who do not use the Internet, or those who do not care.

The Panopticon effect of social media has far-reaching impacts on contemporary movements. Identity is created by liking and sharing information about a protest; and those with whom such information is shared become the guards and watchers as individuals augment their identities with actual attendance. Our study of the White Paper Protest revealed that attendees had mixed motivations: some were there as authentic supporters of the cause, some were there to seek first-hand information, and the rest were exhibiting bandwagon behaviour. Even though there were mixed motivations, they were there on the ground, and they would be known by their acts, even if no one was actually watching.

This Panopticon-like space influences the interactions of people even as they move in and out of multiple communities and identities. Although they are not bounded by one community or organisation, there is an induced state of consciousness serving to remind people to follow through on what they have supported online with offline actions.

Media theorists such as Benkler (2006) and Shirky (2008) argue that, contrary to what many other scholars believe, interactions on the Internet are in fact dominated by a "power law distribution" (Shirky 2008: 125). Gerbaudo (2012: 145) described such organisation as "liquid," arguing that new, softer forms of leadership arise as a result, making use "of the interactive and participatory character of the web 2.0 environment". This was also our observation: only a core group of activists were responsible for organising and promoting the protest, but a large outer circle supported the protest by sharing, commenting and liking. Collective action in the liquid assembly in this context had both traditional and new elements: there is still a core group of organisers, activists and mobilisers, as has been the case for many forms of collective action—but the outer circle beyond this core group is large and fluid, supported by the participatory elements of new media and driven by a loose sense of connectedness and belonging.

Conclusion

In this chapter we have synthesised findings from the three cases from 2011–2013 to present three theoretical propositions on the role of social media and social movements. We began with a general election and ended with a protest against population policy in Singapore. The nature of the cases is highly interrelated: the deliberation and discourse on issues which emerged in 2011 during the general election gained momentum in the events of 2012, and when the Population White Paper was released in 2013, the issue of foreign labour evolved into protests and a social movement. Whilst social media intensified and mediated the interactions and discourse between people, they were only part of an environment that brought people into the streets. This environment is mediated by the 'weak publics' of social media, the nature of online enclaves and interactions functioning in both the online and offline environments, the structural attributes of the social media space, and the types of organisation that is facilitated by the participatory characteristics of social media.

From these cases we proposed new insights into the ways social media function as weak publics; the importance of understanding online enclaves, which, although they are not always obvious, have distinct social norms and behaviours; and the role of social media in social movements, specifically going beyond their obvious roles of information dissemination and mobilisation.

References

Bauman, Z. (2001) *The individualized society*, Cambridge: Polity Press.

Benkler, Y. (2006) *The wealth of networks: How social production transforms markets and freedom*, New Haven: Yale University Press.

Bentham, J. (1843) *The works of Jeremy Bentham (Vol. 1)*, Edinburgh: William Tait.

Berger, S. (2004) "Worldwide: Few dare to raise their voices at the Singapore Speakers' Corner," *The Daily Telegraph* 28 August. Available from: http://www.webcitation.org/5t3jtEYoh.

Bimber, B., Flanagin, A., & Stohl, C. (2005) "Reconceptualizing collective action in the contemporary media environment," *Communication Theory*, vol. 15, no. 4, pp. 365–388.

Brignall, T. (2002) "The new Panopticon: The Internet viewed as a structure of social control," *Theory and Science*. Available from: http://theoryandscience.icaap.org/content/vol003.001/brignall.html.

Campbell, J. E. & Carlson, M. (2002) "Panopticon.com: Online surveillance and the commodification of privacy," *Journal of Broadcasting & Electronic Media*, vol. 46, no. 4, pp. 586–606.

Chatman, E. (1991) "Life in a small world: Applicability of gratification theory to information-seeking behavior," *Journal of the American Society for Information Science*, vol. 42, no. 6, pp. 438–449.

Foucault, M. (1977) *Discipline and punish: The birth of the prison*, New York: Pantheon.

Fraser, N. (1990) "Rethinking the public sphere: A contribution to the critique of actually existing democracy," *Social Text*, no. 25/26, pp. 56–80.

Gamson, W. A. (1992) "The social psychology of collective action," in A. D. Morris & C. Mueller (eds.), *Frontiers in social movement theory*, Yale University Press: New Haven, CT, pp. 53–76.

George, C. (2005) "The Internet's political impact and the penetration/participation paradox in Malaysia and Singapore," *Media, Culture & Society*, vol. 27, no. 6, pp. 903–920.

George, C. (2006) *Contentious journalism and the Internet: Towards democratic discourse in Malaysia and Singapore*, Singapore: Singapore University Press and University of Washington Press.

Gerbaudo, P. (2012) *Tweets and the streets: Social media and contemporary activism*, London: Pluto Press.

Goh, D. & Pang, N. (2012). Online and ontrack? Political parties' use of websites and Facebook during Singapore's 2011 general elections, *International Communication Association (ICA)*, 24–28 May 2012, Phoenix, Arizona.

Goh, D., Pang, N., & Ang, P. H. (2013). "Where they agree: How media exposure, political cynicism and supporting online deliberation influence consonance in online and offline public opinion," *International Communication Association Pre-Conference*, 17–21 June 2013, London.

Goh, D. & Pang, N. (forthcoming). "Protesting the Singapore government: The role of collective action frames in social media mobilization," *Telematics and Informatics Journal*.

Habermas, J. (1962 trans. 1989) *The structural transformation of the public sphere: An inquiry into a category of bourgeois society*, Cambridge: Polity.

Hashmeta (2014) "Social media landscape in Singapore" 30 August. Available from: http://www.hashmeta.com/social-media-singapore-infographic/.

Hebenstreit, J. (2014) "Cyberbalkanization—The local fragmentation of the global village," in *Proceedings of the 2nd Conference for eDemocracy and Open Government (CeDEM) Asia*, 4–6 December, City University of Hong Kong, Hong Kong.

Kirk, M. (2014) "How Singapore got hooked on the Internet of public shame," *The Atlantic Cities* 2 April. Available from: http://www.theatlanticcities.com/arts-and-lifestyle/2014/04/how-singapore-got-hooked-internet-public-shame/8777/.

Lee, F. (2014) "Action repertoire in the Umbrella Movement," *Occupy Central Panel of the 2nd Conference for eDemocracy and Open Government (CeDEM) Asia*, 4–6 December 2014, City University of Hong Kong, Hong Kong.

Lim, C. (2011) *A watershed election: Singapore's GE 2011*, Singapore: Marshall Cavendish Editions.

Marwell, G. & Oliver, P. (1993) *The critical mass in collective action: A micro-social theory*, Cambridge: Cambridge University Press.

Mason, P. (2012) *Why it's kickstarting off everywhere: The new global revolutions*, London: Verso.

MDA. (2010) *"MDA's registration form for class licensable broadcasting services"*. Available from: https://mdaonline.mda.gov.sg/onlineservices/forms/RegFrmCRelgPolContJan2010.pdf.

MDA. (2013) "Online news sites to be placed on a more consistent licensing framework as traditional news platforms," Press release. Available from: http://www.mda.gov.sg/AboutMDA/News ReleasesSpeechesAndAnnouncements/Pages/NewsDetail.aspx?news=4.

Pang, N. & Goh, D. (2012). "Blogs and the rhetorical public sphere," *International Communication Association Pre-Conference*, 24–28 May 2012, Phoenix, Arizona.

Pang, N. & Goh, D. (2014) "There to say 'no'? A study of collective action at Singapore's Speakers' Corner," *Association for Education in Journalism and Mass Communication (AEJMC)*, 6–9 August 2014, Montreal.

Putnam, R. (2000) *Bowling alone: The collapse and revival of American community*, New York: Simon and Schuster.

Reuters. (2013) *"Free my Internet: Hundreds march in Singapore against website licensing scheme,"* June 8. Available from: http://rt.com/news/singapore-website-protest-bloggers-419/.

Rheingold, H. (1993) *The virtual community*. Available from: http://www.rheingold.com/vc/book/.

Rodan, G. (1998) "The Internet and political control in Singapore," *Political Science Quarterly*, vol. 113, no. 1, pp. 63–89.

Shirky, C. (2008) *Here comes everybody: The power of organizing without organizations*, New York: Penguin Press.

Tang, L. & Yang, P. (2011) "Symbolic power and the internet: The power of a 'horse'," *Media, Culture & Society*, vol. 33, no. 5, pp. 675–691.

Tata Communications. (2014) *Global study confirms that Singaporeans are the most emotionally connected to the Internet*, 30 September. Available from: http://www.tatacommunications.com/article/global-study-confirms-singaporeans-are-most-emotionally-connected-internet#.VI6U8TGUd8E.

Tufekci, Z. & Wilson, C. (2012) "Social media and the decision to participate in political protest: Observations from Tahrir Square," *Journal of Communication*, vol. 62, no. 2, pp.363–379.

Wojcieszak, M. & Rojas, H. (2011) "Correlates of party, ideology and issue based extremity in an era of egocentric publics," *The International Journal of Press/Politics*, vol. 16, no. 4, pp. 488–507.

18

SOCIAL MEDIA AND CIVIL SOCIETY ACTIONS IN INDIA

Rajesh Kumar

Introduction

In India, having a conversation on social media is the new *mantra* for success—be it business or governance, political parties or politicians. Social media is also 'setting the agenda' for traditional media, such as television and newspapers (Rodrigues and Ranganathan 2015). The key ingredient of such a framework is to not only ensure information dissemination but to also facilitate its sharing and encourage participation that generates conversation and comments. While discussing 'social media and civil society action in India', this chapter will be concentrating on *expressive social media* which are generally referred to as Social Networking Sites (SNSs) and microblogging services (e.g. Twitter). SNSs have taken off globally since 2006 and have empowered hundreds of millions of users to share content among online communities and create an Internet society. It has been found that about two-thirds of all active Internet users have spent time managing a social networking profile, and more than 80 per cent have visited friends' social network pages, with microblogging services used by 51.9 per cent of active internet users globally (Universal McCann 2013). While the growth in SNSs new users in North America has started to level off, it is growing substantially in other regions. Many top SNSs, such as Facebook and MySpace, made efforts to become more culturally relevant in markets outside the U.S. and thus demonstrated rapid growth in their global user bases (ComScore 2013). They are generating high interest in Asia where the SNS phenomenon is flourishing. India has 243.2 million Internet users (19 per cent of the total population) and 106 million (8 per cent of total population) active social media users (Naidu 2014). Of active Internet users, 44.6 per cent in India are using microblogging services (Universal McCann 2013).

SNSs and microblogging services are being used by the common people for information sharing and also for generating consciousness about different issues and concerns of public interest. News of the shooting and bombing in Mumbai, India, in 2008 was first reported via Twitter and Flickr, before any of the mainstream media had reported on the event. *The Telegraph* reported that, during the attacks, there were approximately 70 eyewitness tweets every five seconds (Deborah 2011). Campaigns such as Batti Bandh; Justice for Jessica, the 2008 Gateway of India rally after the Mumbai attack; and, most recently, It Is My Arunachal: Dream on China, have leveraged the existing network on social media websites (Thirani 2011). Civil society protests in India—from justice to the victims of Godhra, to those living around the Koodankulam nuclear facility (in the southern Indian state of Tamilnadu), to those affected by the Armed Forces Special Powers Act (AFSPA) in Manipur—are occupying significant space in social media and are keeping democracy alive in India. Within this context, this chapter attempts to understand and analyse a civic action in India, namely India Against Corruption (IAC), which is considered to be largely driven by social media.

Social Media: A Force Multiplier for Civil Society Actions

The uses of social media during the Arab Spring present an interesting set of cases for examining theoretic perspective on the relationship between social media and mass action (for e.g. Bimber et al. 2005; Flanagin et al. 2006; Segerberg and Bennett 2011). A significant portion of early research and analysis indicated that social media played an important role in the collective actions that resulted in the overthrow of the governments, for example, Egypt and Tunisia (Iskander 2011; Kavanaugh et al. 2011; Khamis and Vaughn 2011). Social media contributed to collective action in four ways (Lynch 2011): (1) by making it easier for disaffected citizens to act publicly in coordination; (2) by creating information cascades that bolstered protesters' perceptions of the likelihood of success; (3) by raising the costs of repression by the ruling regimes; (4) by dramatically increasing publicity through diffusion of information to regional and global publics. All of these functions were not served by one specific social media platform at a given point in time and in a given context. In fact, different social media platforms provided a variety of facilitations that were important at a given point in time. At one time they provided forums for early critiques of the regimes, and at another they helped in forming public opinion and providing logistical assistance to those organising protests against the regime (Aouragh and Anderson 2011; Howard et al. 2011).

The historic developments and transformations that have taken place in Egypt and Tunisia showed that the digital sphere, which cannot be wholly regulated or shut down, has become a potent platform for protests (Thirani 2011; Wilson and Dunn 2011). In Yemen, for example, as the Egyptian revolution was going full steam, a 24-year-old youth, Al-Razaq Al-Azazi, started a Facebook group called Let's Change the President, which he later renamed Revolution Against Ignorance in preparation for pro-democracy demonstrations. More than 1,200 people defied the government and accepted the site's invitation aptly named Yemeni People Uprising, challenging the three-decade-long regime of their government (Michael 2011).

When Japanese journalist Kosuke Tsuneoka was kidnapped in Afghanistan, he used Twitter to send out the message. Tsuneoka had been held for five months by Islamic militants but got access to his Twitter account when his kidnappers asked him to show them how to use their mobile phones. He was released two days after the tweet was sent (Deborah 2011). Yet another example of social media strength: before the media even got a sniff of the news about Osama Bin Laden's death, on Twitter an unknown user broke the news to the world when Sohaib Athar, an information technology consultant living in Abottabad, started tweeting when he noticed some unusual activity in his town (Deborah 2011).

Kumar and Thapa (2014), in a study titled "Social Media as a Catalyst of Civil Society Movements (CSMs) in India," aimed to identify whether social media are potent tools for catalysing CSMs. The users surveyed expressed a minimal influence of social media tools upon them, yet there was evidence of optimism about their role in CSMs. Users surveyed gave definite pointers so as to infer that social media may be of great use not only in informing them about the onset of a particular civil society initiative/movement but also for catalysing such movements. Many were optimistic that there is enough scope for growth in the Indian Internet market. As per the estimates, an Internet user in India spends, on average, 13 hours per week online and this number is likely to reach 16 hours per week. The time spent online will largely be spent on social media, photo/video sharing, e-commerce and also on utilities/banking/bill payments (Aggarwal 2013).

Media are potent tools for disseminating information but they are not limited to dissemination—they invariably shape our outlook on the world and our perception of reality. Scholars have debated the influence of media in determining our perception of reality through various studies, such as agenda-setting theory, framing, priming, gatekeeping, uses and gratification theory (U & G), individual difference theory, expectancy-value theory, and cute cat theory of digital activism. Uses and gratification theory directly places power in the hands of the audience. Rather than assuming that media messages have direct, uniform effects on those who consume them, the U & G perspective proposes that receivers make deliberate, intentional decisions about the media messages they expose themselves based on personal needs and desires (LaRose et al. 2001). Individual difference theory also stipulates that different people react differently to the same stimuli: people go for selective exposure, selective perception, and selective retention in accordance with their established convictions and beliefs. They also tend to 'read into' the message and perceive whatever suits them. Expectancy-value theory (Palmgreen and Rayburn 1984), on the other hand, proposes that media use is accounted for by a combination of perception of benefits offered by the medium and the differential value of these benefits for the individual audience member. Yet another theory, cute cat theory of digital activism, developed by Zuckerman (2008), posits that most people are not interested in activism. Rather, they wish to use the Web for mundane activities, including surfing for pornography and 'cute cats'. Within the ambit of the theories detailed above (some of them propounded before the onset of social media), the role of social media in civil society actions or movements may be discussed and understood. It may also be noted that it is the volume of potential participants, unencumbered by time and space, coupled with interactivity, which distinguishes social media from other media.

People pay significant attention to the opinion and mental states of others when judging and determining their own behaviour (Malle et al. 2001). Individuals try to understand people's motives and the degree of intentionality before expressing their opinion for an event, issue, or situation (Lagnado and Channon 2008). People also use new media platforms to acquire information about others (Westerman et al. 2008) and use it to shape and modify interpersonal impressions, even among those who are already acquainted offline (e.g. DeAndra and Walther 2011). Thus, social media has a potential to impact people's perception and opinion regarding social and political issues. It may also change the way people express themselves and participate in social and political issues and concerns.

Social Media for Social and Political Mobilisation in India: The IAC Movement

In India, social media have been providing a valuable tool for political and social organisation and also for social activism and mobilisation of mass opinion on issues of public interest. For voicing concern on issues such as corruption among public functionaries and political dispensation, social media offer great potential for mobilising people for participation in social movements. It is also useful to the leaders who organise such movements or emerge from such movements. Here an attempt will be made to explore the role of social media in India's widely participated mass movement known as India Against Corruption (IAC), organised in 2011. It is pertinent to understand the prelude to this massive mass protest, largely catapulted by social media. Following major corruptions and scandals reported by media and political groups in opposition, the then Indian government drafted a version of a Lokpal Bill in 2010 (for creating an institution to monitor/restrict corrupt practices in public funded organisations and by public functionaries). A Group of Ministers (GOM) also considered this draft bill for tackling corruption (PIB, Govt. of India 2011). However, social activists and civil society groups considered the proposed bill as weak, as it did not cover the prime minister, members of parliament, and cabinet ministers. The simmering discontent turned into a mass agitation and protests in the year 2011 led by a 74-year-old civil activist Anna Hazare of Ralegan Siddhi, a small village in the state of Maharashtra, India. Hazare has been a mass organiser and had previously organised successful mass protests and efforts for decreasing alcoholism and ensuring water access for individuals in rural areas (Sawyer 2011). He has also been instrumental in advocating for the Freedom of Information Act in India since 2003, which eventually was passed in 2005 (AnnaHazare.org). He has been leading anti-corruption protests for two decades. However, the 2011 anti-corruption movement, organised under the banner of India Against Corruption (IAC), was the largest one led by him. IAC activists were of the opinion that the Lokpal Bill proposed by the then government was too weak because the provision of ombudsman made under it could not investigate actions of elected officials. The government's argument was that an ombudsman should not be given powers to investigate elected leaders because it would make him or her too powerful and would weaken the democratic structure (The Economist 2011). In spite of series of talks with IAC functionaries, the then government failed to arrive at some consensus with regard to the structure and form of the Lokpal Bill. Demanding a stronger bill, Hazare and his team members from IAC launched a hunger strike on 5 April 2011. Mass protests erupted in support of IAC. People gathered in large numbers at Jantar Mantar and later on in Ramlila Maidan, New Delhi, the national capital. Protesters were pressurizing the then Indian government for forming a Joint Drafting Committee for a Lokpal Bill with five ministers and five civil society members. This civic action or movement sparked extensive discussions across news and social media. Large number of people also came out to the streets in support of IAC movement (Khorana and Ramaswami 2011). After four days of Hazare's fasting, the government agreed to form a joint drafting committee, and Hazare ended his fast. After witnessing so many ups and downs, the Lokpal Bill was finally passed by the Indian parliament in December 2013.

Anna Hazare has been fighting against corruption for a long time and has gone on a Fast unto Death campaign many times in his life. But the reach, publicity, and fame that the Lokpal Bill gave to him were unbelievable (Prabhudesai 2011). This could not have been possible without the SNSs. The second fortnight of August 2011 saw one of the largest mobilisations of people in recent years against corruption in India. The struggle led by Anna Hazare dominated the media all through the fortnight. A new feature during the movement was the participation of people through SNSs, which helped people to mobilise in different corners of the country in support of Team Anna. Twitter, Facebook and other SNSs and blogs have also played a significant part in bringing people together in peaceful demonstration, candle protests and so on. Team Anna may have been the first major beneficiary of this technology (Viswanathan 2011). More than 150 Facebook pages related to Anna Hazare and India Against Corruption (IAC) were created and used almost round the clock for days. The official IAC Facebook page has managed to attract more than 3.2 *lakh* fans so far (Ohri 2011). According to Buzzref.com, the IAC Facebook page received more than 71,000 'likes' and 13,000 'comments' for a mere 170 posts uploaded in the month of August 2011. On 14 April 2011, an IAC post on Facebook, "Aage Bado Anna Hazare, Ham Tumhare Sath Hain [move forward Anna, we are with you]" gathered 127,396 'likes' (Prabhudesai 2011). Not only Facebook but Twitter was also abuzz with messages showing support for Anna Hazare's campaign. "Anna Hazare" and "Jan Lokpal" became the most discussed subject on Twitter in India, at that point of time. YouTube too was not far behind. Hundreds of videos were uploaded in support of Anna Hazare's campaign, when the campaign was in full swing (Prabhudesai 2011).

IAC movement used all the key media tools ranging from electronic media, social media, and websites to mobile phones. A 16-member team of IAC based in Mumbai had the task of sending the messages about the movement to one million cell phone users across India who had registered on a telephone number advertised on newspapers and networking sites. One million cell phone users received two SMS every day from IAC. In the 'missed call campaign', citizens were asked to give a missed call to the number 022 61550789 for supporting IAC. Nearly 25 million people gave a missed call to the number. The IAC official website www.indiaagainstcorruption.org also provided contact details of volunteers and event schedule in all cities. IAC also used this media to counter misleading claims of government and other actors. New/Digital media because of its qualities of speed and reach became a key tool for information dissemination for this movement. A national daily, *The Times of India*, had also launched an online campaign—ACT (Against Corruption Together), where number of voters increased from 0.4 million to 1.2 million in just three days with almost 14,000 votes being added every hour. No social movement in last three decades in India had witnessed such huge mobilisation for an issue of public interest (Desai 2011).

India Against Corruption (IAC) organisers and supporters used social media to disseminate relevant information quickly and mainly to organise mass protests. Common people also used social media to show support for IAC and Anna Hazare, indicated on Facebook by 'likes' on posts. In the first four days of its existence, IAC had 116,000 fans on its community Facebook page (Khorana and Ramaswami 2011). Common people also created many other Facebook pages and provided momentum to the movement. Individual social media users debated the relevant issues, posted statuses, and uploaded videos and photos throughout the movement. According to one estimate, the total online support for the movement was around 1.5 million people (Kurup D 2011). Facebook hosted multiple Anna Hazare-related pages in English and Hindi, with tens of thousands of followers and supporters. The official IAC Facebook page had more than 500,000 followers as of February 7, 2012 (India Against Corruption Facebook Page: www.facebook.com/ IndiACor). Users could follow and access information about the anti-corruption movement through applications for smart phones and other mobile devices. The IAC smart phone application had as many as 50,000 users (Google Play 2012). The organisation used all these outlets to publish photos of Anna Hazare fasting, pro-Lokpal rallies, and examples of corruption. During this social media campaign, Hazare gained support from other prominent Indian activists, as well as the general populace. The intensity of protests can be gauged by the fact that in the first six months of 2011, the Indian government requested 358 removals from Google, mostly from Orkut and YouTube, the majority of such requests pertained to social media content criticizing the government (The Times of India 2011). However, Facebook posts and news reports showed that this anti-corruption movement was centred in urban areas. The Facebook demographics suggested that the movement engaged urban men and women but left large segments of the population out of the ambit of debate which perhaps led to withering out of the campaign (India Facebook Statistics 2012).

The massive use of social media in the Lokpal movement was a trend setter and could be seen as a successful experimentation for a common cause. People could use social media content to gauge the status of the movement and to identify the goals it seeks to attain. Moreover, the movement which was initiated by the social media influenced the mainstream media as well and it carried the news and activity of IAC with added intensity and frequency. User activity peaked as social momentum grew during the various action phases of the movement; however, it sharply decreased following some form of governmental action. Positive government action increased user activity for a short period of time when Facebook users discussed the government action on the issue. However, government actions and initiatives also halted or reduced the protest actions on ground as social activists waited for the government to fulfil a promise or for some progress in desired direction. This limitation of social media for civil society action was well reflected throughout the IAC protests and agitations in 2011.

A study commissioned by U.S. Government Office of South Asia Policy (Bong et al. 2012: 30), titled *Analyzing Social Media Momentum: India's 2011–12 Anticorruption Movement*, analysed the content related to IAC movement posted on Facebook. It says:

> Government actions taken to repress the movement were significant in the natural log of comments model regression, and they correlated with an increase in the number of comments. Negative government action was not significant in the natural log of likes model. This difference makes sense when we consider the nature of the like action. A Facebook post detailing an unfavorable government action would garner fewer likes than a neutral or positive government action simply because movement supporters would disagree with the activity and therefore decline to like it. Thus, a post about a negative government action would not be expected to induce a large number of likes but would more likely lead to an increase in the number of comments as Facebook users discuss the implications of the action. Contrary to positive government action, which may lead to temporary lulls in user activity, negative government actions seem to act as catalysts, increasing social media momentum and triggering further

on-the-ground responses if the negative action is not effective in forcing the movement to change direction or fail at achieving its goals.

Positive and negative actions of the government also influenced mass activity on social media. For example, the police arrest of Hazare in August 2011 provided a big push to Facebook activity and boosted protests on ground as well. However, when the Lok Sabha passed the Lokpal Bill on 27 December 2011, the common people's activity and reactions on social media decreased substantially, so much so that the movement organisers had to use social media to tell the people that the movement was reorganising and shifting focus. Thus, the government's positive action on the legislation decelerated movement support and created an identity crisis for IAC leaders who in turn changed the goals and direction of the movement. Tracking activity related to specific posts could help the movement to better define its message and purpose and better use themes that resonate most with social media users. Overall, social media proved as an excellent organising tool during IAC movement. The content and focus of the posts provided a daily insight into the function of the movement and the message it was trying to advance. The dexterity with which IAC organisers used social media for mass mobilisation and opinion formation may be an example worth following by such civil society movements in future.

Conclusion

Civil society actions in India can still be attributed to the traditional mass communication tools. However, it is also worth noting that traditional media such as television, radio and newspapers are largely influenced by what appears in social media, a phenomenon made visible during the India Against Corruption (IAC) movement in 2011. Most of the prominent news channels in India have created their Twitter hashtags aiming to involve people in news gathering or for gathering feedback pertaining to issues and topics of public interest. Over the past two decades, communication and information infrastructure has spread enormously in India and so are its users. Although it is yet to reach a scale in percentage basis comparable to many developed nations, the population measured quantitatively is significantly higher (third largest in the world). The full horizon of opportunities has yet to be explored, as there is enough space for innovations leading to greater access for users. If the government of India and respective state governments and the governance model bring forth a situation where social media use is facilitated by introducing and expanding new technology into far-flung areas of the country, we may have a scenario where social media could be a force multiplier for civil society initiatives. The 'Digital India' project planned by the present government of India aims to connect every citizen through broadband services, more so through smartphones. This may empower a big chunk of population and may also boost digital activism of the type witnessed during India Against Corruption (IAC) movement. It's worth mentioning here that users are not merely absorbing entities: they also participate in disseminating information. And social media are known for their ability to enable the dissemination of information with just one click. Perhaps the term 'social media' is a summation of the terms social and media—the media which provides the opportunity of socializing in a real time basis. Unlike traditional mass media products, which are remotely produced and brought to us by a broadcast mechanism, social media has a potential edge over other such media by socializing the content in terms of contribution, sharing and use.

RAJESH KUMAR

References

Aggarwal, S. (2013) India Internet outlook. Available from: http://techcircle.vccircle.com/2013/02/01/2013-india-internet-outlook/

AnnaHazare.org. *Biography*. Available from: http://www.annahazare.org/biography.html

Aouragh, M. and Anderson, A. (2011) The Egyptian experience: Sense and nonsense of the Internet revolution. *International Journal of Communication* 5, pp. 1344–1358.

Bimber, B., Flanagin, A. J., and Stohl, C. (2005) Reconceptualizing collective action in the contemporary media environment. *Communication Theory* 15(4), pp. 365–388.

Bong, S., Chung, K., Parkinson, K., Peppard, A., Rabbach, J., and Thiher, N. (2012). *Analyzing Social Media Momentum India's 2011–12 Anticorruption Movement*. Report for the U.S. Government Office of South Asia Policy, Madison, WI: Robert M. La Follette School of Public Affairs. Available from: http://www.lafollette.wisc.edu/research-public-service/publications/analyzing-social-media-momentum-india-s-2011-12-anticorruption-movement

ComScore (2013) Available from: http://www.comscore.com/Insights/Presentations-and-Whitepapers

DeAndra, D. C. and Walther, J. B. (2011) Attributions for inconsistencies between online and offline self-presentations. *Communication Research* 38, pp. 805–825.

Deborah, M. (2011) *Social media and the new wave of journalism*. Available from: http://thenextweb.com/socialmedia/2011/07/27/social-media-and-thenew-wave-of-journalism

Desai, S. (2011) Renegotiating democracy, *The Times of India*, August 12, New Delhi, India.

Flanagin, A. J., Stohl, C., and Bimber, B. (2006) Modeling the structure of collective action. *Communication Monographs* 73, pp. 29–54.

Google Play (2012). Available from: https://play.google.com/store

Howard, P. N., Agarwal, S. D., and Hussain, M.M. (2011) When do states disconnect their digital networks? Regime responses to the political uses of social media. *The Communication Review* 14(3), pp. 216–232.

India Facebook Statistics (2012). Available from: http://webcache.googleusercontent.com/search?q=cache:QHIDs7DpuKgJ:www.socialbakers.com/facebookstatistics/india+socialbakers,+India,+Facebook+statistics&cd=1&hl=en&ct=clnk&gl=us&client=firefox-a

India Against Corruption Facebook Page (2012) Available from: http://www.facebook.com/IndiACor

Iskander, E. (2011) Connecting the national and the virtual: Can Facebook activism remain relevant after Egypt's January 25 uprising? *International Journal of Communication* 5, pp. 1225–1237.

Kavanaugh, A., Yang, S., and Sheetz, S. (2011) Between a rock and a cell phone: Social media use during mass protests in Iran, Tunisia and Egypt. ACM *Transactions on Computer-Human Interaction*. doi: 10. 1145/0000000.0000000

Khamis, S. and Vaughn, K. (2011) Cyber activism in the Egyptian revolution: How civic engagement and citizen journalism tilted the balance. *Arab Media & Society* 13. Available from: http://www.arabmediasociety.com/?article=769

Khorana, S. and Ramaswami, H. (2011). *New technologies, Gandhian activism, and democracy: Re-examining civil society*. Australian Political Science Association Conference, Canberra, Australia.

Kumar, R. and Thapa, D. (2014) Social media as a catalyst for civil society movements in India: A study in Dehradun city, *New Media and Society*. Published online before print 24 February 2014, doi: 10.1177/1461444814523725

Kurup, D. (2011). *How Web 2.0 Responded to Hazare*. Available from: http://www.thehindu.com/news/states/karnataka/article1685157.ece

Lagnado, D. A. and Channon, S. (2008) Judgments of cause and blame: The effects of intentionality and foreseeability. *Cognition* 108, pp. 754–770.

LaRose, R., Mastro, D., and Eastin, M. S. (2001) Understanding Internet usage: A social cognitive approach to uses and gratifications. *Social Science Computer Review* 19(4), pp. 395–413.

Lynch, M. (2011) After Egypt: The limits and promise of online challenges to the authoritarian Arab state. *Perspectives on Politics* 9(2), pp. 301–310.

Malle, B. F., Moses, L. J., and Baldwin, D.A. (2001) The significance of intentionality, in Malle B. F., Moses, L. J., and Baldwin, D. A. (eds.) *Intentions and Intentionality: Foundations of Social Cognition.* Cambridge, MA: MIT Press, pp. 1–24.

Michael, I. N. (2011) *Revolution in the age of Facebook.* Available from: http://artvoice.com/issues/v10n7/getting_a_grip

Naidu, P. (2014) India has 243.2M Internet users and 106M active social media users. Available from: http://www.business2community.com/world-news/india-243–2m-internet-users-106m-active-social-media-users-0934513#e7jxF6w6ROi5pVot.99

Ohri, K. (2011) How powerful is Anna Hazare on Facebook and Twitter? Available from: http://www.afaqs.com/news/story.html?sid=31413

Palmgreen, P. and Rayburn, J. D. (1984) Merging uses and gratifications and expectancy-value theory. *Communication Research* 11(4), pp. 537–562.

PIB, Govt. of India (2011) *Government accepts recommendations of GoM on corruption.* Available from: http://pib.nic.in/newsite/erelease.aspx?relid=75965

Prabhudesai, A. (2011) *Social media catapults Anna Hazare's campaign into a global phenomenon!* Available from: http://trak.in/tags/business/2011/04/08/anna-hazare-jan-lokpal-bill-social-media-coverage/

Rodrigues, U. M. and Ranganathan, M. (2015) *Indian news media: From observer to participant.* New Delhi: Sage India, pp. 148–170.

Sawyer, J. (2011). *The amazing rise of Anna Hazare, India's Gandhi-like protest leader.* Available from: http://www.theatlantic.com/international/archive/2011/12/the-amazingrise-of-anna-hazare-indias-gandhi-like-protest-leader/249542/

Segerberg, A. and Bennett, W.L. (2011) Social media and the organization of collective action: Using Twitter to explore the ecologies of two climate change protests. *The Communication Review* 14(3), pp. 197–215.

The Times of India (2011). *Kapil Sibal's Web censorship: Indian govt wanted 358 items removed.* Available from: http://articles.timesofindia.indiatimes.com/2011–12–07/internet/30485700_1_removal-requests-orkut-social-networking

The Economist (2011). *Protests in India—Jail the messenger.* Available from: http://www.economist.com/blogs/banyan/2011/08/protests-india

Thirani, N. (2011) *Can the Twitterati change the world?* Available from: http://www.timescrest.com/society/can-the-twitterati-change-theworld-4768

Universal McCann (2013) *Wave 7 cracking the social code: The story of why.* Available from: http://wave.umww.com/assets/pdf/wave_7-cracking-the-social-code.pdf

Viswanathan, S. (2011) *Print media do better than TV: Coverage of Hazare fast.* Available from: http://www.thehindu.com/opinion/Readers-Editor/article2423886.ece

Westerman, D., Van, D.H.B., and Klein, K. A. (2008) How do people really seek information about others? Information seeking across Internet and traditional communication channels. *Journal of Computer-Mediated Communication* 13, pp. 751–767.

Wilson, C. and Dunn, A. (2011) Digital media in the Egyptian revolution: Descriptive analysis from the Tahrir data sets. *International Journal of Communication* 5, pp. 1248–1272.

Zuckerman, E. (2008) *The cute cat theory of digital activism.* Available from: http://www.worldchanging.com/archives/007877.html

19

CYBERACTIVISM IN CHINA
Empowerment, Control, and Beyond

Rongbin Han

Introduction

With the rapid expansion of the Internet and social media, scholars have debated on the sociopolitical impact of such technological advancements. Those who are optimistic claim that the new digital tools have empowered social actors and fundamentally transformed the relationship between the governing and the governed. Authoritarian regimes, in particular, now increasingly face the 'dictator's dilemma' between imposing control over the digital media and embracing the new technologies to keep up with the rest of the world. As Shirky (2011: 36) puts it, "with the spread of digital media, a state that is accustomed to having a monopoly on public speech finds itself called to account for anomalies between its view of events and the public's." However, there are also more skeptical views towards the impact of digital media. For instance, Morozov (2011, also see Hindman 2009), among others, questions the idea of the digital media as serving as a democratising force, and highlights the way in which the technology may help entrench dictators, suppress dissidents, and impede democratisation.

China is an interesting case in this regard, as the country has experienced rapid ICT development while maintaining strong authoritarian rule. As Figure 19.1 shows, China's Internet population had reached 632 million (46.9 per cent of the population) by June 2014, and millions of Chinese are online daily, searching for information, entertaining themselves, socializing, and expressing their opinions. In particular, social media platforms like blogs, the Twitter-like microblogs, and online forums have opened considerable space for cyberactivism, allowing Chinese citizens to express, organise, and mobilise. Given the constraints on public participation and expression, the expectation has been that the Internet and social media will serve as a liberalising and democratising force, as in the case of Arab Spring (Howard and Hussain 2013). This is why in China, Internet users are often called 'netizens': the term implies not only the online identity, but also some form of citizenship not found offline. Yet, the Communist Party and the authoritarian state, or the party-state, seems to be able to reap the benefits of the new technologies without jeopardizing its own existence.

To what extent and in what ways has the rise of cyberactivism challenged the Chinese authoritarian regime? How has the party-state attempted to overcome the 'dictator's dilemma' (Boas 2000)? Building on existing literature and the author's own research, this chapter explores cyberpolitics in China through examination of the challenges

Chart 1: Most Frequently Used Online Services in China (June 2014)

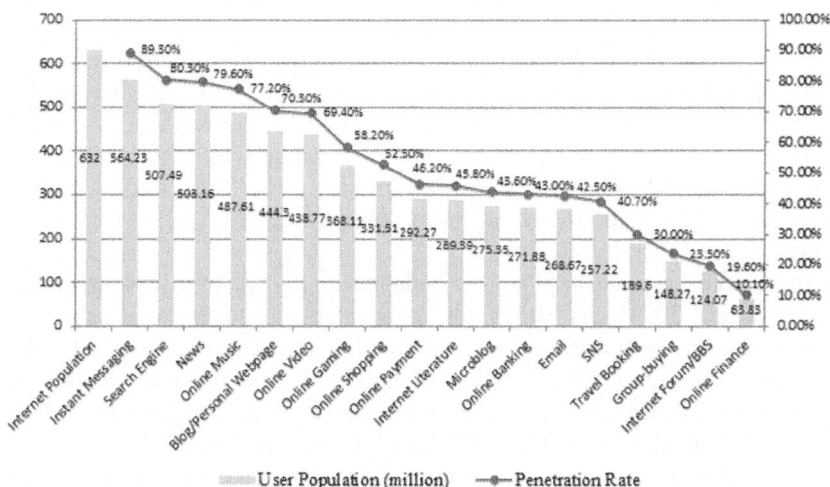

Figure 19.1 Most Frequently Used Online Services in China (June 2014)

brought about by the Internet and social media as well the party-state's adaptation. I argue that challenges brought about by cyberactivism towards the party-state is relatively unthreatening because on the one hand, anti-regime dissident activism is weak and seriously contested, and on the other hand, multiple forms of state adaptation, particularly the efforts to accommodate cyberactivism, help maintain its resilience.

The following sections will first survey the literature, then assess the impact of digital media by examining its challenges towards the regime and state responses to such challenges, and finally the chapter will conclude with suggestions for potential future research projects.

Cyberactivism in China: The Big Picture

Approaching the topic with distinctive theoretical frameworks, methodological approaches, and practical concerns, current studies on cyberpolitics in China can be categorised into three groups. The first group of studies takes a skeptical perspective and questions the political impact of the Internet and social media. Often based on content analysis and survey data, these studies find that the majority of Chinese netizens are simply not politically motivated, just like users in many other societies (Damm 2007; Leibold 2011). A survey done by the Chinese Academy of Social Sciences (Guo 2007) even suggests that the majority of Chinese support a 'managed internet' (3 per cent) and want the state to 'manage' online expression (84.8 per cent).

The second group focuses on the empowering effects of the Internet. Besides providing citizens with the space for freer public expression and some agenda-setting power (Hassid 2012; Tang and Sampson 2012), the new technology has also enhanced intra- and interconnectedness of civil groups (Yang 2003, 2007), facilitated popular protests and dissident mobilisation (Thornton 2008; Chase and Mulvenon 2002), helped citizens

hunt down corrupt officials (Gao and Stanyer 2014), and even influenced policy making and implementation (Zheng 2008; Zheng and Wu 2005). Moreover, netizens have
also contested state control over online expression. They have creatively circumvented
the Great Firewall to visit blocked sites (Mou et al. 2014), discussed sensitive topics
under the radar using creative cyber language (Esarey and Xiao 2008; Xiao 2011; Shirk
2011; Yang 2009), and occasionally forced the state to scale back censorship (Li 2011;
Rosen 2010; Chao and Dean 2009). Furthermore, netizens also engage in a variety of
creative cyberactivism (Herold and Marolt 2011; Liu 2010; Voci 2010), which contribute to the rise of 'a rich and lively internet culture' (Yang 2011; 2012) that contests the
party-state norms (Lagerkvist 2010).

The third group of studies explores state adaptation to explain why the regime remains
resilient (Nathan 2003). As Shirky (2011) suggests, censorship and propaganda are
obvious avenues for authoritarian regimes to cope with the 'dictator's dilemma'. The
Chinese party-state has established systematic control over the Web through network
infrastructure, legal and administrative means, and automatic and manual surveillance
(Harwit and Clark 2001; Han 2012; Zheng 2008). To censor more effectively, the party-
state has delegated responsibilities to intermediary actors like service providers (MacK-
innon 2011; Zuckerman 2010), and selectively targeted different content by tolerating
general criticism while silencing collective mobilisation (King et al. 2013). Besides
outright censorship, the state has also adapted its propaganda strategies by increasing
online presence (Tang et al. 2013), adopting popular cyber culture (Lagerkvist 2007:
53–78), and sponsoring Internet commentators (the "fifty-cent army") to manufacture
seemingly spontaneous support (Hung 2010; Han 2012). Such state adaptation suggest
that the Internet's impact on authoritarian regimes depends on not only on technology, but also political organisation and strategy (Diamond 2010) and that authoritarian
regimes can still 'call the shots' (Kalathil and Boas 2003: 136; Morozov 2011).

These studies have provided unique visions of cyberpolitics in China. Yet, disagreements remain, largely due to the lack of meaningful cross-group dialogue. Studies recognising the political inactiveness of netizens dismiss cyberactivism too easily. Studies
on cyberactivism often assume netizens as being politically active and regime challenging, and do not differentiate actors, targets, and goals in cyberactivism. Studies
highlighting state adaptation tend to treat the party-state as unitary, focus narrowly on
censorship and propaganda, and fail to consider state adaptation in relation to the challenges. Therefore, to achieve a more balanced and accurate understanding of Chinese
cyberpolitics, I propose a multi-actor, multi-dimensional framework in the next section,
which reconciles existing views when evaluating the impact of cyberactivism and state
adaptation.

Cyberactivism and State Adaptation with Chinese Characteristics: A Multi-Actor, Multi-Dimensional Perspective

Since existing studies often highlight only certain aspects of cyberpolitics, a proper
multi-actor, multi-dimensional framework may combine their strengths while avoiding
the limitations. Figure 19.2 illustrates an attempt to construct such a framework. My
basic assumption is that Chinese cyberspace is pluralised, and neither the state nor the
society should be treated as a monolithic entity. Based on that, I examine the diversity
of cyberactivism and breadth of state adaptation. I argue that the regime's resilience
is not a result of perfect control, but builds on the weaknesses of anti-regime activism

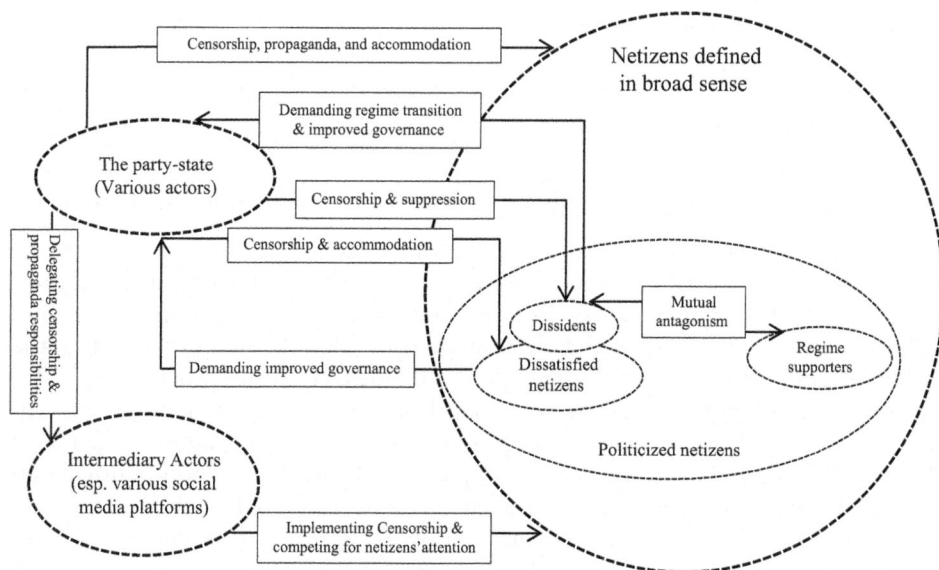

Figure 19.2 A Multi-Actor Multi-Dimensional Framework of Cyberpolitics in China

and a wide array of state adaptation. First, though Chinese netizens can be mobilised, there is no shared agenda of regime transition. Other than dissent groups, netizens are of diverse political orientations, many only demand improved governance, and some even prefer the regime to dissidents. Second, the party-state is fragmented and neither the censorship nor online propaganda is centrally administrated, resulting in severe limitations of such state adaptation. In addition, state response to cyberactivism needs to be differentiated as the party-state has selectively targeted dissidents and collective mobilisation, while trying to accommodate cyberactivism that demands improved governance.

Intermediary actors, particularly service providers, play an important mediating role. Though netizens have access to diverse online services, cyberactivism primarily happens on social media platforms where users can communicate, coordinate, and collaborate. Microblogs and forums are particularly crucial for cyberactivism. For instance, of the 217 corruption cases exposed by netizens between 2004 and February 2013, forums and microblogs account for 59 per cent and 24 per cent respectively (Du and Li 2014). News portals are important because they not only allow users to comment on news, but also incorporate other social media functions like blogging, microblogging, and online forums. As multinational giants like Facebook and Twitter are blocked by the Great Firewall, it is Chinese conglomerates like Tencent, Baidu, and Sina that dominate the market, each often providing multiple services. For instance, Tencent owns the most popular SNS site (Qzone) and instant messengers (QQ and Wechat). Baidu has the largest search engine and a popular forum (Tieba). Sina runs a major news portal and the most influential microblogging platform, Weibo. These companies not only help the party-state achieve its ICT developmental goals but also play an important role in cyberpolitics: (1) they have put the regime in a better situation to control the Web as they are easier to control than foreign IT giants; and (2) as the state has delegated censorship and propaganda responsibilities to them, they can preserve or even facilitate cyberactivism if they choose to. So though discussion below does not single out the role of intermediary actors, it is important to bear them in mind when examining both cyberactivism and state adaptation.

The Challenge of Cyberactivism towards the Authoritarian Regime

To assess the power of the Internet and digital media in the Chinese context, it is imperative to first look at in what ways cyberactivism has challenged the authoritarian regime. It is true that like Internet and social media users elsewhere, most Chinese netizens are concerned with consumerism, lifestyle, and private life rather than public or political affairs (Damm 2007; Leibold 2011; Ministry of Culture 2013). However, Chinese netizens are far from apolitical. Rather, they are more vocal, critical, and more likely to participate in collective action than non-netizens (Lei 2011; Hung 2010; Tang and Sampson 2012; Zheng 2008). In effect, even non-political netizens can be mobilised. More than once, gamers have protested when the state bans or imposes restrictions on foreign games like *World of Warcraft* (Chao et al. 2010). Similarly, when China delayed the market entry of iPhone 6, netizens complained on microblog, asking the Ministry of Industry and Information Technology not only to let in iPhones immediately but also to unblock Google services (MIIT Microblog 2014).

Yet, Chinese netizens are not pursuing regime change. For instance, the party-state's mouthpiece *People's Daily* has an Online Public Opinion Monitoring Center that tracks popular online topics on public affairs. An analysis of the 580 topics the centre collected between 2005 and 2014 (People's Daily Online Public Opinion Monitoring Center 2005–2014) shows that they are mostly about specific rights, grievances, and scandals. Though cyberactivism related to such issues may question the regime's legitimacy, it is qualitatively different from *dissident activism* that seeks regime transition. In general, dissident activism, although it spreads widely online, is of limited influence because it is largely restricted to the dissident groups. Due to state censorship, cyberactivism in China takes artful and playful forms (Yang 2009). For dissidents, outright anti-regime activism is difficult and attracts suppression. Transmitting dissent messages with popular cyberculture helps them evade censorship (as the 'cute cat theory' suggests, using popular web tools makes dissidents more immune to state reprisals because shutting down such applications may provoke a public outcry) and reach a wider audience (see Zuckerman 2008). But the move also results in many average netizens not getting the messages or encourages slacktivism that involves little commitment and has little real impact (Christensen 2011; Morozov 2009), thus fail to construct the 'shared awareness' (Shirky 2011) often seen as necessary for regime change.

Moreover, anti-regime activism has met its resistance. Chinese netizens are divided in terms of their political orientations (Wu 2014) and dissidents are not always more popular than the party-state. For instance, Han (2012) finds a group of netizens voluntarily defends the authoritarian regime against dissidents. These netizens, who call themselves the 'voluntary fifty-cent army' (as opposed to the state-sponsored 'fifty-cent army'), acknowledge the regime's contribution to national unity, social stability, and economic development and consequently, they worry about potential costs and uncertain future of regime change. Referencing the turmoil that accompanied the collapse of the Soviet Union and the Arab Spring, as well as governance deficits in democracies like India, they argue that the authoritarian regime is not the worst option. This nationalistic-realistic view is not a direct result of state sponsorship, but nonetheless echoes state propaganda, defends the regime, and adds to its legitimacy. Han's research echoes findings in survey studies done by Shi (2008) and Guo (2007), suggesting the regime still enjoys considerable legitimacy among citizens.

As a result, although general criticism is common and probably tolerated (King et al. 2013), it is far from sufficient to mobilise for regime transition. This was demonstrated by the fruitless Jasmine Revolution, in which only literally a handful of 'revolutionaries' protested on Beijing's Wangfujing Street, surrounded by hundreds of police, journalists, and thousands of bystanders (Branigan 2011). When the police took the protesters away, not a single bystander showed any sympathy or interest in the cause of the protesters, revealing the limited support base of anti-regime activism.

State Responses: Control, Propaganda, and Accommodation

The Chinese party-state is known for its capacity to adapt (Nathan 2003; Shambaugh 2008; Stockmann 2013) and it has made serious efforts to tame the Internet and social media, as revealed above. However, with only a few exceptions like Noesselt (2014), current studies tend to focus on state adaptation in the realms of censorship and propaganda, which are crucial but far from sufficient to explain authoritarian resilience in the digital era. This section elaborates why we shall look beyond censorship and propaganda and explores how the party-state has attempted to accommodate online activism to improve its governance, thus its legitimacy.

Censorship and Propaganda

There is no doubt that the Chinese state has devised a comprehensive censorship system, which is probably the world's most sophisticated (OpenNet Initiative 2005). Though scholars have detailed how the system functions (Harwit and Clark 2001, Zheng 2008; MacKinnon 2009; King et al. 2013), its effectiveness remains in question. Some suggests that it is sufficient to control (Boas 2006), others see it as full of loopholes and even counterproductive (Esarey and Xiao 2008; Tong and Lei 2013). Both arguments are valid, but incomplete. The censorship system is complicated, yet constantly outsmarted by netizens (Esarey and Xiao 2008; Mou et al 2014). Moreover, as it is not centrally administered and multiple state agencies with different and even conflicting priorities are involved, the system often fails to produce an optimal outcome for the regime as a whole. For instance, local officials have used censorship to cover up scandals. An Internet police officer in Hainan Province allegedly took bribes from counterparts in other local governments for removing negative postings about them (Xi and Zhang 2014). Relying on intermediary actors like service providers to enforce censorship also allows these actors to push the boundary for business or normative concerns. When asked how they would deal with censorship directives, an editor from a major news portal said that they would not delete the content until the last second so that more netizens can read it (Interview in Beijing, 6 May2010).

Why, then, is imperfect control sufficient? First, as explained earlier, anti-regime activism is relatively weak. Second, by selectively targeting collective mobilisation expression (King et al. 2013) and dissident activism, the party-state partially avoids the dilemma implied by the 'cute cat theory'. For instance, expression related to dissent groups like democratic activists and Falungong is strictly forbidden (thus, censorship is often unobservable because such content often cannot be published in the first place), and dissidents are often severely punished. Among the 54 detained cyberactivists listed in an Amnesty International (2004) report, almost all were charged with 'subversion', 'distribution of Falungong material', or 'leaking state secrets'. Such selective repression not only has dissident voices 'nipped in the bud' but also avoids any public outcry because average netizens are largely unaffected.

Besides censorship, the regime has also adapted its propaganda strategies. While enabling freer expression, the Internet and social media platforms also allow the regime to promulgate its own discourse. To increase its influence online, the party-state has encouraged state media outlets, like *Xinhua News Agency* and *People's Daily*, to set up online platforms and granted them the monopoly of news production (other online news services are only allowed to 'reprint'; see State Council Information Office and Ministry of Information Industry 2005). The state has also pushed state-run media to occupy popular social media platforms. According to the *2013 New Media Development Report*, traditional media outlets, often under tighter state control, have set up over 110,000 accounts on Sina Weibo by the end of 2012 (Tang et al 2013: 18). The report states,

> the rise of Central media microblogs has changed mainstream media's tardiness and muteness in responding to hot-button issues and greatly enhanced their capacity to guide popular opinion online.

Besides, the state has also innovated in propaganda tactics. For instance, Lagerkvist (2007) finds the regime embracing 'ideotainment' strategies that mix popular web culture with ideological constructs and nationalistic propaganda. The 'fifty-cent army' (Hung 2010; Han 2012), as mentioned above, is another such instance when the state takes advantage of anonymity in online expression to manufacture pro-government voices under the disguise of average users. Since state propaganda has lost its credibility, hiding state identities and acting like netizens may help the state manipulate popular opinion in some cases.

However, there are limitations to state adaptation in propaganda. For instance, though state media outlets have set up accounts on Sina Weibo, they cannot prevent critical opinion leaders from gaining popularity. Take Han Han as an example. The bestselling author and rebel blogger has over 41 million followers, far outnumbering any state agency. Even subtle strategies like the deployment of the 'fifty-cent army' often prove ineffective or backfire. Supposedly a covert force, the 'fifty-cent army' often gets exposed because they are poorly trained or rewarded. Moreover, like censorship, the system is also fragmented, with local state agencies prioritizing goals other than preserving the regime's legitimacy. In effect, local governments often expose the 'fifty-cent army' themselves because they treat it as routine propaganda work rather than something to hide in dark. All such evidence reveals that state adaptation in its propaganda strategies is of limited effect in maintaining its legitimacy.

Accommodation

State censorship and propaganda innovation cannot sufficiently explain authoritarian resilience, suggesting we look beyond these realms. Scholars studying contentious politics in China suggest that popular protests can help improve policy implementation, and thus enhance the regime's legitimacy (O'Brien and Li 2005). Since netizens often target specific governance deficits, accommodating cyberactivism and responding to the problems (Hassid 2013), however involuntarily, may help increase the regime's transparency, accountability and responsiveness. In this sense, the Internet and social media can bring "limited" democracy that enhances rather than erodes the regime's legitimacy.

The state accommodates cyberactivism actively in multiple ways. First, it has set up e-government platforms to engage the public and experiment with new ways of social management (Schlæger and Jiang 2014). Launched in 1999 to improve government administrative capacity and provide public services online (Qiang 2007), the Government Online Project has resulted in 56,348 government websites by 2014 (CNNIC 2014). Though they have not forged organisational reform, e-government projects have enhanced control over state agents, improved public services, and expanded citizen outreach (Lollar 2006; Schlæger 2013; Qin et al 2014). In particular, government websites often have petition channels, which do not automatically solve problems, yet force the government to respond to citizens' concerns, at least in a superficial way (Hartford 2005).

More importantly, the state also engages the public on popular social media platforms. By October 2013, there were over 100,000 government official accounts on Sina Weibo alone, representing 66,830 state agencies and 33,321 officials (People's Daily Online Public Opinion Monitoring Center 2013). Tencent boasts 160,000 verified governmental accounts on its microblogging platform, and another 3,000 on WeChat (Tang et al. 2014). State agencies also appear on popular Internet forums. Tianya.cn—China's most popular Internet forum with nearly 100 million registered users by February 2015—claims to host over 500 government institutions, which responded to 2,259 complaints in 2013 (Tianya 2014). Besides cosmetic effects and propaganda functions, such channels encourage state-society interaction and often help improve governance in one way or the other.

The current Xi Jinping-Li Keqiang leadership is aggressive in incorporating certain types of cyberactivism. Take online anti-corruption as an example. Research suggests that to reap the benefits of free media without risking overthrow, it is rational for the authoritarian regime to tolerate exposure of corruption to a certain level rather than completely unleash or suppress it (Lorentzen 2014). If this argument holds, the regime would be more cautious about online anti-corruption activism because it is uncontrollable. This explains why scholars find that anti-corruption activism has only achieved limited success in China (Ang 2014; Gao and Stanyer 2014; Sullivan 2014). However, with the new leadership prioritizing anti-corruption (between November 2012 and 2014, 68 corrupt officials at the deputy minister level or above were removed, which is astonishing considering that only 145 such high-ranking officials fell in the previous sixty-three years; Wu and Qian 2015), it is logically incompatible to continue hold back anti-corruption activism online. As a result, the state began to aggressively incorporate it. In April 2013, the Central Commission for Discipline Inspection (CCDI) and Ministry of Supervision (MOS) ordered major news and commercial websites to set up special 'Internet-supervision' channels for netizens to tip off corruption. In September 2013, CCDI and MOS jointly established a portal website (ccdi.gov.cn) by merging several existing online anti-corruption platforms by various party-state agencies to promulgate laws and policies, and promote public engagement. The website allows citizens to report corrupt officials, anonymously if they choose to, and follow up their reports. Official reports claim that netizens have embraced the initiative with enthusiasm: online tip-offs quadrupled from 200 to 800 daily after the portal was launched (Wang 2014). Though further study is necessary to see how sincere or effective the move is, it is obviously strategic for the regime to show its willingness to accommodate rather than standing against the public.

Conclusion

Current studies disagree on the impact of the Internet and social media on Chinese politics. Instead of negating their contributions, this chapter builds on them and fits them into a new framework that highlights the pluralisation of cyberactivism and the breadth of state responses. I argue that though digital media, particularly social media platforms like microblogs, forums, and news commentary channels, has empowered social actors in China, the nature and scale of such empowerment are worth reckoning. Yes, despite general political inactiveness, Chinese citizens have used digital media tools to lodge complaints, defend rights, and demand better governance. However, the pluralisation of cyberactivism and netizen groups, exacerbated by state censorship, has prevented social media platforms from becoming hotbed for anti-regime mobilisation.

In terms of state adaptation, the chapter echoes authoritarian resilience literature that emphasizes the adaptability of the party-state. However, I propose a broader understanding of state adaptation beyond censorship and propaganda because accommodating cyberactivism plays a crucial role in the regime's attempt to alleviate the dictator's dilemma. Moreover, when examining state adaptation to control the Web, I argue that its strength lies less in its rigorousness than its ability to selectively target dissident activism and collective mobilisation.

For those concerned with cyberpolitics and democratisation in China, there are mixed signals. To a large extent, this chapter echoes the mutual empowerment argument that emphasizes the liberalising rather than democratising effects of digital media (Zheng 2008). The analysis suggests that the potential democratic transition depends on not only the state's capacity to control, but also its ability to improve governance as well as the struggle between anti-regime activism and its opponents. The tentative conclusion could be the starting point for several future projects. First, differentiating and comparing cyberactivism more systematically can contribute to the understanding of Chinese cyberpolitics as well as the literature on authoritarian resilience. In particular, any research on the competition between dissident activism and its opposition will help assess the empowering effects of the digital media more accurately. Second, since the state-society interaction online is mediated by intermediary actors, more close examination and comparison of different digital platforms in terms of their role in cyberactivism and state adaptation will be promising. Third, it is still unclear whether cyberactivism that is not an extension of offline mobilisation has any significant impact beyond the virtual space. Since Chinese netizens demonstrate no shared awareness of regime-transition, will activism bounded online change their attitudes and subsequently behaviours in the long run? Finally, with a broader view of state adaptation, projects exploring multiple forms of state responses to digital media and the effectiveness of such responses are surely worth pursuing. Despite the different focuses, all these potential projects will improve our understanding of authoritarian resilience and state-society relations in non-democratic regimes.

References

Amnesty International (2004) *China: Controls Tighten as Internet Activism Grows*. Available at: http://goo.gl/Zc9ENf

Ang, Y. Y. (2014) "Authoritarian Restraints on Online Activism Revisited: Why 'I-Paid-A-Bribe' Worked in India but Failed in China," *Comparative Politics*, 47 (1), pp. 21–40.

Boas, T. C. (2000). "The Dictator's Dilemma? The Internet and U.S. Policy Toward Cuba," *The Washington Quarterly*, 23 (3), pp. 57–67.

Boas, T. C. (2006) "Weaving the Authoritarian Web: The Control of Internet Use in Nondemocratic Regimes," in J. Zysman and A. Newman (eds.) *How Revolutionary was the Digital Revolution: National Responses, Market Transitions, and Global Technology*, Stanford, CA: Stanford University Press, pp. 361–378.

Branigan, T. (2011) "China's Jasmine Revolution: Police but No Protesters Line Streets of Beijing," *The Guardian*, 27 February. Available at: http://goo.gl/7bwcG4

Chao, L. and Dean, J. (2009) "Chinese Delay Plan for Censor Software," *The Wall Street Journal*, 1 July.

Chao, L., Ye, J. and Back, A. (2010) "Video Declares 'War' on Chinese Internet Censorship," *The Wall Street Journal—Asia*, 12 February.

Chase, M. S. and Mulvenon, J. C. (2002) *You've Got Dissent*, Santa Monica, CA: Rand Corporation.

Christensen, H. S. (2011) "Political Activities on the Internet: Slacktivism or Political Participation by Other Means?" *First Monday*, 16 (2). Available at: http://firstmonday.org/article/view/3336/2767

CNNIC (2014) *Zhongguo Hulianwang Fazhan Zhuangkuang Tongji Baogao (July 2014)* (*Survey Report on the Development of China's Internet [July 2014]*). Available at: http://www.cnnic.cn

Damm, J. (2007) "The Internet and the Fragmentation of Chinese Society," *Critical Asian Studies*, 39 (2), pp. 273–294.

Diamond, L. (2010) "Liberation Technology," *Journal of Democracy*, 21 (3), pp. 69–83.

Du, Z. and Li, X. (2014) "Woguo Wangluo Fanfu de Zhuyao Tezheng: Jiyu 217 ge Anli de Shizheng Fenxi" (The Characteristics of Internet Anti-Corruption: An Empirical Analysis of 217 Cases), *Zhongguo Xingzheng Guanli* (*Chinese Public Administration*), 4, pp. 35–39.

Esarey, A. and Xiao, Q. (2008) "Political Expression in the Chinese Blogosphere," *Asian Survey*, 48 (5), pp. 752–772.

Guo, L. (2007) *Surveying Internet Usage and Impact in Seven Chinese Cities*, Beijing: Center for Social Development, Chinese Academy of Social Sciences.

Gao, L. and Stanyer, J. (2014) "Hunting Corrupt Officials Online: The Human Flesh Search Engine and the Search for Justice in China," *Information, Communication, & Society*, 17 (7), pp. 814–829.

Han, R. (2012) *Challenging the Regime, Defending the Regime: Contesting Cyberspace in China*, Ph.D. Dissertation, Berkeley: University of California.

Hartford, K. (2005) "Dear Mayor Online Communications with Local Governments in Hangzhou and Nanjing," *China Information*, 19 (2), pp. 217–260.

Harwit, E. and Clark, D. (2001) "Shaping the Internet in China: Evolution of Political Control over Network Infrastructure and Content," *Asian Survey*, 41 (3), pp. 377–408.

Hassid, J. (2012) "Safety Valve or Pressure Cooker? Blogs in Chinese Political Life," *Journal of Communication*, 62 (2), pp. 212–230.

—— (2013) "Chinese Government Responsiveness to Internet Opinion: Promising but Dangerous," Available at: http://ssrn.com/abstract=2308813

Herold, D. K. and Marolt, P. (eds.) (2011) *Online Society in China: Creating, Celebrating, and Instrumentalising the Online Carnival*, New York: Routledge.

Hindman, M. (2009) *The Myth of Digital Democracy*, Princeton: Princeton University Press.

Howard, P. N. and Hussain, M. M. (2013) *Democracy's Fourth Wave? Digital Media and the Arab Spring*, Oxford: Oxford University Press.

Hung, C.-F. (2010) "China's Propaganda in the Information Age: Internet Commentators and Weng'an Incident," *Issues & Studies*, 46 (4), pp. 149–181.

Kalathil, S. and Boas, T.C. (2003) *Open Networks, Closed Regimes: The Impact of the Internet on Authoritarian Rule*, Washington DC: Carnegie Endowment for International Peace.

King, G., Pan, J. and Roberts, M.E. (2013) "How Censorship in China Allows Government Criticism but Silences Collective Expression," *American Political Science Review*, 107 (2), pp. 1–18.

Lagerkvist, J. (2007) *The Internet in China: Unlocking and Containing the Public Sphere*, Phd Thesis, Lund: Lund University.

—— (2010) *After the Internet, before Democracy: Competing Norms in Chinese Media and Society*, Bern: Peter Lang.

Lei, Y.-W. (2011) "The Political Consequences of the Rise of the Internet: Political Beliefs and Practices of Chinese Netizens," *Political Communication*, 28 (3), pp. 291–322.

Leibold, J. (2011) "Blogging Alone: China, the Internet, and the Democratic Illusion?" *The Journal of Asian Studies*, 70 (4), pp. 1023–1041.

Li, H. (2011) "Parody and Resistance on the Chinese Internet," in D.K. Herold and P. Marolt (eds.) *Online Society in China: Creating, Celebrating, and Instrumentalising the Online Carnival*, New York: Routledge, pp. 71–88.

Liu, F. (2010) *Urban Youth in China: Modernity, the Internet and the Self*, New York: Routledge.

Lollar, X.L. (2006) "Assessing China's E-Government: Information, Service, Transparency and Citizen Outreach of Government Websites," *Journal of Contemporary China*, 15 (46), pp. 31–41.

Lorentzen, P. (2014) "China's Strategic Censorship," *American Journal of Political Science*, 58 (2), pp. 402–414.

MacKinnon, R. (2009) "China's Censorship 2.0: How Companies Censor Bloggers," *First Monday*, 14(2). Available at: http://firstmonday.org/article/view/2378/2089

—— (2011) "China's 'Networked Authoritarianism'," *Journal of Democracy*, 22 (2), 32–46.

MIIT Microblog (2014) *Guanzhu 2014 Guoji Xinxi Tongxin Zhan (Attention to PT/EXPO COMM China 2014)*. 23 September. Available at: http://goo.gl/YkSy8b

Morozov, E. (2009) "The Brave New World of Slacktivism," *Net Effect*. Available at: http://goo.gl/obQ3IV

Ministry of Culture (2013) *2012 Zhongguo Wangba Shichang Niandu Baogao (2012 Survey Report on China's Internet Café Industry)*. Available at: http://goo.gl/yHVCen

Morozov, E. (2011) *The Net Delusion: How Not to Liberate the World*, London: Penguin Books.

Mou, Y., Wu, K., and Atkin, D. (2014) "Understanding the Use of Circumvention Tools to Bypass Online Censorship," *New Media & Society*, pp. 1–20.

Nathan, A. (2003) "Authoritarian Resilience," *Journal of Democracy*, 14 (1), pp. 6–17.

Noesselt, N. (2014) "Microblogs and the Adaptation of the Chinese Party-State's Governance Strategy," *Governance*, 27 (3), pp. 449–468.

O'Brien, K. and Li, L. (2005) "Popular Contention and Its Impact in Rural China," *Comparative Political Studies*, 38 (3), pp. 235–259.

OpenNet Initiative (2005) *Internet Filtering in China in 2004–2005: A Country Study*. Available at: http://goo.gl/Pzbfd1

People's Daily Online Public Opinion Monitoring Center (2013) *2013 Nian Xinlang Zhengwu Weibo Baogao (2013 Sina.com Government Weibo Account)*. Available at: http://goo.gl/sZHAZh

—— (2005–2014) *Renminwang Yuqing Jianceshi Anliku (People's Daily Online Public Opinion Monitoring Center Case Library)*. Available at: http://goo.gl/5ngClx

Qiang, C.Z.-W. (2007) *China's Information Revolution: Managing the Economic and Social Transformation*, Washington DC: World Bank.

Qin, X., Xue, D., and Zheng N. (2014) "Zhengfu Guanwang 2.0 Shidai: Wangmin Xuqiu Gengjia Duoyuanhua" (Government Websites 2.0: Netizen Demands More Pluralized), *Diyi Caijing Ribao (China Business News)*, 8 August.

Rosen, S. (2010) "Is the Internet a Positive Force in the Development of Civil Society, a Public Sphere, and Democratization in China?" *International Journal of Communication*, 4, pp. 509–516.

Schlæger, J. (2013) *E-Government in China: Technology, Power and Local Government Reform*, London: Routledge.

Schlæger, J. and Jiang, M (2014) "Official Microblogging and Social Management by Local Governments in China," *China Information*, 28 (2), pp. 189–213.

Shambaugh, D. L. (2008) *China's Communist Party: Atrophy and Adaptation*, Berkeley: University of California Press.

Shi, T. (2008) "China: Democratic Values Supporting an Authoritarian System," in Y.-H. Chu, L. Diamond, A. J. Nathan and D.C. Shin (eds.) *How East Asians View Democracy*, New York: Columbia University Press, pp. 209–237.

Shirk, S. L. (ed.) (2011) *Changing Media, Changing China*, New York: Oxford University Press.

Shirky, C. (2011) "The Political Power of Social Media," *Foreign Affairs*, pp. 28–41.

State Council Information Office and Ministry of Information Industry (2005) *Hulianwang Xinwen Xinxi Fuwu Guanli Guiding (Administrative Regulations on the Internet News and Information Services)*. Available at: http://goo.gl/MSohc6

Stockmann, D. (2013) *Media Commercialization and Authoritarian Rule in China*, Cambridge: Cambridge University Press.

Sullivan, J. (2014) "China's Weibo: Is Faster Different?" *New Media & Society*, 16 (1), pp. 24–37.

Tai, Z. (2006) *The Internet in China*, London: Routledge.

Tang, L. and Sampson, H. (2012) "The Interaction between Mass Media and the Internet in Non-democratic States: The Case of China," *Media, Culture & Society*, 34 (4), 457–471.

Tang X. et al (eds.) (2013) *Zhongguo Xinmeiti Fazhan Baogao (2013) (Annual Report on Development of New Media in China (2013)*, China: Social Sciences Academic Press.

—— (2014) *Zhongguo Xinmeiti Fazhan Baogao (2014) (Annual Report on Development of New Media in China (2014)*, China: Social Sciences Academic Press.

Thornton, P. (2008) "Manufacturing Dissent in Transnational China: Boomerang, Backfire or Spectacle?" in K. O'Brien (ed.) *Popular Protest in China*, Cambridge Mass: Harvard University Press, pp. 179–204.

Tianya (2014) *2013 Nian Tianya Yuqing Yingdui Nengli Bangdan (Tianya Public Opinion Response Capacity Ranking 2013)*. Available at: http://goo.gl/DXKLqx

Tong, Y. and Lei, S. (2013) "War of Position and Microblogging in China," *Journal of Contemporary China*, 22 (80), pp. 292–311.

Voci, P. (2010) *China on Video: Smaller-Screen Realities*, Milton Park: Routledge.

Wang, S. (2014) "Shubiao Zhitong Zhongjiwei shi Ruhe Liancheng de?" (How Linking to CCDI through A Click is Made Possible?), *Xinjingbao (The Beijing News)*, 3 September.

Wu, A. X. (2014) "Ideological Polarization Over a China-as-Superpower Mindset: An Exploratory Charting of Belief Systems among Chinese Internet Users, 2008–2011," *International Journal of Communication*, 8, pp. 2243–2272.

Wu, G. and Qian, W. (2015) "Dahu Dashuju: Chuandi Naxie Xinxi" (Big Data on Tiger Hunting: What Messages Conveyed), *Jiancha Ribao (Procuratorial Daily)*, 13 January.

Xi, Y. and Zhang, W. (2014) "Wangjing Huilu Wangjing: Ti Lingdao Shantie" (Internet Police Bribing Internet Police: Deleting Posts for Local Leaders), *Nanfang Zhoumo (Southern Weekend)*, 17 April.

Xiao, Q. (2011) "The Battle for the Chinese Internet," *Journal of Democracy*, 22 (2), pp. 47–61.

Yang, G. (2003) "The Co-Evolution of the Internet and Civil Society in China," *Asian Survey*, 43 (3), pp. 124–141.

—— (2007) "How Do Chinese Civic Associations Respond to the Internet? Findings from a Survey," *The China Quarterly*, 189, pp. 122–143.

—— (2009) *The Power of the Internet in China: Citizen Activism Online*, New York: Columbia University Press.

—— (2011) "Technology and Its Contents: Issues in the Study of the Chinese Internet," *The Journal of Asian Studies*, 70 (4), pp. 1043–1050.

—— (2012) "Lightness, Wildness, and Ambivalence: China and New Media Studies," *New Media & Society*, 14 (1), pp. 170–179.

Zheng, Y. (2008) *Technological Empowerment: The Internet, State, and Society in China*, Stanford: Calif.: Stanford University Press.

Zheng, Y. and Wu, G. (2005) "Information Technology, Public Space, and Collective Action in China," *Comparative Political Studies*, 38(5), pp. 507–536.

Zuckerman, E. (2008) *The Cute Cat Theory Talk at ETech*. Available at: http://goo.gl/1VsQgh

—— (2010) "Intermediary Censorship," in R.J. Deibert, J.G. Palfrey, R. Rohozinski and J. Zittrain (eds.) *Access Controlled: The Shaping of Power, Rights and Rule in Cyberspace*, Cambridge, Mass.: The MIT Press, pp. 71–85.

20

VOICING DISCONTENT IN SOUTH KOREA

Origins and Channels of Online Civic Movements

Maurice Vergeer and Se Jung Park

Introduction

The presence of social movements is an indication of how civic engagement is working in a society, and judging from the increase in civic organisations in South Korea, the country is moving towards consolidating democracy. To support their rights and voice their concerns the people in South Korea have taken to the streets for a number of social problems, using the Internet and social media to organise events and mobilise participants. Among the most notable movements are the Candlelight protests, for instance, on the import of U.S. beef (2008) with an estimated attendance of seven hundred protesters and the Sewol ferry disaster (2014) with an estimated attendance of over a million protesters.

The main aim of this chapter is to analyse social movements in the context of South Korea, a relatively young democracy that has embraced information and communication technology. First, the chapter will give a brief overview of modern history of South Korea and discuss why people in South Korea are particularly tech savvy and how technology is being used in the country. South Korean society is characterised as having relatively low trust in political institutions and large businesses, due to insufficient governance. This conflicts with Korea's cultural heritage because Confucianism—which focuses heavily on wisdom and mutual respect, developing personal networks consisting of meaningful strong ties—is a major foundation of Korean culture. Second, the chapter will discuss how a number of social movements in South Korea use the Internet, a section focusses attention to government regulations that affect the use of the Internet by Korean people and politicians.

South Korea's Path to Wealth and Democracy

The development of South Korea towards a democratic and free state was drastically delayed by the Japanese occupation from 1910 until the end of World War II, as well as by the Korean War (1950–1953) that divided the country into the Democratic People's

Republic of Korea (a.k.a. North Korea) and the Republic of Korea (a.k.a. South Korea). After the Korean War, South Korea developed as a country under military ruling. The development of a modernized South Korea started in the late 1960s of the last century, under president Park Chung-hee when, for instance, the economic conglomerates known as *chaebŏl* began to flourish. *Chaebŏl* consist of relatively small, family owned companies, which through their company networks gain enormous economic power on the South Korean market as well as on the global playing field (Fukuyama 1996). Some of the largest conglomerates in the communications market (e.g. Samsung, LG, and SK) are now major players locally as well as globally (see Figure 20.1).

The economic politics laid the foundation of South Korean unprecedented explosive growth in economy: average yearly GDP per capita growth rate of 9.8 per cent between 1971 and 2012 (OECD 2014). However, this growth came at the expense of citizens due to Park Chung-hee's aggressive control (1962–1979) using military coercion toward citizens and suppression of democratic values (Fukuyama 1996). In the context of this chapter, the more interesting fact is that Park contributed to building the currently famous communication infrastructure in South Korea. Still, there are many moderating factors for the Internet to democratize Asian politics, such as political culture, regulatory regimes, and unequal access to the information technology (Kluver and Banerjee 2005: 33).

Within a few decades, South Korea went through an impressive process of economic and political transformation. Presently, South Korea has global players in the automobile market (e.g. Hyundai and Kia) and communications market (e.g. Samsung, LG).

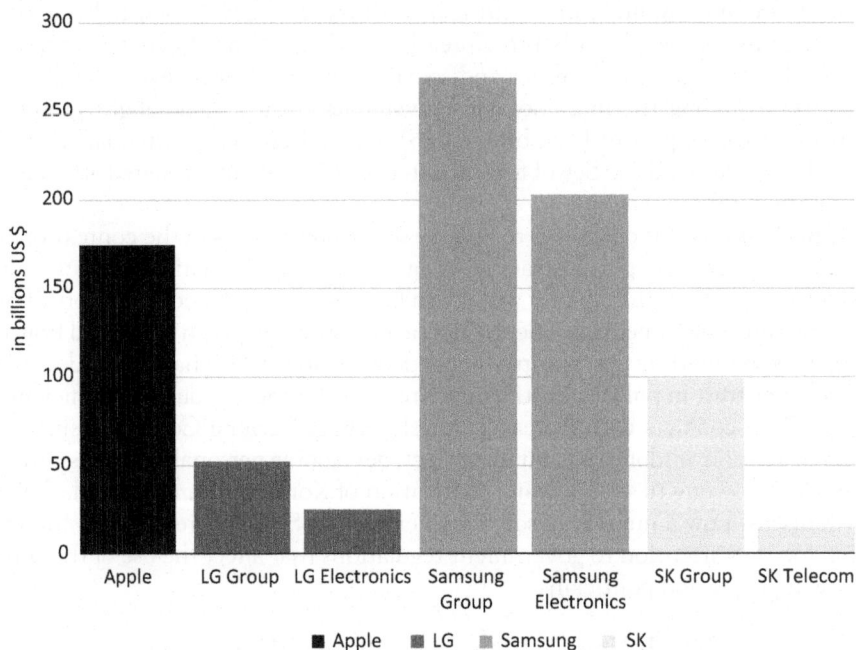

Figure 20.1 2013 Revenues of *Chaebŏl* and Their South Korean Communications Subsidiaries Compared to Apple
Sources: Samsung (2014), SK (2014), LG (2014), KT (2014), Apple (2014).

In terms of adoption of new technology (e.g. smartphones, e-money, social media), South Korea has even surpassed Japan. However, partly due to this rapid industry development, the consolidation of democracy safeguarding people's general well-being and freedom was regularly put to the test, even in the 21st century. The fact that the number of civic organisations has increased over the past decades suggests that there is still quite some discontent among Korean people (Park, Lim, Sams, Nam, and Park 2011), due to corruption, nepotism in government and industry, disregards for employee welfare by *chaebŏl* companies.

Web Culture in South Korea

South Korea is considered the most wired country in the world (see Figure 20.2), outranking many advanced countries. Extremely fast broadband access is widely available,

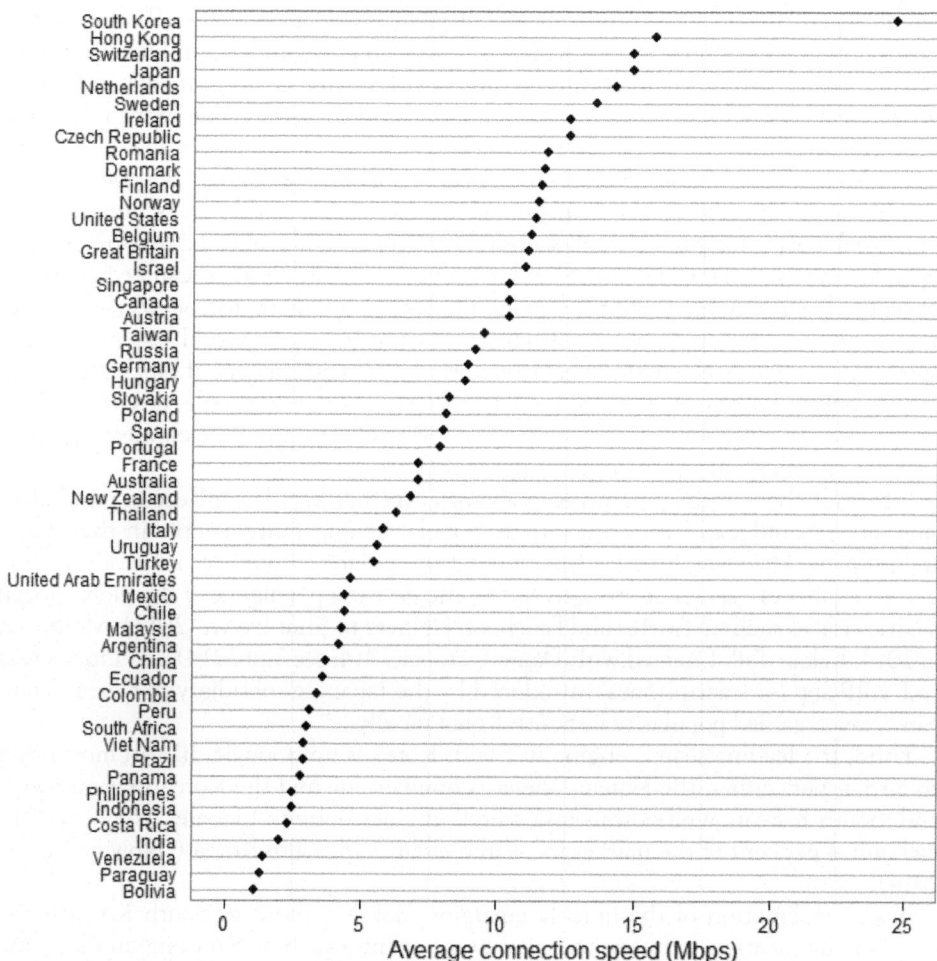

Figure 20.2 Internet Connection Speeds in Countries, Second Quarter of 2014
Note: Data retrieved from Akamai report (Akamai 2014).

and wireless and mobile communication are ubiquitous, as indicated by high adoption rates and use of mobile television and electronic money, such as the T-Money service (Kim, Tao, Shin, and Kim 2010) remove this because it was already mentioned earlier in the sentence. People watching TV on their smart phones while commuting on the subway is quite common. Wired communication is commonly used for shopping, entertainment, and news. Another popular pastime activity for younger people is to play all sorts of computer games in PC Bangs (PC rooms often open 24/7) for a very small fee (Huhh 2008). This has led to a vibrant million dollar professional industry of e-sports in South Korea, where players attain celebrity status (Seo 2013; Dhoedt 2013). The popularity of computer games also led to young Koreans becoming addicted to computer games and the Internet (Heo, Oh, Subramanian, Kim, and Kawachi 2014).

South Korea has a leading role in Internet development and is characterised by a cultural homogeneity, with only 2.5 per cent of the population being foreigners in 2013 (United Nations 2014). These factors have resulted in a distinct South Korean Web culture; even though in recent years global platforms such as Facebook and Twitter have become widely used, South Korea is not entirely dependent on global services. Indeed, the country has a long history with national Korean social media and search engines. First, Cyworld (owned by SK Communications) was the dominant social network in South Korea for over a decade, until the competition from Facebook in recent years has imposed a serious decline in Cyworld's popularity. Compared to other social network sites Cyworld has several unique features, such as Cyworld's 'minihompy', which is a mini-homepage, a small section on the page which allowed users to create a living room with avatars, furniture, and gadgets. These virtual items can be bought for a small amount of money, and SK Communications was among the pioneers to implement and generate large revenues from micro-transactions. Cyworld was particularly known for using *Ilchon*, which reflects a traditional Korean concept of kinship to set up online social relations; an *Ilchon* is a relationship between two people, unique to those two people. The disclosure of information on Cyworld between these connected people could be specified differently for each *Ilchon* relation.

A second characteristic South Korean social media, Me2day, a Korean microblogging service similar to Twitter, was quite popular among young people in their teens and twenties. However, Me2day was closed down in late 2013 due to its steady decline in the number of users that was affected by the growing popularity of the global social media services such as Twitter and Facebook ("Naver to Shut Down" 2013). Moreover, in 2014, Kakao Talk (merged with Daum October 2014; see Tay 2014) and Line, a text and VoIP app for smartphones, introduced by the Japanese subsidiary of Korean company Naver, gained popularity in South Korea rapidly.

Third, the leading search engine in South Korea is not Google, like in most other countries, but, rather, the Korean Naver is number one and the Korean Daum is second. South Korean Web portals and search engines outrank Google, which in 2014 had only 4 per cent of the market for search engines in South Korea ("Now or Naver" 2014).

A key explanation of the quickly emerging mobile culture in South Korea is the large communication industry occupied by companies such as Samsung and LG, and SK telecom provider, who's Nate On—an online messenger—was extremely popular among young Koreans. Given the nation's strong reliance on the ICT industry, particularly Samsung, South Korea is sometimes referred to as the Republic of Samsung

(Harlan 2012). Indicative for Samsung's economic power in South Korea is its revenues of 216.7 billion U.S. dollars in 2013 (Samsung 2014) which is 17 per cent of South Korea's GDP of 1,304.6 billion U.S. dollars in 2013 (Worldbank 2014). Samsung's political power is exemplified by Samsung's former chairman Lee Kun-hee's special amnesty of his embezzlement and tax evasion conviction in order for him to retain his International Olympic Committee membership to campaign for the city PyeongChang to host the 2018 Winter Olympics (Sang-hun 2009).

Apple's iPhone, one of the most advanced and iconic smart phones, was launched in South Korea in November 2009, over two years later after its U.S. introduction (Garner 2009). This delayed introduction was due to strict regulations on location-based services by the Korean Communication Commission. At the same time, the late arrival protected the large market shares of local smart phones brands (e.g. Samsung, LG) on the Korean's internal smart phone market ("iPhone Pipe Dreams" 2008). Before Android phones and Apple's iPhone came to the Korean market, local smart phones brands already had contained proprietary software, resulting to Koreans being familiar with smart phones early on. Even though Samsung has used Google's Android software for their popular smart phone models, their newest products (from smart phones to UHD television sets) use their proprietary software Tizen, again distancing themselves from Google's Android dominance. Whether Samsung's Tizen will be successful depends not only on having a large consumer base (which they have) but also on apps available for Tizen. Even if Samsung succeeds to create a high adoption rate for Tizen, it is unclear whether this will lead to a specific web culture distinct from the Apple and Android ecology.

Sociopolitical Relations in South Korean Culture

The infrastructure of networked communication in South Korea is manifold and consists of both national and global social media services. This infrastructure is widely used by the Koreans to discuss politics and social issues, and to share political news about recent developments. In these discussions, it is common to express discontent towards the government or the ruling party and to make fun of politicians in power through political parody.

The use of social media in South Korea for political engagement as well as for socialising in everyday life must be understood in light of key characteristics of social relations in South Korean culture. First and foremost, South Korea is a collectivist society where family integrity, group membership, and social interactions are considered essential (Choi, Kim, Sung and Sohn 2011). This collectivism corresponds with high context culture, meaning that it involves indirect, ambiguous and harmonious communication between people (Ji, Hwangbo, Yi, Rau, Fang, and Ling 2010). Accordingly, communication is closely related to interpersonal trust, which is an key factor in South Korean society.

In spite of this characteristic collectivism and the high level of interpersonal trust, South Korea is not resistant of emancipatory developments, which is indicated by gender equality, personal autonomy, lifestyle tolerance, and people's voice. The so-called Asian values thesis, as voiced by retired Prime Minister of Singapore Lee Kuan Yew (Zakaria 1994), suggests that Asian collectivistic cultures are resistant of liberal democratic development. This thesis suggests that Asian cultures, in contrast to Western cultures, where modernization of societies leads to liberal democracy and individualism, seems more resistant toward these developments. However, several comparative studies suggest that Asian countries do not differ significantly from Western, but that some Asian countries are probably at different levels of development (Dalton and Ong 2005; Welzel 2011). According to these findings, South Korea is about halfway in the ranking of subscribing to emancipative values, and thus surpassing several western countries (Welzel 2011: 19).

The effect of the Internet on the development towards democracy is depended on at least three key factors: political culture, regulatory regimes, and access information technology (Kluver and Banerjee 2005: 35). South Korea has a multiparty system, with one ideological dimension of conservatism, which focuses on modernization and social stability, versus progressivism, which emphasizes social welfare, humanism and egalitarianism. The Conservative Party, which politically oppressed social movements in the past, to date has been more powerful to than the progressive political parties. This political culture of low trust in political institutions might explain the vibrant social movements in South Korea.

Korean politics is at times unstable, polarized, and emotional, demonstrated by occasional scuffles between members of parliament and a major bribery incident which involved the Grand National Party in 2012 (Kim 2012). These incidents, in addition to the failure of the government to lead South Korea out of the economic crisis of 1997, may explain the decreased trust in politics among South Koreans. Figure 20.3 illustrates the Korean people's declining trust in political institutions and shows that the confidence in political institutions was relatively high in the 1980s, but the degree of trust subsequently decreased. The decrease in trust was particularly significant during the economic crisis of the late 1990s, with the1997 economic crisis as it peak.

This crisis was a result of excessive outstanding bank loans to business conglomerates (*chaebŏl*; e.g. Kia, LG, Samsung, Hyundai) to increase their economic competitiveness on the global market. These loans eventually became a national challenge, passed on from the private companies of South Korea to the citizens. When unable to pay back their loans, the conglomerates appealed to Korean citizens to donate their privately owned gold jewellery to the government to pay of the International Monetary Fund (IMF) loan. The Korean citizens responded to this appeal by donating more than 20 billion U.S. dollars to the Korean companies ("Koreans Give up Their Gold to Help Their Country" 1998). This remarkable individual sacrifice for a collectively perceived greater good is indicative of Koreans' commitment to the collective interest over the individual interests. As a parallel to this engagement of Korean citizens to contribute stability when the nation is in a economic crisis, the Koreans also take responsibility by engaging in civic movements when they observe that the Korean government fails. As seen in the Figure 20.3, the confidence in political institutions slightly increased after the economic recovery, but remains relatively low.

Political trust is however not necessarily related to social trust (Kim 2005). Political trust, particularly in new democracies, depends largely on the performance of political institutions. South Korea has a long history of oppression, a short history of democracy, in addition to several political scandals and abuse of political power. Considering these factors, it is not surprising that political trust is fairly low in South Korea compared to other democratic countries: South Korea ranks 23rd of 52 worldwide countries (see Figure 20.4). Moreover, zooming into East and South-East Asian countries (see Figure 20.5) South Korea is characterised by lower levels of confidence in political

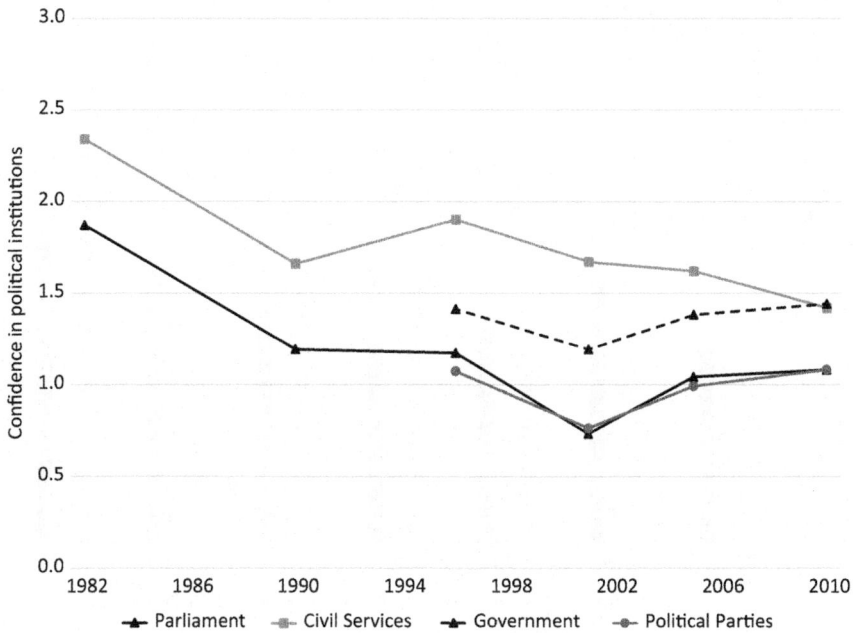

Figure 20.3 Level of Confidence in Political Institutions in South Korea
Note: Data analysis performed on World Values Survey (www.worldvaluessurvey.org). Dataset: WVS_Longitudinal_1981–2014_spss_v_2014_06_17_Beta.sav, wave 6 2010–2014. Answer categories: 0 = 'None at all', 1 = 'Not very much', 2 = 'Quite a lot', 3 = 'A great deal'.

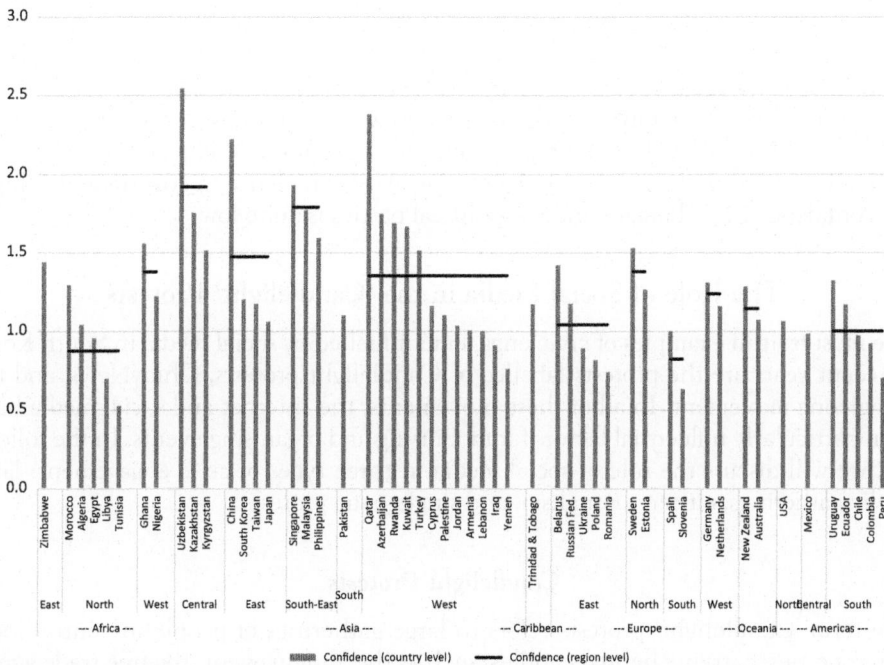

Figure 20.4 Confidence in Political Institutions in Countries and Regions
Note: Data analysis performed on World Values Survey (www.worldvaluessurvey.org). Dataset: WVS_Longitudinal_1981–2014_spss_v_2014_06_17_Beta.sav, wave 6 2010–2014. Average of three measurements of confidence in Government, Political parties and Parliament. Answer categories: 0 = 'None at all', 1 = 'Not very much', 2 = 'Quite a lot', 3 = 'A great deal'.

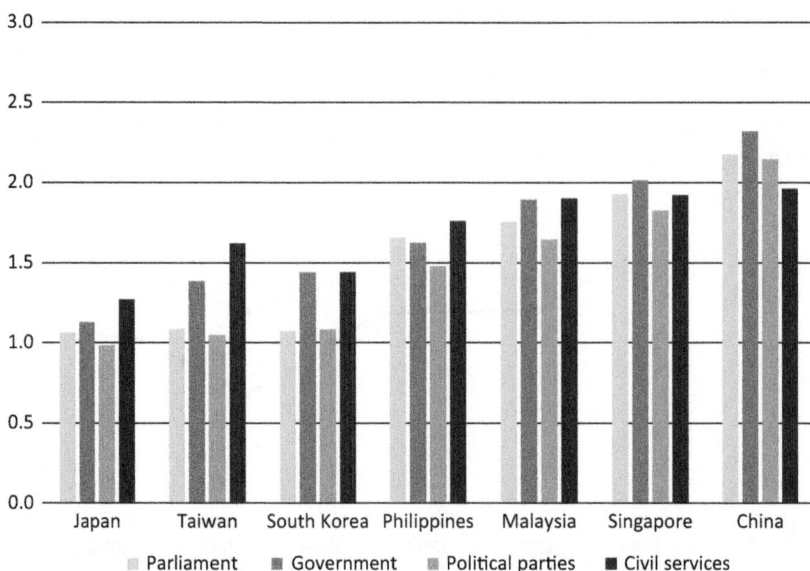

Figure 20.5 Average Level of Confidence in Political Institutions across East and South-East Asian Countries

Note: Data analysis performed on World Values Survey (www.worldvaluessurvey.org). Dataset: WVS_Longitudinal_1981–2014_spss_v_2014_06_17_Beta.sav, wave 6 2010–2014. Answer categories: 0 = 'None at all', 1 = 'Not very much', 2 = 'Quite a lot', 3 = 'A great deal'.

institutions, similar to Taiwan and Japan. Among the countries in these regions with significantly higher levels of confidence are the Philippines, Malaysia, Singapore, and China. It is worth noting that although the level of confidence in government is high, the confidence in parliament and the political parties is quite low.

The Role of Social Media in the 'Candlelight' Protests

The most fruitful examples of civic engagement fuelled by social media in South Korea in recent years are the protests labelled as Candlelight protests, OhmyNews, and the Gangjeong movement. In all of these movements, the Internet and social media have been particularly influential factors for mobilising and organising events. In the following, we will discuss the role of social media in three types of civic engagement: large public gatherings, citizen journalism, and single-issue protests.

Candlelight Protests

The term 'Candlelight' protests refers to large gatherings of people in central locations of cities, carrying lighted candles, such as the Yangju event, the free trade agreement, and the Sewol ferry disaster. The civic engagement in South Korea is not always protest against its own government or the general establishment—sometimes such actions also oppose foreign governments. For example, there are two recent cases involving protests against the U.S. in South Korea, of which the first Candle-light protest—the Yangju event in 2002—was a response to a tragic accident where two teenage females were killed by a U.S. army vehicle (You, Lee, and Oh 2014). The subsequent acquittal by a U.S. court caused a lot of controversy and animosity of Koreans towards Americans. The second Candlelight protest featured a similar expression of anti-American sentiment (cf. Shin and Izatt 2011). It took place in Seoul from May through July 2008 and lasted for over 100 days, attracting more than tens of thousands people at its peak. This protest was in opposition to President Lee's intention to lift the ban on U.S. beef import. This ban was imposed due to the outbreak of mad cow disease in the U.S., and the protesters were concerned that the import would damage Korean economy and endanger the health of Koreans. An extensive analysis of this protest by Seongyi and Woo-Young (2011) provided several interesting findings. First of all, the Internet played a significant role. Internet cafés, existing ones and those dedicated particularly to this protest, particularly on Daum. net, were populated mostly by youngsters and mostly by female teenagers. Further-more, participation in these cafés took place mostly in existing entertainment groups of celebrities and K-Pop groups, showing that the function of theses cafés serves mul-tiple purposes. Seongyi and Woo-Young (2010: 248) argue that these entertainment cafés show more exuberant activities due to the tightly connected participants with a common interest and a common history. In the past, teenagers showed disinter-est in politics, due to Confucianism beliefs, the ruling by an military authoritarian regime and the competitive education system which demands long hours of studying. However, during the Candlelight protest, young people, specifically young, empow-ered females, concerned about health issues, became politically active. During the protests the Internet was used as a core tool for information acquisition, political awakening, and networking among peer group (Seongyi and Woo-Young 2011). For teenagers, the Internet was considered a superior source of information, leaving tra-ditional media far behind. Furthermore, the Internet was deemed trustworthy, again surpassing traditional media by a long stretch. The Internet and social media enabled initially politically disconnected Korean teenagers to participate and contribute to protests and public concerns.

One of the more recent Candlelight protests concerned the Sewol tragedy. On 16 April 2014, nearly 300 people, mostly schoolchildren, died in a ferry accident on a trip to Jeju Island. It resulted in repeated protests about the failing of the state's emergency control system, incorrect reports on the numbers of casualties, and the improperly operating coast guard, refusing assistance from Japan at the scene. Also, the position of President Park was discussed; it was rumoured she was absent for seven hours during the time the rescue operation took place (Klug 2014). Later in this chapter, we shall see that president Park's complaints about and attempts to curtail these the Internet rumours created controversy on Internet regulation and election laws in South Korea.

Citizen Journalism: OhmyNews

South Korea is characterised by a malfunctioning newspaper market, not least because the three major newspapers with a significant major market share are conser-vative and also have strong relations with those in power, known as political paral-lelism (Kim and Hamilton 2006). This political parallelism is further reinforced by government-supported propagation of the Internet (instigated by President Kim Dae Jung administration 1998–2003).

As a response to this malfunction, as well as a result of the unemployment among journalists and the economic crisis in the press, many journalists turned to the Internet as a platform to disseminate news. Moreover, the Internet became a safe arena for progressive intellectuals, active on highly connected progressive websites (Park and Park 2013). As such, these groups created a common enemy: the conservative newspaper *Chosun Ilbo*. From this Oh Yeon Ho created OhmyNews, adopting the slogan 'Every citizen is a journalist'. OhmyNews was an alternative medium, in the meaning that it published stories on issues largely ignored by the traditional news media. Studies show that about 50,000 citizens have contributed to OhmyNews, and that the website has over two million visitors on an average day (Kim and Hamilton 2006; Kern and Nam 2009). In comparison, two of the largest South Korean newspapers have a fairly similar readership, with a circulation of 2.3 million (*Chosun Ilbo*) and 2.2. million (*JoongAng Ilbo*) on an average daily basis (OECD 2010).

OhmyNews played a key political role during the 2002 presidential elections, when the news site supported the progressive candidate Roh Moo-hyun by giving him a platform to present his ideas and ambitions. Until then, Roh Moo-hyun had been largely ignored by the traditional—meaning the conservative—media. Roh's subsequent election as president elevated OhmyNews quickly as an influential news organisation. In addition to contribution to Roh's election, OhmyNews was also a key factor in organising the aforementioned Candlelight protests on the U.S. beef imports.

One of the more recent and in-depth analyses of a social movement in South Korea dealt with the Chopae Internet community that called for the closing of *Chosun-ilbo*, a conservative newspaper with a significant market share (Choi and Park 2013). Chopae, a Twitter community on Twitaddon.com, was analysed with a mixed method approach. Twitaddon.com and Twtkr.com operate as Twitter portals that provide easy access to specific Korean topical communities on Twitter. A content analysis showed that the community focused on four themes; the first and largest theme concerned the large anti-sentiment against the government, the G20 meeting and large conglomerates (i.e. *chaebŏl*). The second main theme involved distrust in the South Korean's government of explanation of the sinking of the South Korean warship Cheonan by the North Korean army, killing 46 seamen (26 March 2010). The third theme involved general rants about the government, while the fourth and final theme referred to critique against the Korean conglomerates' reckless expansion as well as advocating consumer rights. Collective action consisted first and foremost of tweeting and retweeting messages about issues as well as the organisation of protests. Retweeting helped to circulate and resonate messages within the community, consolidating members' thoughts but also expanding the audience. If hyperlinks were included in the tweets they were mostly from online based news media, whereas traditional news media were neglected, considered to be unreliable (Choi and Park 2013). Twitter was also used to plan offline activities, such as organising lectures with public figures, planning boycotts, and spreading leaflets. Rather than turning into an echo chamber (cf. Sunstein 2009) this community seems vibrant both online and active offline, and in turn, the time-consuming offline activities indicate that this movement is contradicting the general perception of online social movements being slacktivism without commitment outside the online context.

Gangjeong Movement

The Gangjeong movement revolves around the controversial governmental plans to build a naval base on Jeju Island. The controversy is related to both environmental issues about the destruction of precious nature, and to sensitive neighbour country issues related to the situation of the planned naval base close to China and Japan, which can be considered a provocative act: several islands and sea borders in the region are being disputed between South Korea, Japan, and China.

These geographical areas are of great economic interests because the Sea of Japan and the East China Sea have rich fishing grounds as well as natural gas reserves and valuable minerals. The website set up to inform about the governments' plans and the opposition against it is in Korean, Japanese and English. This suggests that the people want to engage more than only South Koreans but appeals to the international community.

In this single-issue protest, social media was used extensively, and particularly the popular global social networking sites were used actively: NoBaseJeju, on YouTube; No Naval Base on Jeju! and Save Jeju Island 생명평화 강정마을, on Facebook; and Save Jeju Now. on Twitter. The impact of these social media accounts are, however, questionable, and their popularity varied, with 182 followers on the Twitter account, 6,092 'likes' on their Facebook page, 2,960 group members, and their YouTube account having four videos, four subscribers, and 455 views. Accordingly, the visibilities of these platforms were relatively small, and this limited impact implies that even though the Internet and social media are very popular in South Korea, not all civic movements are successful in utilizing them. Nevertheless, the Gangjeong movement stands out as an example among the Candlelight protests and the OhmyNews, of civic engagements in South Korea in which social media has been a key part of the movements' activity.

Internet Regulation and Election Laws

In spite of the above examples of civic engagement in social media, the Korean government has imposed several hindrances to free speech and imposed regulations to curtail the privacy of users in online environments. First, the election laws have been used to restrict free speech is social media, such as the attempt to reduce the freedom of OhmyNews when its live broadcasting of an interview with the politician Roh Moo-hyun, was deemed illegal because the online news site was not considered a news medium by the National Election Committee. The Constitutional Court however later ruled that OhmyNews was a regular news media outlet and therefor decided that the live broadcast was in fact legal (Shin 2005: 44–45).

A second example of the hindrance of free speech in South Korea is the prohibition against the use of pseudonym on social media, which was imposed in 2007. The real-name verification procedure was made mandatory and forced users to sign up with an authentic name and ID in order to use a social media platform. The law against anonymous user-generated content was legitimized by claims that real-name verification reduces anonymous criticism on politicians. As a result of this law, the global social media network and video sharing service YouTube decided to discontinue their Korean language version, even though the international English version of YouTube was still accessible in South Korea. Again, the Constitutional Court ruled the regulation unconstitutional in 2012 (Ramstad 2012).

A third significant incident of restrictions of freedom of speech was when President Park complained about insults and rumours about her on the Internet in 2014, and her complaints resulted in the monitoring of social media. The rumours referred to the before-mentioned event when President Park was accused of being missing for seven hours on the day of the Sewol ferry disaster. The fact that President Park Geun-hye is the daughter of President Park Chung-hee (1962–1979), considered a repressive ruler and dictator, made the situation worse and increased the public's suspicion when prosecutors decided to monitor social media. Even though officials of the most popular social media app in South Korea, Kakao Talk, stated that messages could only be monitored by court order, many Koreans decided to switch to another social media app, mostly to Telegram, located in Germany, having encryption and no servers in South Korea ("South Koreans Boycott" 2014). Shortly after this incident, Kakao Talk introduced an encrypted mode as a strategy to regain legitimacy as a free and unmonitored social media service.

A fourth example illustrating the restrictions on social media in South Korea is the conservative government's arrest of the blogger with the pseudonym Minerva—the goddess of wisdom—in 2009. The blogger Minerva wrote about South Korea's economy and provided advice on how to prepare for the deepening economic crisis (Schwartz 2009). Minerva's predictions about the economy turned out to be quite correct, and his posts therefore attracted hundreds of thousands of page views on Daum's Agora. This subsequently attracted the attention of the South Korean press, who started to speculate about the true identity behind the pseudonym Minerva, which again resulted in even more people reading his posts. Particularly, his post on the planned acquisition of Lehman Brothers holdings by the Korea Development Bank was widely read and was even considered to be a threat to the public interest. This led to his arrest in early January 2009; the prosecutors had obtained the IP address from Daum, and his anonymity no longer protected his freedom of speech. Rather, the blogger Minerva was charged of "spread[ing] a false rumor maliciously intending to damage the public interest" (Schwartz 2009: para. 29) and risked an 18 months jail sentence. He was however found innocent late April 2009.

Last but not least, in preparations for elections, the use of social media was banned from political campaigning by the National Election Commission in fear of overheated campaigns as well as spreading false information about candidates. In 2012, this regulation was discontinued after the Constitutional Court ruled the ban should be lifted ("Twitter Ruled Legal for Election Campaigns" 2012).

In sum, the above discussion demonstrates recent dilemmas in the civic movement's use of social media and how these relate to freedom of speech issues. On the one hand, South Koreans embrace new media technology and engage in protests and public debates about political and social issues. On the other hand, the conditions for freedom of speech are unstable, and occasionally challenged by the authorities due to their need to monitor, regulate, and restrict.

Conclusion

This chapter shows that South Korea, consolidating its democracy and a global front-runner in Internet adoption, has a vibrant scene of social movements. It demonstrates the significant role of the Internet and social media to diffuse information among Koreans that subsequently took to the streets demanding action by the Korean government.

Even though civic movements were already present in South Korea for some time, these were mostly kept alive by older generations. By contrast, younger people were largely disconnected and disinterested from politics before the popularity of social media. Due to the development of social media, youngsters became more engaged in politics and began to express themselves enabled in online communities, and use social media to create communities of special interest around a social issue, or create petitions through posting and motivating people to sign up for the petitions. Even though conservative political forces in South Korea still dislike social movements and its direct impact on policy making is still debated, it appears that social movements have created a solid foundation offline as well as online.

References

Akamai (2014) *Akamai's State of the Internet*. Retrieved from http://www.stateoftheinternet.com/resources-connectivity-2014-q2-state-of-the-internet-report.html

Apple (2014) *Apple Financial Information*. Retrieved from http://investor.apple.com/financials.cfm

Choi, S. and Park, H. W. (2013) "An Exploratory Approach to a Twitter-Based Community Centered on a Political Goal in South Korea: Who Organized It, What They Shared, and How They Acted", *New Media & Society*, 16(1), 129–148. doi:10.1177/1461444813487956

Choi, S.M., Kim, Y., Sung, Y., and Sohn, D. (2011) "Bridging or Bonding?", *Information, Communication & Society*, 14, pp. 107–29 doi:10.1080/13691181003792624

Dalton, R.J. and Ong, N.-N.T. (2005) "Authority Orientations and Democratic Attitudes: A Test of the Hypothesis", *Japanese Journal of Political Science*, 6(2), pp. 211–231. doi:10.1017/S1468109905001842

Dhoedt, S. (2013) *State of Play*. Retrieved from http://watch.stateofplaydoc.com/

Fish, E. (2009) "Is Internet Censorship Compatible with Democracy? Legal Restrictions of Online Speech in South Korea", *Asia-Pacific Journal on Human Rights and the Law*, 10, pp. 43–96 doi:10.1163/138819010X12647506166519

Fukuyama, F. (1996) *Trust: Human Nature and the Reconstitution of Social Order: The Social Virtues and the Creation of Prosperity*, New York: Free Press.

Garner, B. (2009, November 22) "iPhone to Launch in South Korea at End of November", *Apple Insider*. Retrieved from http://appleinsider.com/articles/09/11/22/iphone_to_launch_in_south_korea_at_end_of_november

Gelfand, M. J., Raver, J. L., Nishii, L., Leslie, L. M., Lun, J., Lim, B. C. et al. (2011) "Differences Between Tight and Loose Cultures: A 33-Nation Study", *Science*, 332, pp. 1100–1104. doi:10.1126/science.1197754

Harlan, C. (2012, December 9) "In S. Korea, the Republic of Samsung", *The Washington Post*. Retrieved from http://www.washingtonpost.com/world/in-s-korea-the-republic-of-samsung/2012/12/09/71215420-3de1-11e2-bca3-aadc9b7e29c5_story.html

Heo, J., Oh, J., Subramanian, S.V., Kim, Y., and Kawachi, I. (2014) "Addictive Internet Use among Korean Adolescents: A National Survey", *PLoS ONE*, 9(2), 1–8. doi:10.1371/journal.pone.0087819

Huhh, J.-S. (2008) "Culture and Business of PC Bangs in Korea", *Games and Culture*, 3(1), pp. 26–37. doi:10.1177/1555412007309525

"iPhone Pipe Dreams." (2008, November 3). Retrieved from http://www.koreatimes.co.kr/www/news/tech/2014/10/133_33792.html

Ji, Y. G., Hwangbo, H., Yi, J. S., Rau, P.L.P., Fang, X., and Ling, C. (2010) "The Influence of Cultural Differences on the Use of Social Network Services and the Formation of Social Capital", *International Journal of Human-Computer Interaction*, 26(11/12), pp. 1100–1121. doi:10.1080/10447318.2010.516727

Kern, T. and Nam, S. (2009) "The Making of a Social Movement Citizen Journalism in South Korea", *Current Sociology*, 57(5), 637–660. Retrieved from http://doi.org/10.1177/0011392109337649

Kim, C., Tao, W., Shin, N., and Kim, K.-S. (2010) "An Empirical Study of Customers' Perceptions of Security and Trust in E-payment Systems", *Electronic Commerce Research and Applications*, 9(1), pp. 84–95. doi:10.1016/j.elerap.2009.04.014

Kim, E. (2012, January 10) "Widening Bribery Scandal engulfs Political Parties before Polls", *Yonhap News*. Retrieved from http://english.yonhapnews.co.kr/national/2012/01/10/37/0301000000AE N20120110004900315F.HTML

Kim, E.-G. and Hamilton, J. W. (2006) "Capitulation to Capital? OhmyNews as Alternative Media", *Media, Culture & Society*, 28(4), 541–560. doi:10.1177/0163443706065028

Kim, J-Y, (2005) "Bowling Together" Isn't a Cure-All: The Relationship between Social Capital and Political Trust in South Korea", *International Political Science Review*, 26, pp. 193–213. doi:10.1177/0192512105050381

Klug, B. F. (2014, October 8) "Japanese Paper: Reporter Indicted in South Korea", *BusinessWeek*. Retrieved from http://www.businessweek.com/ap/2014-10-08/japanese-paper-reporter-indicted-in-south-korea

Kluver, R. and Banerjee, I. (2005) "The Internet in Nine Asian Nations", *Information, Communication & Society*, 8, pp. 30–46. doi:10.1080/13691180500066847

"Koreans Give Up Their Gold to Help Their Country" (1998, January 14) *BBC*. Retrieved from http://news.bbc.co.uk/2/hi/world/analysis/47496.stm

KT (2014) *KT Summary Balance Sheet—Global No.1 KT*. Retrieved from http://www.kt.com/eng/ir/ finance_01.jsp

LG (2014) *LG 2013 Final Consolidated Interim Financial Statements*. Retrieved from http://www.lg. com/global/investor-relations/reports/financial-statements

"Naver to Shut Down Me2Day Next Year" (2013) *Telecompaper*. Retrieved from http://www.telecom paper.com/news/naver-to-shut-down-me2day-next-year--977842

"Now or Naver" (2014, March) *The Economist*. Retrieved from http://www.economist.com/news/ business/21597937-home-south-koreas-biggest-web-portal-has-thrashed-yahoo-and-kept-google-bay-now-its

OECD (2010) *News in the Internet Age New Trends in News Publishing*", Paris: OECD Publishing. Retrieved from http://dx.doi.org/10.1787/9789264088702-en

OECD (2014) *Gross Domestic Product (GDP)*, Paris: OECD Publishing. Retrieved from http://dx.doi. org/10.1787/dc2f7aec-en

Park, S. J. and Park, H. W. (2013) "Mapping Citizen Journalism in South Korea", *Interconnections: Exploring Relationships through Networks and Hyperlinks*. Retrieved from http://cajs.tsukuba.ac.jp/ monograph/articles/05_201303/ CAJS_Monograph_No5.pdf#page=58

Park, S. J., Lim, Y. S., Sams, S., Nam, S. M., and Park, H. W. (2011) "Networked Politics on Cyworld: The text and sentiment of Korean political profiles", *Social Science Computer Review*, 29(3), pp. 288–299.

Ramstad, E. (2012, August 24) "South Korea Court Knocks Down Online Real-Name Rule", *Wall Street Journal*. Retrieved from http://online.wsj.com/news/articles/SB100008723963904440829045 77606794167615620

Samsung (2014) *2013 Samsung Electronics Annual Report*, Seoul, South Korea: Samsung. Retrieved from http://www.samsung.com/us/aboutsamsung/investor_relations/ financial_information/ annual_ reports.html

Sang-hun, C. (2009, December 30) "Korean Leader Pardons Samsung's Ex-Chairman", *The New York Times*. Retrieved from http://www.nytimes.com/2009/12/30/business/global/30samsung.html

Schwartz, M. (2009) "The Troubles of Korea's Influential Economic Pundit", *WIRED*. Retrieved from http://www.wired.com/2009/10/mf_minerva/all/

Seo, Y. (2013) "Electronic Sports: A New Marketing Landscape of the Experience Economy", *Journal of Marketing Management*, 29(13–14), pp. 1542–1560. doi:10.1080/0267257X.2013.822906

Seongyi, Y. and Woo-Young, C. (2011) "Political Participation of Teenagers in the Information Era", *Social Science Computer Review*, 29(2), pp. 242–249. doi:10.1177/0894439310363255

Shin, E. H. (2005) "Presidential Elections, Internet Politics, and Citizens' Organizations in South Korea", *Development and Society*, 1(34), 25–47.

Shin, G.-W. and Izatt, H. J. (2011) "Anti-American and Anti-Alliance Sentiments in South Korea", *Asian Survey*, 51(6), 1113–1133. doi:10.1525/as.2011.51.6.1113

Shirky, C. (2011) "The Political Power of Social Media—Technology, the Public Sphere, and Political Change", *Foreign Affairs*, 90, pp. 28–39.

SK (2014) *SK Financial Information*. Retrieved from http://www.sk.com/Corporation/Finance

"South Koreans Boycott Kakao Talk Social Media Service after President's Rumour Complaints" (2014, October 6). *South China Morning Post*. Retrieved from http://www.scmp.com/news/asia/article/1610202/south-koreans-boycott-kakao-talk-social-media-service-after-presidents

Sunstein, C. (2009). *Republic.com 2.0*. Princeton, NJ: Princeton University Press.

Tay, D. (2014, October 1) "Daum and Kakao Merge, Massive Valuation Puts Them Head-to-Head with Naver-Line", *Tech in Asia*. Retrieved from http://www.techinasia.com/daumkakao-merges-massive-valuation/

"Twitter Ruled Legal for Election Campaigns" (2012, December 30) *The Chosun Ilbo (English Edition): Daily News from Korea*. Retrieved from http://english.chosun.com/site/data/html_dir/2011/12/30/2011123001539.html

United Nations (2014) *World Statistics Pocketbook. 2014 edition*, New York: United Nations. Retrieved from http://unstats.un.org/unsd/pocketbook/

Welzel, C. (2011) "The Asian Values Thesis Revisited: Evidence from the World Values Surveys", *Japanese Journal of Political Science*, 12(1), pp. 1–31. doi:10.1017/S1468109910000277

Worldbank (2014). *World Development Indicators*. Retrieved from http://databank.worldbank.org/data/views/reports/tableview.aspx

You, K. H., Lee, M., and Oh, S. (2014) "Exploring the Relationship Between Online Comments Usage and Civic Engagement in South Korea", *Asia-Pacific Social Science Review*, 14(1). Retrieved from http://www.ejournals.ph/index.php?journal=dlsu-apssr&page=article&op=view&path%5B%5D=7650

Zakaria, F. (1994, April) "A Conversation with Lee Kuan Yew", *Foreign Affairs* (1994, March/April). Retrieved from http://www.foreignaffairs.com/articles/49691/fareed-zakaria/a-conversation-with-lee-kuan-yew

21

NATIONALIST AND ANTI-FASCIST MOVEMENTS IN SOCIAL MEDIA

Christina Neumayer

Introduction

There is a rich body of research on the interaction of social media and political move-ments across the world—examples include student protests, the Arab Spring, and the Occupy movement (Bruns et al. 2013; Castells 2012; Dahlgren 2013). Most of these studies focus on the radical Left and popular movements, the emancipative potential of social media, and activists' social media strategies and tactics. However, nationalist and right-wing movements on social media are usually discussed as a separate entity or subcategory of alternative discourse on the Web (Atton 2006; Cammaerts 2009; Wojcieszak 2010), not taking into account the similarities of their tactics. Although some argue the necessity of including groups with nationalist and racist values in the study of alternative media and counterpublics (Atton 2004; Brouwer 2006; Warner 2002), there have been few attempts to understand how this might be done.

This chapter is based on an analysis of social media communication during national-ist and anti-fascist protests in Germany. It seeks to understand how the antagonistic relationship between fascist and anti-fascist movements is expressed in social media. The chapter outlines the case, introduces an analytical framework, highlights similari-ties between the social media tactics of the two oppositional political positions, and argues that these similarities are important for understanding the antagonism of nation-alist and anti-fascist activists in social media.

Counterpublics, Antagonism, and Social Media

Conceptualising both nationalist and anti-fascist movements as counterpublics (Brou-wer 2006; Fraser 1990; Negt and Kluge 1972; Warner 2002) has the advantage of reflecting the relational perspective present in social media use. This relational compo-nent is apparent not only in the self-representation and interaction of nationalist and anti-fascist activists in social media but also in the larger media ecology within which social media are embedded. The relationship to mass media is relevant for the margin-alised, oppressed, and oppositional self-representation in social media experienced by both sides. Long before the age of social media, Habermas (1962) criticised commer-cial influence on media institutions, which prevents the public sphere from its ideal realisation. One threat of commercialisation is that the media, which should inform citizens so that they can engage in informed discussion, focus on advertising and consumer values, privileging consumption over political action on the part of the citizen. Similar criticism of how commercialisation restricts political engagement is raised in relation to social media (Fuchs 2011; Scholz 2008).

The concept of 'counterpublics' is based on the idea of unbalanced power relations in mass culture (Warner 2002). Counterpublics challenge these power relations, making marginalised and critical voices heard. Conceptually speaking, a public becomes a counterpublic on account of its resistance to domination. The counterpublics in the present study are in line with 'subaltern publics' (Fraser 1990) or counterpublics (Brouwer 2006; Warner 2002) that emphasise oppositional interpretations of identities, interests, and needs among members of subordinated groups. The counterpublics dealt with in this chapter, then, include subaltern publics representing the interests of the political left as well as publics that are antidemocratic, anti-egalitarian, and exclusive but help "expand the discursive space" (Fraser 1990: 124). Oppositionality in a counterpublic is "a position of rejection, resistance, or dissent" and emerges when "social actors perceive themselves to be excluded from or marginalized within mainstream or dominant publics and communicate about that marginality or exclusion" (Brouwer 2006: 197). The identity construction of neo-fascist movements, skinheads, and other antidemocratic groups as marginalised and negatively presented takes place in a similar manner (Hunt et al. 1994: 185) as for anti-fascist and anarchist movements.

Relatively unregulated (apart from corporate players), social media offer a wide range of opportunities for activists to negotiate and maintain meaning by turning them into publics of produsage (Bruns 2007). Many activists today have their own arsenal of social media platforms, facilitating the possibility of engaging a wide range of heterogeneous networked individuals (Svensson et al. 2015). Using social media, different political positions and forms of communication are articulated simultaneously. Due to their relationality, the oppositional and marginalised nature of counterpublics is conditioned by the social media ecology, including relationships between various independent, commercial, and public media. Social media enable not only carefully planned self-representation through blogs, Facebook pages, YouTube videos, and Twitter feeds but also messy and unpredictable communication via Facebook comments, tweets, comment boards, and YouTube videos recorded on mobile phones during protests.

Methodological Approaches and Empirical Material

This study draws on a data set composed by online communication concerning three interrelated events: (1) Two nationalist demonstrations in Dresden on 13 and 19 February 2011, accompanied by large counter-protests, with around 20,000 participating anti-fascists, members of NGOs and civil society, who sought to block the neo-Nazi march, and (2) a nationalist demonstration carried out in Leipzig in preparation for the above events, accompanied by blockades and counter-protests organised by a civil society network and anti-fascist activists. Since 2009, Dresden, the capital of Saxony, has become important to the political, legal, and social discussion surrounding neo-Nazi marches. The nationalist demonstration took place for the third time on 13 February, a memorial day for the World War II bombing of Dresden, used by nationalist groups for historical revisionism and victimisation of Germany. The events received attention from the news media and alternative media and were a trending topic on Twitter.

Table 21.1 Fascists and Anti-Fascists' Marginalisation and Oppositionality

	Oppositional to	Dominated by	Addressee	Form of communication	Platforms
Nation-alists	Democrats, anti-fascists, Left	Democracy, anti-fascists, mass media, police	Public, other nationalists, anti-fascists, mass media	Self-representation, confrontation, discussion, comment	YouTube, Facebook, Twitter, blog
Anti-fascists	Nationalists, fascists, state	Fascists, mass media, police	Public, other anti-fascists, nationalists, mass media	Self-representation, confrontation, discussion, comment	YouTube, Facebook, Twitter, blog

The data set used in this study includes various online communication forms retrieved before, during, and after the anti-fascist protests against the nationalist demonstration. The data set is a selected part of a larger empirical material of communication concerning anti-fascist protests in Leipzig in 2010 and Dresden in 2011, composed of the following: Twitter (6,262 tweets), Facebook (7 groups/events), YouTube (45 videos, 9,820 comments), online news articles (1,140 articles, 4,121 comments), and 14 blogs and websites. The data were exported into a spreadsheet separating the units of text by variables such as date, author, comment, and addressee (if applicable), supported by a script developed for this purpose. Video data were imported into the qualitative analysis software TAMS analyser (see Neumayer 2013: 45–56). Additionally, analysis was informed by memos written by the author concerning informal interviews and observations during the events. Speech acts on various online media platforms served as an archive from which the author sampled and analysed until the point of saturation (Charmaz 2006) to identify similarities and patterns. The author translated speech acts into English from their German originals. To protect the original authors' comments, posts, and tweets, we do not provide further details on user accounts, and their texts are made untraceable by translating them. The analysis is structured in accordance with various expressions of oppositionality and marginalisation, as shown in Table 21.1.

The dominators can be summarised as the antagonistic other (fascists vs. anti-fascists), authority and the state (police, justice, state), and the mainstream media. In the following, I discuss how oppositionality to each of these dominators is expressed in social media.

Resisting the Antagonistic Other

The antagonistic relationship between the nationalist groups and anti-fascists is historically grounded. This constellation is unlikely to ever turn into agonism (Mouffe 2005), where different political positions are respectfully discussed with the other side. The antagonistic other is often portrayed as a dominant oppressor that must be resisted.

According to both sides in the conflict, social media (in contrast to mass media) provide an apparently open space in which these marginalised positions can be openly expressed. Similarly, Cammaerts (2009) in a study of Belgian extreme-right discourse identifies a double standard: hate speech and expression of extreme political opinion in blogs and forums claiming freedom of speech as well as demanding censorship of mainstream media and journalists who do not share their opinion. Although we usually discuss these attributes in relation to freedom of expression for the political Left, this idea is evident in the self-representation of oppositional groups on both ends of the political spectrum.

The nationalist groups in particular ground their marginalisation historically by using a rhetoric of victimisation, including elements of nationalist propaganda from World War II Germany (Braunthal 2009). This idea of victimisation is expressed in different forms in publicly available social media. The threshold of acceptability in public discourse decreases in circumstances that suggest intimacy and security. Facebook groups, for example, provide a feeling of intimacy and privacy in their apparently closed space. Although any Facebook user can view the comments in a public Facebook group or event, it is considered a place for the like-minded. The language used varies from formal to extremely informal, reflecting the counter-mainstream idea and allowing the expression of marginalised political opinion. Comments in the Facebook event page for the nationalist demonstration in Dresden range from 'despite all those blockades and the agitation against us, we'll show that we can remember the victims of the bomb terror with dignity and respect!!' to 'Damn allies! The war is lost, and those swine bomb us! And we're the war criminals?!? Fuck you! It's a pity we didn't bomb the USA' [Facebook, event page]. The tone clearly indicates a feeling of intimacy and expected support from like-minded Facebook group members. This behaviour supports the idea of echo chambers (Sunstein 2009) and polarisation of similar political opinion. This becomes even more evident in the antagonism carried out in the nationalist and anti-fascist protests as the two ends of the political spectrum collide. Confrontation with the opposing political perspective radicalises one's own political perspective (Wojcieszak 2010).

Despite the apparently unregulated space created by social media, corporate owners do enforce a certain degree of regulation. The nationalist Facebook page concerning the 13 February demonstration had already been removed due to its violation of Facebook's terms of service. Similarly, the blog for the nationalist Right to a Future (*Recht auf Zukunft*) mobilisation was shut down by the authorities due to its violation of German law. In the reactions on other social media platforms, it is clear that the shutting down of the blogs and Facebook pages reinforces the perception that the opposing other has sought to suppress the voice of the nationalist activists, and that the activists must resist domination by 'the democrats'. The effortlessness of creating a new Facebook group nevertheless reinforces the liberating idea of social media. This liberating idea is especially used in the nationalists' representation in opposition to the democrats and the system in general. The nationalist groups claim to represent the opinion of 'the people' rather than the intellectual elite dominated by the 'democrats'. Their enemy is an entire system of oppression, one that produces problems for nationalist Germans, such as immigration—or in their own words, "cultural annihilation by multiculturalism and mass immigration" (Altermedia, 17/10/2010: http://altermedia-deutschland.info/content.php). Despite these anti-democratic values, they argue that social media can allow them to overcome the lack of freedom of speech caused by the mass media and its allies, the anti-fascists.

At the other end of the political spectrum, the radical anti-fascist group Red October (*Roter Oktober*, 17/10/2010: http://1610.blogsport.de/) uses its mobilisation blog not only to attack the neo-Nazis: "The intellectual arsonist is the lovely Christian Democratic Union," a political grouping that includes the German conservative party. The blogs are mainly used for self-representation of the group's actions and ideology. In the mobilisation for the anti-fascist counter-protests, the diversity of groups and political positions becomes clear, with each mobilising on their own blog or website. Nazi-Free Dresden (*Dresden Nazifrei*), for example, addresses a large group across the political spectrum, but there are calls for more radical actions on anti-fascist websites and blogs. Whereas Leipzig Takes a Seat (*Leipzig nimmt Platz*) mobilises for non-violent civil disobedience, Red October calls for radicalised forms of action. Actors include the Church, which calls for symbolic action such as silent vigils against the neo-Nazis. Each of these actors address very different audiences that could not be mobilised with the same arguments or calls for similar actions (e.g. anti-fascist activists versus the Church). In social media, however, they can create their own spaces for addressing certain audiences to mobilise against the neo-Nazis. Due to the common enemy (interview with Mouffe, in Cammaerts and Carpentier 2006), they coalesce into apparent unity in the protest events yet diversify again after the events, creating a variety of blogs and websites.

The antagonistic relationship and the unity formed against the enemy during the events become particularly evident on Twitter. "Anti-fascists Twitter with #L1610! Nazis Twitter with #RaZ10!" (Twitter, 15/10/2010) was announced on Twitter before the day of demonstrations in Leipzig to clearly separate the opposing groups using different hashtags. In all of the demonstrations, the unity formed against the neo-Nazis was channelled into one hashtag representing opposition to the common enemy. This also included people who did not physically participate in the events but who offered tweets of solidarity: "I can't be there today but I'm thinking of you #L1610 please take a seat!" (Twitter, 16/10/2010). Similar posts were present on the Facebook event page of Nazi-Free Dresden. The solidarity tweets can be described using the concept of 'mundane citizenship' (Bakardjieva 2012). Although not physically present, citizens of Dresden/Leipzig could follow the events from a distance by using the Twitter stream, sometimes expressing solidarity with the cause by engaging in the conversation. They consequently expressed their political opinions and sought to be part of the event by supporting the cause in their everyday interactions. Through these interactions they became part of the social media representation of the anti-fascist protests.

Twitter and other social media platforms, such as blogs and Facebook groups, were used not only to follow actions within the groups but also to observe actions of the conflicting party, to monitor its behaviour. The anti-fascists and political Left hold a clear advantage inasmuch as they are usually considered to be early adopters of technology (Croeser 2015: 36) compared to their opponents. The representation of the events on Twitter made the sovereignty of the anti-fascist activists apparent: "#RaZ10 #L1610 they probably need all 35 people in the streets, nobody left for tweeting" (Twitter, 16/10/2010) or "What? A Spelling mistake? [. . .] If Der Führer gets to know . . . LOL #L1610 #RaZ10" (Twitter, 16/10/2010). These tweets make the playful character of Twitter and social media use in general evident. Although clearly conflict-oriented, the tweets use humorous language to create comic relief in the demonstrations.

Awareness of being identified with a certain hashtag and profile and consequently of being observed was used tactically: "Nazis still hallucinating. There has never been a Nazi-rally in [name of location]. Who still believes these idiots?" (Twitter, 16/10/2010).

Compared to Facebook groups, Twitter is sometimes regarded as public, and tweets are usually carefully phrased—often humorous, which is also an attempt to gain publicity. Nevertheless, the publicity of Twitter and the possibility of following and interfering with the hashtag was used tactically to confuse and to plant incorrect information, which raised questions about the credibility of social media. Despite the possibility of everyone contributing to a Twitter hashtag stream, credible and trustworthy information was restricted to certain profiles, such as that of the organiser of the counter-protests: "Please do not believe Nazi-infos. We check all information and publish reliable information here #L1610" (Twitter, 16/10/2010).

The question of credibility becomes even more obvious on platforms that allow for direct interaction between the antagonistic groups. A video taken on a mobile camera displaying a violent attack by nationalist protesters on the Praxis alternative living project during the events in Dresden was published on YouTube. The various political positions represented in the comments are reflected in the users' opinions concerning the video: "What happened before? I read that someone threw firecrackers out of the house" and "Have you seen that a Nazi reposted your video and said that it was leftist anarchists who attacked the Praxis? Can you do something about that?" (comments on YouTube). Although video is one of the most persuasive methods of documenting activities, the credibility of what it documents and what information it deliberately omits is open to question. Questioning authorship and the particular timeframe that was recorded represents one tactic for questioning the credibility of user-generated content. These tactics for changing the facts by altering a video's meaning in accordance to one's political position suggest that user-generated 'news' and 'truth' are not necessarily the same thing—even if such users often claim to be counterparts to the supposedly corrupted mass mediated content.

Many of these tactics can, however, only be identified when taking the larger media ecology into account. The YouTube video about the attack was also discussed on the alternative media platform IndyMedia as a way to identify neo-Nazis involved in the attack: "[User 5]: Minute 2:30 with "Good Night Left Side"-jacket. He also showed up at the gathering at the central station. [photos]" (comment on IndyMedia). This article received the most comments of those published on IndyMedia concerning the events. The aim of the comments is clearly to collectively identify the neo-Nazis who were involved in the attack on the house. As a result, video can be a powerful tool of contestation. This becomes particularly clear in this constellation in which two counterpublics with opposite political positions are in conflict with each other, with each using social media to produce its own interpretation of the same events.

Opposition to Authority and the State

Despite the apparent conflict of neo-Nazis against anti-fascists, both ends of the political spectrum are also in opposition to authority and the state. In social media, this struggle against authority gains expression in the creation of space for alternative political perspectives, open criticism against both the antagonistic other and authority, particularly the police. In relation to this, we can look at the Facebook group with the most members—Nazi-Free Dresden. Some users regard the Facebook page as a less censored alternative to the mobilisation website, which authorities can shut down in response to the anti-fascists' acts of civil disobedience. One of the most-liked comments states: "Are we all criminals? [. . .] Shutting down our website didn't help last year either.

[. . .] Help us prevent this: Civil disobedience is legitimate and not criminal!" [Facebook group, Nazi-Free-Dresden]. The Nazi-Free Dresden website was unavailable on several occasions, prompting numerous comments on the Facebook page, the place where supporters could express their otherwise marginalised opinions and mobilise for civil disobedience.

Nevertheless, core activists from the more radical end of the spectrum are critical of Facebook and Twitter due to their commercial foundations: "#Twitter seems to have disabled many Twitter-clients. Just in time for #19februar. Is this what capitalist democracy looks like? #linke" [Twitter, 19/02/2011]. Consequently, despite the possibility of mobilising a broad alliance against the neo-Nazis, social media also carries disadvantages for groups that radicalise their actions with a further anti-capitalist ideology (Neumayer and Svensson 2014).

The police were also identified as an ally of the opponent, especially by activists whose repertoire includes property damage and violence. Activists are aware of being monitored by the antagonistic other as well as by the police. Consequently, surveillance of anti-fascists who act in civil disobedience is a clear expression of power relations between the legal forces and the political activist groups that wish to express disagreement with the Nazi marches. The publicity produced in social media at once supports the political claims through mobilisation and increases the level of insecurity when acting in civil disobedience. In high-risk situations such as blockades, activists explicitly asked people not to tweet information, but to instead use less traceable communication technologies. Social media are thus suitable for mobilising supporters and showing solidarity, yet their public nature can be counterproductive in acts of civil disobedience (see Mercea 2011; Neumayer and Stald 2014). Power relations between the police and activists are presented as stable and dominating activists' behaviour. Authority and police are thus presented as part of the power that the groups seek to resist, as expressed in social media comments: "German police help fascists" (YouTube, comments section) and "Not unusual alliance: neo-Nazis and police unite to fight democracy #19februar #polizeigewalt" (Twitter, 19/02/2011).

Similar claims are made on the other end of the political spectrum: "Egyptian situations in Dresden—political power and police reach out to criminals" (Fight for an Alley of Truth mobilisation blog; JLO Sachsen 2011). Slogans such as 'Don't leave 13 February to the democrats' appear on the nationalist groups' mobilisation blogs, travel through the social media ecology, and appear in highly symbolic and professional mobilisation videos on YouTube. Although the nationalists call for the use of social media, they claim that the Internet in general is owned by the political Left. They use the term *Weltnetz* instead of 'Internet' to highlight their distance from the ideology of the Internet and their focus on German national identity.

The nationalist mobilisation blog Right to a Future claims that "on 16 October: Demonstrate with us against arbitrary police action and public force!" The crimes of the 'democrats' and the police as well as Right to a Future's own marginalisation due to the dominance of democracy must be resisted to permit a more prosperous future for Germans. The apparent openness of social media nevertheless has its limits: The blog was shut down due to its violation of German law, though only after the events took place. Similarly, other users mark as spam comments with nationalist and racist undertones or that glorify the National Socialist regime. Moderating by peers often has a time delay, and as such is not always carried out immediately. The different forms of censorship and moderation, however, feed the nationalist groups' arguments concerning their marginalised position in relation to authorities that prevent them from their right to free expression.

Countering Mainstream Media

The way the media portray radical groups on both ends of the political spectrum nurtures the groups' portrayals of being marginalised and oppositional. By using the frame of violence to describe the nationalist demonstrations and counter-protests, mainstream media present the alliance of New Right and neo-Nazis as a relatively homogenous group of radicals, extremists, and troublemakers, with little information concerning their actual political cause. Newspaper headlines read as "This Saturday: Are Riots and Chaos Threatening Dresden?" (Fleischer 2011) and "Leipzig's Most Dangerous Demonstration Weekend" (Wittig 2011). Nevertheless, violence and property damage become forms of radicalised action to gain visibility in mass media. This tactic represents an "extreme speech act—a crying out for visibility" (Cammaerts 2012: 112) in the media-saturated environments of the digital age, a reaction to the decreasing newsworthiness of regular protest. For some activist groups, these tactics serve to radicalise their political positions and generate radical identities in their struggles (Juris 2005).

In contrast, making visible the violent actions of the opponent through social media has become a powerful form of resistance for oppositional groups. Mass media often focus on violence and 'dramatize' it to increase newsworthiness (Gusfield 1994: 71; Juris 2005). Similarly, uses of frames of violence to present events triggers the use of social media as a space in which alternative perspectives can be constructed, in particular at the less radical end of the political spectrum, where visibility and traceability in social media platforms does not imply exposure to police surveillance. In contrast, symbolic acts are represented as successful resistance if they reach an adequately high number of participants to support newsworthiness. Emphasis is placed on changing the mainstream news media discourse, especially in relationship to violence: "RT @name: Video about Nazis raid against Praxis [link to YouTube] police only watching #19februar #dresden #nazis" (Twitter, 19/02/2011). The main criticism is that police are observing the events without helping the people who are being attacked. Counterpublics create these alternatives to mass media in order to contest the mainstream discourse. This user-generated video was indeed subsequently taken up by many mainstream media to report on the events, though often in the general context of violent clashes between neo-Nazis and anti-fascist activists.

Social media are used both to correct and to criticise mass media: "Dear Aljazeera, please send us reporters, our media are either censored by the state or pimp their ratings #19februar #policeviolence" (Twitter, 19/02/2011). The marginalised position of the anti-fascist actions is expressed with reference to the powerful mass media's production of a mainstream that is not in the protesters' interests. Social media practices should thus not only be understood with reference to the mobilisation of action frames but also with reference to the production and maintenance of meaning (Benford and Snow 2000: 613), not the least through representation and visibility. Social media—in these events often connected to alternative online media—played a role in providing alternative stories and images to those that emerged in traditional mass media. Examples include YouTube videos documenting police violence or violent action initiated by the neo-Nazis to produce a counter narrative to the violent image of the anti-fascist activists presented by the mainstream media. The main critique is that 'left extremists' are blamed for all violence (even though police use tear gas, pepper spray, and water guns) and that no distinction is made between the two antagonistic groups: "Over 200 participants in the demonstrations injured by the police; neo-Nazi attacks are not prosecuted, and the police only say in their press releases (which are uncritically accepted by the media), that there were 80 injured police officers" (Facebook, Nazi-Free Dresden).

On the other end of the political spectrum, the mass media are presented as powerful actors and allies of the opponents, in this case the anti-fascists. An article on the nationalist alternative media platform Altermedia claims to provide a different perspective on the events and includes accounts of "violent activists breaking through police barricades" to "disturb the stationary demonstration by the political right" (Altermedia, 17/10/2010: http://altermedia-deutschland.info/), burning rubbish bins, and throwing bricks at police. Social media are seen as a space in which to address these issues and to produce an apparently uncensored alternative. Comments to the call for action claim that Twitter, Facebook, and other places for sharing images and videos should be used to give a 'true' impression of the events from the otherwise-marginalised nationalist perspective.

Social media also influence on mass media. This was particularly true for Twitter during these events, as the service offered new ways of organising, coordinating, informing, and producing counter-publicity that subsequently became part of mass media headlines. The mainstream media discourse described use of Twitter in a playful, humorous, and performative manner, excluding actual political statements, which is counterproductive to the activists' aim of producing publicity for a political cause: "February 19 on Twitter: Discontent, a little bit of international standing and Justin Bieber" (DNN online 2011). Journalists also used Twitter as a source concerning the protest events: "RT @name: Was anyone hit by a pepperball? #19februar (I am writing an article about it right now)" (Twitter, 19/02/2011). As a result, social media cannot be considered platforms for either the mainstream or counterpublics but rather serve both—thereby maintaining and disseminating mass-mediated discourse, at the same time providing a platform for the production of alternative, radical discourse.

Conclusion

The idea that social media provide room for counterpublics to express their political opinions, create alternatives, contest the mainstream, and assist in protest events is present at both ends of the political spectrum. The underlying liberating and subversive idea of social media (see Curran et al. 2012; Turner 2006) is also used in the representation of the nationalist groups with reference to the right of free speech for otherwise-marginalised positions. Consequently, nationalist rhetoric and discourse in social media shows similarities to that of their anti-fascist counterparts. Social media used in resistance is thus only partially dependent on a group's political ideology in any absolute sense and has more to do with a group's role as a counterpublic. In other words, an essential factor is a group's political position vis-à-vis other political players, other social and ideological formations, and the mainstream discourse.

The tone used to express oppositionality and the awareness of the publicity and traceability of social media differs according to the level of intimacy social media suggest. Facebook groups suggest a high level of intimacy with like-minded peers to support one's own political position (Wojcieszak 2010). Informal and radicalised comments are openly posted within this apparently like-minded group. Similarly, informal comments can be found in the YouTube comments sections, often as ongoing discussions between two or more participants, again highlighting their intimate character. In comments sections, however, antagonistic political positions collide so that peer censorship, by marking comments as spam, occurs. The YouTube videos themselves range from user-generated documentation of police violence to professionally produced and highly symbolic mobilisation videos that become part of the public representation of the groups, linked to their blogs. Like the blogs, the mobilisation videos address different actors across the political spectrum, calling for different actions—something that becomes particularly clear during the counter protests. Different social media call for actions against the neo-Nazis using different levels of radicalisation, creating a mosaic of mobilisation calls against the common enemy.

Social media can potentially facilitate the production of visibility, which can be counterproductive. For example, the traceability and publicity of in-group discussion means that various speech acts become a visible part of the counterpublics' appearance. This traceability can be used strategically for counter-publicity but can also be counterproductive due to the risk of surveillance by potentially hostile authorities. Activists who use radicalised forms of expression are aware of these risks and are sometimes also critical of the commercial ownership of social media. Social media can thus be appropriated by activists at either end of the political spectrum yet simultaneously support existing power relations and hierarchies (see Feenberg 2010).

To understand the social media practices of groups that identify themselves as oppositional and marginalised, one must consider the media ecology that activists navigate and their power relations with other political players and the mass media. Although there are many differences between groups at the two ends of the political spectrum on account of their divergent values, they nevertheless use similar tactics and media practices on account of their common position as counterpublics and their resultant oppositionality to the prevailing system. The two radical ends of the political spectrum do not, however, agree as to the identity of the mainstream itself. Their subordinate status relative to the dominant public is, according to Warner, expressed through a "hierarchy of the media," including "speech genres" (Warner 2002: 119).

The counterpublics focused on in this study not only transcend rational-critical debate but also are also publics of conflict and confrontation, forming alliances and contesting the mainstream in a dialectical relationship. To a degree, the radical counterpublics adapt due to their contrasting political values, yet their social media practices are highly dependent on their positions as counterpublics, i.e. as marginalised, excluded, and underrepresented—as oppositional to the mainstream.

References

Atton, C. (2004) An Alternative Internet, Edinburgh: Edinburgh University Press.
—— (2006) "Far-right Media on the Internet: Culture, Discourse and Power," New Media & Society 8(4), pp. 573–587.
Bakardjieva, M. (2012) "Mundane Citizenship: New Media and Civil Society in Bulgaria," Europe-Asia Studies 64(8), pp. 1356–1374.
Benford, R. D., and Snow, D. A. (2000) "Framing Processes and Social Movements: An Overview and Assessment," Annual Review of Sociology 26(1), pp. 611–639.
Braunthal, G. (2009) Right-wing Extremism in Contemporary Germany, New York: Palgrave Macmillan.
Brouwer, D. C. (2006) "Communication as Counterpublic," in G. J. Shepherd, J. S. John, and T. Striphas (eds.), Communication as . . . Perspectives on Theory, London: Sage, pp. 195–208.

305

Bruns, A. (2007) "Produsage: A Working Definition," *Produsage.org*, URL http://produsage.org/node/9

Bruns, A., Highfield, T., and Burgess, J. (2013) "The Arab Spring and Social Media Audiences: English and Arabic Twitter Users and Their Networks," *American Behavioral Scientist* 57(7), pp. 871–898.

Cammaerts, B. (2009) "Radical Pluralism and Free Speech in Online Public Spaces: The CFase of North Belgian Extreme Right Discourses," *International Journal of Cultural Studies* 12(6), pp. 555–575.

—— (2012) "Protest logics and the mediation opportunity structure," *European Journal of Communication* 27(2), pp. 117–134.

Carpentier, N., and Cammaerts, B. (2006) "Hegemony, Democracy, Agonism and Journalism: An Interview with Chantal Mouffe" *Journalism Studies* 7(6), pp. 964–975.

Castells, M. (2012) *Networks of Outrage and Hope: Social Movements in the Internet Age*, Cambridge: Polity Press.

Charmaz, K. (2006) *Constructing Grounded Theory: A Practical Guide through Qualitative Analysis*, London: Sage.

Croeser, S. (2015) *Global Justice and the Politics of Information: The Struggle over Knowledge*, New York: Routledge.

Curran, J., Fenton, N., and Freedman, D. (2012) *Misunderstanding the Internet, Communication and Society*, London: Routledge.

Dahlgren, P. (2013) *The Political Web: Online Civic Cultures and Participation*, New York: Palgrave Macmillan.

DNN online. (2011) "Der 19. Februar bei Twitter: Unmut, ein wenig Weltgeltung und Justin Biber." http://www.dnn-online.de/dresden/web/dresden-nachrichten/detail/-/specific/Der-19-Februar-bei-Twitter-Unmut-ein-wenig-Weltgeltung-und-Justin-Biber-4291119670

Feenberg, A. (2010) *Between Reason and Experience: Essays in Technology and Modernity*, Cambridge: MIT Press.

Fleischer, N. (2011) "Droht Dresden jetzt das Krawall-Chaos?" http://www.bild.de/regional/dresden/neofaschismus/droht-dresden-jetzt-das-krawall-chaos-15979682.bild.html

Fraser, N. (1990) "Rethinking the Public Sphere: A Contribution to the Critique of Actually Existing Democracy," *Social Text* 25/26, pp. 56–80.

Fuchs, C. (2011) "Web 2.0, Prosumption, and Surveillance," *Surveillance & Society* 8(3), pp. 288–309.

Gusfield, J. R. (1994) "Reflexivity of Social Movements," in H. Johnston, E. Larana, and J. R. Gusfield (eds.), *New Social Movements: From Ideology to Identity*, Philadelphia: Temple University Press, pp. 58–78.

Habermas, J. (1962) *Strukturwandel der Öffentlichkeit. Untersuchungen zu einer Kategorie der bürgerlichen Gesellschaft*, 1990 ed., Frankfurt am Main: Suhrkamp.

Hunt, S. A., Benford, R. D., and Snow, D. A. (1994) "Identity Fields: Framing Process and the Construction of Movement Identities," in E. Larana, H. Johnston, J. Gusfield (eds.) *New Social Movements: From Ideology to Identity*, Philadelphia: Temple University Press, pp. 185–208.

JLO Sachsen. (2011) "Ägyptische Verhältnisse in Dresden – Politische Machthaber und Polizei Hand in Hand mit Kriminellen!" http://www.jlosachsen.de/

Juris, J. S. (2005) "Violence Performed and Imagined: Militant Action, the Black Bloc and the Mass Media in Genoa," *Critique of Anthropology* 25(4), pp. 413–432.

Mercea, D. (2011) "Digital Prefigurative Participation: The Entwinement of Online Communication and Offline Participation in Protest Events," *New Media & Society* 14(1), pp. 153–169.

Mouffe, C. (2005) *The Return of the Political*, London: Verso.

Negt, O., and Kluge, A. (1972) *Öffentlichkeit und Erfahrung: Zur Organisationsanalyse von bürgerlicher und proletarischer Öffentlichkeit*, Frankfurt am Main: Suhrkamp.

Neumayer, C. (2013) *When Neo-Nazis March and Anti-Fascists Demonstrate: Protean Counterpublics in the Digital Age*, doctoral thesis, Copenhagen: IT University of Copenhagen.

Neumayer, C., and Stald, G. (2014) "The Mobile Phone in Street Protest: Texting, Tweeting, Tracking, and Tracing," *Mobile Media & Communication* 2(2), pp. 117–133.

Neumayer, C., and Svensson, J. (2014) "Activism and Radical Politics in the Digital Age: Towards a Typology," *Convergence: The International Journal of Research into New Media Technologies*, online before print, pp. 1–16. doi:10.1177/1354856514553395

Scholz, T. (2008) "Market Ideology and the Myths of Web 2.0," *First Monday* 13(3), http://firstmonday.org/article/view/2138/1945

Sunstein, C. R. (2009) *Republic.com 2.0*, Princeton: Princeton University Press.

Svensson, J., Neumayer, C., Banfield-Mumb, A., and Schossböck, J. (2015) "Identity Negotiation in Activist Participation Online," *Communication, Culture & Critique* 8(1), pp. 144–162.

Turner, F. (2006) *From Counterculture to Cyberculture: Stewart Brand, the Whole Earth Network, and the Rise of Digital Utopianism*, Chicago: The University of Chicago Press.

Warner, M. (2002) *Publics and Counterpublics*, New York: Zone Books.

Wittig, A. (2011). "Leipzigs gefährlichstes Demo-Wochenende. http://www.bild.de/regional/leipzig/dereinsatz-plan-des-polizei-chefs-14309010.bild.html

Wojcieszak, M. (2010) "'Don't Talk to Me': Effects of Ideologically Homogeneous Online Groups and Politically Dissimilar Offline Ties on Extremism," *New Media & Society* 12(4), pp. 637–655.

Part III

POLITICAL CAMPAIGNS

22

FROM EMERGING TO ESTABLISHED?

A Comparison of Twitter Use during Swedish Election Campaigns in 2010 and 2014

Anders Olof Larsson and Hallvard Moe

Introduction

Much as with the Internet during the 1990s, it is often suggested that social media services such as Twitter provide novel arenas for communication about political issues, in addition to contact between citizens and politicians (e.g. Chadwick, 2008). Indeed, a great deal of scholarship has examined the supposed parliamentary-political potentials of Twitter, and most research has been fashioned as single country or election case studies. While these foci can certainly provide the level of in-depth results necessary to grasp the initial tendencies of the adoption new media platforms, the need for comparative work across political elections is apparent (e.g. Bruns and Stieglitz, 2012).

This chapter presents a study gauging developments in political Twitter use during two Swedish parliamentary elections—2010 and 2014. Results from the Swedish context allow us to study these developments in what could be labelled a democratically advanced setting, given high levels of Internet use and voter attendance. Arguably, such an empirical setting could be interesting with regards to seeing early changes in user patterns (Rogers, 2003). Specifically, our interest lies in studying processes of the 'not-so-new' phenomenon of social media in an electoral context, that is to study to what extent the use of Twitter moves from being a novelty to become a staple of political communication.

Our analysis is based on tweets including the most prolific hashtags for each of the two (2010 and 2014) elections. The featured approach builds on the study of several recent election campaigns in Scandinavia (see Larsson and Moe, 2012, 2013; Moe and Larsson, 2012). Our basic assumption is that during the period of study, Twitter went from creating 'buzz' as a novel channel in 2010 to becoming something of a staple of

5

political campaigning by 2014, with more established patterns of use—more mature, more everyday, perhaps even mundane—amongst politicians, campaigners, activists and for politically-inclined citizens.

We call this assumed evolution a move from *emerging* to *established*. To define what we mean by these terms, we introduce a conceptual analytical frame that compares five criteria which point to different aspects of political Twitter use. In addition to improving our understanding of the changing patterns of Twitter use for political communication, the chapter suggests a framework for diachronic comparisons of uses of specific media services or online communication platforms.

A Framework for Studying Developments in Twitter Use

Various online platforms and services rise and fall rapidly. As a result, the Internet has interested researchers for more than two decades—a fascination that has resulted in a plethora of different approaches to the study of online political communication. More generally, understanding and modelling the developments of a medium is a key exercise in media and communication studies. Indeed, Rogers's (2003) classic study of the diffusion of innovations has triggered a wide variety of analyses of the spreading of different media (e.g. Nam and Barnett, 2010) similar to the one undertaken here.

Within media history, we can distinguish between three different analytical scales corresponding to macro-, meso- and micro-historical perspectives (following Drotner 2011, 119). The first, represented by such diverse contributions as McLuhan (e.g. 1965) or Habermas's (1962 [1990]) early work on the public sphere, is interested in the overall relations between the media and society over long stretches of time. Staying at the institutional or sender-side, a meso-historical approach typically zooms in on one medium during a particular period of change, an example being Eisenstein's 1979 book on the printing press (Drotner 2011, 125). With a micro-perspective, studies have tended to zoom in further on one media institution, one program format, or the use practices of one particular group over a short time span.

While the approach developed for the present study does not make claims at media history, Drotner's categorisation is helpful to situate our interest. We focus on how one particular media service—Twitter—as represented by those who use it for political communication, changes over a relatively short period of time. As such, our approach rests somewhere between the analytical scale of a meso- and a micro-historical approach as we seek to test our assumption that the use of Twitter in Swedish politics changed from emerging to established between the election campaigns in 2010 and 2014.

To operationalise the assumed change, we identify five criteria: (1) volume of tweets and users, (2) degree of dependence on mainstream media, (3) relations between most and least active users, (4) use of Twitter's dialogic modes of address (@replies) and redistribution (retweets) among the most prolific users, in addition to (5) the ability for non-elite users to make an impact. In what follows, we describe these criteria and how they help us test and define the assumed move from emerging to established.

Volume of Tweets and Users

While Twitter is currently among the more well-known social media services available, adoption rates are not as high as one might expect. Indeed, figures indicate that in 2010 between 1 and 8 per cent of Swedish Internet users were making some sort of use of Twitter (Larsson and Moe, 2012). More recent studies suggest that about 2 per cent of the Swedish population maintain some form of activity on Twitter, with type and frequency of activity varying considerably (Brynolf, 2013). Thus, while 90 per cent of Swedes have access to the Internet at home (Carlsson and Facht, 2014), Twitter use must be regarded as somewhat low.

As such, while a general increase of user base as well as usage might be expected, we should be careful not to overestimate the spread of Twitter use. For example, a study on Twitter use during two Norwegian elections—the 2011 regional and 2013 national elections—found the number of tweets with election hashtags to have doubled in the month-long period leading up to the latter of these two compared to the first (Larsson and Moe, 2014). While these elections differed in terms of size and scope, and are not directly comparable with our current cases, the Norwegian context can serve as an example of these developments.

In an operationalised sense, then, a first, basic criteria of a move from emerging to established would be changes in the numbers of users and tweets for the particular case under study, from one election to the next. An increase in each of these numbers would indicate a development towards established uses.

Dependence on Mainstream Media

Research has suggested that much political Internet use in general (Lilleker and Jackson, 2010), as well as social media use, tends to follow events covered in the mainstream media—especially towards the end of election periods (e.g. Larsson and Moe, 2013). Such findings are complemented by a more specific claim made by Jungherr (2014) who, in his study of the 2009 German federal elections found that Twitter usage levels increased especially during "media events that allowed for the public discussion and negotiation" (Jungherr, 2014, 247), such as televised political debates. While it is difficult to precisely detail what would indicate an independent 'Twitter agenda' as opposed to an agenda dictated by established media outlets, we nevertheless seek to make inroads by tracing upsurges in Twitter use in relation to election-related media events. The second criteria, then, is dependence on, or reactive use in relation to, mainstream media. While the research discussed above suggests that more often than not, mainstream media outlets appear to have clear influences on hashtagged Twitter activity, we might also find reverse or mixed tendencies in our data (e.g. Wallsten, 2007).

Relations between Active and Less Active Users

Given certain technical and editorial obstacles, partaking in mediated political discussions has traditionally been subject to judgments made by gatekeepers. The Internet supposedly makes it easier for groups hitherto unengaged in political debates to take part to higher extents. The result should be participation from a greater number of people, and a more even distribution between active users and the rest.

Inspired by Nielsen (2006), we test this empirically by comparing the distributions of tweets sent by all users for both elections and divide them into three groups based on frequency of activity (lead users, highly active and least active users). This does not allow us to track whether or not specific citizens change from disengagement to engagement over time. Still, on a general level, if we look at these relations over time, we should expect a trend towards more evenly distributed patterns as Twitter goes from being the arena of a relatively few techno-savvy early adopters to becoming more widely used among a more diverse group.

As such, this third criterion considers user patterns between very active and less active users. A tendency towards more evenly distributed patterns would signal a move towards established use.

Use of Redistributional Modes of Communication

The fourth criterion considers the uses of retweets (the redistribution of a tweet sent by some other user). Focusing on the very top users, we obtain information from their public profile pages on Twitter to see what types of users appear to enjoy higher levels of popularity in this regard—and what types of users are more frequent in redistributing. While we assume that, given their role in public life, politicians, journalists, and other societal elites might enjoy such leverage to larger degrees than average citizens, we might also see some developments regarding these uses from one election to another (see Larsson and Moe, 2014).

While such a focus on high-end users undoubtedly limits our general explanatory possibilities, top users have been shown to stand for a considerable portion of activity within Twitter (Bastos et al., 2013) and could therefore be seen as especially interesting, "particularly during periods of election campaigns" (Stieglitz and Dang-Xuan, 2012, 2). As previous scholarship has largely shown that societal elites tend to be well-represented amongst high-end users, primarily as being on the receiving end of re tweets, we suspect that such actors—including politicians, journalists and celebrities—will be highly represented.

As for those users who are primarily active as senders of retweets, we suggest that they—conversely to what was discussed above—mostly can be described as 'non-elites'. As comparably low-level politicians (and those supporting them) have been found to be especially active on social media (Larsson and Kalsnes, 2014), we choose to define 'non-elites' rather broadly—in order to also include those political actors who might be somewhat well-known, but who did not, at the time of each election, enjoy incumbency status or hold seats in parliament. As such, we expect that the top senders of retweets will primarily self-identify as what we here understand as 'non-elites' (e.g. anonymous users, citizens, lower-level politicians).

The fourth criterion covers uses of specific modes of communication on Twitter. In line with a rich-get-richer-effect and the normalisation thesis (e.g. Klinger 2013), we assume that elites that dominate offline over time will adopt the modes of communication to dominate the arena of Twitter as well. This would signal a move towards established user patterns.

Ability for Non-Elite Users to Make an Impact

The potential for any user to make an impact also tells us something about the robustness of the Twittersphere. The bigger and deeper the sphere becomes, with more users, more offline celebrities, and more established modes of communication in accordance with the former four criteria, the harder we would expect it to be for a new user, followed by few and sparsely networked, to make an impact in the sense of having their message redistributed via retweets and/or discussed via @replies.

The final criterion, then, has less to do with quantitatively measuring developments than examining significant individual cases of Twitter use where scarcely networked non-elite users managed to gain attention (via retweets) to stand out in the Twittersphere during the election campaign periods. Fewer examples would signal a move towards a more streamlined and established Twitter use.

Data and Method

For both rounds of data collection, we employed what is often referred to as a hashtag-based approach (see Larsson and Moe, 2014), using the YourTwapperKeeper tool to archive the main thematic hashtags for each election. YourTwapperKeeper employs the Twitter stream and search APIs to collect public tweets and corresponding metadata. Data collection was performed in similar ways for both periods, starting one month before each respective election day and terminating three days after that same day on both occasions (for 2010: August 19—September 22, Election day on September 19; for 2014: August 14—September 17, Election day on September 14).

Data analysis was performed using statistical techniques available in Excel and SPSS. Furthermore, Gawk scripts were utilised to control data quality, filter the data sets, and extract information from them (e.g. Bruns, 2011). With regards to the identities of high-end Twitter users, their profile pages were visited and the self-disclosed information provided there was taken into account.

Results and Discussion

Volume of Tweets and Users

First, with regards to our initial assumption regarding increases of tweets sent as well as users involved, Table 22.1 provides descriptive statistics.

While the data presented in Table 22.1 might not be rich in detail, the results must nevertheless be called clear. From 2010 to 2014, the volume of tweets more than doubled, while the increase in users involved proved even larger. More than five times as many individual users chose to tweet with the selected hashtag in 2014 compared to 2010. Thus, this must be described as a definite growth in popularity, perhaps as a result of the general spread of the service among the populace and/or of increased use of hashtags in mainstream media outlets (see, e.g. Halavais, 2014).

While use has indeed increased, some users are more persistent in their tweeting than others. Table 22.2 provides an overview of the most active users of Twitter, in terms of sending undirected Twitter messages during both periods under study.

Table 22.2 seems to suggest a dominance of journalists and media organisations for both years, with individual journalist making a clearer mark on the 2010 distributions. Such a shift from accounts operated by individuals to those operated by organisations

Table 22.1 Volumes of Tweets Sent and Users Involved for #val2010 and #val2014

	#val2010	#val2014	Change
N of tweets	99,832	248,091	+ 148,259 (248.5 per cent)
N of users	8,987	48,784	+ 39,797 (542.8 per cent)

Table 22.2 Top Senders of Undirected Twitter Messages in #val2010 and #val2014

#val2010 top undirected senders	N of tweets	Type	#val2014 top undirected senders	N of tweets	Type
all_insane	1,932	Political satire	Denfinarasismen	1,270	Right-wing, anonymous
blogfia	618	Political blogger	niklassvensson	935	Journalist
AnnikaBeijbom	616	Liberal politician	MartinMoberg	680	Social Democrat supporter
Nemokrati	550	Anonymous	LeoBergmanz	475	Social Democrat politician
Pihlblad	544	Journalist	socialdemokrat	445	Social Democrats
Juditburda	392	Conservative politician	svtdinrost	441	PSB election feature
vpressfeldt	352	Student	Nyheterna	409	Commercial news program
MuzafferUnsal	345	Conservative politician	DagensArena	384	Left-progressive online news
mickep2	312	Journalist	AndersWester1	377	Right-wing supporter
skogskant	312	Anonymous	Fnordspotting	368	Political blogger

could be interpreted as a sign of Twitter becoming institutionalised or established: while use of Twitter in 2010 could be described as an individual initiative of media profession-als, the situation four years later sees their respective media houses taking to this service to larger degrees instead.

Political supporters and party accounts of various persuasions are also represented. This tendency is primarily seen for #val2014, where anonymous right-wing supporters emerge as highly active in this regard. Focusing on the most active sender of undirected messages during this latter election, the Twitter handle *denfinarasismen* (Swedish for 'the acceptable racism') would suggest a non-mainstream standpoint on one of the hot topics in current Swedish societal debate: immigration policy (see also Larsson, 2014).

The only official party account found for both elections is @socialdemokrat, oper-ated by the largest opposition party in 2010 and in 2014, the Social Democrats. For the latter election, Social Democrat supporters and individual politicians show up as well, giving merit to the claim that challengers will make use of online media to higher degrees than incumbents (e.g. Graham et al, 2013).

In sum, we find tweet volume as well as user numbers to have risen considerably during the period of study. This would, in isolation, signal a move towards establishing Twitter as a part of the arsenal of online platforms for political communication during election campaigns. Looking at the top senders of undirected messages, though, the impression is of a mixed bag—including anonymous accounts and political supporters— though the apparent development from individual journalist accounts in 2010 to media organisation accounts in 2014 could be taken as a tendency towards more established uses. Similarly, the presence of a party account (@socialdemokrat) could be seen as a sign of the increased perceived importance of Twitter also for firmly established actors—perhaps especially in challenger positions, as was the case for the latter of the two studied elections.

Dependence on Mainstream Media

The influence of mainstream or established media on Twitter can be assessed by study- ing the timelines of Twitter traffic, the idea being that if a media event became popular on the service under study, this would provide a visible upsurge in social media activ- ity during the same timeframe. Figure 22.1 provides such timelines for both elections, effectively allowing us to gauge these influences.

The solid grey line in Figure 22.1 denotes activity for the 2010 hashtag, while the darker dotted line does so for the 2014 events. Accounting for obvious differences with

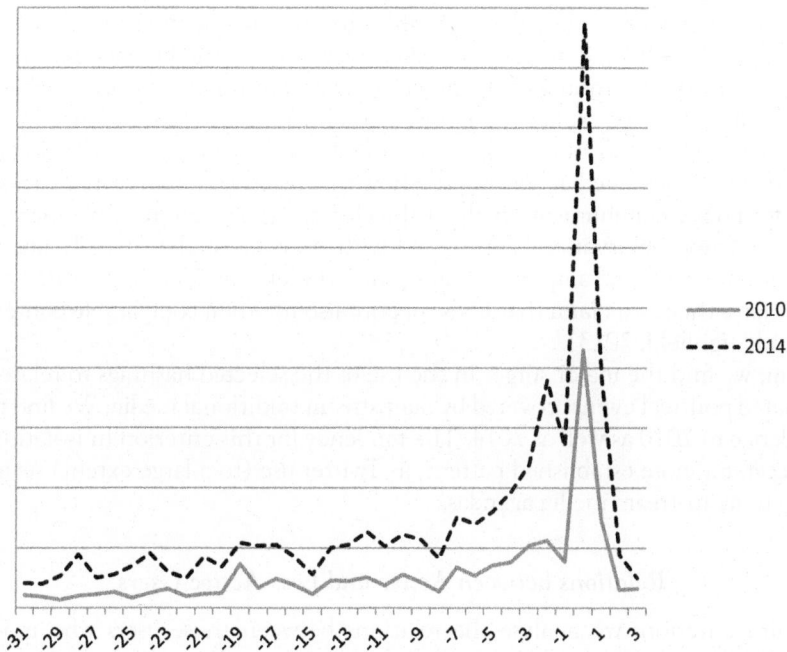

Figure 22.1 Distribution of Tweets over Time, Comparison of #val2010 and #val2014, 31 Days Prior to Election Day to 3 Days after Election Day; 2010 N = 99,311, 2014 N = 248,091

regards to volume of tweets, both timelines reach their highest peak during Election day. While the other peaks as visible in Figure 22.1 must be described as smaller in comparison, they nevertheless result in distinguishing marks for each line. With this in mind, the dependence on established mass media appears to take on similar forms for both elections. Consider the peaks visible in both lines at the -2 mark, indicating two days before the elections. Traditionally, this marks the day when the final debate between the leaders of all parliamentary parties is broadcast on SVT, the main Swedish public service television broadcaster. A significant event in contemporary election campaigns, it makes a clear mark also in Twitter traffic for both campaigns.

Similar tendencies can be discerned also when looking at other peaks visible in Figure 22.1. As an example from 2010, the increase visible at the -19 mark takes place on September 1 and corresponds to a debate between the Social Democrat and Conservative party leaders featured in the *Aktuellt* evening news, broadcast on the previously mentioned SVT network. Here, hashtag users react to and comment on the arguments proposed by the politicians, suggesting largely reflective tendencies. For example, hashtag users quote the party leaders in their tweets, effectively spreading what is said on screen to a potentially new forum. Besides such engagement with the actual content of the debate, comments are also posted regarding the appearances of the politicians, and, from each side of the political fence, who could be said to be the 'winner' of the televised event. For 2014, a similar televised debate involving the leaders of the two main parties appear to cause the upsurge that occurs one week from election day—at the -7 mark in Figure 22.1. Similarly, on the -19 mark, an upsurge in 2014 activity is made by Twitter users commenting on SVT's traditional party leader interview program, on that date with the Swedish Democrats' leader. Messages range from expressions of disappointment with the journalists to attempts at discussing rhetoric, and specific questions directed at the politician. Even though the broadcaster presents its own hashtag at the beginning of the program, at no point in the nearly hour-long segment is Twitter activity explicitly addressed or drawn into the discussion.

Such observations do not speak to the longitudinal flow of issues between social media and traditional media, but they do show that peaks in activity among those using Twitter for public communication about the election stem from reactive use related to television. These observations correspond with previous studies, largely finding that "the Internet reflects and amplifies other events" (Lilleker and Jackson, 2010, 93) rather than initiates them—a claim that finds support also in other, comparable contexts (e.g. Bruns and Highfield, 2013).

In sum, we find the major surges in the use of the selected hashtags to relate closely to mediated political events covered by mainstream traditional media. We find this correspondence in 2010 as well as 2014. The tendency for this criterion in isolation, then, is one *against* a more established pattern, as Twitter use (to a large extent) seems to be reactive to mainstream media agendas.

Relations between Active and Less Active Users

As a third criterion, we analyse the relations between those users who most often tweet employing the selected hashtags, and those who only rarely choose to take part in that manner. The term 'active' is here reserved as a label for the act of tweeting itself. Indeed, while other uses of Twitter, such as reading the messages sent by others, can trigger activities outside the platform (offline conversations or actions, or online communication via other services), this definition and delimitation of active senders allows for a focus on specific roles taken on Twitter. By examining the relations between these user groups, we take one step beyond more general volume measurements, gaining a better understanding regarding different patterns of use.

Figure 22.2 details the relative intensity with which users of the studied hashtags took part in tweeting about each election. Figure 22.2 is inspired by Nielsen's '90–9–1 rule', which suggests that more often than not, online communities can be assumed to be made up of three overarching user groups with regards to each participant's activity in the specified community (Nielsen, 2006). Ninety per cent of users belong to the least active group, contributing rarely, while the upper 10 per cent of users are divided into 9 per cent of highly active and a top 1 per cent of lead users, the latter contributing almost continuously. Figure 22.2, then, shows the result of analyses utilising computer scripts to detail the volume of tweets sent by each identified user group. While the percentages suggested by the 90–9–1 rule should not necessarily be expected to hold true in all empirical settings, this form of user group division can nevertheless be helpful in understanding the development of Twitter use.

Employing the scheme suggested in the legend, we can conclude that hashtagged Twitter activity during the two elections appears to have been dominated by the two more active groups. For both campaigns, a small 1 per cent minority produces 31.3 per cent (2010) and 31.4 per cent (2014) of the total amount of messages. This is not only an enormous volume but also a remarkably stable ratio. The corresponding numbers for the other two user groups show similar stability, though with a slight increase in the part produced by the least active group (from 29.5 per cent to 32.6 per cent).

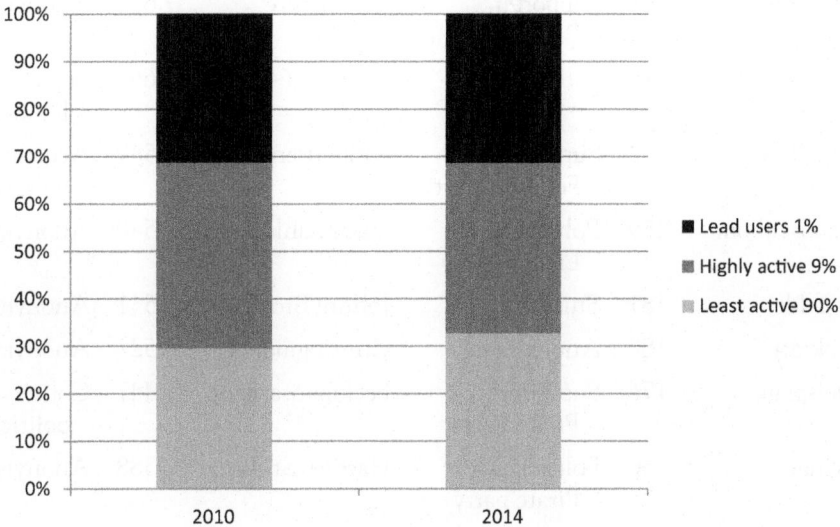

Figure 22.2 Distribution of Activity among Three User Groups (1 per cent lead users, 9 per cent highly active users, and 90 per cent least active users) as Percentages of the Total Number of Tweets Sent; 2010 N = 99,348 Tweets, 9,285 Users: 2014 N = 248,091 Tweets, 48,784 Users

In sum, the distribution of activity between most, less, and least active users remains the same in 2010 and 2014. We assumed that a development towards a more even distribution between the different groups would indicate a more mature or established use, since the dominance of techno-savvy early adopters would be diminished when larger user groups grew accustomed to the norms of the service, employing hashtags more actively. Our findings do not confirm such an assumption: a small group of very active users still make up a third of the Twitter messages for both hashtags, and the presence of a larger group of less active users cannot be found in this analysis. In isolation, then, our analysis on this third proposed measure points *against* a more established pattern of use.

Use of Redistributional Modes of Communication

Criterion four is about redistribution and who the top users who sent and received comparatively greater amounts of retweets are. Table 22.3 deals with the first of these groups.

While the presence of anonymous or non-elite users is felt in 2010, this tendency is enhanced in 2014, when several high end retweeters provide no or only very little information regarding their roles in civil society. As with our previous comparison of top @reply senders, we find some similarities between users and elections: specifically,

Table 22.3 Top Senders of Retweets for #val2010 and #val2014

#val2010 top retweeters	N	Types	#val2014 top retweeters	N	Types
Annoula64	3,969	Supporter, Pirate Party	nyborjaren	7,684	Anonymous
all_insane	1,179	Satirical	Annoula64	667	Supporter, Pirate Party
dreadnallen	302	Supporter, Feminist Party	gotlandsenahand	589	Account removed
AnnikaBeijbom	259	Politician, Liberal party	mattiasahlstrom	540	Anonymous
vpressfeldt	181	Student	JohnnyBrottom9	531	Anonymous
Nemokrati	180	Anonymous	Cruisingman88	522	Anonymous
MrQuispiam	176	Supporter, Pirate Party	beckmansasikter	447	Conservative politician
Falkvinge	150	Politician, Pirate party	Harriet_Sthlm	388	Anonymous
annatroberg	146	Politician, Pirate party	Perkibaby	383	Anonymous
leoerlandsson	145	Supporter, Pirate Party	AnnaEvaL	375	Anonymous

the user @Annoula64, a supporter of the Pirate Party, emerges as energetic in this regard for both hashtags. Beyond the activity undertaken by this user, this type of frequent activity related to the Pirate Party appears to have diminished in the 2014 election, giving room instead to the aforementioned anonymous users, as well as traces of activities undertaken by an established politician—@beckmansasikter, a parliamentary representative from the conservative party.

Table 22.4 provides an overview of those users who received the most attention in this regard within both hashtags.

Amongst the users receiving frequent retweets, we clearly see how the dominance of journalists and Pirate Party associates in 2010 appears to have been broken in the period leading up to the 2014 elections. Indeed, while the Pirate Party account is featured also among the 2014 roster of high-end users, and while two journalists did make their mark in this regard (@niklassvensson and @Pihlblad), the distribution for 2014 appears as more varied than for 2010. Much as for top @reply receivers discussed previously, we see media organisations, rather than a multitude of journalists, emerge as

Table 22.4 Top Receivers of Retweets for #val2010 and #val2014

#val2010 top retweeted	N	Types	#val2014 top retweeted	N	Types
piratpartiet	1,228	Pirate Party	niklassvenson	9,338	Journalist
Pihlblad	521	Journalist	socialdemokrat	6,302	Social Democratic party
emanuelkarlsten	392	Journalist	RebeccaWUvell	3,643	Liberal debater, PR consultant
mickep2	335	Journalist	Expressen	2,426	Tabloid
SDopping	324	Journalist	svtdinrost	2,366	PSB election feature
danielswedin	318	Journalist	jonssonjessica	2,174	No personal info on profile page
nikkelin	310	IT Consultant	MXCartoons	1,474	Anonymous, Immigration critic
Falkvinge	309	Politician, Pirate Party	ozznujen	1,419	Comedian
annatroberg	307	Politician, Pirate Party	Pihlblad	1,418	Journalist
UlfBjereld	305	Professor of Political Science	piratpartiet	1,350	Pirate Party

successful in gaining retweets. Moreover, the presence of a well-known comedian—@ozznujen—reflects another tendency identified by similar research, where celebrities gain leverage in online political discussions (see Larsson and Moe, 2014).

In sum, discussing the fourth criterion, we find offline elites and elite Twitter users to get the most attention—more evidently so in 2014 compared with 2010. On the sender side, though, we still find less well-known users. In isolation, criterion four, concerning the use of redistributional modes of communication, signals a move towards more established patterns of use.

Ability for Non-Elite Users to Make an Impact

Finally, we address the fifth criterion, which relates to the possibilities of non-elite users to break through and get wide attention in the Twittersphere.

Based on Table 22.4, we identify what is here regarded as two non-elite users who succeeded in getting their tweets redistributed to high degrees in 2014. First, the person (or perhaps persons) responsible for the @MXCartoons account provides a statement, basically saying that the tweets will feature "common sense over political correctness," which is crystallised by largely discussing and criticising Swedish immigration policy. Second, the influence of the user @jonssonjessica appears to have emanated from one tweet only. This particular tweet was sent on election night—lamenting the fact that the incumbent liberal-conservative government appeared to have lost the popular vote. We have found similar examples in other contexts. During the 2013 Norwegian election campaign, one such well-formulated and aptly-timed tweet from a non-elite user, otherwise not central to the hashtagged Twitter debate, gained wide attention—if only briefly (Larsson and Moe, 2014). Apart from these two examples, the top list of retweeted users from both election periods under study show only well-known figures.

This final criterion deals with individual examples of lesser-known users with few followers and a sparse network who managed to break through and get heard in the Twittersphere by way of extensive retweeting. Though we identify only a limited number of such examples, we would argue that they illustrate how the Swedish political Twittersphere still lacks the volume and intensity that would hinder the emergence of someone coming out of nowhere, so to speak. The fact that both our examples are from the 2014 data, while we find no similar episodes in 2010, strengthen the impression that the fifth criterion in isolation shows that Twitter use in our context has not moved towards an established pattern of use.

Conclusion

This chapter has presented findings of a comparative study of political Twitter use during two consecutive election campaigns in Sweden, with the aim of providing insights into how such use develops over time. As an analytical framework, we identified five different criteria, which in sum should enable a scrutiny of the extent to which, and how, Twitter use went from emergent status in 2010 to more established in 2014.

We found the first criterion—volume of tweets and users—to signal a move towards established use. The second criterion, covering reactive use in relation to mainstream media, pointed in the opposite direction, as it depicted Twitter as an emerging platform in the sense of still depending to a large extent on the agenda of televised political events. Similarly, our third feature, which looked at the distribution of activity among different user groups, found no change from 2010 to 2014, which is an argument against any notion of a more established pattern of use. Fourth, when looking at the use of dialogic and redistributional modes of communication, we identified a move towards more established patterns of use. This was somewhat contradicted by the final criterion, which identified individual successes at getting heard across the Twittersphere from a position outside the densely networked elite of users. Taken together, our criteria do not allow for a clear answer to whether or not Twitter use has moved towards a more established mode between the two Swedish elections. However, the findings on several criteria that show strong similarities between 2010 and 2014 suggest that we should be careful not to overstate the role of Twitter during election campaigns: it remains hard to grasp its uses, and it seems that important aspects remain in an emergent status.

Applying the approach presented here—a set of criteria which can be used to assess the developmental stage of specific online communication platforms in the context of a wider national media ecology—to other cases, in other cultural and political contexts, based on other technological groundings, and in other time periods, would help us to develop better knowledge of the mechanisms at work when new media platforms turn into staples of everyday political communication.

References

Bastos, M. T., Raimundo, R.L.G., and Travitzki, R. (2013) Gatekeeping Twitter: Message Diffusion in Political Hashtags. *Media, Culture & Society*, 35: 260–270.

Bruns, A. (2011) How Long Is a Tweet? Mapping Dynamic Conversation Networks on Twitter using Gawk and Gephi. *Information, Communication & Society*, 15(9): 1–29.

Bruns, A., and Highfield, T. (2013) Political Networks on Twitter. *Information, Communication & Society*, 16(5): 667–691.

Bruns, A., and Stieglitz, S. (2012) Quantitative Approaches to Comparing Communication Patterns on Twitter. *Journal of Technology in Human Services*, 30: 160–185.

Brynolf, H. (2013) Twitter Census: En rapport om Twitter i Sverige. Stockholm: Intellecta Corporare.

Carlsson, U., and Facht, U. (2014). *MedieSverige 2014*. Gothenburg: Nordicom Sverige.

Chadwick, A. (2008) Web 2.0: New Challenges for the Study of E-democracy in an Era of Informational Exuberance. *I/S: Journal of Law and Policy for the Information Society*, 4: 9–42.

Drotner, K. (2011) *Mediehistorier*. København: Samfundslitteratur.

Graham, T., Broersma, M., Hazelhoff, K., & van 't Haar, G. (2013). Between Broadcasting Political Messages and Interacting with Voters. *Information, Communication & Society*, 16(5): 692–716.

Habermas, J. ([1962] 1990). *Strukturwandel der Öffentlichkeit. Untersuchungen zu einer Kategorie der bürgerlichen Gesellschaft*. Frankfurt: Suhrkamp.

Halavais, A. (2014). Structure of Twitter: Social and Technical. *Twitter and Society*. K. Weller, A. Bruns, J. Burgess, M. Mahrt, and C. Puschmann (eds.). New York: Peter Lang, 29–42.

Jungherr, A. (2014) The Logic of Political Coverage on Twitter: Temporal Dynamics and Content. *Journal of Communication*, 64: 239–259.

Klinger, U. (2013) Mastering the Art of Social Media. *Information, Communication & Society*, 16: 717–736.

Larsson, A. O. (2014) Everyday Elites, Citizens or Extremists? Assessing the Use and Users of Non-Election Political Hashtags. *MedieKultur. Journal of Media and Communication Research*, 56: 61–78.

Larsson, A. O., and Kalsnes, B. (2014) 'Of Course We Are on Facebook'—Social Media Adoption in Swedish and Norwegian Parliaments. *European Journal of Communication*, 29(6): 653–667.

Larsson, A. O., and Moe, H. (2012) Studying Political Microblogging: Twitter Users in the 2010 Swedish Election Campaign. *New Media & Society, 14*: 729–747.

Larsson, A. O., and Moe, H. (2013) Twitter in Politics and Elections—Insights from Scandinavia. *Twitter and Society*. A. Bruns, J. Burgess, K. Weller, et al. (eds.). New York: Peter Lang.

Larsson, A. O., and Moe, H. (2014). Triumph of the Underdogs? Comparing Twitter Use by Political Actors during Two Norwegian Election Campaigns. *SAGE Open*, October–December 2014: 1–13.

Lilleker, D. G., and Jackson, N. A. (2010) Towards a More Participatory Style of Election Campaigning: The Impact of Web 2.0 on the UK 2010 General Election. *Policy & Internet, 2*: 67–96.

McLuhan, M. (1965) *Understanding Media: The Extensions of Man*. New York: McGraw-Hill Paperbacks.

Moe, H., and Larsson, A. O. (2012) Twitterbruk under valgkampen 2011. *Norsk medietidsskrift, 19*: 151–162.

Nam, Y., and Barnett, G. A. (2010) Communication Media Diffusion and Substitutions: Longitudinal Trends from 1980 to 2005 in Korea. *New Media & Society, 12*: 1137–1155.

Nielsen, J. (2006). *Participation Inequality: Encouraging More Users to Contribute*. Retrieved from http://www.useit.com/alertbox/participation_inequality.html

Rogers, E. M. (2003) *Diffusion of Innovations*. New York: Free Press.

Stieglitz, S., and Dang-Xuan, L. (2012) Social Media and Political Communication: A Social Media Analytics Framework. *Social Network Analysis and Mining, 3*: 1277–1291.

Wallsten, K. (2007). Agenda Setting and the Blogosphere: An Analysis of the Relationship between Mainstream Media and Political Blogs. *Review of Policy Research, 24*(6): 567–587.

23

SOCIAL MEDIA IN THE UK ELECTION CAMPAIGNS 2008–2014

Experimentation, Innovation, and Convergence

Darren G. Lilleker, Nigel Jackson, and Karolina Koc-Michalska

Introduction

Digital and social media platforms and applications have been placed at the heart of debates around political communication for at least the last two decades. The cyberoptimist perspective that technology would be democratising gave way to more pessimistic views. Pessimism was validated by empirical findings which largely demonstrated that access to resources and popularity in the real world was mirrored in online environments and that there were few indications that online political communication attracted a wider or different audience than, say, specialist television documentaries (Ward et al., 2003). Cyberoptimists were proven inaccurate in their predictions because the Internet is a pull medium, with users selecting what they wish to see, and users sought personal gratifications when seeking content. Given that politics is only of interest to a minority, few political websites gain hits and only prominent media outlets and political celebrities gain significant attention.

Social media may be in the process of reinvigorating a more positive perspective of the role digital media can play in democracies. The ability for any individual or organisation to connect to a diverse community, share or create content on any topic, and for that to be seen across a network suggests such sites can raise political awareness, encourage information seeking, and so act as a pathway to participation (Rojas & Puig-i-Abril, 2009). Yet, to invigorate engagement with electoral politics, political parties or candidates need to be active players in social media environments. We argue that it is normatively good for democracy that citizens should be permitted to interact with political representatives and co-create politics within official and unofficial spaces, and because social media have provided a low-cost means where party campaigning and citizen co-creation can converge, a new and interactive paradigm of political communication could be emerging. We therefore adopt a methodology for assessing quantitatively the extent that UK political parties permit co-creation and adapt to the communication norms of social media while also exploiting its potential for meeting campaigning aims.

Political campaigns in the UK in many ways are a blend of traditions from European party systems, with some aspects influenced by the more U.S. candidate-centered model. There are two reasons for this. First, the UK features a 'first-past-the-post' system, where candidates stand for election as individuals in constituencies, and where the candidate who has most votes is elected, encourages a more individualistic style of campaigning at the local level (Southern & Ward, 2011). Second, since the Thatcher era, British politics has adopted a more presidential style, placing party leaders central to the campaign. That said, Web-based campaigning largely follows a party-centric model where the party rather than the leader has a set of domains across platforms (websites and linked presences on Facebook, Twitter, and YouTube, mainly), though some local candidates independently create their own presences across the Internet. UK campaigns therefore have potential to be innovative in their use of social media and to present voters with multiple means of interacting with the individuals and their parties who seek their vote.

In order to explore the adoption and use of social media during election campaigns in the UK, this chapter draws on three data sets. First, a longitudinal analysis of website and Web presence features which allows us to track the use of the Internet by the major political parties across the local elections of 2008, subsequent European parliamentary election (2009), general election (2010), and the most recent contest, the 2014 European parliamentary election. The parties selected for analysis represent a cross-section of the UK political scene. Labour were the party of government from 1997–2010 and, subsequently, the main opposition, the Conservatives, were in opposition until 2010 and subsequently major partners in a coalition with the third largest party in terms of popular vote, the Liberal Democrats. The Green Party has a long history as a campaigning organisation but only gained their first MP in 2010. However, they have always had representation in local councils and the European Parliament. The UK Independence Party (UKIP) has been a serious contender in local and European Parliament elections, gaining second place in the popular vote 2009 and first in 2014. Subsequent to the 2014 contest, UKIP gained two MPs through defections from the Conservatives, though both forced by-elections and gained their own mandate. The final party, the British National Party (BNP) has no parliamentary representation but stands in all four nations of the UK (England, Northern Ireland, Scotland, and Wales) and most of the seats within parliament across those nations. These smaller parties have all had significant impact on the news agenda. Specifically, UKIP due to its populist conservative and Eurosceptic stance coupled with media friendly pseudo-events, and the BNP for its controversial far right, neo-fascist platform. The BNP has also historically been innovative in their use of forums to bind their supporters together into party-focused communities (Lilleker & Jackson, 2011); the BNP had two MEPs until 2014.

The second data set is from interviews with party strategists who were asked to prioritise different elements in order to define a 21st-century professional campaign. This chapter draws only on data that compare the prioritisation of different media use (online and offline) to identify how social media are embedded strategically within a campaign. Finally, the chapter draws on data from social media pages that detail the usage of Facebook, Twitter, and YouTube by the six major parties. Here we assess how social media offers each party reach and how reach (in terms of followers and page views) corresponds with strategies. This analysis focuses on the aftermath of the European elections and provides insights into the role social media might play in the UK general election in 2015. It follows a brief summary of research on Web campaigning in the UK up to 2008 and the role the Internet has been argued to play as a campaign tool.

UK Online Election Campaigning: Slow on the Uptake

One chapter of the Political Communications study of the 1997 general election asked if the contest was the first Internet election, with the response being no (Ward & Gibson, 1997). Reviewing Internet use, Ward and Gibson noted UK parties were recognising the Internet's potential for increasing internal party debate and connecting better to members. However, while debate was facilitated, party websites were utilised primarily as a tool for downward information dissemination. There was evidence of equalisation, with parties having similar or equal quality websites independent of their resources, but limited Internet use by the electorate hindered technology being exploited to its fullest extent (Gibson & Ward, 1998). By 2001, party websites looked better and were more user friendly, with easy-to-navigate menus, less dense text, and more pictures and videos. However, the content was largely 'shovelware', material from leaflets and other documents stored online in case anyone wanted to view them. Largely, there seemed no great sense of design strategy, with no evidence of the production of targeted content relevant to those who might visit a party website and so providing what they might want to find (Gibson et al., 2003; Gibson, Ward, & Lusoli 2002).

The European parliamentary Elections of 2004 offered little evidence that the Internet was becoming a serious electoral battleground. Evidence showed that the online campaign, or rather the lack of a campaign, largely reflected the apathy of national politicians and the media with the second-order election (Lusoli & Ward, 2005). Parties provided informational content mirroring the, by then, longstanding tradition of shovelware content. Although perhaps a lower resourced campaign would be expected of a second-order contest (Maier, Strömbäck, & Kaid 2011), the 2005 general election campaign also relied largely on television and news management with little development in the use of digital technology (Jackson, 2007). We therefore find that there was little sense across the contests 1997–2005 that the Internet was going to fulfil the potential to provide a more level playing field where all parties and citizens could co-create a cyber-campaign. There was, however, evidence that supporter mobilisation was increasingly a function of Web presences (Norris & Curtice, 2008) and weblogs became a feature, so allowing flexibility in messaging and provided a means for parties to gain feedback on some aspects of policy or their campaign (Jackson, 2006). In the UK, as across Europe, this cautious approach by the parties was natural given that only a small percentage of voters used the Internet as a source of political information (Lusoli, 2005).

Although many individual MPs may have seen benefits from a more personalised campaign and so developed an Internet presence, this was also unrealised. Using the catchy title 'from weird to wired', one of the first studies of UK MPs shows few dabbled with the Internet (Ward & Lusoli, 2005). One or two pioneers metaphorically dipped their toe into online campaigning, creating weblogs (Stanyer, 2006), developing websites (Norton, 2007), and interacting with constituents via email (Allan, 2006), but these were exemplars outside of the norm. Furthermore, as most MPs' websites were paid for out of their parliamentary communication budget, they could not be used for election campaigns. A few used them to highlight their achievements in parliament on behalf of their constituency or to explain their voting record (Lilleker, 2005). However, beyond isolated examples, there seemed to be little to indicate that the Internet was taken seriously as a campaign tool.

The Evolution of Online Campaigning 2008–2014

Of course, one cannot ignore the fact there were innovations and that parties were experimenting with a range of features that may appear basic now but at the time were providing data that would shape later behaviour. Party e-newsletters, and the finding that their subscribers wanted not just to read but also to give feedback, showed there might be rewards from offering greater involvement through interactivity (Jackson & Lilleker, 2007). Examples from campaigns in other nations also appeared to lead innovation in the UK. Howard Dean's campaign in the U.S. in 2004 paved the way for crowdsourcing donations. The campaigns in 2007 in France by Ségolène Royal taught of both the potentials and pitfalls of co-creation through her harnessing a personal blogosphere and producing a co-authored manifesto. Similarly, Nicolas Sarkozy's adventures in Second Life, where he offered French citizens a chance to test drive his leadership, showed the values of having an interactive dimension to the campaign (Lilleker & Malagón, 2010). These innovations influenced those UK parties who sought ways to appear modern, innovative, and to gain greater attention and support. Uncharacteristically, this meant that the contests for the local councils in 2008 and the 2009 European parliamentary election became testing grounds for innovations in online campaigning, with interactive opportunities emphasised to an unprecedented and unexpected degree.

Our research captured data from the Web presences constructed by the six UK parties described earlier for the 2008 local elections, 2009 and 2014 European elections, and the 2010 general election. The research involved a content analysis, or feature analysis, of websites; a method pioneered by Gibson and Ward (2000) when analysing party and candidate websites at the turn of the century. The method initially detects the presence or absence of features, with a coding scheme updated to include links to and content on social media platforms. This non-intrusive method treats Web presences as a strategic artefact, designed in order to provide experiences for visitors (from informative to interactive) and provide a feature count for each party, which aids simple comparison. Intercoder reliability tests of 86 per cent to 100 per cent demonstrate the reliability of the counting procedures between the researchers. The presence of features in and of themselves tells little; the function is important. The team produced a range of measures that were tested with experts in digital communication design in order to determine the function and extent of functionality. The features were rated for direction of communication (monologue, two-way feedback, or participatory) and for the level of user control (rated 1–10); so, for example, press releases, a common feature of early websites, were one-way and offered minimal control, read or not. In contrast, a social media profile where comments were allowed is participatory and permitting the maximum level of user control where they might like, share, comment, or enter into conversation with the profile host or other visitors. The expert testing of attributed scores ensure the validity of the measurement tool. Averages for each party's Web presences were created to permit simple comparability; the data for average direction of communication and user control for each contest are presented graphically in Figures 23.1 and 23.2.

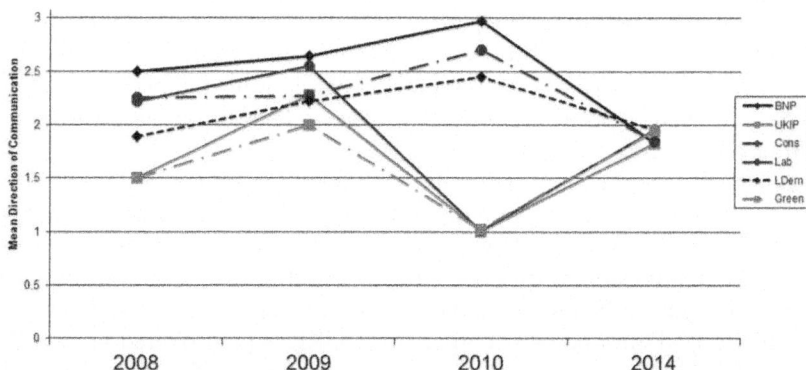

Figure 23.1 Direction of Communication between Parties and Their Voters (one-way, two-way, or participatory) Compared across Contests 2008–2014, Mean Scores

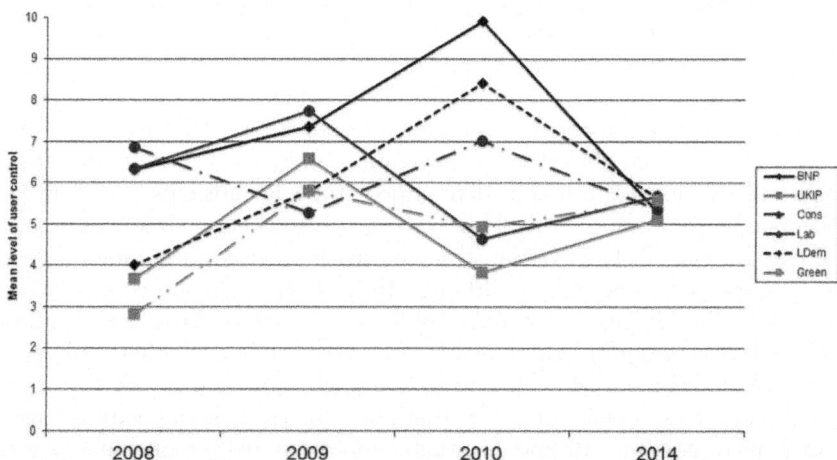

Figure 23.2 Level of User Control over Communication between Parties and Voters (*low* 1–10 *very high*) Compared across Contests 2008–2014, Mean Scores

The local election contest of 2008 saw some interesting campaign innovations. The contest coincided with the widespread societal adoption of MySpace and Facebook and the introduction of Web 2.0 as a concept explaining interactive communication. Parties adopted a range of features that fitted into the Web 2.0 framework, so building architecture for websites that permitted participation. However, largely the parties themselves had no representation within the interaction. The parties provided a news feed, invited responses via email or online forms, and allowed comments, yet they did not respond to questions publicly and rarely monitored social media platforms. For some parties, in particular the BNP, the MySpace profile had no content and users of the platform were allowed to join, post a hostile remark, and then leave. Hence, the conclusion was that UK political parties actually resided within Web 1.5. This suggested that while their online presences offered the look and feel of Web 2.0, providing space for visitors to correspond, the parties largely retained the control offered by tech-nologies underpinning the Web 1.0 era of online communication. This halfway-house approach led many visitors to use social media profile walls for 'graffiti'; they posted a comment that could be positive or hostile and seemed never to return, perhaps because not gaining a response.

This approach remained for the European parliamentary election in 2009. The Web presences built for the contest emphasised resource inequalities, with the major parties innovating in more sophisticated ways than minor or fringe parties. However, when comparing the features used, their functionality and the level of control awarded to site visitors in terms of being able to post, comment, and interact, it was actually the far-right fringe BNP and populist conservative UKIP which offered visitors the most freedom, followed by Labour, the then party of government. We suggested, therefore, a strategic focus on Internet campaigning was emerging (Jackson & Lilleker, 2010). The fringe parties were ambitious to increase their vote share and opened up their site to their supporters. Labour similarly offered a more interactive experience in an attempt to limit their decline at the next general election. Drawing on the innovations of Dean and Obama in the U.S., parties appeared to be exploring the potential of technology to enhance the relationship with their grassroots and so used the online environment as a greenhouse for nurturing support (Albrecht, 2007).

Perhaps it was the influence of the 2008 Obama campaign for the U.S. presidency that led some parties to reconsider their adherence to the Web 1.5 mode of campaign-ing; perhaps it was a combination of desperation and caution surrounding the close 2010 general election contest that determined strategies; insights from party strate-gists suggested something of both. However, the divergence in strategies was striking (Lilleker & Jackson, 2011). UKIP largely eschewed any social aspects, focusing on older voters not expected to be online, although they did have some members who regu-larly blogged. The Greens, constrained by resources, offered little onsite interaction but provided some engaging features, such as a customisable video that could be shared via Facebook. Labour retreated somewhat, although the 'Change We See' campaign permitted supporters to upload pictures that encapsulated Labour's achievements over their 13 years of government and the #Labourdoorstep Twitter campaign was impor-tant in mobilising their activists. However, these were minor innovations compared to the Obama-style social network created by the Conservative Party (myConservatives. co.uk) and the Liberal Democrat's Forum (LibDemAct). These allowed visitors who wished to sign up to write directly to the websites, creating content and shaping the experiences of future visitors. The Greens, Labour, Conservatives, and Liberal Demo-crats also utilised Facebook, Twitter, and YouTube to create multiple points of entry and participation in their campaign. Yet, the British National Party offered an even more participatory experience. Their website consisted of participatory architecture that gave members a role in creating the campaign. Around 1,500 members, using pseudonyms, contributed detail on local campaigns, supportive examples for the anti-immigrant and homophobic platform, and attacks on the other parties. The BNP avoided other social networks and controlled joining and posting, but the party was the closest to a Web 2.0 campaign. They embraced the philosophy of the social Web by creating their own social media platform while other parties relied on the free platforms.

Given this level of innovation, one might expect further advances between 2010 and 2014. In contrast, as shown in Figures 23.1 and 23.2, we find in 2014 almost com-plete convergence around a mixed communication strategy that offers varying levels of control and varying directions of communication. The differences are minor; for example, the Liberal Democrats did not have an online shop, the Green Party only had an online mechanism for volunteering, and the BNP and UKIP did not encourage emails to the party. More importantly, all interactive elements were gone from the sites, so for party websites user control became very low and the communication one-way or in places two-way. Rather, the free spaces offered by the Facebook, Twitter, and You-Tube platforms were utilised exclusively to allow participatory communication and for visitors to have control over communication. Therefore, social media, by 2014, were the one place where supporters could interact with one another and, in theory, with the party. Only the BNP site allowed comments to their news section that features weblog tools. All the other parties encouraged sharing their pages and joining their presences on social media platforms. The retrenchment could be a reflection of the second-order status of the European parliamentary election. However, it might also suggest recognition that the website had greater use for supporters, allowing them to donate, download material for printing, or promoting the party online. Social media, in contrast, may attract a looser support base into a community that can then be mobilised. The functionality is similar to the bespoke social network created by Obama (Woolley, Limperos, & Oliver, 2010), but costs little, does not require large levels of resources for monitoring, as some believe social media to be anarchic and uncontrollable anyway so would not expect all comments to be on message (for discussion, see Papacharissi, 2002). The website, however, remains simple, clean of clutter, and largely utilised to disseminate simple messages and brand information in the form of images, soundbites, and policy promises. This strategy may reflect the priorities UK party strategists place upon different platforms and media.

Social Media: Just Another Mass Medium?

The data for this section draw on a survey, conducted either face-to-face, via telephone, or in one case via email with the individuals responsible for designing and overseeing the campaign strategy for the 2014 European parliament and 2015 general election strategies for each of the major UK parties. The BNP refused to respond, so there are no data on that party. The interviewees' specific job titles differed across parties, from party leader to communication and campaign manager; however, each had a unique perspective on where their party stood in relation to voters and the challenge they faced at forthcoming electoral contests, the objectives the party had set, and how these were best achieved. For each means of communication they gave a score from 1 to 5, denoting its relative importance and so allowing means to be derived which are compared in this case across parties. The means were generated from two distinct sets of questions, one set on priorities for the 2014 European parliamentary election; the second for the forthcoming general election, in the case of advertising this is cumulative for prioritising print, online, and television advertisements.

The mean scores, shown in Table 23.1, offer some indications of the different priorities parties have when viewing different methods for communicating to and with their potential voters. Face-to-face communication is the priority for all, but there are divergences across traditional and social media. Major parties see news (an up-to-date presence in the media and having an impact on the agenda) as of significant importance; the two minor parties recognise the difficulty in achieving positive or balanced news coverage. The two parliamentary opposition parties, Labour and the Greens, although

Table 23.1 Parties' Preferred Priorities of Methods for Communication with Their Voters in the 2014 EP Campaign and General Election Campaign 2015, Mean Scores

	News	TV spots	Other ads	Website	Email	Face-to-face	Facebook	Twitter	YouTube
Cons	4.5	4.0	3.7	4.5	2.0	5.0	3.0	3.0	3.0
Lab	5.0	4.5	4.2	5.0	4.0	5.0	4.0	4.0	4.0
LibDem	5.0	3.0	3.2	4.0	5.0	5.0	4.0	3.0	3.0
UKIP	3.0	1.5	1.0	1.0	3.0	5.0	1.0	1.0	1.0
Green	3.0	1.0	2.0	5.0	5.0	5.0	3.0	4.0	5.0

the latter only has one MP, both rate social media as highly important; UKIP, due to their more conservative, older and working class target electorate, prefer a ground or street-level campaign. Labour appear to be prioritising all forms of communication, perhaps as they are trying to build positive awareness for their relatively new leader and have struggled to build a strong public image despite them earning a respectable standing in the polls.

Overall, however, there is a general pattern across the UK parties. The gold standard for communication is face-to-face, hence the importance of canvassing and, within the marginal constituencies, local and national party luminaries are highly visible throughout a campaign (Lilleker, 2005). The second priority is likely to be mass media, and in particular, appearances on regional and national news, so suggesting these give the party and its candidates prominence as well as allowing them to set the news agenda. Third is email, particularly as a tool for interparty communication. Social media reinforces these activities but only the Green party place it as a highly important medium, notwithstanding the prioritisation of face-to-face communication. For most parties there is a respect for the role of social media in a campaign; however, there is a level of uncertainty as to the potential advantages and disadvantages of social media campaigning.

Caught in the Social Web: Party Use of Facebook, Twitter, and YouTube

Table 23.2 shows the reach the six parties enjoy, with this representing the number of 'likes' (on Facebook fan pages), followers (on Twitter), and subscribers (to YouTube channels). Reach is important as it suggests, at the very least, the number of people willing to receive direct communication from each party, including having material pushed at them.

The numbers represent the immediate audience each party can reach by social media but not the networks they might have access to, or reach into, should their online supporters like and share the party posts, videos, and images. The picture is disparate to some extent, with the likes, followers, and subscribers largely mirroring recent electoral results. We therefore see the Conservatives and UKIP having the largest following on Facebook, Labour beating the Conservatives on Twitter slightly with the Liberal Democrats, Greens and UKIP with half their following and with little between them. UKIP

Table 23.2 Social Media Reach by Party during the 2014 EP Campaign; Facebook Likes, Twitter Followers, YouTube Subscribers; Absolute Figures

	Facebook fans	Posts	Twitter followers	Tweets	YouTube subscribers	Videos
Cons	223,180	(29)	113,649	(59)	6,953	(3)
Lab	176,979	(33)	141,419	(335)	7,360	(3)
LibDem	97,219	(26)	65,878	(482)	3,328	(11)
UKIP	219,285	(46)	62,494	(265)	19,802	(1)
Green	67,068	(46)	63,842	(578)	2,522	(17)
BNP	151,837	(86)	7,813	(181)	5,656	(9)

won on YouTube with the rest of the parties having under 10,000 subscribers. The BNP had a strong following on Facebook but was hardly visible on Twitter. Largely, politics as usual (Margolis & Resnick, 2000) is supported here, with the current hype around, and support for, UKIP being mirrored online with the two traditional rivals for government in close proximity to them depending upon the channel. The question is whether there are alternative explanations for the levels of support.

In terms of the effort parties make in communicating via these platforms, there seems to be no correspondence between the number of posts, tweets, or videos and the likes, followers, or subscribers earned. The figures in brackets in Table 23.2 denote effort in terms of material created during the 2014 European parliamentary election campaign when one might expect activity to be at its greatest. Therefore, in terms of the adage that producing content equally might generate a following, that would seem an erroneous hypothesis. Particularly, the Green Party created most content for both Twitter and YouTube but did not have an equitable level of following.

In terms of the type of content, all parties treated social media as a news feed. The profiles across platforms were largely a repository for videos, or with Twitter, links to a video, the latest line from the party leader, or updates about events and inviting members. The exception was the BNP who selected news stories and put their nationalist spin on these, so pushing an image of representing and defending Britishness. The party only shared material from their leader's pages or profiles, or for the major parties other prominent spokespersons.

Facebook offers the opportunity to see the extent of likes, shares, and comments received as well as whether the party or any notable and obvious figure from the party responds. Table 23.3 shows the numbers of posts by the party during the four-week period of the 2014 European parliamentary election campaign, and the average number of likes, shares, and comments per post. The only observation that can be made from this data is that, unless the party was a member of the coalition (the Conservatives and Liberal Democrats), the size of support was also an indicator of the level of expected activity. UKIP gained most votes at the 2014 European parliamentary election and earned a larger and much more vibrant online community than any of the other parties, suggesting a simple correlation between electoral and social media support for that party. We also find that activities that required least effort were the most popular: a

Table 23.3 Parties' Reach and Visible Support on Facebook during the 2014 EP Campaign; Absolute Figures

	Posts to the page	Likes of posts average per post	Shares of posts average per post	Comments on posts average per post
Cons	29	356	142	197
Lab	33	1,270	508	329
LibDem	26	317	126	115
UKIP	46	1,988	1,325	1,093
Green	46	663	265	57
BNP	86	1,547	859	161

large number liking, a smaller number sharing and yet fewer commenting. The commenting figure is, however, spurious, as on some posts there are numerous interactions between a small number of participants as opposed to a stream of comments from different individuals. The most striking finding is that at no time did the party respond (or rather the individual or individuals who manage the Facebook profile and speak as the party) nor did any of the top party personnel feature responding to posts or comment posted by their supporters. Even when, as in the case of the Conservatives, many of those who liked their page commented that they were unconvinced by Conservative party promises and would vote for UKIP, there was no attempt by the party to prevent this erosion of votes. The party activity seemed to encourage graffiti and only due to the energy of those who commented, some form of interest was sustained. It may be that parties viewed these pages simply as a means to gather data about their supporters and their opinions, and that had unique value. However, as noted in empirical studies, it would appear they were missing a trick in not communicating back and building relationships with their online supporters (Jackson & Lilleker, 2009).

The UK Social Media Campaign: Evolution and Devolution, Never Revolution

The history of online campaigning, albeit covering only 17 years, overall demonstrates a greater sense of caution than a desire to be innovative. In this respect, UK parties demonstrate similar caution to their EU counterparts (Lusoli, 2005) barring some notable exceptions. Where there is innovation towards more interactive modes of communication, it mirrors findings from the U.S., where 'controlled interactivity' is argued to dominate (Stromer-Galley, 2014). The decade of reliance on shovelware perhaps indicates that UK parties see voters and supporters as individuals who need informing and persuading in equal measure but not talking with online. This may be an indication that all parties are unsure of the impact of interaction, how to deal with the demands of their online community of loose supporters, and are concerned about the extent that the party may have to accommodate them more at the expense of constitutionally defined decision-making processes (Lilleker, Pack, & Jackson, 2010). Innovation appears to have been ushered in on the back of influences from across the channel and then from over the Atlantic, but it was short-lived. It was also unsuccessful, with the myConservatives social network having very few members and even less activism (Lilleker & Jackson, 2010: 135); suggesting the O'Reilly adage 'build it and they will come' (O'Reilly, 2007) is reliant on context.

It is therefore unsurprising that parties turn to free platforms, as they require little effort, low-level monitoring, and are places where the people already go. As one veteran campaigner commented, "The website is a side street, people only go there to visit someone when invited; Facebook and Twitter are the high street, everyone passes through nowadays, and if you do something interesting people may stop to take a look". While there still needs a pull to any profile there is some logic to the statement. Unsurprisingly, parties have mixed views on social media as a priority channel but all, except UKIP, rate it as an above average priority. Importantly, UKIP used social media extensively and gathered a significant following. So despite these media being a low priority in the lead up to the 2014 contest this perception may change for the 2015 general election when their goal is to increase their representation in the national parliament. Of the 50 parties that stood across the UK for election to the European Parliament, 26 had a Facebook profile, 29 used Twitter, and 32 had a YouTube channel. These figures suggest that social media is embedded in UK campaigning and is a de rigueur feature for any party seeking to be taken seriously and seeking to reach out to the electorate.

Yet, in truth, little beyond adoption of these platforms is innovative. Social media are simply used to replicate tasks of old media; it is a form of online advertising with some elements of recruitment built in. There are few attempts to convert supporters into more active advocates or campaigners despite visitors' apparent willingness to like, share, and comment on the material of the party. Even more surprising, many comments are never responded to and remain unread. Perhaps Facebook, in particular, is perceived as a place for supporters to keep in touch with what the party is doing and with one another; however erroneous that perception might be. Therefore, while UK parties have embraced social media and use them regularly, their use remains in the realm of Web 1.5. They facilitate participatory interaction but seldom participate themselves. Hence, we might view the UK party experience with social media as one of cautious experimentation, followed by some innovation but ending with convergence around the most basic usage. This is not a normative judgement and criticism, but it does raise a question; is this appropriate usage of social media, or at least appropriate for a political party, and if not what is an effective model of usage that may lead to a more social, interactive and accessible form of politics? The medium may have changed but the political mind-set has not, it may be fear of losing control of communication, having to answer the tough questions in public or it may be a more primal fear that politicians experience (Stromer-Galley, 2000). In setting out why politicians must be independent legislators and not delegates, Edmund Burke (1890, p. 474) argued,

> When the leaders choose to make themselves bidders at an auction of popularity, their talents, in the construction of the state, will be of no service. They will become flatterers instead of legislators; the instruments, not the guides, of the people.

Perhaps for many politicians the fear is that moving closer to their online supporters will lead to just such impulses. Hence, communication remains two-way at best, private and under the control of UK parties even when they colonise platforms designed for social interaction and conversation.

References

Albrecht, S. (2007) "Weblog campaigning in the German Bundestag Election 2005," *Social Science Computer Review*, 25(4), pp. 504–520.

Allan, R. (2006) "Parliament, elected representatives and technology 1997–2005—Good in parts?" *Parliamentary Affairs*, 59(2), pp. 360–365.

Burke, E. (1890) *Reflections on the revolution in France*. London: Macmillan.

Gibson, R. K., Margolis, M., Resnick, D., & Ward, S. J. (2003) "Election campaigning on the WWW in the USA and UK: A comparative analysis," *Party Politics*, 9(1), pp. 47–75.

Gibson, R. K., & Ward, S. J. (1998) "UK political parties and the Internet 'politics as usual' in the new media?" *The Harvard International Journal of Press/Politics*, 3(3), pp. 14–38.

Gibson, R., & Ward, S. (2000) "A proposed methodology for studying the function and effectiveness of party and candidate Web sites," *Social Science Computer Review*, 18(3), pp. 301–319.

Gibson, R., Ward, S., & Lusoli, W. (2002) "Online campaigning in the UK: The public respond," Paper presented to American Political Studies Association, Boston, 29 August–1 September 2002.

Jackson, N. (2006, July) "Dipping their big toe into the blogosphere: The use of weblogs by the political parties in the 2005 general election," *Aslib Proceedings*, 58(4), pp. 292–303).

Jackson, N. (2007) "Political parties, the Internet and the 2005 General Election: Third time lucky?" *Internet Research*, 17(3), pp. 249–271.

Jackson, N. A., & Lilleker, D. G. (2007) "Seeking unmediated political information in a mediated environment: The uses and gratifications of political parties' e-newsletters," *Information, Community and Society*, 10(2), pp. 242–264.

Jackson, N. A., & Lilleker, D. G. (2009) "Building an architecture of participation? Political parties and Web 2.0 in Britain," *Journal of Information Technology & Politics*, 6(3–4), pp. 232–250.

Jackson, N., & Lilleker, D. G. (2010) "Tentative steps towards interaction: The use of the Internet in the British European Parliament Election 2009," *Internet Research*, 20(5), pp. 527–544.

Lilleker, D. G. (2005) "Local campaign management: Winning votes or wasting resources?" *Journal of Marketing Management*, 21(9–10), pp. 979–1003.

Lilleker, D., & Jackson, N. (2011) *Political campaigning, elections and the Internet: Comparing the US, UK, France and Germany*. London: Routledge.

Lilleker, D. G., & Jackson, N. A. (2010) "Towards a more participatory style of election campaigning: The impact of Web 2.0 on the UK 2010 general election," *Policy & Internet*, 2(3), pp. 69–98.

Lilleker, D. G., & Malagón, C. (2010) "Levels of interactivity in the 2007 French Presidential candidates' Websites," *European Journal of Communication*, 25(1), pp. 25–42.

Lilleker, D. G., Pack, M., & Jackson, N. (2010). "Political parties and Web 2.0: The liberal democrat perspective," *Politics*, 30(2), pp. 105–112.

Lusoli, W. (2005). "A second-order medium? The Internet as a source of electoral information in 25 European countries," *Information Polity*, 10(3), pp. 247–265.

Lusoli, W., & Ward, J. (2005) "Politics makes strange bedfellows: The Internet and the 2004 European Parliament Election in Britain," *The International Journal of Press/Politics*, 10(4), pp. 71–97.

Maier, M., Strömbäck, J., & Kaid, L. L. (eds.) (2011) *Political communication in European parliamentary elections*. Farnham: Ashgate.

Margolis, M., & Resnick, D. (2000) *Politics as usual: The cyberspace revolution*, Thousand Oaks, CA: Sage.

Norris, P., & Curtice, J. (2008) "Getting the message out: A two-step model of the role of the internet in campaign communication flows during the 2005 British general election," *Journal of Information Technology & Politics*, 4(4), pp. 3–13.

Norton, P. (2007) "Four models of political representation: British MPs and the use of ICT. *The Journal of Legislative Studies*," 13(3), pp. 354–369.

O'Reilly, T. (2007) "What is Web 2.0: Design patterns and business models for the next generation of software," *Communications & Strategies*, 65(1), pp. 17–37.

Papacharissi, Z. (2002) "The virtual sphere: The internet as a public sphere," *New media & society*, 4(1), pp. 9–27.

Rojas, H., & Puig-i-Abril, E. (2009) "Mobilizers mobilized: Information, expression, mobilization and participation in the digital age," *Journal of Computer-Mediated Communication*, 14(4), pp. 902–927.

Southern, R., & Ward, S. J. (2011) "Below the radar? Online campaigning at the local level in the 2010 election," in D. Wring, R. Mortimore, & S. Atkinson, S. (eds.) *Political communication in Britain: The leader debates, the campaign and the media in the 2010 general election*, Basingstoke: Palgrave, pp. 218–240.

Stanyer, J. (2006) "Online campaign communication and the phenomenon of blogging: An analysis of web logs during the 2005 British general election campaign," *Aslib Proceedings*, 58(5), pp. 404–415.

Stromer-Galley, J. (2000) "On-line interaction and why candidates avoid it," *Journal of Communication*, 50(4), pp. 111–132.

Stromer-Galley, J. (2014) *Presidential campaigning in the Internet age*. Oxford: Oxford University Press.

Ward, S., & Gibson, R. (1997) "The first Internet election? UK political parties and campaigning in cyberspace," in I. Crewe, B. Gosschalk, & J. Bartle (eds.) *Political communications: Why labour won the general election of 1997*, London: Frank Cass, pp. 93–112.

Ward, S., Gibson, R., & Lusoli, W. (2003) "Online participation and mobilisation in Britain: Hype, hope and reality," *Parliamentary Affairs*, 56(4), pp. 652–668.

Ward, S., & Lusoli, W. (2005) "'From weird to wired': MPs, the Internet and representative politics in the UK," *Journal of Legislative Studies*, 11(1), pp. 57–81.

Woolley, J. K., Limperos, A.M., & Oliver, M. B. (2010) "The 2008 presidential election, 2.0: A content analysis of user-generated political Facebook groups," *Mass Communication and Society*, 13(5), pp. 631–652.

24

COMPULSORY VOTING, ENCOURAGED TWEETING?

Australian Elections and Social Media

Tim Highfield and Axel Bruns

Introduction

As the various chapters in this volume demonstrate, the use of social media platforms for political purposes—from commentary and analysis to activism and more tangential discussions—covers a wealth of contexts and forms. Such a diverse range of approaches to the political on social media is apparent even in election settings, which might be expected to feature only a few obvious themes. In this chapter, we examine patterns in social media activity around Australian elections; our analysis focuses primarily on the 2013 federal election, but we contextualise this study within our extended research into Australian politics on social media, including elections at the federal and state levels since 2007. We approach Australian elections on social media from three perspectives. First, we discuss the evolution of the use of online platforms during elections, for campaigning and citizen commentary alike. Second, we consider how politicians and their parties employed social media during the 2013 election, focusing on Twitter. Third, we examine how citizens engaged with the election and the voting experience by identifying practices of tweeting on election day itself. The specific context of Australian politics, including compulsory voting for citizens on the electoral roll, makes this case notably different from other Western democracies, where Twitter is not adopted to the same extent, a wider range of parties and ideologies might be present in the political spectrum, and voting is optional.

Social Media and Australian Politics

Social media platforms and their predecessors, such as blogs, have had an at times uneasy integration into the Australian political and media landscape. The early political blogs were mostly the work of citizen experts and political activists offering their own analyses of economic issues, policies, and polling data. This new group of voices contributing to political discussions online and commenting on mainstream coverage of politics was not always viewed positively by the established news media (Highfield & Bruns, 2012). While blogging and similar approaches to presenting opinions and analysis were eventually adopted and co-opted by the Australian mainstream media (Garden, 2014), for politicians they went largely unembraced. Indeed, it took social media, in particular Twitter and Facebook, for Australian politicians to take to the Internet as a means for communicating with the electorate online (whether in dialogue with voters or simply sharing their press releases and public appearances).

A further disparity around social media adoption was seen in the respective integration of online platforms into election campaigns by the main political parties. The 2007 federal election, for instance, saw the Australian Labor Party (ALP) pursue a youth-oriented campaign focused on its new leader, Kevin Rudd—using a 'Kevin07' branding strategy—that in part included online social networking strategies on Facebook and MySpace. During the same election, the conservative Liberal Party—which had been in power since 1996—was less engaged with the Internet as a campaign tool, and while the party posted some material on YouTube, its strategy here was inconsistent (see Flew, 2008). The following federal election, in 2010, was notable in part because of the leadership spill in the ALP which saw Prime Minister Kevin Rudd deposed by his deputy, Julia Gillard. This happened before the campaign was announced and occurred almost literally in the middle of the night. Its suddenness meant that developments were covered by journalists and other observers on Twitter as they became known, and before mainstream media could interrupt their regularly scheduled programming. The spill underlined the emerging importance of Twitter to the Australian political and media landscape (see also Jericho, 2012), with politicians, journalists, celebrities, and ordinary citizens making use of the platform to cover the ensuing election (Burgess & Bruns, 2012).

Following the 2010 federal election, which resulted in a hung parliament led by the ALP, with Gillard as Prime Minister, Twitter in particular became a popular platform for the ongoing discussion of Australian politics. The 2010 election had received centralised coverage by Twitter users employing the #ausvotes hashtag, and after the election, the online commentariat took to using #auspol as the central marker for day-to-day political discussions. Similar hashtags were adopted for state-level discussions, including #qldpol for Queensland politics and #wapol for Western Australian politics, and elections in these states following the #x-votes template (Bruns & Highfield, 2013; Highfield, 2013). The exception is Victoria, where day-to-day politics uses the #springst hashtag, due to the common use of 'Spring Street' (the location of the Victorian parliament) to refer to Victorian politics. While such popular markers can become swamped by tweets from a small group of dedicated or antagonistic Twitter users whose activity far outweighs other users' contributions (akin to the 'political junkies' described by Coleman, 2006), political topics are also addressed by the wider population, even if they are not employing these hashtags. Regular political topics also received their own, specialised hashtags, including #qt (for Question Time during parliamentary sessions), #qanda for the Australian Broadcasting Corporation (ABC)'s Q&A political panel show (Given & Radywyl, 2013), and #spill (or #libspill) for leadership challenges.

The ritualisation of Australian political coverage on social media is demonstrated through the adoption of recurring jokes, references, and tropes when discussing politics. Constant speculation about Kevin Rudd challenging Julia Gillard to regain the ALP leadership and become Prime Minister again was accompanied by hashtags such as #respill, #kevenge, and #ruddmentum; these peaked during an unsuccessful challenge in February 2012, a rumoured challenge in March 2013 and finally during a successful challenge in June 2013. Following this final leadership spill, Rudd became Prime Minister for a second time. (Similar ritualised hashtags have also accompanied speculation about the Liberal party during 2014 and 2015, from #libspill to #returnbull, reflecting rumours of Malcolm Turnbull's interest in challenging Tony Abbott for the Liberal leadership—a challenge which finally succeeded in September 2015.)

As with 2010, the change in ALP leadership occurred just before an imminent federal election, and this was the context for the 2013 campaign. The Liberal Party, led by Tony Abbott since December 2009, had been obtaining strong results in opinion polls, and changing from Gillard to Rudd was seen as a possible approach for the ALP to reverse this trend and stay in power. Two parties or party blocs that are the only groups likely to have the numbers to form government—the left-of-centre ALP and the essentially permanent Coalition between the conservative Liberal Party and the rural-focused National Party (which in the state of Queensland have merged into the Liberal National Party, LNP) dominate Australian politics. However, smaller parties and independent candidates can be competitive in individual electorates and in the Senate. The long-established Australian Greens, several new entrants including the Palmer United Party, Katter's Australia Party, the Pirate Party, and the WikiLeaks Party, and a number of minor, often conservative and right-leaning parties, therefore also contested the 2013 election.

The Australian parliamentary system is based on the Westminster system. At the federal level, there are two houses of parliament: the House of Representatives, where members represent local electorates, and the Senate, where members represent states—but there are some notable differences to the election process. Australia uses preferential voting; with votes for minor candidates distributed to other candidates following the voters' stated preferences until one candidate has more than 50 per cent of the vote. This applies for each electorate, and a similar system is used for the Senate except that the vote here is to elect multiple Senators. Government is then formed by the party with a majority of seats in the House of Representatives, either in its own right or in coalition with other parties, and the leader of that party becomes Prime Minister. The other major distinctive aspect of Australian elections is that voting is compulsory for eligible citizens aged 18 and over: anyone registered on the electoral roll who does not vote in an election that they are supposed to can receive a fine. This results in a higher voter turnout than in other Western democracies and contributes to the familiarity and ritualisation of election experiences in Australia. It also implies at least a passing engagement with politics, even if only to criticise this necessity.

Australian Election Campaigns on Social Media

There has been widespread adoption of online platforms for sharing commentary, content, and experiences, both publicly and among a more select audience with social media increasingly integrated into the Australian political and media landscapes. Politicians and their parties run Twitter accounts and Facebook pages as part of their online presences, while YouTube, Instagram, and other content-sharing channels have also been employed for political purposes. Social media make politicians accessible to a wider audience, connecting them in additional ways—using popular channels—to citizens online. Depending on their individual strategies, this means that politicians can present a particular persona or combat a common perception of their character. During the latter stages of his first period as Prime Minister, and especially after being deposed by Julia Gillard, Kevin Rudd had been described as micromanaging and difficult, his real self very different to his media image and distant from his party and the electorate (Wilson, 2014). Before the 2013 ALP leadership spill and as a newly reinstalled Prime Minister, Rudd started posting selfies on social media in an attempt to seem more personable and down to earth than his opponents had previously depicted him. These attempts were not necessarily successful, though: Rudd's selfies, including a post-shaving photo complete with small cuts, were also widely criticised and satirised as examples of Rudd's purported narcissism (Chen, 2015; Manning & Phiddian, 2015).

While not the only platform used for this purpose, Twitter has become an established medium for political discussions in Australia, with journalists, commentators, politicians, analysts, lobbyists, activists, and citizens all active participants. There has also been a standardised approach to discussing Australian politics on Twitter through the adoption of common hashtags: the #ausvotes hashtag used in 2010 and then again in 2013 provides a starting point for our studies into social media and elections. Since 2010, though, the scope of our research has expanded beyond hashtags alone to also track user accounts and mentions of candidates and parties. While the following analysis focuses on the 2013 federal election, this work builds on methodologies and findings developed from research into the 2010 federal election and state elections in Queensland and Western Australia in 2012 and 2013, respectively.

During the 2013 election, we used YourTwapperKeeper to capture data from the Twitter API, representing specified hashtags (including #ausvotes), and tweets by and @mentioning candidates' accounts (for a full description of our methods from previous elections, see Bruns & Highfield, 2013). In total, during the 2013 election campaign, we tracked the Twitter accounts of some 454 sitting members and candidates across the 150 Australian federal lower house electorates and the eight state and territory senate contests, and captured some 694,000 tweets @mentioning or originating from these accounts between 4 August and 8 September 2013. The data set was variously filtered to isolate periods of interest, topics, and individual users, with the text and media content of relevant tweets studied to provide further context and explanation of the patterns identified here.

We observed regular patterns in Australian election coverage on social media, and these appear to apply internationally, too. Tweeting using the main election hashtag gradually increases during the campaign, with spikes coinciding with the major broadcast events: in particular, televised debates involving party leaders, a trait not unique to Australia (see, for instance, Larsson & Moe, 2013). There is then a marked increase in tweeting in the days leading up to the vote itself, while election day results in a clear peak in related social media activity. However, this spike in tweeting is a result of several different user practices that coincide on election day, all related to the voting context but reflecting personal experiences as well as engaging with the results at large.

#ausvotes tweeting during the 2013 election followed this pattern: The election was called on 4 August, with the vote on 7 September 2013, and over the four weeks of the campaign the gradual increase of activity saw peaks on days with televised debates and the ALP's campaign 'launch' (which came a week before the vote). The tweeting increased in the days leading up to the election. Yet the hashtag does not represent the entire election coverage on Twitter: while it provides a useful marker for related content, it is not universally used in election tweets, or by candidates actively participating on Twitter. While #ausvotes provides an initial context for the election, by demonstrating when there was peak interest or activity, analysis needs to look further to determine *how* social media were used during the campaign, rather than just *when*.

Tweeting about and by Candidates in the 2013 Election

One way of doing so is to track @mentions of the main candidates, to see which political figures are attracting attention (whether positive or negative) and in what contexts. The Australian electoral system is parliamentarian and constituency-centered, unlike, for instance, the U.S. presidential system. However, the popular media portrayal of Australian elections, including the social media attention directed towards candidates, shows that there is a presidential-style focus on the leaders of the two major parties, well ahead of other candidates and sitting politicians.

Figure 24.1 shows the @mentions (including @replies and retweets) of the Twitter accounts of the most party leaders during the campaign, including Rudd and Abbott as well as Clive Palmer and Christine Milne, respectively the leaders of the Palmer United Party and the Australian Greens. The mentions of Rudd and Abbott far exceeded those of the other accounts, although their fortunes fluctuated against one another: spikes again accompanied televised debates between the two leaders, but other events also provoked increased mentions, such as gaffes like Abbott remarking that a Liberal candidate had 'sex appeal'.

Although the focus of Twitter coverage was directed towards Rudd and Abbott as the two leaders contesting to become Prime Minister, this prominence is not only a

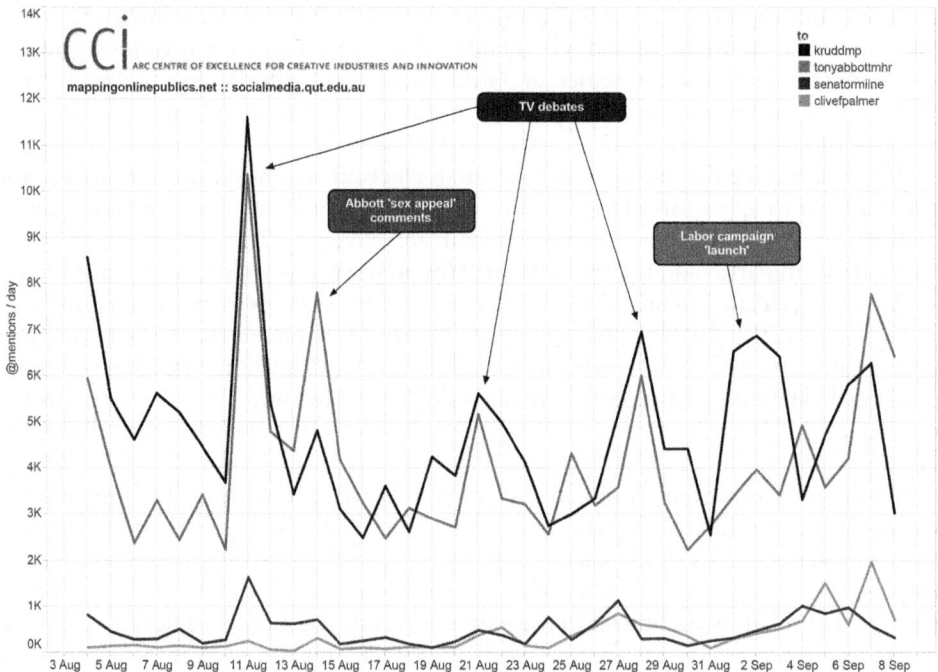

Figure 24.1 @mentions of Party Leaders, 4 August to 8 September 2013

response to tweeting activity by the politicians in question. During the campaign, Abbott and Rudd each posted only around 100 tweets, with their deputies and other prominent members of their respective parties being considerably more active on Twitter. Figures from both sides, including Malcolm Turnbull and Julie Bishop (Liberal) and Anthony Albanese and Penny Wong (ALP) doubled and even tripled their leaders' total campaign tweets. However, even Albanese, the most active representative from either major party, posted fewer than 500 tweets during the 35-day campaign; in comparison, the Greens leader Christine Milne tweeted over 1,300 times during this period.

Such divergent activity patterns amongst the leading politicians did not result in significantly different numbers of retweets received by their tweets. While Twitter users tweeted about the major candidates regularly and at substantial volume throughout the election period, as Figure 24.1 shows, their choices to rebroadcast what the politicians posted was based less on the prominence of the account and more simply a response to specific moments or comments. Tony Abbott received the most daily retweets on the day the election was called, but during the rest of the campaign retweets of his and Kevin Rudd's posts were much more limited, generally remaining at below 100 retweets per day (and therefore astonishingly low, given that each leader's account was @mentioned some 4,200 times per day, on average). The only other significant peaks in the daily number of retweets were received by Greens leader Milne and by ALP Senator Penny Wong, and both remained isolated incidents; ordinarily, even highly active Twitter user Milne received fewer than 20 retweets per day.

The brief spike in retweets for Wong's account is worth noting, however, as it represents a rare incident of a senior politician stepping outside their carefully stage-managed campaign role and responding forcefully to an ordinary Twitter user. Wong (the first Australian federal politician to be openly in a same-gender relationship) tweeted an off-the-cuff response to a user registering their opposition to same-sex marriage, and this response, which also quoted the original tweet (which itself was later deleted), was then widely spread by other Twitter users, receiving over 500 retweets in one day:

> Gee, highly original. Hope your one follower enjoyed it. RT @[redacted]: @SenatorWong marriage is for Adam & Eve, not Adam & Steve.

Throughout the rest of the campaign, Wong was not retweeted especially widely, but this comment clearly cut through and travelled beyond her follower list, due to its relevance to the election and the long-running debate about gay marriage legislation in Australia but especially also because of its particularly straight-talking style.

Figure 24.1 also demonstrates that, while Rudd and Abbott were the most mentioned politicians during the election, other major figures also maintained presences on Twitter without being particularly active. This includes several senior frontbenchers of the Liberal Party, which in previous state elections had adopted a so-called small-target strategy of not using social media widely in order to avoid gaffes and to control its message (Highfield, 2013). However, the prominent figures were present on Twitter and the combined @mentions for ALP and Liberal candidates exceeded any other party by 50,000 tweets even without counting @mentions of Rudd or Abbott. Nevertheless, the total tweeted output *by* each party's candidates shows that the Liberal Party (and its coalition partners) were still considerably less active than either the ALP or the Greens. The 131 ALP candidates on Twitter were responsible for nearly 17,000 tweets during the campaign, while the 80 Greens candidates contributed just under 12,000 tweets. No other party exceeded 10,000 tweets; the next highest total was from the Pirate Party, contesting its first federal election with seven tweeting candidates and becoming the only other party to contribute more than 5000 tweets, while the cumulative activity of the 82 tweeting Liberal Party candidates totalled over 4,000 tweets.

These patterns are in keeping with general trends from Australia and overseas. Previous elections have seen ALP politicians and candidates as more active and more represented on social media than their conservative opponents, for instance. Similarly, analyses of Twitter-based political commentary in various European countries have found that Green parties have taken to social media as popular communication and campaigning tools (Ausserhofer & Maireder, 2013). In countries such as Australia, where the Greens are a relatively minor party and do not attract the support, attention, or funding of the major parties, social media can offer a means for sharing information and attracting voters that might not be available through traditional media channels. Furthermore, both the Greens and the Pirate Party have clear connections with internet-related issues and policies, and so their use of social media demonstrates their familiarity with online communication and platforms.

Candidate strategies on Twitter during the 2013 election reflected a mix of party promotion and engagement with issues and discussions across party lines. Extracting the @mentions of other candidates from tweets posted during the campaign, there was some clustering along party lines. Greens candidates, for instance, repeatedly @mentioned one another—and especially Christine Milne, the party leader, and Adam Bandt, the sole Greens member in the House of Representatives—in their tweets, as a means of responding to comments by fellow candidates and promoting the party. Cross-party connections were still apparent, particularly when topical interests converged or for specific rivalries and contests. The bridging role of Greens Senator Scott Ludlam, between the Greens and the Pirate Party, resulted from his visibility in debates around Internet policy, for instance. While ALP and Liberal candidate strategies focused on @mentioning other candidates from their parties, there was also substantial tweeting directed at their opposition. Kevin Rudd and Tony Abbott were often mentioned in tandem, and there were similar connections between other major figures in both parties; Treasurer Wayne Swan and Shadow Treasurer Joe Hockey, for example, were also closely linked through @mentions. Finally, close contests in individual electorates also made for connections between opposing candidates. Most notably, the Liberal member for Indi, Sophie Mirabella, was @mentioned repeatedly in tweets by rival independent candidate Cathy McGowan (who went on to win the seat).

While @mentions showed candidates' willingness to engage opposition members, whether in civil debate or by criticising and attacking them, their retweeting patterns exhibited very different tendencies. The retweet network generated from candidates reposting tweets by other candidates is seen in Figure 24.2; this network clearly demonstrates that retweeting is a party-oriented strategy. Clustering is highly focused on parties, with distinct groups of ALP, Liberal, Greens, Pirate Party, and Palmer United Party candidates. These candidates predominantly only retweeted their fellow party candidates, promoting their messages and campaigns. Although generally retweets may serve various purposes and are not necessarily an endorsement of another Twitter user's views, for the candidates studied here retweeting outside of the party was not a common approach, most likely in order to avoid the risk of appearing to promote a rival's messages.

The patterns of activity and attention around candidates on Twitter suggest that social media, while adopted by the various parties, occupy different places in campaign

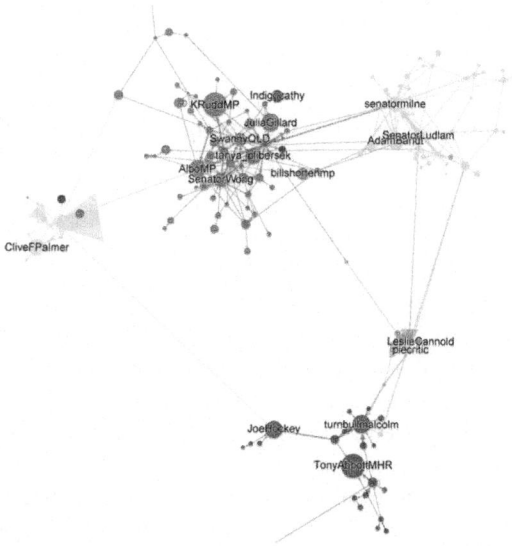

Figure 24.2 Network of Retweets between Candidates, 4 August to 8 September 2013

strategy for different parties, as well as for citizens. The major parties are present on Twitter, but actual tweeting activity highlights a wide gulf between ALP and Liberal Party. ALP candidates tweeted throughout the election campaign while Liberal candidates were much less active. Instead, smaller parties such as the Greens and the Pirate Party posted more often on Twitter, using social media as an outlet for their messages. Yet this activity also over-ascribes prominence to these parties, in particular the Pirate Party. Despite being very active on social media, the Pirate Party did not attract a substantial share of the vote. Its tweeting is more representative of the importance of the Internet to its policies and interests than of the size of its support base.

Twitter activity thus provides an important perspective on the public discussions and campaigns taking place during elections, but it is not the campaign itself; tweeting during the 2013 Australian federal election skewed towards an urban electorate, with the metropolitan areas of the major Australian cities most represented here. Twitter activity is also not demonstrative of each party's fortunes in the election: the Liberal Party's strategy of lower levels of activity, avoiding gaffes, and focusing on the party leadership team might have resulted in far fewer tweets than for other parties, but they were also successful in winning the election overall. The ALP's strategy was less focused, in comparison; while many candidates were active, there was a lack of coordination across the leadership team (and despite his well-established social media presence, Kevin Rudd himself was not particularly active on Twitter during the campaign). The Greens' high levels of tweeting might also have had negative effects: increased activity does not mean increased support and engagement, and the sheer output of tweets by Christine Milne in particular might have been excessive for followers.

Most fundamentally, what our observation of activity patterns during the 2013 election indicates is that there is an almost complete disconnect between the tweeting activities of election candidates on the one hand, and the volume of @mentions they receive on the other. Many Twitter users in Australia who did engage with the election evidently simply used the Twitter handles of politicians like Kevin Rudd and Tony

Abbott as alternatives for their names, without necessarily following these leaders' tweets, and certainly without bothering to retweet their messages on a day-to-day basis.

Election Day on Twitter: Tweeting while Australia Votes

These patterns of politician activity and user interaction on social media provide one picture of Australian elections, but politicians are not the only participants in the campaigns or in the Twitter discussions. Tweeting directly at or about candidates is just one way that Australians might engage with elections on social media. Previous studies of election coverage on Twitter have noted the patterns of activity resulting in peak tweeting on election day itself. Examining election-day tweets for the 2013 election in more detail finds that this spike is the result of several different practices over the course of the day, using Twitter for different purposes as the nation goes to the polls. For the analysis of these practices, we return our focus to the #ausvotes hashtag.

Three distinct phases of election-day tweeting are apparent within the Australian context. Figure 24.3 shows the total tweets per hour tagged with #ausvotes on 7 September 2013—the date of the federal election. There is a regular level of tweeting activity during voting period itself, from 8 a.m. to 6 p.m., with the end of polling and the start of the analysis and vote counting serving as the catalyst for increased tweeting. A third phase accompanies the official results and, especially, the victory and concession speeches made the respective leaders of the major parties.

These three phases each feature their own particular practices and purposes for election-day tweeting. The day starts with tweets about the individual and personal experience of voting, at the micro-level of the election. After the polls close, there is a shift to more analytical tweets, moving from the personal to a greater mix of the individual's own electorate with nationwide predictions and results. Finally, the official results and leaders' speeches are accompanied by a predominantly reactionary mode of tweeting, where users provide live responses to the broadcast media coverage of

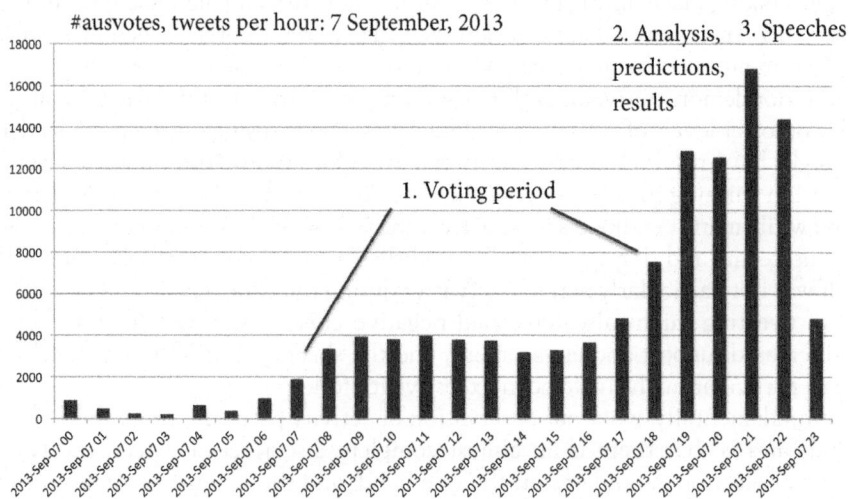

Figure 24.3 #ausvotes Tweets per Hour, 7 September 2013

election night, including live tweeting the speeches. The election-day-tweeting model also exhibits a narrowing of the scope of the comments posted during the day. While there is a general, shared context of the election, the first phase features a wide range of topics as users provide their own personal thoughts on voting and campaigns, specific to them. The shift to the analytical discussion and, later, the live tweeting of results, though, sees the common context become substantially more focused: commentary becomes less individualised, instead reflecting responses to mass broadcasts.

The first phase of election-day tweeting, the personal experience, sees a mix of political commentary and individual reports on the democratic act of voting. In the context of a compulsory voting system in particular, actually going to a polling place and filling in a ballot paper is a necessary activity for enrolled voters. This obligation is reflected in tweets during this period—criticising the requirement that an individual has to interrupt their day to vote, ignoring the fact that this is a privilege not available to many people around the world—which represents quite a grudging engagement with the election. Other tweets feature partisan commentary, promoting parties and candidates at the local and national level in a last-minute campaign push at a time when formal political advertising in broadcast media is embargoed. Tweets might also reflect the temporary intrusion of the political into an individual's usual weekend and social media activities; their messages might not normally have any political content, but their brief participation in the election allows a mix of the everyday and politics, even if the content is only along the lines of 'just voted. #dutyfulfilled #ausvotes'.

The voting experience also informs various political rituals which play out both physically and on social media. There are aspects of election days which are well-established routines for Australian voters: voting takes place on Saturday, with polling places at local schools and community centres often accompanied by fundraising barbecues (sausage sizzles) and cake stalls (Meikle, Wilson, & Saunders, 2008). These rituals have been recognised and underlined on social media, with several independent projects running online on election days to document the election day experience and to provide information for people still to vote. Projects such as *Booth Reviews*, *Democracy Sausage*, *Snag Votes*, and *The Hungry Voter* respond to the compulsory voting context by variously soliciting feedback on the voting experience and making information about polling places available to people still to vote. *Booth Reviews* asks for crowd-sourced voter feedback about the experience and facilities at individual polling places, whereas the other projects named above reflect directly the rituals of Australian elections. They offer information specifically about the food available at polling places, putting user contributions on collaborative maps and promoting further participation to improve the accuracy of the information. Although a user tweeting about the availability (or lack thereof) of 'democracy sausage' at their local polling place might not be offering any political opinions or campaigning, they are still engaging with the election itself by documenting their experience of voting. Such tweets might also include general election hashtags such as #ausvotes in addition to the project-specific #snagvotes, for example. Conversely, #democracysausage and its ilk have also become de facto markers and punch lines for election coverage in general, providing commentary without necessarily contributing information to the relevant projects.

The personal experience in the first phase of election-day voting may also be separate to others' experiences, with @mentions, @replies, and retweets not widespread—and certainly less focused on prominent accounts. During the second phase, though, as the focus of tweets moves from the individual experience to the wider coverage of the election with predictions, analyses, and initial results, different information flows are apparent. Established media and political actors become central figures in the election coverage on Twitter, demonstrated through high levels of @mentions. This pattern is enhanced by some broadcasters, such as the ABC, which use common hashtags like #ausvotes rather than their own channel-specific election hashtags. Similarly, journalists and accounts for local news stations will retweet the relevant comments posted by their parent media organisations, further centralising established media accounts. For the journalists, politicians, and pundits appearing on election night broadcasts, their presence will also lead to increased levels of @mentions, as users employ Twitter handles as shorthand for their full names.

This second phase is not entirely broadcast–oriented, though; local results and candidates remain important, but they are also incorporated into the overall narrative of the election results, and are at times even referred to on air as they report new exit polls or counting updates from local polling places. This phase then bridges the personal model of election day and the mass, common context of the official results tally on election night. In the final phase, then, the focus is narrower still, as users respond to the major results and the specific media coverage being observed. There is now a shared focus by a mass audience on a small handful of actors—and especially on the leaders of the Liberal Party and the ALP—rather than a distributed coverage of the voting experience. Attention is directed towards these key figures, as users live–tweet the speeches and offer short, immediate analyses of the remarks and the future implications of the election results.

The election-day tweeting practices then suggest a general transition from personal to popular contexts over the course of the day, as social media discussions ultimately coalesce around a common focus on the results and speeches. While election commentary mixes political and personal views throughout, with responses to the results including personal opinions as well as partisan slogans, the early tweets are more uniquely individual in their content: one person's voting experience will not be the same as another's. By the time of the speeches, however, the individual context is subsumed by a shared response to a common topic. There is a further participatory aspect during these latter phases, though, similar to other media events, as social media users comment on broadcasts as they happen and offer analysis, invective, and pithy one-liners (see, for example, Harrington, 2013).

What Australian election-day tweeting practices demonstrate, then, is that some aspects of the traditional politics-media dynamic are reinforced on social media. The role of traditional media sources for both providing and amplifying information is central—even if users do not mention media accounts, they are responding to elections as media events. Analysts, commentators, and politicians appearing in the broadcast coverage might not simultaneously tweet, but they still receive high numbers of @mentions from other users due to the practice of using Twitter handles rather than proper names. This further positions these established gatekeepers as central figures, even if they are only being invoked in the social media discussion rather than actively participating.

This is not to say that the traditional political and media voices are the only actors of note; newer and alternative voices can also achieve prominence and the Twitter discussions, both during elections and in more everyday political contexts are a mixed space of the old and the new. However, it is clear that established political figures are still central to these discussions, even with inconsistent use of social media by politicians and parties. While their accounts are @mentioned by other users, they are not universally tweeting on election day itself. Last-minute social media campaigning is not a common strategy, as candidates make appearances at local polling places to promote their causes in person rather than on Twitter.

The tweeting practices of the Australian electorate highlight that elections and political discussions are not the sole preserve of the political elite. The election context affords a wide range of subjects in social media discussions that might be tangential to the actual democratic process. Similarly, election-day tweets are not necessarily 'serious' in tone, with humour and sarcasm, in text and in image-based memes and macros, present in online commentary around the vote. While a common hashtag like #ausvotes acts as a central marker to denote election-related coverage, what the election day practices make clear is that there are several different approaches to discussing the election that are connected by these hashtags, and which otherwise might not intersect. Hashtags can serve useful curatorial purposes, but they may also suggest the existence of a more unified discussion than the diverse and distinct tweeting patterns that are actually found in the Australian context.

Conclusion

The use of Twitter by many Australians for ongoing communication, including regular political discussions, has led to the development of rituals and standard practices around social media and media events, inviting diverse kinds of participation on social media. In addition to contributions by the politically engaged, election days also see increased activity from casual contributors, whose interest or participation within political themes is limited to the period in which they are required by law to be involved due to the compulsory voting context. Secondary hashtags, around sub-themes, issues, and rituals, hook into these different practices and audiences, from tweeting about food availability at polling places to discussing specific parties or electorates.

In this chapter, we have primarily focused on the use of Twitter during the 2013 Australian federal election, by politicians and citizens alike. Of course, Twitter is not representative of the Australian population at large, or indeed of Australians on social media: other platforms, including Facebook and Instagram, are used for election campaigning and commentary, for documenting and sharing the experience of voting, and for reacting to events as they occur. However, Twitter has seen a relatively widespread uptake in Australia (see Bruns, Burgess, & Highfield, 2014), and so the practices observed here do demonstrate behaviours by more people than just the traditional political elite. Twitter is a space in which Australian politicians, journalists, and ordinary citizens are present, and can potentially interact as well as providing their own interpretation of political topics. At the same time, though, the mediation of politics takes place across multiple platforms, involving diverse actors who also participate on more than one platform themselves. Australians are willing to use social media platforms for political discussion and engagement. Building on the findings from Twitter to examine how this takes place across the wider media ecology is the next major step for our research.

Acknowledgments

Preliminary findings from the individual election studies drawn on here were presented at several conferences, including ECREA Istanbul 2012, ANZCA Fremantle 2013, AoIR Denver 2013, and Social Media and the Transformation of Public Space Amsterdam 2014. This research was supported by the Norwegian Research Council project

The Impact of Social Media on Agenda-Setting in Election Campaigns, the ARC Future Fellowship project Understanding Intermedia Information Flows in the Australian Online Public Sphere, and an ATN-DAAD collaboration project with Ludwig-Maximilians-Universität Munich.

References

Ausserhofer, J., & Maireder, A. (2013) "National politics on Twitter: Structures and topics of a networked public sphere," *Information, Communication & Society*, 16(3), pp. 291–314.

Bruns, A., Burgess, J., & Highfield, T. (2014) "A 'big data' approach to mapping the Australian Twittersphere," in P. L. Arthur & K. Bode (eds.), *Advancing Digital Humanities: Research, Methods, Theories*, Houndmills: Palgrave Macmillan.

Bruns, A., & Highfield, T. (2013) "Political networks on Twitter," *Information, Communication & Society*, 16(5), pp. 667–691.

Burgess, J., & Bruns, A. (2012) "(Not) The Twitter election: The dynamics of the #ausvotes conversation in relation to the Australian media ecology," *Journalism Practice*, 6(3), pp. 384–402.

Chen, P. J. (2015) "New media in the electoral context: The new normal," in C. Johnson & J. Wanna (eds.), *Abbott's Gambit: The 2013 Australian Federal Election*, Canberra: ANU Press, pp. 81–94.

Coleman, S. (2006) "How the other half votes: Big Brother viewers and the 2005 general election," *International Journal of Cultural Studies*, 9(4), pp. 457–479.

Flew, T. (2008) "Not yet the Internet election: Online media, political commentary and the 2007 Australian federal election," *Media International Australia Incorporating Culture and Policy*, (126), pp. 5–13.

Garden, M. (2014) "Australian journalist-blogs: A shift in audience relationships or mere window dressing?" *Journalism*, (online first), first published on 1 December 2014. doi:10.1177/1464884914557923.

Given, J., & Radywyl, N. (2013) "Questions & answers & tweets," *Communication, Politics & Culture*, 46. Retrieved from www.rmit.edu.au/browse;ID=t8dzoos720ck1.

Harrington, S. (2013) "Tweeting about the telly: Live TV, audiences, and social media," in K. Weller, A. Bruns, J. Burgess, M. Mahrt, & C. Puschmann (eds.), *Twitter and Society*, New York: Peter Lang, pp. 237–247.

Highfield, T. (2013) "National and state-level politics on social media: Twitter, Australian political discussions, and the online commentariat," *International Journal of E-Governance*, 6(4), pp. 342–360.

Highfield, T., & Bruns, A. (2012) "Confrontation and cooptation: A brief history of Australian political blogs," *Media International Australia*, (143), pp. 89–98.

Jericho, G. (2012). *The rise of the fifth estate: Social media and blogging in Australian politics*. Melbourne: Scribe.

Larsson, A. O., & Moe, H. (2013) "Twitter in politics and elections: Insights from Scandinavia, in K. Weller, A. Bruns, J. Burgess, M. Mahrt, & C. Puschmann (eds.), *Twitter & Society*. New York: Peter Lang.

Manning, H., & Phiddian, R. (2015). "Nearly all about Kevin: The election as drawn by Australian cartoonists," in C. Johnson & J. Wanna (eds.), *Abbott's Gambit: The 2013 Australian Federal Election*, Canberra: ANU Press, pp. 161–187.

Meikle, G., Wilson, J., & Saunders, B. (2008) "Vote/Citizen," *M/C Journal*, 11(1). Retrieved from http://journal.media-culture.org.au/index.php/mcjournal/article/viewArticle/20.

Wilson, J. (2014) "Kevin Rudd, celebrity and audience democracy in Australia," *Journalism*, 15(2), pp. 202–217.

25

NOT JUST A FACE(BOOK) IN THE CROWD

Candidates' Use of Facebook during the Danish 2011 Parliamentary Election Campaign

Morten Skovsgaard and Arjen van Dalen

Introduction

Great expectations surfaced in the build up to the 2011 Danish parliamentary election campaign, with blunt predictions such as: "We will experience a digital revolution in the election campaign" (Lotte Hansen, PR consultant and former spin doctor, in Andreassen, 2011, para. 1). These predictions were expressed following a phase of fast adaption to the digital age. The Internet penetration and Facebook usage in Denmark was among the highest in the world (Internet World Stats, 2012; Socialbakers, 2012).

In spite of such 'digital revolution' expectations, the political parties were not totally convinced that social media were the most efficient way to communicate with voters. Already early in the election campaign, it was reported by the newspapers *Information* and *Jyllands-Posten* that the third biggest party in parliament, Danish People's Party, did not even have a public Facebook profile. According to the party's manager of press relations, they preferred personal dialogue with citizens on the streets or at public meetings.[1]

Social media have become an integral part of election campaigns in the Western world (Enli & Moe, 2013), but they have not revolutionised political campaigning, and the prediction of a digital revolution is thus exaggerated. Social media should not be discarded as insignificant in election campaigns, rather they should be considered one among several tools politicians resort to when they want to reach potential voters (Towner & Dulio, 2012: 99). Candidates utilise a mix of campaign channels such as advertisements, mass media, live debates, direct contacts on the streets or at people's front doors, and social media (Kleis Nielsen, 2012: 17). There are also significant individual differences in the degrees to which the candidates embrace social media as new digital tools for political communication (Skovsgaard & van Dalen, 2013). The diversity of candidates' use of social media in election campaigns contradicts the idea of an 'across the board' digital revolution and calls for more detailed analysis of who uses social media, to what extent, and for what reasons.

In this chapter we embark on a detailed analysis by combining a survey of the candidates for the 2011 Danish parliamentary election with their actual posting behaviour on Facebook during the campaign. Integrating these two data sources gives us the opportunity to explore who uses Facebook and for which reasons. Our study shows that social media should be seen as one among several tools in the campaign tool box. Campaigning on Facebook is particularly important for a select group of candidates—in particular younger candidates, who do not have easy access to the mass media and who primarily campaign to get attention for themselves rather than for the party. We first briefly describe the Danish electoral system, and the main sources of political information for Danes, to provide necessary context for our study.

Danish Electoral System and the Growing Importance of Social Media

After the bourgeois coalition had enjoyed three rather comfortable election wins and 10 years in government, the 2011 election was decided by a small margin, and the centre-left coalition replaced the bourgeois government. The prospect of a close race resulted in an election campaign with high incentives to actively campaign on both sides of the political spectrum.

In the Danish multiparty system, elections are proportional, which gives candidates a double incentive to campaign. At the same time they compete to maximise their own parties' share of the total number of votes (interparty competition) and to maximise their own number of votes to beat their fellow candidates from the same party in the race for the party's seats in parliament (intraparty competition). With 784 candidates from nine parties of very different size in parliament (plus 20 independents) running for office, there is considerable variation in the incentive structure as well as the campaign strategy and resources among the candidates. This can be expected to affect to what degree and for what purposes the candidates use the different campaign channels—including social media.

According to Internet World Stats (2012), almost three million Danes use Facebook, which is equal to approximately 63 per cent of the population. Despite a high Facebook use, traditional mass media are still the most important source to political communication in Denmark. The Danes considered television the most important and trustworthy source of information in the 2011 election campaign (Hoff et al., 2013: 13). The Danish media system is characterised by an early professionalisation of journalism (Hallin & Mancini, 2004). Politics is generally covered in accordance with a media logic where institutional news values determine what is covered and how it is covered. This means that election coverage in the Danish media are not biased based on political leaning, but rather that there is an uneven access to the mass media between incumbents and challengers, and between powerful candidates and less powerful candidates (Albæk et al., 2010; Hopmann et al., 2011).

Prior to the 2011 election, several political campaign leaders remarked that in spite of increased importance of social media, the channel was still of less importance compared to the mass media, which still set the agenda (Nyegård Espersen, 2011). In addition, direct contact with voters was mentioned as a means of campaigning with more relevance than social media use. Danish politicians acknowledge that elections cannot be won by media spin alone. A tactical ground war, where parties strategically plan to get in personal contact is indeed a central part of winning campaign strategies around the world (Kleis Nielsen, 2012). These ground wars are not yet as professionalised and strategically planned, as in the U.S. Nevertheless, Danish parties are also becoming more tactical in their personal contacts with voters (Nyegård Espersen, 2011).

In terms of being a source of campaign information, the importance of social media is growing even though other sources are still more important. According to surveys, almost one in five Danish voters gets political information from and engages in political debate on social media. There are, however, some segments that are more politically active on social media than others, and certain types of engagement are more common than others. First, young people are most politically active on social media and thus more likely to engage with politicians. Second, those who are already engaged in politics offline and who already were directly or indirectly related to the politicians' network were more likely to connect with politicians online (Normann Andersen & Medaglia, 2009: 110). Third, the most typical form of engaging with politics on social media is to 'like' or read posts, while actively searching for information or commenting on politicians' posts is still less common (Hoff et al., 2013). In the next part, we will discuss more closely how social media is used in recent Danish election campaigns.

Key Advantages of Social Media in Danish Election Campaigns

Social media have a number of advantages as a campaign tool compared to other campaign channels, and in a Danish political context, three advantages are particularly relevant. First, there is a remarkably *lower entry barrier* compared to more costly campaign channels. While candidates have to pay large sums for advertising, all it takes to campaign on social media is a profile on Facebook or Twitter which serve as a platform from which any candidate can communicate unlimited. To design and maintain a professional social media profile might require both time and resources, but compared to the costs of spots on television or radio these costs are minimal. This makes Facebook an attractive campaign channel for Danish candidates who generally work with small budgets.

The second advantage is that social media is a platform where the political candidates have *more control over their message* than when they campaign through the mass media. By-passing the mass media is particularly attractive in Denmark, since Danish journalists are more critical towards politicians than their colleagues in several other European countries (Skovsgaard et al., 2012; van Dalen, 2012). In the context of the mass media, the candidates do not control how they are portrayed and they seldom come across with their messages without interference as the journalists will decide the framing of the story. Not least because journalists have a preference for conflict and negativity (e.g. Baum & Groeling, 2010; Soroka, 2014), social media has the advantage of being an arena where the candidates have more autonomous control over their message.

A third advantage is that social media are well-suited for *personalised and candidate-centred campaigns*, meaning that candidates primarily want to promote their own candidacy rather than the party. Such a personalised campaign is particularly important for Danish candidates who are engaged in intra-party competition for a seat in parliament, and need to mobilise potential voters (Skovsgaard & van Dalen, 2013). Social media offer ample opportunity for direct contact between the individual politician and potential voters (e.g. Druckman et al, 2007; Van Santen & Van Zoonen, 2010). Compared to canvassing, candidates will potentially reach more people on social media in an instant than they can shake hands with during a whole day on the street. Still, a kind of direct contact with potential voters can be maintained on the social media.

Politicians may engage in debate and respond directly to questions or comments from citizens, which is not possible when they campaign through the mass media.

Compared to social media, traditional mass media have advantages when the goal is to get in contact with the broader population (Maarek, 2011). Since people who follow politicians on Facebook are often already supporting them (Normann Andersen & Medaglia, 2009), candidates preach to the already converted on social media, which, of course, is problematic if the goal is to win over voters (Karlsen, 2011). Through mass media candidates can reach supporters and opponents as well as undecided voters. Although media exposure would be beneficial for all candidates, not everyone is able to make use of this to the same extent. Due to institutionalised news values, the mass media tend to cover already powerful and high-profiled candidates, at the expense of less influential and less profiled candidates (e.g. Hopmann et al., 2011; van Dalen, 2012).

A survey among the candidates for the 2011 election in Denmark pinpoints newsworthiness as an important factor explaining how Danish candidates use social media and traditional media (Skovsgaard & van Dalen, 2013). The survey identified three different groups of politicians on the basis of their media use; the first group emphasised traditional mass media while also giving some priority to social media. The second group almost disregarded national media and focused more on social media in addition to local and regional newspapers. The third group did not find any of the campaign channels very important, which indicates that they hardly campaigned at all. A characteristic of the second group, the candidates who emphasise social media more than mass media, was that they were less 'newsworthy', and that they use social media to compensate for the lack of access to mainstream media. Among the typical traits were that the group using social media most actively were less experienced, and more likely to be challengers compared to candidates who emphasise traditional mass media above social media. The candidates who focus mainly on the national news media use social media mostly as a supplementary channel; first and foremost intended as a means to gain coverage in traditional media (Skovsgaard & van Dalen, 2013).

Survey measures rely on the respondents' self-reported perceptions of their behaviour rather than actual behaviour, and studies have found significant inconsistencies between self-reported behaviour and actual behaviour (Olsen, 1998). Based on these findings, this study will combine the survey data with analysis of the candidates' actual use of Facebook. The rationale for choosing Facebook is its position as the dominant social network site in Denmark,[2] and in turn, its unique status in terms of reaching voters and its related popularity among Danish politicians (Hansen & Kosiara-Pedersen, 2014).

As we demonstrated above, the widespread usage of Facebook combined with the easy access, control over the message, and the personalised and direct mode of communication make the social media site a potentially useful campaign channel for candidates. There were, however, significant differences between how various groups of politicians—depending mostly on their competitive position—used Facebook according to the survey. Based on this backdrop, we will investigate the following questions: First, what characterises the candidates who are most likely to have a public Facebook profile? To what degree do individual differences demonstrate patterns related to age, incumbency status, and personalised campaigning, and chances of being elected? Second, how does the use of Facebook compare to traditional campaigning such as canvassing and interviews in broadcast media, and which candidates are most likely to use each of these forms of campaigning? Third, *what motivates politicians* to use social media, and to what degree do politicians use their public Facebook profile mainly for a personalised campaign or mainly for reaching a broader audience? Through studying these questions, this chapter will provide detailed insight into candidates' use of Facebook in the Danish election campaign. Before we proceed to the analysis, we will present the data and the method of the study.

Data

The above research questions will be analysed on the basis of a combination of two datasets from the 2011 Danish parliamentary elections. The first dataset is a collection of all updates on the public Facebook pages of candidates who were running for a party in the 2011 election campaign (van Dalen et al., 2014).[3] The limitation to public profiles is a result of Facebook's privacy policy, and as a result we do not study the politicians' private profiles.

Out of the total number of 784 candidates, 217, or 28 per cent, of the Danish candidates had a public Facebook profile and posted at least one message during the 2011 campaign. The campaign ran from 26 August, when the prime minister called the elections, until election day, on 15 September. Over this period all status updates by the candidates were collected. These 6,388 status updates include 2,805 simple status updates, 1,872 links, 1,143 pictures, 545 videos, and 23 other types of updates.

This dataset was merged with the responses of 375 of the same candidates to a questionnaire including questions about their professional background, the election campaign, and motivations to use social media (see Elmelund-Præstekær & Schumacher, 2014; Skovsgaard & van Dalen, 2013). Data collection took place in October and November 2011, as part of the Comparative Candidate Survey project.[4] Response rate for the survey is 49 per cent and the respondents are representative of candidates' age, gender, and party affiliation, but it is worth noting that new candidates responded more frequently than established candidates. Combined, these two data sets will provide insight into the politicians' activity and motivations for using Facebook, as well as differences between various groups of politicians.

Characteristics of the Most Active Politicians

On average, candidates with an active public Facebook profile posted 29 updates during the three weeks parliamentary election campaign, but there was substantial variation between the individual candidates. While 44 per cent of the candidates posted less than once a day, the most active candidate posted 179 updates in total. To identify shared characteristics of the most active candidates we identified the ten most active candidates (Table 25.1).

A key characteristic of the most active candidates was that they had personal strategies, rather party-centred strategies; among the 10 most posting candidates the number of new candidates was fairly equal to the number of established candidates. Four candidates are from government parties and six candidates from opposition parties. The second most posting candidate was incumbent Prime Minister Lars Løkke Rasmussen from the liberal party, Venstre. Another party leader, Johanne Schmidt Nielsen from the left-wing party, Enhedslisten, is in fourth place. The candidate with most posts on his public Facebook profile was Uffe Elbæk, a former journalist who ran for the social

Table 25.1 Politicians with Most Posts on Public Facebook Profile during 2011 Parliamentary Election Campaign in Denmark

Politician	Party	Incumbent?	Party leader	Posts
Uffe Elbæk	B—Radikale Venstre	No	No	179
Lars Løkke Rasmussen	V—Venstre	Yes	Yes	151
Mette Abildgaard	C—Det Konservative Folkeparti	No	No	121
Johanne Schmidt-Nielsen	Ø—Enhedslisten	Yes	Yes	110
Kirsten Hasberg	K—Kristendemokraterne	No	No	92
Manu Sareen	B—Radikale Venstre	No	No	88
Torsten Schack Pedersen	V—Venstre	Yes	No	82
Morten Østergaard	B—Radikale Venstre	Yes	No	79
Ellen Trane Nørby	V—Venstre	Yes	No	78
Kim Raben	F—Socialistisk Folkeparti	No	No	77

Note: Campaign lasted from 26 August to 15 September 2011 (21 days).

liberal opposition party, Radikale Venstre. His nine updates on average per day during the campaign are exceptionally high. It is more than double the updates compared to number six on the top 10 of the most posting candidates.

Of the 10 most posting candidates, three were not elected into parliament. Thus, being highly active on Facebook is no guarantee for electoral success. This finding corroborates with a study of the effects of online campaigning in the Danish 2011 parliamentary election that found no effect of online campaigning on personal votes in the election when controlling for campaign resources, and the active use of other campaign channels (Hansen & Kosiara-Pedersen, 2014).

Table 25.2 demonstrates the number of candidates of each of the nine parties who had a public Facebook profile. The parties can be divided into three groups; for three smaller parties outside government, more than 40 per cent of the candidates have a public profile. This is followed by the two governing parties Det Konservative Folkeparti and Venstre, as well as the main opposition party (Socialdemokratiet), with around 30 per cent of candidates with a public profile. Finally, for three parties (Enhedslisten, Dansk Folkeparti, and Kristendemokraterne) less than 15 per cent of candidates have a public Facebook profile. For those candidates who actually have a public Facebook profile, there are no large differences between parties in numbers of updates. The mean number of posts per active candidates is 29, and most parties are not far from that average apart from Dansk Folkeparti, whose candidates are less active with an average of 10 posts.

A mix of three factors seems to explain the difference in presence on Facebook. First, the high activity on Facebook among smaller opposition parties could be a way to compensate for the difficulties they might have of accessing the mass media. Due to the news values of power and relevance, mass media pay most attention to politicians

Table 25.2 Number of Posts per Party on Public Facebook Profiles during 2011 Parliamentary Election Campaign in Denmark

Party	% of candidates who have active public profile	No. of posts per active candidates[1]
F—Socialistisk Folkeparti (92)	45.70 per cent	32.95 (18.7)
I—Liberal Alliance (74)	43.20 per cent	20.88 (13.2)
B—Radikale Venstre (75)	42.70 per cent	35.00 (34.5)
C—Det Konservative Folkeparti (86)	31.40 per cent	26.19 (26.4)
A—Socialdemokratiet (93)	29.00 per cent	30.26 (17.1)
V—Venstre (93)	28.00 per cent	35.04 (34.0)
Ø—Enhedslisten (92)	14.10 per cent	37.85 (29.9)
O—Dansk Folkeparti (92)	10.90 per cent	9.60 (9.9)
K—Kristendemokraterne (87)	9.20 per cent	24.13 (30,5)
All candidates (784)	27.70 per cent	29.44 (25.4)

Note: [1]Mean number of posts with standard deviation between brackets. Campaign lasted from 26 August to 15 September 2011 (21 days).

who are either in parliament or who are expected to win the elections (Hopmann et al., 2011). A public Facebook page can be a means to by-pass the traditional media and directly be in contact with potential voters, but it can also be a way to catch attention from journalists who are often in the social networks of politicians.

A second possible explanation is related to the candidates' target groups for their campaign and the demographics of their potential voters. Liberal Alliance and Det Radikale Venstre are among the parties whose voters are politically most active online.[5] The party whose voters are least likely to search for political information online (Dansk Folkeparti) is among the least active Facebook parties. Candidates from Dansk Folkeparti with a public profile post significantly less than candidates from other parties.

Third, incentives to invest in a (personalised) campaign can also account for some of the differences in active Facebook use across the parties. The only party which organises most of their candidate lists with a closed list (Enhedslisten) is also a party where many candidates do not have a public Facebook profile. This is despite the fact that voters from Enhedslisten are as likely to search for political information online as voters of the parties with the most active candidates on Facebook. Candidates for Enhedslisten have a fixed place on the party list, which means that their campaigns have little influence on whether they are elected or not. Candidates from other parties can make it into parliament despite their low place on the party list by attracting personal votes. Accordingly, they may benefit personally from campaigning on Facebook, by motivating people to vote and bond with supporters. For candidates for Enhedslisten this incentive to use Facebook to run a personalised campaign is weaker, which seems to be reflected in the results.

357

The party with the lowest presence (Kristendemokraterne) was below the electoral threshold in all of the opinion polls leading up to elections. It thus had a very small chance to make it into the parliament and thereby few incentives to campaign on Facebook.

Facebook in the Campaign Mix

In order to contextualise the role of Facebook in relation to the total campaign mix, we have compared the use of public social media profiles to participating in interviews on radio and television and canvassing, i.e. personal meetings with voters on the street, because these were regarded as important campaign channels by Danish campaign professionals (Nyegård Espersen, 2011).

Candidates are more likely to participate in interviews (71.4 per cent), or meet voters on the street (94.3 per cent), than to have a public Facebook profile (72.3 percent). Table 25.3 demonstrates that there were no significant gender differences in the preferences for these various campaign tools. Age was however a significant factor; Facebook is particularly relevant for young candidates, while older candidates are less likely to have a public profile. In comparison, age had no influence on the degree of interviews and canvassing.

Moreover, the analysis demonstrated that motivation to run an individual campaign is a key explanation for politicians' active public Facebook use. Candidates indicated on a scale from 0 to 10 whether they mainly campaign to get as much attention for themselves (0) or for the party (10). Candidates are less likely to engage in all three

Table 25.3 Explaining the Use of Different Campaign Channels

	Public Facebook profile B (SE)	Interviews on radio and television B (SE)	Canvassing B (SE)
Gender	.25 (.27)	.03 (.27)	2.96 (.65)
Age	−.05 (.01)***	−.01 (.01)	.01 (.02)
Campaign mainly for party	−.12 (.04)**	−.10 (.04)*	−.20 (.09)*
In parliament	.50 (.47)	2.54 (1.03)*	.32 (1.06)
Constant	1.57* (.51)**	2.15 (.52)***	3.64 (1.05)**
n	325	325	317
Nagelkerke R square	.15	.11	.08
Correctly classified	72.6 per cent	71.4 per cent	94.3 per cent
−2 log–likelihood	348.620	351,639	129.283

***$p < .001$, **$p < .01$, *$p < .05$.

campaign activities when they campaign for the party rather than for themselves. Even though campaigning for oneself and for the party is not mutually exclusive, this finding indicates that the individual campaign is a more important driver for engaging with all these campaign channels than the party campaign.

Candidates who defend a seat in parliament are not more likely to have a public Facebook profile than new candidates. These candidates are, however, more likely to appear in interviews, most likely because they are powerful elite sources and thus fulfils key news values. Canvassing is, however, done by almost all candidates and is not related to either being a newcomer or an established politician. The fact that new forms of campaigning do not replace but rather supplement old forms might explain why canvassing is in general still more popular among the candidates than campaigning via social media (Kleis Nielsen, 2012). Research has shown that the direct meeting with voters has a considerable effect on turnout (e.g. Gerber & Green, 2000), and this effect is acknowledged by the party organisations (Nyegård Espersen, 2011).

Public Facebook Profiles, Personalised Campaigning

Candidates who have a public Facebook profile do indeed see social media first and foremost as a campaign channel to run a personalised campaign. The main motivations to use social media are to present oneself and to have direct contact with voters (see Table 25.4). Reaching as many voters as possible is less important than running a personalised campaign, but still motivates two-thirds of the candidates. About half of the candidates use social media to organise the campaign, while gaining visibility in traditional mass media is the least important of the six reasons.[6]

Younger candidates are not only more likely to use Facebook; their motivation to use Facebook also differs from older candidates. Younger candidates are more motivated to use social media to have direct contact with voters than older candidates, while gaining media attention through social media is significantly more important for established candidates than for newcomers. Moreover, half of the candidates, with an overrepresentation of established candidates, state the aim to *appear modern* as a motivation for social media use. This finding confirms a recent study that found that British MPs regard Twitter as a "bandwagon they need to jump on" (Jackson & Lilleker, 2011: 86).

Table 25.4 Motivation to Use Facebook and Twitter for Candidates with Public Facebook Profile during the 2011 Parliamentary Election Campaign in Denmark

Make oneself and ones points of view visible	86 per cent
Communicate directly with voters	84 per cent
Reach as many voters as possible	65 per cent
Appear modern	51 per cent
Organise campaign	46 per cent
Gain visibility in traditional media	38 per cent

Note: N = 87 (minimal), based on candidates with a public Facebook profile who filled out the candidate survey.

Chances of Being Elected and Public Facebook Use

Perceived chances of being elected impact on the candidates' use of Facebook. Table 25.5 shows that candidates who believed they were very likely to win a seat in parliament were also most likely to use Facebook actively. This is hardly surprising, because the ones who were very confident of being elected are the high-profile politicians with the largest campaign resources, as well as being the most profiled in news media (Skovsgaard & van Dalen, 2013).

Disregarding the group of candidates who were very confident to win, the group of candidates who from the beginning thought that it was an open race for a seat in parliament is most likely to have a Facebook profile and to frequently update their profile during the campaign. Moreover, this group were even more active on Facebook than the candidates who thought they were likely to win, although differences were not significant. A key reason for this tendency could be that candidates who thought that they were in an open race for a seat in parliament know they had a lot to gain but also a lot to risk in the campaign and thus were highly motivated to campaign but lacked the more established candidates' access to mass media. Consequently, they have a double incentive to be on Facebook.

Conclusion

Although Facebook has gained a prominent position as a communication channel in Danish politicians' campaigns, our study shows social media should be seen as one among several tools in the campaign tool box. The number of candidates who engage in interviews with mainstream media and go out canvassing during election campaigns still exceeds the number of candidates who have a public Facebook profile. Almost half of the candidates with an active Facebook profile posted updates less than once per day on average, while only six candidates posted more than four updates per day in average during the three week campaign.

Digging deeper, we see that in the Danish campaign context Facebook campaigning on social media such as Facebook can be seen as a supplement, but not the most important tool for incumbent candidates and parties who have relatively easy access to

Table 25.5 Explaining the Use of Public Facebook Profiles by Chances to be Elected during the 2011 Parliamentary Election Campaign in Denmark

	Public Facebook profile %	Number of posts M (S.D)
Thought I had no chance (n = 121)	17 per cent	3.85 (10.99)
Thought I had small chance (n = 98)	30 per cent	6.49 (13.23)
Thought it was an open battle (n = 29)	41 per cent	13.93 (34.52)
Thought I was likely to win (n = 48)	36 per cent	11.79 (20.16)
Thought I was certain to win (n = 16)	63 per cent	32.38 (35.13)

mainstream mass media. For candidates without such resources and access to the mass media, who are involved in an open battle and pursue a personalised campaign, social media present a welcome opportunity to campaign and reach more voters.

The relatively small competing parties have the biggest proportion of candidates with a public Facebook profile. This finding confirms the idea that social media might be used as compensation for lack of exposure in the mass media. Given that mass media's news values favour the biggest and most powerful parties, these smaller parties have the clearest incentives to be on Facebook. By the same logic, parties with the lowest incentive to be on Facebook due to low intraparty competition, due to minimal chances of reaching the two per cent threshold to win seats in parliament, or due to an older target group in the electorate, have the lowest proportion of candidates with a Facebook profile.

The main motivation among candidates to campaign on Facebook is to promote themselves and their opinions, and communicate directly with voters, or in other words to personalise their campaign. Apparently, one thing is that candidates say that they use Facebook to personalise the campaign and another is what they actually do. A study of candidate updates in the 2011 parliamentary election in Denmark shows that candidates hardly separate themselves from the party line when they campaign on Facebook (van Dalen et al., 2014). And other studies, though not of this particular election, show that politicians communicate directly with voters to a very limited extent (Duvander Højholt & Kosiara-Pedersen 2011; Goldbeck et al., 2010; Grant et al., 2010; Jackson & Lilleker, 2011).

However, the results in this chapter show that younger candidates are more eager to engage with voters while older candidates are more inclined than young candidates to say that they are on Facebook to appear modern and to gain visibility in the mass media. Despite the discrepancy between what candidates say and what they do, these results also indicate that the younger generation of candidates in their campaigns are more inclined to utilise the special features that Facebook and other social media offer. This could be an indication that future Danish candidates will integrate social media more in their campaign mix and utilise the strengths of this communication channel to complement the other communication channels in their campaign.

Notes

1 "DF: Forsamlingshus ikke Facebook," *Jyllands-Posten*, September 2, 2011. "Kommunikation: DF gider ikke Facebook," *Information*, September 2, 2011.
2 www.infomedia.dk/media/77918/sociale-medier-2013-danskernes-holdning-til-og-brug-af-sociale-medier-yougov-smpdk-2013.pdf
3 The Facebook profile data were collected by Zoltan Fazekas, Department of Political Science and Public Management, University of Southern Denmark.
4 The survey data were collected by Christian Elmelund-Præstekær, Department of Political Science, University of Southern Denmark, as part of the Comparative Candidate Survey.
5 We analysed online activity of voters for different parties with data from the 211 Danish election studies (Stubager et al., 2013).
6 When interpreting these data, one has to take into account that that these are self-reported motivations. It cannot be ruled out that social-desirability influenced the answers. The finding that half of the respondents with a Facebook profile admit to be on Facebook in order to appear modern suggests that social desirability did not lead to completely idealised answers.

References

Albæk, E., Hopmann D. N., & de Vreese, C. H. (2010) *Kunsten at Holde Balancen. Dækningen af Folketingsvalgkampe i Tv-nyhederne på DR1 og TV2 1994–2007 [The Art of Staying on Balance: Coverage of Parliamentary Elections in Television News at DR1 and TV2 1994–2007]*, Odense: Syddansk Univesitetsforlag.

Andreassen, A. M. (2011, 4 April) "Lotte Hansen: Vi får en Digital Revolution ved Valget" [Lotte Hansen: There Will Be a Digital Revolution during the Elections]. http://journalisten.dk/lotte-hansen-vi-far-en-digital-revolution-til-valget

Baum, M. A. & Groeling. T. J. (2010) *War Stories*, Princeton: Princeton University Press.

Druckman, J. N., Kifer, M. J., & Parkin, M. (2007) "The Technological Development of Congressional Candidate Web Sites," *Social Science Computer Review*, 25(4), pp. 425–442.

Duvander Højholt, L. & Kosiara-Pedersen, K. (2011) "Forandrer Facebook Partiernes Forhold til Vælgerne?" [Does Facebook Change Parties' Relation to Voters?], *Tidskrift Politik*, 14(3), pp. 57–66.

Elmelund-Præstekær, C. & Schumacher, G. (2014) "Én for Alle og Alle for én? Mønstre i og Effekter af Partiintern Uenighed blandt Folketingskandidaterne ved 2011-valget" [One for All and All for One? Patterns and Effects of Party Internal Disagreement among Candidates for Parliament in the Danish 2011 Election] *Politica*, 46(3), pp. 296–322.

Enli, G. & Moe H. (2013) "Introduction to Special Issue: Social Media and Election Campaigns—Key Tendencies and Ways Forward," *Information, Communication & Society* 16(5), pp. 637–645.

Gerber, A. S. & Green D. P. (2000) "The Effects of Canvassing, Telephone Calls, and Direct Mail on Voter Turnout: A Field Experiment," *American Political Science Review*, 94(3), pp. 653–663.

Goldbeck, J., Grimes, J.M., & Rogers, A. (2010) "Twitter Use by the US Congress," *Journal of the American Society for Information Science and Technology*, 61(8), pp. 1612–1621.

Grant, W.J., Moon, B., & Busby Grant, J. (2010) "Digital Dialogue? Australian Politicians' use of the Social Network Tool Twitter," *Australian Journal of Political Science*, 45(4), pp. 579–604.

Hallin, D. & Mancini, P. (2004) *Comparing Media Systems: Three Models of Media and Politics*, Cambridge: Cambridge University Press.

Hansen, K. M. & Kosiara-Pedersen, C. (2014) "Cyber-Campaigning in Denmark: Application and Effects of Candidate Campaigning," *Journal of Information Technology & Politics*, 11(2), pp. 206–219.

Hoff, J., Jensen J. L., Klastrup, L., Schwartz, S., & Brügger, N. (2013) *Internettet og Folketingsvalget 2011*, Copenhagen: Danske Medier. http://www.fdim.dk/sites/default/files/mediearkiv/rapporter/fdim_valgrapport2011.pdf

Hopmann, D.N., de Vreese, C.H., & Albæk, E. (2011) "Incumbency Bonus in Election Coverage Explained: The Logics of Political Power and the Media Market," *Journal of Communication*, 61(2), pp. 264–282.

Internet World Stats (2012) http://www.internetworldstats.com/stats4.htm

Jackson, N. & Lilleker, D. (2011) "Microblogging, Constituency Service and Impression Management: UK MPs and the Use of Twitter," *The Journal of Legislative Studies*, 17(1), pp. 86–105.

Karlsen, R. (2011) "A Platform for Individualized Campaigning? Social Media and Parliamentary Candidates in the 2009 Norwegian Election Campaign," *Policy & Internet*, 3(4), article 4.

Kleis Nielsen, R. (2012) *Ground Wars: Personalized Communication in Political Campaigns*, Princeton: Princeton University Press.

Maarek, P.J. (2011) *Campaign Communication & Political Marketing*, Oxford: Wiley-Blackwell.

Normann Andersen, K. & Medaglia, R. (2009) "The Use of Facebook in National Election Campaigns: Politics as Usual?" *Electronic Participation*, LNCS(5694), pp. 101–111.

Nyegård Espersen, I. (2011) Valg på alle Hylder [Elections All Around]. *Journalisten*. http://journalisten.dk/valg-pa-alle-hylder

Olsen, H. (1998) *Tallenes Talende Tavshed: Måleproblemer i Surveyundersøgelser*, København: Akademisk Forlag.

Skovsgaard, M., Albæk, E., Bro, P., & de Vreese C. H. (2012) "Media Professionals or Organizational Marionettes? Professional Values and Constraints of Danish Journalists," in D. H. Weaver & L. Willnat (eds.), *The Global Journalist in the 21st Century*, London: Routledge, pp. 155–170.

Skovsgaard, M. & van Dalen, A. (2013) "Dodging the Gatekeepers?" *Information, Communication & Society*, 16(5), pp. 737–756.

Socialbakers (2012) *Denmark. Facebook Statistics.* http://www.socialbakers.com/facebook-statistics/denmark

Soroka, S. N. (2014) *Negativity in Democratic Politics: Causes and Consequences*, Cambridge: Cambridge University Press.

Stubager, R., Hansen, K. M., & Andersen, G. J. (2013) *Krisevalg. Økonomien og Folketingsvalget 2011* [Crisis Election: The Economy and Parliamentary Election 2011], Copenhagen: Jurist- og Økonomforbundets Forlag.

Towner, T. L. & Dulio, D. A. (2012) "New Media and Political Marketing in the United States: 2012 and Beyond," *Journal of Political Marketing*, 11(1–2), 95–119.

Van Dalen, Arjen (2012) "Structural Bias in Cross-national Perspective. How Political Systems and Journalism Cultures Influence Government Dominance in the News," *International Journal of Press/Politics*, 17(1), pp. 32–55.

Van Dalen, A., Fazekas, Z., Klemmensen, R., & Hansen, K. M. (2014) "Policy Coherence on Facebook: Agendas, Coherence and Communication Patterns in the 2011 Danish Parliamentary Elections," *Working Paper*, University of Southern Denmark: Centre for Journalism.

Van Santen, R. & Van Zoonen, L. (2010) "The Personal in Political Television Biographies," *Biography*, 33(1), pp. 46–67.

26

SOCIAL MEDIA INCUMBENT ADVANTAGE

Barack Obama's and Mitt Romney's Tweets in the 2012 U.S. Presidential Election Campaign

Gunn Enli and Anja Aaheim Naper

Introduction

Recent U.S. presidential campaigns have been symbolic for social media and politics on a global scale. In particular, the 2008 Obama campaign marked a shift from the old paradigm of information dissemination and persuasion via the mass media to a new paradigm of controlled interactivity via digital media (Stromer-Galley 2014: 14). The social media element of the 2008 Obama campaign became a global phenomenon, and inspired politicians and staffers around the world to engage with voters through user-generated content and interactive features.

The aim of this chapter is to investigate how U.S. presidential candidates used Twitter when the first phase of novelty had passed and 'the dust had settled' after the 2008 Obama campaign. Focusing on the theory of the incumbent advantage, which is one of the most well documented features of U.S. elections (Erickson 1995; Ansolabehere, Snowberg, and Snyder 2006; Jamieson 2013), this chapter will investigate to what degree the theory has relevance when transferred to social media. What kind of incumbency advantages did Obama have in relation to his challengers in the context of social media? To what degree is this advantage in social media comparable with the incumbency advantage resulting from coverage in mass media?

The analysis draws on a quantitative content analysis of the 3,420 tweets posted during the U.S. election campaign of 2012 on the Twitter accounts of Democrat President Barack Obama and Republican candidate Mitt Romney. Among the two teams' several accounts, the accounts chosen for this study are @BarackObama and @MittRomney, because they can be classified as *candidate accounts*, opposed to *team accounts*, such as, for example, @Obama2012 and @TeamRomney. Importantly, however, the distinction between candidate accounts and team accounts must not be confused with indication of authorship, as none of the accounts published tweets on a regular basis written by the candidates. Staffers as a rule wrote the tweets posted on both types of accounts, the candidates themselves wrote only a fragment of the updates, and they were particularly promoted as 'authentic' (Enli 2015). The analysed material was collected over the course of the election year, from the primaries to election day.

This chapter has five main parts. The first discusses characteristics of the U.S. political system, United States politics, and the implications of these characteristics for the relations between the media and politics. The second part reviews research literature on political communication and social media. The third part outlines the historical development of online campaigning and social media campaigning in the U.S. The fourth part will present the key findings in the comparative study of the tweets posted on the candidate accounts for Obama and Romney, while the last part concludes and pinpoints key arguments.

Political Marketing and the U.S. Political System

The United States is the heartland of political marketing. This is the nation where political spin, political advertising, and branding of politicians originated and have their main foundation. According to Maarek (2011: 7), "there can be no doubt that the genesis of modern political marketing is entirely rooted in the history of political communication in the United States". Maarek defines political marketing as a form of political communication that has migrated from the U.S. to other parts of the world. The terms 'political marketing' and 'political communication' are often used with overlapping meanings; however, there are distinctions. Political communication may best be defined as an umbrella term that includes political marketing but also other forms of communication outside the realm of commercial sales logics. A key aspect in definitions of political marketing is that tools and strategies from commercial marketing are transferred to the political arena, such as the idea of elections as analogue to commercial sales, and that politicians resemble salesmen (Scammell, 1999; Street 2003; Ormrod et al, 2013).

The United States' dominant role in political marketing can be explained by the political system and the media system as well as by economic factors: First, the election system in the U.S. is characterised by primaries in the early stages of presidential election campaigns. The presidential primaries run from January to June every four years, whereas the actual campaign starts only mid-July after the appointment of the candidates by their party conventions and runs until the first Thursday in November. In contrast to, for example, the party-centred West-European style of campaigning, the U.S. style is remarkably candidate-centred as the campaign organisation is built on the individual candidate, almost from scratch (Plasser and Plasser 2002). Because the politicians need a full-scale campaign to launch their candidacies already in the primaries, this system encourages the production of enormous amounts of political marketing. In turn, this overflow of content produced to promote political candidates results in an innovative development of new methods for political marketing.

Second, the U.S. is characterised by a tradition of election for all public offices, which roots back to its origins as an independent country: "As soon as the United states came into existence, it became routine to hold elections for most major public offices, from the local sheriff, major, or judge, to the president" (Maarek 2011: 9). For this reason, as soon as railroad tracks were laid across the country, potential presidents entered trains to meet their voters. For example, Abraham Lincoln delivered speeches from the rear platform of the campaign train. The third reason for U.S.'s leading role in political marketing is related to the fact that mass media, primarily TV, was spread significantly faster in North America than in other parts of the world. Likewise, the Internet was also launched in the U.S., and North Americans were among the key groups of early adopters of the new technology in the early 1990s (Winston and Walton 1996: 79). In the context of an election campaign, the Internet was first taken into use in 1996, and since then its share of political communication has never ceased to grow (Chadwick 2006: 151; Maarek 2011: 11; Stromer Galley 2014: 14).

The media's impact on election campaigns is often discussed with reference to U.S. politicians' performances in the media. The TV debates between presidential candidates Richard Nixon and John F. Kennedy in 1960 have, for instance, become emblematic for the 'television age' of politics (Polsby and Wildavsky 2002; Donaldson 2007; Maarek 2011). In the next section, we will discuss to what degree the U.S. has also become a point of reference in the more recent field of social media and politics.

Social Media and Politics in the United States

The U.S. is the second largest democracy in the world, after India, and the most influential one. The United States' influence in world politics has historical and political reasons, but also the media and cultural industries have contributed to making the U.S. powerful. Being a global exporter of film and TV, America has been accused of cultural imperialism, meaning that its cultural values and political ideas have been exported via mediated representations (Schiller 1976). Ideas of American politics have not least been exported through film and TV series about U.S. presidents, celebrity endorsements, and the portrayal of politics in TV series, such as *The President*, *The Good Wife*, and *House of Cards* (see, e.g. Van Zoonen 2005). After his 2008 election campaign, President Obama had status as a celebrity politician, a status that was also used against his candidacy in a TV commercial promoting an opponent, Republican candidate John McCain, with the catchphrase: "He's the biggest celebrity in the world. But is he ready to lead?" (quoted in Plouffe 2009: 279).

A large share of currently successful social media networking sites have their origins in the U.S., and dominant social media firms, such as Facebook and Twitter, have their headquarters and major ownership interests located in the United States. Since 2009, Facebook is by far the most used social media site in the U.S. In 2014, the number of users had reached 71 per cent of the online adult United States population and 58 per cent of the total adult population. The equivalent numbers for Twitter is 23 and 19 per cent, respectively, and although more than half of the users utilise multiple social media sites, Facebook acts as 'home base' (Duggan et al. 2015b).

The demographics of social media use is much debated, and the usage was originally associated with young people. A recent trend in the U.S. is that Facebook use among seniors (65 and older) is increasing, and that women are more likely to use Facebook compared to men (Duggan et al. 2015a). A parallel trend is that Twitter use is still most popular amongst young adults and that the use increases in several demographic groups: men, whites, college graduates, high-income, and urbanites (Duggan et al. 2015a). In terms of the relationship between social media, politics, and engagement, these groups are politically more engaged than the average population.

The growth in social media use was noticed by marketers and PR consultants as well as by political communication strategists. The Web was included in political campaigns already from mid-1995; however, in hindsight, both the 1996 and the 2000 U.S. election campaigns was more 'false starts' than full-blown online campaigns. For example, the presidential websites in 1996 included only simple feedback options, such as signing up to volunteer and registering to vote, which is a prerequisite for participation in U.S. elections, and the websites were infrequently updated. In fact, the websites were simply digital versions of campaign literature produced for the offline campaign, and levels of interactions between candidates and voters were very limited and restricted. In addition, the 2000 campaign was an experimental phase in digital media strategies, and the insurgent campaigns with less to lose but much to gain was spearheads in this phase (Stromer-Galley 2014). Front-runner campaigns, however, were reluctant to include citizen-driven efforts, and the 2000 were campaign was a TV-politics-as-usual event. Only 1 in 10 Americans used the Internet for information about the campaign (Chadwick 2006: 152–155).

The shift towards online campaigns in the U.S. was the 2004 presidential election cycle, represented by the Democrat candidate Howard Dean's innovative use of digital media, and blogs in particular. The Internet usage for news and information had doubled since 2000 and reached two-thirds per cent of American adults, according to Pew Research Center (2015). The campaign represented a shift in fundraising by using online tools to enable supporters to donate small amounts, often repeatedly. Still, the Dean campaign had weighty flaws and particularly failed to structure the enthusiasm of the supporters into a productive work for the campaign (Kreiss 2012).

The 2008 presidential campaigns expanded the paradigm of digital technology-driven campaigning, not least because of the 10 per cent increase in Internet adoption since the 2004 election, the launch of the first iPhone in 2007, and the 'participatory turn' resulting partly from new interactive technology (Enli 2007; Stromer-Galley 2014). In the 2008 U.S. presidential election cycle, strategies for online campaigning and social media had become elementary across every campaign. The Obama campaign nevertheless went a step further than the Clinton campaign, as Obama's highest paid employee was the e-campaign strategist, and the campaign was networked and not compartmentalised (Stromer-Galley 2014: 110). The Obama campaign tapped into a participatory culture by establishing an image of the candidate as tech-savvy and cutting-edge through YouTube, Facebook, and the organisation site MyBo (my.BarackObama.com). The 2008 Obama campaign is often regarded as a breakthrough for social media and politics because it efficiently created enthusiasm and massively involved supporters. In the next section, we will build on this historical backdrop and investigate the role of social media in the 2012 U.S. presidential election campaigns, where Republican Mitt Romney challenged the incumbent candidate Barack Obama.

The Incumbent Advantage in Social Media

Part of the explanation for the 2008 Obama campaign's success in social media was the candidate's appeal as an outsider, an insurgent, and an unlikely winner. This anti-establishment appeal was compatible with the image of social media as an alternative to mainstream media, and the candidate image and the social media image seemed to be interconnected. The outsider image was however less prominent both for the candidate and the medium in the 2012 campaign. Obama had lost some of his appeal as fresh and different, while social media had become an integrated part of the media system, and an obligatory part of the campaigns.

In spite of social media's character as a standard and conventional part of a campaign, there were significant differences between the Obama team and the Romney team in their social media performance. The Obama campaign had *incumbent advantage*, not only as an elected politician but also as a 'social media politician'. Previous research has investigated the impact of television on the incumbent advantage, with diverging results. Erikson (1995: 415) argued that "the entrenching of incumbency seems to have coincided with the rise of television," and in general, incumbents receive more media coverage than their opponents do. Recent studies are reluctant to single out TV as the key cause of incumbent advantage, but argue that campaigns have an effect on the incumbency advantage (Ansolabehere, Snowberg, and Snyder 2006). In relation to social media, incumbency advantage has been debated, and several studies have pointed to the opposite effect; that the challenger benefits from new campaign tool, as they change the rules of the game (Jackson and Lilleker 2009; Druckman et al., 2007; Larsson and Kalsnes 2014). However, none of these studies have analysed the U.S. presidential elections.

This study is primarily based on an analysis of empirical data, but as a supplement, we will draw on insights from existing research. One crucial insight is that the 2012 Obama campaign benefitted from experiences and resources from past campaigning. First, according to a comparative study of the two candidates' Twitter use during the 2012 U.S. presidential election cycle, the Obama campaign was significantly more efficient and professionalised than the Romney campaign (Bruns and Highfield 2013). Second, several studies have pinpointed that the staffers in the Obama campaign had more a autonomy in relation to the political leadership compared to Romney's staffers and were thus able to respond more quickly, and even in real time, to unfolding commentary, to more efficiently micro-target voters, and to adjust campaign strategies according to recent developments (Jamieson 2013; Kreiss 2014). A third relevant finding in previous research is that the Obama campaign benefitted from the cumulated numbers of fans and followers from one campaign—and political term, to the next campaign. While Romney's account had 1.8 million followers, Obama's had 22 million followers on 6 November 2012 (Bimber 2014: 138). An explanation for this remarkable difference is that Obama's supporters were considerably more likely, according to demographic measures such as age, lifestyle, and ethnicity, than Romney's supporters to be using Twitter regularly.

Method

The methodological strategies of this study are based on the results of a pilot study where we compared data collected manually and automatically over a limited period (one week). During the same period, about 30 per cent more relevant tweets were collected with the manual method than the automatic API-based methods. For this chapter, we rely on the manually collected tweets from the above-mentioned twitter accounts, @BarackObama and @MittRomney.

There are advantages and limitations of both the manual and the automatic collection methods. A limitation with the most common APIs for collecting tweets automatically is that they are unable to collect the total universe, and the studies using this method are thus designed to capture a comprehensive (if not representative) sample of tweets which relate to the event under investigation (Bruns 2012). Because of the massive amount of tweets posted during the U.S. presidential election campaign in 2012, the automatic collection of data would not provide a sufficient sample. As the manual collection turned out to capture a more refined sample, we chose this method for this particular analysis.

Consequently, we collected tweets manually, in spite of its challenges. First, the risk of missing individual tweets from the dataset because of occasionally selective display of tweets, and that the collector is inattentive. Yet, in this study, the manual collection of tweets was reliable according to the intercoder reliability test (89 per cent correspondence). Second, manual collection of tweets is time-consuming; the researcher monitored the Twitter accounts in real time, minimum twice every day, and systematically archived the material.

Findings

Identical Dramaturgy, But Different Volume

In total, the research period encompasses the entire campaign cycle, from 1 January to election day on 6 November 2012; divided into four research periods: (1) the primaries (1–31 January), (2) the convention (1–15 May), (3) the summertime (15 June–15 July), and (4) the get-out-the-vote phase (1 September–6 November). Although the four periods are not symmetrical, they are valid because the collected data are weighted to be statistically comparative. During this election cycle, the two campaigns followed an identical dramaturgy, but as seen in Figure 26.1, the number of tweets posted on @BarackObama (3,095) was significantly higher than that posted on @MittRomney (325) throughout the election cycle. The average difference was 1:9, with a peek in the last month before the election.

After Obama's victory in the 2008 election, the Republicans claimed to have heightened their awareness around the importance of social media (Bimber 2014). Still,

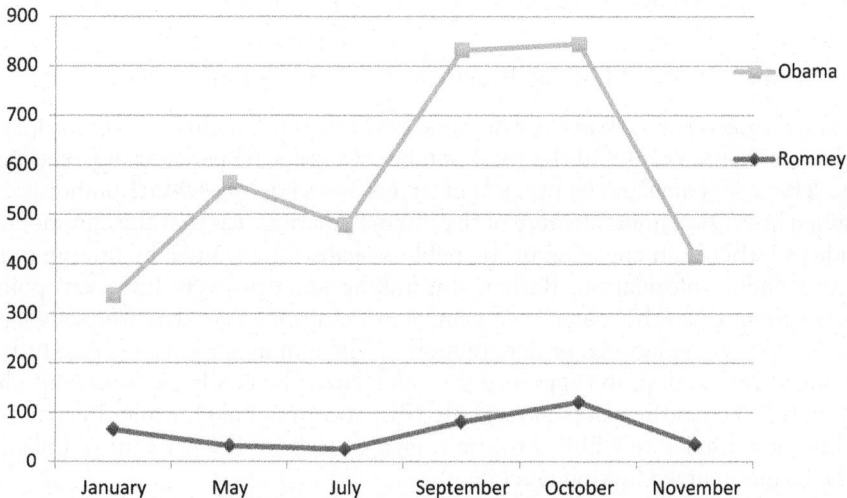

Figure 26.1 Tweets Posted on the Accounts @BarackObama and @MittRomney in the 2012 Election Campaign, Absolute Figures

the amount of tweets indeed was higher in the Democrat Obama's account than in the account of Republican Romney. This does not contest the Republicans claim, as the Romney campaign posted more tweets on the *team account* than *candidate account*. However, they presumably failed to optimise the number of users reached, as the team accounts in general had considerably fewer followers than the candidate accounts. Moreover, the Obama campaign generated more synergy effects between the related accounts, such as @Obama2012, @ObamaForAmerica, @TruthTeam, @MichelleObama, and @JoeBiden by extensive retweeting and use of mentions, compared to the Mitt Romney campaign (Bruns and Highfield 2013).

The fact that updating the candidate's social media accounts was outsourced, in line with a range of other campaign activities, was made explicit when tweets posted on @BarackObama refers to Obama in third person, as 'him' or 'Obama'. In contrast, the Mitt Romney account refers to the candidate in first person, as, for instance, in this tweet: "@BarackObama wants to raise taxes on the middle class. I want to bring tax rates down to put people back to work" (10.10.12). In general, the tweets posted on Mitt Romney's account were written in a more personal and intimate tone than tweets posted on Barack Obama's account, characterised by a more distant and public voice, as for example: "President Obama is fighting to double U.S. exports" (12.09.12). The different rhetoric and linguistic style is clearly related to Obama's role as the incumbent, which enables him to tweet with more authority and status than his opponent.

The status as the incumbent president also increased the appeal of the, very few and thus exclusive, tweets posted on Obama's account that were actually authored by the president himself. The signature 'bo' identifies the exclusive tweets, and as explained in the account profile, these tweets are signed to prove that Barack Obama and not staff members wrote them. In our study, we found that 'bo" tweets only make up about 1 per cent of the total tweets posted on the Obama account. Yet, this exclusiveness and the paradox that the U.S. president is expressing himself in a mundane format, brings a certain appeal—or aura—to the tweets. As a result, both the formal and distanced staffer tweets, and the folksy and personal 'bo' tweets potentially had a unique appeal because they were posted on the account of the incumbent president.

Common Internal Linking Practices, But Various Intermedia Linking

The candidate accounts @BarackObama and @MittRomney included a significant share of links (see Figure 26.2). On the total number of tweets, 63 per cent of tweets posted on the @BarackObama and 66 per cent of tweets posted on the @MittRomney account contained links. A common feature of the linking practices was that they promoted the candidates rather than engaging in the public debate, for example, by linking to news stories or public information. Rather, the linking practices were introvert, pointing the users primarily to the teams' own campaign websites, where they were encouraged to sign up to vote, volunteer, or donate money. The aim might have been to turn user engagement into action, in support of the candidate. The challenger's account almost exclusively linked to the campaign website (91 per cent of links), while the incumbent account, more moderately linked to the campaign website (54 per cent of links), and thus had a more mixed linking practice.

The second largest category for both accounts was the links to pictures and videos, which more specifically included the campaigns' social media channels; for instance Twitpic, YouTube, or Instagram. This category demonstrated a significant difference

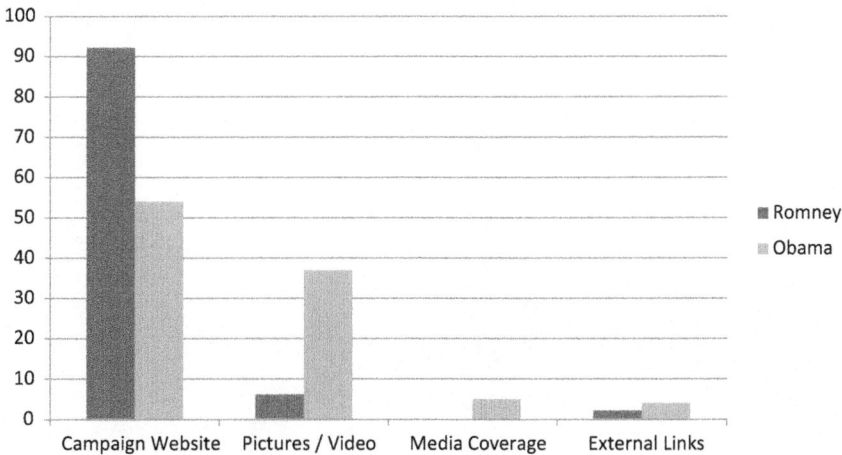

Figure 26.2 Links in Tweets Posted on @MittRomney and @BarackObama in the 2012 Election Campaign, by Percentage, N=3,420

between the incumbent and the challenger account, as @BarackObama directed the users to the campaign's other social media content more than five times as often as @MittRomney. This shows that the Obama campaign was more focused on multidirectional and network effects of social media than of the more one-sided focus in the campaign website.

The linking practice coded as 'media coverage', which includes links to mainstream media' coverage of the campaign and the candidate, was used only to a limited degree and only by the incumbent candidate. Among the links on @BarackObama, 4 per cent directed the users to for example online news and TV shows, typically, when the candidate appeared on live shows on CNN or MSNBC. The finding that no equivalent links were posted on @MittRomney in the studied period, might indicate that the president were given more opportunities to promote his candidacy than the opponent, or that the social media staffers in the Romney campaign did not recognise the potential in intermedia agenda setting.

Lack of Dialogue, But Incumbent Centred

The main features for dialogue in Twitter are mentions (@), requests for replies, and hashtags (#). Related to the distinction between political communication and political marketing, we could categorise one-way-communication of campaign tweets as a marketing tool, and the dialogic use of twitter as a communication tool. Yet, there would always be overlaps between the two, and to initiate dialogue might be a marketing strategy to build symbolical alliances with the users more than an aim to initiate a deliberative political debate.

Neither of the candidates' accounts gave much priority to initiating dialogue, whether for marketing or deliberative purposes. As we see in Figure 26.3, requests for replies were almost non-existing. To the degree that they were used, it was by the incumbent account; however, less than one per cent the tweets posted on @BarackObama asked

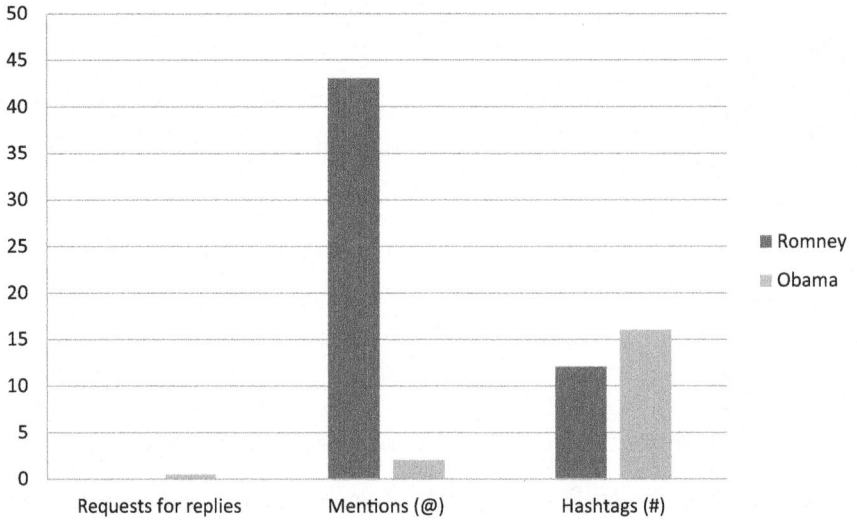

Figure 26.3 Use of Common Twitter Features by Presidential Candidates in the 2012 Election Campaign, by Percentage, N = 3,420

for replies. All of these were posted in the first phases of the election cycle, indicating that an early motivation for dialogue, faded away as the campaign intensified.

Typically, the Obama team requested replies by urging users to 'share your story', that is to relate their private stories to issues currently on the public agenda. This way, the replies indirectly served as adverts, because the shared stories featured by the campaign mainly commented on the president's accomplishments.

There are, as demonstrated in Figure 26.3, large differences between incumbent's and the challenger's use of the feature '@-mentions', which implies the degree to which they mentioned other Twitter users. The @-mentions used by the @BarackObama account were limited to addressing the Twitter accounts ran by the campaign team, and were thus introvert and self-promoting. As for the challenger, the use of mentions was strikingly high in comparison; the candidate account of Mitt Romney used mentions in a little less than half the tweets posted in the period, and of these, the majority were mentions of @BarackObama. Accordingly, the incumbent candidate was the centre of attention, and the object for many of the tweets posted on the challenger's account, while the incumbent seemingly ignored the attacks from the opponent. That way the Obama team could focus on promoting their candidate, rather than being distracted by confrontations with the Romney team.

A Twitter feature which was fairly equally used by both presidential candidates was hashtags (#), which links tweets together in a thematically oriented thread. Still, only 16 per cent of the Obama account's tweets included this feature, and none included multiple hashtags, which is a common practice among Twitter users. The majority of the hashtags posted in the incumbent's account was generic related to the election or to political issues, and #MarriageEquality was, for example, frequently used during the debates about gay marriages. Romney's account included fewer hashtags than Obama's account, but they were more polemic and often critical towards the incumbent candidate, as, for example, the hashtag #CantAfford4More.

In sum, the reluctant use of Twitter features indicates that both campaigns aimed for accessible tweets as they serve the purpose of political marketing better than complex tweets. The avoidance of dialogue also supported the clear-cut and unambiguous style preferred by marketing, and served the purpose of securing campaign staffers control of the account without time-consuming engagement.

Attacking the Incumbent

The focus in each tweet selected for this study was analysed, and tweets were coded according to a predefined codebook. The results are visualised in Figure 26.4 below, which shows that the main difference between the Obama account and the Romney account can be explained at least partly by their positions as incumbent and challenger.

First, nearly half of tweets posted on the @MittRomney account were concerned with 'attacking opponents', meaning that tweets were attacking Obama's leadership. Examples of tweets in this category are "Bringing America back on track" (05.11.2012), and "I have a clear and unequivocal message: With the right leadership, America is coming roaring back" (03.11.2012). In comparison, the tweets attacking opponents posted on the Obama account were primarily directed at Mitt Romney and made up 10 per cent of the total amount. Nearly five times as many attacks directed at the incumbent were posted compared to attacks on the challenger.

Second, about one third of all tweets posted on the Obama account were categorised as 'mobilisation', meaning that the tweets encourages actions in the line of donating, supporting, voting, or volunteering. The clearly most important objective of these tweets is encouragements to vote or to register to vote (39 per cent of tweets coded as 'mobilisation'). Likewise, encouragements to volunteer for the campaign were frequent,

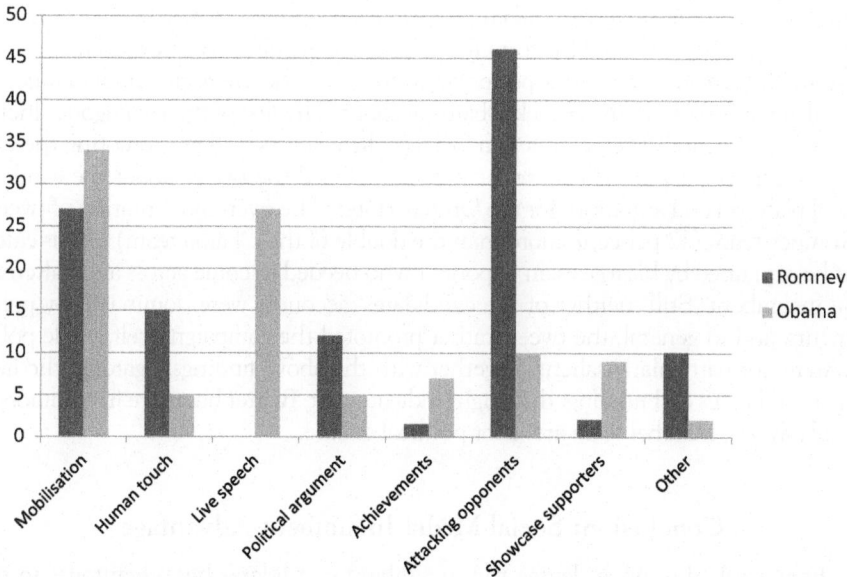

Figure 26.4 Tweets Posted on @BarackObama and @MittRomney, by Theme, in the 2012 Election Campaign, by Percentage, N = 3,420

and among these tweets, individual voter mobilisation on the ground was emphasised. This included hosting election events in private houses, signing up to connect with other Obama supporters in your neighbourhood, or arranging low scale election events. Even though the Mitt Romney account also tweeted to mobilise votes, the focus were less oriented towards mobilising grass-root actors.

Donations from supporters are essential for U.S. presidential candidates. Presidential campaigns have become progressively more expensive, and the 2012 campaigns were the, until then, most costly in history with a total spending estimated to $6 billion. In both the Obama campaign and the Romney campaign, more than $1 billion were raised and spent. Twitter was actively used for generating donations by both campaigns, but their strategies were different; the @BarackObama account frequently encouraged the followers to donate specific and small amounts, such as this tweet: "If you pitched in $5 or $10, it helped. 97.77% of donations in August were $250 or less, for an average of $58.31" (10.09.12). Emphasising that even small contributions count, the threshold for donating was lowered and supporters with average or low income could easily contribute. In contrast, the @MittRomney' account appealed to donators less frequently, and never referred to specific amounts, or argued that even small amounts mattered. This strategy is reflected in the donations to the 2012 presidential election campaigns; donations under $200 made up over two-thirds of the total donations to Obama and a quarter of the donations to Romney (Bimber 2014; Gerodimos and Justinussen 2014). Moreover, the divergent strategies demonstrated that Obama had a more adjusted strategy for the social media logics of donations, which is typically oriented at maximising the number of small-scale donations rather than to appeal to exclusive elites of big-spender donators.

A third finding in the thematic content analysis is that the Obama team used Twitter as platform for 'live tweeting' of the President's speeches. Just over a quarter of the tweets posted on Barack Obama's account, in contrast to no tweets posted on Mitt Romney's account, were coded as 'live speech'. The difference demonstrates that the incumbent candidate included official performances and political speeches in the twitter feed, and thus transferred his formal role and social status to a new arena.

Last, the Mitt Romney account posted more tweets in the categories 'human touch' and 'political arguments' than the Barack Obama account. The first of these categories included tweets about the candidates' families and their colleagues, as well as promoting the candidates as 'ordinary people'. The second category included the tweets about the candidate's political platform and ambitions for the United States. The overrepresentation of tweets by the Romney team (12 per cent, more than the double of the Obama team) in this category might be explained by his role as an opponent who needed to come across as an alternative to the incumbent. Still, neither of the candidates' accounts were dominated by political arguments, and in general, the tweets rather promoted the campaign itself, while political issues were not particularly salient. Together with the above findings regarding the lack of dialogue, and focus on branding, this might indicate that Twitter has more in common with political adverts, than being an arena for political debate.

Conclusion: Social Media Incumbent Advantage

This chapter asked to what degree the incumbent candidates has advantages in social media election campaigns, by comparing the Twitter presence of incumbent Barack Obama and challenger Mitt Romney during the 2012 presidential election campaigns in the U.S. The article draws on a quantitative content analysis of 3,420 tweets posted on the candidate accounts @BarackObama and @MittRomney.

The comparative analysis pinpointed significant differences, indicating that there might be a tendency of incumbency advantage in social media campaigning. First, the most obvious difference was related to *the accounts' volume and potential impact*. The Obama account posted nine times as many tweets as the Romney account, and (potentially) reached over ten times as many followers with each tweet. The actual impact of a high volume of tweets and a high user reach on actual voting behaviour is very hard to measure, not least because it would depend on the user's political preference before they were exposed to the tweets. We know that young people are more active on twitter, and that Democrats and Independents are more active users than Republicans are, so it is likely that the tweets posted by the Obama campaign simply confirmed the preferences of the users exposed to the tweets rather than convincing new voters.

Second, the analysis documented that the use of social media has become a standard element in U.S. presidential election campaigns from 2008 onwards, and that the political campaigns use social media for *marketing and branding purposes*. In turn, this implies that the interactive features are used primarily to promote the candidate and to spread the campaign messages. Social media's potential for political debate and dialogue between users is not prioritised by the campaigns, and the aspect of message control still seems to be a key aim for the campaigners. Consequently, the incumbent's social media team might have an advantage in being more experienced and well-resourced, and in turn have more marketing power.

A third key finding was a tendency of *social media incumbency advantage*, meaning that the sitting president had a number of advantages within the hierarchy of Twitter that served to Obama campaign's advantage. Even though the incumbency advantage resulting from social media is of a very different character the one related to the mass media such as TV, this analysis found that the sitting president had a set of advantages within the logic of social media. For example, while airing-time for TV commercials can be bought, the social media requires an additional type of 'capital', namely user-engagement networked communication that requires a critical mass of followers and a prominent place in the power hierarchy on Twitter. The incumbency advantage in social media to some degree contradicts the idea of social media as the underdog-friendly arena where David beats Goliath. Of course David's slingshot has a chance, but Goliath's army has the upper hand. Rather, in the attention economy of social media, the incumbent will often have the upper hand.

References

Ansolabehere, Stephen, Eric C. Snowberg, and James M. Snyder (2006) "Television and the Incumbent Advantage in U.S. Elections" *Legislative Studies Quarterly*, Volume 31, Issue 4: 469–490.

Bimber, Bruce (2014) "Digital Media in the Obama Campaigns of 2008 and 2012: Adaptation to the Personalized Political Communication Environment" *Journal of Information Technology & Politics*, Volume 11, Issue 2: 130–135.

Bruns, Axel (2012) "Journalists and Twitter: How Australian News Organisations Adapt to a New Medium," *Media International Australia*, Volume 144: 97–107.

Bruns, Axel, and Tim Highfield (2013) "May the Best Tweeter Win: The Twitter Strategies of Key Campaign Accounts in the 2012 US Election," in C. Bieber and K. Kamps (eds.) *The United*

States Presidential Election 2012: Perspectives from Election Studies, Political and Communication Sciences. Wiesbaden: V. S. Verlag.

Chadwick, Andrew (2006) *Internet Politics: States, Citizens, and New Communication Technologies.* New York: Oxford University Press.

Donaldson, Gary A. (2007) *The First Modern Campaign: Kennedy, Nixon, and the Election of 1960.* Latham, MD: Rowman & Littlefield.

Druckman, J. N., M. J. Kifer, and M. Parkin (2007) "The Technological Development of Congressional Candidate Web Sites" *Social Science Computer Review*, Volume 25, Issue 4: 425–442.

Duggan, M., N. B. Ellison, C. Lampe, A. Lenhart, and M. Madden (2015a). "Demographics of Key Social Networking Platforms," Pew Research Center: Internet, Science & Tech, 9 Jan. 2015. Retrieved from http://www.pewinternet.org/2015/01/09/demographics-of-key-social-networking-platforms-2.

Duggan, M., N. B. Ellison, C. Lampe, A. Lenhart, and M. Madden (2015b). "Social Media Update 2014," Pew Research Center: Internet, Science & Tech, 9 Jan. 2015. Retrieved from http://www.pewinternet.org/2015/01/09/social-media-update-2014.

Enli, G. (2007) *The Participatory Turn in Broadcast Television*, PhD Thesis, Oslo: Faculty of Humanities, University of Oslo.

Enli, G. (2015) *Mediated Authenticity: How the Media Constructs Reality*, New York: Peter Lang.

Erikson, Stephen C. (1995) "The Entrenching of Incumbency: Reelections in the U.S. House of Representatives 1790–1994" *The Cato Journal*, Volume 14 (Winter): 397–420.

Gerodimos, R. and J. Justinussen (2014) "Obama's 2012 Facebook Campaign: Political Communication in the Age of the Like Button" *Journal of Information Technology and Politics*, Volume 12, Issue 2: 113–132. DOI:10.1080/19331681.2014.982266

Jackson, N. A. and D. G. Lilleker (2009) "Building an Architecture of Participation? Political Parties and Web 2.0 in Britain" *Journal of Information Technology & Politics*, Volume 6, Issue 3: 232–250.

Jamieson, K. H. (2013) *Electing the President: 2012 Insiders' View.* Philadelphia: University of Pennsylvania Press.

Kreiss, Daniel (2012) *Taking Our Country Back: The Crafting of Networked Politics from Howard Dean to Barack Obama.* Oxford: Oxford University Press.

Kreiss, D. (2014). "Seizing the Moment: The Presidential Campaigns' Use of Twitter during the 2012 Election Cycle," *New Media & Society* [online first]. DOI: 10.1177/1461444814562445.

Larsson, A. O. and B. Kalsnes (2014) "'Of Course We Are on Facebook': Use and Non-Use of Social Media among Swedish and Norwegian Politicians" *European Journal of Communication*, Volume 29, Issue 6: 653–667.

Maarek, P. (2011) *Campaign Communication and Political Marketing.* Malden: Wiley-Blackwell.

Polsby, N. W. and A. B. Wildavsky (2002) *Presidential Elections: Strategies and Structures of American Politics.* Laham, MD: Rowman & Littlefield.

Scammell, M. (1999) "Political Marketing: Lessons for Political Science," *Political Studies*, Volume 47, Issue 4: 718–739.

Schiller, H. I. (1976) *Communication and Cultural Domination.* New York: International Arts and Sciences Press.

Stayner, J. (2013) *Intimate Politics: Publicity, Privacy, and the Personal Lives of Politicians in Media-Saturated Democracies.* Cambridge: Polity.

Stromer-Galley, Jennifer (2000) "On-line Interaction and Why Candidates Avoid It" *Journal of Communication*, Autumn 2000: 11–132.

Stromer-Galley, Jennifer (2014) *Presidential Campaigning in the Internet Age.* Oxford: Oxford University Press.

Street, J. (2003) "The Celebrity Politician: Political Style and Popular Culture," in J. Corner and D. Pels (eds.) *Media and the Restyling of Politics.* London: Sage, pp. 85–98.

Ormrod, R. P., S.C.M. Henneberg, and N. O'Shaughnessy (2013) *Political Marketing: Theory and Concepts.* Los Angeles: Sage.

Pew Research Center: Internet, Science & Tech. (2015). "Internet Use over Time." Retrieved from http://www.pewinternet.org/data-trend/internet-use/internet-use-over-time/.

Plasser, F. and G. Plasser (2002) *Global Political Campaigning: A Worldwide Analysis of Campaign Professionals and Their Practices*. New York: Praeger.

Plouffe, D. (2009) *The Audacity to Win: How Obama Won and How We Can Beat the Party of Limbaugh, Beck, and Palin*. New York: Penguin Books

Van Zoonen, L. (2005) *Entertaining the Citizen: When Political and Popular Culture Converge*. Laham, MD: Rowman & Littlefield.

Winston, B. and P. Walton (1996) "Netscape. Virtually free" *Index of Censorship*, Volume 25, Issue 1: January/February.

27

THE 2012 FRENCH PRESIDENTIAL CAMPAIGN

First Steps into the Political Twittersphere

Françoise Papa and Jean-Marc Francony

Introduction

The French 2012 presidential election was marked by the emergence of Twitter as a tool which appeared, in the eyes of commentators, to be the main innovation of the campaign. Twitter was especially promoted by the candidates' teams and the media, who made 'real time' a new imperative in the media coverage of the campaign. The first result of this trend was a sharp increase in the publishing activity on Twitter, growing as election day and its uncertain result approached. Activists and, more broadly, the supporters of candidates invaded the space of debate on Twitter. This activism, which took various forms, reflected the vitality of social networks and their now inevitable role in public debate. The more traditional spaces of online information and political debate, such as websites and blogs, were overshadowed by Twitter, a reactive medium allowing for instantaneous communication which proved complementary to traditional mass media, and particularly to television.

This raised new questions for the field of political communication and the analysis of public opinion (Gerstlé & Magni Berton, 2014). The spread of Web 2.0 environments facilitated the emergence of new forms of interaction through networking, shaking up hierarchies and traditional institutional boundaries. In particular, traditional media were no longer the sole conduit for candidates aiming to control their end-to-end communication, which in turn also explains (at least partially) their enthusiasm for social networks. The logic of *eventization* (Couldry, Hepp, & Krotz, 2010) also contributed to the success of Twitter, as the 'mainstream' media were permanently on the lookout for content exchanged on social networks that might make news. Finally, Twitter created a space where public figures could be permanently visible commenting on news in real time, and at the same time creating live stories around themselves.

During an election campaign, participation in public debate first entails the mobilisation of partisan systems associated with the candidates. This so-called institutional activism aims to set the framework for interactions and modes of contribution to the public debate, in which activists, political supporters, and citizens are encouraged to participate. These institutional arrangements are generally associated with the Twitter accounts of the candidates as well as with those of their campaign teams and parties. They can be linked, to varying degrees, to spaces facilitated by communities with similar viewpoints, which are indicative of changes in the forms of activism and political debate brought about by online communication (de Zúñiga et al., 2009; Monnoyer-Smith & Wojcik, 2014).

The first challenge, for each candidate, is to obtain the participation of numerous publics and hence expand the dominant public sphere. In an *attention economy*, this also means pre-empting a communication space which becomes essential for the media through its activity and popularity. To gain influence, the organisation of this space is essential: this involves the organisation of activists on the network to multiply their impact on citizens and relies on agents with specialised skills in the facilitation and organisation of communities. Mediators that come from media or politics are enlisted to relay influence in the public sphere. We analyse these forms of network activism in this chapter.

Our analysis of the activity on Twitter that we recorded continuously over four months of the presidential campaign (from mid-January 2012 to mid-May 2012) allowed us to characterise the networks of relations and actors as well as their modes of expression on social networks. We present below the main findings from this case study.

Twitter Invites Itself to the Campaign

In 2012, the main concerns of the French in the lead-up to the election were the economic and financial crisis with its impact on employment, purchasing power, pensions, the education system and health care. On the eve of the first round of the election, the credibility ratings for François Hollande (Socialist Party—*Parti Socialiste*, or PS) were high in relation to his policies to reduce unemployment and social inequality and to re-enforce the defence of social rights. As for the candidate Nicolas Sarkozy, the incumbent French president (of the main right party—*Union pour un Mouvement Populaire*, or UMP), his credibility ratings remained high in areas such as law and order and the fight against illegal immigration. Fifteen days before the first round, pollsters' forecasts gave the socialists 45 per cent per cent of the vote. In the second-round run-off election, Hollande continued to be seen as the likely winner despite a rise in the popularity of Nicolas Sarkozy. However, the outcome remained uncertain due to uncertainty about the second-round voting intentions of the supporters of the four candidates who had received a substantial share of the vote (all over 14 per cent) at the first round.[1]

Sarkozy was squeezed between Hollande on his left, who was leading the race, the French Nationalist Party (*Front National*, FN) led by Marine Le Pen on his right, and François Bayrou, the candidate of the *Mouvement Démocratique* (MoDem), in the centre. As for François Hollande, he had to deal with the growing popularity of Jean-Luc Mélenchon, the candidate representing the radical left, *Le Front de Gauche* (FDG), while his main political allies in the environmental party (*Europe Ecologie Les Verts*, EELV) collapsed in the polls. The mobilisation of support with the aim of influencing the electorate would therefore play a major role in keeping Hollande's lead or, conversely, in reducing the gap between Nicolas Sarkozy and his main opponent.

These two candidates were not confronted by any specific events that were likely to have significant impacts on the balance of power over the campaign. Each candidate had to impose their agenda on the media to obtain the broadest possible coverage of their campaign. This period was punctuated by rallies, primarily in support of the candidates, and their appearances and statements in the media especially during their daily commutes and visits as well as in debates organised by the television channels.

As far as the use of social networks was concerned, all of the presidential candidates had expanded their communication to the Web and social networks, with varying levels of success. Their Twitter and Facebook accounts were linked to their official campaign sites; they were permanently connected and were able to cater to all types of usage, notably mobile use. The candidates also professionalised their use of social networks in general, with the help of teams of professional Web specialists and activists. This was done to varying degrees depending on their resources: both Sarkozy and Hollande officially declared having dedicated two million out of approximately 21 million euros to their Web campaign.

Our analysis of their editorial activity was based on a Twitter data set which focussed on the candidates' campaign accounts. We continuously collected—within the limits of what the Twitter Application Programming Interface would provide—a body of nearly two million tweets produced by, sent to, or mentioning at least one of the candidates. This collection provided a framework which was completed by studies of specific micro-events throughout the campaign—such as televised debates, identified by their hashtags, which generated large audiences.

Publication Activity Strongly Influenced by the Main Events of the Campaign

Within the limits of the representativeness of the data, the analysis of posting activity over the election period provided a clear picture of the dynamics of the campaign and showed how the candidates' communication built up over time. In particular, it highlighted the intensification of Sarkozy's communication activities between the two rounds of the election.

It was notable that the candidates' communication patterns were far from identical, notably as far as intensity is concerned; the resources mobilised differed, their audiences were not the same, reflecting the differences in their positions of the contest. The volume of publication activity varied with key moments that marked the activities of the candidates in social networks. The entry into the campaign is signalled by mass conventions in which candidates give speeches on their programmes: those of François Hollande (Le Bourget, 22 January 2012) and Nicolas Sarkozy (Villepinte, 11 March 2012) triggered considerable posting activity on Twitter. The campaign events which followed (Hollande scheduled 12 rallies, Sarkozy 10) correspond to moments of high activity on Twitter.

Generally speaking, there is a direct relationship between campaign events covered by the media and publishing activity on Twitter. This mainly concerns the televised debates between candidates (four debates took place over the last month of the campaign) and public rallies broadcast on television. These events strongly mobilised social networks and led to battles or 'retaliation parties' between supporters and opponents of the candidates, whose performances were commented upon in real time.

The key moments of the campaign were also linked to the media agenda that was sometimes imposed on the candidates or even thwarted their communication. A tragic episode, the Merah case[2] illustrated the emergence of news in the presidential campaign, which temporarily resulted in a dramatic reduction of posting activity on Twitter, the accounts of the candidates having been put on standby.

The study of content over this period confirmed that Twitter was fully involved in the information cycle, alongside the mass media. The media events and the volume of activity on Twitter were linked, regardless of whether the event was imposed on the candidates or whether it was generated as part of their communication strategies. Twitter was an echo chamber and an extension of the public media space that candidates aimed to use to their best interests.

Finally, by virtue of the event creation logic, actors developed viral strategies, the purpose of which was to cross over into the mainstream media in order to be more widely disseminated. These observations confirmed the analyses establishing the role of Twitter as a backchannel to live television, an extension of large-audience television, and an element in creating live audiences in real time (Harrington et al., 2012; Highfield et al., 2013).

A contextualisation of posting activity on Twitter in relation to external media events during the campaign or to specific events in the electoral contest (such as chat shows) more accurately captures these interrelationships. The examination of interactions between a televised debate and simultaneous content production on Twitter shows a relationship between the words spoken by a candidate and the increase in posts on Twitter reacting to them. The activity on Twitter is closely correlated to microsequences in the broadcast which crystallise opposition, and opinions that find their echo in the mobilised network. Twitter was also an indicator of the sensitivity of audiences to certain topics of discussion, which do not all generate the same volume of messages.

Differentiated Modes of Use

Far from being a forum disconnected from institutional points of view, or from the supporters' points of view, Twitter was used both by candidates and supporters' organisations whose online interventions helped structure the exchange. The analysis of interactions and communication provides information on the intensity and the modes of participation in the public debate as well as on the involvement of participants.

Posting activity on Twitter was effectively based on the political agendas of the candidates, but their investment in the social network was variable and unequal. These differences are a logical extension of their previous positions (Papa, 2007; Francony & Papa, 2014; Greffet & Wojcik, 2008) and of the communication habits of the parties that support them (Theviot, 2013). So, Facebook was at the core of Sarkozy's Web communication activities, while Twitter was used mostly as a channel for the dissemination of information, with very little interactivity. His strategy was to present himself first and foremost on his Facebook page.[3]

Hollande communicated mainly via dedicated websites (francoishollande.fr and toushollande.fr) to which the cloud of Socialist Party websites was linked, and via Twitter. Twitter was used in service of Hollande's communication and the mobilisation of his supporters: it provided convenient tools to relay his campaign in a more interactive way with the aim of involving supporters and facilitating their online participation in the campaign and on the ground. Hollande entrusted a community manager to coordinate a team of Web content curators. Their tasks were to aggregate the messages that supporters were invited to post and to organise responses to the statements of other candidates. Romain Pigenel, in charge of the digital mobilisation during the campaign, explains this strategy:

> One can join the "TousHollande" sphere by creating an account on the website and connecting your personal blog or Twitter account. From that moment on, the platform supports several functions. First, to make the community of bloggers that support François Hollande (which is up to this point scattered and non-quantifiable) visible, and enable them to know each other. Second, to highlight their posts without interfering with the official communication disseminated through François Hollande's institutional website. Third, to create motivation and emulation by publishing rankings of the most effective and influential twittos and bloggers in the campaign. Fourth, to discover and empower via these rankings, the twittos and bloggers of great value that are outside the usual groups of the Socialist Party. Then, last but not least, to make innovative tools available to this community to facilitate their action and make their support public.
>
> (Pigenel, 2011: para. 4)

The National Front, for its part, based its communication around its candidate, Marine Le Pen, by meshing a multitude of websites around the official campaign website and its Facebook accounts. These websites were run by supporters who could register their blogs, and be labelled with an official logo as a participant in *La Toile Bleu Marine* ('Blue Marine Network'). This organic set-up evolved over the duration of the campaign. Its focus was on the interconnection of existing resources on the Web, and to a large extent it ignored Twitter, which was not used much by the voters and supporters of Marine Le Pen.

These differences can be explained in part by the structure of the various supporter networks and the number of active connections in the each of them. Posting activity over the campaign was organised through the intervention of key actors such as network facilitators, community managers, activists, and to a lesser extent the supporters of the candidates.

To compare the total activity of the candidates, we studied the number of posts produced over time (based on calculations of hourly presence ratios and average flow intensity). Over the 15 days preceding the first ballot, the volumes of posts emphasised strong commitment by the supporters of the MoDem and the environmental group EELV, and a modest share of the Socialist Party.

The various categories of accounts studied (candidate, community, and party) do not contribute equally to the debate for each candidate. As stated before, Hollande's community manager benefited from significant autonomy in managing communication, notably within the 'TousHollande' environment. Sarkozy's personal Twitter account played the premier role and was the most active account (in the number of posts and in the frequency of its use) in the campaign; his very centralised and vertical communication approach was centred largely on his personal charisma and strong personality.

The activity of the different networks was not homogeneous over the period. Though the activity of the Socialist candidate was globally stable, the results of the first round of the election had a notable impact on the activity of the other candidates' campaigns. There was a significant increase in the UMP's activity over the two weeks between rounds, whereas almost symmetrically there was a corresponding collapse in the activity of both the MoDem and the EELV, with the radical left FDG decreasing as well, though less markedly. The period between the first and second rounds led to a polarisation of discussions, focussing on the battle between Sarkozy and Hollande.

Twitter quickly became an important tool in deploying the strategies of the candidates whose objectives were to reach media saturation through the permanent occupation of the Twittersphere by means of a continuous production of messages. It became clear that there was a need to organise the monitoring of content on the network in order for the candidates to be able to react through communication or through their campaign teams. This was also necessary in order to keep a close eye on events and to ensure the mobilisation of their Twitter followers and supporters.

To understand the candidates' communication strategies during the campaign, we identified and characterised the key participants in the discussion on Twitter. Mapping their networks of relationships allowed us, in a second phase, to analyse the forms of mobilisation of activists on Twitter.

A Forum for Debate Structured by Supporter Networks

Candidates made up the core of the study, from which we characterised the political affiliations and political preferences of the contributors to the discussions on Twitter. Whenever it was possible we did this by using the biographies posted on Twitter accounts, so that we were able to identify the core contributors and their political affiliations. We looked for "remarkable" contributors that we characterised in terms of their communication activity in relation to their position in the network (notably their connector function, which was identified from the analysis of retweets).

We then built up a representation of the interactions between these points, and studied the graphs built from the relationships expressed in the tweets. Thus we identified affinities between individuals of the same political affiliation and/or relationships between those with opposing views. We have also made visible the relations of these core actors and the clouds of points that we were not, at first, able to position explicitly on the political spectrum. Our hypothesis, continuing from the pioneering work of Adamic (Adamic and Glance 2005), was that there were similar opinions between these categories of actors.

An earlier analysis of tweets mentioning a political party and associated accounts during an election period, carried out by Feller et al. (2011), aimed to update the participants' network structure with the exchanges sorted along the lines of their political preferences and their subjects of discussion. This study, following on from the work of Conover et al. (2011), confirmed that Twitter users interested in politics tend to follow peers who share the same opinions, although according to Bode et al. (2011) and An et al. (2011), Twitter and other social networks provide opportunities to access more diverse political opinions.

The map of relations that we established confirmed the results of this earlier research, and confirmed the phenomenon of political polarisation on Twitter. The forum of relations that developed on Twitter over the 2012 campaign was, at first analysis, structured by the proximity of the political opinions of the Twitter users, whose activity in the network, however, remained far from uniform or homogeneous. These disparities were not specific to the theme that drives conversations, in our case politics; whatever the interests under discussion, only a minority of Twitter users produce content for a wide audience, while most of them only follow conversations, or interact within limited groups of acquaintances.[4] Variations occur in the intensity of activity, the type of activity, and the structure of the networks of relationships that develop around or concern a candidate.

We referred earlier to the different positions of the candidates, and their impact on the use of social networks: a comparison of the structures of the networks of relationships of each candidate, based on the retweet activity analysis between two rounds of the presidential election, is significant in this respect. For example, the communication strategies deployed by Hollande have a star-shaped configuration whose centre has two parts: @TousHollande and @fhollande were in a reciprocal relationship. This core ensures the cohesion of the whole set-up, so that the clouds of official websites of the Socialist Party link to this double heart. The EELV and FDG set-ups also have star-shaped structures that are focused solely on their candidates who ensure, alone, the cohesion of their systems. On the other hand, the relationship between the accounts of Sarkozy and the UMP, his own party, was very distant, as the candidate only rarely relayed any of the party's content.

Some common factors appeared, however: whatever the structure adopted, community managers are located at the interface of three subnetworks (party, candidate, communities) and ensure a link between them. Some of them (R. Pigenel—PS; A. Champremier-Trigano—FDG) also engaged publicly through their own Twitter accounts. These results are consistent with the work of Ausserhofer and Maireder (2013) and emphasise the importance of professional politicians and political communication in the facilitation and organisation of political exchanges on Twitter. Finally, relationships appeared between the campaign networks, a fact which addresses the strategic need that requires 'bridges' between the candidacies, and a discursive reality involving the opposing discourses in the construction of an identity and unique position for each candidate.

A Forum That Structures the Political Debate

During the campaign, the political Twittersphere is mainly structured by the publishing activities of supporters and of political institutions, but it is also a forum that provides structure. In our analysis of publishing activity, we identified circles of participants with increasing levels of involvement in debates (see Figure 27.1).

Our analysis of retweets highlighted the support logics at work in the Twittersphere over the election campaign. First, the existence of politicised cores with networks supporting the candidacy indicated a high level of activity as well as the efficient relaying carried out by community activists. Second, it revealed the logics of reciprocity at work within these communities, which in turn shows the internal cohesion of the group. This cohesion was such that the community structure—identified using social network analysis methods—persisted even when the nodes associated with candidates and the institutional systems that support them (community managers, party venues, etc.) were eliminated from the retweet graph.

Twitter has also proven to be an organising tool for mobilising and influencing beyond the core supporters, particularly during key moments of the campaign, such as during televised debates that offer opportunities for online expression remarkable in both volume and intensity. It also helped organise the work of supporters in the field and incite people to participate both in candidates' rallies and in public debates. Finally, Twitter contributed to the construction of a common discourse around the candidates.

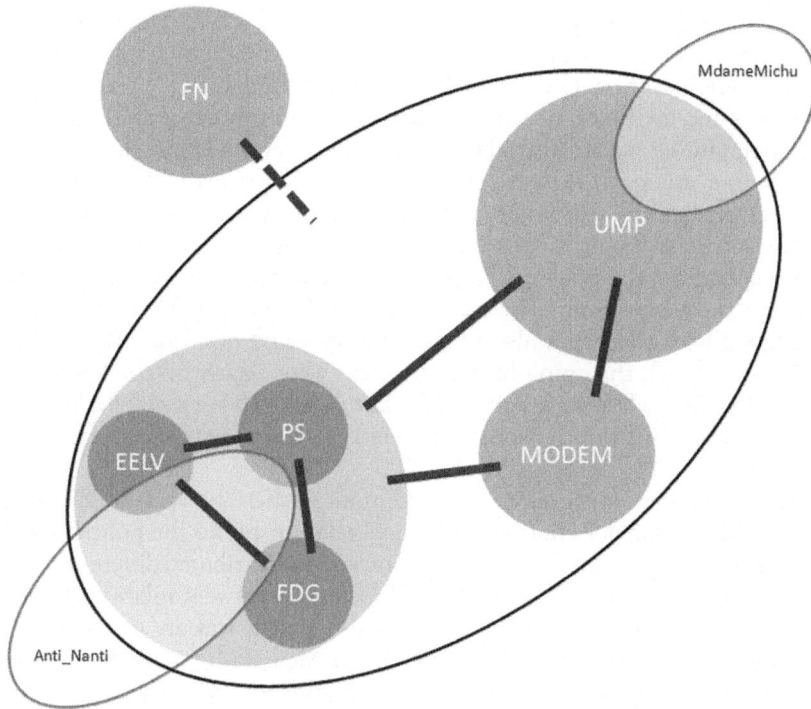

Figure 27.1 Diagram Illustrating the Political Polarities Identified from the Analysis of Content on Twitter over the 2012 Campaign

In the vicinity of clearly defined political communities, we identified another two very cohesive communities. These communities with similar opinions had developed their own posting activities but were not apparently significantly linked to any political party, though they did channel some of the editorial activity. Further analysis of these structures showed that each has a strong identity, based on the left-right political divide.

Channelled by the specific hashtags #Anti_Nanti (AgainstNob), #MdameMichu (MrsBrown), and attributed to accounts of the same names, @Anti_Nanti and @Mda-meMichu function as an antagonistic dipole. Without claiming any partisan label, each community has emerged through its opposition to the ideological positions of the candidates of the adverse party, rather than through the affirmation of what characterised their preferred candidates. Despite this off-party positioning, an analysis of the community structure of MdameMichu revealed three sub-communities close to the UMP political machinery. The largest group (52.4 per cent) was the first circle centred on the MdameMichu account, in which public figures from the entertainment world had a special place. The second group (29 per cent) were young right-wing activists and members of youth organisations (JeunePop, UNI, etc.), and was organised around several UMP activists, acting as community managers. The third group (18.6 per cent) corresponded to the interfaces with other supporter networks. From the political categorisation we conducted on a thousand accounts, it appeared that 88 per cent of actors in the community core showed a tendency to support the UMP. More generally, those with strong involvement in the network were engaged in a form of proclaimed radical anti-left militancy, as shown by the analysis of their biographies.

Using the same method for reconstructing upstream retweet graphs, we also found four sub-communities within Anti_Nanti whose members had more diverse party affiliations. The four groups were distributed as follows: 30 per cent MoDem, 29 per cent PS, 13.6 per cent UMP, and 9 per cent FDG. The largest group (45.7 per cent) was not centred on Anti_Nanti. It included several accounts that expressed opinions to the left, ranging from the Socialist Party further left to the FDG, with various levels of radicalism in their expression. The second group (27.6 per cent) was driven by a core clearly aligned with the FDG, also very active on social networks. Within the third group (19.9 per cent), the opinions of individuals were clearly on the left but with no claims of belonging to left-wing parties. The last group (6.8 per cent) did not maintain close connections with the network and seemed rather to play a peripheral interface role with others.

Although they share a common 'anti' orientation, these two communities differ in two respects: their core does not have the same relationship to the political machines, and their members, aggregated in sub-communities, are distributed differently across the political spectrum. For the UMP, the lack of reciprocal retweet relations between the campaign organisation and MdameMichu suggests that it was an autonomous set-up, although interlinking was very strong between the MdameMichu network and institutional clouds around the UMP candidate. The analysis shows a very strong representation of UMP supporters within the MdameMichu community. In a different manner, Anti_Nanti feeds on the activities of the left-wing networks, and especially the FDG candidate. This diversity of relayed content positioned the group that aggregated it as an interface of left-wing opinions for both the PS and the EELV, federating opinions directed against the incumbent president Nicolas Sarkozy and his party.

These results, although partial, support the observation that there has been a progressive diversification in the forms of political engagement and participation on the Web over the past decade. In the context of the election, this non-institutional use of Twitter is less a response to the need for more extensive and diversified information than to the need to monitor political news, the need for self-expression, and the need to construct of a collective identity. The analysis of messages exchanged in these communities, as well as of the way they were formalised, confirms this.

Enunciation Modes That Are Both Significant and Remarkable

Twitter logic tends to reduce the diversity of the publication forms produced by its users. This normative logic is reinforced by the strategic goals of communication, whose aim is to address the broadest possible audience. Consequently, looking for patterns in the forms of expression as well as in the structure of the interventions enables us to understand the mechanisms and tactics that are being used, and hence to obtain a better understanding of the contribution of Twitter as a communicative environment. It also facilitates the characterisation of the actors and their roles in structuring the Twittersphere in the context of the event.

First, this normalisation intervenes in the way that the actors involved in the political debate are referenced. Referring to individuals by using their Twitter username enables users to fuel the public flow of information which is associated with them. This way of referencing an individual with no possible ambiguity was widely favoured during the campaign when designating the candidates in tweets. This contributes to the association of the various publication forums with the candidates, and in this way sets up the political reference area for the campaign on Twitter.

Over and above the normative aspects, the linking of an account to another account, perceived as the transposition of interpersonal relationships into the Twittersphere, promotes the idea of proximity. This aspect is integrated into the communication strategies of the leading candidates who associate their names with accounts likely to speak out for them.

Spontaneous indexing supported by hashtags is another element of this normalisation. As far as the nomination of candidates is concerned, here it is necessary to distinguish between the strict patronymic constructions that are formally equivalent to the addresses of accounts (#hollande, #sarkozy), and the qualifying constructions (nicknames, diminutives, etc.) which provide scope for more creativity. Creativity is rather expressed through various constructions representing positive voting instructions (#lepenvite, #avecsarkozy, #votezmélenchon) or negative statements (#stopsarkozy, #nohollande). Another type of construction aims to build aphorisms, puns and other slogans, essentially disqualifying the concerned candidates (#lolhollande, #lafrancemolle).

Second, standardisation is also involved in structuring messages. The order of the components of a message, partly inherited from the recommendations of use and the evolution of Twitter, provides a widely adopted framework for Twitter users. One of the most important aspects concerns the author citation and reference mechanism that can be considered as a generalisation of the republication mechanism. Unlike verbatim republication through "button" retweeting, citation allows the inclusion of external elements such as reported speech or fragments of tweets that can also be considered as elements of speech.

Throughout the campaign, we found that the quotes and retweets were particularly stable markers for identifying the elements of the candidates' political communication. Implemented by the campaign teams and close circles around the supporters, these messages build the longest chains of retweets. Diffusing especially effectively throughout the networks of supporters, they help convey the elements of speech essential to the persuasive communication of the candidates. We also measured a very strong correlation between candidates' citations and the simultaneous presence of hashtags encouraging people to vote.

During televised debates, the production of this type of message is remarkable, both by the published content and the timing of publication. In addition to the language elements that are taken directly from the candidates' discourse, extracts of programmes, blogs, interviews and URLs pointing to multimedia documentary resources and related to the candidates' speeches are also made available. The astonishing speed (less than one minute) between giving the speech and the dissemination of the tweets suggests that these often complex elements may be prepared beforehand. Sometimes, some messages allowed other candidates to enter into the ongoing debate on the TV show, although they were not physically present on the set, thereby enabling their reintroduction into the public discussion.

Based on the structure of the quote they complement, we identified the structure of the comments which enabled the authors of the tweet to position themselves in relation to its content. Comments played a significant role, equivalent to those of the quotes which they can complete or complement or to which they can reply. The length of tweets does not allow for long development in the comments; rather, it provides support or conversely sanctions the quoted content using incisive language or one good word.

The candidates' words were widely commented upon on Twitter: the comment, though it remains the prerogative of politicians, journalists and experts, was also largely used by supporters in a fashion more or less coordinated with the campaign. Therefore, during the televised debates, many comments were produced both to bring new or contradictory elements to the subjects under discussion and to respond to quotes published by the opposing camps. Twitter was used to re-enforce the persuasive communication of the candidates by disseminating quotes from the candidates' speeches, by producing ready-made arguments and by enriching the messages with Web content.

Twitter also provided a forum of expression unique in both form and mode. Sheltering their editorial activity behind an avatar whose virtual identity is easily understandable, the 'antis' have channelled and stimulated the expression of opinions free of the constraints of form and language, moving towards transgressive forms of political expression. This expressivist new form of activism helps diversify political discussion on the networks by setting free individual speech. Throughout the campaign, Anti_ Nanti and MdameMichu functioned like fora where almost instantaneous responses to the events of the campaign were organised and where messages disparaging political opponents were generated. Types of expression, like lampooning, emerged which were far from, if not in breach of, the institutional political speeches of the candidates and their political setups. As a transgressive genre both polemical and incisive, the objective of a lampoon is to get people to react and to cause an event (Hastings et al. 2009), whilst official campaigning devices remain regulated by their political machinery: they are now articulated with spaces where opinions can be given in discursive forms favouring comments to simple quotes, and where, often, invective competes with caricature.

Conclusion

During the 2012 presidential election, candidates' communication strategies evolved and integrated Twitter as a new tool and a new space. This feature was used in particular with the aim of saturating media space during the key events in the candidates' agendas. The effectiveness of these devices relied heavily on the involvement of the Web professionals with whom parties or candidates surrounded themselves.

We have highlighted the fact that the space of political debate on Twitter is structured in line with the communication strategies of the institutional actors involved in the election campaign, but also under the influence of *ad hoc* communities that are opportunistically associating themselves closely with the political event. Our study shows, however, that there remain significant differences between partisan institutional organisations: these differences lie in the organisational cultures of the parties, and the need to adapt to a configuration of communication where candidates are supported by a federal structure of supporter groups, but where a posture of strong leadership remains possible.

The Twittersphere has emerged as a new territory for politics to colonise, bringing with it new forms of implications for supporters and a new audience to conquer. The community managers were key players in the structuring of the audience, facilitating community activists around the institutional organisations of their candidates. Their role was also found to be that of an interface with peer communities that had similar opinions but were not linked to the institutional frameworks. The communities observed around MdameMichu or Anti_Nanti are illustrative of these aggregation phenomena.

Analysis of the content posted by the members of these two communities showed that their comments are not led by the candidates' official communication activities. Nevertheless, the spontaneity of these networks can be questioned considering the fact that key players in the active core of these communities have a strong commitment to a candidate or party. This type of intervention in the area of political debate, apparently disconnected from partisan institutional arrangements, has several advantages: it can access a public resistant to all active support whilst developing a political discourse, and broaden the modes of political expression through less conventional forms and content. Advancing 'masked', in a sense, may ultimately be, as one of the riposte strategies, a way of ensuring the broader dissemination of proposals and ideas for a candidate. This may re-enforce a sense of belonging to a community of ideas, identify contributors who may ultimately join the official supporter structures, and in this way collect resources that could potentially be mobilised in the political contest.

Activism on social networks, in whatever forms it takes, challenges the regulatory principles of the electoral contest as applied for example to equal access to the media for all candidates. It opens up new questions about the conditions of democratic public debate, and therefore about the factors which contribute to the development of political opinion, notably as it appears on Twitter as a poorly regulated space still marked by uneven social take-up.

Notes

1 The results of the first round confirmed an advantage to the left, with a combined vote share of 44 per cent. Hollande received 28.6 per cent of the vote, Sarkozy 27.2 per cent, Le Pen 17.9 per cent and Mélenchon 11.1 per cent. In the second round Hollande won with 51.6 per cent of the vote against 48.4 per cent for Sarkozy.

2 The case involved three gun attacks targeting French soldiers and Jewish civilians in March 2012. In total, seven people were killed and five others were injured. The perpetrator, Mohammed Merah, a 23-year-old French petty criminal of Algerian descent, was shot and killed after a 30-hour siege with police. Merah attacked French Army personnel reportedly because of their involvement in the war in Afghanistan. Merah admitted anti-Semitic motivations and said he attacked the Jewish school because "the Jews kill our brothers and sisters in Palestine."

3 The number of people who had 'liked' Nicolas Sarkozy on Facebook by the eve of the first round of the presidential election was 689,344, whereas François Hollande had only around 350,000 fans. In France, Facebook has 26 million monthly active users; Twitter, 2.3 million.

4 "Nearly six out of 10 active Twittos reported reading Twitter accounts (other than their own) at least once every two days (59%), 31% several times a day. However, only a third (33%) issue tweets at least once every two days, only 13% emit tweets several times a day. Twitter therefore appears more as a means of communicating information" (Ipsos, 2013: para. 4).

References

Adamic, L.A., and Glance, N. (2005). "The Political Blogosphere and the 2004 U.S. Election: Divided They Blog." Proceedings of the Third International Workshop on Link Discovery, Link-KDD '05, pp. 36–43. New York, NY, USA: ACM.

An, J., Cha, M., Gummadi, K., and Crowcroft, J. (2011). "Media Landscape in Twitter: A World of New Conventions and Political Diversity." Proceedings of the Fifth International AAAI Conference on Weblogs and Social Media, pp. 18–25. Barcelona, 17–21 July 2011.

Ausserhofer, J., and Maireder, A. (2013). "National Politics on Twitter." *Information, Communication & Society*, 16(3), 291–314.

Bode, L., Hanna, A., Sayre, B., Yang, J. H., and Shah D. V. (2011). "Mapping the Political Twitterverse: Finding Connections Between Political Elites." Political Network Paper Archive. Carbondale, IL: Open SIUC.

Conover, M. D., Ratkiewicz, J., Francisco, M., Goncalves, B., Flammini, A., and Menczer, F. (2011). "Political Polarization on Twitter." Proceedings of the Fifth International AAAI Conference on Weblogs and Social Media, pp. 89–96. Barcelona, 17–21 July 2011.

Couldry, N., Hepp, A., and Krotz F. (eds). (2010). *Media Events in a Global Age*. London: Routledge.

De Zúñiga, H. G., Puig-I-Abril, E., and Rojas, H. (2009). "Weblogs, Traditional Sources Online and Political Participation: An Assessment of How the Internet Is Changing the Political Environment." *New Media & Society*, 11(4), 553–574.

Feller, A., Kuhnert, M., Sprenger, T. O., and Welpe, I. M. (2011). "Divided They Tweet: The Network Structure of Political Microbloggers and Discussion Topics." Proceedings of the Fifth International AAAI Conference on Weblogs and Social Media, pp. 474–477. Barcelona, 17–21 July 2011.

Francony, J. M., and Papa, F. (2014). "Twitter en campagne," in J. Gerstlé & R. Magni Berton (eds.), *2012, La Campagne Présidentielle*, Paris: L'Harmattan, pp. 87–102.

Gerstlé, J., and Magni Berton, R. (dir) (2014). *2012, La campagne présidentielle*. Paris: L'Harmattan, coll. Communication, Politique et Société.

Greffet, F., and Wojcik, S. (2008). "Parler politique en ligne: une revue des travaux français et anglo-saxons." *Réseaux*, 26(150), 19–50.

Harrington, S., Highfield, T., and Bruns, A. (2012). "More than a Backchannel: Twitter and Television" in José Manuel Noguera (ed.) *Audience Interactivity and Participation*. Brussels: COST Action ISO906 Transforming Audiences, Transforming Societies, pp. 13–17.

Hastings, M., Passard, C., and Rennes, J. (2009). "*Les mutations du pamphlet dans la France contemporaine.*" in Mots. *Les langages du politique*, 91.

Highfield, T., Harrington, S., and Bruns, A. (2013). "Twitter as a Technology for Audiencing and Fandom: The #Eurovision Phenomenon." *Information, Communication & Society*, 16(3), 315–39. doi:10.1080/1369118X.2012.756053

Ipsos (2013) Ipsos Survey 2013. http://www.ipsos.fr/decrypter-societe/2013-04-25-usages-et-pratiques-twitter-en-france

Monnoyer-Smith, L., and Wojcik, S. (2014). "La participation politique en ligne, vers un renouvellement des problématiques?" in *La participation politique en ligne: Politics as usual? Participations* (2014) N° 8, 2014/1.

Papa, F. (2007). "Événements médiatiques en ligne: vers de nouveaux dispositifs d'intermédiation." *Enjeux et usages des TIC. Médias et diffusion de l'information, vers une société ouverte*. Athènes: Ed Gutenberg, pp. 47–58.

Pigenel, Romain. (2011). "Pourquoi @TousHollande?" *Variae.com* 1 Sep. 2011.

Theviot, A. (2013). "Ignorer les potentialités du Web 2.0: une campagne 1.5? Analyse comparative des stratégies (participatives en ligne du PS et de l'UMP pendant la campagne présidentielle de 2012." In *GIS Démocratie et Participation*. http://www.participation-et-democratie.fr.

28

THE EMERGENCE OF SOCIAL MEDIA POLITICS IN SOUTH KOREA

The Case of the 2012 Presidential Election

Lars Willnat and Young Min

Introduction

South Korea ranks among the most Internet-connected nations in the world, with slightly more than 92 per cent of its 50 million citizens online (Internet Live States 2014). As in other democracies with well-developed online environments, digital media have played an important role in South Korea's local and national elections. During the 2011 mayoral election in Seoul, for example, Twitter users overwhelmingly supported the opposition candidate Park Won-soon, which contributed to his unexpected victory in a highly competitive race (S.-Y. Lee 2012). Similarly, during the legislative election in April 2012, which was considered a bellwether for the presidential election later that year, nearly half of the 1,090 candidates used Twitter as part of their campaign strategy (W. Chang & Ryu 2013).

This sudden rise of social media as a strategic campaign tool was no coincidence. Beginning with the 2007 presidential election, the Korean National Election Commission placed a 180-day ban on the display and distribution of election-related information through the Internet and social media before elections. However, in December 2011, the Constitutional Court ruled that the ban was unconstitutional and infringed upon free expression, thus allowing candidates' use of all available digital media throughout the upcoming election year (Ser 2011). This ruling marked an important turning point in South Korean politics. Politicians could now mobilise younger citizens who often could not be reached through traditional media (D. Chang & Bae 2012). Candidates also could reach far more citizens through the Internet as more and more citizens accessed social networking services through their smartphones. As a result, the main political candidates in the 2012 presidential election mounted aggressive online campaigns, using a wider range of social media than in previous elections.

Given the important political changes in South Korea's digital media environment, this chapter aims to analyse the political role of social media, particularly their function as newly emerging channels of political learning and participation during the 2012 presidential election. We will start with a brief overview of South Korea's digital media environment, the political context of the 2012 presidential election campaign, and the main candidates' social media strategies. This will be followed by an empirical analysis of how social media were used during the 2012 presidential election in South Korea.

The analysis draws on data from an online survey we conducted shortly before the election in December 2012 with a national sample of 1,063 Koreans. The survey focused on how citizens used social media to gather election information and their overall level of political engagement. To provide a wider context for the South Korean survey results, we will compare them with findings of an identical survey we conducted shortly before the 2012 U.S. presidential election with a national sample of 1,064 U.S. citizens. Because most of the questions in the Korean and U.S. survey were identical, we were able to compare the findings of both.

These comparisons, upon which most of our analyses are based, were done to provide a contextual baseline for the analysis of the Korean findings on social media use in politics. These findings would have been difficult to evaluate without knowing how much citizens in other media-rich nations rely on social media during political election campaigns. The fact that both presidential elections happened around the same time in two highly developed countries that share several political characteristics makes such comparisons even more valuable in our eyes. Overall, we believe that this cross-national comparison of social media users will help to more accurately gauge the political role that social media played during South Korea's 2012 presidential campaign.[1] The chapter will conclude with a final discussion of the current role of social media in South Korean politics.

The 2012 South Korean Presidential Election

The 2012 South Korean presidential election was held on 19 December 2012. According to the National Election Commission, more than 30.7 million people or 75.8 per cent of eligible voters (aged 19 or over) cast their ballots ("Presidential Election Turnout at 75.8%" 2012). This record turnout was 12.8 per cent higher than the last presidential election in 2007, due mainly to increased participation among voters between 20 and 40 years.

Six candidates officially sought office in 2012. They included Park Geun-hye of the ruling Saenuri Party, Moon Jae-in of the main opposition Democratic United Party, and four other minor candidates. Park is the daughter of Park Chung-hee, who seized power in a 1961 military coup and ruled as autocratic president until his death in 1979. A legislator since 1998, Park's work has always been evaluated in light of her father's legacy. Among her supporters, she is seen today as a principled, determined leader who endured extreme personal tragedy. Her critics, on the other hand, mostly view her as a symbol of Korea's authoritarian past (Rauhala 2012). By contrast, challenger Moon was a former human rights lawyer once jailed for leading student protests against the elder Park's authoritarian rule. Moon later served as chief of staff for President Roh Moo-hyun, who was in office from 2003 to 2008. As a consequence, both candidates' political careers were deeply connected with Park's father, a fact that quickly became the focus of the 2012 election campaign (Choe 2012).

Both candidates agreed on the need for economic democratisation, extensive political reforms, and greater engagement with North Korea. Park employed a more pro-business approach and focused on continued economic growth. Moon campaigned for more liberal policies such as universal social-welfare systems, regulating big corporations, and a closer embrace of North Korea (Colapinto 2012). These relatively large political differences, however, were not much debated during the election campaign. Instead, the candidates focused on mutual accusations and personal attacks throughout the campaign ("Presidential Election Campaigns Turn Negative" 2012).

While Moon was especially popular among younger voters, many of Park's constituents were older and more conservative (Yoon 2012). Opinion polls consistently indicated a small lead for Park throughout the election year, but Moon gradually eroded this gap as the campaign drew to a close. Nevertheless, the bitter contest ended with a narrow 3.6 per cent margin of victory for Park, making her South Korea's first female president (H.-J. Kim & Klug 2012).

The Rise of Social Media in South Korean Politics

At the time of the presidential election in December 2012, about 82 per cent of South Korea's 50 million citizens had access to the Internet, with slightly more males (53 per cent) than females online. The vast majority (83 per cent) of Internet users also read newspapers online and almost 6 in 10 netizens (55 per cent) said they used social media within the past year. About 9 in 10 (94 per cent) of social media users were members of networking services such as Facebook, 25.5 per cent used microblogs such as Twitter, 23.1 per cent used blogs, and 22 per cent participated in so-called *minihompy* (personal webpages that feature personal profiles, background music, photo albums, etc.; Lim et al. 2013).

Like many other developed nations in Asia, South Korea saw a significant surge in social media users in 2012. The total number of Korean Facebook users, for example, surpassed 10 million, an increase of 47 per cent in one year (Socialbakers 2013). Similarly, the number of Korean Twitter users surged from 780,000 in September 2009 to 6.4 million in May 2012—up more than eightfold (Twitter Korean Index 2012). This rapid adoption of social media was partly credited to the wide adoption of smartphones among Koreans seeking Internet access through mobile devices. By the end of 2012, more than 90 per cent of social media users were accessing social media through their smartphones (Lim et al. 2013).

Because of Koreans' preference for mobile Internet applications, one of the most popular services was KakaoTalk, a multiplatform texting service that allows free messaging. KakaoTalk attracted a huge following of all ages during the 2012 election, as many Koreans used it to receive real-time text messages from the main political candidates. By early December 2012, more than 441,000 Koreans received so-called Ka-talks from Park and about 305,000 citizens 'friended' Moon through this service (Im 2012; M.-J. Lee 2012).

Overall, Koreans clearly were well-connected throughout the 2012 presidential election, with many taking advantage of the new social media services offered by the political candidates. In turn, this allowed the candidates to creatively use social media to increase their name recognition, empower previously disengaged young voters, and build political momentum.

Candidates' Social Media Strategies

While previous election campaigns in South Korean revolved mostly around Twitter, the 2012 presidential campaign used a variety of social media that allowed candidates to circumvent traditional media and reach voters directly (Park & Cho 2013). The two main candidates, Park and Moon, strategically connected with citizens and sought more personal and reciprocal interactions with online 'followers' or 'friends', thus enthusiastically embracing the direct reach of social media.

Both campaigns were built on a variety of social media platforms that included blogs, Twitter, Facebook, KakaoTalk, *minihompy*, Plickers, Opencast, and YouTube (Park & Cho 2013). Park, for example, posted videos on her YouTube channel (www.youtube.com/user/pgh545) that discussed her private life and delivered numerous campaign messages designed to improve her political image. Alongside her campaign's official Twitter account (@at_pgh), Park maintained a personal account (@gh_park) mostly for retweeting the campaign's official posts. Similarly, Park's Facebook account was used mainly to provide additional publicity for official campaign messages (Keum 2014).

Moon also actively used Twitter, Facebook, and YouTube. His YouTube channel Moon Jae-in TV (www.youtube.com/user/moonriver365) featured audio and video podcasts, which were particularly popular among young citizens (H.-N. Jeon 2012; Min 2014). These podcasts resulted in numerous comments on other social media and links to them were frequently shared and retweeted.

Both campaigns also were fairly successful in soliciting campaign donations from Korean citizens through digital media. Social media served as key drivers for such donations by rapidly sharing fund raising campaigns across online communities. The first creative user of this strategy was Moon, who asked his social media followers to invest in the Moon Jae-in Ivy Fund. Through this unconventional method of crowd-funding, Moon raised more than 30 billion won ($27.8 million) from 40,000 'investors', who he promised to pay back after the election with an interest rate of 3.1 per cent per year (Ser 2012; Song 2012). Park quickly mounted a similar effort with her Park Guen-hye Promise Fund and raised 25 billion won ($23.1 million) from 11,800 social media followers in less than 52 hours (B.-Y. Jeon & Lee 2012). The minimum investment in these funds was 10,000 won ($9), but no upper ceiling was set.

Yet, the campaign strategies of the two main candidates were also characterised by some key differences. Because the main targets of social media strategies were young voters, a group that traditionally shuns politics as well as news originating from mainstream media, social media were more important to Moon, whose main constituents were young and liberal (Choi & Shim 2014). Park focused more on strengthening her image as a strong, dependable politician with older citizens, who still could be reached through television and traditional newspapers.

As a result, Moon relied much more heavily on Twitter than Park, who he quickly surpassed in total number of followers and tweets posted (Park & Cho 2013). During the campaign's final stage, Moon's two Twitter accounts (@moonriver365 and @mooncamp1219) attracted 374,317 followers, compared to Park's 261,685. More importantly, Moon's followers were more likely to retweet political messages than Park's followers. And unlike Park, Moon often tweeted about personal observations, the campaign, and his planned policies (Park & Cho 2013), which made his posts much more interesting to the average voter.

Moon's Facebook page also attracted more fans than Park's. By early December 2012, Moon's page had received 77,663 'likes' compared to Park's 20,280 (Im 2012). To make his page more attractive to potential voters, Moon's staff regularly uploaded multimedia messages about campaign activities and Moon personally posted messages to his time-line (Keum 2014).

Overall, both presidential candidates successfully integrated social media into their campaigns to directly reach voters with their messages. Neither Park nor Moon, how-ever, took full advantage of the technological and political potential of social media. Both failed, for example, to develop a comprehensive plan for how different social media could be integrated into one coherent campaign strategy. As a result, each medium was used in isolation. More importantly, their strategies mostly ignored ways to empower citizens to organise themselves into small or large voluntary groups—a strategy that Barack Obama's presidential campaigns successfully employed in 2008 and 2012. While social media became central for more customised and tailored political campaigns in South Korea, in many ways they remained top-down channels to transmit messages to voters (Park & Cho 2013).

Studies on Social Media Effects in the 2012 Presidential Election

A significant number of studies have explored the impact of Internet use on political attitudes and behaviors in South Korea (for an overview, see Choi & Shim, 2014). Yet, there are only a few studies with a specific focus on the impact of social media on political participation and voting behavior. Among those few, however, there are noticeable findings about social media as a factor that might engage citizens politically (D. Chang & Bae 2012; S.-Y. Lee 2012). In particular, so-called 'proof of vote' images posted on social media during Election Day have received a great deal of scholarly attention. According to Seo and Lee (2012), voter 'selfies' contributed to a greater turnout among fellow SNS users during South Korea's 2010 parliamentary elections. Similarly, the 'proof of vote' images of celebrities and opinion leaders were retweeted widely during Seoul's 2011 mayoral election and significantly boosted young voters' turnout at the polls (S.-Y. Lee 2012).

According to W. Chang and Ryu (2013), political Twitter campaigns also had sig-nificant effects on the results of the 2012 legislative election. The length of the Twitter campaign, the number of followers, and the number of retweets were found to be signifi-cant predictors of a candidate's vote share. These findings indicate that social influence on political behavior can be diffused through online social networks and, in turn, can have real effects on politics.

At the same time, social media also have been shown to contribute to a growing ideo-logical divide among Koreans. According to S.-S. Lee (2013), social media use increased the intensity of political polarisation during the 2012 presidential election. Based on a national survey conducted immediately after the election, the author found that social media users were significantly more likely to hold extreme attitudes compared to non-users. In another study, Moon supporters perceived mainstream news media to be hos-tile toward their candidate, while social media were seen as more friendly toward Moon. Meanwhile, Park advocates were more likely to judge social media opinion toward their candidate as antagonistic (Y. Lee, Jeong & Min 2013). Thus, use of social media might have significant polarising effect by intensifying the ideological divide between conser-vative and liberal voters in South Korea.

Overall, it appears that social media use is associated with political attitudes and behaviors among the Korean public. However, exactly how citizens use social media for political purposes and what consequences it may have remains a relatively open question that requires more detailed exploration. In the following sections, we will address this question with new survey data collected shortly before the 2012 South Korean presidential election.

2012 Pre-Election Survey Findings

The following section will first describe how Korean citizens used social media to obtain information about the political candidates and the election campaign itself. We will focus specifically on the use of Facebook, Twitter, and YouTube, yet also evaluate the utilisation of more localised networks such as KakaoTalk. We will also discuss how Koreans felt about social media as a political information tool and how much they participated politically during the campaign using such media. In the last section, we will analyse whether social media use might have been associated with higher levels of political participation during the campaign and, ultimately, a higher likelihood of voting for either candidate.

As explained earlier, we will compare the Korean survey findings with findings obtained in a similar survey conducted in the United States shortly before the 2012 presidential election. The goal of this comparative analysis is to provide a more comprehensive understanding of how frequently Koreans used social media to learn about the 2012 election campaign and the main candidates and what effects this usage might have had on their political attitudes. Due to President Obama's extensive use of social media in the 2008 and 2012 election campaigns—and the widespread adoption of such digital networks among the American public—the political use of social media among Americans should serve as a valid benchmark against which the Korean findings can be judged and evaluated.

As expected, our survey findings indicate that the Internet has become a major source for political news among audiences in South Korea and the United States. Most Koreans (49 per cent) saw the Internet as the most important news source for information about the 2012 presidential election, closely followed by television (46 per cent). In the United States, the pattern was reversed as 54 per cent named television as the most important information source and only 35 per cent mentioned the Internet. The growing importance of online news is underscored by the fact that about half of all Korean and American respondents said they did not read printed newspapers (46 per cent Korea vs. 54 per cent U.S.) or listen to radio news (54 per cent Korea vs. 48 per cent U.S.).

Possibly as a result of the perceived importance of the Internet as a news source, Koreans were significantly more likely than Americans to use the Internet for gathering news and information about the presidential campaign. During the month prior to the election, 59 per cent of Korean respondents used the Internet at least once a day to get campaign information, compared to only 35 per cent of Americans. One reason for this finding might be the fact that the Korean media are dominated by public broadcasters, which are less critical in their political reporting than the commercial broadcasters in the United States.

The speculation that the traditional news media in South Korea are perceived as politically biased is supported by the fact that most Koreans considered social networking sites much more important for politics than Americans did. As Table 28.1 shows,

Table 28.1 Importance of Social Media for Politics among Korean and U.S. Citizens (in per cent)

		Very important	Somewhat important	Not very important	Not important
Keeping up with political news on SNS	Korea	10.0	47.2	29.7	13.1
	USA	20.1	27.9	21.8	30.2
Expressing my feelings and opinions on political issues on SNS	Korea	13.7	46.2	27.1	13.1
	USA	16.2	29.2	21.7	32.8
Discussing political issues with others on SNS	Korea	13.7	45.7	26.9	13.7
	USA	15.1	27.3	24.7	32.9
Finding people on SNS who share my views about important political issues	Korea	13.4	46.0	27.8	12.8
	USA	13.1	29.0	24.6	33.2

while about 6 in 10 Koreans believed that social media are 'somewhat' or 'very important' to stay abreast of political news (57 per cent vs. 48 per cent in U.S.), express political feelings and opinions (60 per cent vs. 45 per cent), discuss politics with others (59 per cent vs. 45 per cent), or find people who share their views on key political issues (59 per cent vs. 42 per cent), significantly fewer Americans believed that social media can assist such actions.

Despite the fact that most Koreans believed that social media have an important political role, they were somewhat less likely than their American counterparts to use social media as a political tool. First, Koreans were less likely than Americans to use social media as part of their daily media routine. While only about 6 in 10 (61 per cent) Koreans said they use social networks such as Facebook or Twitter, about 8 in 10 (81 per cent) Americans reported such use. The findings also indicate that most (79 per cent) Koreans spent less than an hour on social media each day, compared to slightly more than half (58 per cent) of Americans. Similarly, only 1 in 10 (10 per cent) Koreans said that they spent between one and three hours on social media, compared to 23 per cent of Americans.

Second, only 19 per cent of Korean respondents used social media as a political information and communication tool, while one-third (33 per cent) of American respondents did so. Similarly, few Koreans followed the candidates on social network sites such as KakaoTalk (6 per cent Park; 6 per cent Moon), Twitter (4 per cent Park; 3 per cent Moon), or Facebook (3 per cent Park; 2 per cent Moon).[2] Finally, posting political messages on social media was equally unpopular in both nations. Fewer than 1 in 10 Koreans and Americans said that they posted election-related messages on social networks such as Twitter or Facebook.

Overall then, Koreans obviously considered social media to have an important role during the 2012 presidential election, but many hesitated to use these media to communicate about politics during the campaign. This, of course, might have been the result of social media being a relatively new form of communication in Korean politics, which many citizens in this young democracy still might have to get used to.

To determine more specifically how Koreans used social media during the 2012 campaign, we asked a series of questions that probed their political use of Facebook, Twitter, and YouTube. As expected, Koreans were less likely than Americans to use Facebook and Twitter to gather and discuss election-related news and information. However, it appears that respondents in both nations equally enjoyed watching political videos on YouTube.

As Table 28.2 shows, 17 per cent of Korean social media users used Facebook at least 'sometimes' to 'get information about the election campaign or the presidential candidates' (23 per cent U.S.), 13 per cent used it to 'discover which presidential candidate your friends will vote for this year' (19 per cent U.S.), and 10 per cent to 'share content related to the presidential election' (22 per cent U.S.). Other political activities on Facebook, such as signing up as a presidential candidate's 'friend', subscribing to political journalists' posts, or posting election-related content or links were even less common than among American social media users.

The most popular political activity on Twitter during the 2012 election was to get news and information about the election or the candidates. Slightly more Koreans than Americans used Twitter as a political information tool (12 per cent Korea vs. 10 per cent U.S.). All other political activities, such as following presidential candidates or political journalists, posting election-related tweets, or retweeting political content were less common. However, differences in the use of these political activities between Korean and American social media users were less pronounced than those observed for similar activities on Facebook.

Table 28.2 Political Activities on Social Media by Korean and U.S. Citizens (in per cent)

	U.S.	Korea
Facebook activities		
Get information about the election campaign or the presidential candidates	23.4	17.2
Discover which presidential candidate your friends will vote for this year	19.4	12.9
Sign up as a 'friend' of a presidential candidate, party, or interest group	15.3	6.0
Subscribe to postings of political journalists, analysts, & commentators	10.8	8.7
Share content related to the presidential election	22.0	10.4
Post content related to the presidential election	21.1	4.9
Post a link about the presidential election	17.1	5.3
Post a wall comment about the presidential election	18.0	6.0
Post a status update that mentions the presidential election	14.2	5.7
Join a political group related to the presidential election	7.5	3.0
Start a political group related to the presidential election	2.5	0.8

	U.S.	Korea
Twitter activities		
Get information about the election or the presidential candidates on Twitter	10.2	12.1
Follow a presidential candidate, party, or political interest group on Twitter	8.8	6.0
Follow tweets of political journalists, analysts, commentators or columnists	8.7	4.9
Post a tweet that mentions the presidential election	8.0	4.3
Post a tweet that included a link to content about the presidential election	5.6	2.5
Reply to tweets about the presidential election	4.9	2.6
Retweet content related to the presidential election	5.3	3.1
YouTube activities		
Watch videos on Park's/Obama's YouTube channel	13.3	12.0
Watch videos on Moon's/Romney's YouTube channel	11.0	12.2
Watch political news and other videos about politics on YouTube	13.8	15.3
Watch official campaign advertisements on YouTube	11.4	17.6
Watch videos about the candidates or the election created by citizens	11.7	7.5
Watch videos about the candidates or the election created by celebrities	—	3.8

Korean and American social media users were most similar in their use of YouTube during the 2012 presidential election. Only a slightly larger percentage of Korean users watched campaign advertisements (18 per cent Korean vs. 11 per cent U.S.) and political videos (15 per cent Korea vs. 14 per cent U.S.) than Americans. In addition, about 12 per cent of Koreans watched videos on Park's and Moon's YouTube channel (similarly, 13 per cent of American users said they watched videos on Obama's YouTube channel, and 11 per cent on Romney's channel). A small percentage (8 per cent vs. 12 per cent U.S.) of Koreans also said they watched political videos created by other citizens.

Because social media use during the campaign might have encouraged concerned citizens to become politically more engaged, we decided to test whether social media use might be associated with higher levels of political efficacy and a greater likelihood to vote on Election Day.[3] While prior research has shown that social media use can be associated with higher political participation in a number of Asian nations (Choi & Shim 2014), it is reasonable to assume that citizens who use social media to discuss politics also feel more efficacious politically because they can actively share their political views with others. Such connectedness, in turn, might bolster feelings of 'having a voice' in the political process, even if such online connections have little 'real' impact on politics. However, even actions that seem trivial online can impact voter behavior. As noted earlier, there is empirical evidence that the 'I voted' pictures, posted on Facebook by people who voted, encouraged at least some social media users who saw the images to vote as well (Bond et al. 2012). Consequently, we also test the possibility that political social media use is associated with a higher likelihood of voting.

The regression model shown in Table 28.3 tests whether there are significant relationships between respondents' political efficacy and likelihood of voting and their (1) demographic characteristics (age, sex, political ideology, income, interest in the election, and frequency of discussing politics with friends and family in person); (2) traditional media use (TV news, newspapers, radio news, online news, and number of political TV debates watched); and (3) political social media use (political information posted online, political information from SNS, political discussion with online friends, political discussion on Twitter or Facebook, and political videos watched on YouTube).[4]

Table 28.3 Predictors of Political Efficacy and Likelihood of Voting among Korean Citizens

	Political efficacy	Likelihood voting
Demographics		
Age	.12***	.11***
Female	−.09***	.04
Education	.15***	.03
Political ideology (conservative)	.03	.03
Income	.05	.06
Interest in election campaign	.33***	.33***
Discuss politics with friends	.09**	.05
Political efficacy	—	.03
Incr. R^2 (%)	22.1***	16.4***
Traditional media use		
TV news	−.04	−.04
Newspapers	.07*	−.14***
Radio news	.04	−.04
Online news	.04	.02
TV debates	.06	.12***
Incr. R^2 (%)	1.1**	2.9***

	Political efficacy	Likelihood voting
Social media use		
Posted political information on SNS	–.08	–.05
Got political messages on SNS	.13***	.03
Discuss politics with friends on SNS	–.01	.05
Political use of Facebook	.10*	.01
Political use of Twitter	–.03	–.05
Political use of YouTube	.03	.01
Incr. R^2 (%)	1.8***	.30
Total R^2 (%)	25.0***	19.6***
N	1,010	1,010

Note: ***$p < .001$, **$p < .01$, *$p < .05$. Cell entries are before-entry standardised beta coefficients.

Overall, the findings indicate that social media use was indeed associated with stronger feelings of political efficacy. Especially those respondents who received political news and information on social media and participated in political Facebook groups were more likely to think their voices and opinions mattered in politics. While these relationships were relatively weak, they remained significant despite the control for respondents' demographics, which turned out to be the strongest predictors of political efficacy (older, educated males interested in the campaign were especially likely to report high levels of political efficacy).

At the same time, respondents' likelihood of voting was not associated with social media use. Rather, it appears that older citizens who were interested in the election and watched the candidates' televised debates were especially likely to vote. Surprisingly, reading printed newspapers more frequently was associated with less enthusiasm for voting on election day, while social media use did not show any correlation at all. Thus, while frequent social media users tended to feel politically more powerful, these feelings of political efficacy might apparently did not combine with social media use to make these citizens more likely to vote for their candidates.

Conclusions

South Korea's 2012 presidential election proved to be a seminal moment for social media in this media-rich nation. For the first time since the emergence of social media as a significant force in modern politics, Korean politicians and voters were completely free to utilise these digital communication tools during a national election campaign. As a result, the main political candidates launched extensive social media campaigns especially targeting young voters who traditionally shun politics and have been difficult to reach with traditional television and newspaper campaign advertisements. Korean netizens, on the other hand, enthusiastically embraced social media to discuss the candidates, the campaign, and key election issues. Given that online political discussions

401

are a relatively new phenomenon in South Korea due to its turbulent political past, it would be difficult to overstate the importance of how communicating and processing political information was changed.

A comparison with U.S. citizens—also in the midst of a presidential campaign at the end of 2012—shows that Koreans depended much more on the Internet for accessing campaign news and information. As discussed earlier, this tendency to rely on online news rather than television for election information—as most Americans do—is probably related to the fact that the dominant public broadcast media in Korea are much less diverse than the commercial broadcast media in the United States. As a result, almost half of Koreans found the Internet to be the most important news source for information about the election campaign. Only about one-third of Americans concurred; they still found television to be their main political news source.

While Koreans clearly preferred the Internet as a source of political news, they appeared to be somewhat less likely than Americans to rely on social media for such news. Although 6 in 10 Koreans used Facebook or Twitter within six months of the election (compared to 8 in 10 Americans), only about 2 in 10 of Korean netizens made daily use of social media for political news. This contrasted with about one-third of Americans who relied on social media for election news. Thus, while most Koreans consider social media to be important political discussion tools, they seem to remain reluctant to take advantage of these new communication forms. This reluctance to use social media during the 2012 campaign was likely due to the fact that such communication is relatively new in South Korea and has yet to be adopted by citizens as a routine information source. In contrast, Americans have had significant experience with political social media during the 2008 U.S. presidential election, which was dominated by Barack Obama's sophisticated Internet strategies that embraced social media as a central campaign tool (see also Chapter 8 in this volume).

It is important to note, however, that most Koreans saw social media as politically important. Consistently, about 6 in 10 Koreans believed that social media are important for keeping up with political news, expressing political feelings and opinions, discussing political issues, and finding people who share their views on important political issues. Americans, on the other hand, were far less enthusiastic about these utilities of social media. Only about one-third of U.S. netizens believed it was important to discuss political issues or sharing political views with others through social media.

Overall, it appears that Koreans tend to believe much more strongly than Americans in the 'political utility' of social media, possibly because it became a widespread tool for citizens and politicians alike during the 2012 Korean presidential campaign. It is therefore not surprising that social media users in South Korea tended to feel politically more efficacious, especially those who exchanged political messages on social media and used Facebook to discuss politics. And while the 2008 U.S. presidential election might have provided Americans with an earlier glimpse at the power of social media during elections, many of them might have become disillusioned with the democratic power of social media during the first four years of the Obama administration. As a consequence, Korean citizens have been much more enthusiastic about the political power of social media than their American counterparts.

At the same time, the findings also indicate that both political efficacy and social media use were not associated with a greater likelihood of voting among Korean citizens. While this is somewhat surprising, we believe that the high participation rate in the 2012 presidential election might have been at least partly responsible for this non-finding. After all, almost 8 in 10 of eligible citizens voted in the hotly contested 2012 election, thus greatly reducing the likelihood that social media might have had any significant additional impact on political engagement or voter turnout.

In the end, the strong emergence of social media in the 2012 Korean presidential election simply marked the beginning of an important trend toward more voter engagement and participation in the campaign itself. While American citizens have been exposed extensively to such engagement efforts during the 2008 and 2012 U.S. presidential election (for example, through Obama's strategy to encourage citizens to become active 'grassroots' campaigners through his social networking communities), most Koreans still have to get used to the idea that they themselves can actively participate in political elections with more than just their vote.

Notes

1 The South Korean survey was conducted online with a representative sample of 1,063 Korean citizens between 23 November and 6 December 2012. The survey, which took about 10 minutes to complete, contained questions that focused on (a) perceptions of the two main presidential candidates (Park Guen-hye and Moon Jae-in), (b) the use of traditional and social media for obtaining election information, (c) the use of social media for discussing the election with friends and relatives, (d) the level of political participation during the six months leading up to the campaign, and (e) voting behaviour. Additional questions probed respondents' political interest and efficacy, plus standard demographic characteristics such as sex, age, education, political ideology, and income. The survey's response rate was 15 per cent. Similarly, the U.S. survey was conducted online with a representative sample of 1,063 U.S. citizens interviewed between 26 October and 6 November 2012. The questions in the U.S. survey were mostly identical to the questions used in the South Korean survey and therefore can be compared directly. The response rate for the U.S. survey also was 15 per cent.

2 The findings also indicate that fewer than 2 in 10 Korean netizens visited either Park's (15.7 per cent) or Moon's (13.5 per cent) campaign website during the last six months of the election. Although this amounts to a fairly impressive use of a new political medium in South Korea, only a very small percentage used the websites to participate in activities such as fundraising (2 per cent both for Park and Moon) or volunteering to support events (3 per cent for Park and 2 per cent for Moon).

3 Political efficacy was measured by combining the agreement scores to the following three statements: "I consider myself well-qualified to participate in discussions about politics"; "Voting provides people with an effective way to influence government"; "I think I am better informed about politics than most people." The resulting scale ranges from 3 (= low efficacy) to 15 (= high efficacy; M = 9.98, SD = 2.28, Cronbach's α = .64). Respondents' likelihood of voting was measured by asking respondents to rate their chances of voting in the presidential election on a scale from 1 (= definitely will not vote) to 10 (= definitely will vote).

4 The variables measuring political use of Facebook, Twitter, and YouTube were created by combining the answers to questions that probed the political use of each social networking site during the six months prior to the election (1 = yes, 0 = no). For 'political use of Facebook', answers to 11 separate questions were combined into an index (M = .81, SD = 1.57, range 0–11, Cronbach's α = .77), for 'political use of Twitter' seven questions were combined (M = .36, SD = .93, range 0–7, Cronbach's α = .72), and for 'political use of YouTube' six questions were combined (M = .69, SD = 1.15, range 0–6, Cronbach's α = .66).

References

Bond, R. M., Fariss, C. J., Jones, J. J., Kramer, A.D.I., Marlow, C., Settle, J. E., & Fowler, J. H. (2012) "A 61-million-person experiment in social influence and political mobilization," *Nature*, 489, pp. 295–298.

Chang, D., & Bae, Y. (2012) *The birth of social election in South Korea, 2010–2012 (fesmedia Asia series)*, Berlin, Germany: Friedrich-Ebert-Stiftung.

Chang, W., & Ryu, S.-J. (2013) "The political effect of social network campaign: Tweeter big data analysis in the 19th national election," *Korean Journal of Political Science*, 47(4), pp. 93–213. (In Korean).

Choe, S.-H. (2012, December 19) "Ex-dictator's daughter elected president as South Korea rejects sharp change," *The New York Times*. Retrieved from www.nytimes.com/2012/12/20/world/asia/south-koreans-vote-in-closely-fought-presidential-race.html?pagewanted=all&_r=0

Choi, J.-H., & Shim, J. W. (2014) "New media and participatory politics: The case of South Korea," in L. Willnat and A. Aw (eds.) *Social media, culture and politics in Asia*, London: Peter Lang.

Colapinto, R. (2012, November 27) "South Korean presidential election starts with surprise," *Atlantic Sentinel*. Retrieved from http://atlanticsentinel.com/2012/11/south-korean-presidential-election-starts-with-surprise

Im, K.-B. (2012, December 4) " 'Ka/Fa/T'-portals, presidential battlegrounds," *Financial News*. (In Korean). Retrieved from www.fnnews.com/news/201212041713225960

Internet Live Stats. (2014) "Internet users by country." Retrieved from www.internetlivestats.com/internet-users-by-country/

Jeon, B.-Y., & Lee, J.-Y. (2012, November 28) "Park Guen-hye and Moon Jae-in, competing for campaign fundraising," *The Kyunghyang Shinmun*. (In Korean). Retrieved from http://news.khan.co.kr/kh_news/khan_art_view.html?artid=201211282009411&code=910100

Jeon, H.-N. (2012, December 2) "Increase in the number of political podcasts," *ZDnet Korea*. (In Korean). Retrieved from www.zdnet.co.kr/news/news_view.asp?artice_id=20121205103052

Keum, H.-S. (2014) "Evaluation of candidates' new media campaign strategies for the 18th presidential election in Korea," *Journal of 21st Century Political Science*, 24(1), *pp. 121–143*. (In Korean)

Kim, H-J, & Klug, F. (2012, December 19) "Park Geun-hye, South Korea presidential candidate, wins election," *The World Post*. Retrieved from www.huffingtonpost.com/2012/12/19/park-geun-hye-south-korea-presidential-election_n_2329931.html

Lee, J.-H. (2013) "Mass media and their political impacts on the 2012 presidential election," *Politics & Information Studies*, 16(1), pp. 113–135. (In Korean).

Lee, M.-J. (2012, November 28) "South Korean tech firms in election mode as vote nears," *Yonhap News*. Retrieved from http://english.yonhapnews.co.kr/news/2012/11/28/21/0200000000AEN20121128001751320F.html

Lee, S.-S. (2013) "Can political communication intensify attitude polarization? An analysis of the 18th South Korean presidential election," *The Korean Journal of Party Studies*, 12(1), pp. 217–242. (In Korean).

Lee, S.-Y. (2012) "SNS election campaigns in the 19th congressional election," in The Korean Society for Journalism & Communication Studies (ed.) *Political communication and SNS*, Paju, Korea: Nanam, pp. 157–188. (In Korean).

Lee, Y., Jeong, S.-H., & Min, Y. (2013) "Hostile media perceptions, third person effects, and political participation: Exploring an interaction influence on voting intention in the 2012 South Korean presidential election," *The Korean Journal of Journalism & Communication Studies*, 57(5), pp. 346–367. (In Korean).

Lim, J.M., Yoo, J.Y., Jang, S.J., Lee, J.H., & Yoo, J.M. (2013) *2013 survey on the Internet usage*. Seoul: Korea Internet & Security Agency (KISA).

Min, Y. (2014). "Intertwining of news and entertainment: The effects of political podcasts in the 2012 Korean presidential election," *The Korean Journal of Journalism & Communication Studies*, 58(4), pp. 70–96. (In Korean).

Park, C.-M., & Cho, J-W. (2013) "A critical review of Twitter political mobilization effect," *The Korean Journal of Party Studies*, 12(2), pp. 187–220. (In Korean).

Presidential Election Campaigns Turn Negative (2012, November 30) *Yonhap News*. Retrieved from http://english.yonhapnews.co.kr/topics/2012/11/30/83/4609010000AEN2012 1130009100315F.html

Presidential Election Turnout at 75.8% (2012, December 19) *The Korea Times*. Retrieved from www.koreatimes.co.kr/www/category/subsection_608_4.html

Rauhala, E. (2012, December 18) "Heads to the polls: As South Koreans vote today, the race between Park Geun-hye and Moon Jae-in looks too close to call." *Time*. Retrieved from http://world.time. com/2012/12/18/the-burden-of-history-a-divided-south-korea-heads-to-the-polls

Seo, H.-J., & Lee, M.-N. (2012) "Young generations' political participation and election culture: An analysis of voting proof shots on Twitter," in The Korean Society for Journalism & Communication Studies (ed.) *Political communication and SNS*, Paju, Korea: Nanam, pp. 189–215. (In Korean).

Ser, M.-J. (2011, December 30) "Ban on SNS campaigning overruled," *Korea Joongang Daily*. Retrieved from http://koreajoongangdaily.joins.com/news/article/article.aspx?aid=2946372

Ser, M.-J. (2012, November 5) "How candidates fund their campaigns," *Korea Joongang Daily*. Retrieved from http://koreajoongangdaily.joins.com/news/article/Article.aspx?aid=2961804

Socialbakers (2013) "10 fastest growing countries on Facebook in 2012." Retrieved from www. socialbakers.com/blog/1290–10-fastest-growing-countries-on-facebook-in-2012

Song, J.-A. (2012, December 16) "South Korean election funds draw a big draw," *The Financial Times*. Retrieved from www.ft.com/cms/s/0/47f18c9e-3d6b-11e2-b8b2-00144feabdc0.html#axzz3Q1r LaBkF

Twitter Korean Index (2012) *Twitter Korean index*. Retrieved from http://tki.oiko.cc/count

Yoon, S.-W. (2012, December 19) "Korea's Park leads close election race, exit polls show," *Bloomberg News*. Retrieved from www.bloomberg.com/news/2012-12–18/south-koreans-go-to-polls-with-turnout-crucial-in-park-moon-vote.html

29

INTERACTIONS BETWEEN DIFFERENT LANGUAGE COMMUNITIES ON TWITTER DURING THE 2012 PRESIDENTIAL ELECTION IN TAIWAN

Yu-Chung Cheng and Pai-Lin Chen

Introduction

The concept of 'global public spheres' arose at the beginning of the 21st century as new communication technologies matured. Sparks (2001) pointed out that the Internet prompts the dissemination of traditional media content across the borders of nations. Volkmer (2003) stressed the significant impact of satellite television channels such as CNN International and Al Jazeera on the flow of political information. The infrastructure of these new media allows an eyewitness view of events taking place in local contexts to spread globally, and shapes a politically relevant 'global' public sphere, even it is divergent and originating from different viewpoints. Castells (2008) also pointed out that the global networks connected by communication technologies shape the new public sphere, as the space of debate on public affairs, so that the debate progresses from the national to the global. Accordingly, this prompts a conversation between global governments and global civil societies.

The aforementioned researchers focus on the expressions and interaction of participants such as news agencies, governments, and nonprofit organisations. However, they ignore the expressions and interaction of individual users in a global public sphere. A result of the rapid spread of global social networking sites such as Twitter and Facebook, more users publish their opinions about global public affairs on these social networking sites. Castells (2009) described this as 'mass self-communication', which allows sending messages from many to many in real time and potentially reaches a global audience. Through sharing and retweeting, these individually published opinions can spread very quickly on social networking sites and influence decision-making on global public affairs. From this observation, we therefore focus on the individual users of social networks, to investigate how social media users influence information flows on global social networking sites during an election.

We take the discussion of the 2012 Taiwan presidential election on Twitter as our case study. This is a major regional political event: not only Taiwanese, but also Chinese and Japanese societies took an interest in this election. Taiwanese users engaged in discussions with members of the local community as well as in information exchange with foreign communities. As global public spheres, social media afford local communities a space for producing and receiving public discourses for and from cross-language communities. Based on this affordance, researchers can compare the different communication patterns between cross-language communities, and explore the potential and limitations of social media as global public spheres.

Taiwan, Japan, and China have an intertwined past, present and future in East Asian politics, diplomacy, economics, and culture. Taiwan was the first colony acquired by the Japanese Empire after the Meiji Restoration. Between 1895 and 1945, Taiwan experienced a leap from medieval feudalism into social, cultural, and economic modernity under Japanese rule. Today, many elderly people are still deeply influenced by their childhood experiences of Japanese culture and education. On the other hand, the majority of the Taiwanese population are of Chinese origin, and Taiwan and China share a common language and a substantial level of cultural similarity. In 1949, the Nationalist Party (Kuomingtang) was defeated by the Communists in Mainland China and withdrew to Taiwan, whose sovereignty had been transferred from Japanese to Chinese authority just four years earlier. The Nationalist-held Republic of China (Taiwan) and the Communist People's Republic of China (PRC) entered into a 40-year stand-off across the Taiwan Strait. It was only in the 1990s, when travel and commercial exchange resumed between Taiwan and China after the end of Cold War, that the cultural and commercial connections between the two began to strengthen again. These intertwining geopolitical histories gave Taiwan cultural proximity to both Chinese and Japanese society (Iwabuchi 2002). Lacking direct interaction with an individual from the other side, such cultural proximity allowed people to experience the daily lives and cultural values of the other side via representations in the form of news reports and drama in the mass media. However, after the rise of global social media, direct communication between members of different language communities has become possible.

In this chapter, we examine the interactions between different language communities to identify and compare discussion topics that are specific to each language community, and we explore the temporal patterns of discussion frequency during the election. This set of analyses focuses on the interactions within a community and on the characterisation of the core participants in the community. Furthermore, we investigate the interactions between communities to identify and characterise the types of participants who bridge different language communities to facilitate cross-language information flows in the social network. Through our analysis of cross-language interactions relating to this election on Twitter, we aim to explore how local communities interact in global social media.

Social Media as Global Public Spheres in Real-Time Events

Global social media such as Facebook and Twitter connect a large number of users online. Most of the time, this vast network consists of numerous loosely connected clusters that are defined by the extent of the daily personal social lives of individual users. However, when provoked by acute events, such as natural disasters (earthquakes, tsunamis, volcanic eruptions, etc.), human disasters (plane crashes, car accidents, school campus shootings, etc.), or other major social events which are difficult to predict (political and sporting events, for example), a large number of social media users will turn to these specific events simultaneously and generate a substantial number of related posts within a short period of time.

General elections are highly relevant as case studies to explore the interactions between such emerging communities on social media. Burgess and Bruns (2012) examined how people participated in discussions during the 2010 election in Australia. They collected all tweets containing #ausvotes during the 38-day period from one month before the election to two days after the election, and found that 22 per cent of tweets were posted on the day of election. Among the 37,000 participating users, 51 per cent (19,000) only posted on the day of election. In other words, more than half of the users expressed their opinions and feelings along with the election broadcast, before the election outcome was known, and earlier in the day, many users tweeted to mark the casting of their vote and encourage others to vote.

Anstead and O'Loughlin (2010) analysed the audience behaviours on Twitter during the candidates' debates on TV in the 2010 UK general election. They called this new audience an 'emerging viewertariat', which means that viewers watch real-time events on TV and give their comments on social media at the same time. These new multi-screen watching behaviours are becoming even more popular for sports, reality TV shows, and political events since the adoption of mobile and tablet devices. Bruns and Burgess (2011) also pointed out that Twitter hashtags could aid the formation of *ad hoc* publics around specific themes and topics. These *ad hoc* publics emerge from within the Twitter community, and hashtags allow a group of users to coordinate information and public debates during public events.

Social media are therefore a kind of instant public sphere. As pointed out by Papacharissi (2010), it makes people feel more comfortable and safe to discuss public affairs in such an online space that mixes the public and the private. This social space allows a blending of the originally separate public and private spheres. Here, citizens can participate in public affairs and control their own public face without losing their private individuality. Therefore, Papacharissi sees the appearance of online social media technologies as recombining the traditional public–private dichotomy, which creates a new civic geography that facilitates the emergence of a new form of social relationships and conversations.

Thus, we take the 2012 presidential election in Taiwan as a case study to explore the interaction between various groups from Taiwan, China and Japan in the global social networking platform, Twitter. The various stakeholders include traditional media, political parties, celebrities, and individual users. By analysing the interactions of cross-language communities, we can further rethink the potential of global public spheres in the social media age.

Data Collection and Challenges in Language Separation

In Taiwan's 2012 presidential election, the incumbent Kuomingtang (KMT) candidate Ying-jeou Ma and the challenging Democratic Progressive Party (DPP) candidate Ing-wen Tsai, who was then the chairperson of the DPP and the first ever female presidential candidate in Taiwan, matched each other in pre-election polls; the third candidate was Chu-yu Soong, who represented the People First Party (PFP). Votes were cast on

14 January 2012, and the official result of the vote count was published at 9 p.m. on the same day. Ma won 51 per cent of the votes (6.89 million) in the election; Tsai came second with 46 per cent of the votes (6.09 million); and Soong received 3 per cent of the votes (0.37 million). With such a tight contest, the election attracted a huge amount of discussion in social media communities.

This study chose the social networking site, Twitter, as our data-collecting platform. Twitter is not among the most popular social networking sites in Taiwan and the PRC. According a GNIP analysis, 0.05 per cent of tweets featured Chinese as the user-selected language in 2012. GNIP showed that Simplified Chinese (ZH) ranked 17th and Traditional Chinese (ZH-TW) ranked 19th of all languages at that time (GNIP 2014). However, Internet censorship in China (Bamman, O'Connor, & Smith 2012) led netizens tending toward free speech to discuss democracy-related issues on Twitter (blocked by the Great Firewall in the PRC), which, unlike Chinese-based social media such as Weibo, is without censorship. According to an observation by a renowned Hong Kong journalist, there are more than one hundred thousand active Chinese Twitter users in the PRC using virtual private network technology (VPN) to access Twitter in order to avoid the Great Firewall (Lüqiu Luwei 2012). Considering that Twitter can serve as a platform for active users in the PRC to exchange information with international users or sources, including those in Taiwan, it is an important site for observing interactions between different Chinese-speaking societies. In contrast to the Chinese speaking societies, Twitter is tremendously popular in Japan, as the amount of Twitter users in Japan (30 million) was the third largest in the world in 2012, behind only the U.S. and Brazil (Semiocast 2012).

Focusing on Twitter, during January 2012 we collected data associated with Chinese-language tweets that were related to the election. Using the Twitter search API, we selected six Chinese keywords to computationally identify election-related tweets: Ying-jeou Ma, Ing-wen Tsai, Chu-yu Soong, Kuomingtang, Min-chin Tang (DPP in Chinese), Chin-min Tang (PFP in Chinese)—the names of the candidates and the political parties they belonged to. Using the names of the candidates instead of their nicknames can avoid the preference bias of nicknames, but it may result in capturing many tweets that reference news stories.

Furthermore, given that Taiwan and Mainland China, the two major Chinese-speaking societies, use Traditional Chinese characters and Simplified Chinese characters respectively, this provided an effective way to separate tweets created by different language users. Hence, we have opted to explore the use of language coding in individual tweets as a way to characterise the social and community identities of the users. Based on these characterisations, we assumed that members of the Taiwanese Twitter community would mostly adopt Traditional Chinese as their writing language, and thus when a tweet was marked with 'iso_language_code: zh-TW' after filtering through the language detection software, there was a high probability that this tweet originated from Taiwanese society. Conversely, when a tweet was marked with 'iso_language_code: zh', it was more likely from Chinese society, including both Mainland China and Chinese users residing overseas.

This language detection process has a limitation of not being able to identify Hong Kong accounts, because news agencies in Hong Kong tweet in Traditional Chinese but ordinary users may tweets in Traditional Chinese or Cantonese—thus making it difficult to computationally separate Hong Kong users from Taiwanese users in the Traditional Chinese Twitter community. In the results of our language detection process, however, Cantonese tweets accounted for less than 1 per cent of the data set, and we did not treat Cantonese as a major language community in its own right.

Tweets in the Japanese language accounted for about one third of the data set. They were collected because the names of the presidential candidates were shown in Kanji characters (sharing a common language code with Traditional Chinese and Simplified Chinese). Japanese Kanji characters represent an ancient culture imported from China; in the Unicode system, Japanese Kanji characters and Chinese characters having the same appearance share the same code, and thus the Twitter search API would collaterally collect tweets in Japanese language with these keyword terms.

Among the 27,968 unique tweets collected during the election (1 to 23 January 2012), we sorted unique tweets into different subgroups based on their respective language codes. Tweets in Traditional Chinese represented 49 per cent of the collected tweets (13,646 tweets in total). Following Traditional Chinese was Japanese (9,548 tweets, 34 per cent), and then Simplified Chinese (4,342 tweets, 15.5 per cent). Tweets in English made up only 1 per cent of total tweets, and fewer than 1 per cent of tweets were in another language or unidentifiable (Cheng & Chen 2014a).

Comparing Tweeting Patterns between Language Communities

Many media commentators thought that the candidates' attitudes toward China would influence the level of support from Taiwanese and Chinese societies (Sullivan 2013). The incumbent president, Ying-jeou Ma, is more China-friendly. He claims that more economic and trade exchange with China is beneficial for Taiwan. But the economic performance during Ma's first term (2008–2012) was not as good as people expected. Some people cited his lack of decisiveness as a reason for the poor economic performance. Many supporters who voted for Ma in the previous election were expected to switch their votes to another candidate (Wang 2011). The rival candidate, Ing-wen Tsai, advocates more autonomy for Taiwan than Ma, to avoid an overdependence on trade exchanges with China. Thus, Tsai is more attractive for people whose political tendency is in favour of Taiwanese independence. The third candidate, Chu-yu Soong, had served a highly regarded governorship of the Taiwan Province in the past, and was the chair of the PFP, a small party split off from the KMT whose attitude toward China is similar to Ma's.

Based on the reports and analysis in traditional mass media, Ma and Tsai were evenly matched in the Taiwanese poll, but the Chinese government and population were thought to support Ma because to his attitude toward China. By analysing the frequency of discussion about the three candidates within the Traditional Chinese community and Simplified Chinese community on Twitter, we can compare the dynamics of preference amongst the two communities. Furthermore, we can also examine whether the attitude of the Chinese community on Twitter is the same as the position of government.

Figure 29.1 shows the changing volume of tweets containing terms associated with a specific candidate in the Traditional Chinese community, mostly comprising Taiwanese Twitter users. The Traditional Chinese community preferred to discuss Tsai over Ma during the election period, but the gap between Tsai and Ma fluctuates with the changing amount of coverage in mass media. Only on 12 January, just before election day, the volume of discussion about Ma surpasses that about Tsai, as certain influential public figures voice their support of Ma in the mass media.

By comparison, Figure 29.2 shows the volume of tweets containing terms associated with the three candidates in the Simplified Chinese community, mostly representing

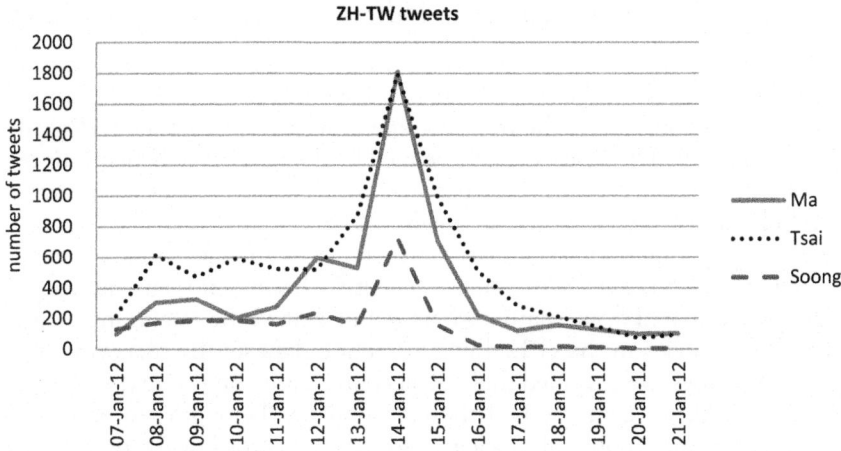

Figure 29.1 Volume of Tweets in the Traditional Chinese Community Relating to Individual Candidates

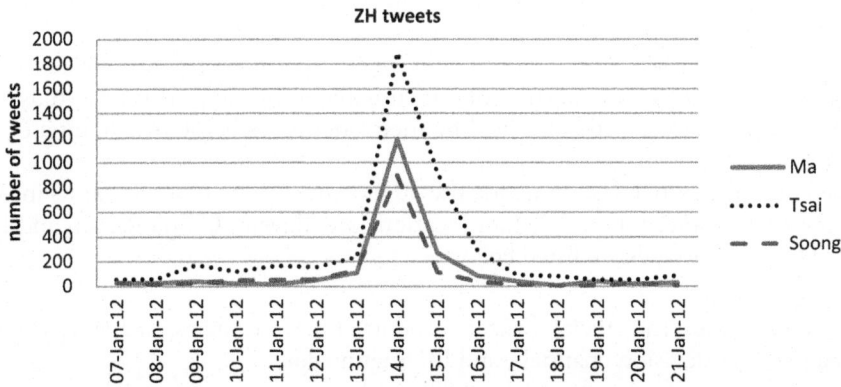

Figure 29.2 Volume of Tweets in the Simplified Chinese Community Relating to Individual Candidates

Twitter users in China, who used VPN to avoid the Great Firewall of the PRC. Unexpectedly, they preferred to discuss Tsai over Ma. This was very different from the focus of the government and the traditional media in China. In addition, by analysing the conversations in the Simplified Chinese community, we found that the Simplified Chinese users were particularly moved by the speech given by Tsai to acknowledge her loss in the election. Video of Tsai's speech on YouTube had been shared many hundreds of times (Cheng & Shih 2014), even in spite of YouTube being officially unavailable in Mainland China, and Twitter users in China noted that this speech was an example of real democracy, which they have not yet experienced. The artist Ai Wei-wei (@aiww), for example, who had the most followers, at almost 130,000, in the Chinese Twittersphere at that time, tweeted 'Tsai won, at least she won me' after he saw the video. Ai's comments were also retweeted many times in the Chinese Twittersphere.

Patterns of User Interactions in Different Language Communities

To find the key users who are the core nodes of interaction within the different language communities, we considered user visibility as a valid indicator. User visibility refers to the visibility of a user within the overall community of participants; technically, the visibility of a specific Twitter user can be defined by the number of @mentions received by that user in the data set, as this is indicative of other users reacting to tweets from that particular user account (Bruns & Stieglitz 2013).

Accordingly, we found 51 user accounts which had been @mentioned over 50 times in the total of 27,968 tweets. We excluded @youtube because it is automatically added when tweets are shared from Youtube.com, and identified the remaining 50 accounts as highly visible nodes in the 2012 Taiwan election data set. By reviewing their user profiles and postings, we classified these 50 accounts based on their type and location. On the one hand, we characterised these accounts as belonging to news agencies, journalists, celebrities, political bloggers, ordinary users, or bots in order to explain why other users retweet and reply to these accounts. On the other hand, we could identify the locations of these accounts and thus place them in four geographic contexts: Taiwan, China, Japan, and Hong Kong. The positions and viewpoints of Hong Kong news agencies are very different from those in Taiwan and China, so we have had to identify Hong Kong users manually amongst the 50 most visible user accounts. Furthermore, some visible accounts in the data set represent the Chinese diaspora living overseas (outside of the Mainland Chinese territory or Taiwan). From the contents of their tweets, we found that they are usually bilingual. In this case study, these Chinese diaspora are usually classified by their origins (as being from China or from Taiwan).

Based on these principles, we divide the 50 most-mentioned user accounts into four locations and six user types. The four locations are Taiwan, China, Japan, and Hong Kong. The six user types are listed below:

1. **News agencies**: the official Twitter accounts of news agencies, such as newspapers, magazines, television channels, and Internet media.
2. **Journalists**: professional media workers such as news reporters, columnists, radio hosts, and Internet media editors.
3. **Celebrities**: influential public figures in various areas, such as politicians (the presidential candidates), artists, writers, and scholars.
4. **Political bloggers**: bloggers who publish their political opinions and comments on current events, serious and satirical alike.
5. **Active users**: ordinary users who actively discuss with and reply to other users.
6. **Bots**: robots which automatically post tweets with certain terms.

The distribution of these six different types of highly visible users across the local Twitter communities of Taiwan, China, Japan and Hong Kong is shown in Table 29.1.

Amongst these 50 accounts, there are seven accounts belonging to news agencies. They are all from Japan, including *Asahi Shimbun* (@asahi_shinsen and @asahi_kokusai, total 567 mentions), one of the three national newspapers with a circulation of more than 7 million; *NHK News* (@nhk_news and @nhk_tonight, total 254 mentions), the national Japanese Broadcasting Corporation with several TV channels; *47 News* (@47newsflash and @47news, total 163 mentions); *Kyodo News*, founded in

Table 29.1 Matrix of User Visibility in Four Local Twitter Communities

Society	News agencies	Journalists	Celebrities	Political bloggers	Active users	Bots	Total	Total percentage
JA	7	4	1	1	1	0	14	28%
CN	0	2	4	3	12	1	22	44%
TW	0	2	3	1	4	1	11	22%
HK	0	1	0	0	2	0	3	6%
Total	7	9	8	5	19	2	50	100%
%	14%	18%	16%	10%	38%	4%	100%	

Note: JA: Japan; CN: China; TW: Taiwan; HK: Hong Kong.

1945 as a nonprofit cooperative organisation; and *Mainichi News* (@mainichijpnews, 54 mentions), one of the oldest newspapers in Japan, founded in 1872.

Also, the most visible user is the Japanese columnist Kaori Fukushima (@Kaokaokao-kao, 638 mentions). Her expertise is in Chinese issues. She was a news correspondent residing in Beijing and had about 32,000 followers on Twitter at that time. Her main tweeting language is Japanese and her comments about China-Taiwan-Japan issues would be trusted and shared in the Japanese community. Thus, Kaori Fukushima and the seven Japanese news Twitter accounts were key nodes in the Japanese community of the whole network during this election (Cheng & Chen 2014a).

Apart from the Japanese community, other visible journalists are two former Chinese reporters and two Taiwanese Internet media editors. The two former Chinese reporters (@wenyunchao, 152 mentions, and @mranti, 138 mentions) worked in Hong Kong and the U.S. at that time and maintained conversations with netizens in China on Twitter. The two Taiwanese Internet media editors (@aboutfish, 112 mentions, and @Portnoy, 69 mentions) curated noteworthy news stories or opinions from the Internet and are influential in the Taiwanese online community.

Celebrities were also influential in the election event. The Twitter accounts of the main candidates Ma (@PresidentMa19, 122 mentions) and Tsai (@iingwen, 57 mentions) were followed by several thousand users. Many followers would retweet their posts. But the account of incumbent president Ma had not followed any accounts. It meant that the candidates in Taiwan did not use social media as tools for mutual communication with voters and instead saw social media as one-way message publishing outlets. Otherwise, artists and writers such as Ai Wei-wei (@aiww, 253 mentions) are visible users in the Simplified Chinese community. Ordinary users regularly asked these celebrities to comment on people and events. In this case, the opinions of celebrities about the candidates would spread rapidly in Twitter communities.

In contrast to the Japanese Community, we found a relatively low visibility for Chinese and Taiwanese news agencies in their respective Simplified Chinese and Traditional Chinese communities. This was probably due to the different communication patterns between language communities. In the 2012 Taiwanese election, users in Taiwan could receive the exact election results from the mainstream media but preferred to discuss and express their own opinions and emotions on social media. Even several of the Chinese websites operated by international news agencies would publish news stories about China and Taiwan on Twitter (Cheng & Chen 2014b), but users in China who cared about Taiwan's election would compare it to their own political situation, so they usually replied and retweeted other users instead of citing tweets from news agencies. Conversely, users in Japan, which was furthest from the location of the election, would depend on reports by the news media to inform them of the results of the Taiwanese election.

Further exploring the six user types in Table 29.1, we can identify two major categories of highly visible users. The first category is the user whose online identity is the same as their offline identity—such as news agencies, journalists, and celebrities. Due to their credibility in the real world, they are likely to be seen as trustworthy sources by social media users when they publish posts under their real names. The second category is the user whose online identity is more famous than their offline identity, such as political bloggers and other active users. They are anonymous in the real world and acquire their reputation through long-term interaction with other users online. Although accounts in these two categories obtain their online credibility in the different ways, they are both amongst the most trusted and most credible sources in social media.

Next, we compared the interaction patterns within different language communities, and a significant finding was that in the Japanese community, news agencies and journalists are major nodes of information dissemination. Thus, the highly visible users belong to this category. This pattern is similar to that in the U.S. and in European societies (Vis 2013). By contrast, the Simplified Chinese community is just the opposite: it did not disseminate the messages of its news agencies. Instead, it interacts directly with celebrities, political bloggers and active users. This implies that news media in China are seen as being less credible than political bloggers and active users. People prefer to retweet the postings from these trustworthy online sources and do not trust the published information from governments and traditional media. This gap may reflect how the different political systems (from democracy to despotism) bring about different cultures of information sharing on the Internet. The Traditional Chinese communities, Taiwan and Hong Kong, are situated somewhere between these two poles.

Exploring Social Networks in Cross-Language Communities

We further used the network visualisation software Gephi to analyse the connection patterns of users participating in the discussion of the 2012 Taiwanese election on Twitter, based on the tweets collected with our keyword search. As boyd, Golder, and Lotan (2010) pointed out, retweeting represents both information dissemination and conversation, which encourages citizens to participate in public affairs. We used retweet conversations to connect each user in the analysis; 5,118 nodes were identified in total. After removal of the nodes with fewer than three connections in the network, 1,310 nodes remained. A social network map was constructed based on the filtered data set (Figure 29.3). Node size is based on betweenness centrality, and node color on degree.

There are two subnetworks in this social network. In the top left corner, there is a relatively isolated network consisting of Japanese users, centred around @koichiuno. This user was identified as Uno Koichi, a Japanese teacher and Japanese-Chinese translator in Taiwan. He ran a blog to introduce interesting things in Taiwan to a Japanese audience. Although @koichiuno was not among the top 50 users in the visibility matrix

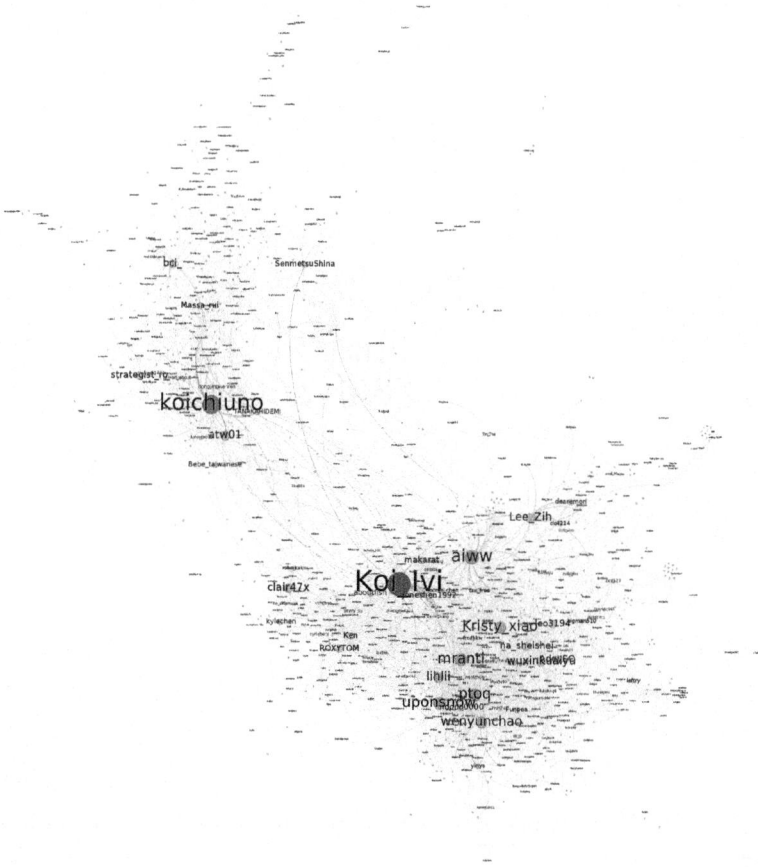

Figure 29.3 Social Network of Retweet Conversations in the 2012 Taiwanese Presidential Election

(with a ranking of 64, and 41 mentions), @koichiuno is a typical bilingual bridging user who can disseminate information from one language community to another.

In the right corner, there is a mixed subnetwork of Simplified Chinese and Traditional Chinese communities. The most notable node is @Koi_lvi. This user was an ordinary user whose real identity could not be verified. @Koi_lvi tweets in both Simplified Chinese and Traditional Chinese and interacts with other users very actively. Other significant nodes were important users from the Chinese community who often expressed their public opinions on Twitter. Their posts were frequently retweeted by other users.

In this analysis, we found that multi-language users make up about 8 per cent of the 9,416 unique tweeting users in the data set. This finding supports our earlier hypothesis that multi-language users are key nodes facilitating the transmission of information between different language communities (Cheng &Chen 2014a).

In another analysis of this Twitter network, we used only @reply conversations in our Gephi analysis. In total, 2,039 nodes were identified; after the removal of nodes with

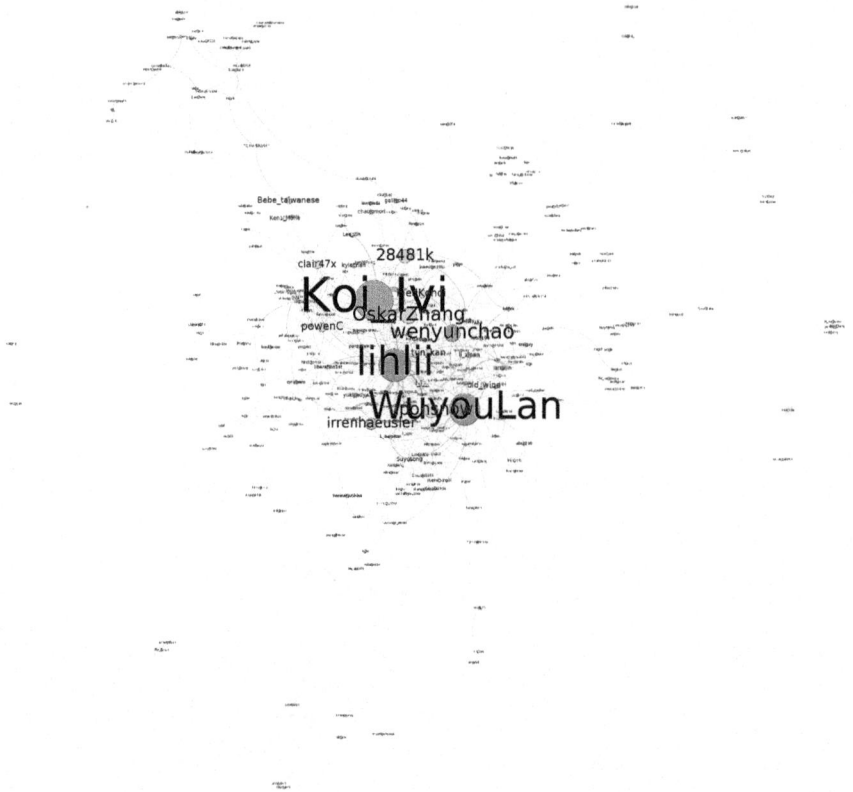

Figure 29.4 Social Network of @reply Conversations in the 2012 Taiwanese Presidential Election

fewer than three @reply connections, 319 nodes remained. A social network map of the @reply conversations was constructed from this filtered data set (see Figure 29.4).

This social network map of @reply relations was very different from the map of retweets (see Figure 29.3). The nodes in the network map of @reply connections represented mostly users in the Simplified Chinese community. Users in the Traditional Chinese and Japanese communities were far less involved. In Figure 29.4, celebrities such as journalist @wenyunchao and artist @aiww are not particularly notable, and the active ordinary users amongst the top 50 most visible users, such as @Wuyoulan (177 mentions), @lihlii (53 mentions), and @Koi_lvi (82 mentions), are the key nodes in this @reply network. As ordinary users, they are not particularly famous, but they talked and replied to other users very frequently. It thus turned out that this network was a space of mutual conversations, instead of representing unidirectional information dissemination.

Conclusion: Emerging Communities in Global Social Media

Global social networking sites can connect a large number of users as global public spheres, so that users from different places can join to discuss public affairs simultaneously.

A key challenge for social media researchers is consequently to distinguish different communities on the same social networking sites, and to compare their communication behaviours. In this case study, computationally distinguishing subgroups by language usage has proven to be an effective methodology, at least for East Asian countries. We successfully distinguished the Twitter users involved in the discussion of the 2012 Taiwanese presidential election into Traditional Chinese, Simplified Chinese, and Japanese communities, and found different interaction patterns within and between these language communities.

Furthermore, we can also distinguish various ways of community formation by the different interaction patterns that we are able to observe in social media. At least three types of communities on Twitter were identified for this election. The first community is composed of all users on Twitter engaged in the discussion of the election during the same period of time. By this definition, the community is made up of all the users we observed in this case study. Due to the popularity of real-time broadcast media, a lot of people can watch the unfolding progress of an event and discuss it on social media at the same time. On social media, users encounter others and exchange their opinions on these moments, but the interaction between them is too short to form a solid community.

The second community is the information dissemination community. It consists of celebrities, news agencies, journalists, online opinion leaders and their followers, as exemplified by the retweet and @reply network in our case (Cheng & Chen 2014a). The relations between these highly visible users and their followers are usually unidirectional: fans and ordinary users follow celebrities, but celebrities do not follow them back. This results in an information-disseminating social network in which a large number of followers retweet posts by those highly connected users (celebrities, news agencies, journalists, online opinion leaders) who are usually the key nodes in this network.

The third community is the conversational community. It is made up of active users, such as those found in the @reply network in our case (see Figure 29.4). The number of users in this community is smaller than that in the first two communities, but users in the conversation community are mutually connected. This makes collaboration, such as mobilising groups or building an online organisation, more possible in this community.

These three types would exist in all social media events. But the relation between the three types is rather liquid, as people can switch their roles from one to another at any time. We suggest that the connection and liquidity of these emerging communities exists because of the potential ability of global social media to connect several thousand people at the same moment. These emerging communities have had a tremendous impact on contemporary society. It will be necessary to further explore various emerging communities in social media through more case studies to understand the potential of social media in shaping collective wisdom and power.

References

Anstead, N. & O'Loughlin, B. (2010) *The Emerging Viewertariat: Twitter Responses to Nick Griffin's Appearance on BBC Question Time*, School of Political, Social and International Studies, University of East Anglia, Norwich. Retrieved from http://www.uea.ac.uk/polopoly_fs/1.147340!Anstead_OLoughlin_BBCQT_Twitter_Final.pdf

Bamman, B., O'Connor, B., & Smith, N. (2012) "Censorship and Deletion Practices in Chinese Social Media," *First Monday*, 17(3). Retrieved from http://firstmonday.org/htbin/cgiwrap/bin/ojs/index.php/fm/article/view/3943/3169

boyd, d., Golder, S., & Lotan, G. (2010) "Tweet, Tweet, Retweet: Conversational Aspects of Retweeting on Twitter," in Proceeding HICSS '10 Proceedings of the 2010 43rd Hawaii International Conference on System Sciences, 6 January, IEEE: Kauai, HI, USA, pp. 1–10.

Bruns, A. & Burgess, J. (2011) *The Use of Twitter Hashtags in the Formation of ad hoc Publics*, in Sixth European Consortium for Political Research General Conference, 25–27 August 2011, University of Iceland, Reykjavik.

Bruns, A. & Stieglitz S. (2013) "Toward More Systematic Twitter Analysis: Metrics for Tweeting Activities," *International Journal of Technology in Social Research Methodology*, 16(2), pp. 91–108.

Burgess, J. & Bruns A. (2012) "(Not) the Twitter Election: The Dynamics of the #ausvotes Conversation in Relation to the Australian Media Ecology," *Journalism Practice*, 6(3), pp. 384–402.

Castells, M. (2008) "The New Public Sphere: Global Civil Society, Communication Networks, and Global Governance," *The ANNALS of the American Academy of Political and Social Science*, 616(1), pp. 78–93.

Castells, M. (2009) *Communication Power*, Oxford: Oxford University Press.

Cheng, Y.-C. & Chen, P.-L. (2014a) "Global Social Media, Local Context: A Case Study of Chinese-Language Tweets about the 2012 Presidential Election in Taiwan," *Aslib Journal of Information Management*, 66(3), pp. 342–356.

Cheng, Y.-C. & Chen, P.-L. (2014b) "Emerging Communities in Social Media during the 2012 Taiwanese Presidential Election: A Big-Data Analysis Approach (in Chinese)," *Mass Communication Research*, 120, pp.121–165.

Cheng, Y.-C. & Shih, S.-F. (2014). *News Sources in Social Media during the 2012 Presidential Election in Taiwan* (in Chinese), in 5th International Conference of Digital Archives and Digital Humanity, 1–2 December 2014, Taipei, Taiwan.

GNIP (10 March 2014) "From A to B: Visualizing Language for the Entire History of Twitter," *GNIP*. Retrieved from https://blog.gnip.com/data-visualization

Iwabuchi, K. (2002) "Becoming Culturally Proximate: Japanese TV Dramas in Taiwan," in *Recentering Globalization: Popular Culture and Japanese Transnationalism*, Durham: Duke University Press, pp.121–157.

Lüqiu Luwei (2012) "Similarity and Difference from This Viewpoint (in Chinese)," in IP Iam Chong (ed.) *Grassroots Revolution: From the Virtual to the Real*. Hong Kong: The UP Publication Limited, pp. 4–7.

Papacharissi, Z. (2010) *A Private Sphere: Democracy in a Digital Age*. Cambridge, UK: Polity.

Semiocast (2012, 31 January) "Brazil Becomes 2nd Country on Twitter, Japan 3rd, Netherlands most Active Country," *Semiocast*. Retrieved from http://semiocast.com/en/publications/2012_01_31_Brazil_becomes_2nd_country_on_Twitter_superseds_Japan

Sparks, C. (2001) "The Internet and the Global Public Sphere," in W. L. Bennett & R. M. Entman (eds.) *Media Politics: Communication in the Future of Democracy*, Cambridge, UK: Cambridge University Press, pp.75–95.

Sullivan, J. (2013) "Taiwan's 2012 Presidential Election," *Political Studies Review*, 11, pp. 65–74.

Vis, F. (2013) "Twitter as a Reporting Tool for Breaking News," *Digital Journalism*, 1(1), pp. 27–47.

Volkmer, I. (2003) "The Global Network Society and the Global Public Sphere," *Development*, 46(1), pp. 9–16.

Wang, C. (2011, 3 November) "2012 elections: Tsai in the Lead, Brain Trust Poll Says," *Taipei Times*. Retrieved from http://www.taipeitimes.com/News/taiwan/archives/2011/11/03/2003517350

30

SOCIAL MEDIA USE IN THE GERMAN ELECTION CAMPAIGN 2013

Christian Nuernbergk, Jennifer Wladarsch, Julia Neubarth, and Christoph Neuberger

Introduction

Concerning election campaigning research, Germany can be considered as a special case for several reasons: first, Germans are rather reluctant to use social media and generally less interested in news-related participation as well as political campaigning online (Hasebrink and Hölig 2013; Bernhard, Dohle, and Vowe 2014). Second, Germans are generally cautious to embrace new and individualised news services broadly. Germany's media system reflects the country's federal structure: a comparably strong regional press market, several regional public broadcasters, regional and national commercial operators, and national press titles shape the media landscape. Traditional mass media have also taken the lead online: Germans seem to be rather loyal to established news sources. Third, Germany's political system is described as a 'party-driven democracy' (Esser and Hemmer 2008) with a fairly stable set of influential parties.

Such structural constraints as well as specific patterns of media use and civic engagement are likely to have an effect on the particular shape of German election campaigning and the significance of social media use in these campaigns. Therefore, this chapter draws a more detailed picture of the role social media played during the German federal election campaign 2013. It provides an overview on the German media and political system and will briefly describe the 2013 campaign cycle developments. From an analytical point of view, different perspectives on social media use in campaigns will be considered: on the one hand, the focus lies on how candidates and parties make use of social media in their campaigns. On the other hand, the dynamics of the networked publics which emerge around these campaigns in social media and which are shaped by citizens as well as campaigners are emphasised.

The German Political System: A Party-Driven Democracy

The electoral context that German voters operate in is quite complex. German electoral law combines principles of proportional representation with elements of a first-past-the-post system (Klingemann and Wessels 2001). The country's mixed-member election system allows voters to cast a nominal and a party vote in national elections. The nominal ballot selects a candidate by plurality vote in single-seat districts. The second ballot is based on a closed party list in each of the 16 federal states. The proportion of this party vote determines the number of seats a party receives in parliament. List-tier allocation only takes place when parties overcome a nation-wide 5 per cent threshold or win three single-seat districts. Each party will get its plurality-won seats plus the seats gained by the proportional rule less the number of plurality-won seats (Klingemann and Wessels 2001). Thus, half of the seats are allocated to district winners. The German system exhibits a high degree of stability regarding turnover in governments and the number of parties in the Bundestag. Germany's voter turnout is also relatively high compared to some other European countries (2013: 71.5 per cent). But younger people and those with lower education are less likely to participate in elections (Partheymüller and Schmitt-Beck 2013: 504). Federal elections take place every four years.

Electoral systems may have an effect on campaign behaviour. In mixed-member systems, Plasser and Plasser (2002) expect mainly party-driven campaigns. Parties alone organise the nomination of candidates for public office in Germany. Thus, candidates will need to serve as team members and are required to cooperate to some extent (Zittel and Gschwend 2008). Parties receiving 0.5 per cent of all votes will receive public funding based on their electoral success. This regulation lessens the dependency on collecting donations during campaigns. Overall, party organisations play an important role in the administration of campaigns and influence policy making and government formation. They also shape political programmes and campaign messages. This is also true for social media: all established parties employ professional staff to manage the party's and leading candidates' different social media channels (Jungherr 2014a).

The right-of-centre Christian Democrats (CDU/CSU) and the left-of-centre Social Democratic Party (SPD) are both known as catch-all parties (*Volksparteien*) in Germany. However, the combined share for both parties has declined from 77.3 per cent of the vote in 1990 to 56.8 per cent in 2009. The liberal Free Democratic Party (FDP), the ecological Green Party (Die Grünen), and the more orthodox Left Party (Die Linke) are smaller parties which were also represented in the 17th Bundestag (2009–2013). Since German unification, an increased level of fragmentation has been observed in the party system (Lees 2012). The newly emerged Alternative for Germany (AfD), a far more Eurosceptic group, gained popularity during the 2013 election campaign and nearly entered parliament.

The German Media System and Patterns of Media Use

Following Hallin and Mancini's framework of comparing media systems, Germany can be considered as 'Democratic Corporatist' by showing a strong involvement of organised social groups in policy (Hallin and Mancini 2004). Generally, the German media landscape is rather diverse with a large number of press titles and a dual system of public and private broadcasting. According to the Federation of German Newspaper Publishers (BDZV), newspaper readers can choose between 351 daily newspapers, 21 weekly titles, and seven Sunday titles with a combined circulation of 21.5 million copies (BDZV 2014). Press and public broadcasting both reflect the regional structure of the federal republic, which still influences the cultural life of Germany. Despite the regionalised newspaper landscape, a small number of publishing houses dominate the press market and a process of concentration has been underway in recent decades (see

Hasebrink and Hölig 2013; Röper 2014). However, compared to other countries, the German press market is still healthy in terms of political diversity (Esser and Hemmer 2008).

Under the German Constitution, broadcasting is controlled by the German states rather than the federal government. As a consequence of this federal model, public service broadcasting and commercial broadcasting are both regulated by an Interstate Broadcasting Treaty. The Treaty describes public broadcasters' duties to fulfil informational and educational purposes. It does not allow sponsored political newscasts. Following these rules, public broadcasters' election news coverage must uphold standards of professional distance and impartiality (Esser and Hemmer 2008). Commercial broadcasting was introduced in 1984. Regulation in this sector is limited in comparison: according to the treaty, commercial channels have no comparable duties to inform and educate the public. Election airtime is granted to parties in commercial as well as in public channels (Esser and Hemmer 2008). While this airtime is generally free (but limited) on public channels, the Interstate Broadcasting Treaty authorises parties to pay a reduced spot rate on commercial channels.

Germany is among the countries with the highest traditional news media consumption. Therefore, a majority of the population is still reached by traditional channels (Hasebrink and Hölig 2013). The representative Reuters Institute news survey lists Germany highest with Japan concerning the use of news from newspapers (63 per cent). It is also one of the top-ranked countries in terms of TV news (82 per cent) and radio news consumption (51 per cent) (Hasebrink and Hölig 2013: 81). The same report also states that Germans are least likely to use online news (66 per cent). Additionally, only one fifth of Germans receive news from blogs and social media (21 per cent). Except for France (20 per cent), all other countries examined in the comparative Reuters Institute survey exhibited higher numbers, ranging from 23 per cent to 51 per cent (Newman 2013: 10). It is likely that this country-specific communicative behaviour and media culture will also shape the application of different election campaign strategies. According to Hasebrink and Hölig (2013), a possible reason for this reluctance to use social media may lie in a German need for "systematic and reliable structures" (Hasebrink and Hölig 2013: 83), which may keep Germans from embracing new technologies at an early stage.

Research on Social Media in German Election Campaigns

The empirical research related to German election campaigns on social media can be classified into two main fields: (1) usage studies, and (2) campaign features. Research on the usage side explores who consumes information on social media, and who participates. Additionally, studies also examine the possible effects of social media use. Further, the empirical work on campaign features researches what social media opportunities are provided, and for what campaign purposes they are designed.

The reluctant social media use in Germany leads to the assumption that social media activities are rather unlikely to play important roles in the country's election campaign strategies. So far, a representative survey on news consumption on the 2013 election showed that the most common media channel for using news on the election campaign was television (66 per cent), followed by newspapers (38 per cent) and the Internet (23 per cent) (Gscheidle and Gerhard 2013: 559). Bernhard, Dohle, and Vowe (2014) reported a similar order concerning media use for political information. The younger generation is more likely to use a wide range of platforms and combines online sources and traditional media (Hasebrink and Hölig 2013). But even among young adults (18–29) the Internet was not more important than television for consuming news on the election campaign (Gscheidle and Gerhard 2013). Overall, social network sites (SNS), like Facebook and Twitter, have not played an exceptional role: only a minority of those who informed themselves about the election campaign on the Internet also relied on these channels (8 per cent; see Gscheidle and Gerhard 2013: 558).

German election campaigners first experimented with social media in 2005. Barack Obama's successful presidential campaign in 2008 was especially influential in terms of promoting the potential uses of (and myths about) social media in political campaigns. Even a crossover of personnel expertise took place when U.S. strategists advised German politicians preceding the 2008 campaign (Lilleker and Jackson 2011). Within the German party-centred system, political parties control official campaign strategies and play the central role. But this structural pattern could be challenged by the personalised and dialogical characteristics of social media (Enli and Skogerbø 2013) which allow candidates to communicate politics more individually. Beyond their official party accounts on social media, German parties do not try to systematically encourage party discipline in social media channels. According to a Tagesschau.de news report, no party had issued guidelines for its members' use of social media in the 2013 election campaign. Thus, there was no official 'overall strategy' on how to use and communicate via social media even in 2013 (Matzen 2013).

However, all parliamentary parties had implemented a range of Web 2.0 features by 2009 (Lilleker and Jackson 2011). Campaign weblogs and supporter networks emerged even earlier, in the 2005 election. But this previous experiment with weblogs was not really substantial. Only a small percentage of German Internet users used weblogs in 2005, and the political blogosphere was still in an early stage of development (see Neuberger, Nuernbergk, and Rischke 2007). Not surprisingly, blogging was then mostly discontinued by politicians after the 2005 election (Bieber 2011).

As a consequence of the impressive Obama campaign, SNSs like Facebook or its German counterpart StudiVZ, YouTube videos, and Twitter received more attention than the traditional campaigning websites in 2009 (Bieber 2011). However, on a national level, these 'interactive activities' did not have a statistical effect on electoral performance (Marcinkowski and Metag 2013). Lilleker and Jackson (2011: 107) described the German parties' Web 2.0 features as "more or less aesthetic tools," and missed "genuine political discussions". Notably, only 21 candidates and 11 Members of the Bundestag (MdBs) were found to be blogging in 2009 (Albrecht 2011). Nevertheless, Albrecht also identified a strong increase in election-related blogs based in civil society. He concluded that this format is relevant for the political periphery rather than for the system's centre.

Since the 2009 election, extensive research was conducted, especially on Twitter (see Jungherr 2014b for an overview). Plotkowiak and Stanoevska-Slabeva (2013) investigated how German candidates used Twitter in 2009. They found that less than one fifth of the 3,500 candidates held an active Twitter account in 2009. Conversations on Twitter were mainly in-group focused and took place between members of the same party. During the same election, Elter (2013) studied seven regional state election campaigns. He found that Twitter was used less than Facebook in these campaigns. Almost all parties received the most 'likes' and comments immediately prior to the election date. Despite this tendency for mobilisation, no patterns of sustainable dialogue were visible. Thimm, Einspänner, and Dang-Anh (2012) described two rather distinct styles of Twitter use during two regional state elections in 2011: a 'personal-interactive' style and a 'topic-informative' one. Politicians tweeting in the first style were characterised as 'networkers' who frequently used Twitter's conversational markers. On the other side of the spectrum were politicians who often used hyperlinks to share information with their own followers but did not engage in conversations. Beside these considerable differences regarding politicians' activities, they observed a preference for non-dialogical styles.

More generally, Jungherr (2014b) stated that Twitter messages with hashtag mentions of political parties followed different temporal patterns than their mentions in traditional media during the 2009 election. Research showed that those actors who were retweeted the most in mentioning political parties during two state election campaigns were leftists, activists, and bloggers (Stieglitz and Dang-Xuan 2012). Similarly, Jungherr's (2013) findings indicated that especially the Pirate Party was comparably more visible on Twitter in the 2009 election than traditional parties. With regard to the 2009 case, these results point to a rather specific user environment in the Twitter publics which emerged during the campaign as it unfolded.

Particularly in the case of German Twitter studies, two typical selection strategies are present: in one approach, studies analyse and track specific accounts or specific outlets. In another approach, topic-related tweets are selected by keywords or hashtags. The case studies on the German election campaign presented below each stand for one of these two perspectives.

Although online election campaigns are well researched, some limitations can be identified. First, most studies concerning campaigns still focus on single *platforms*. Second, much previous research focuses on the online activities of established political *actors*. In doing so, the substantially new aspect of the networked public sphere remains hidden: the participation of non-established actors outside of the control of campaign headquarters, MPs' offices, or the editorial offices of mass media. Third, so far most studies have concentrated on a single *topic*. For this reason, a comparison of topics could hardly be drawn. More generally, a focus on the strategic use of social media in election campaigns dominates, whereas research in this field interrogates the extended participatory structures only much more rarely.

The 2013 Campaign Cycle

The 2013 federal election took place on 22 September 2013. The conservative CDU/CSU nearly won an absolute majority of seats but still needed a coalition partner to govern in the new term. The liberal FDP failed to re-enter parliament for the first time since 1949. The newly emerged Alternative for Germany (AfD) came very close to entering parliament but finally fell below the 5 per cent hurdle. SPD, Greens and Leftists each re-entered parliament, but with mixed results.

In 2013, all established parties could build on previous experience with communities on social media. Hence, campaign planners were able to manage them more efficiently and knew how to utilise social media in a realistic manner in the pursuit of their main campaign goals. Therefore, differences regarding social media were also prevalent in this campaign cycle. But as in earlier election campaigns, some events mainly took place to generate media attention and coverage (see Jungherr 2014a). For example, the challenger Peer Steinbrück (SPD) organised a Twitter Townhall which was not primarily meant to be an interactive forum. It was rather an attempt to illustrate the candidate's affinity for digital media. On different SNS, especially two symbolic gestures quickly gained visibility: Angela Merkel's signature hand gesture of a rhombus (<>), which was also used on a giant campaigning billboard in Berlin, and Steinbrück's middle finger (#stinkefinger). The challenger's gesture was printed before in a pictorial interview in the *Süddeutsche Zeitung Magazin* (Seifert 2013).

A first synopsis of the 2013 campaign by Jungherr (2014a) indicated that especially the supporter network platforms were more professionally integrated into the overall campaign framework. They were used to organise local campaigns in the constituencies. Additionally, donations were more successfully collected than in previous elections. This may have helped to boost the AfD which also quickly obtained visibility in social media and the comment sections of news websites. Furthermore, both leading parties CDU/CSU and SPD produced professional media content, which they distributed across different social media channels.

Two empirical case studies will be presented in the following to further examine the role of social media in the 2013 campaign. The first study analyses different social media and examines how they mirror election content. The aim of this research was to overcome the limitations mentioned above. A second case study explores how politicians used Twitter in their individual campaigns and to what extent they interacted with citizens.

Study 1: Dynamics of Topics, Parties and Candidates in Social Media

This study presents results from a broad-based social media monitoring that encompasses the period between 16 May and the election date, 22 September 2013. It does not focus on a specific platform but rather on content relevant to the federal election—topics, candidates and political parties. The study compares Twitter as a microblogging service, selected weblogs, and the forum *meta.tagesschau.de*, which is used to comment on the online articles of Germany's highest-reach television news broadcast, *Tagesschau* (see full report: Wladarsch et al. 2014). In this context, the following research questions will be addressed: Which agenda did social media have during the election campaign 2013? How did the agenda concerning topics, political parties, and candidates change over time? What are the differences between the three platforms? Who are the influential players in social media, in terms of generating the highest resonance?

The digital database of online articles allows an automatic data collection and analysis. Thereby, quite a large number of cases can be handled. However, the methods used have hardly been tested yet and lack established standards (Jungherr 2014b; Kaczmirek et al. 2014). Thus, the following study also has to be interpreted on the basis of these constraints.

Data collection was realised by the internally developed software tool SMART Prototype. The software is able to handle a large volume of unstructured data (e.g. text body, status updates) and related metadata (e.g. author, amount of comments/retweets) from a broad variety of social media platforms. On *meta.tagesschau*, all articles and comments were tracked. For blogs, a preselection had to be made due to the vast population. Those blogs highly relevant for political and economic communication in Germany had to be identified. Therefore, several blog rankings and blog awards were used as indicators (e.g. Ebuzzing, Virato, Google Page Rank). Using these criteria, a selection of 76 blogs was made. In order to determine relevant topics on Twitter, a broad tracking of the political campaign was necessary. For this, a keyword-based way of data tracking was used to in principle include any account. In the run-up to the tracking, a keyword list was defined which finally contained 350 words as indicators for political communication (e.g. names of all parties and politicians, political topics, general words in the context of elections).

In a second step, articles on different topics relevant to the analysis were extracted from these data. Sixteen topics of relevance to the voters' decision (as indicated in surveys) or much discussed on social media were selected. Every topic was operationalised by several keywords.[1]

Which agenda did social media have during the election campaign 2013? The number of cases differs very substantially between the three platforms (see Table 30.1), which can be explained by the platforms' different functions: tweets are quickly written

Table 30.1 Amount and Shares of Articles on Different Topics

	Twitter		Blogs		meta.tagesschau	
	amount	share in %	amount	share in %	amount	share in %
NSA affair	217,600	39.0	3,465	40.5	16,588	38.0
Energy transition	65,818	11.8	611	7.1	1,449	3.3
Candidates' TV debate	60,529	10.8	157	1.8	375	0.9
Taxes	53,709	9.6	792	9.3	2,112	4.8
Mollath[2]	30,730	5.5	294	3.4	280	0.6
Syria crisis	24,445	4.4	1,453	17.0	17,321	39.7
Minimum wage	23,036	4.1	246	2.9	520	1.2
Floods in Central Europe	18,852	3.4	246	2.9	963	2.2
European crisis	16,309	2.9	442	5.2	548	1.3
Euro Hawk[3]	12,923	2.3	72	0.8	1,550	3.6
Road tolls	11,764	2.1	63	0.7	626	1.4
Pensions	11,455	2.1	515	6.0	830	1.9
Tax evasion	8,597	1.5	172	2.0	368	0.8
Loaning of party votes	1,976	0.4	10	0.1	100	0.2
'Amigo' affair[4]	470	0.1	14	0.2	6	0
Criticism of Europe	65	0	4	0	6	0
Total	558,278	100	8,556	100	43,642	100

Note: multiple topics can be assigned to one article.

and forwarded, whereas postings on blogs are much more detailed and discussed over a longer period of time. Comparing the agenda across the topics, some differences can be noticed. Media-driven events and topics with reference to the Internet generate a higher resonance on Twitter than on other platforms. Topics of great social or political significance (e.g. Syria crisis, taxes) are much discussed on blogs and especially *meta. tagesschau* and are less tied to specific events. In this context it must be taken into account that *meta.tagesschau*'s agenda is pre-determined by the *Tagesschau*'s online articles and thus follows an editorial selection of topics. Analysing the topic dynamics on a daily basis, two special peculiarities can be noticed. First, Twitter and the comments on *Tagesschau* articles respond quickly and intensively to events, whereas blog postings are less linked to topicality and tend to be commented on over a longer period of time. Second, the analysed dynamics of topics can be grouped into (at least) two types: the first group includes dynamics with one or more strong peaks (e.g. TV debate, flood, NSA affair, Syria crisis). Those topics are especially driven by important events (mostly reported by media). Their dynamics are very similar across the platforms. The second group can be characterised by topics that are discussed continuously on a more or less constant level; these topics are all economically, socially or politically relevant over the long term, and less tied to major events (e.g. energy revolution, taxes, pension). Thus, the platforms' dynamics are quite heterogeneous.

How visible are political parties on the three platforms? Table 30.2 shows large differences between the three platforms. On Twitter mostly small parties (Alternative for Germany, Pirate Party) are mentioned, whereas on blogs left parties (Greens, Left Party, Social Democrats) predominate. Only on *meta.tagesschau* do the proportions correspond roughly to the weighting of the popular vote.

How visible are the top candidates on the three platforms (see Table 30.3)? In general, the Chancellor Angela Merkel was mentioned much more often than her challenger Peer Steinbrück across all platforms. Furthermore, concerning the proportions on a daily basis it can be noticed that media performances generated the highest

Table 30.2 Amount and Shares of Party Mentions

	Twitter		Blogs		meta.tagesschau	
	amount	share in %	amount	share in %	amount	share in %
CDU	309,897	13.6	1,174	12.2	2,712	16.7
CSU	165,744	7.3	465	4.8	1,223	7.5
SPD	358,419	15.7	1,643	17.1	3,593	22.2
FDP	315,117	13.8	945	9.8	2,245	13.8
Greens	294,084	12.9	2,207	23.0	2,693	16.6
Left Party	166,726	7.3	1,699	17.7	1,753	10.8
AfD	223,040	9.8	915	9.5	1,371	8.5
Pirate Party	450,789	19.7	562	5.8	628	3.9
Total	**2,283,816**	**100**	**9,610**	**100**	**16,218**	**100**

Note: Multiple parties can be assigned to one article.

Table 30.3 Amount and Shares of Candidate Mentions

	Twitter		Blogs		meta.tagesschau	
	amount	share in %	amount	share in %	amount	share in %
Only Angela Merkel (CDU)	339,200	73.7	1,585	72.8	6,122	80.4
Only Peer Steinbrück (SPD)	88,780	19.3	296	13.6	767	10.1
Both	32,359	7.0	295	13.6	723	9.5
Total	460,339	100	2,176	100	7,612	100

resonance. Thus, a large dependency on journalism and the three examined platforms can be confirmed.

Who are the influential players in social media, in terms of generating high resonance? Resonance was measured by the count of retweets (Twitter), or the amount of comments generated (blogs). For each topic, the top 10 accounts were identified to examine whether the resonance depended on topics. Amongst the most influential Twitter accounts, there are particularly many accounts of political parties, famous politicians, mass media, and interest groups. Hence, tweets sent by individual (ordinary) citizens did not generate high resonance. Comparing the 16 topical rankings, only a few consistencies can be determined. Thus, Twitter accounts that are influential across topics cannot be identified on the basis of the topics examined, quite contrary to the top blogs. Here, several blog names (e.g. *wiesaussieht.de*, *spiegelfechter.com*, *starkemeinungen.de*) are to be found across many topical rankings. This finding suggests that an elite has emerged within the German blogosphere—much as it has in the U.S. (Hindman 2009). However, it has to be considered that only 76 blogs were analysed, due to the pre-selection.

Study 2: Twitter as a Campaigning Device? German MdBs' Adoption of Twitter

The second study analyses the activities of Members of the German Bundestag (MdBs) on Twitter before and during the 2013 election campaign. The aim of this study lies in investigating whether politicians simply integrate Twitter into their established set of campaigning strategies, or whether they adapt their strategies somehow to the interactive and participatory environment provided by Twitter. To what extent the empowering potential of social media is challenged by the social-political reality of political campaigning is still a relevant empirical question (Larsson and Svensson 2014). By focusing on German MdBs, this study examines whether the political elite is engaged in a basic dialogue with citizens. It addresses the following research questions: Does the dominance of certain parties on Twitter reflect their electoral strength in the German Bundestag? Who are the primary addressees of the MdBs' Twitter communication?

A comparative synopsis of earlier research mainly ascertained that resourceful opposition parties are also predominant on Twitter (Jungherr 2014b). According to Jungherr's research summary, there is also "little evidence of Twitter being an enabling device for dialogue between politicians and other Twitter users, not part of the political elite" (2014b: 48).

For the purposes of this study, data from all official Twitter profiles of German MdBs were retrieved using the Twitter API.[5] Beside the MdBs' tweets, all users who were mentioned in these messages using the @name as a marker of addressivity have been recorded. For comparative reasons, two weekly timespans were selected to study MdBs' activities and their conversations with other actors: the data were retrieved for a first timeframe six months before the election day (20 to 26 March 2013), and for a second timeframe close to the election (15 to 21 September 2013). The first timeframe could still be described as a period of 'routine' politics outside the election. We identified Twitter accounts held by MdBs through systematic manual searches and cross-checking of different sources: All official MdB websites and the additional profile information for each MdB provided at the website of the Bundestag were reviewed. Thus, 338 tweeting MdBs out of 620 were identified by September 2013. Among these is Angela Merkel's opposition challenger Peer Steinbrück, whereas the Chancellor herself does not have an account. 193 MdBs also had a verified profile, according to Twitter. The tracking resulted in 4,244 tweets for the March period. In the September timeframe, MdBs posted 7,736 tweets altogether. All tweets were included in a quantitative content analysis. This analysis was conducted to classify political content and forms of political campaigning. Furthermore, all users marked by using the @reply or RT @ operator in a message were classified by their actor type as citizens, politicians, or media actors. The coding was conducted by undergraduate student coders and two researchers. A reliability assessment achieved acceptable results on the coding of different forms of campaigning (Holsti's coefficient: .71–.85) and good results on the classification of actor types (.81–.96).

The tracking of Twitter profiles allowed us to determine the number of active members during both periods: even though a majority of German MdBs was found to have an account on Twitter, just one third of all MdBs also composed tweets during the timeframes analysed. In the March period, 208 MdBs contributed tweets (34 per cent). Only a small increase was found for the September period, with 221 MdBs composing messages (36 per cent). However, the tweeting activity of those using the service almost doubled closer to the election (March: 20.4 tweets on average; September: 35.0 tweets). The Greens exhibited the highest share of actively tweeting Members in their parliamentary group (68 per cent in September, $n = 68$), followed by the Left Party (44 per cent, $n = 75$), and the FDP (42 per cent, $n = 93$). The 'catch-all' parties SPD (31 per cent, $n = 146$) and CDU/CSU (24 per cent, $n = 237$) followed last.

If the number of composed tweets is counted per political party, differences tend to diminish in September between the Greens and the conservative CDU/CSU of Chancellor Merkel. As Table 30.4 shows, the mean use of Twitter was significantly different in September, whereas MdBs' use of Twitter did not differ by party during the routine period in March. Especially Members of the CDU/CSU and Greens exhibit a clearly increased posting rate close to the September election. Overall, Twitter activity by party only partially reflects their electoral strength in parliament. The strongest deviation was visible for the Greens party.

Graham et al. (2013) have demonstrated that averages on a party group level could be somewhat misleading given the divergence in posting rates among politicians in the UK. In the case of German parliamentarians, our study confirms that the distribution of composed tweets is also not egalitarian. But as Table 30.5 shows, election

Table 30.4 Distribution of MdBs' Tweets Compared to Party Strength in the Bundestag

	Distribution of seats (in %, n=620)	Tweets		Distribution of tweets (in %)		Mean per MdB		Median per MdB	
	2009–2013	MAR	SEP	MAR	SEP	MAR	SEP	MAR	SEP
CDU/CSU	38.2	1,096	2,174	26	28	20.3	38.1	8.0	26.0
SPD	23.5	1,027	1,402	24	18	23.9	31.2	14.0	19.0
FDP	15.0	538	998	13	13	15.4	25.6	8.0	13.0
Greens	11.0	1,058	2,330	25	30	25.2	50.7	10.5	33.0
Left Party	12.1	525	777	12	10	15.4	23.5	10.5	16.0
Total	–	4,244	7,736[a]	–	–	20.4	35.0	10.0	24.0

[a] Also includes independent MdB Wolfgang Neskovic.
September: $F = 2.477$, $df = 5$, $p < .05$; March: n.s.

Table 30.5 Weekly Rate and Distribution of Tweets

Number of published tweets per week	Number of MdBs publishing tweets		Share of MdBs publishing (in %) ...		Number of tweets		Share of all tweets (in %)	
	MAR	SEP	MAR	SEP	MAR	SEP	MAR	SEP
1	18	5	8.7	2.3	18	5	0.4	0.1
2–9	84	58	40.4	26.2	399	295	9.4	3.8
10–49	89	114	42.8	51.6	2,001	3,096	47.1	40.0
50–99	12	31	5.8	14.0	809	2,174	19.1	28.1
100 or more	5	13	2.4	5.9	1,017	2,166	24.0	28.0
Total	208	221	100	100	4,244	7,736	100	100

campaigning has mostly led to an overall increased posting rate. Thus, the comparison of different periods exhibits a slightly more moderate distribution close to the election in September.

In September, the parties also differed regarding their distribution rate (Cramer's V = .291, $p <. 01$, Chi-square = 18.7, $df = 5$): The Greens exhibited the most visible presence on Twitter. Up to 94 per cent of their MdBs with posting activity published ten or more tweets per week. Other parties only reached values between 56 per cent and 74 per cent.

Not surprisingly, the results of the content analysis clearly demonstrate a turn towards campaigning-related Twitter activities closer to the election: Political campaigning was subject of 39 per cent of the self-composed tweets in September ($n = 4,441$), whereas earlier in March only one fifth (20 per cent, $n = 2,371$) of tweets

Table 30.6 @replies and Retweets in MdBs' Tweets by Parties (in %)

	@replies MAR (n = 2,295)	@replies SEP (n = 2,875)	Retweets MAR (n = 774)	Retweets SEP (n = 1,912)
Political actors	49.2	44.5	61.6	60.5
Journalistic actors	9.3	14.1	15.6	15.8
Ordinary citizens	35.0	36.8	12.9	18.4
Other	6.4	4.7	9.8	5.3

contained campaigning for party-related events, activities or information. Here, the periods differ significantly (Phi = .202, p <. 001, Chi-square = 276.7, df = 1). Likewise, efforts to mobilise (e.g. calls for votes) clearly increased (March: 3 per cent, n = 2,380; September: 10 per cent, n = 4,476; Phi = .112, p <. 001, Chi-square = 86.2, df = 1). Calls for donations were almost entirely absent from MdBs' messages. More generally, a decreasing amount of communication focusing on private life was observed in September (March: 18 per cent, n = 2,902; September: 4 per cent, n = 4,649; Cramer's V = .241, p < .001, Chi-square = 439.5, df = 2). With the ballot box in sight, messages which focused on specific policies were also posted significantly less (March: 72 per cent, n = 1,880; September: 23 per cent, n = 3,779; Phi = -.474, p <. 001, Chi-square = 1,275.3, df = 1).

Regarding the Members' primarily interaction partners, the content analysis reveals that the most apparent actor types were other political actors. This is especially true in the case of retweets (see Table 30.6). Overall, this pattern remains rather stable across the comparison of both periods. Interestingly, ordinary citizens received more attention via the @reply operator than by being retweeted through politicians' accounts. Mainly journalistic actors were more often involved in Twitter conversations closer to the election.

Additionally, findings indicate that the examined parties also differed regarding their Members' interaction partners on Twitter. Only the Green Party was mentioning other politicians in a majority of the cases in both periods. A network analysis perspective could provide further insights into the selected interaction partners according to partisan lines.

Conclusion

Germany's politicians and campaign planners have experimented with social media since the 2005 election. Although they have learned to manage communities and different platforms, their messages do not necessarily flow across social media offhandedly. Most of the politicians' engagement could be characterised as symbolic action. Therefore, the dialogic characteristics of social media remain largely unused. Not surprisingly, gestures and iconic images often go viral, whereas key policy messages commonly remain unshared by the masses. However, from a political actor's perspective, the distribution of non-viral content can also be functional in an age of hybrid media (see Chapter 1 by Chadwick, Dennis, and Smith in this volume). Virality is not a necessary condition for agenda-building or political influence.

Both case studies have shown that especially smaller parties take the opportunity to engage in social media (Study 2) and thus gained visibility (Study 1) on Twitter. However, smaller as well as larger parties do not engage broadly in dialogue with citizens. The analysis of politicians' Twitter networks has shown that the most visible interaction partners were political actors. Although citizens were mentioned to some extent, the impression prevails that the political Twittersphere is mainly dominated by the political and media elite. One explanation lies in the generally reluctant use of social media in Germany. User surveys have demonstrated that only a small number of citizens are actively engaged with political content and participate in the political periphery. Concerning the topic dynamics, the results indicate that traditional media are amplified by social media, especially in the context of major events.

The limitations of existing studies have revealed that there is a need for comparative studies on several dimensions (topics, actors, platforms, countries, time). So far, little is known about differences and commonalities among countries in social media use in general and for political purposes. Therefore, longitudinal data as well as systematic international comparisons would be desirable.

Previous campaign developments do not indicate that social media will broadly reshape Germany's next election campaigns online. Certainly there is a trend towards pluralisation and personalisation in politics. But all parties—established or not—will have to deal in the long run with the country's specific media landscape, which is still substantially driven by traditional actors. It is no accident, then, that especially social media have become a preferred space for extra-parliamentary, extremist positions and media criticism in Germany. Aside from this trend, the ongoing adoption of social media is rather unlikely to change reluctant political participation behaviour. In addition, unless social media platforms like Facebook also do not afford dialogue and deliberation in a substantial way, it is unlikely that dialogic approaches will become a major element of professional campaign strategies. However, it is clear that social media will continue to play an important role in upcoming elections—but with various approaches and goals.

Notes

1 To define the keywords, every topic was analysed by content-based dimensions to cover all relevant aspects. Across topics, all keywords are more or less on the same level of abstraction. Additionally, different ways of writing were considered. When the focus is on a single person or organisation in a scandal (e.g. Mollath), the name is a reliable keyword. The number of keywords used ranges from one (Mollath) to 15 (Euro Hawk).
2 Gustl Mollath is the victim of a juridical error.
3 Euro Hawk is an unmanned reconnaissance plane.
4 Political affair of the Bavarian conservative party: Bavarian parliamentarians misused public finances to employ relatives.
5 The retrieval process was jointly organised within a DAAD/ATN-funded research cooperation aiming to compare Australian and German Twitter activities ('Mapping Networked Politics'). The public streaming API was used to gather the data published by a specific set of *accounts*. Due to this approach and the small amount of tweets posted by German MdBs during the two weeks selected, no API-related limitations are to be expected.

References

Albrecht, S. (2011) "Wahlblogs revisited: Nutzung von Wahlblogs im Bundestagswahlkampf," in E. J. Schweitzer & S. Albrecht (eds.) *Das Internet im Wahlkampf: Analysen zur Bundestagswahl 2009*, Wiesbaden: VS Verlag für Sozialwissenschaften, pp. 181–200.

Bernhard, U., Dohle, M., & Vowe, G. (2014) "Wie werden Medien zur politischen Information genutzt und wahrgenommen? Online-und Offlinemedien im Vergleich," *Media Perspektiven*, (3), pp. 159–168.

BDZV (2014) "Zahlen—Daten—Fakten," in BDZV (ed.), *Zeitungen 2014/15*, Berlin: ZV Zeitungs-Verlag Service GmbH, pp. 339–364.

Bieber, C. (2011) "Der Online-Wahlkampf im Superwahljahr 2009," in E. J. Schweitzer & S. Albrecht (eds.) *Das Internet im Wahlkampf: Analysen zur Bundestagswahl 2009*, Wiesbaden: VS Verlag für Sozialwissenschaften, pp. 69–95.

Elter, A. (2013) "Interaktion und Dialog? Eine quantitative Inhaltsanalyse der Aktivitäten deutscher Parteien bei Twitter und Facebook während der Landtagswahlkämpfe 2011," *Publizistik*, 58(2), pp. 201–220.

Enli, G. S., & Skogerbø, E. (2013) "Personalized Campaigns in Party-Centred Politics," *Information, Communication & Society*, 16(5), pp. 757–774.

Esser, F., & Hemmer, K. (2008) "Characteristics and Dynamics of Election News Coverage in Germany," in J. Strömbäck & L. L. Kaid (eds.), *The Handbook of Election News Coverage around the World*, New York, NY: Routledge, pp. 289–307.

Graham T., Broersma M., Hazelhoff K., & van't Haar G. (2013) "Between Broadcasting Political Messages and Interacting with Voters," *Information, Communication & Society* 16(5), pp. 692–716.

Gscheidle, C., & Gerhard, H. (2013) "Berichterstattung zur Bundestagswahl 2013 aus Sicht der Zuschauer," *Media Perspektiven*, (12), pp. 558–573.

Hallin, D. C., & Mancini, P. (2004) *Comparing Media Systems: Three Models of Media and Politics*, Cambridge: Cambridge University Press.

Hasebrink, U., & Hölig, S. (2013) "Lagging Behind or Choosing a Different Path? Information Behaviour in Germany," in D. Levy & N. Newman (eds.), *Reuters Institute Digital News Report 2013*, Oxford: University of Oxford, pp. 81–83.

Hindman, M. (2009) *The Myth of Digital Democracy*, Princeton: Princeton University Press.

Jungherr, A. (2013) "Tweets and Votes, a Special Relationship: The 2009 Federal Election in Germany," in I. Weber, A.-M. Popescu, & M. Pennacchiotti (eds.), *PLEAD 2013: Proceedings of the Second Workshop, Politics, Elections and Data*, New York, NY: ACM, pp. 5–14.

Jungherr, A. (2014a) "Die Rolle des Internets in den Kampagnen der Parteien zur Bundestagswahl 2013," in M. Beckedahl (ed.), *Jahrbuch Netzpolitik*, Berlin: Newthinking.org, pp. 34–40.

Jungherr, A. (2014b) "Twitter in Politics: A Comprehensive Literature Review," *Social Science Research Network*. Available at: http://dx.doi.org/10.2139/ssrn.2402443

Kaczmirek, L., Mayr, P., Vatrapu, R., Bleier, A., Blumenberg, M., Gummer, T., Hussain, A., Kinder-Kurlanda, K., Manshaei, K., Thamm, M., Weller, K., Wenz, A., & Wolf, C. (2014) *Social Media Monitoring of the Campaigns for the 2013 German Bundestag Elections on Facebook and Twitter*, Köln 2014 (GESIS Working Papers 2014 | 31). Available at: http://www.gesis.org/fileadmin/upload/forschung/publikationen/gesis_reihen/gesis_arbeitsberichte/WorkingPapers_2014–31.pdf

Klingemann, H.-D., & Wessels, B. (2001) "The Political Consequences of Germany's Mixed-Member System: Personalization at the Grass Roots?" in M. S. Shugart & M. P. Wattenberg (eds.), *Mixed-Member Electoral Systems: The Best of Both Worlds?* Oxford: Oxford University Press, pp. 279–296.

Larsson, A. O., & Svensson, J. (2014) "Politicians Online—Identifying Current Research Opportunities," *First Monday*, 19(4). doi: http://dx.doi.org/10.5210/fm.v19i4.4897

Lees, C. (2012) "The Paradoxical Effects of Decline: Assessing Party System Change and the Role of the Catch-All Parties in Germany Following the 2009 Federal Election," *Party Politics*, 18(4), pp. 545–562.

Lilleker, D. G., & Jackson, N. A. (2011) "Elections 2.0: Comparing E-Campaigns in France, Germany, Great Britain and the United States," in E. J. Schweitzer & S. Albrecht (eds.), *Das Internet im Wahlkampf: Analysen zur Bundestagswahl 2009*, Wiesbaden: VS Verlag für Sozialwissenschaften, pp. 96–116.

Marcinkowski, F., & Metag, J. (2013) "Lassen sich mit dem Internet Wählerstimmen gewinnen?" *Publizistik*, 58(1), pp. 23–44.

Matzen, N. (2013) "Im Social Web angekommen," *tagesschau.de*, 22.08.2013. Available at: http://www.tagesschau.de/wahl/parteien_und_programme/socialmedia-wahlkampf100.html

Neuberger C., Nuernbergk C., & Rischke, M. (2007) "Weblogs und Journalismus: Konkurrenz, Ergänzung oder Integration?" *Media Perspektiven*, (2), pp. 96–112.

Newman, N. (2013) "Executive Summary and Key Findings," in D. Levy & N. Newman (eds.), *Reuters Institute Digital News Report 2013*, Oxford: University of Oxford, pp.9–16.

Partheymüller, J., & Schmitt-Beck, R. (2013) "Eine, soziale Logik' der Demobilisierung: Einflüsse politischer Gesprächspartner auf Wahlbeteiligung und-enthaltung bei der Bundestagswahl 2009," in B. Weßels, H. Schoen, & O. W. Gabriel (eds.), *Wahlen und Wähler: Analysen aus Anlass der Bundestagswahl 2009*, Wiesbaden: Springer VS, pp. 496–513.

Plasser, F., & Plasser, G. (2002) *Global Political Campaigning: A Worldwide Analysis of Campaign Professionals and Their Practices*, Westport: Praeger.

Plotkowiak, T., & Stanoevska-Slabeva, K. (2013) "German Politicians and Their Twitter Networks in the Bundestag 2009 Election," *First Monday*, 18(5). doi: http://dx.doi.org/10.5210/fm.v18i5.3816

Röper, H. (2014) "Zeitungsmarkt 2014: Erneut Höchstwert bei Pressekonzentration," *Media Perspektiven*, (12), pp. 254–270.

Seifert, J. (2013) "Middle Finger Criticized in German Campaign," in *DW*, 14.09.2013. Available at: http://www.dw.de/middle-finger-criticized-in-german-campaign/a-17088391

Stieglitz, S., & Dang-Xuan, L. (2012) "Political Communication and Influence through Microblogging: An Empirical Analysis of Sentiment in Twitter Messages and Retweet Behavior," in R. H. Sprague Jr. (ed.), *HICSS 2012: Proceedings of the 45th Hawaii International Conference on System Science*, Washington, DC: IEEE Computer Society, pp. 3500–3509.

Thimm, C., Einspänner J., & Dang-Anh, M. (2012) "Twitter als Wahlkampfmedium," *Publizistik*, 57(3), pp. 293–313.

Wladarsch, J., Neuberger, C., Brockmann, T., & Stieglitz, S. (2014) "Der Bundestagswahlkampf 2013 in den Social Media. Themen, Parteien, Spitzenkandidaten und Resonanz auf Twitter, Blogs und meta.tagesschau," *Media Perspektiven*, (9), pp. 456–474.

Zittel, T., & Gschwend, T. (2008) "Individualised Constituency Campaigns in Mixed-Member Electoral Systems: Candidates in the 2005 German Elections," *West European Politics*, 31(5), pp. 978–1003.

31

COMPARING FACEBOOK AND TWITTER DURING THE 2013 GENERAL ELECTION IN ITALY

Luca Rossi and Mario Orefice

Introduction

The 2013 Italian general election has been labelled by many media and communication scholars as the "the first Twitter Italian general election" (Vaccari & Valeriani 2013: 1026). In this chapter we describe the 2013 electoral campaign from a social media perspective, comparing the use of Facebook and Twitter during months leading to the election. In so doing, we will show how different social media present different perspectives when it comes to political communication and how these perspectives can be fully be understood only if social media are framed within a *continuum* together with traditional mass media.

When discussing the electoral use of social media, it is necessary to contextualise such use within the general adoption of digital media in the country of reference. Internet use in Italy is limited, even if it is possible to see a growing trend over the years. In 2012, 62.1 per cent of the population used the Internet at least once a week, with the same value reaching 63.5 per cent in 2013 (Censis 2013). It is interesting to note that data about the daily use of the Internet show a stronger trend increasing from 43.9 per cent of daily Internet users in 2012 to 51.6 per cent in 2013 (+7.7; Demos & PI 2013). The growth in Internet access seems to be coupled with an interesting change of user habits. In particular, while 86.4 per cent of Italians still indicate television as their preferential source of information (Censis 2013) a significant portion of online users say they combine television with Facebook or Twitter. Specifically, the 2013 survey indicated that Twitter was a "news and information channel" for 6.3 per cent of the users (+3.8 compared to 2012). Similar uses of Facebook increased from 26.8 per cent in 2012 to 37.6 per cent a year later (+10.8). These data suggest a scenario where large parts of the population currently remain outside of the digital debate. At the same time, data show a stable increasing trend over the years, and it is now safe to say that social media do play a relevant role in contemporary Italian political communication, both in qualitative and quantitative terms. From a quantitative perspective, the months leading up to the 2013 national election saw a high level of activity by new political actors entering the arena and old parties redefining their traditional communication strategies. In the remainder of this chapter, we will first explore existing research regarding social media and electoral communication. Subsequently, we introduce and present the data collected during the election period. Finally, we discuss these data within the wider frame of contemporary political communication defined as *circular* and *hybrid* (Chadwick 2011; Bentivegna & Marchetti 2014).

Social Media for Political Election Research

On a general level, one can identify two complementary approaches to the analysis of social media use during election periods. The first line of research, coherent with classical studies on political communication, focuses on the use of digital media by political parties or politicians. The second research area pays more attention to the study of grassroots communications arising before or between elections.

These different research areas, that obviously see many middle-ground approaches, are largely rooted in two substantially different research questions. On the one hand, scholars investigating how political parties and politicians use digital media typically describe the new forms of political communication and analyse whether or not social media innovate the interaction dynamics between politicians and citizens (Mori 2011; Pira 2012; Vergeer & Hermans 2013; Morcellini 2013). On the other hand, scholars interested in grassroots communication typically investigate if social media-based conversations can be used to study and describe the ongoing political debate produced online by ordinary citizens (Bentivegna 2014, Larsson 2014). In this latter area of research the approach is often non-deterministic, thus digital media are usually described as a new possibility to observe political discussions that would happen anyway just in different media. This second approach, usually based on large collection of social media data, has seen the participation of many disciplines trying to use Twitter, or data gathered from some other social media platform, in order to investigate people's political opinions and sentiments (Ceron et al. 2014). A side-track of these studies is represented by research that attempts to use social media data in order to predict election results (Tumasjan et al. 2010; Sang & Bos 2011; Caldarelli et al. 2014). While the goal is undoubtedly ambitious, the actual possibility of making such forecasts has been strongly criticised by many authors (Metaxas, 2011; Jungherr et al. 2012; Gayo-Avello et al. 2011). Beside the inconclusive academic debate about election results' predictability, there is no denying that this line of research has provided an opportunity for scholars to observe an emergent communicative structure of large-scale political communication, as well as the growth of new global protest movements that have emerged over the last years (Lotan et al. 2011; Valeriani 2011; Castells 2013).

Despite the fact that these two research lines have fundamental differences in terms of specific foci and theoretical backgrounds, they largely rely on the same type of data (mostly from Twitter)—even if these data are collected differently. Beside some exceptions where data collection is based on a pre-defined list of Twitter accounts (Vergeer & Hermans 2013), the vast majority of researchers collect what could be referred to as topical data (Bruns & Moe 2013) produced over a single or multiple hashtags (Tumasjan et. al 2010; Larsson 2014; Caldarelli et al. 2014). While a detailed analysis of the perils of Twitter data collection is not the goal of this chapter (see Bruns & Burgess 2012; Gaffney & Puschmann 2013; Morstatter et al. 2013 for further discussion on this topic), we still want to emphasise that when working with topical data we are collecting messages that have been written explicitly to take part in a larger conversation potentially involving anyone interested in the same topic (Bruns & Moe 2013). Within the context of the present chapter, this means that a set of hashtags centred on the names of parties or political leaders (e.g. #M5S for the Italian Five Star Movement or #Berlusconi) will produce a candidate/party-centred data. On the opposite gathering data using hashtags referring to electoral process (such as #elezioni2013 for the Italian case) will produce a wider collection of topics potentially linked to the election. It could be easy to assume that data collected through a list of politicians' name hashtags would be a subset of the data collected through more general hashtags, but due to the unstructured nature of hashtags, we cannot take that for granted. As noted by Bruns & Burgess (2011), when single users add a specific hashtag to their messages they virtually engage with an audience, outside of their own network, that is potentially interested in the topic.

Compared to the large and growing corpus of Twitter-based research, literature investigating how Facebook is used during political campaigns is surprisingly limited. Beside a peak of scientific interest following 2008 U.S. presidential election that resulted in a significant amount of studies (Johnson & Perlmutter 2010; Vitak et al. 2011; Carlisle & Patton 2013), politological research based on what is currently the largest online social network is relatively rare. Since technical difficulties that researchers have to face when they try to collect Facebook data have surely had an impact in terms of quantity of studies available (for more detailed description of these issues, see Giglietto et al. 2012), Facebook-based research has always shown a different focus. This strand of research seems to have a broader social media perspective focusing on how political communication or user-generated contents are spread through multiple platforms— Blogs, Facebook, YouTube (Woolley et al. 2010). At the same time, much political communication research focusing on Facebook, as it happened also for Twitter later in time, has from the very beginning tried to understand whether social media could function as tools for increasing political participation and engagement (Vitak et al. 2011; Kushin & Yamamoto 2010).

In this chapter we use both Facebook and Twitter data to describe the 2013 Italian general election. By using a multiple data approach we try to produce a comparative analysis that has few precedents. At the same time, by adopting a multiple data approach, we claim that every single social media plays a specific role within the complex phenomenon of political elections. Every type of data, from Facebook to Twitter, constitutes, by definition, only a partial representation of the communication happening during an electoral campaign. Through the comparison of multiple data sources we can provide a better understanding of the whole campaign (from a communication perspective) as well as valuable information about the role played by different social media within it.

Both Facebook and Twitter data used in this chapter have been collected from January 2013 to February 2013 using Blogmeter (2013) acquisition tools. Technical details of these tools are discussed in a recent work by Boccia Artieri (2013). Facebook data are obtained through Facebook public API while Twitter data are obtained through a combination of Twitter REST and Streaming API. For both Facebook and Twitter data, we defined an initial set of keywords using names of all the principal politicians running for the election.

For Facebook, we collected 'Engagement' and PTA data (People Talking About) about the public pages of the selected politicians. Engagement value represents the total number of *likes* + *comments* + *shares* obtained by a page and PTA is a broader metric that counts every kind of interaction a user can perform with a public page (e.g. like a page, post on the page wall, like a post, comment on a post, share a post). While Engagement is a cumulative metric, PTA counts single user's interactions thus it is not affected by high level of activity of some users (if a user comments many times in one day it will still counts as one).

For Twitter data, we collected every mention of a politician that was present in our list. Twitter mentions are all the tweets that explicitly mention, within the body text, an existing Twitter user by writing the @ symbol followed by the username.

Multiple Platforms for Multiple Realities

Tables 31.1 and 31.2 give us a first glimpse of how different political leaders performed on different social media. Looking at the Facebook data (Table 31.1) the former comedian Beppe Grillo had the highest level of Engagement and PTA value during the campaign. It should be noted that Beppe Grillo's page counts a level of activity extremely higher than any other politician, posting, on average, 23 updates (videos, status, or pictures) every day reaching, by the end of the two months campaign, the number of 1,306 updates, more than six times the updates written by Nichi Vendola who ranked second.

Table 31.1 Top 5 Political Accounts on Facebook for Level of Engagement and People Talking About (PTA)

Facebook (1 January–24 February 2013)	Engagement	PTA	Status updates
Beppe Grillo	5,933,393	207,264	1,306
Silvio Berlusconi	1,141,932	55,241	122
M5S	1,044,878	49,278	81
Rivoluzione Civile (RC)	753,810	32,390	11
Nichi Vendola	667,008	41,163	221

Table 31.2 Top 5 Political Accounts on Twitter for Number of Direct Mentions (absolute values)

Twitter (1 January– 24 February 2013)	Mentions	Unique authors	Ment/Auth
Pierluigi Bersani	300,667	48,249	6.23
Mario Monti	276,127	65,514	4.21
Oscar Giannino	225,997	34,853	6.48
Beppe Grillo	212,371	58,296	3.64
Fare	129,312	21,198	6.10

While this is undoubtedly a relevant data to describe Beppe Grillo's Facebook strategy it is important to point out how there is no direct connection between the number of PTA and the number of updates published by a page, since PTA does not measure only interactions with the 'content' (likes, shared, comments) but also interactions with the page (check-in, mentions, etc.). Moreover, it is worth noticing that while most candidates had a Facebook page exclusively dedicated to their political activity, Beppe Grillo opened his page before he entered the political arena. Despite the change of 'public role', he kept the same Facebook page. Beppe Grillo's party, the Five Star Movement (M5S), also has another very popular page that ranked third just behind Silvio Berlusconi official page. Fourth is the left-wing party Rivoluzione Civile (Civil Revolution) which was created just before the election to gather votes of left-wing electors that had a very limited success. Fifth, we see the personal page of Nichi Vendola, leader of the left-wing party Sinistra Ecologia e Libertà (Left, Ecology, and Freedom). At the same time, it is interesting to notice the absence both of Partito Democratico (PD; Democratic Party, the centre-left party that actually won the election) and Scelta Civica (Civic Choice), a centre party led by former prime minister Mario Monti, who was expected, by many analysts, to obtain a better result.

While both PD's leader (Pierluigi Bersani) and Scelta Civica's leader (Mario Monti) had active pages at the time of study, they were absent from the Facebook rankings presented in Table 31.1. Table 31.2 shows how these two leaders were respectively the first and the second with the highest number of Twitter mentions. Due to the aforementioned differences in available data, Twitter scores are more affected by differences in content production rates; that means that a small number of hyperactive users might be able to produce a large amount of data. Thus, it is important to observe the number of mentions paired with the number of unique users. In fact, while Pierluigi Bersani engaged lower numbers than Mario Monti, the ones engaged seem to be more active in this sense with an average value of 6,23 mentions per user. Among the top five most mentioned Twitter accounts, we can observe both the account of the centre-right coalition 'Fare per fermare il declino' (Act to stop the decline) and the account of its leader, the journalist Oscar Giannino, are present among the top five accounts.

These kinds of data that connect either to parties or to individual politicians suggest the complexity of contemporary political communication, where individual leaders might attract audiences larger than their respective parties. These developments represent a substantial problem for data aggregation and interpretation. If, on the one side, we frame this as a specific characteristic of contemporary political debate, where citizens and individual politicians are able to connect and discuss without the symbolic mediation of traditional parties (Anduiza et al. 2009), on the data-collection side we should keep in mind how this might relate to different pre-existing backgrounds of every candidate. In this case, both Oscar Giannino and Beppe Grillo had established popular Twitter and Facebook accounts before they entered the political arena, so their followers can only be partially understood as uniquely political.

Besides showing the difference between political performances on Facebook and Twitter, the two tables show, when compared with Table 31.3, how neither Facebook nor Twitter data can be compared with the actual election results.

While this is not surprising, as a low correspondence between election success and social media success has been observed before, the observed differences between Facebook and Twitter should be explored further. We will investigate these differences

Table 31.3 Official Results of 2013 Italian General Election—Votes for the Candidate

Politician (Supporting Party)	Camera	Senato
Pierluigi Bersani (PD + SEL)	29.54 per cent	31.60 per cent
Silvio Berlusconi (PDL)	21.56 per cent	22.30 per cent
Beppe Grillo (M5S)	25.55 per cent	23.79 per cent
Mario Monti (SC)	8.30 per cent	9.13 per cent
Antonio Ingroia (RC)	2.25 per cent	1.79 per cent
Oscar Giannino (FARE)	1.12 per cent	0.90 per cent

Source: Ministry of the Interior (2015).

through two hypotheses used to consider the nature of social media data and social media use during political elections.

Facebook and Twitter during Political Elections

Our first hypothesis is that different performances are direct results of different communication strategies as performed by political parties or leaders on the various social media platforms. While parties undoubtedly communicate differently on different social media, it also seems that social media use exhibits specific 'local culture' (Marwick 2011) that might favour certain parties. This could be due to specific demographics (such as age, gender, race, or socioeconomic state) associated with certain social media and it could be described as a platform-size form of the so-called echo-chamber effect. The idea that social media might act as political echo chambers by reinforcing already existing opinions and offer few opportunities for actual debate has been previously discussed extensively (Gilbert et al. 2009; Yardi & boyd 2010). While this is a well-known risk, the phenomenon has only been analysed in detail within single social media (Twitter, Blogs, etc.) and little is known of echo-chamber effect on a larger level. The different level of success that parties obtain moving through different social media may suggest that not only an echo-chamber effect can take place within a specific platform but that specific social media can be used more within a specific part of the population generating platform-size echo-chamber effects. Within this perspective, the observed difference between Partito Democratico (successful on Twitter and not on Facebook) and the Movimento 5 Stelle (successful on Facebook and not on Twitter) could be explained by the different political preferences of the average user of each platform. While this is an intriguing hypothesis that challenges the assumption of even adoption of social media we currently do not have a proper understanding of social media demographics (Sloan et al. 2015) to confirm it.

A second hypothesis that could explain the data we collected assumes that different social media are used by citizens for different purposes and goals and that this produces a specific (biased) representation of the political arena. While such a multi-goals approach is visible in some research (Metaxas & Mustafaraj 2012), difficulties in collecting comparable data have reduced the diffusion of this idea in favour of a more simple assumption that the large number of participants on a single social media platform (usually Twitter) might be a reliable representation of a digital public sphere (Caldarelli et al. 2014).

In order to explore these potential different functions, we visualised the evolution of collected data over the time that collection took place (see Figures 31.1 and 31.2).

Twitter data (see Figure 31.1 and Figure 31.3) show a peak of communication at the very beginning of the campaign with tweets about Scelta Civica (Label 1 on

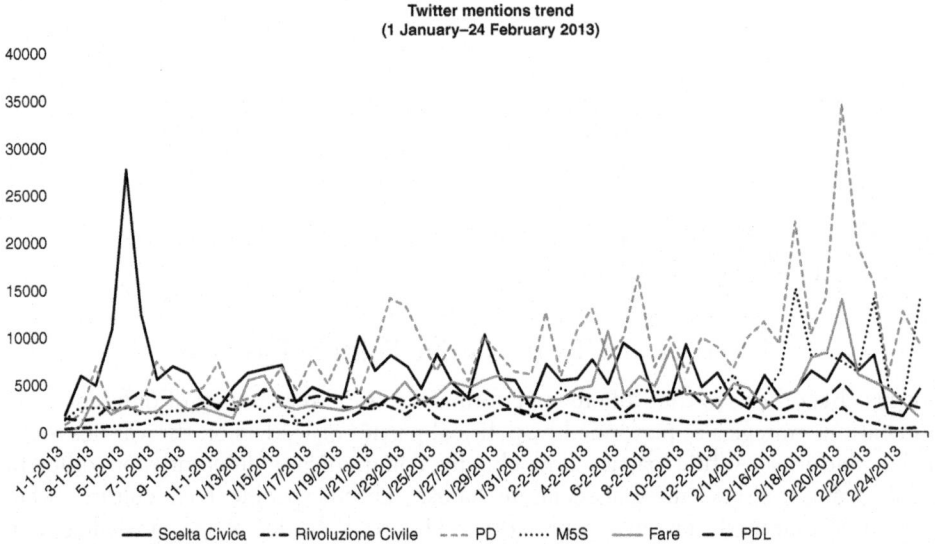

Twitter mentions trend
(1 January–24 February 2013)

Scelta Civica — Rivoluzione Civile --- PD ...... M5S — Fare -- PDL

Figure 31.1 Daily Volume of Twitter Mentions

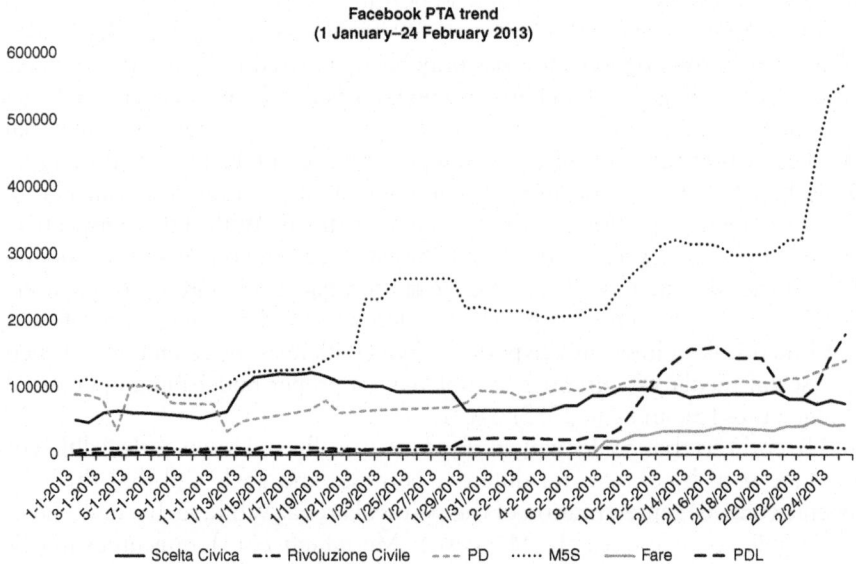

Facebook PTA trend
(1 January–24 February 2013)

Scelta Civica — Rivoluzione Civile --- PD ...... M5S — Fare -- PDL

Figure 31.2 Daily Volume of People Talking About

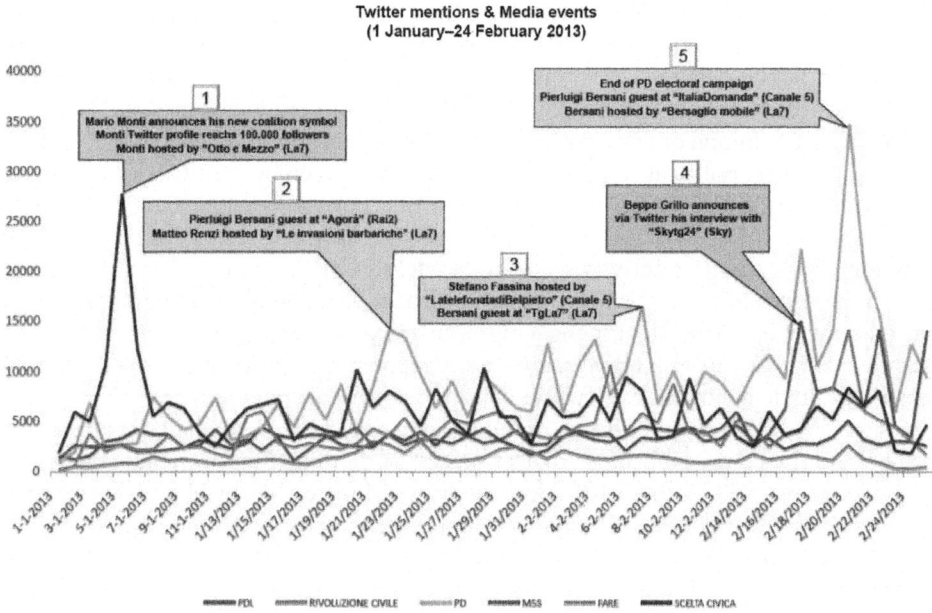

Twitter mentions & Media events
(1 January–24 February 2013)

Figure 31.3 Media Presence of Political Leaders Superimposed to the Volume of Twitter Mentions

Figure 31.3). This is mainly due to the statement made by the then Prime Minister Mario Monti announcing his candidacy for the 2013 elections. The campaign went on with few notable events mostly related to the largest centre-left party Partito Democratico (Labels 2–3–5 on Figure 31.3). While we will discuss most of the these data in the following paragraphs, it is interesting to point out the peak of Twitter data about 'Fare per fermare il decline', a minor centre-right party that are visible few days before the elections. These peaks are due to a huge scandal that involved Fare's candidate— the economic journalist Oscar Giannino—being found guilty of having falsified his résumé by adding fake academic titles.

Facebook data (see Figure 31.2) show a very different scenario. Throughout the studied period, the data suggest clear trends of growth and decline. The Five Star Movement (M5S) shows a continuous dominance in terms of People Talking About that became extreme after January 23, exactly one month before election day. In comparison to Twitter, Facebook trends do not seem related to any specific event that takes place during the campaign. It is worth noticing that while most parties had an electoral campaign organised through a plurality of communication channels (TV presence, public debates, blogs, and social media) the M5S decided to not appear on TV. This sort of mass media-absence of the M5S was accompanied by an extremely active campaign on the ground with meetings and rallies in a number of Italian cities. This media strategy proved to be effective since mass media had to report about these offline political activities anyway, and since these offline meetings and rallies were the source of a large number of videos diffused online through Facebook and YouTube. As of this writing, it is possible to find about 351,000 videos on YouTube regarding the 2013 Beppe Grillo election tour.

Comparing Twitter and Facebook trends and assuming a media-specificity perspective—as stated before—one can observe that if Facebook shows how parties might be able to engage in public debates—with different rates of success—with clearly identifiable growth towards the end of the campaign, Twitter seems to produce bursts of communication exhausted in one or few days. A possible interpretation of this behaviour is that, in our data, Twitter political communication is mainly driven by political debate taking place on Television or by other media-based events (Larsson & Moe 2012; 2013; Lietz et al. 2014).

More precisely, Twitter activity seems to be clearly dependent on what is broadcast through mainstream media. Indeed, during political campaigns such channels offer a large amount of opportunities for engaging as an active audience with electoral content (Highfield et al. 2013). This claim can be easily supported by observing how Figure 31.3 maps every single major peak of Twitter activity with highly recurrent presence of politicians on TV talk shows. With this in mind, large and strategic media presence seems to be behind the comparably large Twitter success of Pierluigi Bersani (leader of Partito Democratico) as well as that of the former Prime Minister Mario Monti. Every peak registered in Twitter data corresponds to a concurrent mass media presence of one of the two leaders. At the same time, it is interesting to notice how the Five Star Movement yielded no significant peaks during the whole campaign—except for two moments close to the election days. As previously suggested, while the official media strategy of M5S was to avoid any kind of mass media presence (no talk shows, no interviews, etc.) towards the end of the campaign Beppe Grillo announced an interview with SkyTG24-news channel of Sky Corp.— but he then decided to cancel the interview after a few days (Label 4 on Figure 31.3). Thus, even if M5S never participated on any TV political debate or talk show, the observable Twitter peaks can still be connected to announced and later cancelled mass media appearances.

While TV doesn't tweet or define how much users should tweet, it seems evident that the broadcasted content provides opportunities and topical resources for Twitter conversation. Some researchers have claimed that Twitter could be understood as an additional communication environment to traditional media in which politicians strengthen their already existing relations with the voters (Bentivegna & Marchetti 2014). Nevertheless the synchronous dynamics that have been pointed out between TV presence and Twitter conversation suggest not only that Twitter agenda is somehow influenced by TV programming but also that politicians have very limited control over digital conversation regarding it. Such a strict dependence of Twitter conversations on TV contents seems to offer an additional perspective to the general assumption that social media challenge traditional intermediation between voters and politicians. While, nowadays, there is undoubtedly space for direct communication between candidates and potential voters and for spontaneous debate emerging with no involvement of traditional mass media, there are also opportunities for autonomous political debates arising from more traditional media products.

Conclusions and Discussion

This chapter has analysed the 2013 Italian election from a social media viewpoint, trying to relate the uses of such services to a more general perspective. First, when social media communications are observed as part of a larger social dynamic, they should be framed within a specific sociocultural context defined by the diffusion of social media and by the actual (observable) social practices. Thus, while social media undoubtedly played a central role in 2013 Italian election, this should be framed within a countrywide context where weekly Internet use is just at 62,1 per cent of population and where social media use is still limited. At the same time, social media should not be perceived as a unique undistinguished environment but rather as a set of platforms and specific techno-social contexts that can be more or less favourable to specific parties, coalitions or other kind of political groups. Finally, we have shown how different social media—Facebook and Twitter in our case—have been used in a different ways, as Twitter showed a more firm relation with television (being used largely as a second-screen tool) while Facebook didn't show this kind of coupling.

At the same time the use of social media to explore political dynamics requires framing of empirical analysis within a larger context of contemporary political systems as has been described by political science. It is therefore necessary to study how social media enable and support deeper changes in the political system and, vice-versa, how social media are affected by these. On a political level the contemporary crisis of political legitimation, as well as the lack of representativity of traditional parties, led to the emergence of new types of political actors (Parkinson 2003; Duso 2003; Barbera 2008) characterised by three major elements: *individualisation, mediatisation and spectacularisation.*

Individualisation: We observe a shift from traditional parties toward 'personal parties' heavily focused on single leaders. In 2013 Italian election we saw three main examples of this, from Silvio Berlusconi's Popolo della LIbertà (PDL), to the Movimento 5 Stelle (M5S) centred on the former comedian Beppe Grillo, and Scelta Civica (SC) led by Mario Monti.

Mediatisation: Political communication is more and more defined by specific media strategies. According to Castells (2000), networked media politics needs to convey simple messages designed according to the preferred social media platform. Within this perspective the large adoption of political-Twitter hashtag made by the Partito Democratico (PD)—#pb2013 (which stands for PierluigiBersani2013),#ItaliaGiusta"(Fair Italy), or #propostashock (shocking proposal)—represent an effective ways to engage within a specific social media platform. In a similar way the large amount of video material and clips produced during M5S's offline campaign proved to fit perfectly into the sharing practices of Facebook and YouTube.

Spectacularisation: Parties' communication strategies will be more and more 'candidate-centred' (Wattenberg 1991) in order to catch media and public attention—as well as votes. These strategies are especially based on the power of an individual politician to set the political and media agenda through the public exposure of specific aspects coming from his or her private (or intimate) life (Helms 2005; Mazzoleni & Sfardini 2009). The greatest example of this in Italian politics has been traditionally Silvio Berlusconi but during the election described in this paper we note that a large part of Beppe Grillo's campaign was based on his personal experiences and on being an outsider in the political arena and therefore different from the rest of the politicians.

While political scientists have largely analysed these characteristics, individualisation, mediatisation and spectacularisation have rarely been taken into consideration when it comes to research from the perspective of media and communication. In contrast, these should be included as necessary background for social media analyses around civic or political phenomena. By doing so we would be forced to frame political usage of social media within a larger perspective that makes no clear separation between social and mass media. It seems difficult to argue for such a separation when, as we have observed in our data, social media appear to be coupled on so many levels with traditional mass media.

A more fruitful approach would be to consider political elections—and political communication in general—existing within what Andrew Chadwick calls a 'hybrid media system'. In particular, he defines the relationship between politics, media and connected audiences as

> the system built upon interactions among older and newer media logics—where logics are defined as technologies, genres, norms, behaviors and organizational forms—in the reflexively interconnected fields of media and politics. Actors in this system are articulated by complex and ever-evolving relationships based upon adaptation and interdependence and simultaneous concentrations and diffusions of power. (Chadwick 2013: 4)

While data show clear evidences of such hybrid system, whether this can be studied from a methodological point of view is still an open question. Nevertheless, we claim that in order to be fruitful, any future analysis of political use of social media should be rooted within a similar theoretical perspective and we are suggesting that the simultaneous analysis of multiple media data (both social media and mass media) could provide the proper methodological approach.

References

Anduiza, E., Cantijoch, M., & Gallego, A. (2009) Political participation and the Internet: A field essay. *Information, Communication & Society, 12*(6), 860–878.

Barbera, A. (2008) La rappresentanza politica: un mito in declino. *Quaderni costituzionali, 4.*

Bentivegna, A. (2014) *La politica in 140 caratteri, Twitter e spazio pubblico.* Milan: Franco Angeli editore. Codice ISBN: 9788891705044.

Bentivegna, A., Marchetti, R. (2014) Prove tecniche di ibridazione mediale. Guardare la Tv e commentare su Twitter. *Comunicazione politica,* 1/2014, 61–78. doi: 10.3270/76588.

Blogmeter (2013) Report on online activity of the most popular candidates for 2013 general election. Full report available at: http://vincos.it/2013/02/25/elezioni-2013-analisi-di-23-milioni-di-conversazioni-e-interazioni-online/.

Boccia Artieri, G. (2013) Un tweet non fa l'elettore. In I. Diamanti, *Un salto nel voto–ritratto politico dell'italia di oggi,* Rome: Editori Laterza, 167–182.

Bruns, A., & Burgess, J.E. (2011) *The use of Twitter hashtags in the formation of ad hoc publics.* In Proceedings of the 6th European Consortium for Political Research (ECPR) General Conference 2011, University of Iceland, Reykjavik.

Bruns, A., & Burgess, J. (2012) Researching news discussion on Twitter: New methodologies. *Journalism Studies, 13*(5–6), 801–814.

Bruns, A., & Moe, H. (2013) Structural layers of communication on Twitter. *Twitter and Society, 89,* 15–28.

Caldarelli, G., Chessa, A., Pammolli, F., Pompa, G., Puliga, M., Riccaboni, M., & Riotta, G. (2014) A multi-level geographical study of Italian political elections from Twitter Data. *PloS ONE, 9*(5), e95809.

Carlisle, J.E., & Patton, R.C. (2013) Is social media changing how we understand political engagement? An analysis of Facebook and the 2008 presidential election. *Political Research Quarterly, 66*(4), 883–895.

Castells, M. (2000) Materials for an exploratory theory of the network society. *The British Journal of Sociology, 51*(1), 5–24.

Castells, M. (2013) *Networks of outrage and hope: Social movements in the Internet Age.* New York: John Wiley & Sons.

Censis (2013) *47th Annual Report on Social Statement of Italy.* Full report available at: http://www.censis.it/10?shadow_ricerca=120989.

Ceron, A., Curini, L., Iacus, S. M., & Porro, G. (2014) Every tweet counts? How sentiment analysis of social media can improve our knowledge of citizens' political preferences with an application to Italy and France. *New Media & Society, 16*(2), 340–358.

Chadwick, A. (2011) The political information cycle in a hybrid news system: The British prime minister and the "bullygate" affair. *The International Journal of Press/Politics, 16*(1), 3–29.

Chadwick, A. (2013) *The hybrid media system: Politics and power.* Oxford: Oxford University Press.

Demos & PI (2013), *Ecco i Cives.Net, la Community Politica. Research focus belonging to 2013 Edition of the Observatory on Social Capital.* Full report available at: http://www.demos.it/a00798.php.

Duso, G. (2003) *La rappresentanza politica: genesi e crisi del concetto* (Vol. 12). Milan: Franco Angeli.

Gaffney, D., & Puschmann, C. (2013) "Data collection on Twitter," *Twitter and Society.* New York, NY: Peter Lang.

Gayo-Avello, D., Metaxas, P.T., & Mustafaraj, E. (2011) Limits of electoral predictions using Twitter., In *Proceedings of the Fifth ICWSM* (pp. 490–493). Palo Alto, CA: AAAI Press.

Giglietto, F., Rossi, L., & Bennato, D. (2012) "The Open Laboratory: Limits and Possibilities of Using Facebook, Twitter, and YouTube as a Research Data Source," *Journal of Technology in Human Services, 30*(3–4), 145–159.

Gilbert, E., Bergstrom, T., & Karahalios, K. (2009) Blogs are echo chambers: Blogs are echo chambers. In *System Sciences, 2009. HICSS'09. 42nd Hawaii International Conference on* (pp. 1–10). Picataway, NJ: IEEE.

Helms, L. (2005) The presidentialisation of political leadership: British notions and German observations. *The Political Quarterly, 76*(3), 430–438.

Highfield, T., Harrington, S., & Bruns, A. (2013) Twitter as a technology for audiencing and fandom. *Information Communication Society,* 1–25. doi:10.1080/1369118X.2012.756053.

Johnson, T.J., & Perlmutter, D.D. (2010) Introduction: the Facebook election. *Mass Communication and Society, 13*(5), 554–559.

Jungherr, A., Jürgens, P., & Schoen, H. (2012) "Why the pirate party won the German election of 2009 or the trouble with predictions," *Social Science Computer Review,* Vol. 30, no.2, pp. 229–234, doi:10.1177/0894439311404119.

Kushin, M.J., & Yamamoto, M. (2010) Did social media really matter? College students' use of online media and political decision making in the 2008 election. *Mass Communication and Society, 13*(5), 608–630.

Larsson, A.O. (2013) Tweeting the Viewer—Use of Twitter in a Talk Show Context. *Journal of Broadcasting & Electronic Media, 57*(2), 135–152.

Larsson, A.O. (2014) Everyday elites, citizens, or extremists? Assessing the use and users of non-election political hashtags. *MedieKultur. Journal of Media and Communication Research, 30*(56), 61–78.

Larsson, A.O., & Moe, H. (2012) Studying political microblogging: Twitter users in the 2010 Swedish election campaign. *New Media & Society, 14*(5), 729–747.

Lietz, H., Wagner, C., Bleier, A., & Strohmaier, M. (2014, May) *When politicians talk: Assessing online conversational practices of political parties on Twitter.* International AAAI Conference on Weblogs and Social Media (ICWSM2014), Ann Arbor, MI, USA.

Lotan, G., Graeff, E., Ananny, M., Gaffney, D., & Pearce, I. (2011) The Arab Spring | the revolutions were tweeted: Information flows during the 2011 Tunisian and Egyptian revolutions. *International Journal of Communication, 5,* 31.

Marwick, A.E. (2011) I tweet honestly, I tweet passionately: Twitter users, context collapse, and the imagined audience. *New Media & Society, 13*(1), 114–133.

Mazzoleni, G., & Sfardini, A. (2009) *Politica pop. Da'Porta a porta'a'L'isola dei famosi.* Bologna: Il Mulino.

Metaxas, P.T., Mustafaraj, E., & Gayo-Avello, D. (2011) How (not) to predict elections. *Privacy, security, risk and trust (PASSAT), 2011 IEEE third international conference on and 2011*

IEEE third international conference on social computing (SocialCom) (pp. 165–171). Picataway, NJ: IEEE.

Metaxas, P. T., & Mustafaraj, E. (2012) Social media and the elections. *Science*, 338(6106), 472–473.

Ministry of the Interior, Ufficio IV–Servizi Informatici Elettorali (2015). "Eligendo, il portale delle elezioni." Available at: http://elezioni.interno.it/.

Morcellini, M. (2013) Una campagna eccezionale. La politica vecchia e nuova alla prova della battaglia elettorale. *Federalismi.it*, 3.

Mori, L. (2011) Partiti, leadership e consenso agli albori del social networking (2005–2010): il caso italiana. *SocietàMutamentoPolitica*, 2(3), 183–197.

Morstatter, F., Pfeffer, J., Liu, H., & Carley, K. M. (2013) Is the sample good enough? Comparing data from Twitter's streaming API with Twitter's firehose. *ICWSM 2013*, 400–408.

Parkinson, J. (2003) Legitimacy problems in deliberative democracy. *Political studies*, 51(1), 180–196.

Pira, F. (2012) *La net comunicazione politica. Partiti, movimenti e cittadini-elettori nell'era dei social network* (Vol. 17). Milan: Franco Angeli.

Sang, E.T.K., & Bos, J. (2011) "Predicting the 2011 Dutch senate election results with Twitter," *Proceedings of the Workshop on Semantic Analysis in Social Media* (pp. 53–60), Association for Computational Linguistics.

Sloan, L., Morgan, J., Burnap, P., & Williams, M. (2015) "Who tweets? Deriving the demographic characteristics of age, occupation and social class from Twitter user meta-data. *PLoS ONE*, 10(3).

Tumasjan, A., Sprenger, T. O., Sandner, P. G., & Welpe, I. M. (2010) Predicting Elections with Twitter: What 140 Characters Reveal about Political Sentiment. *ICWSM 2010*, 178–185.

Vaccari, C., & Valeriani, A. (2013) Follow the leader! Direct and indirect flows of political communication during the 2013 general election campaign. *New Media & Society*. doi:10.177/1461444813511038.

Valeriani, A. (2011) Bridges of the Revolution Linking People, Sharing Information, and Remixing Practices. *Sociologica*, 5(3), 1–27.

Vergeer, M., & Hermans, L. (2013) "Campaigning on Twitter: Microblogging and online social networking as campaign tools in the 2010 general elections in the Netherlands. *Journal of Computer Mediated Communication*, 18(4), 399–419.

Vitak, J., Zube, P., Smock, A., Carr, C. T., Ellison, N., & Lampe, C. (2011) It's complicated: Facebook users' political participation in the 2008 election. *CyberPsychology, Behavior, and Social Networking*, 14(3), 107–114.

Wattenberg, M. P. (1991) *The rise of candidate-centered politics: Presidential elections of the 1980s*. Cambridge, MA: Harvard University Press.

Woolley, J. K., Limperos, A.M., & Oliver, M. B. (2010) The 2008 presidential election, 2.0: A content analysis of user-generated political Facebook groups. *Mass Communication and Society*, 13(5), 631–652.

Yardi, S., & boyd, d. (2010) Dynamic debates: an analysis of group polarization over time on Twitter. *Bulletin of Science, Technology & Society*, 30(5), 316–327.

32

SOCIAL MEDIA AND ELECTION CAMPAIGNS IN SUB-SAHARAN AFRICA

Insights from Cameroon

Teke Ngomba

Introduction

Within the last four years, election campaigns in some African countries such as Nigeria (2011), Ghana (2012), Kenya (2013), and South Africa (2014) have been followed by extensive commentaries on the appropriation of social media by politicians in these countries (Ogunlesi 2013; Mutiga 2013; Ndlela, Chapter 33 in this volume). On the surface, these regularly cited, high-profile instances of social media use by politicians in these countries give the impression that all the continent's politicians are hopping onto social media platforms in massive numbers.

The reality, however, is more nuanced both within and between countries. This point is illustrated by an article in the influential pan-African magazine *Jeune Afrique* titled, 'Twitter: Why are Francophone African leaders this lousy?' arguing that some politicians in French-speaking countries in sub-Saharan Africa (SSA)—compared to their English-speaking counterparts—are even 'allergic' to social media (Olivier 2013). This argument is in line with the Cameroonian experience thus far with regards to politicians' use of social media (especially in the context of election campaigns).

This chapter examines this phenomenon by going beyond the 'usual suspects' of Kenya, Nigeria and South Africa when it comes to studying issues concerning the political appropriation of the Internet or social media in SSA. It discusses how Cameroonian politicians have used social media during recent election campaigns. Drawing on mainstream newspaper coverage of recent election campaigns in Cameroon and an analysis of how three candidates used Facebook during the 2013 legislative and municipal elections, this chapter demonstrates and explains the tepid adoption of social media by Cameroonian politicians thus far, and reflects on what the Cameroonian experience suggests in relation to scholarly efforts to understand the relationship between developments in the media sector and changes in campaign communication.

While there is a significant volume of research on politicians' use of social media in American and European contexts (e.g. Gibson et al 2014; Jungherr 2014), we know little about the use of social media in politics on a global level. The existing research is thus far from representative, and, SSA is one region with wide gaps in our understanding of the uses and impacts of social media during election campaigns. The research gap is explained by lack of studies mainly due to the novelty of the phenomenon. Furthermore, even in countries with access to social media, it is terribly difficult to obtain updated, reliable, and verifiable statistics (see Balancing Act 2014: 46–48).

In the case of Cameroon, the lack of research is particularly eye catching, and has been commented on by van Reijswoud (2014: 32), who underlines that, "the use of social media and other Web 2.0 tools in general and for socio-political [activities] in particular, has not been systematically researched" and that there is indeed, "hardly" any data available. This means that unlike how things operate in Europe or North America, in Cameroon, as in most of SSA, there is currently more journalistic and other public commentary on social media and elections than theoretically informed and methodologically rigorous peer-reviewed academic research.

These commentaries (and the few pieces of academic research) have shown that with an increasing number of Africans—especially youth—gaining access to the Internet thanks in large part to mobile Internet connectivity, popular social media sites like Facebook, LinkedIn, YouTube and Twitter have risen to be among the most visited sites in several countries (Balancing Act 2014: 8). Taking note of this, politicians have in recent elections across SSA used social media as part of their campaign communication strategies.

The few instances of significant uses of social media in recent election campaigns across SSA have shown that scope and technical sophistication aside, in terms of overall patterns, African politicians have been using social media more or less like their counterparts in Europe and North America. Their social media platforms have, for instance, been used mainly to disseminate information rather than to engage in dialogue with ordinary citizens (see Steenkamp and Hyde-Clarke 2014).

Overall, the general picture emerging is that, on average—and beyond a few high-profile exceptions like Guillaume Soro (President of the National Assembly in Côte d'Ivoire), President Uhuru Kenyatta of Kenya, and President Paul Kagame of Rwanda—the use of social media by politicians in SSA is still tepid. Earlier observations of the Cameroonian scene have also confirmed the presence of these central patterns: a generalised low use of social media by politicians; in case of use, a preference for 'broadcasting' information rather than engaging in interactions with ordinary citizens; and last, the tendency for social media profiles to be abandoned shortly after elections (Tande 2011; Langmia 2013; van Reijswoud 2014).

Given the paucity of empirical research on politicians' uses of social media during election campaigns in Cameroon, and in a bid to extend understanding of this phenomenon, this chapter examines how three candidates used Facebook during the 2013 legislative and municipal elections in Cameroon.

Cameroon: Key Background Information

Following the reintroduction of multiparty politics in 1990, Cameroon, with a population of about 22.5 million, has been experiencing significant political, socioeconomic and technological changes. Prominent among these has been the liberalisation of the media landscape. As a result, Cameroon now has a burgeoning media system characterised by an interesting mix of forcefully emerging modern media of communication and persistent forms of indigenous communication. One of these modern means of communication—the Internet—was introduced in Cameroon in the late 1990s. In October 2014, the Ministry of Post and Telecommunications indicated that about 6.5 per cent of Cameroonians had access to the Internet and an estimated 15.2 million Cameroonians were mobile phone subscribers. While this Internet penetration rate is modest, the fact that more and more ordinary Cameroonians are gradually gaining access to the Internet through their mobile phones has spurred some media and political attention on the political affordances of the Internet (van Reijswoud 2014).

These discussions took a major turn in 2011 when one of the 23 presidential candidates, Kah Walla, gained significant media attention following her strategic appropriation of online campaigning, notably through a splashy website, YouTube channel, and Facebook page. These strategies led Kah Walla to become the first Cameroonian politician to demonstrate a focused and proactive appropriation of social media during election campaigns (Tande 2011; Ngomba 2014). At that time, however, it was estimated that less than 500,000 Cameroonians were using Facebook. With an understanding that the number of Cameroonians using different social media will increase after the 2011 presidential elections, many observers expected the next general elections in Cameroon to feature a significant use of social media, especially after the 'Kah Walla phenomenon'.

Current statistics on actual use of social media in Cameroon are hard to come by, but recent estimates indicate that Facebook, Twitter, and LinkedIn are the most popular social media platforms in Cameroon (van Reijswoud 2014). By the legislative and municipal elections on 30 September 2013, it was estimated that there were about 760,000 Facebook users in Cameroon (van Reijswoud 2014: 12). As concerns Twitter, the 2012 study *How Africa Tweets*, which analysed geo-located Twitter traffic for three months, recorded 30,444 tweets from Cameroon. This pales in significance to the 'output' from other countries such as South Africa (5,030,226), Kenya (2,476,800), and Nigeria (1,646,212; Portland Communications 2012: 5). While these data are not conclusive about the actual number of active Twitter users in Cameroon, they nonetheless suggest that there may now be several hundreds of thousands of active Twitter users.

It is against this background of a modest but perceptible increase in access to the Internet and social media, and an anticipation of more political uses of social media, that the most recent legislative and municipal elections took place in September 2013. These elections therefore provide a good opportunity to examine Cameroonian politicians' use—or non-use—of social media in the context of election campaigns. Such analyses also offer the opportunity to see if, in the context of a changing media ecology, there have been corresponding major changes as far as the central practices of campaigns in Cameroon are concerned. Since the official reintroduction of multiparty politics in Cameroon in 1990, two central practices have characterised the conduct of election campaigns in the country: the widespread distribution of money and other material goods to the electorate and the prioritisation of door-to-door campaign strategies over media-based initiatives (see Ngomba 2012).

These campaign practices and the existing analyses have thus far taken place prior to the spread of social media across Cameroon. The increasing use of social media platforms by Cameroonians especially within the last two to three years, therefore, leaves room to question whether recent campaign practices are different from those of the past, especially given the possibility to directly target potential voters through social media. Briefly, how have Cameroonian politicians used social media during recent election campaigns? Overall, is there any significant change in campaign practices in Cameroon in the context of the spread of social media amongst the electorate? These are the core issues addressed in this chapter through the examination of how three politicians used social media in the 2013 legislative and municipal elections.

Data and Methods

On 30 September 2013, thousands of candidates took part in the legislative and municipal elections in Cameroon, which are party and list based.[1] Twenty-nine political parties representing 212 lists competed for 180 seats in the National Assembly; and 35 political parties, representing 751 lists, competed for the control of Cameroon's 360 councils. For both elections, candidates are elected through a mixed single round ballot comprising a majority and proportional representation system. So the way the system is designed, individual candidates (and thus personal attributes of candidates) are important during campaigns but only under the banner of political parties, since they have to campaign for a party list. This means that that in many cases candidates simultaneously adopt both a personalised and party-based campaign strategy.

The main selection criterion for this study has been mentions of a candidate's campaign activities online and on social media in selected news reports. I used this approach because I assumed that, as they have done in past elections, newspapers will regularly report on parties' and candidates' campaign communication strategies. This information about different campaign communication strategies will then help to situate the discussions of the use or non-use of social media within a broader perspective of communicative ecologies present during campaigns. Briefly, by looking at all relevant news reports about candidates' campaign communication strategies, it will be possible to get a good idea of which kinds of communication strategies are common and prioritised and which are absent, thus side-lined in the context of mediated and non-mediated communication possibilities. Furthermore, based on past research (Ngomba 2012), I assumed that most candidates may not use social media, and that any candidate effectively using social media will most likely feature in media reports since this will be newsworthy given the novelty this will represent in the Cameroonian context (Ngomba 2014).

Based on the above, I chose five of the six dailies in Cameroon (the state-owned bilingual newspaper *Cameroon Tribune* and the private dailies *Le Messager*; *Le Jour*; *La Nouvelle Expression* and *Mutations*—all published in French) and one bi-weekly (*The Post*, the main English language newspaper in Cameroon). The timeframe selected was the coverage of the campaigns during the official two weeks of the campaigns plus one day after the elections (15 September 2013 to 1 October 2013). Unfortunately, as indicated in Table 32.1, a few issues of the selected newspapers could not be obtained in time before this analysis, but, this notwithstanding, the issues available are substantial enough to give a representative view of the mainstream print media coverage of the election campaigns.

For the issues obtained, all reports focusing on the elections were read and divided into the following sections: news and features, interviews, opinion pieces (this includes things like editorials or commentaries by journalists or external contributors), and documents (this includes things like ministerial orders, campaign manifestos or press releases). Table 32.1 gives an overview of the number of reports published for each category, per newspaper, excluding the issues of the newspapers that could not be obtained.

Table 32.1 List of Newspapers and Reports

Newspaper	News and Features	Interviews	Opinion Pieces	Documents	Total
Cameroon Tribune	295	61	29	17	402
Le Messager*	78	13	5	3	99
Le Jour**	87	3	19	3	112
La Nouvelle Expression***	110	7	3	3	123
Mutations	124	17	14	3	158
The Post****	55	2	7	0	64
Total	**749**	**103**	**77**	**29**	**958**

*Excluding the issues of 16 September, 17 September, and 1 October.
**Excluding the issue of 16 September.
***Excluding the issue of 1 October.
****Excluding the issue of 16 September.

All of the 958 reports were read and coded with a particular focus on the campaign communication strategies mentioned in the report. On the basis of these, all the reports mentioning social media were read thoroughly to sort out any candidate identified as having a focused online campaign strategy. As it turned out, very few mentions were made of social media in these reports. Just eight reports mentioned social media: one from *Le Jour* (27 September p. 5); one from *Le Messager* (27 September p. 7); two from *La Nouvelle Expression* (26 September p. 4). and four from *Cameroon Tribune* (18 September p. 4; 24 September p. 11; and 26 September p. 11).

Of these reports, just two focused on social media use in the campaigns. These include a feature report and an interview published by *La Nouvelle Expression* of 26 September 2013. Actually, the angle of the feature report was on the fact that candidates for the elections were *not* making much use of social media; and, a similar angle was used in the interview with the president of the union of online journalists in Cameroon: why politicians are not making much use of social media.

Just two candidates were specifically mentioned as having a focused online campaign strategy: Albert Dooh-Collins of the ruling Cameroon People's Democratic Movement (*Cameroon Tribune* of 26 September and *Le Jour* of 27 September) and Joshua Osih of the main opposition party, the Social Democratic Front (*Cameroon Tribune* of 26 September). Both were candidates for the legislative elections in Douala, Cameroon's economic and media capital. Although other candidates such as Olivier Bile of the Union for Fraternity and Prosperity and Ayah Paul of the People's Action Party were mentioned as being 'regularly present on Facebook' (*La Nouvelle Expression* of 26 September), an examination of Ayah Paul's Facebook page, for instance, shows that during the entire official two week campaign period, only one post was made on his page: the party's manifesto posted on 15 September 2013. His Twitter page as of 10 November 2014 had just 55 followers and four tweets—the first sent on 8 December 2010 and the last on 14 December 2010. So, he had used it for just one week, four years ago.

In addition to selecting Joshua Osih and Dooh-Collins, I added one other opposition candidate, Kah Walla of the Cameroon People's Party, even though she was not singled out as having a social media strategy in these reports. I added her because in 2011, as mentioned earlier, she was prominent as one of the candidates for the presidential elections, thanks in a large part to her pioneering use of social media. Since she was a candidate for the municipal elections in 2013 (also in Douala) it seemed interesting to examine if and how she used social media.

Only the Facebook pages of these candidates have been examined principally because, from all available estimates, Facebook is the most popular social media platform in Cameroon. Furthermore, the three candidates did not really use Twitter. While Joshua Osih has a relatively active Twitter profile, updated during the 2013 election campaigns, a comparison of his Facebook profile with his Twitter profile shows that both contained very much the same material within the campaign period. Dooh-Collins does not have a Twitter account and the four Twitter profiles associated with Kah Walla all date back to her 2011 presidential campaign and the only one with tweets (@kahwallaamis) was last updated on 18 August 2011—about two months before the presidential election.

Since all three candidates used Facebook, their profiles were checked and all the postings published from 1 to 29 September 2013 were collected and analysed. This covers the two weeks before the official campaigns and the two weeks of the official campaigns (15–29 September). In particular, the goal was to analyse what characterised the postings, including the mode and level of interactivity in these online platforms as seen through the numbers of Likes, Comments, and Shares. As Gerodimos and Justinussen (2014) pointed out, there is currently 'little empirical work on engagement through social media' especially on how people are using 'social buttons' such as 'Like' as 'metrics of civic engagement.' By looking at such engagements on these candidates' pages, it is hoped that a further empirical angle from SSA can be added to preliminary examinations of such forms of online engagements. The postings were categorised under the following headings:

- Campaign manifesto/slogan/poster.
- Announcements about upcoming campaign activities or events (e.g. holding of rallies, media appearances).
- Reports on campaign activities (these include pictures, videos or texts about past campaign activities).
- Campaign rhetoric (this includes brief commentaries about the candidate; his or her policies; or about other competing candidates or parties and their policies).
- Internal media linkage (this includes a link or information about another party or candidate-controlled site containing information about the candidate or his or her party).
- External media linkage (this includes a link or information about the candidate or his or her party published elsewhere).
- Others (any other posting which does not fit any of the categories above).

In addition, the number of Likes, Comments, and Shares for each posting was recorded and an average obtained. A more focused analysis of the most Liked, Shared, and Commented postings as well as the candidates' commenting patterns is presented below.

Findings

The three candidates used Facebook, but they joined the social network at different times; Kah Walla's Facebook profile[2] was created on 19 July 2011, about three months before she took part in the 2011 presidential elections. Joshua Osih's profile[3] was established on 5 September 2013, which is 10 days before the official start of campaigns for the Legislative and Municipal elections. As for Dooh-Collins, he established his Facebook profile[4] on 21 September 2013, about one week *after* the commencement of the election campaigns, and barely eight days before its end.

While Kah Walla's and Joshua Osih's cases align with the tendency for politicians in Africa to gain an online presence only shortly before elections, Dooh-Collins's case suggests that the decision to use Facebook came as an afterthought. This may also explain what has happened after the elections: as of 10 November 2014, their respective Facebook pages show that Joshua Osih last posted on his Facebook page on 5 November 2014, Kah Walla on 7 November 2014, and Dooh-Collins on 7 October 2013—more than a year ago (and just after the elections).

With regards to the number of posts and the level of interaction exhibited, as seen in Table 32.2, Joshua Osih had the most active presence on Facebook and also garnered more interactions (with an average of two posts per day) during the period studied. He similarly outperforms the other candidates with each of his posts garnering on average about 28 Likes; 13 Comments, and was Shared about three times.

'Liking' emerges as the most popular form of online interaction on these candidates' Facebook profiles eclipsing 'more active' modes of participation like commenting and sharing information with others. For some, this pattern may be a pointer towards a manifestation of one of the travails of digital political participation as encompassed in the notion of 'slacktivism' (Morozov, 2011). While this can be an important pointer, as others have shown, 'Likes' are actually important when perceived as affective endorsements of a politician and his or her assertions or actions (Gerodimos and Justinussen 2014).

Since the focus was on counting the number of Likes, Comments and Shares for each post, it is hard to make a definite assessment on who were those taking part in these forms of interactions: whether for instance, the same people 'Liking' were also those Commenting and Sharing. Also, this approach makes it difficult to assess whether only a few people dominated the discussions through several comments. In scanning through all the comments to see if there was any trace of this for instance, it emerged that only in Kah Walla's profile was there a clear case of this. All seven comments on her post of 17 September 2013, for instance, were from one individual. But this is an

Table 32.2 Overview of Facebook Posts and Interactions

Candidate	Total Posts	Total Likes	Total Comments	Total Shares	Comments by Candidates
Joshua Osih	54	1,477	691	166	45
Kah Walla	11	154	35	15	2
Dooh-Collins	8	85	18	5	3

exception which underscores the need for caution in drawing conclusions from quantitative overviews of Comments or Likes per post.

What is possible to ascertain, however, is the kinds of comments made by the candidates themselves beyond the posts on their walls. The dominant types of comments from the candidates are messages to express gratitude to commenters for their support, and an exhortation for them to vote for the candidate on election day. All of Dooh-Collins's messages are in these category, as is one of the two comments from Kah Walla (the other is a response to a commenter who wanted to know why her party was not represented nationally). For Joshua Osih, who is far more active, the dominant types of comments are: 'thank you' messages, exhortations to vote and assuring commenters that there will be less rigging during the elections. In fact, more than half of Osih's comments fall into this third category (25 out of 45). He nonetheless gets into a discussion with other commenters on a range of issues including the situation of health care in Cameroon, the place of youths in the SDF party and how best to curb corruption. These latter discussions are more in tune with regularly expressed desires for more deliberative democratic interactivity between politicians and citizens in online spaces.

But, these few instances notwithstanding, there is an overwhelming tendency for the candidates to engage in *courtesy* rather than *deliberative* engagements with commenters. The preference for this form of engagement resonates with the overall nature of the posts from candidates during the period under study. As shown in Table 32.3, the candidates also adopted a 'broadcast' style with regards to the utilisation of Facebook: a tactic we have seen in previous studies from other regions of the world (see Gerodimos and Justinussen 2014). The candidates' posts consisted mostly of information about their manifestos, announcements about campaign-related events and reports about campaign activities (often using pictures rather than texts).

As seen in Table 32.3, Joshua Osih had the most diversified posts covering all the different categories. Furthermore, unlike Dooh-Collins and Kah Walla, Joshua Osih's posts had a 'personal touch' to them via his use of campaign rhetoric and 'personalisation' of

Table 32.3 Types of Posts

Category	Dooh-Collins	Kah Walla	Joshua Osih
Campaign manifesto, slogan, or poster	3	2	5
Announcement about campaign activities	3	–	14
Reports on campaign activities	1	9	22
Campaign rhetoric	–	–	5
Internal media linkage	1	–	4
External media linkage	–	–	2
Others	–	–	2
Total Posts	**8**	**11**	**54**

announcements about campaign activities. On the former, for instance, on 22 September 2013, he posted this Facebook update:

> The minimum wage in Cameroon is about 28,300 frs, the lowest in the continent. But in neighboring Chad—which was receiving food aid from us few years back, the minimum wage is 85 thousand. My dear brothers, it is time for these miseries to end in Cameroon. (Joshua Osih, 22 September 2013)

None of the other candidates used such personal rhetorical strategies. While the available data are indeed minimal to make any firm conclusions, it is clear from Joshua Osih's postings, both in terms of scale and content, that he personally managed his Facebook profile, took his engagement on Facebook seriously, and perhaps understood more than his counterparts the informal nature of communication on Facebook. These latter points are seen, for instance, in the way he tended to combine announcements about campaign activities and invitations to these. On 22 September 2013 for instance, he wrote that

> we are waiting for many of you, my very dear ones: Dear Friends, we have a rally this evening at 8 pm at the Douala polytechnique entrance, part in Bessengue. We are waiting for many of you. (Joshua Osih, 22 September 2013)

Given that Facebook is a 'personal medium', suitable for personalised communication, it is fairly remarkable that none of the candidates significantly personalised their posts. Rather, they posted impersonally and focused on 'official business', such as campaign reports, announcements, policies, and so on. No candidate for instance, posted personal pictures showing them doing domestic chores, or spending time with their families—things for which Facebook is known and, as previous research has shown, politicians like Barack Obama have appropriated strategically (see Gerodimos and Justinussen, 2014). Further research on this, combined with interviews with the politicians, will be useful to throw more light on the prevalence and rationale of this strategy because while this may suggest a desire to construct a public image of seriousness, it may be a shortcoming as politicians fail to make a more 'personal connection' with potential voters—a move which, as will be indicated below, is vital for electoral success.

On the topic of 'personal touch' and engagement, one of the central issues regarding online political interactivity concerns attempts to understand what kinds of content citizens either engage with or ignore on politicians' social media profiles. Given the exploratory nature of this study, I looked at the most Liked, Shared, and Commented posts of the candidates to see if this can suggest anything provisionally. Given that he had more diverse posts, the case of Joshua Osih may be more instructive in orienting us towards what kinds of contents citizens are prone to engage with on politicians' social media pages. As seen below, the most Liked, Shared and Commented post from Osih are all campaign rhetoric, suggesting that posts with a more personal voice of the candidate can generate more engagement. As indicated earlier, content coded under 'campaign rhetoric' include brief commentaries about the candidate, his or her policies, or about other competing candidates or parties and their policies.

Most Liked Post: A statement saying if elected, he will propose a law to oblige all civil servants to be treated in hospitals in Cameroon in a bid to force the government to construct good hospitals and stop the tendency for medical evacuations abroad for civil servants (posted, 21 September, 114 Likes).

Post with Most Comments: A statement, summarising an interview he granted a journalist, castigating the government for the poor state of public schools (posted, 26 September, 54 Comments).

Most Shared Post: A statement castigating the minimum wage in Cameroon and declaring that it is time to change this (posted, 22 September, Shared by 30 people).

Overall, the findings presented above suggest that by privileging reportage on campaign-related events and courtesy engagements over more interactive approaches in their Facebook posts, the candidates demonstrated that the 'broadcast mentality' of how politicians have approached social media in different political contexts also resonates in Cameroon. Beyond this, and importantly, the findings clearly demonstrate the non-prioritisation of Facebook as an effective campaign communication outlet.

Why this non-prioritisation? Often, issues such as limited access to the Internet or lack of financial and human resources are offered as explanations for the limited use of the Internet or social media by politicians and parties in SSA. While these are of course important, the Cameroonian case suggests that we need to move beyond offering technical and financial constraints as explanations of this phenomenon. As indicated earlier, arguably, a major (if not *the* major) reason why social media, like all other media, are not prioritised by parties and politicians in Cameroon during campaigns is because politicians believe that they are not effective tools for securing electoral victory—the major focus of virtually all politicians. Radio for instance, has more reach than the Internet, but also is not prioritised.

This is not to suggest that the media do not matter, only that they matter less as compared to non-mediated campaign strategies. In fact, during the 2013 Legislative and Municipal election campaigns, candidates and parties used a variety of communication strategies, both mediated and non-mediated. The ruling CPDM, for instance, paid for the publication of its manifesto in private newspapers; its candidates used the free time available on the state broadcaster for all competing parties to pass on its messages, but even with all its financial might and enormous human resources, the official method of campaigning approved and recommended by the party hierarchy in 2013 as well as in all previous elections was door-to-door campaigning.

The 958 reports examined for this study indicate that, overwhelmingly, all the competing parties and candidates prioritised and extensively used non-mediated campaign communication strategies, especially door-to-door strategies. Headlines such as 'The Door-to-Door Chorus' (*Mutations* of 19 September 2013), 'East: The Opposition Opts for Door-to-Door' (*La Nouvelle Expression* of 18 September 2013), 'Centre: Priority on Proximity' and 'Extreme North: Door-to-Door in Yagoua' (*Cameroon Tribune* of 18 September 2013) all capture the inherent tendencies in contemporary election campaigns in Cameroon and show that the arrival and relative spread of social media has not changed the country's central campaign dynamics. These tendencies, as Ngomba (2012) has argued, have led to the rather paradoxical situation that developments in the media sector have been accompanied not by a prioritisation of mediated campaign strategies, but rather an overwhelming adoption of door-to-door campaign strategies across all political parties. As Ngomba (2012) showed, and as the reports mentioned above indicate, this prioritisation of what are generally termed 'proximity strategies' is anchored in the belief that they are more effective (for a discussion of a similar paradox in Taiwan, see Schafferer, 2009: 390; for Latin America, see Szwarcberg 2014).

These proximity campaigns also 'align' with the communication culture of a preference for face-to-face communication in Cameroon (Mbaku 2005:172), a practice that provides politicians and other elites with the opportunity to distribute money and other things like rice, soap and salt to the electorate. Campaign news reports with headlines such as 'Corruption Is Doing Well' (*La Nouvelle Expression* of 20 September 2013) and 'CPDM Campaign: El Hadj Nana Bouba Argues Gastronomically' (*Le Messager* of 20 September 2013) point to the continuous presence of these practices that are in line with arguments highlighted earlier about the political instrumentalisation of clientelism and patronage during election campaigns in Cameroon and most of SSA.

Conclusion

The central purpose of this chapter has been to provide an overview and a new empirical contribution to the discussions about the use of social media by political parties and candidates during election campaigns in SSA. Looking at how three politicians in Cameroon used Facebook in the context of the 2013 legislative and municipal election campaigns, the chapter has shown that the candidates adopted a 'broadcasting' approach with regards to their use, and focused their interactions on courtesy rather than deliberative engagements.

Overall, these findings suggest a non-prioritisation of social media as an effective campaign tool in Cameroon. This contrasts sharply with the significant prioritisation of non-mediated campaign communication strategies that are perceived to be more effective. So, while commentators tend to criticise politicians and parties for side-lining social media in Cameroon (see, for instance, Tande 2011), the experiences of politicians 'on the ground' make these criticisms seem uninformed. The Cameroonian case suggests that, as in Taiwan (Schafferer 2009), beyond issues of access, financial capabilities of parties/politicians or the regulatory framework governing campaigns, the perception of the effectiveness of a medium significantly influences the extent to which it can be adopted and prioritised within a campaign strategy. For Cameroonian politicians, while the costs of adopting a media-based campaign strategy are certain, its benefits, compared to other strategies, are not (see Cardenal 2011 for a discussion of this in relation to parties' use of the Internet in Spain and Catalonia).

How this will play out in the years ahead is a matter of opinion, but given the increase in social media use in the region, and that the diaspora can now vote in referenda and presidential elections, it is possible that by the 2018 presidential election, parties and candidates will make more use of social media. Whether this potential increase in use of social media by parties and candidates will result in actual changes in the patterns of this use will remain to be seen. But the experiences of more established democracies with a longer history of the use of the Internet in campaigns seem to suggest a need for cautious optimism (see Gibson et al. 2014).

Accordingly, it seems likely that, as with radio, television and newspapers, social media will continue to play only a marginal role in election campaigns in Cameroon for a very long time. On the other hand, Cameroonian politicians will most likely continue to prioritise proximity-based campaign communication strategies—strategies that underscore a fundamental issue in electoral politics: namely that personal relations and personal contact matters significantly. This is why even in the United States, known for its pace-setting role as far as the use of social media in campaigns are concerned, the reality is that instead of diminishing, direct contact with the electorate, referred to as the "ground war," has instead *increased quite dramatically,*" especially since 2000 (Beck and Heidemann 2014: 271, emphasis added). These 'ground wars' have been and will arguably continue to be for a long time again, the defining feature of election campaigns in Cameroon even as we witness the gradual but continuous spread of social media across the country.

Notes

1 For legislative and municipal elections in Cameroon, parties compile lists of candidates based on the number of available seats per constituency. The electorate in a constituency vote for a list of candidates proposed by competing political parties without indications of preference for any candidate on the list.
2 http://www.facebook.com/kah.walla
3 http://www.facebook.com/OsihJoshua
4 http://www.facebook.com/alberdoohcollins

References

Balancing Act (2014) *The Sub-Saharan African Media Landscape: Then, Now and in the Future.* Available at: http://www.balancingact-africa.com/sites/balancingact-africa.com/files/products/1.%20SSA%20Media%20Landscape.pdf

Beck, P. and Heidemann, E. (2014) "Changing Strategies in Grassroots Canvassing: 1956–2012," *Party Politics,* 20(2), pp. 261–274.

Cardenal, A.S. (2011) "Why Mobilize Support Online? The Paradox of Party Behaviour Online," *Party Politics,* 19(1), pp. 83–103.

Gerodimos, R. and Justinussen, J. (2014) "Obama's 2012 Facebook Campaign: Political Communication in the Age of the Like Button," *Journal of Information Technology and Politics.* DOI:10.1080/19331681.2014.982266.

Gibson, R.; Römmele, A., and Williamson, A. (2014) "Chasing the Digital Wave: International Perspectives on the Growth of Online Campaigning," *Journal of Information Technology and Politics,* 11(2), pp. 123–129.

Jungherr, A. (2014) *Twitter in Politics: A Comprehensive Literature Review.* Available at: http://ssrn.com/abstract=2402443

Langmia, K. (2013) "*Social Media Technology and the 2011 Presidential Election in Cameroon*". Paper Presented at the International Conference on ICT for Africa, February 20–23, Harare, Zimbabwe.

Mbaku, J. (2005) *Culture and Customs of Cameroon.* Westport, CT: Greenwood Press.

Morozov E. (2011) *The Net Delusion: How Not to Liberate the World.* London: Allen Lane.

Mutiga, M. (2013) "The Campaign Revolution: On the Road with Kenya's Candidates," *Portland* (The Quarterly: Africa Edition). Available at: http://www.portland-communications.com/publications/the-quarterly-africa/the-campaign-revolution-on-the-road-with-kenyas-candidates/

Ngomba, T. (2012) *Political Campaign Communication in sub-Saharan Africa: The Cameroonian Experience in a Global Perspective,* PhD Dissertation submitted to the Faculty of Arts, Aarhus University, Denmark.

Ngomba, T. (2014) "Cameroon's Female Obama? Deconstructing the Kah Walla Phenomenon in the Context of the 2011 Presidential Election in Cameroon". In Stova, M. and Ibroscheva, E (eds.) *Women Politicians and the Media in Emerging Democracies.* New York: Bloomsbury, pp. 149–166.

Ogunlesi, T. (2013) "Youth and Social Media in Nigeria," *Rhodes Journalism Review,* 33, pp. 20–22.

Olivier, M. (2013) "Twitter: Pourquoi les Dirigeants Africains Francophones Sont-ils si Nuls?" Available at: http://www.jeuneafrique.com/Article/ARTJAWEB20130821183201/

Portland Communications. (2012) *How Africa Tweets.* Available at: http://www.portland-communications.com/wp-content/uploads/2013/05/Twitter_in_Africa_PPT.pdf

Schafferer, C. (2009) "Evolution and Limitations of Modern Campaigning in East Asia: A Case Study of Taiwan". In Johnson, D. (ed.). *The Routledge Handbook of Political Management*. New York: Routledge, pp. 370–392.

Steenkamp, M. and Hyde-Clarke, N. (2014) "The Use of Facebook for Political Commentary in South Africa," *Telematics and Informatics*, 31(1), pp. 91–97.

Szwarcberg, M. (2014) "Political Parties and Rallies in Latin America," *Party Politics*, 20(3), pp. 456–466.

Tande, D. (2011) *2011 Presidential Election: How Candidates Are Navigating the Social Media Land-scape*. Available at: http://www.dibussi.com/2011/09/cameroon-election-social-media.html Van Reijswoud, V. (2014) *Social Media in Cameroon: State of Play and Perspectives*. Yaounde: Friedrich Ebert Stiftung.

33
SOCIAL MEDIA AND ELECTIONS IN KENYA

Martin Nkosi Ndlela

Introduction

The political communication landscape in Kenya, as in other sub-Saharan African countries, is undergoing tremendous changes due to multifaceted processes of globalisation, particularly the changing stratifications in information and communication technologies. New technologies such as the Internet, mobile telephones, and tablets are inevitably shaping contemporary forms of political communication, be it political campaigns, mobilisation, participation, monitoring, or civic engagement. Social media platforms embedded in these new technologies create complex dynamics to forms of citizen engagement and participation in political processes. Political actors, citizens, and civic organisations in Kenya are increasingly seeking to maximise their political communication by adopting new information and communication technological spaces, including social media platforms. This chapter takes a step towards untangling the implications of social media to elections in Kenya. It explores the inherent potential embedded in social media, and provides illustrative examples on how social media was used or misused during 2013 elections in Kenya. The chapter tackles the question of social media influences on election processes in an emerging and unstable democracy. It also discusses the limitations associated with social media in the Kenyan context.

The Kenyan Political Context: Liberalisation and Democratisation

Literature on the impact of new technology on society, in our case elections, emphasises the importance of contextual and institutional factors in explaining different effects of new technologies in different countries (Karlsen 2010; Anstead and Chadwick 2008; Plasser and Plasser 2002). The impact of new technology is affected by contextual, historical, and cultural factors which vary between campaign environments (Karlsen 2010). Christensen (2011a: 157) also reminds us of the importance of sociopolitical context in any analysis of social media and the importance of maintaining a critical, contextualised perspective on the relation between technology and politics at the local, national, and transnational levels. As such, social media use in elections shape, and are shaped in interplay with, the changing campaigning environment in Kenya.

Social media use in election processes in Kenya should be examined against a backdrop of the country's struggles for democratisation since the wave of democratisation swept across sub-Saharan Africa in the early 1990s. The period witnessed a series of developments on the African continent suggesting a massive return to liberalised forms of politics (Olukoshi 1998). The wave of democratisation ushered in a new period of governance in Africa, with a number of countries shifting away from authoritarian one-party systems, military dictatorships, or other forms of communist totalitarianism to open systems of governance (Murunga and Nusong'o 2007). The transition period was expected to usher a new system of government characterised by competitive multiparty elections, associated freedoms of association and expression, opening up of political communicative spaces as well as institutional reforms. Kenya officially moved away from a one-party rule and introduced a multiparty system in 1992. It however took another 10 years to remove the ruling Kenya African National Union (KANU) and its incumbent leader Daniel arap Moi, who had been in power since 1978. While political liberalisation processes opened up spaces for political pluralism and competitive elections, several obstacles lay in the path of democratisation. Fragmented opposition parties, strong ethnic loyalties, weak institutions of governance, and inadequate media system prevailed. Hence, the transition of power in 2002 from KANU to the opposition alliance, the National Alliance Rainbow Coalition (NARC), led by Mwai Kibaki, ushered in a new era in the Kenyan politics, albeit for only a short time. A split in NARC led to the formation of other entities such as NARC–Kenya led by the incumbent President Kibaki and the Orange Democratic Movement, a loose coalition of opposition leaders. Intense competition for power, rivalry between candidates and their supporters, ethnic divide, shifting alliances, and violence have characterised Kenya's electoral processes and its struggles for democracy. As such, elections in Kenya, just as in the rest of sub-Saharan Africa have acquired a reputation for violence (Goldsmith 2014). The violence surrounding the elections raise concerns about how to sustain citizen engagement with elections (Smith 2009).

The 2007 elections were heavily contested, accompanied by physical violence, loss of life, destruction of property, displacement, and gross violation of human rights. The election outcome was disputed on various grounds, including accusations of vote rigging, intimidation of voters, vote buying, or even unfair electoral framework. The post-election violence resulted in over one thousand deaths, and an estimated 500,000 were displaced from their homes. According to the UN High Commission for Human Rights (OHCHR 2008), the patterns of violence in 2007 were either a spontaneous reaction to election results, organised attacks against targeted communities, or organised retaliatory attacks. As Sommerville (2011) notes, as the violence escalated the planned and organised nature of the attacks on particular communities became clear. The violence had a strong ethnic dimension, pitting the Kalenjin and Luo supporters of the main opposition leader Raila Odinga against the mainly Kikuyu supporters of the President Kibaki. The interethnic violence which erupted after the disputed elections of 2007 captured the attention of both the international media and human rights organisations, culminating with charges being brought against prominent Kenyan politicians and former rivals, Uhuru Kenyatta and William Ruto at the International Criminal Court (ICC). As Cheeseman et al. (2014) note, Ruto, then with the Orange Democratic Movement (ODM), was singled out for allegedly mobilising anti-Kikuyu attacks at in the Rift Valley, while Kenyatta was alleged to have organised revenge attacks against Odinga's Luo and Kalenjin supporters in Nakuru and Naivasha. The 2013 elections were thus held amidst fears of a return of 2007 violence. However, they turned out to be peaceful, free, and fair, even though the election results were challenged in court. Kenya remains a deeply divided and ethnically polarised country. It has experienced ethnically driven politics, where issues of ethnicity and linguistic belonging are an overwhelming predictor of voting patterns. The structure of ethnic groups is a formative influence on vote choices (Bratton et al. 2012).

Political Communicative Spaces in Kenya: The Growth of New Media

The mainstream media have played a key role in mediating the Kenyan electoral processes. Kenya has a modern and developed communication system, with pluralism in broadcasting and the print media as well as being an East African hub for international media organisations. However, the Kenyan media system use English as the primary language of communication, with few outlets using local languages. Swahili and other vernacular languages are used mainly in radio stations and some newspapers. The linguistic factor inevitably restricts access to the mass media in Kenya. Other factors, such as the availability of electricity and the coverage of broadcasting signals, have also limited the coverage and consumption of mass media. The Kenyan media ranks fairly well in the freedom of expression index, with journalists enjoying a large measure of freedom in newsgathering and reporting (Reporters Without Borders 2014). The mainstream mass media still maintain an important position in the Kenyan political public sphere. However, the mass media have their limitations in political communication. They tend to be elitists and their messages go through journalistic filtering mechanisms. There is often a time delay between when a message is formulated and when it is actually received by the audiences. The mass media tends to limit the number of public voices and have a predisposition towards one-way forms of communication, where messages flow from politicians to the public via the media.

Social media characteristics affect the political communication process in different ways. First, social media are not elitist driven and provide possibilities for new forms of public participation. Second, messages can be shared with receivers without the aid of intermediaries. Third, there is no time delay in message sharing. Fourth, social media offer possibilities for a multitude of voices. Finally, social media provides opportunities for different directions of informational flow. Social media have various configurations, some of which enable different means of political communication, on a one-to-one or one-to-many basis and in different media platforms. Commenting on the situation in Australia, Bruns and Highfield (2013) observe that commenting on politics now takes place across a multiplatform media ecology, as social media are integrated into mainstream media coverage. The same trend can be noted in Kenya, where social media commentary has at times ended up as articles in the mainstream media and vice versa. The new platforms add new dimensions to political communication by shifting the configurations of power, giving anyone with access the opportunity to create and share content. They offer immediate interactivity in both production, dissemination and consumption of political messages. A simple 'retweet' or 'share' button creates a message spiral in different media platforms.

The last years have seen tremendous growth and uptake of new media in Kenya. According to the report by Apoyo Consultoria (2011), access to voice services has been growing rapidly in recent years due to the development of mobile networks, with four companies providing mobile services in Kenya. Internet Live Stats (2014) show that Kenya has an Internet penetration of 36.7 per cent, with users accessing Internet at home via computer or mobile devices, and the percentage is higher if one includes access to the Internet via workplaces or Internet cafes. A report from the International

Telecommunications Union (ITU; 2014) shows that mobile broadband remains the fastest growing market segment, and it is growing fastest in developing countries. The report also notes that in developing countries mobile-cellular penetration will have reached 90 per cent by the end of 2014. Digital divide is still a major factor in Kenya, where many people do not have access to mainstream media, let alone social media platforms. However, the gap is narrowing especially in the mobile telephone sector.

Kenya has witnessed a substantial increase in the mobile cellular sector, notably an increase in the number of smart phones. All of these statistics point to a rapidly changing social media landscape. While the social media landscape in general is awash with different platforms, those commonly used in Kenya are Facebook, Twitter, YouTube, and more recently WhatsApp. Even though these platforms have different characteristics, they facilitate political communication and mobilisation, thus enabling shift in the way political information is produced, mediated, and received. Social media are undoubtedly influencing the Kenyan political public sphere by creating new spaces and forms of communication, citizen engagement, and participation in political processes.

Social media are increasingly becoming an important communication tools in the Kenyan political public sphere, facilitating, for example, communication between the politicians and the electorate, as well as allowing users to generate discussions on political issues. Dahlgren (2005) describes a functioning public sphere "as a constellation of communicative spaces in society that permit the circulation of information, ideas, debates—ideally in an unfettered manner—and also the formation of political will" (Dahlgren 2005: 148). Dahlgren also delineates three constitutive dimensions for conceptualising the public sphere, namely the structural, representational and interaction dimension. The structural dimension pertains to formal institutional features, including media organisations. This dimension directs attention to issues such as the political economy of media organisations, ownership structures, control and the legal framework regulated access to the media including associated freedom of expression. The structural dimension also includes issues of inclusion and exclusion in the public sphere. In the representational dimension, Dahlgren (2005) focuses on issues of media output for political communication including fairness, accuracy, plurality of views and agenda setting. According to Dahlgren, the dimension of interaction has to do with citizens' encounters with the media—a communicative process of making sense, interpreting and using the output, as well as interaction between themselves.

Social media in Kenya arguably reconfigures the issues raised by Dahlgren (2005). It can be argued that social media have implications on the structural, representational and interactional dimensions of the political public sphere by expanding and pluralising communicative spaces. These changes are also noted by Blumler and Gurevitch (2001), who in relation to the Western democracies have noted how the massive growths in media outlets and channels have influenced the traditional systems of political communication. Social media have a created multipublic sphere of political communication. This stratification conforms to Fraser's (1992) conceptualisation of the public sphere as a multiple-segmented sphere. Keane (2000) also conceptualises the public sphere as multiple and multilevel overlapping public spheres at local, regional, and international levels. The social media increases the plurality of communicative spaces. These spaces facilitating information flows and participation in political issues.

For participants in the political communication process, be it politicians, civic organisations, or citizens, access to social media technologies such as mobile telephones, especially smartphones, is enabling, at least according to the theoretical foundations behind the *liberation technologies/ technologies of liberation* thesis. As expounded by Diamond (2010: 70):

> Liberation technology is any form of information and communication technology (ICT) that can expand political, social, and economic freedom. In the contemporary era, it means essentially the modern, interrelated forms of digital ICT—the computer, the Internet, the mobile phone, and countless innovative applications for them, including "new social media" such as Facebook and Twitter.

As noted by Christensen (2011b), "the liberation technology view is one in which there is a causal relation posited among specific forms of technology, the expansion of rights, and other forms of economic and social development" (Christensen 2011b: 237). The following sections will discuss how different participants in Kenya used social media in the political communication process during the 2013 elections.

The Use of Social Media by Politicians

New technologies are increasingly changing the manner in which politicians communicate with their constituencies, especially for electoral campaigning. As noted above, the expansion of social media is changing the political communicative spaces in Kenya. The successful uses of social media in diverse countries, most notably the U.S. presidential election in 2008 and the claims of social media use in what is now referred to as the Arab Spring in 2011, have prompted politicians in Africa into harnessing new social media tools for political mobilisation processes. As Askanius and Østergaard (2014: 1) observe,

> surrounded by the hype and buzzwords such as the 'Twitter or Facebook revolution', media and communication technologies have been celebrated as vehicles for rapid political mobilization and alleged to have made a considerable impact on political life, agency and the public sphere.

The hype of social media use in elections is also becoming a visible component of political campaigning and mobilisation in African countries, as "politicians and political groups have quickly realised the potential of social networking sites as campaign tools" (Borah 2014: 201). With the increasing accessibility of smart phones and mobile Internet, new communicative spaces have emerged and politicians are eager to tap the opportunities provided by new technologies. Kenyan political parties and candidates are harnessing the social media platforms as tools for canvassing votes, promoting their ideas. In the Kenyan general elections in 2013, several political positions were contested for—president, senators, county governors, and members of parliament. As noted above, the key contenders in the 2013 elections were the Jubilee Coalition, led by presidential candidate Uhuru Kenyatta with his running mate Samuel Ruto, and the CORD coalition (Coalition for Reforms and Democracy), led by Raila Odinga with his running mate Kalonzo Musyoka.

Politicians across the political divide adopted different strategies in their utilisation of social media tools. The social media strategies for campaigning range from carefully planned usages to simply maintaining a presence. These strategies differ according to the type of social media used and the attributes of the social media platform used. Odinga (2013) observes that during the 2013 presidential elections in Kenya, "some parties emphasized on the participatory aspects of new technologies in communicating with voters and monitoring of public opinion, whilst others focused on the possibility of a top-down information dissemination" (Odinga 2013: 18). In another study, Wasswa (2013) notes that the 2013 presidential candidates in Kenya integrated social media into their campaigns, using the platforms mainly for sharing information on campaign activities, debates on issues, the sharing of photos, videos and links, updating their followers, soliciting funds, and countering propaganda.

While both coalitions tried to harness the existing social media tools such as Facebook and Twitter on the campaign trail, this chapter provides examples of social media use by politicians linked to the Jubilee Coalition. For their enthusiasm in using social media presidential candidate, Uhuru Kenyatta and his Jubilee Coalition team were referred to as 'digital'. Social media platforms such as Facebook, Twitter, YouTube, and Scribd were integrated in the 2013 campaign trail. Within the Facebook platform, Uhuru Kenyatta adopted different strategies such as profiling non-governmental organisations linked to him and pages dedicated to individual profile. The Facebook profile UHURU Kenyatta 2013 (founded in January 2013) is premised along non-government organisation lines and not individual candidate Uhuru Kenyatta or his coalition. The page is registered as a non-government organisation, focusing on engaging, empowering, and celebrating Kenyan young people. It seeks to empower youth for life and nation building. The community was used as one of the campaign platform for the Jubilee Coalition of Uhuru Kenyatta and Samuel Ruto. The campaign messages are simply and subtly and written predominantly in English. The messages focus on a developmental and social change premises.

In another Facebook profile, Uhuru Kenyatta is aimed at individual branding (as of September 2014 the profile had over 1.2 million 'likes'). The profile provides details about the 'individual'—his educational background, relationship status, life events, religious inclinations and other individual attributes. This profile provides links to a personal website (www.uhuru.co.ke), which provides other possibilities for being connected, getting involved through participating in events, hosting events, or simply volunteering. The election campaigns methods used in the Uhuru Kenyatta Facebook profile exploit visual imagery accompanied by simple textual messages, providing information on the location of events or thanking the participants to previous meetings and events. Photo imageries, showing huge crowds attending rallies addressed by Uhuru Kenyatta and Jubilee Coalition leaders or representing key segments of the electorate, such as the youth, elderly, chiefs, farmers, other ethnic minority groups, immigrant communities are used extensively. The diversity is clearly intended to reinforce the popularity of the presidential candidate Uhuru Kenyatta and his Jubilee Coalition across the geographical and cultural breadth of Kenya. The candidate and his coalition are presented as inclusive and representative of the Kenyan society.

The Facebook profile also incorporates Uhuru Kenyatta TV: a collection of election campaign video clips posted to YouTube. These clips include campaign speeches from Uhuru Kenyatta and key candidates from his coalition. The coalition's manifesto, campaign launch and other speeches by the Jubilee Coalition leaders are published in the Uhuru Kenyatta TV. Other videos in the collection address policy issues in the areas of education, agriculture, health, sports and arts. Some videos portray the Jubilee coalition as a transformation force, or the 'digital team,' as they referred to themselves.

Another social media platform used by the Kenyan politicians during the 2013 elections is Twitter. Even before the 2013 elections, some Kenyan politicians were amongst the top Twitter users in Africa (Smith 2012). In its Africa network series, *The Guardian* (UK edition) observed that with more and more voters online, leaders are turning to Twitter to get their political message across (Smith 2012). The main presidential candidate in the 2013 elections, Uhuru Kenyatta and Raila Odinga are amongst Africa's top 10 tweeting politicians. The *Sahan Journal* also notes that,

> as Twitter usage continues to expand in Africa, presidents and politicians in the continent are leveraging the unique power of the micro-blogging site to disseminate their political agendas, instantly communicate with a vast majority of people, recruit citizens to help in their campaigns, and create a space for dialogue and participatory. (*Sahan Journal* 2013: para. 1)

The *Sahan Journal* also notes that Uhuru Kenyatta gained more than 76,000 Twitter followers between January 1 and 31 March 2013 (at the height of the elections). His deputy, Samuel Ruto, was also an avid tweeter during the elections.

An analysis of the social media profiles of key Kenyan politicians such as Uhuru Kenyatta, Raila Odinga, William Ruto, and Musalia Mudavadi show that social media were in various ways incorporated into the overall political campaigning, for dissemination messages or simply informing on past and forthcoming events. It can be concluded that social media are increasingly becoming an important component of the Kenyan political public sphere. Every election time triggers an exponential growth in the use of different media platforms for galvanising votes, organising events through social media, interacting with opinion influencers and engagement with key political issues or simply using online platforms to support offline campaign activities.

It is however important to mention that social media are not replacing traditional forms of campaigning, which in Kenya are still dominated by face-to-face platforms such as public meetings or rallies organised by the parties. Some sections of voters in Kenya, as in other parts of Africa, value predominantly oral communication, mediated through television, radio or face-to-face. Political rallies are used to bridge the linguistic barriers. As noted by Odinga (2013), a large percentage of Kenyans do not understand the country's two official languages, English and Swahili. For parliamentary and local elections, the face-to-face interactions are mainstream modes of campaigning, especially to voters in rural and peri-urban areas.

Political Engagement—Citizens and Social Media Use

To those citizens with access to the Internet, social media have made possible access to alternative communicative spaces 'relatively free' from political and professional mainstream media domination. Several uses of social media can be deciphered in connection with the elections, such as election monitoring, interaction with politicians, and conversations on politics. For voters in Kenya, the conduct of elections and its outcomes has always been a site of contention. Allegations of election rigging, manipulation of votes have undermined the credibility and fairness of the elections in Kenya. As Cheeseman et al. (2014) observe, "the months leading up to the Kenyan elections of March 2013 there was much concern—both within Kenya itself and internationally— that political competition would trigger a fresh wave of violence" (Cheeseman et al.

2014: 2). Memories of the 2007 elections were still fresh and the political atmosphere tense. New media technologies, especially social media offered Kenyans unique opportunities for monitoring the conduct of elections. As Diamond (2010: 70) writes,

> liberation technology enables citizens to report news, expose wrongdoing, express opinions, mobilize protest, monitor elections, scrutinize government, deepen participation, and expand the horizon of freedom.

The decentralised nature of social media applications, including the cheaper variants of text messaging via mobile telephone, when deployed properly, can cover vast geographic areas, and facilitate election monitoring. The 2013 elections, therefore, saw the deployment of different tools, including social media, to the monitoring of electoral conduct in the form of crowdsourcing. Crowdsourcing is defined as "an online, distributed problem-solving and production model that leverages the collective intelligence of online communities to serve specific organizational goals" (Brabham 2013: xix). The term itself can be applied to a range of activities where services, ideas and contributions are solicited from other people sharing the same cause. The crowdsourcing approach enables very localised and relevant information to be collected. One example of such crowdsourcing tool is the Ushahidi (n.d.; Swahili word for 'witness' or 'testimony') platform, which was launched in Kenya in 2008 to enable Kenyans to report and map incidents of violence via SMS or the Web. The motivations behind the Ushahidi lies in the disconnection between what the media and official were reporting and other eyewitness accounts. As one of the core-founders of Ushahidi vividly pointed out in her blog, "we believe that the number of deaths being reported by the government, police, and media is grossly underreported. We also don't think we have a true picture of what is really going on" (Kenyan Pundit n.d.: para. 7). The Ushahidi platform was meant to enable everyone on the ground to report on election conduct via SMS messages or submit a report via the Web. The Ushahidi platform offered opportunities to citizens to play a greater role in election coverage and monitoring, penetrating even those areas where journalists had limited access. Crowdsourcing through platforms like Ushahidi indicate the growing possibilities of social media. These citizen-centered initiatives sought to empower the electorate, and compel government institutions to be more transparent, open and accountable. The watchdog role often associated with mainstream journalism was thus extended to social media platforms, where ordinary citizens (witnesses) could act as citizen journalists.

Other examples of crowdsourcing involved individuals setting up, for example, Facebook pages dedicated to sharing experiences and witness accounts on election conduct. During the 2013 elections, Facebook communities like Elections Iwitness Kenya (n.d.) were established with the sole objective of sharing information and knowledge about elections. The community encourages the participants to "give your recollections on the elections, what you saw and heard that was wrongfully or intentionally done to bar free and fair elections. For example bribery, multiple ballot papers given to one person, doctored documents (results), etc." (Elections Iwitness Kenya n.d., section 'About', para. 1). Another Facebook community of the Elections Kenya official fanpage, whose stated mission was to bring 'sanity in elections, education and stopping tribalism'. Facebook group Kenya Elections 2013 describes itself a group of concerned global citizens whose main objective is to inform, debate and get in step with the unfolding of the national election.

Social media were used by groups in Kenya, to gather and share election informa-tion, and to provide commentary on the freeness and fairness of the electoral processes. Diamond (2010) argues that digital cameras combined with sites such as YouTube cre-ate new possibilities for exposing and challenging abuses of power. For example, inci-dents of violence during the 2007–2008 elections were captured on mobile cameras and later uploaded to YouTube, thereby generating public attention. As noted by Marchant (2013), when applied to election monitoring, crowdsourcing has the potential to foster citizen engagement with the information—to dispute, confirm or acknowledge its exis-tence, and, thus, has the potential to contribute to empowerment and participation in electoral processes (Marchant 2013:13). Other uses of social media by citizens include general interactions with politicians. These interactions are expressed through various forms such as 'retweets', 'following', 'likes', and 'commentary' on social media postings by politicians.

Limitations of Social Media in Elections

Social media have heralded new communicative spaces for political engagement in Kenya. The number of politicians and citizens using social media for election purposes is continually increasing. However, there are some limitations in terms of both access to and application of the new communicative spaces. The social media's participative function in the Kenya political public sphere is arguably hampered by issues of accessibility, both in terms of the availability of prerequisite technologies and related costs. Limited access to social media affects the plurality and diversity of views in the social media arena. It should be noted however that the presence of a few opinion leaders in the social media arena have some a potential of influencing offline interactions.

Another limitation pertains to the abuse of social media for spreading hate speech and inciting violence. Evidence from the 2007 election violence in Kenya show that social media were used by politicians and individuals to incite violence. Several groups in civil society expressed concern that the violence surrounding the 2007 elections had some parallels with the genocide in Rwanda in the early 1990s, when politicians used media to incite hatred and violence against specific ethnic groups and communi-ties. The UN Office of the High Commissioner for Human Rights (OHCHR 2008) fact-finding mission, after the 2007 election violence, identified hate speech as an area of concern. It recommended the establishment of a regulatory framework against hate-speech (OHCHR 2008). The National Cohesion and Integration Commission (NCIC), established after the 2007 post-election crisis, was mandated to develop guidelines for media houses on hate speech. Hate speech is covered by the National Cohesion and Integration Act of 2008. Specifically, Section 62 (1) stipulates that any person who utters words intended to incite feelings of contempt, hatred, hostility, vio-lence or discrimination against any person, group or community on the basis of ethnic-ity or race, commits an offence. The electoral violence during and after the 2007 led to the development of various strategies and tools for monitoring hate speech, particularly in the electronic media, including social media. One initiative for monitoring hate speech in social media, is the Umati project run by the iHub, an innovation hub for the technology community in Kenya. Umati emerged also out of the concern that mobile and digital technologies have played a central role in the 2007–2008 post-election violence.

Conclusion

Any new communication technology has the potential of changing political communication patterns and structures, thereby changing the public sphere, its contents and participants. In Kenya, social media are increasingly becoming important for politicians and citizens alike. As noted in this chapter, politicians in Kenya have begun experimenting with social media platforms, notably Facebook, Twitter, and YouTube, as campaign tools during elections. These platforms have been used for mobilising supporters, organising rallies and meetings, reporting on past events, and communication with supporters. They have also been used for individual or party profiling, illustrating the diversity of support base through powerful visual imageries. Self-promotion or praising their coalition partners also features in the social media texts.

Another dimension of social media use during elections pertains to monitoring the conduct of politicians during elections, as individuals and civil society organisations share the burden of reporting abuses, violent acts, corruption cases and other vices likely to diminish the integrity of the elections or, in the worst case scenario, lead to a repeat of the 2007–2008 post-election violence. The use of social media for election monitoring purposes is a vivid example of the changing power constellations in the Kenyan political public sphere. Used appropriately, social media platforms have an empowering and 'liberating' potential. The range of possibilities extends beyond the capabilities and limitations of mainstream media in developing societies such as Kenya.

References

Anstead N. and Chadwick, A. (2008) Parties, election campaigning and the Internet: Toward a comparative institutional approach, in A. Chadwick and P N Howard (eds) *The handbook of Internet politics*, New York: Routledge.

Apoyo Consultoria. (2011) *Study on ICT access gaps in Kenya*. Nairobi: Communications Commission of Kenya.

Askanius T. and Østergaard L S. (2014) *Reclaiming the public sphere: Communication, power and social change*. London: Palgrave Macmillan.

Blumler J G. and Gurevitch M. (2001) The New media and our political communication discontents: Democratizing cyberspace. *Information, Communication & Society* 4: 1–13.

Borah P. (2014) Facebook use in the 2012 USA presidential campaign. In: Pătruţ B and Pătruţ M (eds) *Social media in politics*. Springer International, 201–211.

Brabham D C. (2013) *Crowdsourcing*. Cambridge, MA: MIT Press.

Bratton M., Bhavnani R., and Chen T-H. (2012) Voting intentions in Africa: Ethnic, economic or partisan? *Commonwealth & Comparative Politics* 50: 27–52.

Bruns A. and Highfield T. (2013) Political networks on Twitter. *Information, Communication & Society* 16: 667–691.

Cheeseman N., Lynch G., and Willis J. (2014) Democracy and its discontents: Understanding Kenya's 2013 elections. *Journal of Eastern African Studies* 8: 2–24.

Christensen C. (2011a) Twitter revolutions? Addressing social media and dissent. *The Communication Review* 14: 155–157.

Christensen C. (2011b) Discourses of technology and liberation: State aid to net activists in an era of 'Twitter Revolutions'. *The Communication Review* 14: 233–253.

Dahlgren P. (2005) The Internet, public spheres, and political communication: Dispersion and deliberation. *Political Communication* 22: 147–162.

Diamond L. (2010) Liberation technology. *Journal of Democracy* 21: 69–83.

Elections Iwitness Kenya (n.d.) http://www.facebook.com/pages/Elections-Iwitness-Kenya/603437 336351660

Fraser N. (1992) Rethinking the public sphere: A contribution to the critique of actually existing democracy. In: Calhoun C (ed) *Habermas and the public sphere*. Cambridge, MA: MIT Press, 109–142.

Goldsmith A A. (2014) Electoral violence in Africa revisited. *Terrorism and Political Violence*: 1–20.

International Telecommunications Union (ITU). (2014) *The world in 2014*. ICT Facts and Figures. Geneva: International Telecommunications Unions.

Internet Live Stats. (2014) Internet users. http://www.internetlivestats.com/internet-users-by-country/

Karlsen R. (2010) Does new media technology drive election campaign change? *Information Polity* 15, 215–225

Keane J. (2000) Structural transformation of the public sphere. In: Hacker K and Dijk J (eds) *Digital democracy: Issues of theory and practice*. London: Sage, 70–89.

Kenyan Pundit (n.d.) http://www.kenyanpundit.com/2008/01/09/ushahidicom/

Marchant E. (2013) *Viability, verification, validity: 3 Vs of crowdsourcing tested in election-based crowdsourcing*. Nairobi: iHub Research.

Murunga G and Nusong'o S. (2007) *Kenya: The struggle for democracy*. London: Zed Books.

Odinga C. (2013) *Use of new media during the Kenya elections*. Uppsala, Sweden: University of Uppsala, Department of informatics and Media, p. 49.

OHCHR. (2008) *Report from the OHCHR fact-finding mission to Kenya 6–28 February 2008*. Geneva: United Nations Office of the High Commissioner for Human Rights.

Olukoshi A. (1998) Economic crisis, multipartyism, and opposition politics in contemporary Africa. In: Olukoshi A (ed) *The politics of opposition in contemporary Africa*. Uppsala: Nordiska Afrikainstitutet.

Plasser F. and Plasser G. (2002) *Global political campaigning*. London: Praeger.

Reporters Without Borders. (2014) *World press freedom index 2014*. Paris: Reporters without Borders.

Sahan Journal. (2013) Top 10 most followed African presidents on Twitter. *Sahan Journal*. http://sahanjournal.com/african-presidents-on-twitter/#.VSJY__msWSo

Smith D. (2012) Africa's top 10 tweeting politicians. *The Guardian*. http://www.theguardian.com/world/2012/oct/30/africa-twitter-blogs-politicians

Smith L. (2009) Explaining violence after recent elections in Ethiopia and Kenya. *Democratization* 16: 867–897.

Sommerville K. (2011) Violence, hate speech and inflammatory broadcasting in Kenya: The problems of definition and identification. *Ecquid Novi: African Journalism Studies* 32: 82–101.

Ushahidi (n.d.) *From crisis mapping Kenya to mapping the globe*. https://tavaana.org/en/content/ushahidi-crisis-mapping-kenya-mapping-globe#_ednref3

Wasswa H W. (2013) *The role of social media in the 2013 presidential election campaigns in Kenya*. Nairobi: University of Nairobi, School of Journalism and Mass Communication.

34

ELECTORAL POLITICS ON SOCIAL MEDIA

The Israeli Case

Sharon Haleva-Amir and Karine Nahon

Introduction

The elections to the 19th Knesset (the Israeli Parliament) were held on 23 January 2013. During the electoral campaign, which began in October 2012, social media and other IT platforms were buzzing with political activity by formal and informal groups, candidates, parties, supporters, and members of the general public. In this chapter, we report and analyse the daily Web and social media use patterns of political actors. Seven main themes arose from our findings: (1) predominantly personal politics; (2) prominence of anonymous and negative campaigning; (3) focus on one platform; (4) symbiotic relationship with traditional media; (5) increased use of custom-made technology; (6) high level of civic engagement; and (7) extensive use of memes and satire. A comparative literature analysis shows that some of these themes are consistent with other global political campaigns. Finally, we discuss the reasons for these behavioural practices.

Social Media and Political Uses

The Internet has created an opportunity to restructure communication between parliamentarians and their constituents (Zittel 2003; Castells 2009). However, studies have repeatedly shown that parliamentarians are still largely focused on promoting themselves through reporting their parliamentarian activities (Williamson 2009b) and using the Web to produce an electorally advantageous impression (Stanyer 2008) rather than truly engaging with the public (Jackson 2003; Vegyte et al. 2008).

The expectations for the first wave of information technology affordances, specifically interactivity, to bridge the gap between politicians and citizens have been mostly disproven (Vergeer et al. 2011). These expectations were renewed, however, with the advent of Web 2.0 and social media. While the Web 1.0 era had been characterised by websites with largely static content and top-down messages, Web 2.0 provided more substantial affordances, such as interactivity, persistence, replicability, scalability, and searchability, as well as a variety of social platforms which enabled users to share content and chat more easily (boyd 2010). This generational transition was hoped to fundamentally change the way politicians communicated with their constituents.

Indeed, a comparative literature survey shows that the use of social media among candidates as well as incumbent parliamentarians has been on the rise in democracies such as Britain (Williamson 2009a), New Zealand (Busby & Bellamy 2011), Australia (Bruns & Burgess 2011), the US (Smith 2014) and Israel (Haleva-Amir 2014a). In the British context, for example, it was suggested that

> by inhabiting the same online spaces as their constituents on a day-to-day basis, MPs will interact with them in much more normal conditions—when the MP is not the privileged voice of authority, but merely one member of a conversation among many. In doing so, perhaps they will get a much more realistic idea of what their constituents actually think. (Colvile 2008: para. 6)

However, this hope was hardly fulfilled, as studies show that politicians use Web 1.0 and 2.0 platforms quite similarly: they focus on delivering messages and promoting themselves rather than on engaging with their constituents (Vergeer et al. 2011; Jackson & Lilleker 2009; Stromer-Galley 2013; Segaard & Nielsen 2013).

Historical Background: Israeli Electoral Web Campaigns (1999–2009)

Israel has an electoral system based on nation-wide proportional representation, where citizens vote for their preferred party and not for any individual candidates. Prior to the elections, each party submits its list of candidates for the Israeli parliament (the Knesset) in order of precedence. The parties select their candidates for the Knesset in primaries or by other procedures. After the elections, the 120 seats in the Knesset are then assigned proportionally to each party that received votes, provided that the party's share of the total votes met or exceeded the electoral threshold (currently 3.25 per cent). Elections must take place every four years unless the Knesset dissolves itself; the budget is not approved by the Knesset within three months of the start of the financial year; or a no-confidence vote has passed and a new government cannot be formed.

The structure of the Israeli electoral system makes the parties very powerful. However, since the 1990s the status of Israeli parties has deteriorated, for several reasons: (1) a loss of public trust (Hermann 2012); (2) the number of interest groups that are outside the traditional parties' control has grown; (3) a move to a primaries system has taken the power away from a small group in each party that used to decide who would be included in the party's candidate list for parliament, and passed it to the larger community of all party members; (4) finally, the global trend focusing on individual political leaders has also impacted the status of parties in Israel (Koren 1998).

The first use of the online medium for political purposes in Israel dates back to 1996: Member of Knesset (henceforth MK) Yael Dayan, who was running for the primary in the Labor party, created an information website. It was only in the 1999 elections, however, that other informational websites appeared: four out of five prime ministerial candidates maintained websites that provided biographical notes and information about their views. In addition, seven out of 31 political parties used websites in the 1999 elections. These provided information about the parties and their prime ministerial candidates' positions on major issues, as well as biographical notes. At this point, websites functioned mainly as digital bulletins, delivering top-down information (Gilboa & Katz 2001). By the 2003 elections, 17 out of 27 parties had an online presence. However, these websites demonstrated a one-sided communication pattern, largely ignoring the Internet's interactive and dynamic potential (Lehman-Wilzig 2004; Serfaty 2010).

The 2006 elections were the first time the online sphere played a significant role in electoral strategies (Atmor 2008). Several behavioural patterns emerged. First, political parties used the Internet to circumvent legal restrictions on campaigning. For example, the law in Israel restricts election propaganda to the 21 days preceding the elections. However, it lacks specific reference to the online sphere, and parties took advantage of this lacuna to engage in propaganda. Second, political parties used websites to recruit members, create supporter databases, enrol volunteers, and raise funds. Third, several MKs and candidates used political blogging as a more personal and less formal tool to communicate—but still not truly interact—with prospective voters (Atmor 2008). Still, features encouraging civic engagement were rarely used in the 2006 elections. For example, the vast majority of party websites provided limited access, if any, to features encouraging discourse and involvement, such as discussion forums or chat spaces.

The 2009 general elections for the 18th Knesset proved a turning point in the Israeli political arena for two main reasons. For the first time, three major Israeli parties—Kadima (centrist), Likud (right wing), and Meretz (left wing)—acknowledged the Internet's importance as a campaigning tool and declared their intention to allocate a considerable portion of their budgets accordingly (Mualem et al. 2008). These intentions, however, were not fully realised as Internet campaigns were often allocated a smaller budget than planned, since the managers of the campaigns did not fully understand and believe in the power of the Internet as a marketing tool (Nahon 2009).

Nevertheless, the 2009 elections showed intensive and extensive Internet use during the various parties' campaigns. Besides the growing availability of broadband connections and other technological developments, which made the Web more accessible and central in voters' lives, the 2009 Israeli elections campaign started shortly after the tremendous success of Barack Obama's 2008 presidential campaign. Obama's success—attributed by many to his brilliant use of the Web (Cain-Miller 2008)—drove local politicians to try and imitate his methods (Bronner & Cohen 2008; Keinan 2008; Pereg 2008) in both municipal and general election campaigns. This intensive use was characterised by seven trends:

1. *Dedicated websites that were abandoned after the elections.* Electoral campaigns in Israel are short-lived and end a few days after the elections. Consequently, a few days after the 2009 elections the parties and many of the elected candidates practically ceased their online activities (Nahon 2009; Haleva-Amir 2011b).
2. *Web tools were used for organisational purposes.* Parties have gradually begun to use web tools for organisational and regular party activities. For example, right-wing party HaBayit HaYehudi (The Jewish Home) was established and organised through the Internet: 10,000 people who participated in an online poll gave it

its name, chose its logo, and suggested 560 electoral candidates, out of whom 40 final candidates were appointed by a special committee (Atmor 2009; Shragai 2008; Lev-On 2011). Atmor (2009) argued that this unprecedented popular involvement was an indirect cause of the party's split a few weeks later. Another party, Israel Hazaka (Strong Israel), held its primaries exclusively online (Wolf 2008).

3. *Multiple and extensive use of social media.* Most of the parties and candidates used numerous social media and other websites simultaneously and linked them together (e.g. Facebook, YouTube, LinkedIn, Flickr, and local Israeli websites, such as The Marker Café). The rich variety of applications was intended to create an atmosphere of vivid and active campaigning. Facebook was the most commonly used social network, followed by the local blogging and social-business networking website The Marker Café (Haleva-Amir 2011a). Half the MKs who had active Facebook profiles by the time the electoral campaign began had joined it during the six weeks before the election. Consequently, most social media campaigns were short-lived and lacked engaging activities, as their Facebook walls were used mainly as billboards (Haleva-Amir 2011b).

4. *Politics turned more personal,* following a global and local trend of leader- and candidate-centred—as opposed to party- and platform-centred—politics (Wattenberg 1992; Galili-Zucker 2004; Rahat & Sheafer 2007). This led to an emphasis on personal websites during elections and primaries, as opposed to previous election periods where the parties' websites had served as the campaign anchor and the focus was on the general election only (Haleva-Amir 2011b).

5. *User-generated content* was increasingly used, independent of the parties. This included such activities as uploading video clips or writing posts. Most of these social media applications were used to attract young voters via their favourite Web applications.

6. *Dynamic campaigns.* Websites used in prior election campaigns had been rather static in nature, as they remained unchanged throughout the campaign and were infrequently updated. In the 2009 campaigns, however, they were dynamic and frequently updated.

7. *Guerrilla websites.* An interesting trend that had begun with the 2006 general election campaign became more salient during the 2009 election campaign. Guerrilla websites were unofficial websites with anonymous operators that railed against politicians. One example was the *Bibi Bluff* website which portrayed Benjamin ('Bibi') Netanyahu, the incumbent prime minister and candidate, as an unreliable politician. Later on, it was revealed that the rival party Kadima had been behind this website (Wolf 2008).

Social Media: The 2013 Election in Israel

The election to the 19th Knesset was held on 23 January 2013. This election was held in a context were social media were already embedded in the daily life of Israeli society, the digital literacy of users and candidates was quite high, and ready-to-use tools shifted the use of social media in elections from depending on professionals only (PR, advertising companies) to independent use. As elaborated below, some of the trends identified in the 2009 election campaign were intensified and enhanced; these included personal politics, using Web tools for organisational purposes, dynamic websites, user-generated content, and guerrilla websites. Others, such as the discontinuation of websites after the elections and the use of multiple social media were reversed. Finally some patterns emerged for the first time, including meme usage and smartphone campaigns.

Intensified Previous Trends: Personal Politics and Anonymous Campaigns

Like the 2009 election, the 2013 election's online campaigns were characterised by a growing use of Web tools for organisational purposes, user-generated content, the presence of guerrilla websites and dynamism. Most party leaders updated their Facebook pages several times a day (Cabir 2012), and the traffic of new political content increased compared with the 2009 campaign. Both the growing role of social media and the deterioration of the status of Israeli parties (as mentioned above) contributed to the intensifying trend of personal politics.

In order to study the uses of social media in the 2013 election, we first examined 122 new candidates in the primaries or general election (51 from this list later became MKs). All candidates conducted online campaigns. Additionally, parties that conducted primary elections published a booklet listing the candidates, their contact information, their emails and Facebook pages (if any). Such online activity, even at a time when candidates were somewhat anonymous, became standard. In a broader sense, this development further deepened the trend towards personalised politics. The rapidly growing number of politicians using new online platforms could be seen as a form of personalisation—the shift of attention from political parties to individual politicians (van Santen & van Zoonen 2010).

Second, two parties (Yesh Atid and HaBayit HaYehudi) did not operate an official Facebook page. Instead, each party's Facebook page was actually its leader's, and the party's website linked to that page (see Figures 34.1 and 34.2).

Figure 34.1 HaBayit HaYehudi Facebook Homepage

Figure 34.2 Yesh Atid Facebook Homepage

This was no mere technicality. The total identification of the party with its leader reflected the continued weakening of parties as major institutions in Israeli politics and society—a process that had begun several decades ago and is evident also in other parliamentary democracies around the world (Bartolini & Mair 2001; Koren 1998). In November 2014 we revisited the Facebook pages of these two parties and found that both of them by now had an official Facebook page separate from their leaders. However, the website of Yesh Atid still linked to the Facebook page of its leader rather than the one affiliated with the party.

Third, the individual crowdfunding trend was also found to be strongly related to the personalisation trend. Donations were raised through popular Israeli crowdfunding websites such as HeadStart and Mimoona. The first crowdfunding initiative was started by Likud's MK Michael Eitan, who used his personal website as a platform for donations for the 2009 elections and collected 53,000 NIS (approximately US$13,500 at current exchange rates). In 2011, Shelly Yachimovich of the Labor Party raised 500,000 NIS from party members and supporters through her personal website (Schneider 2011). In the 2013 election it became common to use crowdfunding for primary and general election purposes. This demonstrates the shift of digital campaigns from amateur to professional digital campaigns. Candidates who lacked enough funding used existing crowdfunding platforms to reach out to the public (e.g. MK Nino Abesadze, journalist Merav Michaeli, and Tamar Zandberg).

A fourth trend that intensified compared to the 2009 election was the use of anonymous campaigns to criticise, stigmatise, and condemn the image and stance of opponents. As mentioned earlier, Israeli law does not specifically address Internet campaigns; this is one of the main reasons why social media were flooded with anonymous negative campaigns in the 2013 election. The main platform for distributing these campaigns was Facebook. Examples include the anti-right The Day after the Elections, the anti-left The Right Block, and the anti-former opposition leader Livni Has Failed (see Figure 34.3 for a number of examples).

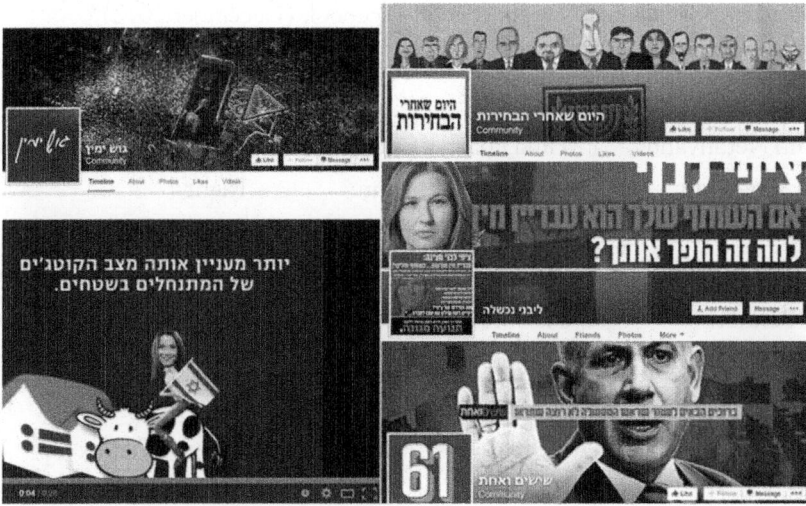

Figure 34.3 Negative Anonymous Campaigns

Changing Trends: From Multiple to Single-Platform Focus

While the 2009 campaigns were characterised as frantic and overextended, involving all popular social media platforms available (Haleva-Amir 2011a; Lev-On 2011; Haleva-Amir 2013), most online campaigns in 2013 focused exclusively on Facebook. By the end of 2012, approximately 70 per cent of the Israeli population of 5.3 million were connected to the Internet, and 71 per cent of those (about half the total population, or 3.8 million) were active Facebook users (Internet World Stats 2013).

Several factors made Facebook an attractive platform for the 2013 election: (1) It is a social network with high traffic and thus high chances of attracting users' attention; (2) its features makes it easy to use by ordinary users and campaigners; (3) its advertising system is highly personalised, allowing politicians to easily reach both large and specific audiences in a way that would have been difficult if not impossible through traditional media—in particular, younger people reported getting their news mainly through social media (Mitchell et al. 2013); and (4) Facebook, like other social media platforms, can bypass regulatory campaign restrictions in the Israeli context. To varying degrees, all those factors are also applicable in election campaigns worldwide, and indeed, the trend of focusing on Facebook is a global one.

Table 34.1 shows the number of Facebook followers of the leaders of the major parties in Israel in December 2012, one month before the election.

For many parties, the campaign budgets allocated to the online channel increased to up to 50 per cent of the total (Haleva-Amir 2013). Campaign managers used Facebook to test public opinion on various issues. For example, Gil Samsonov, the Facebook campaign manager of Halikud-Beitenu (a party bloc of Likud and Israel Beitenu), opined that "Facebook is a cruel courthouse, it knows you, judges you, reaches a verdict and sentences you as a matter of minutes" (Haleva-Amir 2014b: 80).

Table 34.1 Party Leaders and Followers on Facebook (December 2012)*

Name	Party	Political positioning	Followers
Benjamin Netanyahu	PM and chair of Likud	Right	386,000
Avigdor Liberman	Chair of Israel Beitenu	Right	118,000
Yair Lapid	Chair of Yesh Atid	Centre	97,000
Shelly Yachimovich	Chair of the Labor Party	Left	56,000
Naftali Bennett	Chair of HaBayit HaYehudi	Right	56,000
Tzipi Livni	Chair of Hatnua	Centre	30,000
Zehava Galon	Chair of Meretz	Left	16,000
Eli Yishai	Chair of Shas	Ultra-orthodox	7,533
Shaul Mofaz	Chair of Kadima	Centre	6,221

* The leader of the ultra-orthodox party, Yahadut Hatora, and the leaders of the Arab parties, Balad and Raam-Taal, did not have Facebook Accounts. Mohammad Barakeh, the leader of the Arab-Jewish party, Hadash, had a regular Facebook account, not a politician page.

New Trends in the 2013 Election

Symbiotic Relationship: Social and Mainstream Media

Social media, particularly Facebook, enabled candidates to avoid inconvenient journalist inquiries. In this campaign, more than ever before, candidates could circumvent traditional media and still reach and address the public directly. This forced journalists to regularly follow candidates' Facebook pages and use them as a primary source for political information. It became common to see journalists quoting statements of candidates from their Facebook pages, turning them into headlines. Social media became the forefront of electoral news, and Internet campaigns gained greater presence in traditional, mainstream media (Caspi 2013). Still, the former needed the latter to reach broader audiences, since only after reaching the traditional media did social media news go viral or spread in further networks on Facebook (Nahon & Hemsley 2013). In other words, the relationship between social and mainstream media became increasingly intimate and reciprocal.

A good example for this symbiotic relationship was Netanyahu's avoidance of debates with his rivals. On 24 December 2012, Shelly Yachimovich of the Labor Party invited the incumbent Prime Minister to a public debate by posting the following message on his and her Facebook walls:

> I invite you to a debate on TV, as is the custom in the western world, and also used to be the custom in Israel. The public is entitled and we [politicians] are obliged to hold an earnest, in-depth discussion of two different worldviews. The only real choice voters have is between you and me. . . . I would like to debate with you and present our opposing views . . . above all: What is the meaning of the state and its roles in our eyes? What are our obligations toward the public? Any other issue that you would like to raise for discussion will be most welcome.

This post was reported immediately in the traditional media. Hours later, the head of the Likud campaign, Gilad Erdan, responded on Yachimovich's wall:

> Hi Shelly, this is Gilad. Do you want a debate? As is the custom in the western world? I'm glad you remembered that it is a part of the game rules, because I wanted to remind you (since you've probably forgotten) that you had previously refused several debate offers while you ran for Labor Party chair. Here is a reminder what your number 2, Buji Hertzog, said about you [link to Hebrew news website]. In any case, what kind of debate do you want? Left wing vs. right-center? Great, but against who exactly? Against Livni? Galon? Lapid? You? Mofaz? When you finish squabbling among yourselves about who represents the left block, post another Facebook status and we will discuss it straight to the point.

Mobile Campaigns and Custom-Made Applications

Another new trend that emerged in the 2013 elections was the use of mobile technologies and custom-made applications in social media campaigns. Candidates used such applications to send text messages to party members and supporters, asking for survey participation or support in primary elections. Furthermore, most prospective voters received text and recorded voice messages to their mobile phones as well as landlines. This upset many and raised questions regarding legitimacy, legality, and privacy (Crystal 2013). For example, a new group in the Likud, The New Likudniks, whose goal is to influence the identity of future Knesset members, initiated a Facebook counter-campaign against two senior Likud MKs— Danny Danon and Dr. Leah Ness—who ran a text message campaign. The New Likudniks wanted to raise public awareness of the importance of the primary election and to increase voter turnout on election day. They created a Facebook page which shared text messages sent by Danon and Ness alongside ironic and mocking replies (Kayris 2012). This campaign demonstrates the civic political and democratic activism that played an important role in the online sphere prior to the elections.

New applications were developed during the election period for the specific purpose of disseminating electoral messages. Some applications were generated to share political messages humorously, or in a unique way, for example by using gamification. For example, Kadima developed two games that were embedded on a Facebook platform. The games (see Figure 34.4) were based on the classic Pac-Man game, and aimed to demonstrate the unfair share of socioeconomic rights and obligations between the secular and ultra-Orthodox groups in Israeli society (Almog 2012). The Labor Party developed Shoogle—Shelly's Google—a search engine for Yachimovich's positions and opinions on various issues such as housing costs, food prices, etc. The Labor Party also developed The Future Timeline, which showed Facebook users what their future would look like if the Labor wins the election.

Civic Engagement for Electoral Purposes on Social Media

The 2013 election campaigns were characterised by higher levels of civic engagement activities, manifested mainly on social media. These activities did not result in a big change in actual voter turnout, which was estimated at 67.8 per cent, only 2.6 percentage points more than the previous elections. Engagement activities were initiated mainly by civil society organisations. For example, The Public Knowledge Workshop,

Figure 34.4 A Game Developed by the Kadima Party

an NGO of programmers, designers and other volunteers, sought to develop applications to promote transparency and allow other democratic gatekeepers (such as journalists and citizens) to use the public information thus made available to increase democratic accountability. Over the three years before the election, the NGO developed websites such as Open Knesset (mainly to monitor legislation as well as other parliamentary activities) and Open Budget (to monitor budget allocation at the macro-level). For the election, The Public Knowledge Workshop developed easy-to-use Internet tools with relevant information regarding parties, candidates and agendas. One of these was The MK Meter, which helped users choose their candidates in the primary elections. Another was The Electo-Meter, an application that matched users' viewpoints with the party they should vote for. Other non-political individuals, activists and celebs opened Facebook pages or created videos in order to raise public awareness of the importance of voting and call for increasing voter turnout.[1]

Individuals and groups also undertook other civic engagement activities. Some of these were part of collaborations between parties, candidates and users, aiming to harness users to campaigns. For example, several private groups were formed on Facebook to aggregate all Facebook activities supporting Shelly Yachimovich while collaborating to form an active "Facebook brigade" (Schneider 2012). The members of such groups would monitor information flows on social media and join discussion threads whenever required to show support, answer questions or thwart attempts to use verbal violence against their candidate. Another example was the call by HaBayit HaYehudi to their Facebook supporters to help the party create campaign clips (Azulay & Yahav 2012). Meretz also used user-generated clips in their official campaign (Ronen 2013a).

Importantly, however, some of the civic engagement activities by individuals and groups were performed independently of parties and candidates. For example, the

Facebook page Naftali Bennett—The Unofficial Page, which was managed by a student supporter, had more followers than the official page of the HaBayit HaYehudi's leader. It was estimated that this unofficial campaign contributed immensely to the official campaign (Mor 2013; Yaron 2013).

Nevertheless, non-coordinated online activity could harm official campaigns and tarnish the party's image by conveying messages not correlated with the formal campaign strategy, and even impose penalties on the party due to violations of election regulations. This was the case when Likud activists ran various grassroots campaigns that damaged their party. One of these informal campaigns was published on the main website of the Likud supporters, and depicted right-wing rival Naftali Bennet in a ghetto, behind a barbed-wire fence, hinting that HaBayit HaYehudi was an Orthodox religious party not suitable for secular voters like those of the Likud (see Figure 34.5).

Another negative—and sexist—campaign referred to the only secular candidate in that party, Ayelet Shaked, calling upon her to 'Be Pretty and Keep Quiet', suggesting that she became a candidate just because of her pretty face since all the others were religious men (see Figure 34.6).

Figure 34.5 Likud Activists Sharing a Negative Advertisement about Naftali Bennet

Figure 34.6 'Be Pretty and Keep Quiet' Negative Campaign

Consequently, the HaBayit HaYehudi party appealed to the Central Election Committee for an urgent injunction warrant against the Likud and also demanded to expose the identity of the people behind the informal campaigns. The Likud, which was not coordinating these campaigns (at least not officially), had to appeal to the committee for an injunction warrant against its own supporters.

Memes, Humour, and Satire

The final common theme, which featured strongly in the 2013 election period, was the use of satire and humour. Israeli cyberspace was filled with memes (cultural artefacts that spread, usually with alteration, from one person to another via the Internet) created and circulated by political actors, TV programmes, and individuals on a daily basis. The enormous flow of memes created rather odd situations in which one could not tell at first sight who was responsible for a specific meme, and whether it was for or against any specific candidate, party or agenda. In many cases memes were not 'signed' by their creators, thus further contributing to the general confusion. For example, a supporter captioned a video of football star Cristiano Rolando, creating a humorous support clip for Naftali Bennett. The clip was uploaded to Bennett's official page once it became viral, but then began receiving angry reactions arguing that Ronaldo had supported Hamas during Israel's attack on Gaza in November 2012 (Operation Pillar of Defense). Consequently, the campaign managers removed the clip from Bennett's official Facebook page (Ronen 2013b).

Yachimovich used her satirical counterpart from Israel's leading TV political satire programme, *Eretz Nehederet* (A Wonderful Country). Kadima leader Shaul Mofaz invited the actor who portrayed his character in the same TV show to a debate (Farbstein 2012). On Facebook, official pages were opened for fictitious characters running for the office of prime minister.[2] These allowed humorous comments, but were primarily used as a critical and satirical tool, which indicated high levels of civic engagement. Simultaneously, fake profiles of real politicians were created. Some of these were declared as satire, but others obfuscated the fact that they were fake accounts and misled voters by their appearance as well as their names (Yaron 2013; Kayris 2012). For example, Netanyahu's fake page was called 'Netanyahu Bibi' (see Figure 34.7a), while his official page was called 'Benjamin Netanyahu' (see Figure 34.7b); the fake page used the same styling as the formal page. Only the humoristic content of the updates, the number of likes, shares and 'people talking about this' revealed the differences between the two pages. The Likud filed an official complaint and asked Facebook to remove the page. The party spokesperson claimed the problem was not the satire, but rather the fact that the page did not clearly state that it was a satire and thereby confused people. The page was removed by Facebook and reopened a few weeks later using a different design (Mor 2012).

Conclusion

This chapter discussed the role of social media in the 2013 election in Israel. In 2013, social media emerged as the main public space where discussions, discourse, deliberations and debates around the topic of the election occurred—for the first time surpassing traditional media in terms of exposure and engagement. However, the potential of new media was still not fully exploited, as candidates and constituents did not engage

Figure 34.7 The Fake and Official Facebook Pages of PM Benjamin Netanyahu

interactively, political messages were mainly one-sided, and constituents' sharing practices supported the echo-chamber theory. Subsequently, in March 2015, Israel held its 20th election (two years earlier than planned). This also allows us to swiftly explore the results of this study in the context of the next election. According to this study, the main themes which characterised the 2013 election included:

1. An emphasis on personal politics. There is an ongoing deterioration in the status of parties, as the entities elected to the Knesset (Hermann 2012). As social media became the main space of political activity, it reflects and accelerates this deterioration process. In the 2013 election, politicians mainly developed their professional Facebook pages, at the expense of their and their parties' websites. In some cases the page of the party linked to that of the leader. In cases where parties did maintain their own Facebook pages, the content was poor and did not receive a great deal of traffic. In 2015, this trend of personalisation intensified further, and the Facebook pages of parties served merely to syndicate the pages of the politicians. This has turned the parties' pages into a shell without substance, while the locus of activity remained on the personal pages.
2. The flood of anonymous and negative campaigns, which characterised the 2013 election, changed in the 2015 elections. Anonymous campaigns were still thriving;

however, there were not anonymous any more, and in many cases were presented as part of the official campaigns. Studies have shown that negative campaigns usually backfire (Nahon & Hemsley 2014). This was the case in both the 2013 and the 2015 elections.

3. Politicians focused solely on the Facebook platform in the 2013 election. While Facebook remained the main platform for political discourse in the 2015 election, another two social media platforms emerged as popular: Whatsapp and Twitter. Whatsapp, an instant messaging platform, is one of the most popular platforms in Israel. It is used frequently to pass social media content between friends and groups. In the 2015 election it played a major role in helping content go viral. While Twitter adoption in Israel is very low (estimations are around 5 per cent), it is used frequently by journalists and, at the time of the 2015 election, by politicians. Nevertheless, Facebook still is the most popular space for political purposes in terms of the number active users and the amount of content produced.

4. The symbiotic relationship between social media and traditional media continued to be prominent in the 2013 and the 2015 elections. Most viral phenomena on social media were covered by mainstream media.

5. The development of custom-made applications, which characterised the 2013 election, happened to a lesser extent in the 2015 election. For example, MK Naftali Bennet requested that users make a rhyme for the phrase 'Bennet is a brother'. This resulted in a viral event where users used an application to rhyme the phrase with insulting words.

6. The 2013 election was characterised by a high level of civic engagement, but it also demonstrated that dialogue is still missing and better communication between political actors and ordinary users is yet to be achieved. In the 2015 campaign, the number of civic engagement projects grew. For example, the initiative of Kikar Hamedina, a website developed by The Public Knowledge Workshop, collects the posts of candidates and politicians on Facebook and provides statistics and patterns about their usage. Another example is Project 61, which accumulated all published polls before the elections and provides an easy way to analyse these polls. Civic engagement initiatives in the 2013 election were mainly used by social media users. However, in the 2015 elections the civic engagement initiatives were more interactive, useful and information-rich, and therefore were also used extensively by professionals such as journalists, campaign managers and politicians.

7. Finally, the extensive use of memes and satire also intensified in the 2015 election. In fact, all the campaigns consisted to a significant extent of videos and images in which politicians themselves played a role. For example, the viral video 'Bibi the Babysitter', with 880,000 views, showed PM Benjamin Netanyahu as a babysitter coming to help a young couple, while warning them not to take the leaders of the other party as babysitters.

Notes

1 www.facebook.com/ILvote2013; www.facebook.com/IL80p; www.youtube.com/watch?v=EJAF4DIUV Ck&feature=youtu.be; http://mizbala.com /?p=59704

2 Some of these are: www.facebook.com/Hugo.Woof; www.facebook.com/MshDzLrswtHmmslh; www.facebook.com/shuali.kabab; www.facebook.com/nofutureforisrael; www.facebook.com/MiriPaskalPM.

References

Almog, N., 2012. Towards the Elections: Kadima Launched Its Version of Pac-Man. *People & Computers*. Available at: http://www.pc.co.il/it-news/106521/

Atmor, N., 2008. The Internet Race: Parties and the Online Campaign in the 2006 Elections. In A. Arian & M. Shamir, eds. *The Elections in Israel 2006*. New Brunswick: Transaction Publishers.

Atmor, N., 2009. 18th Knesset Elections Online Campaign: A Moment before the Elections. *The Israeli Democratic Institute*.

Azulay, M. & Yahav, T., 2012. HaBayit HaYehudi: Facebook's Friends to Produce Campaign Clips. *ynet*. Available at: http://www.ynet.co.il/articles/0,7340,L-4319300,00.html

Bartolini, S. & Mair, P., 2001. Challenges to Contemporary Political Parties. In L. Diamond & R. Gunther, eds. *Political Parties and Democracy*. Baltimore: JHU Press, pp. 327–344.

boyd, danah, 2010. Social Network Sites as Networked Publics: Affordances, Dynamics and Implications. In Z. Papacharissi, ed. *A Networked Self: Identity, Community, and Culture on Social Network Sites*. London: Routledge.

Bronner, E. & Cohen, N., 2008. Israeli Candidate Borrows a (Web) Page From Obama. *The New York Times*. Available at: http://www.nytimes.com/2008/11/15/world/middleeast/15bibi.html

Bruns, A. & Burgess, J., 2011. #ausvotes: How Twitter Covered the 2010 Australian Federal Election. Available at: http://search.informit.com.au/documentSummary;dn=627330171744964;res=IELHSS

Busby, C. & Bellamy, P., 2011. *New Zealand Parliamentarians and Online Social media*. New Zealand Parliament's Parliamentary Library. Available at: http://www.parliament.nz/en-nz/parl-support/research-papers/00PLSocRP11021/new-zealand-parliamentarians-and-online-social-media

Cabir, O., 2012. The Social Knesset: Our Politicians Still Don't Understand Facebook. *Calcalist*. Available at: http://www.spot.im/embed/%D7%9B%D7%9C%D7%9B%D7%9C%D7%99%D7%A1%D7%98%D7%98%D7%9B%D7%A0%D7%95%D7%9C%D7%95%D7%92%D7%99

Cain-Miller, C., 2008. How Obama's Internet Campaign Changed Politics. *The New York Times: Bits Blog*. Available at: http://bits.blogs.nytimes.com/2008/11/07/how-obamas-internet-campaign-changed-politics/

Caspi, D., 2013. Put Some Tippex on These Elections. *ynet*. Available at: http://www.ynet.co.il/articles/0,7340,L-4332129,00.html

Castells, M., 2009. *The Rise of the Network Society: The Information Age: Economy, Society, and Culture* (Volume I, 2nd Edition with a New Preface edition). Chichester: Wiley-Blackwell.

Colvile, R., 2008. How MPs Can Use the Internet to Become More Relevant. *Conservative Home*. Available at: http://www.conservativehome.com/platform/2008/02/robert-colvil-3.html

Crystal, M., 2013. Calls and Text Messages from Bibi and Shelly—Harassment under the Protection of Law. *ynet*. Available at: http://www.ynet.co.il/articles/0,7340,L-4334127,00.html

Farbstein, R., 2012. Recruited Country: Shaul and Mariano, Shelly and Chelly. *Holes in the Net*. Available at: http://www.holesinthenet.co.il/holesinthenet-media-story-30010

Galili-Zucker, O., 2004. *Tele-Politicians: New Political Leadership in the West and in Israel*. Tel Aviv: Tel Aviv University.

Gilboa, E. & Katz, Y., 2001. The Media Campaign: The Shift to Alternative Media. *Israel Affairs*, 7(2), pp. 223–244.

Haleva-Amir, S., 2011a. Online Israeli Politics: The Current State of the Art. *Israel Affairs*, 17(3), pp.476–485.

Haleva-Amir, S., 2011b. Present—Absentees: MKs Usage of Personal Internet Tools. In E. Cohen & A. Lev-On, eds. *Connected: Politics, Technology and Society in Israel*. Tel Aviv: Israeli Political Science Association, pp. 211–261.

Haleva-Amir, S., 2013. MKs Usage of Personal Internet Tools, 2009: On the Verge of a New Decade. *World Political Science Review*, 9(1). Available at: http://www.degruyter.com/view/j/wpsr.2013.9.issue-1/wpsr-2013-0010/wpsr-2013-0010.xml

Haleva-Amir, S. 2014a. *Personal Web Applications in the Service of Knesset Members: Personal Israeli Politics in the Digital Era*. PhD Dissertation. Haifa, Israel: University of Haifa.

Haleva-Amir, S. 2014b. "Political Communication: Online Campaigns in the Elections for the 19th Knesset," in R. Mann & A. Lev-On (eds.) *Annual Report: The Israeli Media 2013 – Agendas, Usages and Trends*, Ariel, Israel: New Media, Society & Politics Institute, 2014, pp. 79–90. Available at: http://aunmedia.org/sites/default/files/research/mediareport2013.pdf

Hermann, T. S., 2012. Introduction. In T. Hermann S., ed. *By the People, For the People, Without the People? The Emergence of (Anti) Political Sentiment in Western Democracies and in Israel*. Jerusalem: Israeli Democracy Institute, pp. 9–39.

Internet World Stats, 2013. *Internet Usage in the Middle East*. Available at: http://www.internetworldstats.com/stats5.htm

Jackson, N., 2003. MPs and Web Technologies: An Untapped Opportunity? *Journal of Public Affairs*, 3(2), pp.124–137.

Jackson, N. A. & Lilleker, D. G., 2009. MPs and E-representation: Me, MySpace and I. *British Politics*, 4(2), pp.236–264.

Kayris, V., 2012. Satire on the Web: Fake Posts and More. *ynet*. Available at: http://www.ynet.co.il/articles/0,7340,L-4296622,00.html

Keinan, I., 2008. Obama's and Netanyahu's Websites. *Room 404*. Available at: http://room404.net/?p=15299

Koren, D. ed., 1998. *The Demise of Parties in Israel*. Tel Aviv: Hakibbutz Hameuchad.

Lehman-Wilzig, S., 2004. Worth an Agora? 2003 E-lection Party Sites and Public Discourse. *Israel Affairs*, 10(4), pp.242–262.

Mitchell, A. et al., 2013. The Role of News on Facebook. *Pew Research Journalism Project*. Available at: http://www.journalism.org/2013/10/24/the-role-of-news-on-facebook/

Mor, G., 2012. Due to Formal Complaint: Satiric Page on Netanyahu has been Removed. *Holes in the Net*. Available at: http://www.holesinthenet.co.il/holesinthenet-media-story-26496

Mor, G., 2013. An Election Post: Naftali Bennett can Create an Obstructive Bloc. *Holes in the Net*. Available at: http://www.holesinthenet.co.il/holesinthenet-media-story-24951

Mualem, M., Zinger, R., & Huri, J., 2008. On-Line Elections: Campaigns Migrate Online. *Walla News*. Available at: http://news.walla.co.il/item/1384636

Nahon, K., 2009. The Future of Online Politics: What Our Elected Representatives Know? *ynet*. Available at: http://www.ynet.co.il/articles/0,7340,L-3750548,00.html

Nahon, K. & Hemsley, J., 2013. *Going Viral*. Cambridge: Polity Press.

Nahon, K. & Hemsley, J., 2014. Homophily in the Guise of Cross-Linking: Political Blogs and Content. *American Behavioral Scientist*, 58(10), pp.1294–1313.

Lev-On, A., 2011. Campaigning Online: Use of the Internet by Parties, Candidates and Voters in National and Local Election Campaigns in Israel. *Policy & Internet*, 3(1), pp.1–28.

Pereg, N., 2008. Everyone Wants to Be Obama: What Do the Big Parties do to Reach Constituents on the Internet. *Globes*. Available at: http://www.globes.co.il/news/article.aspx?fbdid=1000407627

Rahat, G. & Sheafer, T., 2007. The Personalization(s) of Politics: Israel, 1949–2003. *Political Communication*, 24(1), pp.65–80.

Ronen, E., 2013a. Citizens for Meretz: Users' Content Was Integrated with the Formal Campaign. *Holes in the Net*. Available at: http://www.holesinthenet.co.il/holesinthenet-media-story-26435

Ronen, E., 2013b. How a Ronaldo Supporting Clip for HaBayit HaYehudi Had Upset Bennett's Boys. *Holes in the Net*. Available at: http://www.holesinthenet.co.il/holesinthenet-media-story-26324

Schneider, T., 2011. Adopted Obama's Technique: Shelly Yachimovich Raised 500,000 NIS in an Online Campaign. *Globes*. Available at: http://www.globes.co.il/news/article.aspx?fbdid=1000685945

Schneider, T., 2012. Spin Machine: 2.0. *The Plog—Tal Schneider's Political Blog*. Available at: http://www.talschneider.com/2012/11/27/spinmachine/

Segaard, S. B. & Nielsen, J. A., 2013. Local Election Blogs: Networking among the Political Elite. *Information Polity*, 18(4), pp.299–313.

Serfaty, V., 2010. Web Campaigns: Popular Culture and Politics in the US and French Presidential Elections. *Culture, Language and Representation*, 8, pp. 115–129.

Shragai, N., 2008. The Jewish Home Party Received Its Name from the Users. *Haaretz*. Available at: http://www.haaretz.co.il/captain/net/1.1362565

Smith, A., 2014. Cell Phones, Social Media and Campaign 2014. *Pew Research Center's Internet & American Life Project*. Available at: http://www.pewinternet.org/2014/11/03/cell-phones-social-media-and-campaign-2014/

Stanyer, J., 2008. Elected Representatives, Online Self-Presentation and the Personal Vote: Party, Personality and Webstyles in the United States and United Kingdom. *Information, Communication & Society*, 11(3), pp.414–432.

Stromer-Galley, J., 2013. The Paradox of Networked Politics: A Critical Examination of Presidential Campaigns in the United States. *Selected Papers of Internet Research*, 3(0). Available at: http://spir.aoir.org/index.php/spir/article/view/839

Van Santen, R. & van Zoonen, L., 2010. The Personal in Political Television Biographies. *Biography*, 33(1), pp.46–67.

Vegyte, N., Malinauskiene, E., & Petrauskas, R., 2008. *E-Participation in Lithuanian Representative Power*. In The Sixth International Eastern European e-Gov Days: Results and Trends. Prague.

Vergeer, M., Hermans, L., & Sams, S., 2011. Online Social Networks and Micro-Blogging in Political Campaigning: The Exploration of a New Campaign Tool and a New Campaign Style. *Party Politics*, doi:1354068811407580.

Wattenberg, M. P., 1992. *The Rise of Candidate-Centered Politics: Presidential Elections of the 1980s*. Cambridge, Mass.: Harvard University Press.

Williamson, A., 2009a. *MPs on Facebook*. London: Hansard Society.

Williamson, A., 2009b. *MPs Online: Connecting with Constituents: A Study into How MPs Use Digital Media to Communicate with Their Constituents*. London: Hansard Society. Available at: http://www.hansardsociety.org.uk/wp-content/uploads/2012/10/MPs-Online-Connecting-with-Constituents-2009.pdf

Wolf, P., 2008. Primaries in "Israel Hazaka": Voting through the Internet. *Walla News*. Available at: http://news.walla.co.il/item/1395335

Yaron, O., 2013. The Facebook Pages That Will Get You through Elections' Week. *Haaretz*. Available at: http://www.haaretz.co.il/news/elections/1.1907623

Zittel, T., 2003. Political Representation in the Networked Society: The Americanisation of European Systems of Responsible Party Government? *The Journal of Legislative Studies*, 9(3), pp.32–53.

35

SOCIAL MEDIA AND THE SCOTTISH INDEPENDENCE REFERENDUM 2014

Events and the Generation of Enthusiasm for Yes[1]

Mark Shephard and Stephen Quinlan

Social Media and Political Campaigns: What We Know, and the New Frontiers

Ever since the 2008 U.S. presidential election, when Barack Obama's campaign demonstrated the potential of social media as a useful tool in political campaigning (Harfoush 2009), the use of social media by political campaigns has become more prevalent cross-nationally (e.g. Chen 2010; Lassen and Brown 2010; Gainous and Wagner 2011; Gibson and McAllister 2011; Sudlich and Wall 2011; Vergeer et al. 2011; Ackland and Gibson 2013; Conway et al. 2013; Vergeer and Hermans 2013). For politicians, social media offers a new means of engaging supporters and also an alternative form of soliciting donations (Davis et al. 2009; Straw 2010; Cogburn and Espinoza-Vasquez 2011). We also know that social media has the capacity to mobilise people to participate politically (Cogburn and Espinoza-Vasquez 2011; Bond et al. 2012) and that it could even be a useful tool in helping predict election outcomes (Tumasjan et al. 2010, 2011; Sang and Bos 2012; DiGrazia et al. 2013; Ceron et al. 2014), although its ability to do the latter is contested (Jungherr et al. 2012). Moreover, considering its extensive usage by journalists and news organisations (Fahri 2009; Bruno 2011), social media has gained an increasingly prominent agenda setting capacity, illustrated at the extremes by the 2011 Irish presidential election, which showed that posts on social media do have the propensity to alter voter behaviour and the result of an election in extreme cases (O'Malley 2012; Hogan and Graham 2013). In sum, with social media now such an integral part of daily life for many people (Eurobarometer Flash 2013; Pew Research Centre's Internet and American Life Project 2014) and many potential benefits accruing from a social media political presence, having some form of social media presence is almost a necessary component of a modern-day campaign.

In spite of the above, research on social media's impact on politics is still relatively in its infancy. In terms of adoption by candidates and politicians, we know that social media are more likely to be used by younger candidates (Lassen and Brown 2010; Strandberg 2013; Larsson and Kalsnes 2014), and more often than not, by newer and progressive parties (Gulati and Williams 2011; Vergeer and Hermans 2013). However, much of our understanding is based on analyses of elections. There has been little analysis of social media during a referendum campaign, which is likely to be different given the idiosyncratic nature of referenda. Unlike elections, in referendums there are only two sides competing for attention, one primary issue is at stake, and voters may be less likely to be as embedded in their preferences than in a general election, thereby increasing the possibility of volatility (LeDuc 2002). Consequently, patterns of behaviour could indeed be different from those found during elections.

The little research that exists has focused on discussion of referenda in online forums and whether such conversations promote deliberation (Quinlan et al. 2015). But there has not yet been any in-depth focus on how social media plays out in a referendum campaign. Additionally, while most existing research on social media and campaigns has tended to explore the reasons underlying a campaign's adoption, and the extent to which voting behaviour is influenced by engagement with these channels, an important dimension has remained largely unexplored, namely, the extent to which campaigns generate enthusiasm and support through these channels, and the patterns underlying this engagement. This chapter seeks to fill this void.

The 2014 Scottish independence referendum provides a unique opportunity to explore the impact of social media as a campaign tool in a referendum. We do so by examining the social media campaigns of the two official protagonists in the independence referendum debate, the 'Yes Scotland' (YS) campaign, which campaigned for a yes vote in favour of Scottish independence, and the 'Better Together' (BT) campaign, which argued for a no vote, and Scotland remaining within the United Kingdom. Our focus is on each campaign's use of two of the most popular social media, Facebook and Twitter. Our analysis is based on a unique set of data that captures the activity of the two campaigns on these two channels over a 14-month period from August 2013 up until the referendum in September 2014. Our objective is threefold: (1) to examine the trends in engagement with social media over the course of the referendum campaign; (2) to establish which campaign generated more enthusiasm online over the course of the campaign; (3) to discuss some of the potential reasons as to why particular patterns took hold.

Our analysis shows that as the campaign progressed, more and more people engaged with the campaign online, with the peak of interest occurring in the final three weeks before the vote. Engagement on social media was particularly salient around the time of two TV debates between the main sides. We also find that the Yes campaign, on the surface at least, generated greater online enthusiasm for its campaign than the No side. We posit a number of potential reasons for this, including some referendum-specific reasons why the Yes side was able to come out on top online.

The chapter proceeds as follows: we first provide an overview of the 2014 independence referendum in Scotland. We then detail our data, followed by an in-depth discussion of our empirical findings. We then discuss a number of potential reasons that could explain why we observed the patterns of behaviour we did, including advancing some referendum specific explanations. The chapter concludes with a summary of our findings and suggestions for future research.

The 2014 Scottish Independence Referendum

The question of Scottish independence first came on to the political agenda with a vengeance as the pro-secessionist Scottish National Party (SNP) won 11 seats in the UK parliament in the 1974 Westminster elections. While the fortunes of the SNP have ebbed and flowed since that election (Cairney 2011), the independence question has remained omnipresent with the presence of the Scottish National Party, resulting in Scotland having a distinct political system (Kellas 1984; McCrone and Paterson 2002; Keating 2010). Although public opinion polls pre-2014 had never shown even close to a majority in favour of Scottish secession (Curtice 2013), the creation of a Scottish Parliament in 1999 provided the SNP with a platform for illustrating competence in governance, demonstrating in small part what might be possible given independence.

The independence question took on renewed significance in the aftermath of the 2011 Scottish parliament elections, when the Scottish National Party were re-elected to power with a majority government. While the SNP's victory appears to have been driven more by Scottish voters' perceptions of the SNP's competence in running the Scottish government rather than any particular burning desire for Scottish independence (Johns et al. 2011, 2013), the majority result provided legitimacy to the granting of an independence vote.

The referendum was confirmed in October 2012 when the UK Prime Minister David Cameron and the Scottish First Minister and leader of the SNP Alex Salmond signed the Edinburgh Agreement, granting the Scottish Parliament the power to hold a referendum by asking a single question of Scottish voters. Even before the signing of the Edinburgh Agreement, both sides had actually launched official campaigns in the summer of 2012. An 18-month intensive campaign was initiated following the announcement of the referendum question in March 2013. The campaign was dominated by a range of issues ranging from Scotland's role in the EU in the event of independence, Trident and nuclear defences, to welfare cuts and austerity. However, the principal issue at hand was the economy with debate between both sides on Scotland's continued use of the British pound in the event of independence, the division of debt between Scotland and the rest of the UK in the event of independence, associated revenues from oil, and the impact independence might have on employment and industry.[2] When asked about being worse off or better off, YouGov polling evidence throughout 2014 consistently showed that more people thought that both Scotland and their own fortunes would be worse off in an independent Scotland.[3]

As to how the public received information, social media was arguably central to the Scottish campaign. There was substantial activity on Twitter and Facebook related to the referendum, particularly in the final 30 days of the campaign. Between 2013 and 2014, there were 5.4 million tweets using the '#indyref' (Cellan-Jones 2014) and hashtags associated with the independence referendum ended up trending heavily in the final week of the campaign, at one stage even comprising eight out of 10 top hashtag trends in Glasgow for example.[4] Meanwhile, on Facebook, there were 10 million interactions alone relating to the referendum in the five weeks preceding the vote.[5]Afterwards, the potency of social media in the campaign was illustrated by research from pollster You-Gov, which suggested that 54 per cent of people got general information on the issues from social media, and when asked what information had influenced their decision in the referendum, 39 per cent said information from social media and the Web (Haggerty 2014). Furthermore, 11 per cent of Scots claimed to have taken part in discussions related to the referendum online, more than those who said they attended a public meeting during the campaign, or indeed joined either of them (TNS Global 2014). Indeed, even if a person tried avoiding social media, by accident or design, what took place online often became the lead story for traditional news media themselves. This was illustrated by numerous occurrences of stories generated by the online abuse meted out to prominent politicians and donors on both sides of the campaign, for example, Nicola Sturgeon (at the time, deputy leader of the SNP, and a key Yes politician) and J. K. Rowling (author and a major No donor).[6] As such, there is a strong case to be made that even if every single member of the electorate was not consuming and/or engaging online, they were nonetheless indirectly confronted with what was taking place online (e.g. Geser 2011; Maireder and Schlögl 2014), heightening the importance of a focus of the online trajectory of both campaigns.

Polls throughout this long campaign consistently showed the No side holding a lead, although this lead began to subside in summer 2014. The final fortnight resulted in a flurry of activity on both sides as the polls started to suggest that the result would be much closer than first thought, with two polls even suggesting that Scotland would vote yes.[7]

However, on 18 September 2014 voters in Scotland went to the polls and were asked: *Should Scotland be an independent country?* Fifty-five per cent of voters in Scotland voted no and in favour of remaining part of the United Kingdom on a high turnout of 84.6 per cent of voters (Electoral Management Board for Scotland 2014). While we know what happened in the polls, we are interested in exploring the state of the two campaigns on social media over the course of the campaign. Was there also a surge to Yes on social media and how might we account for this?

Data and Measures

Our analysis is based on the tracking of social media activity of the two main campaigns in the 2014 Scottish referendum, namely the Yes Scotland campaign that argued for a yes vote in the referendum, and the Better Together campaign, which campaigned for a no vote. We monitored each campaign's official Facebook and Twitter accounts, choosing these two forms of social media as we expected them above all others to be most likely to engender the widest connection to, and interest from, the public. For Facebook, we specifically monitored the number of likes each campaign's Facebook page received and the number of people talking about each campaign's page.[8] For Twitter, we collected the number of Twitter followers each account boasted as well as the number of tweets it had posted by that particular day. Our unique set of data was collected each weekday during the period August 2013 until the end of September 2014.

We suggest that these metrics can be divided into different themes, namely those indicating support/interest in the campaigns and those illustrating a deeper engagement with the campaign. Liking the Facebook page of the campaign or following one of the campaign's Twitter accounts are indicators of support or interest in that campaign. On the other hand, our intensity/engagement measures require a greater level of effort either on the part of the campaign, as measured by the number of tweets emanating from it's account, or on the part of the user. We measure the general public's intensity engagement by examining how much the Facebook page of each campaign was 'talked about'. This metric measures how much people are interacting with each of the campaign's pages, for example by commenting/sharing a wall post, or tagging a photo.

Empirical Analysis

A review of the wealth of data over the fourteen-month period has enabled us to iden-tify three distinct patterns of behaviour during the campaign depicted in our figures by three different shaded background blocks. The first of these periods runs from the Sum-mer of 2013 until November 2013, and the launch of the Scottish government's White Paper on Scottish Independence, a period which is characterised by offline hegemony for BT and a mixed online battle. The second is the period between November 2013 and May 2014, a period in which the Yes campaign pulled ahead noticeably from the BT campaign online. And finally, a third period, which runs from May 2014 until poll-ing day, 18 September 2014, in which we observe an online tsunami of support for the Yes campaign.

Period I: Fairly Close Social Media Horse Race
(August to November 2013)

Figure 35.1 charts the extent of support (total numbers of Facebook likes and Twitter followers) for the two campaigns between August 2013 and September 2014. Overall totals of Facebook likes for both the Yes Scotland (YS) and Better Together (BT) campaigns increased by approximately 30,000 between August and November 2013 (approximately 76,000 to 106,000 for YS and approximately 66,000 to 96,000 for BT). For the first period (August 2013 to November 2013), the volume of Facebook likes and Twitter followers was quite similar for both campaigns, albeit there was one noticeable blip on Facebook in mid-September 2013, suggesting a change in momentum towards BT. As Figure 35.1 illustrates, the BT campaign did manage to reduce the gap in Face-book support marginally right after the one year mark from the referendum. This 'year to go' milestone coincided with the launch on 19 September 2013 of a campaign called

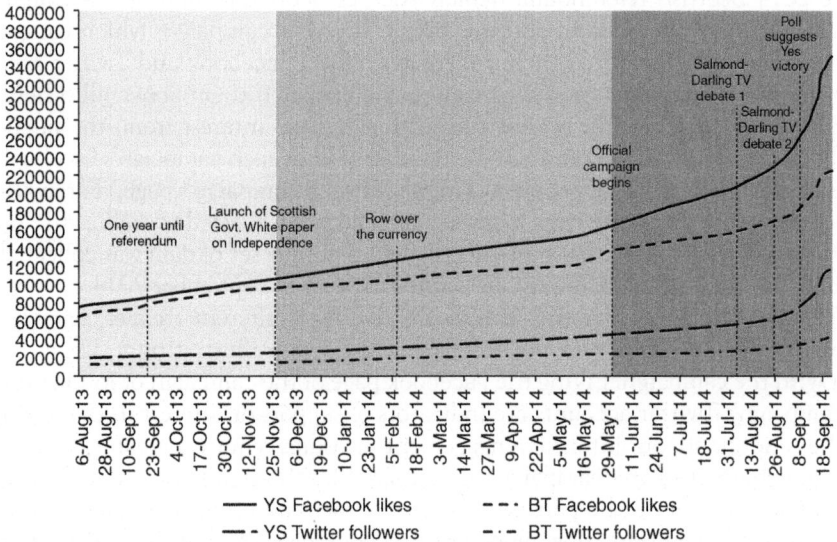

Figure 35.1 Facebook and Twitter Support Totals for Both Campaigns (August 2013 to September 2014)

'Mid-Morning Sessions', the purpose of which was to encourage BT supporters to step up their online activities by referring their friends on Facebook and Twitter to the BT campaign. However, closure in the gap was short-lived, and the YS campaign maintained its lead through this period (undulating and varying between just under 6,000 likes difference in mid-September 2013 and just under 10,000 likes difference in both August and November 2013).

On Twitter, YS also had noticeably more followers on Twitter than BT, and unlike Facebook likes, Twitter followers showed evidence that online support for YS was consistently pulling ahead of the BT campaign as YS pulled in twice as many new followers as BT over this period. In August 2013, YS had just over 21,000 followers versus just under 13,000 for BT. By the end of November, YS had over 26,000 followers compared with just over 15,000 for BT.

Figure 35.2 explores the differences in support for the two campaigns between August 2013 and September 2014. The figure depicts the difference in the number of likes between the Yes Scotland campaign's Facebook page and the Better Together campaign's Facebook page (as illustrated by the solid black line). It also shows the difference in the number of Twitter followers for each campaign, illustrated by the black dotted line. We see that the Yes Scotland campaign had an advantage in the number of Facebook likes and Twitter followers it had for it's campaign from the outset. While this was an advantage that the Yes Scotland campaigns were never to lose throughout the entire campaign, as Figure 35.1 shows, in this early period of the campaign, the differences between the two campaigns was quite marginal, suggesting a close horse race.

Figures 35.3 and 35.4 depict level of engagement with the two campaigns according to the number of tweets on Twitter and the 'talked about' metric on Facebook, respectively.

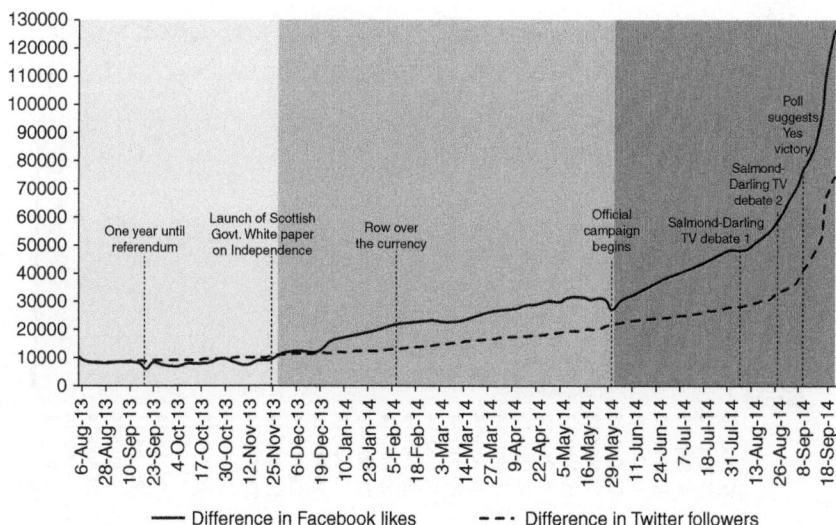

Figure 35.2 Differences in Facebook and Twitter Support Levels for Both Campaigns—YS Campaign Total Minus BT Campaign Total (August 2013 to September 2014) Note: A positive score indicates an advantage for YS campaign. The direction of scoring is purely arbitrary.

Interestingly, BT were consistently ahead of YS in the number of tweets that were posted between August 2013 and November 2013. That said, the margin of difference was consistently being closed by YS, so that a BT advantage of more than 1,200 extra tweets per day in August 2013, was almost halved by the end of November 2013 (see Figure 35.3).

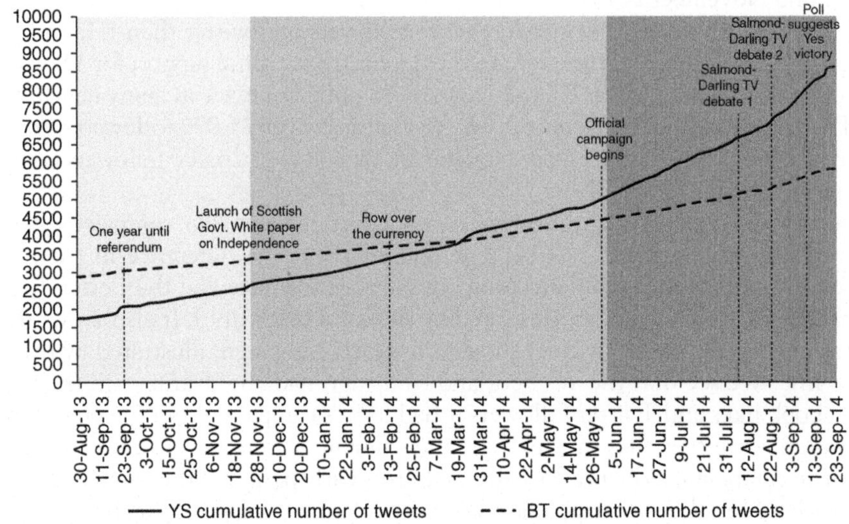

Figure 35.3 Social Media Intensity of Engagement by the Campaigns: Number of Cumulative Tweets from Each Campaign (August 2013 to September 2014)

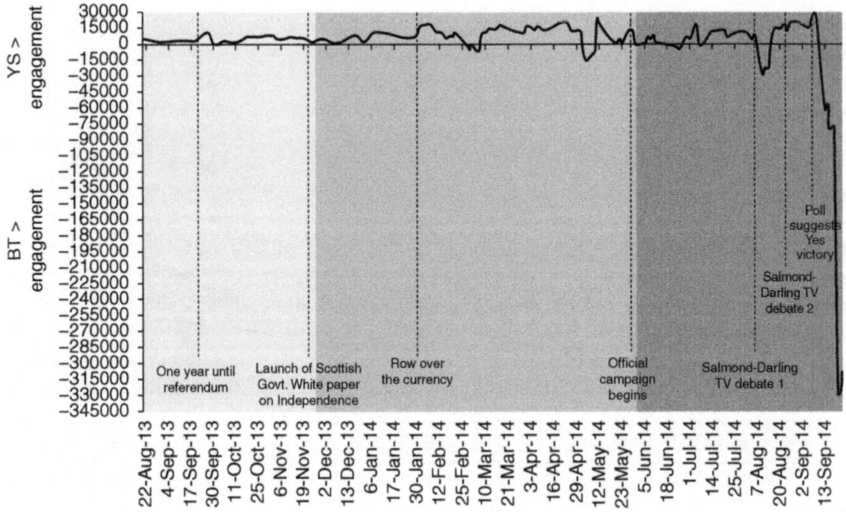

Figure 35.4 Social Media Intensity of Engagement by the Public with Social Media Campaigns: Difference In the Number of People Talking about Each of the Campaigns (August 2013 to September 2014).

Note: A positive score indicates an advantage for YS campaign. A negative score indicates an advantage for BT campaign. The direction of scoring is purely arbitrary.

Conversely, the Facebook 'talked about' metric was invariably a few thousand more in favour of YS than BT (for example, in August 2013 YS were at approximately 8,000 compared to approximately 5,000 for BT), except on a couple of occasions in early October 2013 when BT surpassed YS. However, proportionately, this lead is arguably more impressive than the lead for 'likes'. Also, compared with the number of Facebook 'likes', the 'talked about' metric is a more precise indicator of how much people are engaging with the campaigns.

Initially, the YS campaign was the more 'talked about', reaching a peak at the time of the UK party conference season in September 2013. However, the BT campaign did appear to gain some short-lived traction in its favour at the beginning of October, when it was making a concerted effort to focus attention on what would happen to the currency and to taxes in an independent Scotland and when it launched several regional campaigns. The YS campaign then succeeded in regaining momentum following the 2013 SNP annual conference.

In sum, the campaign period from August 2013 until November 2013 suggests a close horse race on social media. While YS were behind (but closing) in terms of the volume of tweets, the other metrics of engagement and support suggest a steady, but slight, lead on average for the YS campaign.

Period II: The Launch of 'Scotland's Future' and the Rise of the Yes Campaign Online despite Dire Warnings over the Currency and EU Membership (November 2013 to May 2014)

The referendum campaign intensified considerably online following the launch of the Scottish Government's White Paper on independence (aka 'Scotland's Future') on 26 November 2013. It is very noticeable from this point that the solid and consistent Yes Scotland (YS) lead in terms of support, at least on Facebook, began to widen. At the launch of Scotland's Future, the YS Facebook page had been averaging around 8,000 more likes than the BT campaign. After the launch the gap between the two campaigns started to grow, and edged up considerably over the next six months, to the extent that by the end of May 2014 YS were ahead of BT by just over 30,000 Facebook likes (see Figures 35.1 and 35.2). The YS campaign also gained more Twitter followers than BT during this period. From the end of November 2013 to the end of May 2014, the gap steadily doubled from a 10,000 advantage over BT to well over a 20,000 lead with YS having nearly double the followers (45,000 to 23,000—see Figures 35.1 and 35.2). This represents an important development in which YS were developing a much larger network of tweeters and re-tweeters of pro-independence campaign messages.

Moreover, by the middle of March 2014, YS started to tweet more than BT for the first time (see Figure 35.3), and this lead continually extended extended. Figure 35.3 charts the number of tweets emanating from each campaign's account and by the end of May 2014, YS had tweeted more than 500 more times than BT (4,930 times compared to 4,393, respectively). The YS campaign was also more consistently 'talked about' on average than the BT campaign during this period (see Figure 35.4). Of the 105 daily data time points we have during this period, the BT campaign was the more talked about on only 13 occasions. Indeed, as the purple line shows for this period, despite two fairly substantial swings towards BT, the overall trend was one of upward growth for YS. On the two main occasions when momentum swung back to the BT camp, this followed concerns raised by European Commission President Jose Manuel Barroso over the possibility of Scottish membership of the EU as well as Chancellor George Osborne insisting that a currency union was not possible in the event of independence (both in February 2014), and the release of a report by Moody's on the challenging financial implications of independence in May 2014.

Period III: Official Campaign Period, Impact of Events, and an Overall Online Tsunami towards Yes (May 2014 to September 2014)

The official campaign period (a 16 week period from 30 May 2014 to 18 September 2014) saw the online and offline campaigns in full swing. Offline activities included: door-to-door canvassing; leafleting; parades; street bands; creative art projects; banners; posters; the sporting of lapel badges and T-shirts as well as countless interventions from industry figures, politicians, and celebrities, and two set piece televised debates between the two campaign leaders. Online campaign activity increased too, especially following the two TV leader debates.

What is most noticeable during the official campaign period is that online support for YS skyrocketed compared with BT (see Figures 35.1, 35.2, and 35.3). The only very slight aberration to this coincided with the first television debate between the two campaign leaders, on 5 August 2014, when an ICM poll for *The Guardian* newspaper found that Alistair Darling (BT) 'won' the debate against Alex Salmond (YS) by 56 per cent to 44 per cent.[9] That said, in terms of Facebook likes YS extended its lead over BT from 27,000 at the end of May 2014 to over 109,000 by the day of the referendum (see Figures 35.1 and 35.2). Similarly, the YS lead in terms of Twitter followers jumped from 22,000 at the end of May 2014 to over 68,000 by the day of the referendum (see Figures 35.1 and 35.2).

In relation to campaign tweets, the final numbers of tweets (8,354 for YS and 5740 for BT) suggested a ratio of 41 per cent for BT versus 59 per cent for YS (see Figure 35.3). The volume of tweeting by YS increased significantly during the official campaign period, and moreover increased more than it did for BT. This arguably matters because if you are giving your supporters comparably more tweets to re-tweet and share on other sites such as Facebook, then your potential for both audience reach and message control is arguably going to be much greater.

Interestingly, before September 2014 very few public opinion polls were in the 40s for Yes, whereas during September only one poll out of 19 was not in the 40s. There was a clear shift in public mood and volume of support for Yes in the final weeks of the campaign, and our online data arguably detect this momentum slightly ahead of time as depicted by the steepening curves of both Facebook likes and Twitter 'followers' during the official campaign period, and in particular following the second TV debate on 25 August 2014, in which Alex Salmond was deemed the winner over Alistair Darling. Arguably compounding the leverage of this second debate performance was the airing of the so-called Patronising BT Lady television commercial in which a hypothetical uninformed middle-class housewife talked herself into voting no. Much parodied (e.g. 'ma fridge magnets told me to vote No'), the commercial was widely derided as being a male creation representing another era.[10]

However not all of the social media metrics pointed so clearly towards a Yes victory, online or in the vote itself. The Facebook 'talked about' metric (see Figure 35.4) was interesting in that despite a general upward trend for YS, there were two clear time points when the momentum swung dramatically back to the BT campaign.[11] The first swing towards BT followed the first leaders' TV debate on 5 August 2015, in which pundits generally thought BT leader Alistair Darling outperformed YS leader Alex Salmond. The second swing towards BT was huge (see Figure 35.4) and occurred during the last week of the campaign. Following public opinion polls suggesting a last minute move towards Yes[12] there was a last minute flurry of activity from the three main Westminster parties and UK party leaders who rushed north to rally the cause in Scotland. What manifested was what the media labelled a 'vow' for more powers to Scotland than the pro-Union side had been willing to countenance beforehand (albeit what this 'vow' meant varied across the parties making up the No camp), as well as an outpouring of warnings from many prominent business and industry players of the implications of a yes vote in the closing days. Ex-Labour prime minister Gordon Brown also delivered what was widely perceived to be the speech of his life in the closing days of the campaign, as the BT campaign finally tried to reclaim brand Scotland through the use of red heart balloons and logos with Scotland written all over them.

Most importantly, what our data show, especially in this final period, is that events very much appear to be driving online activities. This finding nicely supports research by others such as Rossman et al. (2014) who found surges in Twitter activities around the time of the TV debates between the two Chancellor candidates in the 2013 German election, a pattern which is very much mirrored in our analysis. Events seemed to drive behaviour, and different events played well in terms of generating support (online at least) for both camps.

Understanding Patterns of Social Media Behaviour in the Campaign

There are a number of possible reasons for Yes having carved a decisive lead online. Our starting framework is that social media in a referendum campaign is likely to result in the Yes side having a positive advantage because the medium favours 'positive messages'. For instance, it is invariably easier to 'like' something with the click of a button on Facebook or retweeting a tweet. Disliking takes more effort. This is arguably even more the case when this also relates to one's own country (e.g. Yes to Independence, or even Yes to Scotland) than to like a negative position (e.g. No to Independence, which could feasibly be perceived, or misperceived, as No to Scotland).

Second, it could be that those backing the Yes side were simply more engaged in their campaign than were the No supporters, and that consequently, Yes supporters may have been more likely than No supporters to express their views in a public forum. A June 2014 poll by TNS Global showed that Yes supporters were three times more likely to have discussed the independence question online (TNS Global 2014), giving credence to this interpretation. Another potential issue to consider is the observation of Michael Keating that the campaign ground war favoured the Yes side because the No campaign included two parties that were weak in Scotland, the Conservative and Liberal Democrats, meaning that much of the ground campaign on the pro-Union side was left to only one of three parties on the BT side, Labour (Keating 2014). It was also difficult for the No side to present coherence given the slightly different flavours of No on offer, not to mention the rather unusual position of having the two main opposing parties at General Elections at the UK level seemingly on the same page as each other in the referendum. Indeed, this was a gift for the Yes side as Labour could be labelled as 'red Tories'.

Third, data show that younger age groups are more likely to be involved online than older age groups. A 2013 Eurobarometer survey, for example, illustrated that 28 per cent of EU citizens on average said they had expressed their view on a public issue online or through social media in the past two years (Eurobarometer Flash, 2013). This figure rose to 39 per cent for individuals under the age of 40. Given that we now know that more young people voted for independence than against it,[13] we might expect greater support and engagement for the YS campaign on average as a result.

Furthermore, in a high stakes election such as the independence referendum in which fear of misinformation was omnipresent, social media offered the capacity for many on both sides to seek out information, although many would argue that social media was a source for misinformation to be spread too. In particular, those advocating independence arguably had a means to by-pass traditional media formats that, to many within the Yes camp, were perceived as inbuilt defenders of the status quo in both name (e.g. *British* Broadcasting Company) and content (see e.g. the protests outside the BBC in the days running up to the referendum). For many on the Yes side in particular, social media became not just a means to share information and to rally the troops to attend and support events[14] but also a means to correct perceived bias in more traditional media formats (see for example, focus group research of Carvalho and Winters (forthcoming).

Conclusion and Discussion

Our chapter has explored the interplay of social media in a referendum campaign. The 2014 Scottish referendum could indeed be classified as 'the first social media referendum'. Our contribution has specifically measured the extent of enthusiasm each campaign generated online and has examined the interplay between events and online support. The chapter shows that the Yes campaign generated a greater degree of enthusiasm online. We speculate as to a number of reasons why that may have occurred including some referendum specific factors ranging from: it is easier to like a positive (vote yes) than a negative (vote no); YS were more engaged online and more united; YS had the benefit of more younger supporters who are more active on average online; and YS turned to social media as a reaction to the perceived bias of the content of traditional news sources. Our analysis also illustrates that certain events in the course of the campaign did appear to have an impact in terms of generating enthusiasm and interest in the online campaigns of both sides including the launch of the White Paper on Scottish independence in November 2013, the TV debates between Alex Salmond and Alistair Darling, and in the final week, the publication of an opinion poll suggesting a yes victory. Accordingly, what we can say is that engagement with online campaigns appears to be driven by events, illustrating that behaviour observed on social media seems to be strongly influenced by specific newsworthy items.

Given the final electoral outcome, three of our online metrics (Facebook likes, Twitter followers, and tweets) were in a converse relationship with what took place in the actual vote. Consequently, one could argue that Facebook likes and Twitter followers and volume of tweets by the two campaigns were not a very good predictor of the final referendum outcome. However, what is more interesting is the nature of the relationship between the shift in online fortunes of YS with the change in offline fortunes of the YS campaign, with our data arguably picking up the upsurge in the Yes campaign before it became apparent offline. Furthermore, our data appear to illustrate the importance of events in determining online political behaviours, at least in a referendum campaign, with particular occurrences generating various online patterns of enthusiasm for both campaigns. Accordingly, the "here and now" character of social media is evident for all to see.

While it is impossible to infer any form of causation without taking into account a multitude of other factors, it is at least noteworthy that increased online activity and overall online trends for the two campaigns often preceded subsequent increased support for Scottish independence in the polls. No may have won the independence referendum, but our data generally suggested momentum was moving to Yes, which it was, and which the final result is testament to if we contrast this with where Yes were a year out from the referendum. Yes went from nowhere to somewhere, and the online data are arguably useful in detecting this development before the opinion polls. Nonetheless, it should be evident that the Yes side's advantage in generating online enthusiasm was not sufficient for victory. While this might at face value indicate that online activity can tell us little about movements in general public opinion, we have at least demonstrated that the surge in support for the yes campaign among the general public was preceded by a rally in support online, which at least suggests that online activity might be able to be used to predict to a certain extent offline activity. Future research is needed to fully understand the trajectory and impact of online support and enthusiasm for political campaigns.

All that being said, our chapter is very much a first cut at investigating this, with our analysis primarily descriptive.

Notes

1 The research for this chapter was conducted as part of a wider social media project on Scottish independence funded by the UK Economic and Social Research Council (ESRC) in conjunction with the Applied Quantitative Methods Network (AQMeN) as part of the Future of the UK and Scotland research programme (www.esrc.ac.uk/majorinvestments/future-of-uk-and-scotland).

2 See for example: Black, A., 'Scottish independence: What is going on in Scotland?', available: www.bbc.co.uk/news/uk-scotland-scotland-politics-26550736

3 See for example: YouGov's economy question polling in 'Scotland trackers—Scottish referendum', available: https://d25d2506sfb94s.cloudfront.net/cumulus_uploads/document/5lijo88bs3/YG-trackers-Scottish-Referendum-150501.pdf

4 Trends 24: Twitter trends (2014). Twitter trends in Scotland: 11 September–18 September 2014 [online], available: http://trends24.in/united-kingdom/glasgow/~cloud (observation during the final week of the referendum).

5 *The Guardian* (2014) 'Scottish independence referendum inspires 10m Facebook interactions', *The Guardian*, 16 September 2014, available: www.theguardian.com/politics/2014/sep/16/scottish-independence-10-million-facebook-interactions

6 See for example: Nicolson, S., 'Scottish independence: A civilised debate?', available: www.bbc.co.uk/news/uk-scotland-27809898; and Stevenson, A., 'The tyranny of the cybernats: Is online aggression hurting Scottish independence?', available: www.politics.co.uk/comment-analysis/2014/08/31/the-tyranny-of-the-cybernats-is-online-aggression-hurting-sc

7 See September 2014 YouGov and ICM polls discussed in: https://yougov.co.uk/news/2014/09/06/latest-scottish-referendum-poll-yes-lead/ ; and Curtice, J., 'ICM put yes ahead—perhaps', available: http://blog.whatscotlandthinks.org/2014/09/icm-put-yes-ahead-perhaps/ respectively

8 The 'Talked About' Facebook metric is a compendium measure of several actions that show engagement with a page, and takes into account the average number of likes per page, number of posts to a page wall, liking/commenting on/sharing a wall post, and phototags.

9 Carrell, S., and Brooks, L. 'Scottish debate: Salmond and Darling in angry clash over independence', available: www.theguardian.com/politics/2014/aug/05/alex-salmond-alistair-darling-scotland-debate-independence

10 See for example, 'Scottish independence no campaign given savage mauling on Twitter, The Best of #PatronisingBTLady', available: www.huffingtonpost.co.uk/2014/08/27/patronisingbtlady-scottish-independence_n_5721048.html

11 Facebook metrics at the time indicated that the largest volume of contributors for both BT and YS were from the under 34s in the Glasgow area. While we cannot rule out the role of contributors from outside Scotland, the metrics suggest that they were not primary forces in driving the swings.

12 Shephard, M. and Quinlan, S. (2014) 'Is the "yes" online tsunami finally paying dividends?', 16 September 2014, available: http://blog.whatscotlandthinks.org/2014/09/yes-online-tsunami-finally-paying-dividends/

13 See for example, Curtice, J. (2014) 'So who voted yes and who voted no?', available: http://blog.whatscotlandthinks.org/2014/09/voted-yes-voted/

14 See Michael Comerford quotes in MacDowall, C. (2014) 'How Twitter is being used in the Scottish independence referendum debate' 9th January 2014', available: http://phys.org/news/2014-01-twitter-scottish-independence-referendum-debate.html

References

Ackland, R., Gibson, R. (2013) 'Hyperlinks and networked communication: a comparative study of political parties online', *International Journal of Social Research Methodology*, 16(3), 231–44.

Bond, R. M., Fariss, C. J., Jones, J. J., Kramer, A.D.I., Marlow, C., Settle, J. E., Fowler, J. H. (2012) 'A 61-million-person experiment in social influence and political mobilization', *Nature*, 489(7415), 295–298.

Bruno, N. (2011) *Tweet first, verify later? How real-time information is changing coverage of worldwide events*, Reuters Institute for the Study of Journalism, University of Oxford, Oxford, UK.

Cairney, P. (2011) *The Scottish Political System Since Devolution: from new politics to the New Scottish Government*, Imprint Academic: Exeter, UK.

Carvalho, E., and Winters, K. (forthcoming) *Perceptions of the independence referendum campaign: No versus yes voters and activists*.

Cellan-Jones, R. (2014) Who has won the social referendum?, *BBC News*, available: http://www.bbc.com/news/technology-29235876

Ceron, A., Curini, L., Iacus, S. M., Porro, G. (2014) 'Every tweet counts? How sentiment analysis of social media can improve our knowledge of citizens' political preferences with an application to Italy and France', *New Media and Society*, 16(2), 340–58.

Chen, P. (2010) 'Adoption and use of digital media in election campaigns: Australia, Canada and New Zealand', *Public Communication Review*, 1, 3–26.

Cogburn, D., Espinoza-Vasquez, F. (2011) 'From networked nominee to networked nation: examining the impact of Web 2.0 and social media on political participation and civic engagement in the 2008 Obama campaign', *Journal of Political Marketing*, 10, 189–213.

Conway, B. A., Kenski, K., Wang, D. (2013) 'Twitter use by presidential primary candidates during the 2012 campaign', *American Behavioural Scientist*, 57(11), 1596–1610.

Curtice, J. (2013) *Who supports and who opposes independence—and why?*, ScotCentre Social Research, available: http://www.scotcen.org.uk/media/1106700/who supports and opposes independence and why.pdf

Davis, R., Baumgartner, J. C., Francia, P. (2009) 'The Internet in U.S election campaigns', in *Routledge Handbook of Internet Politics*, Routledge: New York, NY, 13–25.

DiGrazia, J., McKelvey, K., Bollan, J., Rojas, F. (2013) 'More tweets, more votes: social media as a quantitative indicator of political behaviour', *PLos ONE*, 8(11).

Electoral Management Board for Scotland. (2014) 'Scottish Independence Referendum: Results', available: http://www.electionsscotland.info/

Eurobarometer Flash (2013) *Europeans' engagement in participatory democracy*, 373, TNS Political & Social, available: http://ec.europa.eu/public_opinion/flash/fl_373_en.pdf

Fahri, P. (2009, April/May) 'The Twitter explosion', *American Journalism Review*, available: http://ajrarchive.org/Article.asp?id=4756

Gainous, J., Wagner, K. (2011) *Rebooting American politics: the Internet revolution*, Lanham: Rowman and Littlefield.

Geser, H. (2011) 'Has tweeting become inevitable? Twitter's strategic role in the world of digital communication', Presented at the Working Paper, available: http://socio.ch/intcom/t_hgeser26.pdf

Gibson, R., McAllister, I. (2011) 'Do online election campaigns win votes? The 2007 Australian "YouTube" election', *Political Communication*, 28(2), 227–44.

Gulati, G. J., Williams, C. B. (2011) Social media in the 2010 congressional elections. *Social Science Research Network*, available: http://papers.ssrn.com/sol3/papers.cfm?abstract_id=1817053

Haggerty, A. (2014) 'Social media more influential information source than newspapers in Scottish independence referendum, YouGov finds', *The Drum: Modern Marketing*, 17 Oct, available: http://www.thedrum.com/news/2014/10/17/social-media-more-influential-information-source-newspapers-scottish-independence

Harfoush, R. (2009) *Yes we did: An inside look at how social media built the Obama brand*, New Riders: Berkeley, CA.

Hogan, J., Graham, S. (2013) 'An examination of Seán Gallagher's presidential campaign in a hybridized media environment', *Irish Communications Review*, 14(1), 30–47.

Johns, R., Carman, C., Mitchell, J. (2011) 'The Scottish National Party's success in winning an outright majority at Holyrood', available: http://blogs.lse.ac.uk/politicsandpolicy/archives/12865.

Jungherr, A., Jurgens, P., Schoen, H. (2012) 'Why the Pirate Party won the German election of 2009 or the trouble with predictions: a response to Tumasjan, A. et al.', *Social Science Computer Review*, 30(2), 229–234.

Keating, M. (2010) *The Government of Scotland*, Edinburgh University Press: Edinburgh, UK.

Keating, M. (2014) 'Foresight: Scotland decides', *Political Insight*, 5(1), 18–19.

Kellas, J. (1984) *The Scottish Political System*, Third Edition. ed, Cambridge University Press: Cambridge, UK.

Larsson, A. O., Kalsnes, B. (2014) '"Of course we are on Facebook": Use and non-use of social media among Swedish and Norwegian politicians', *European Journal of Communication*, 29(6), 653–667. DOI: 10.1177/0267323114531383

Lassen, D. S., Brown, A. R. (2010) 'Twitter: The electoral connection', *Social Science Computer Review*, 23, 1–18.

LeDuc, L. (2002) 'Opinion change and voting behaviour in referendums', *European Journal of Political Research*, 41(6), 711–29.

Maireder, A., Schlögl, S. (2014) '24 hours of an #outcry: the networked publics of soco-political debate', *European Journal of Communication*, 29(6), 687–702. DOI: 10.1177/0267323114545710

McCrone, D., Paterson, L. (2002) 'The conundrum of Scottish independence', *Scottish Affairs*, 40 (June 2002), 54–75.

O'Malley, E. (2012) 'Explaining the 2011 Irish presidential election: culture, valence, loyalty or punishment?', *Irish Political Studies*, 27(4), 635–55.

Pew Research Centre's Internet and American Life Project (2014) *Social media use over time*, available: http://www.pewinternet.org/data-trend/social-media/social-media-use-all-users/

Quinlan, S., Shephard, M., Paterson, L. (2015) 'Online discussion and the 2014 Scottish independence referendum: flaming keyboards or forums for deliberation?', *Electoral Studies*, 38, 192–205.

Rossman, J., Gummer, T., Wolf, C., (2014) 'Twitter im Wahlkampf', in *Zwischen Fragmentierung und Konzentration: Die Bundestagswahl 2013*, Baden-Baden: Nomos, pp. 61–72.

Sang, E., Bos, J. (2012) 'Predicting the 2011 Dutch Senate election results with Twitter', in *Proceedings of the 13th Conference of the European Chapter of the Association for Computational Linguistics*, Avignon, FR, 53–60.

Strandberg, K. (2013) 'A social media revolution or just a case of history repeating itself? The use of social media in the 2011 Finnish parliamentary elections', *New Media and Society*, 15(8), 1329–47.

Straw, W. (2010) 'Yes we did? What Labour learned from Obama', in Gibson, R., Williamson, A. and Ward, S., eds., *Putting the small 'p' back in politics?*, Hansard Society: London, 43–50.

Sudlich, M. L., Wall, M. (2011) 'Wow a 140 characters campaign: Twitter usage in the 2011 Irish general Election'. Paper presented at the European Consortium for Political Research conference, Reykjavík, 25–27 Aug. 2011.

TNS Global. (2014) 'Scottish opinion monitor: Referendum effect set to increase political activity, but trust in main parties is low', 17 Oct. 2014, available: http://www.tnsglobal.com/uk/press-release/scottish-opinion-monitor-referendum-effect-set-increase-political-activity-trust-main

Tumasjan, A., Sprenger, T. O., Sander, P. G., Welpe, I. M. (2011) 'Election forecasts with Twitter: How 140 characters reflect the political landscape', *Social Science Computer Review*, 29, 402–18.

Tumasjan, A., Sprenger, T. O., Sandner, P. G., Welpe, I. M. (2010) 'Predicting elections with Twitter', in *Proceedings of the Fourth International AAAI Conference on Weblogs and Social Media*, available: http://www.aaai.org/ocs/index.php/ICWSM/ICWSM10/paper/viewFile/1441/1852.

Vergeer, M., Hermans, L., Sams, S. (2011) 'Online social networks and micro-blogging in political campaigning: the exploration of a new campaign tool and a new campaign style', *Party Politics*, 19(3), 477–501.

Vergeer, M., Hermans, L. (2013) 'Campaigning on Twitter: microblogging and online social networking as campaign tools in the 2010 general elections in the Netherlands', *Journal of Computer Mediated Communication*, 18, 399–419.

36
THE USE OF TWITTER IN THE DANISH EP ELECTIONS 2014

Jakob Linaa Jensen, Jacob Ørmen, and Stine Lomborg

Introduction

This chapter analyses the use of Twitter in the Danish election campaign for the European Parliament 2014. It is among the first attempts to analyse political use of Twitter in Denmark, as well as among the first studies of nationally based social media communication in a wider context of a transnational political event, the European Parliament (EP) election of 2014. How and to what extent is the EP election discussed on Twitter among Danish parliament candidates, voters, and other actors? Who are the dominant actors and which discussion patterns and networks are established? Employing descriptive measures and network analysis of the conversation structure, we identify central actors to the Danish portion of this election, leading us to a qualitative analysis of the dialogue and content characterising the debate surrounding two important, yet different, candidates.

The European Parliament Elections and Denmark

Elections to the European Parliament have taken place every four years since 1979. In Europe in general, the voter turnout has been lower than in national and local elections. Furthermore, overall European turnout has decreased over time, from 62 per cent in 1979 to 43 per cent in 2009 and 2014. There are large national differences: in countries with compulsory voting, like Belgium, turnouts are usually above 90 per cent; some countries in central and Eastern Europe report voting attendance below 30 per cent. Although Denmark traditionally has featured relatively high turnouts in national elections, 80–90 per cent, this general European trend can also be found here with turnouts typically 30 per cent lower than during national elections. At the first EU election in 1979, turnout was at 48 per cent, and at the 2014 election 56 per cent. In that respect, the slightly rising turnout in Denmark over time is against the general European trend, although the turnout remains significantly lower for EU elections than for national and local elections (European Parliament, 2009).

The Campaign of 2014

The EU and the European Parliament have often expressed a strong interest in making voters more interested in European affairs and raising the voter turnout (Rittberger, 2005; Hix, Noury, & Roland, 2007). New media have been perceived as a tool for enhancing interest and participation. According to the European Parliament itself, the 2014 campaign was the breakthrough for virtual and viral campaign strategies (European Parliament, 2014). There were more than one million tweets featuring the election hashtag #EP2014, and Twitter directly contributed to the campaign by hosting a banner on their mobile app, urging people to vote.

In Danish politics, even though the Internet has been used in election campaigns since 1997, with social media entering the fray 10 years later, the national election campaign of 2011 was the first where a majority of politicians and candidates used social media. Further, more than one-third of Internet users, about 30 per cent of the voters, used social media in relation to this election (Linaa Jensen, 2013). Therefore, it seems fair to say that from a Danish perspective, the EP election of 2014 was the first with a huge potential for social media for creating interest in the election and facilitating political debates.

Precisely 100 Danish candidates ran for the election in 2014, distributed among seven parties and one movement: the left-wing parties of the Socialist People's Party (SPP) and the Social Democrats (SD); the centre party, the Danish Social Liberal Party (SLP); and the right-wing parties of the Liberal Party (LP), the Conservative People's Party (CPP), Liberal Alliance (LA), and the Danish People's Party (DPP). Further, the cross-political but left-wing-dominated organisation the People's Movement Against EU ran for election.

Regarding social media, many candidates, especially the top candidates, relied on the traditional campaign offices of their parties and their communication advisors. The top candidates, along with the younger cohort of secondary candidates, were particularly well represented on social media. About half of the candidates had a Twitter profile (the focus of this chapter) and the vast majority had a Facebook profile. In the following sections, we will present specific results pertaining to the Twitter use of these and other politicians.

Methods

This chapter focuses on Twitter for three reasons. First, even though Facebook is a much more popular social medium in Denmark (more than three million users compared to 200,000 Twitter users), the Danish Twitter users feature highly influential individuals like journalists, politicians, and opinion leaders, thus making it a potential tool for agenda setting and, as such, interesting from a research perspective.

Second, Twitter is well suited for studying conversations around key issues and events, like elections. The ability to link tweets through hashtags (#s) enables the formation of *ad hoc* publics (Bruns & Moe, 2013), where Twitter users can engage with a common topic without being directly affiliated with each other beforehand.

Third, more generally, one might expect that Twitter's short-form posting format, unidirectional and non-personal networking and its 'public by default' character to a greater extent than other social media enable users to connect with distant, but like-minded, others.

For data collection, we included the tweets of all Twitter accounts belonging to candidates and parties. Further, relevant hashtags for the Danish context were included. With these guidelines, the data consisted of tweets from 56 candidates, seven political parties, one popular movement (The People's Movement Against EU), running for election. The data also include tweets with the hashtag #ep14dk, the more-or-less official hashtag for the election, #dkpol, the general hashtag for political discussions in Denmark, and #dkmedier, the general hashtag for media-related discussions in Denmark.[1] The latter two are included in order to archive as many relevant tweets as possible. We acknowledge that some tweets with such overall hashtags might be not relevant for this study.

Data collection was done using the online tool yourTwapperKeeper, archiving all tweets on a local server. The period of harvesting ran from 14 April 2014 to 31 May 2014, with election day taking place on 25 May.

By including hashtags as well as posts sent from individual accounts, we aimed at catching relevant posts outside the sphere of the candidates and other actors but still relevant in the election campaign debate. Subsequent script-based data cleaning ensured that no tweets were included in the final archive more than once.

As for our analysis, our efforts fall in three steps: first, we describe the level of engagement, the number of tweets, and tweeters and other overall patterns of Twitter use during the campaign. Second, we employ a network analysis in order to identify the most active and central candidates, based on posts, retweets, and mentions sent from their accounts. In the subsequent qualitative content analysis, we go in more depth with two central candidates, their use of Twitter, and the conversational patterns of the discussions surrounding these candidates.

Descriptive Analysis

During our studied period, 73,089 tweets related to the election campaign were sent. The tweeting activity increased as election day approached. Indeed, 33 per cent of all tweets were sent in the last week prior to the election, culminating during election day May 25 as the most active date (12.6 per cent of all tweets sent). About half of all tweets were retweets (39,081).

The 73,089 tweets were sent by 11,101 accounts (mean: 6.58 tweets sent, median: 2 tweets sent). About half of the accounts (5,434) only sent one tweet related to the EP election during the period, and almost 9 out of 10 accounts sent less than 10 EP-related tweets. This is illustrated in Table 36.1. The relationship between tweets and accounts is very skewed and roughly follows the Pareto principle, with 20 per cent of accounts sending about 80 per cent of all tweets (Newman, 2005). This suggests that relatively few accounts were instrumental in upholding Twitter conversations about the EP elections, echoing similar findings from national elections on Twitter in Scandinavia (Larsson & Moe, 2013)

Focusing on the most active accounts, it is apparent that accounts affiliated with political actors in Denmark play a prominent role in the Twitter conversations. In the top we find in particular EP candidates, lobbyists (like Je5perl, the chairman of the IT-Political Association of Denmark) official EP accounts (like EPiDanmark), and media professionals (like DRValg and EU_tropolis). For the following analysis, we focus specifically on the candidates and parties running for election.

Table 36.1 Distribution of Twitter Accounts According to the Number of Tweets Sent by Each Account Related to the 2014 EP Election

Tweets sent	*1 tweet*	*2–9 tweets*	*10–50 tweets*	*>50 tweets*	*Total*
Number of accounts	5,434 (approx. 49 per cent)	4,310 (approx. 39 per cent)	1,146 (approx. 10 per cent)	206 (approx. 2 per cent)	11,101 (100 per cent)

There were 100 candidates running for the election coming from seven parties and one popular movement (http://epvalg14.euo.dk/kandidater/alle/). In total, 45 candidates (45 per cent of all) employed Twitter accounts during the campaign, and all parties, apart from the Danish People's Party, maintained a central party account on Twitter as well. The vast majority accounts, 36 accounts, are within the top 10 per cent of most active accounts (tweeting more than 10 times about the election) and about half, 22 accounts, are within the top 2 per cent (tweeting more than 50 times). Thus, the politicians that did contribute to Twitter, for the most part, constituted central actors in the Twitter conversation around the EU elections.

Party Accounts

There is great variation in the presence and activity of candidates across parties. Table 36.2 provides an overview of the number of accounts and Twitter activity affiliated with each political party and movement. The number of accounts signals the party's readiness to interact on Twitter. Having an account enables you to tweet, of course, but even more importantly, it enables other Twitter users to engage with you by recirculating your messages (through retweets) and directing messages to you (through @mentions).

The Socialist People's Party, the Social Democrats, and the Danish Social Liberal Party maintain the greatest presence on Twitter. Especially the two latter (who constitute the current government coalition) stand out, since all their candidates had an active Twitter account during the campaign. In the bottom of the list we find the two liberal parties, The Danish Liberal Party and Liberal Alliance, as well as the right-wing party, the Danish People's Party, who all have less than a third of their candidates on Twitter. Accordingly, the socialist and centre-left parties appear to be more oriented towards Twitter as a medium in the campaign than the right-wing parties.

The activity of the parties tells us something about how much each candidate and party seeks to contribute to the conversation about themselves and other parties. When we aggregate tweets on party level, the Danish Social Liberal Party remains by far the most active, with 1,990 tweets. This is largely due to one candidate, Karen Melchior, who sent out more than a 1,000 tweets during the campaign and was the second most active of all accounts in the dataset (only surpassed by ep14dk who predominantly retweeted others). The Social Democrats and Socialist People's Party are also in top in terms of activity, but so is the Conservative People's Party.

Most parties had a single candidate, who provided the majority of all their tweets. These turn out to be for the most part lower-level politicians that have not established a strong figure in public yet (i.e. Kathrine Alexandrowiz from SD, Karen Melchior from

Table 36.2 Twitter Activity of Political Parties

Political party/ movement (abbreviation)	Candidate with Twitter accounts	Tweets sent by candidates	Most active candidate (tweets in parentheses)
The Social Democrats (SD)	9 (100 per cent)	880	Kathrine Alexandrowiz (339)
The Socialist People's Party (SPP)	9 (ca. 43 per cent)	483	Margrethe Auken (149)
The Danish Social Liberal Party (SLP)	8 (100 per cent)	1990	Karen Melchior (1,018)
The People's Movement Against EU	7 (ca. 33 per cent)	280	Party Account (91)
The Conservative People's Party (CPP)	6 (ca 55 per cent)	527	Nichlas Vind (329)
The Danish Liberal Party (LP)	5 (ca. 30 per cent)	137	Jens Rohde (91)
Liberal Alliance (LA)	4 (ca 40 per cent)	296	Niels Westy (151)
Danish People's Party (DPP)	4 (ca 36 per cent)	327	Morten Messerschmidt (196)

Note: Parties were allowed to list maximum 20 candidates to the election. Most parties listed fewer. The list of accounts includes the main account of the party (if such existed).

SLP, Nichlas Vind from CPP, and Niels Westy from LA). This underscores the opportunities of Twitter to engage in public debate, particularly for politicians who might not have the same access to traditional media or large town-hall meetings as the top candidates. Interestingly, only two of the leading candidates, Margrethe Auken from SPP and Morten Messerschmidt from DPP, were top contributors from their respective parties.

The Social Liberal Party had many active candidates; they are the most active party even without Melchior. Because they were a kind of 'Twitter first mover' among Danish political parties and since they cater specifically to the well-educated part of the population, it is not surprising that they maintain a strong position both in terms of presence and activity during the campaign. The Social Democrats, the traditionally grand party in national and EP elections with a strong party organisation and currently heading the government coalition, might also be expected to have a noticeable presence on Twitter.

From this analysis of the presence and activity of parties, it is clear that even though politicians play an active role in the EP 2014 debate in general, there are variations across parties. To look closer at how central various candidates were in the conversations around the election, we now turn to a network analysis of the interactions between the politicians and the greater public on Twitter.

Network Analysis

In this section, we analyse the interactions between candidates and party accounts on one hand and regular users on the other hand. The conversation network consists therefore of those tweets where one user either recirculates other users' messages (by retweeting) or addresses other users directly (by mentioning). To analyse this, we mapped the whole network of mentions and retweets using the software Gephi. The actors (or nodes) represent Twitter user accounts while the ties (edges) are tweets by one account mentioning (appearing in Twitter as '@[account name]') or retweeting ([appearing as 'RT @[account name]') another account.

Thus, mentions and retweets are treated as a similar form of communication between users in this analysis; together they comprise a conversation network. To assist interpretation, we have labelled the user accounts with an in-degree (Wasserman & Faust, 1994) greater than 500, meaning that more than 500 other users have mentioned the accounts or retweeted their messages once or more during the study period. The result is shown in Figure 36.1. Accordingly, these actors occupy a central position in the conversation network, because they attract the attention of the greatest number of other actors in the network. The relative distance between the actors in the network signals the similarity in list of actors interacting with them. Thus, if two accounts are positioned close to each other, they share many of the accounts pointing to them through either retweets or mentions, and vice versa.

The conversation network (see Figure 36.1) reveals a network of dense interactions forming a tight central community around almost all the labelled actors. This means that these actors both are referenced by many users each and by a large share of the same users.

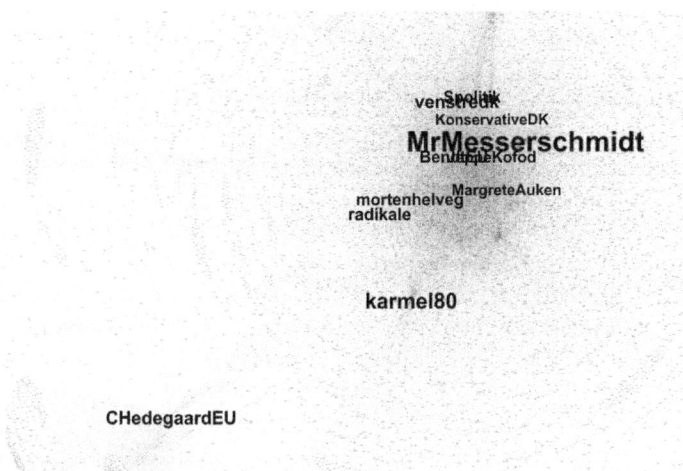

Figure 36.1 Conversation Network with >500 In-Degree Accounts Labelled

However, two labelled accounts stand out. One (karmel80) is slightly below the dense cloud of interactions and seems to be affiliated with both the central community and with another community (visible by the heavy amount of interactions extending both towards and away from the central community). We return to karmel80 shortly. The other actor (CHedegaardEU) is visible in the lower left corner. CHedegaardEU, was EU Commissioner for Climate Action, Connie Hedegaard, appointed by the former Danish government. She turns out to be closely affiliated with cross-European politicians and international lobbyists and less so with the Danish EP candidates or parties. She is indeed an EU politician (from the Conservative People's Party) but not a candidate for the election. The Twitter conversation around her mostly concerns broader EU issues and not the Danish election campaign. As such, even though she is a central actor in the general Twitter conversation about EU matters, her presence here is not relevant for our current efforts, and we will therefore exclude her for our subsequent analyses.

To assist the interpretation of the network visualisation we have listed particularly relevant centrality measures for the remaining 10 actors with in-degree greater than 500 in Table 36.3.

Table 36.3 includes many of the central actors in the election campaign—the leading candidates from the Danish People's Party (MrMesserschmidt), the Danish Social Liberal Party (mortenhelveg), the Socialist People's Party (MargreteAuken), the Conservative People's Party (BendtEU), and the Social Democratic Party (JeppeKofod). We also see party accounts for the Social Democrats (Spolitik), Conservatives (KonservativeDK), the liberal party (venstredk), and the social liberals (radikale), and one ordinary candidate for the Danish Social Liberal Party, Karen Melchior (karmel80). However, no candidates from the Danish Liberal Party—the biggest party in the Danish Parliament—could be found in the network. As mentioned earlier, their leading candidate (Ulla Tørnæs) did not have a Twitter account at all, and the party was the least active of all Danish parties on Twitter.

When we take both the network in Figure 36.1 and Table 36.3 into consideration, two actors in particular stand out: MrMesserschmidt and karmel80. The leading candidate for the Danish People's Party Morten Messerschmidt (MrMesserschmidt) obtains a particularly important position in the network, leaving the party in an unprecedented central position in the political landscape on Twitter. The in-degree scores show that Morten Messerschmidt garnered interest from the largest public (2010 unique accounts mentioned him throughout the period). Furthermore, his high PageRank score—a widely used measure for how popular the accounts interacting with him is—suggests that he also managed to attract the attention of more influential accounts than the rest. When measuring the number of other accounts with which he is connecting Messerschmidt appears as the most popular actor in the network, connecting both highly important and less noticeable nodes.

Karen Melchior (karmel80) also occupies a central position in the network. Melchior is seen slightly below the centre of the network connecting to both the center of the network and of a separate, ICT-related cluster. She plays a bridging function in the network because she connects a range of otherwise weakly connected nodes to the network (Granovetter, 1983). This is also supported by her high betweenness centrality score (the highest in the network), suggesting that she performed the most important function as connection point between actors in the whole network. Melchior also managed to attract the attention of 1,343 unique accounts and was the most active tweeter in the network (writing more than 1,000 tweets related to the campaign). A peculiar

Table 36.3 Centrality Measures for EP Candidate Twitter Accounts with In-Degree >500 (Highest values highlighted)

Politician/ party [@account]	Description (party abbreviations in parentheses)	In-degree of account	Mentions of account] in total	Tweets by account	Page Rank[2]	Between-ness centrality[3]
MrMesserschmidt	Leading candidate (DPP)	**2010** **accounts**	5,353 mentions	196 tweets	**0.024**	2021,929
karmel80	Candidate (SLP)	1343 accounts	**6,745** **mentions**	**1,018** **tweets**	0.017	**3459,921**
venstredk	Party Account (LP)	945 accounts	2,019 mentions	10 tweets	0.011	77,706
radikale	Party Account (SLP)	813 accounts	2,328 mentions	330 tweets	0.008	493,0908
mortenhelveg	Leading candidate (SLP)	776 accounts	2149 mentions	140 tweets	0.009	350,849
BendtEU	Leading candidate (CPP)	753 accounts	1915 mentions	60 tweets	0,009	253,905
Spolitik	Party Account (SD)	704 accounts	1,469 mentions	16 tweets	0.006	251,931
JeppeKofod	Leading candidate (SD)	635 accounts	1,610 mentions	94 tweets	0.009	415,376
MargreteAuken	Leading candidate (SPP)	589 accounts	1,123 mentions	149 tweets	0.007	915,768
KonservativeDK	Party Account (CPP)	541 accounts	1,401 mentions	103 tweets	0.004	214,312

finding here is that she achieves a much better PageRank than both the leading candidate of her party (Morten Helveg) and the official party account (radikale), meaning that Melchior reaches a broader group of influential accounts than these two.

Apart from these two extraordinary accounts, there are a few noticeable features of this elite group. The liberal party account achieves a high in-degree level even though they contributed very little (only 10 tweets) and received a poor betweenness score,

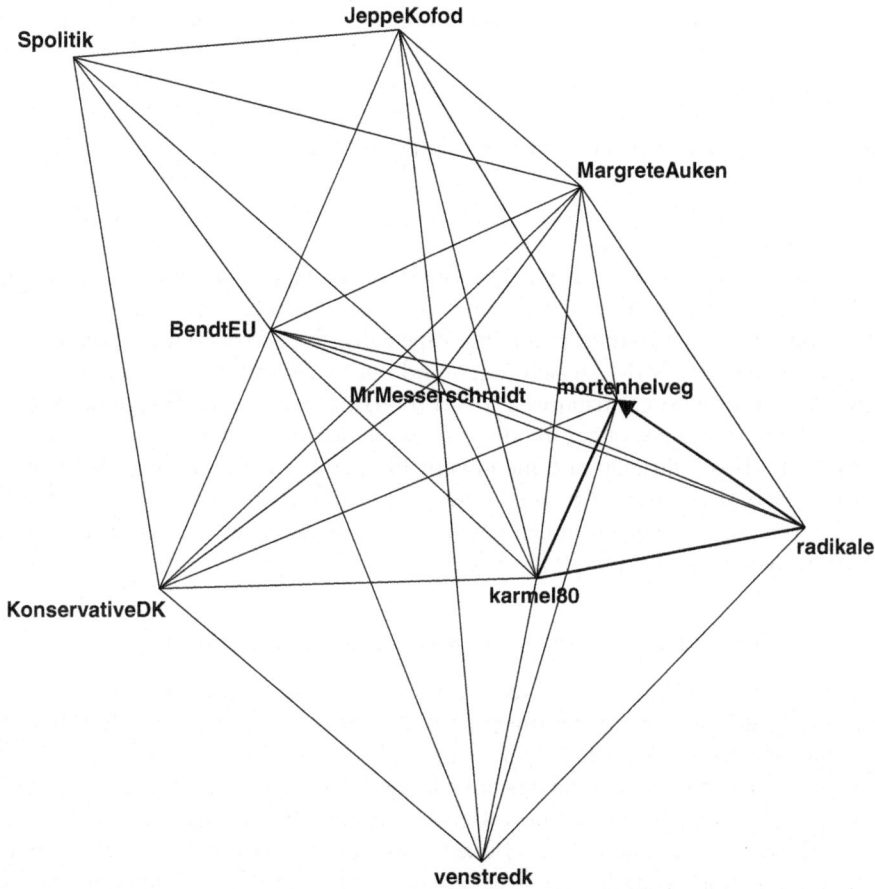

Figure 36.2 Network of Interactions between >500 In-Degree Accounts (edges are weighted by amounts of retweets and mentions)

suggesting that they played a diminutive role in sustaining communication throughout the network. They were frequently addressed but almost never responded. The remaining accounts seem to cluster somewhat in the middle of the network around Messerschmidt and all contribute quite a lot to the conversation. To get a clearer picture of the relationship between the elite we visualised solely the ties between them in Figure 36.2.

The partial (elite) network proves to be quite different from the full network. BendtEU is the most central measured by in-degree with everybody apart from venstredk referring to him, followed by MrMesserschmidt with everybody apart from venstredk and BendtEU referring to him. The Danish Social Liberal Party (radikale, mortenhelveg, karmel80) form a coherent network of consistent internal linking in the triad, known in the literature as homophily (Wasserman & Faust, 1994). The thickness of edges here reveals high degrees of reciprocal mentioning, especially between radikale and mortenhelveg. Whereas Melchior functions as a bridge between a cluster of IT-policy actors and other tweeters outside the political domain, Helveg predominantly attracts the attention of loyal party troopers. Likewise, the conservative dyad of KonservativeDK and BendtEU also forms a small internal community in the network. In comparison, karmel80 does not occupy a central position in the political elite network outside this Social Liberal triadic cluster. She is the least popular politician; only MrMesserschmidt and MargreteAuken mention her apart from her party allies—even though she reaches out to almost everybody else. This type of aspirational linking where a person lower in the hierarchy (in this instance the political elite) links to others higher up without receiving reciprocal ties has been observed in the network literature on multiple accounts (see discussion in Ørmen, 2012).

Taken together, the network analysis has identified a Twitter conversation network around the election that predominantly revolves around the leading candidates and parties with one particular outlier, karmel80. Especially, the two accounts operated by politicians karmel80 and MrMesserschmidt stand out as central cases. Karmel80 is a very active politician who contributes a lot to the conversation and bridges connections between different types of actors in the network. MrMesserschmidt on the other hand is an established politician and incumbent EP member with a strong media persona. In these ways, these two politicians showcase different prototypes—in a structural sense—of Twitter use in an election campaign. Therefore, we now go a bit deeper into the conversations surrounding these two accounts.

Beyond Tie Structures: Conversation and Content

In this section, we aim to take a close look at the content and degree of reciprocity in conversation of the tweets that form the @mention networks of MrMesserschmidt and karmel80. Specifically, we explore (a) the degree of conversation in the Twitter communication of which the two candidates are part (whether the candidates are engaged in ongoing political dialogue with fellow users or whether Twitter mainly serves other purposes for the candidate) and (b) the characteristics of the content of their respective Twitter communication: what do they tweet about, and how are they depicted in tweets mentioning them?

As already touched upon in the previous section, what is distinct about MrMesserschmidt's conversation network is the relatively moderate tweeting activity by the user himself, combined with a very lively and widespread conversation around him. For karmel80, the picture is different: she is highly active in tweeting herself and she also receives many mentions, although from a comparably smaller set of users (with 1,343 accounts mentioning her and 6,745 mentions of her in the data set). Hence, she appears to be more committed to reciprocity in conversation. These basic tendencies indicate different types of engagement and perhaps different degrees of authority in the network for the two candidates. The qualitative content analysis allows us to examine what the figures are actually hiding along the lines of authority and engagement.

When looking at the candidates' tweets intended to initiate conversation with others, it is evident that karmel80 is far more likely to initiate conversations with others than is MrMesserschmidt: almost all her tweets have an addressee, and on several occasions she seeks to leverage her Twitter network to inform her political agenda (e.g. asking their advice on what is important when discussion EU and politics of education. Furthermore, almost half of her tweets (445) are RTs of others' tweets, including not only tweets directly related to her own campaign (e.g., media presence) and that of her party but also political 'food for thought' and humouristic tweets generated by others. Through this practice of retweeting, irrespective of immediate relevance to her campaign, she acknowledges and sanctions the contributions of others to the overall conversation (cf. Lomborg, 2012, 2014). Overall, karmel80's conversational inclinations on Twitter indicate that a prime purpose of her presence is to have a political discussion and engage others in it too.

MrMesserschmidt also has some tweets with addressee, but it is not his predominant type of activity. He mainly tweets about his media presence and about his election campaign, including RTs of other users advertising his media presence. That is to say, MrMesserschmidt's Twitter profile is very much a vehicle for self-promotion in other media.

When looking at the content of the two candidates' tweets beyond self-promotion, both candidates address political topics and issues that were on top of the election agenda. MrMesserschmidt's tweeting is largely concentrated on these topics, which are typically framed as critical remarks addressed at candidates from pro-EU parties. A few of these tweets are part of regular debate with specific candidates (e.g., Ida Auken May 7 and Jeppe Kofod May 9). This indicates a very purposeful engagement with Twitter to promote topics that are key to his election campaign and thereby sharply profile and position himself in the political landscape. In contrast, karmel80 additionally tweets about a wide set of political topics, including educational politics, data security, discrimination, and gender equality and the overall importance of EU for Denmark. Furthermore, the political topics are debated not primarily with other candidates but more often with ordinary Twitter users who have no official political or commercial affiliation. Her involvement on Twitter may be said to reflect a broader purpose: namely, to debate the role of EU politics along more general lines, again underlining her use of Twitter for the purpose of leveraging political discussion.

Given that the nationally held elections are for a transnational political body and that at least some candidates are already members of the European Parliament, one might expect to find that they tweet in diverse languages, even if pro-European candidates may be more likely to locate themselves in an international network on Twitter. Analysing the two candidates' language use on Twitter, we find that both are primarily oriented towards the Danish national scene. However, whereas MrMesserschmidt only tweets in Danish, and karmel80 mainly tweets in Danish, she also retweets and responds to tweets in other European languages, including English, German, French, and Swedish. This mix of languages gives her account a more distinct international profile and suggests that she actively attempts to link the national and the transnational political discussion.

Finally, both candidates to varying degrees embrace the 'personal' style of communication on social media by offering tweets of a more private nature (Lomborg, 2014). MrMesserschmidt sends three discernible personal tweets related to the campaign, for example, a tweet about relaxing at the workplace of his partner. For karmel80, personal tweets focus on for instance the Eurovision song contest, a highly and internationally tweeted event (Highfield, Harrington, & Bruns, 2013). Her way of personalising tweets does not so much concern the topics that she tweets but more her conversational style, which is light and informal and sometimes humorous, echoing what appears to be the accepted style of regular Twitter users in Denmark (cf. Lomborg, 2014).

Overall, the content and directionality of the candidates' own tweets elaborate the finding from the network analysis that MrMesserschmidt is very much tied to a political elite network. He shows limited investment in dialogue on Twitter and mainly uses Twitter as a channel for political promotion and positioning vis-à-vis other candidates by tweeting about his campaign. By contrast, karmel80 seems oriented towards political discussion in the broad sense, bridging between the political elite and the regular Twitter user by way of her conversational engagement.

To complement and further contextualise the analysis of the candidates' tweets, it is crucial to look at how others try to engage, frame, and position the candidates. Hence, we looked at the @mentions of MrMesserschmidt and karmel80 with regard to their content and style.

The discussion mentioning MrMesserschmidt involves a wealth of users, featuring not only the political elite network and the mass media but also local Danish People's Party supporters and other regular Twitter users. While all kinds of individuals try to initiate conversation with MrMesserschmidt, he prioritises to engage with the political and media establishment. This finding echoes the tendency of hierarchical linking mentioned in the network analysis above.

Concerning the content of tweets mentioning MrMesserschmidt, the majority are tweets discussing specific political matters: the dominant subject matter is the Unified Patent Court, but MrMesserschmidt is also addressed regarding social dumping, border control, the Banking Union, and LGBT rights. In addition to substantial political debate, there is quite a large group of tweets that could be said to be more person focused. These involve satirical commenting on his choice of clothes at media appearances, his election tour bus, and his musical productions. In some instances these tweets take the form of personal attacks from critics as well as supportive messages.

When looking at the RTs involving MrMesserschmidt, many of these receive a number of additional RTs. The tweets receiving the most RTs are critical of him and his candidature, and they come from both political opponents and regular Twitter users. For instance, the Social Democrat BennyEngelbrech tweets that MrMesserschmidt has apparently flip-flopped on the issue of the Unified Patent Court, a tweet that is retweeted 115 times. In comparison, MrMesserschmidt's own tweets are typically retweeted only a handful of times and typically by his few eager Twitter supporters. The exceptions here are MrMesserschmidt's own tweet of the election results ('4 mandater') and his tweet calling for people to vote, which receive RTs from critics and supporters alike. There are only few RTs of the personal tweets about MrMesserschmidt. Hence, the framing of MrMesserschmidt is predominantly negative but sober in the sense that his political success at the election is acknowledged, and personally focused tweets are not deemed worthy of a RT.

Turning to karmel80, her @mentions reflect what was also seen in the analysis of her own tweets, namely a lively conversation characterised by brief exchanges. Given the large topical scope of karmel80's own tweets it is perhaps surprising that the topical focus of her mentions are quite narrowly focused on the Unified Patent Court as well as ICT- and data politics (e.g. data protection, the EU data retention directive, and various applications that raise questions of digital surveillance). This functions to position Karmel80 as a candidate with specific focus on advancing an ICT-political agenda in the EU, a central element of her campaign. Further, she received many mentions about her election campaign. In addition to @mentions related to the elections, many address karmel80 with other issues, some of which are politically related, while others seem to concern personal coordination (e.g. meet-ups with friends). Hence, her Twitter mentions underscores the impression of a candidate with a highly expansive, activated, and lively Twitter network that is leveraged for her campaign, but which also stretches beyond the campaign into everyday life.

In contrast to MrMesserschmidt, there are no negative tweets mentioning karmel80. Moreover, many international Twitter users ask karmel80 about her election results and extend their support for her candidature. That is to say, she appears as uniformly sanctioned as someone to listen to and possibly vote for by her Twitter network. Almost all mentions are factual rather than personal, contrary to MrMesserschmidt. This popularity in the network to some extent spilled over to the election result, which was surprisingly good for a secondary candidate from one of the smaller parties, although it did not secure karmel80 a seat in the parliament.

Finally, when looking at the RTs in which karmel80 is mentioned, the picture is very diverse. In contrast to MrMesserschmidt, each RT only travels a limited way. In terms of content, her network retweets her regarding issues of ICT policy, as well as her comments on the election in other countries. Furthermore, her Danish network retweets tweets from her about non-political issues, again indicating that she is considered part of a Twitter network that is not issue specific and reaches well beyond the political elections.

A final note regarding the content: the political debate related to both candidates appears to be very sober and focused on topic rather than person. This is interesting, given the character of the platform used for discussion. Twitter is to a large extent person-centred in that it is built around individual profiles, with brief and informal exchanges among them and no centralised editing and moderation of communication. This result is remarkable also since MrMesserschmidt is established as a controversial figure in Danish politics. However, it appears as if the network of users discussing the elections regulates and polices itself. For instance, the few users attacking MrMesserschmidt through offensive tweets are not retweeted, but rather ignored: this collective 'muting' of inappropriate tweets, in turn, serves to ensure that disagreement does not turn into verbal fights.

Conclusions

In this chapter we have analysed a national Twitter network in an international context, the debate surrounding the EP elections of 2014. While though Twitter is still a small phenomenon in Denmark, we have seen that it is widely used among politicians, candidates and other societal elites. Most main candidates and almost all parties had Twitter accounts, that were used with varying frequency. The most frequent users constituted a mix of established politicians and young upcoming candidates, showing that Twitter can be a medium for both well-known and unknown candidates, contrary to early hypotheses that the Internet mainly benefitted those who did not normally get access to established media (see for instance Davis, 1999).

Although focused on an international event, the EP election, the network did not show strong coherence with international actors and debates; language- and topic-wise, the debate was focused on Denmark, with the Danish EU Commissioner Connie Hedegaard and the debate surrounding her constituting an important exception. Thus, even though the debate of the EP election has a potential to facilitate a move towards a joint European public sphere, the case of Denmark indicates that debates remain within the national domain. Future analysis, encompassing debates of more countries will reveal, whether this tendency is general or particular to Denmark.

The Twitter network of the debates revealed, however, that some of the dominant candidates in the general election also achieved central positions in the network.

A surprising conclusion is that MrMesserschmidt, the top candidate from the Danish People's Party, a party that has been discursively marginalised in other election campaigns, take the most central position in the network.

The other dominant candidate, karmel80, is a totally different case. An upcoming candidate of the Danish Social Liberal party, she used Twitter as a way of getting known by a wider audience. Further, her conversation patterns and topics of discussion were more conversational and combined everyday talk and political discourse, compared to MrMesserschmidt who mainly used Twitter as a mass medium, for self-promotion and raising awareness about his presence in other media.

Even though we have identified two very distinct types of Twitter politicians, further empirical work is needed to examine the relations between structural positions in the conversational network and purposes of politicians' communication on Twitter.

Notes

1 For the cross-national study we also archived tweets with several pan-European hashtags, like #EU, #EPP, #EP14, and #EU2014. However, we deemed them not necessary in this study as explorative readings demonstrated that the Danish tweets including such generic hashtags also included more specific Danish hashtags or accounts and thus were included in the study.
2 PageRank is an alternative measure to estimate an account's centrality in the network. It a build-in feature in Gephi using the methodology outlined in Brin and Page (1998). It is an effective way to estimate the importance of a given account by calculating the importance of all the accounts mentioning that particular account.
3 Betweenness centrality is an indicator of a node's, here a person's, centrality in the network. Mathematically it denotes the number of shortest paths from other nodes that pass through the present node. A high betweenness centrality indicates that a person has a large influence on transfers through the network. The concept was developed by Freeman (1977).

References

Brin, S., and Page, L. (1998) "The Anatomy of a Large-Scale Hypertextual Web Search Engine." Seventh International World-Wide Web Conference (WWW 1998), 14–18 April 1998, Brisbane, Australia.

Bruns, A. & Moe, H. (2013) Structural Layers of Communication on Twitter. In: Weller, Katrin, Bruns, Axel, Burgess, Jean, Mahrt, Merja, & Puschmann, Cornelius (Eds.) *Twitter and Society*. New York: Peter Lang, pp. 15–28.

Davis, Richard (1999) *The Web of Politics*. New York: Oxford University Press.

European Parliament (2009) http://www.europarl.europa.eu/aboutparliament/da/000cdcd9d4/Valg deltagelse-(1979–2009).html

European Parliament (2014) http://www.elections2014.eu/da/news-room/content/20140603STO48801/ html/Sociale-medier-under-EP-valgene-virtuel-kampagne-virkelig-effekt

Freeman, L. (1977) A Set of Measures of Centrality Based on Betweenness. *Sociometry*, 40, 35–41.

Granovetter, M. (1983) The Strength of Weak Ties: A Network Theory Revisited. *Sociological Theory(1)*, 201–233.

Highfield, T., Harrington, S., & Bruns, A. (2013) Twitter as a Technology for Audiencing and Fandom: The #Eurovision Phenomenon. *Information, Communication & Society*, 16(3), 315–339.

Hix, S., Noury, A. G., & Roland, G. (2007) *Democratic Politics in the European Parliament*. Cambridge: Cambridge University Press.

Larsson, A. (Forthcoming) Going Viral? Comparing Parties on Social Media during the 2014 Swedish Election. *Convergence: The International Journal of Research into New Media Technologies*, pre-print version. Available at: http://www.academia.edu/10383362/Going_Viral_ Comparing_Parties_on_Social_Media_During_the_2014_Swedish_Election

Larsson, A. & Moe, H. (2013) Twitter in Politics and Elections: Insights from Scandinavia. In: Weller, K., Bruns, A., Burgess, J., Mahrt, M., & Puschmann, C. (Eds.) *Twitter and Society*. New York: Peter Lang, pp. 321–330.

Linaa Jensen, J. (2013) Politisk deltagelse online i folketingsvalget 2011. In: Jensen, J.L., Hoff, J., & Klastrup, L. *Internettet og folketingsvalget 2011*. Copenhagen: Danske Medier.

Lomborg, S. (2012) Becoming a 'Tweep': Networks of Affiliation and Relational Pressures on Twitter. *OBS—Observatorio*, 6(1), 111–127.

Lomborg, S. (2014) *Social Media—Social Genres : Making Sense of the Ordinary*. London: Routledge

Newman, M.E.J. (2005) Power Laws, Pareto Distributions and Zipf's Law. *Contemporary Physics 46*, 323–351.

Rittberger, B. (2005) *Building Europe's Parliament: Democratic Representation beyond the Nation State*. Oxford: Oxford University Press.

Wasserman, S. & Faust, K. (1994) *Social Network Analysis: Methods and Applications*. Cambridge: Cambridge University Press.

Ørmen, J. (2012) The Issue Network as a Deliberative Space: A Case Study of the Danish Asylum Issue on the Internet. *CEU Political Science Journal*, 7(1), 1–31.

37

TWITTER IN POLITICAL CAMPAIGNS

The Brazilian 2014 Presidential Election

Raquel Recuero, Gabriela Zago, and Marco T. Bastos

Introduction

The turnout in the 2014 election in Brazil was among the highest ever, with over 140 million voters heading to the polls and voting for president, senators, deputies, and governors. The election resulted in intense political campaigning from August to October of 2014, when candidates resorted to television, radio, and the Internet to engage and mobilise potential supporters. While in 2010 social media played a minor role in the political debate (Amoris et al. 2012), in 2014 the political campaigns were expected to hinge on social media affordances, particularly Facebook and Twitter, which have been strongly growing in usage in the country. Social media appear as the most accessed category of websites in Brazil (ComScore 2014). In 2013, Facebook had 66 million unique users in the country whereas Twitter had 11 million. These numbers put Brazil among the top nations using each of the websites.

The 2014 presidential election was a milestone for Brazil's social media ecosystem. It was the first time that all candidates for president created official accounts dedicated to partisan politics both on Twitter and Facebook. Social media were also used as a backchannel for the debates hosted on television, with 'official' hashtags proposed by the networks for the events, and massive monitoring of tweets while the debates occurred. In this context, social media played an important role as a backchannel for discussing the candidates and their political agendas. In this chapter we discuss the intersection between the political campaigns and the audience participation enabled by social media, showing how Twitter both shaped and echoed the campaigns of presidential candidates.

The Brazilian Political Context

Brazil has been a democracy for less than 30 years. Like many of its Latin American neighbours, Brazil was under a military regime from 1964 until 1984. In 1984, protesters across the country took to the streets, fuelled by an economic crisis, and demanded fully democratic elections in what is known as the Diretas Já movement that initiated the re-democratisation process. The new constitution was enacted in 1988 and the first direct presidential elections since the 1950s took place in 1989. The free-market advocate Fernando Collor de Mello (National Reconstructive Party; PRN) won the presidential election and started in office with widespread popular support but was impeached in 1992 by the lower house of the Brazilian Congress in the midst of a corruption scandal.

After Collor's impeachment, vice-president Itamar Franco, also from PRN, assumed the presidency until the end of the mandate. Later, former finance minister Fernando Henrique Cardoso was elected. Maintaining a budget surplus and holding down inflation, Cardoso was elected for two terms as president with the PSDB (Brazilian Social Democracy Party). This period of relative economic stability continued with the election of Luis Inácio Lula da Silva from the PT (Workers' Party), who continued the strategies of former governments and implemented several social welfare programs to combat extreme poverty, which developed mass consumption in a country with a highly imbalanced social development. Brazil's current president is the successor and protégée of Lula, Dilma Rousseff, the 35th president and only the third president directly elected since Collor in 1989. In 2014, Rousseff was elected for a second term.

The Brazilian Political System

Brazil is a federal presidential constitutional republic constituted of 26 states administered by governors. The federal government has three independent branches: executive, legislative, and judicial. The legislative comprises the National Congress, with both an upper chamber, the senate, where each state has three representatives, and a lower chamber, with deputies elected based on the population size of each state and the percentage of votes each party receives. The judiciary is the single branch of government whose highest members are not directly elected but nominated by the executive.

Executive power is exercised by the president as the head of the government and the representative of the state but also includes state governors and city mayors. President, governors, and mayors are directly elected by vote on a multiparty system. Brazilian general elections take place every four years, and the population votes for president, senators, federal deputies, governors, and state deputies. The current president can be re-elected for a second term, and voting is compulsory for citizens between 18 and 60 years old (it has been so since 1932). Individuals between 16 and 18 years can register to vote if they want. Seniors above 60 years also have the option of voting or not voting. Compulsory voting takes place since the promulgation of the first electoral code in the country, in 1932. A second-round runoff election may take place if one candidate for president, state governor, or mayor in cities with more than 200,000 inhabitants does not receive 50 per cent +1 of the total number of valid votes (absolute majority).

Political Campaigns and Social Media

Political campaigns in Brazil are funded from both private and public sources. Television and radio time are allocated to each candidate during the campaigns based on their coalition's share of seats in the National Congress. In 2014, Dilma Rousseff was provided the larger share of TV time due to her party coalitions, with 11 minutes and 24 seconds, followed by Aécio Neves, with four minutes and 35 seconds, and Eduardo Campos, with two minutes and three seconds. All other candidates had one minute or less. Campaigns of major candidates are heavily dependent on private funding due to the rising costs of political campaigns (Souza 2012). These costs may include merchandising, rallies, travelling costs, publicity, and other activities. There is no limit to how much money each candidate may use for their campaign. Candidates are since 1994 obliged to have their campaign accounts checked by the Superior Electoral Court (TSE), however.

Although the influence of mandatory political propaganda on television and radio during the campaign period is also a point of contention in the literature, Da Silveira and De Mello (2011) found evidence that TV propaganda played a critical role in the gubernatorial election outcomes in Brazil, with a larger impact among poor and less educated households. According to the authors, the amount of time received by each candidate on TV is likely to have a strong impact on the results. Singer (2001) also agrees that the media have a strong influence on voters' behaviours and points out that the media are also shaping democracy in the country. Despite the sizable body of literature on the role played by the media in the presidential elections since 1989, research covering the interplay between media, political campaigns, and voter behaviour in Brazil is still sparse (Mundin 2010).

The same can be said about studies discussing campaigns and social media's influence on Brazilian elections. Very few works cover this influence, most after 2008 (Amoris et al. 2012), and even fewer focus on Twitter (Bertol, Bacaltchuck, & Mezzaroba 2011). Most directly relevant to this chapter, Cremonese (2012) discussed Twitter's impact on the 2010 presidential election, pointing to its role as a participatory tool for civic engagement. Bachini (2012), examining political strategies on Twitter, argued that opposition parties tend to use the tool in a more participatory way than ruling parties.

The role of social media in political campaigning in other countries, however, has been extensively studied in the past few years, particularly on Twitter (see Bruns & Burgess 2011; Burgess & Bruns 2012; as well as the other chapters in Part III of the present volume). Aragón et al. (2012, 2013) studied Twitter's role during the Spanish elections and found results similar to what Bachini argued: parties tended to use the tool as a one-way communication tool rather than a participatory tool. Burgess and Bruns (2012) examined the use of Twitter for political campaigns and elections and argued that Twitter's structure allows the formation of 'ad hoc publics', or publics that can share public debates through hashtags and mentions, contributing to political participation.

Other studies have pointed to a strong relationship between social media channels and traditional media, which is also unexplored in Brazil. Kalsnes, Krumsvik, and Storsul (2014) pointed to the strong relationship between television and social media during the campaigns in Norway, describing social media as backchannel. A similar relationship was explored by Towner and Dulio (2011) in the 2008 U.S. elections. but for Facebook and focusing on voter behaviours.

In the remainder of this chapter we explore this dimension of the public sphere, which is at the same time detached from the traditional debate on public opinion and the public sphere and critical to the formation of new, dispersed, and often politically polarised politics in Brazil, and we further discuss the candidates' strategies on Twitter.

Methodology

Data for this study was collected using yourTwapperKeeper (yTK), which connects to the Twitter Streaming API and archives tweets relevant to the research. We used yTK to collect tweets from each of the candidates' official accounts on Twitter and to collect all mentions of each of the accounts. The data were collected from July to October 2014. In this study we focus only on a data set of mentions of and activity by the official accounts from 1 August (when candidates started campaigning more strongly) to 26 October (the second-round polling day). The only exception is the candidate Marina Silva, for whom we only started collecting data after a plane crash that killed the then candidate of PSB, Eduardo Campos; data collection for this candidate thus started only after 13 August 2014.

The official accounts were selected based on the following criteria: (1) accounts were recognised by Twitter as 'verified' with the sign used by the company to indicate an official account. This was the case for the top contenders. (2) Accounts were acknowledged by the campaign material as 'official'. (3) Accounts were used by the campaign as official (mentioned by other accounts). Since there were several 'fake' Twitter accounts, we manually checked all accounts that made reference to the candidates to make sure we were collecting the stream of data associated with the official campaign of each of the candidates. Table 37.1 shows the data collected in the period and the candidates for each party.

Data collection was divided into three parts. We collected data for all candidates during the first round and for the runoff candidates during the second round. From this

Table 37.1 Data from Official Twitter Accounts of Presidential Candidates (accounts in bold indicate runoff candidates with data through both rounds)

Party	Candidate	Account	Mentions	Tweets	Unique users
PSDB	**Aécio Neves**	**@aecioneves**	**1,089,116**	**1,600**	**393,646**
PT	**Dilma Rousseff**	**@dilmabr**	**914,859**	**1,358**	**429,829**
PSB	Marina Silva	@silva_marina	505,675	1,711	228,524
PSOL	Luciana Genro	@lucianagenro	162,173	2,311	162,173
PSDC	Everaldo	@Everaldo_20	16,103	401	10,993
PV	Eduardo Jorge	@eduardojorge43	821	932	463
PRTB	Levy Fidélix	@levyfidelix	35,594	348	24,911
PCO	Rui Pimenta	@ruipimenta29	474	251	304
PSTU	Zé Maria	@zemaria_pstu	4,022	462	2,343
PCB	Mauro Iasi	@MauroIasi	2,110	224	1,289
PSC	Eymael	@eymaeloficial	8,261	4,722	5,864

data set we selected the 10 most retweeted tweets mentioning each candidate as well as their 10 most active retweeters (users who frequently retweeted their content), and the accounts that most often cited the official accounts. We analysed the content of each tweet, and the profiles of the accounts involved in cross-mentioning and retweeting activity. Second, we collected weekly follower data from the official Twitter accounts of each candidate from August to October 2014. Third, we monitored Twitter hashtags and keywords associated with the debates and major campaign events and noted user participation through participant observation of Twitter feeds during the debates and major election events (such as the public, real-time vote count published by the Superior Electoral Court).

The data on the 10 most retweeted tweets provide insights on the repercussions of each campaign and on how users perceived the candidates online. We manually classified the accounts that made the most retweeted tweets in the following categories:

Campaign: the tweet was posted by a campaign account (a Twitter account directly involved in the campaign, such as the candidate's official account, the party's official account, or accounts created by campaign staff).

News: the tweet was posted by a news organisation. These tweets are usually part of the live coverage of debates and campaign events.

Celebrity supporters: the tweet was posted by a user with more than 10 thousand followers who supported the candidate.

Ordinary supporters: the tweet was posted by an everyday account that supported the candidate, but the user is not popular (mostly such accounts had fewer than two thousand followers, but all accounts with fewer than 10 thousand followers were considered in this category).

Fake/humouristic: the tweet is a joke posted by a fake or humouristic account.

Opponents: the tweet was posted by a political adversary or an account affiliated with the political opposition.

Results of the Election

The first round of the 2014 general Brazilian election took place on 5 October 2014, followed by the second round on 26 October. Brazilians voted for president, federal deputies, senators, governors, and state deputies. For the purposes of this study, we focus only on the presidential vote, which included 11 candidates. The campaign started officially on 6 June, with free television and radio airtime starting on 19 August. The onset of the presidential race included current president Dilma Rousseff from the Workers' Party (PT), senator Aécio Neves from the Brazilian Social Democracy Party (PSDB), current governor of the state of Pernambuco Eduardo Campos from the Brazilian Socialist Party (PSB), Luciana Genro from the Socialism and Freedom Party (PSOL), Everaldo Pereira from the Christian Social Party (PSC), Eduardo Jorge from the Green Party (PV), José Eymael from the Christian Social Democratic Party (PSDC), José Maria de Almeida from the United Socialist Workers' Party (PSTU), Levy Fidélix from the Brazilian Labour Renewal Party (PRTB), Rui Pimenta from the Workers' Cause Party (PCO), and Mauro Iasi from the Brazilian Communist Party (PCB).

Of the 11 candidates, only three received more than 10 per cent of the intended vote in the opinion polls, namely, Dilma Rousseff, Aécio Neves, and Eduardo Campos.

Luciana Genro, Everaldo Pereira, and Eduardo Jorge followed with 1 per cent of votes. Amongst the three more popular candidates, Dilma Rousseff was the first in the polls, followed by Aécio Neves and Eduardo Campos (see Figure 37.1). The presidential race changed greatly after the fatal plane crash of PSB candidate Eduardo Campos on 13 August, only six days before the radio and TV campaign started (BBC, 2014a). Campos had just given his first national television interview for *Jornal Nacional* (on Globo Network) the night before, and was flying in a private jet to attend another interview in Santos City. Campos's vice-presidential candidate, former senator Marina Silva, was soon announced as the new candidate.

The general commotion about Campos's death and announcement of Silva's candidacy contributed to give the party more visibility. While at the time of the accident Campos had less than a 10 per cent share in the opinion polls, polls following the crash showed Silva at more than 21 per cent. In fact, Silva quickly became a strong candidate with polls constantly showing her growth and advancement over the favourite candidate, president Dilma Rousseff. But by the middle of September, after a sequence of debates on TV and on social media, the polls indicated that Silva's candidacy was plummeting while Neves's was taking off. Part of the decline of Silva's campaign was credited to the several changes in her government plan and positions throughout the campaign, mostly caused by internal disputes within the Socialist Party (BBC, 2014b). Neves, on the other hand, remained the strongest option for those opposed to the Workers' Party, which had been in power for the last 12 years. At the end of the first round Neves amassed 34 per cent of the vote, and Dilma Rousseff had 42 per cent of the vote. Silva fell short with only 21 per cent of the vote, and the rest of the candidates combined gained less than 5 per cent of the vote.

During the second round, the campaign intensified and became increasingly polarised. Due to the growing opposition between the two presidential candidates, Neves (PSDB) and Rousseff (PT), social media and mainstream media experienced increasing levels of partisan politics. The population at large became intensely involved, and the flow of news associated with the election on social media was unprecedented. Neves received support from defeated first-round candidates, including Eduardo Jorge (PV), Levy Fidélix (PRTB), Everaldo (PSC), and Marina Silva (PSB).

Since mid-October, election polls showed voters divided between the two remaining candidates. The first second-round polls gave an edge to Neves (PSDB), closely followed by Rousseff (PT). However, after 15 October, the lead changed back to Rousseff, followed closely by Neves. On 23 October, another poll showed Neves taking the lead again. These results only changed in the final polls, which showed Rousseff as the frontrunner, for the first time beyond the margin of error. These oscillations in the polls were arguably an effect of the multiple debates between the two candidates, promoted by television networks and transmitted online (Tavares et al. 2014). On 26 October, Dilma Rousseff (PT) was re-elected with 51.6 per cent of the total number of valid votes, with little more than 54 million votes against 51 million for Neves (48.3 per cent), one of the smallest margins in Brazilian election history. She was immediately announced as the next president by the Superior Electoral Court (TSE 2014).

The 2014 Presidential Campaign on Twitter

Although all candidates had dedicated Twitter accounts prior to the general election, account activity was minimal to non-existent (Aecio Neves's Twitter account did not

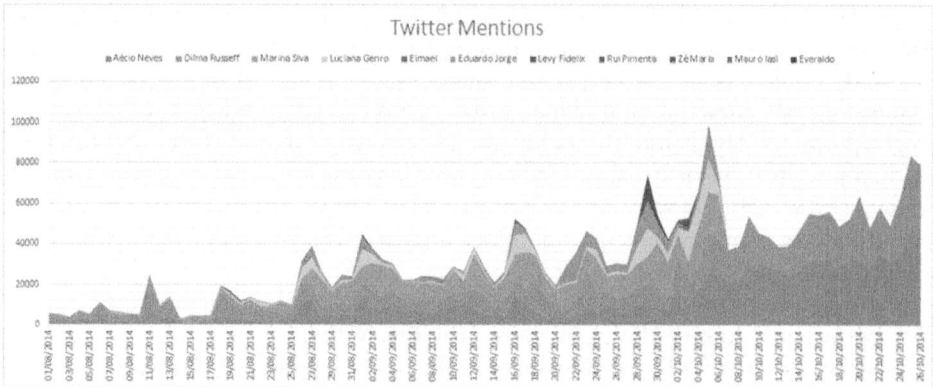

Figure 37.1 Number of Mentions per Candidate per Day

post any tweets in the run-up to the election). Twitter was a central backchannel for the discussion. During the election period, we collected more than five million tweets related to the event, and voter participation increased as the final round approached. There were peaks of participation during major campaign events, particularly during the debates broadcast on television. Figure 37.1 shows the daily number of Twitter mentions for each the candidates' 'official' accounts between 1 August and 5 October (first round) and 6 October and 26 October (second round).

The spikes shown in Figure 37.1 indicate the date of the debates on TV, with the first round debates having occurred on 26 August (Bandeirantes Network), 1 September (SBT Network), 16 September (Aparecida TV), 28 September (Record Network), and 2 October (Globo Network). Debates for the second round occurred on 14 October (Bandeirantes Network), 16 October (SBT Network), 19 October (Record Network), and 24 October (Globo Network). Each debate had an 'official' hashtag assigned by the broadcaster. Only candidates from parties with a seat in the Congress were invited for the debates (thus, only PSDB, PT, PV, PSOL, PRTB, and PSC). The exception is the candidate from PSDC (Christian Party) who was also invited for the debate on the Aparecida TV (the Christian Network). Supporters of the leading candidates (PT, PSDB, and PSB) also introduced their own set of hashtags in support of their candidates, and promoted several *tuitaços* (coordinated mass manifestation on Twitter), thus pushing hashtags such as #Aecio45 (in support of Neves), #DilmaMaisEmprego (more jobs with Dilma Rousseff), #SouMarina40 (I'm with Marina), which often showed up amongst Brazilian Twitter's trending topics.

Figures 37.1 and 37.2 show how Twitter and TV were intertwined during the elections, as the increase in the number of mentions coincides with the debate dates. This is a strong indication that visibility on TV has considerable impact on Twitter mentions. During the first debate, Rousseff (PT) and Neves (PSDB) increased their number of mentions by 238 per cent and 300 per cent, respectively, while Silva (PSB) increased her mentions by 141 per cent.

The relative figures are even higher for independent candidates, with Genro (PSOL) increasing her mentions by 1,105 per cent, Eduardo Jorge (PV) by 830 per cent, and Pastor Everaldo (PSC) by 435 per cent. The same pattern is observed in the follower

Tweets per day

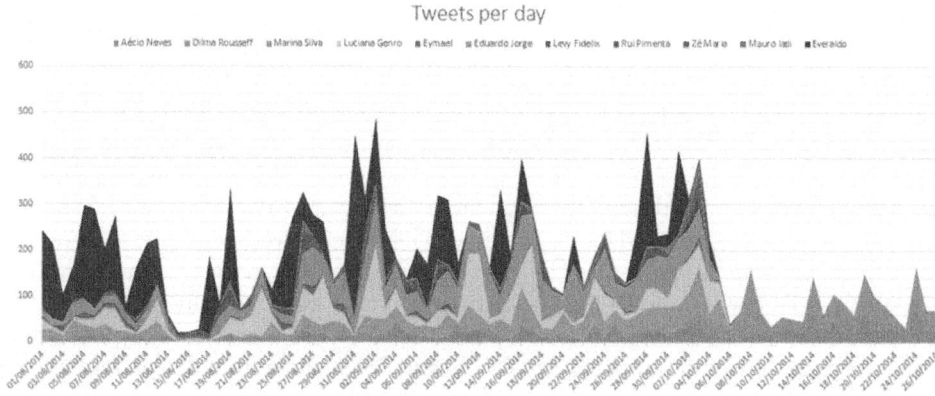

Figure 37.2 Number of Tweets per Candidate per Day

growth. The traction gained online by independent candidates is potentially a result of their growing Twitter follower numbers during the debates (even though their usernames did not appear on screen during these events). During the first round, independent candidates such as Jorge and Genro reported the most impressive follower growth, while established contenders such as Rousseff (PT) only grew their audience by 5 per cent. On the other hand, Neves (PSDB) grew his following considerably during the second round (by 94 per cent), from 107,000 to 208,000 followers. Rousseff kept a lower growth rate during the second term and added only 80,000 followers (2.9 per cent) to her 2,835,164 followers, likely due to the fact that her account was long-established and already had much larger following than the accounts of her adversaries.

We also mapped the Twitter activities of each of the official accounts of the candidates (see Figure 37.2). While Rousseff (PT) and Neves (PSDB) posted 1,358 and 1,600 tweets between 1 August and 26 October (both rounds), they were surpassed by the account of Eymael (PSC), who posted 4,722 tweets, Jorge (PV) with 2,630 tweets, Genro (PSOL) with 2,311 tweets, and Silva (PSB) with 1,711 posted during the first-round period only. Although the number of tweets posted does not correlate with audience interactivity (@mentions received), it seems to indicate that Twitter provided a more participative platform for campaigning, especially for minority parties with less time on TV and radio. Additionally, our data show that the most participative candidates online were those with less time on TV and radio (PRTB, PV, PSOL). Minority political parties engaged more intensely with their Twitter followers during the campaign, especially during television debates. During the second round, participation by the major candidates increased heavily, indicating that they adopted a stronger presence on Twitter.

Retweet Behaviour

We further analysed the retweets from each data set (retweets by the candidates and retweets mentioning the candidates) to try to uncover part of the candidates' strategies on Twitter. Here, we examine more closely the data from the three major candidates (Neves, Rousseff, and Silva), and discuss more generally the less popular candidates.

Retweet behaviour among the accounts was very different. The Neves (PSDB) account, for example, had the lowest percentage of retweets amongst its tweets, with only 3.7 per cent of the total number of tweets, while Rousseff (PT) had 8.7 per cent and Silva (PSB) 12.5 per cent. While these accounts privileged their own content rather than that of others, Silva and Rousseff also gave visibility to tweets from celebrity supporters and partisan accounts. These numbers are rather different from those for the less popular parties, even though they had more Twitter activity (as Figure 37.2 shows).

Of the tweets posted by PSTU, for example, 35.4 per cent were retweets; so were 32.5 per cent of PCO's and 21 per cent of PCB's tweets. These parties retweeted more ordinary supporters, celebrity supporters and news tweets, giving more visibility to other users' content. This retweet strategy may also have helped to keep the account more active when the party had fewer resources. PSOL, PV, and PSDC differ from this pattern as they have a larger number of tweets and a smaller percentile of retweets (6.1 per cent, 10.4 per cent, and 1.3 per cent, respectively), and thus are also privileging their own content and being largely active during the campaign. When retweeting, they seem to have used the same strategy as the more popular parties, retweeting celebrity supporters, news, and campaign accounts. In this case, it seems that these parties (with fewer resources than the major parties) invested more of their campaigning efforts in Twitter, hoping to gain and keep more visibility through social media. PRTB is the exception, with a small amount of tweets and a small amount of retweets (7.2 per cent), mostly of ordinary supporters.

The most active retweeters of candidates were ordinary supporters and partisan campaign accounts (e.g. @psdbba for Neves, @ptbrasil for Rousseff, @40presidente for Silva). Interestingly, some of the top retweeters were not supporters but opponents of the candidates, which is indicative of the non-endorsement nature of their retweets, especially in relation to Rousseff's account. Their actions, however, still increased that account's visibility.

Mentions

Our data show that most mentions of Neves (PSDB) came from partisan campaign Twitter accounts and news organisations. Mentions of Rousseff (PT) are considerably more diverse, although they also included partisan campaign accounts, news organisations and comedians (humourous accounts). Mentions of Silva (PSB) follow a similar pattern. Partisan Twitter accounts were particularly prevalent in mentions of candidates affiliated with minority parties, and candidates who participated on broadcast debates were also the object of the tweets posted by humouristic and fake accounts. Eduardo Jorge (PV) and Levy Fidélix (PRTB), in particular, were the objects of a number of humoristic Twitter accounts, from fakes to Web celebrities.

These data show that news organisations played an important role in providing visibility to the candidates on Twitter. However, this influence seems to be tied to the presence of the candidates during the debates. Candidates from PSTU, PSDC, PCB, and PCO received far fewer tweets from the mass media, while candidates from PT, PSDB, PSB, PSOL, PRTB, and PSC were the objects of a much greater number of tweets. The PSDB campaign seems to have relied more heavily on gaining visibility through retweets from other partisan campaign accounts. A large majority of its retweets fall within this category.

Nonetheless, Neves's tweets were replicated by a much smaller user base compared to the messages tweeted by Rousseff (PT) or Silva (PSB). Conversely, the messages by Rousseff (PT) and Silva (PSB) attracted more celebrities and elite users, who helped spread their tweets, compared to those of Neves (PSDB). Perhaps expectedly, candidates of minority parties received less media coverage and more exposure from partisan Twitter accounts, which is indicative of the grassroots nature of their campaigns.

We also examined the 10 most retweeted messages mentioning each of the candidates. We analysed the political affiliation of the source of the tweet and the users who retweeted it, and found that the most retweeted messages for the top three contenders were from their own official accounts, followed by celebrity supporters and news organisations. Tweets from official accounts mostly focused on positive messages about the candidates, with a fitting example coming from Neves's (PSDB) account:

> @AecioNeves: We continue to believe, as I always have, that it is possible to give the country decent and efficient government #Aecio45

This sentence is actually a verbatim reproduction of the candidate's campaign slogan.

Tweets from the mass media focused mostly on Rousseff's (PT) account, were predominantly negative, and largely retweeted by the opposition. A fitting example is the most retweeted tweet from the mass media:

> @OGloboPolitica: Audience laughs when @dilmabr says inflation is under control [link]

The tweet refers to the live broadcast of one of the presidential debates, where the president was constantly asked about the prospects of inflation in the country, and stressed the audience's disbelief of the president's response.

Celebrity tweets proved to cut both ways. For example, one of the most retweeted messages citing Rousseff showed filmmaker Oliver Stone supporting her platform:

> @TheOliverStone: #Brazil don't forget to vote for President #DilmaRoussef @dilmabr on Sun 26/10. Do not go backwards to the past!

Also through Twitter, Silva (PSB) received the support of international celebrity and vocal environmentalist Mark Ruffalo, who posted a video on YouTube supporting her candidacy based on her environmental platform. However, upon being informed of her position about marriage equality, Ruffalo publicly withdrew support by tweeting

> @MarkRuffalo: @silva_marina Are you pro marriage equality?

The message was one of the most retweeted in our Silva data set (over 2,000 retweets as of 7 November).

It is also important to highlight the occurrence of opposing views within some of the most retweeted tweets associated with the candidates. This was particularly the case with PRTB's candidate Levy Fidélix. During one of the broadcast presidential debates, Fidélix voiced several strong, often offensive, and potentially libellous opinions against LGBT rights that were met with a strong response on Twitter. The second most retweeted message mentioning the candidate read:

> Opinion my ass . . . there should be no place for homophobia. If you are homophobic you should go to jail! @LevyFidelix should be arrested!

Several similar tweets were among the most retweeted in his data set, together with a long list of derogatory jokes about the candidate.

Conclusion

Our data show a massive use of Twitter during the 2014 presidential election in Brazil, both by voters (through mentions) and by candidates (through tweets). Usage increased as an effect of major campaign events, particularly broadcast presidential debates. Twitter played a critical role as a backchannel during television debates by allowing voters to discuss the unfolding debate and enabling non-participating candidates to contribute their remarks using the 'official' debate hashtags. Mainstream media in Brazil proved to have a fairly acute understanding of the formation of *ad hoc* publics and advocated the use of hashtags dedicated to the debates even before the debates went to air. This is consistent with previous research covering the relationship between social media and mainstream media (Bruns & Burgess 2011; Towner & Dulio 2011) and indicates the existence of an intricate ecosystem between social and traditional media in electoral campaigns (Kalsnes, Krumsvik &, Storsul 2014).

The debates around the several hashtags proposed by candidates and television networks seem to contribute to the formation of *ad hoc* publics (Bruns & Burgess 2011). These publics not only allowed candidates who did not appear at these events to participate and gather attention from the conversation, but also provided a space for these conversations to happen (Cremonese 2012), thus generating a spike in mentions for the candidates.

Also consistent with previous research (Aragón et al. 2013; Bachini 2012), we found considerably different strategies associated with Twitter from each of the political parties campaigning. Top contenders resorted to the platform less often, while candidates with less free time on television and radio found on Twitter a valuable communication channel. Perhaps surprisingly, these strategies changed considerably in the second round, when the two remaining contenders resorted heavily to Twitter. PSOL and PV, for example, are minority parties with some of the most active accounts in our data set. While the growth of their mentions seems to be directly connected to participation in television debates, they were also very successful at campaigning on Twitter. In relative terms, they proved able to grow their audiences at a much greater rate than the top contenders. Eduardo Jorge from PV increased his following from a few hundred to more than 100,000 followers over the period, and together with other independent candidates received a large proportion of mentions (see Figure 37.1). These grassroots strategies were also more informal, and most of the retweets relied on partisan supporters rather than on campaign accounts managed by public relation teams.

The differences between the social media strategies adopted by the two top contenders point to the interplay between social media and politics in Brazil. The PSDB (Brazilian Social Democracy Party) campaign deployed dedicated Twitter accounts to retweet the content of the main account, a strategy that walks a fine line towards astroturfing by drawing on a relatively small user base to retweet the main account and provide more exposure to the candidate. Overall, official tweets comprised most of the most retweeted messages for the PSDB campaign. The party also emphasised the role of celebrity supporters, although the official account of Neves was much less active on Twitter compared to those of the other candidates, only showing strong activity during the second round. On the other hand, the PT (Workers' Party) Twitter data show a shared space with news about the current government, which offered an important selling point as its candidate was the incumbent president. Although the account was active long before the campaign started, celebrity supporters, news outlets and partisan campaign accounts played an important role in mentioning Rousseff and increasing her exposure. PT's candidate account was the second most cited, and the one with the largest number of unique users citing it (see Table 37.1). Nonetheless, the account was on average also less active compared to the other candidates, growing only during the second round.

This chapter has presented an overview of the relationship between social media and political campaigns in Brazil. Further research will be able to shed light on other aspects not covered here, such as the role of Facebook in elections, the use of social media in political campaigns in other countries, or the connections between voting behaviour and Twitter use. Social media may play an even more crucial role in future elections in Brazil, especially in the minor election rounds in 2016, when campaign funding will be more limited.

Note

This chapter is a research output from the project Mapeando as conversações em rede das Eleições Presidenciais de 2014, funded by CNPq (National Scientific Development Council) under the number 408650/2013-3.

References

Amoris, V., Gollner, A. P., Goulart, E., and Pessoni, A. (2012) "Marketing politico e redes sociais: reflexos nas eleições 2010 à presidencia da República," in A. Queiroz, C. Françoso, P. Tomaziello, and R. Macedo (eds.) Comunicação política e eleitoral no Brasil: Perspectivas e limitações no dinamismo politico, Americana, SP: Politicom. pp. 140–157.

Aragón, P., Kappler, K., Kaltenbrunner, A., Neff, J., Laniado, D., and Volkovich, Y. (2012) "Tweeting the campaign. Evaluation of the Strategies performed by Spanish Political Parties on twitter for the 2011 National Elections, " Internet, Politics, Policy 2012, Barcelona.

Aragón, P., Kappler, K., Kaltenbrunner, A., Neff, J., Laniado, D., and Volkovich, Y. (2013) "Communication dynamics in Twitter during political campaigns: The case of the 2011 Spanish national election," Policy & Internet, 5(2), pp. 183–206.

Bachini, N. (2012) "As cibercampanhas no Brasil: uma análise dos Twitters de Dilma, Serra e Marina em 2010," Ponto-e-Vírgula, 12(1), pp. 135–164.

BBC (2014a) http://www.bbc.com/news/world-latin-america-28778604

BBC (2014b) http://www.bbc.co.uk/portuguese/noticias/2014/10/141003_marina_queda_ru

Bertol, S., Bacaltchuck, B., and Mezzaroba, M. (2011) "A Campanha Eleitoral na Internet: Uma análise do Twitter dos candidatos à presidency Dilma Rousseff e José Serra," Democracia Digital e Governo Eletrônico, 3(5), pp. 172–185.

Bruns, A. and Burgess, J. (2011) "#ausvotes: How Twitter covered the 2010 Australian federal election," Communication, Politics & Culture, 4(2).

Burgess, J. and Bruns, A. (2012) "(Not) the Twitter election: The dynamics of the #ausvotes conversation in relation to the Australian media ecology," Journalism Practice, 6(3).

ComScore (2014) 2014 Brazil digital future in focus, http://www.comscore.com/por/Insights/Presentations-and-Whitepapers/2014/2014-Brazil-Digital-Future-in-Focus-Webinar

Cremonese, D. (2012) "Política on-line: a utilização do Twitter como ferramenta de capital social nas eleições presidenciais de 2010," Sociedade e Cultura, 15(1), pp. 135–149.

Da Silveira, B. S., & De Mello, J.M.P. (2011). "Campaign advertising and election outcomes: Quasi-natural experiment evidence from gubernatorial elections in Brazil," *Review of Economic Studies*, 78(2), pp. 590–612.

Kalsnes, B., Krumsvik, A.H., and Storsul, T. (2014). "Social media as a political backchannel: Twitter use during televised election debates in Norway," *Aslib Journal of Information Management*, 66(3), pp. 313–328.

Mundin, P. (2010) "Cientistas Políticos, Comunicólogos e o Papel da Mídia nas Teorias da Decisão do Voto," *Revista Política Hoje*, 19(2).

Singer, A. (2001) "Midia e Democracia no Brasil," *Revista USP*, 48.

Souza, C.R. (2012) "Parties and electoral campaigns financing in Brazil: A review of legislation," in *Proceedings of XXII IPSA World Congress of Political Science*, Madrid.

Tavares et al. (2014) "Dilma X Aécio: A eleição que divide o Brasil," *Revista Época*, http://epoca.globo.com/tempo/eleicoes/noticia/2014/10/bdilma-x-aeciob-eleicao-que-divide-o-brasil.html

Towner, T. and Dulio, D. (2011) "The Web 2.0 election: Does the online medium matter?," *The Journal of Political Marketing*, 10(1 & 2), pp. 165–188.

TSE (2014) http://www.tse.jus.br/noticias-tse/2014/Outubro/presidente-do-tse-anuncia-que-dilma-rousseff-foi-reeleita-presidente-da-republica

INDEX

Note: Italicized page numbers indicate a figure on the corresponding page. Page numbers in bold indicate a table on the corresponding page.